Core Text Series

- Written with authority by leading subject experts
- Takes a focussed approach, leading law students straight to the heart of the subject
- Clear, concise, straightforward analysis of the subject and its challenges

Series Editor: Nicola Padfield

Company Law: Alan Dignam and John Lowry

Constitutional and Administrative Law: Neil Parpworth

Criminal Law: Nicola Padfield

Employment Law: Robert Upex, Richard Benny and Stephen Hardy

European Union Law: Margot Horspool and Matthew Humphreys

Evidence: Roderick Munday

Family Law: Mary Welstead and Susan Edwards

Intellectual Property Law: Jennifer Davis

Land Law: Kevin Gray and Susan Francis Gray

Medical Law: Jonathan Herring

The Law of Contract: Janet O'Sullivan and Jonathan Hilliard

The Law of Trusts: James Penner

The Legal System: Kate Malleson, Richard Moules

Tort: Stephen Hedley

For further information about titles in the series,
please visit www.oup.co.uk/series/cts

OXFORD
UNIVERSITY PRESS

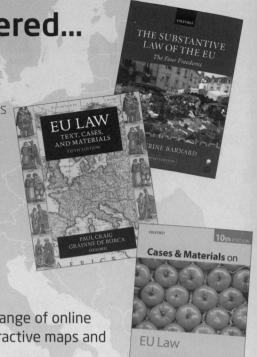
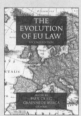

CORE TEXT SERIES

European Union Law

Seventh Edition

MARGOT HORSPOOL

Emeritus Professor of European and Comparative Law at the University of Surrey;
Fellow in European Law of the British Institute of International and Comparative Law;
Visiting Professor, Queen Mary University, London

MATTHEW HUMPHREYS

Professor of Law and Head of School, Kingston Law School, Kingston University

Series Editor
NICOLA PADFIELD

OXFORD
UNIVERSITY PRESS

OXFORD
UNIVERSITY PRESS

Great Clarendon Street, Oxford, OX2 6DP,
United Kingdom

Oxford University Press is a department of the University of Oxford.
It furthers the University's objective of excellence in research, scholarship,
and education by publishing worldwide. Oxford is a registered trade mark of
Oxford University Press in the UK and in certain other countries

Fourth Edition Published 2006
Fifth Edition Published 2008
Sixth Edition Published 2010

Impression: 1

British Library Cataloguing in Publication Data

Data available

Library of Congress Cataloging in Publication Data

Data available

ISBN 978-0-19-963981-6

Printed in Great Britain by
Ashford Colour Press Ltd, Gosport, Hampshire

MARGOT

Ter herinnering aan mijn moeder, *Johanna van Ling (1908–1997) and
to Isabella, Amelia, Jude, Opre and Johan, Europeans of the new Millennium.*

MATTHEW

For Emma and Sam, Beth and Henry.

Foreword to the sixth edition, at the time of the coming into force of the Lisbon Treaty

Much has changed in the field of EU law since the publication of the fifth edition of this book—most of all, as a result of the Lisbon Treaty coming into force.

On the simplest level, the structure of the Treaties has been changed and the Articles have been renumbered. But the substantive changes are extensive and their consequences are potentially far-reaching.

What was formerly the Third Pillar (Freedom, Security and Justice—formerly Justice and Home Affairs) has been removed from the loose structures of inter-governmental negotiation, and brought within the discipline of the 'Community system'. Proposals in this field of activity will now be fully subject to parliamentary and judicial control, although public understanding is not made any easier by the proliferation of opt-outs. Indeed, the number and complexity of Protocols and Declarations make the legal regime extremely confusing, even for experts.

Two consequences of Lisbon have been less widely noticed and commented upon than they should have been, in Britain at any rate.

The first is the importance attached by the Treaty on European Union to the principles of conferral, subsidiarity and proportionality. All proposals must now pass these tests which are, in principle at least, judicially enforceable. Judicial enforcement is, however, the ultimate sanction. Of greater practical importance will be the disciplines imposed on the political institutions, especially the Commission.

The second consequence, intimately connected with the first, is the role given to national Parliaments as guardians of these principles in the evolution of EU proposals. The Council, as an institution, represents the *governments* of the Member States and is closely involved in the evolution of legislative proposals. The Lisbon Treaty presupposes that national Parliaments may, and sometimes will, raise objections to proposals that have found favour with their governments. The political consequences are potentially far-reaching.

In addition, the Treaty recognises, for the first time, the existence of regional Parliaments with legislative powers. Admittedly, they are only to be consulted by national Parliaments, and then only 'where appropriate'. But the recognition that EU proposals may be of legitimate concern to democratically accountable actors below the level of the Member States is also a recognition that respect for subsidiarity is not the exclusive prerogative of national institutions.

Looked at from this point of view, the Lisbon Treaty is not a further step towards a 'European super-state', but rather a step towards a Europe that recognises and protects the variable geometry of its constituent parts. For one observer at least, it is a pity that the Lisbon Treaty marks the end of the 'European Community'—a title that is less ambitious than 'European Union', but perhaps more truly reflective of what we would like to build.

David Edward
Edinburgh
25 June 2010

Foreword to the first edition

The law of the European Union has evolved considerably both in scope and importance since the early days. The rapidly changing legal landscape has made it one of the most interesting fields of law for the student, the teacher, the practitioner and even the legal philosopher. Once perceived as a curiosity of only marginal interest to all but the specialist, it has become of central importance for many aspects of the national legal scene, so that the lawyer who dismisses Community law as an irrelevance does so at his—and his insurer's—peril. This risk is all the greater because much of Community law is hidden behind national legislation.

In the early days, when lawyers asked what EC law was about, one could simply recommend them to read the Treaty. Its structure was straightforward and so, for the most part, were its terms. This is still good advice, for the Treaty remains the primary source of law and it is impossible to understand Community law without knowing one's way round the Treaty. But the treaty structure has been complicated by the addition—without a clear indication of their inter-relationship—of the Single European Act, the EU Treaty and now, increasingly, Third Pillar Conventions. The EC Treaty itself has been radically amended, and there has been an explosion of secondary legislation, much of it highly technical.

Some of the new texts seem designed to paper over political differences rather than to set out in a coherent way the legal rules and institutional relationships that form the basis of the European Union. To an increasing extent, the Court of Justice is called upon to complete or explain legislative uncertainties. So, simply to read the texts would give a very incomplete understanding of their legal effect. They must be set in their historical and political context and the special methods of interpreting multilingual texts must be mastered.

This presents a challenge to the student and the teacher. The contours of the Community legal system change so rapidly that textbooks quickly become out-of-date. The student should, in any event, be exposed to more than one view of how the law has evolved, and how it should be read, understood and applied.

Margot Horspool's new book presents EU law, not as a static body of legal rules, but as a dynamic system, evolving as much through case law and academic discussion as legislative activity. It offers a comprehensive guide to the Union and Community system, looking at the institutional structure and processes as well as the substantive and procedural law. A particular strength of the book is that it encourages the reader to adopt a pro-active, reflective approach through the inclusion, at the end of each chapter, of self-test capsules of questions and points for discussion.

This book is a worthy addition to the valuable contribution that University College London has already made to the study of European law in the United Kingdom.

Judge David Edward
Court of Justice of the European Communities
Luxembourg
3 September 1998

Preface

This book is intended as an introductory text to European Union law. Successive Treaties follow the initial ones, the impact of European Union law has expanded even further than before. It is becoming practically impossible for law students, and increasingly difficult for legal practitioners in many areas, to do without at least a basic knowledge of European law. This book hopes to serve as a guide and as a basis for further studies of the subject. For a more extensive knowledge of any of the areas of European law dealt with in this book, reference should be made to:

(a) the original sources of European Union legislation

(b) the case law of the Court of Justice and the General Court

(c) textbooks on European law

(d) casebooks on European law

(e) European (and sometimes national) law journals

(f) Internet sources, in particular the Europa website

(a) Original sources

European Union primary legislation is to be found in the various Treaties. There are original versions of the treaties available in all 23 official languages of the Union, but the most useful texts are those in the collections of statutes, which also contain the most important secondary legislation (published in the 23 languages of the Union).

Halsbury's Statutes volumes 51 and 52; N. Foster *Blackstone's EU Legislation* (Blackstone, latest edition), Rudden & Wyatt *EU Treaties and Legislation* (OUP, latest edition), Butterworths Student Statutes: Gale: *EC Law* (Butterworths, latest edition).

European Union secondary legislation (Regulations, Directives, Decisions) is published in the *Official Journal of the European Union* (L Series). The C Series contains proposals for legislation.

Regulations are numbered giving the number first, followed by the year of publication, e.g. Regulation 1612/68; Directives indicate the year of publication first, followed by the number, e.g. Directive 64/221. The same applies to Decisions.

(b) Case law of the European Courts

European Court cases are referred to by number, followed by the year. Cases before the General Court of the European Union (formerly the Court of First Instance) are preceded by a T, and cases before the Court of Justice of the European Union are preceded by a C. Readers should note the distinction between General Court and Court of Justice cases only starts with the establishment of the Court of First Instance in 1989, and cases before that date have no letter prefix. Appeals are marked P, interim measures are marked R.

There are two sets of court reports published in English. The European Court Reports (ECR) is the official reporter of cases before the Court of Justice of the European Union and publishes all such cases. Reference will usually be made to these reports. The All England Law Reports have published EU law reports since 1995 and reference will be made to them where appropriate. The most widely used unofficial reporter is the Common Market Law Reports (CMLR). This series publishes the principal judgments of the Court of Justice, competition decisions taken by the European Commission, important judgments on Union law by courts of the Member States and other important communications. Reference will be made to this series particularly in respect of national cases which are not reported in the European Court Reports. Important judgments of the Court are also reported in the Times Law Reports (TLR), the Independent, the Financial Times and the Industrial Relations Law Report (IRLR).

(c) Textbooks

There are a number of textbooks which may be referred to for more extensive treatment of the subjects in this book. It is best mainly to consult books published since the ratification of the Lisbon Treaty, but some earlier books are still useful:

Craig & de Búrca, *EU Law, Text, Cases and Materials* (5th edn, Oxford: OUP, 2011)

Woods & Watson, *Steiner & Woods EU Law* (11th edn, Oxford: OUP, 2012)

Hartley, *The Foundations of European Union Law* (7th edn, Oxford: OUP, 2010) (very good on institutional and constitutional law)

Douglas-Scott, *Constitutional Law of the European Union* (London: Pearson, 2002). New edition due for publication 2013.

Kapteyn & Verloren van Themaat, *Introduction to the Law of the European Union and the European Communities,* edited by L Gormley (4th edn, Kluwer, 2009)

Weatherill, *Cases and Materials on EU Law* (10th edn, Oxford: OUP, 2012)

Dougan et al., *Wyatt & Dashwood's* European Union Law (6th edn, London: Sweet & Maxwell, 2011)

Worthy of special mention is H.G. Schermers and D. Waelbroeck, *Judicial Protection in the European Union* (6th edn, Kluwer, 2001)

A good cases and materials plus textbook published in the US is: Bermann, Goebel, Davey & Fox, *European Union Law* (3rd edn, Thomas Reuters Westlaw, 2011)

(d) Casebooks

Because of the rapid development of EU law, the most recent casebooks are the most useful, such as:

Weatherill, *Cases and Materials on EU Law* (10th edn, Oxford: OUP, 2012)

(e) Law journals

The principal English language journals that publish articles on European Union law include:

Common Market Law Review (CMLRev)

European Law Review (ELRev)

European Competition Law Review (ECLRev)

International & Comparative Law Quarterly (ICLQ)

European Journal of International Law (EJIL)

Journal of Common Market Studies (JCMS)

Legal Issues of European Integration (LIEI)

Yearbook of European Law (YEL)

A major headache caused by both the Treaties of Lisbon and Amsterdam is the renumbering of the Articles of the Treaty on European Union and of the European Community Treaty, now the Treaty on the Functioning of the European Union. A table of equivalences of the old and the new articles charting both alterations is included in the Online Resource Centre. The book uses the new numbers throughout, but frequently refers to older numbers in brackets.

(f) Internet sources

The most useful website is that of the European Union itself: <www.europa.eu>, on which most of the materials referred to in (a) and (b) may be found. In addition, all the latest developments are also reported there.

Acknowledgments

The most important of the changes to the text for the sixth edition related to the ratification of the Treaty of Lisbon, a major reform of the Treaties, albeit not in the form of the originally envisaged 'Constitution'. For the seventh edition, we have retained the scope of the book and updated the law. We would like to thank Alexis Cooke, Rupert Dunbar, Tony Harris and Clare Williams for the various contributions made to helping with these updates. Alexis Cooke and Justine Stefanelli have a specific credit for the work on the persons chapters. Siri Harris has a specific credit for the competition chapter.

We would also like to express our gratitude to the numerous individuals who have assisted and contributed to the different editions of the book: Vera Sacks, Niamh Moloney, Antonio Bavasso, Nicolas Emiliou, Mark Attew, David O'Keeffe, Jennifer Davis, Rosalind Malcolm, Melanie Baier-Goessl and Tim Sinnamon.

Finally, Margot would like to thank her family, in particular her son David who applied his editorial experience to his reading of the entire text of the first edition, and her husband Christopher, who put up bravely with my mental and physical absences when working on this book in all its editions, with remarkably few complaints. Matthew would like to thank his family and in particular Ian, for all their support and Charlaine Harris for a really excellent series of entertaining books about vampires in Louisiana: the absolute antidote to European Union treaty renumbering headaches.

London
March 2012

New to the 7th edition

- Post-Lisbon developments considered in detail with reference to Eurozone problems and the UK approach to Treaty amendments in the European Union Act 2011 (the 'referendum lock') (Chapters 1 and 2).

- Analysis of EU and international interaction in the fields of the environment (Chapter 15), the increasingly clarified High Representative role (Chapter 3), and the application of international law in the EU courts (Chapter 5).

- Update on Comitology process (Chapter 5).

- New supremacy cases in France and Germany (Chapter 7).

- Consideration of new European Court case law in the field of the Four Freedoms, with increased consideration given to the proportionality principle in the area of the free movement of goods (Chapter 10).

- Extensive consideration of the expansion of the concept of citizenship, in particular by the application of Directive 2004/38 and its interpretation by the European Court (Chapters 12 and 13).

- Consideration of the role played by national courts and the European Court in the area of competition (Chapter 14).

- Consideration of access to justice in the field of environment (Chapter 15).

- Development of the general principle of non-discrimination (Chapters 6 and 16) in further case law on specific forms of discrimination.

Contents

Table of Abbreviations

Throughout this book, a number of abbreviations are used to save space and to make the text more concise:

AG	Advocate General
CFI	Court of First Instance (now General Court)
CFSP	Common Foreign and Security Policy
COR	Committee of the Regions
COREPER	Committee of Permanent Representatives
DG	Directorate General
EC	European Community
ECA	European Communities Act 1972
ECB	European Central Bank
ECHR	European Convention for the Protection of Human Rights and Fundamental Freedoms
ECJ	European Court of Justice
ECR	European Court Reports
ECSC	European Coal and Steel Community
ECtHR	European Court of Human Rights
EEA	European Economic Area
EEC	European Economic Community
EESC	European Economic and Social Committee
EFTA	European Free Trade Association
EMI	European Monetary Institute
EMU	Economic and Monetary Union
EP	European Parliament
ERM II	Exchange Rate Mechanism
EU	European Union
Euratom	European Atomic Energy Community
FCC	Federal Constitutional Court (*Bundesverfassungsgericht*)
GATT	General Agreement on Tariffs and Trade
IGC	inter-governmental conference
IP	intellectual property

MEP	Member of the European Parliament
NATO	North Atlantic Treaty Organisation
OECD	Organisation for Economic Co-operation and Development
OEEC	Organisation for European Economic Cooperation
OJ	Official Journal of the European Communities
QMV	qualified majority voting
SEA	Single European Act
TEU	Treaty on European Union
TFEU	Treaty on the Functioning of the European Union
VAT	Value Added Tax
WTO	World Trade Organisation

Table of Cases

Numerical list of European Cases

Court of Human Rights

National Courts

France

Germany

Table of European Legislation

European Secondary Legislation; Decisions, Directives, Regulations, Opinions

Decisions

Table of Other Legislation

1 Introduction

1.1 Since its inception in 1952, the European Union has come a long way; it has matured and developed from a Community of like-minded states into a Union of a greater diversity of states, with a comprehensive legal system which is increasingly penetrating the national legal systems of Member States. However, the original Community was set up for sound political reasons which since then have undergone profound changes. As a result, the Community, which has now finally become the European Union after the ratification of the Treaty of Lisbon, has developed and has turned into something quite different from the model to which many originally aspired. In the middle of the cold war the founding fathers could have had little idea that the Union would expand in the way it has. From the six original members, the European Union now counts 27 Member States, after 10 more joined in May 2004, and Romania and Bulgaria joined on 1 January 2007. Ten of these 12 states are in Central and Eastern Europe and have discarded their old Communist regimes, turning into democracies with the qualifications to join the Union. The inevitable shift in political base and objectives caused by expansion as well as other factors should always be borne in mind when studying the development of the Union legal system. It will explain why there was a need—and indeed a desire—for creativity in the interpretation of Community law in the early days and at certain levels, interspersed thereafter with periods of caution and reticence at times. The shift can also help to explain some of the interventionist decisions of the Court of Justice of the European Union (CJEU), formerly the European Court of Justice. Union law will, in the end, only work with the cooperation of all the Member States and their national institutions, governments and courts.

1.2 Why was the Community set up, and set up in the way it was? The idea of a 'united Europe' has a long history. 'Europe' was already conceived of as an entity in Greek and Roman times. Roman citizenship is often taken as the inspiration for the modern idea of European citizenship. It was Cicero, himself a lawyer, who claimed that the proudest boast of an individual in the Roman Empire was *civis Romanus sum,* and the aspiration is that one day the European citizen will regard the accolade of European citizenship with the same respect and pride, as Advocate General Jacobs said in Case C–168/91 *Konstantinidis v Stadt Altensteig* (1993): *civis Europeus sum* (see **6.65**). The modern ideal is based on an idea of common civilisation, common origins, a common spiritual heritage and common ways of thinking. Philosophies and spiritual ideas always transcended national borders, as do science, culture, painting, music and so on. In Roman times, in the Middle Ages, and subsequently, free movement of persons was something to which at least educated people were accustomed, but others, too, travelled surprisingly widely. Obstacles to such travel, and to the free movement of goods, date from relatively recently. The concept of a unified Europe has been put into practice on several later occasions to a greater or lesser extent, but it has never endured. Before the twentieth century, however, conquest was generally the driving force behind attempts at unification. The Carolingian Empire under Charlemagne fell apart after his death and the peace of Verdun in 843, although, as the Holy Roman Empire, it continued to exist in one form or another until the beginning of the nineteenth century. Napoleon, too, succeeded for a short time in bringing most of Europe under his authority, and in modern times Hitler partially succeeded, but for an even shorter period. However, the contemporary idea of a united Europe is a different one. In the nineteenth century, Europe saw itself as the centre of civilisation and the major European powers were the most powerful in the world. After the Congress of Vienna in 1815, following the final defeat of Napoleon, these great powers regulated European affairs between them, organising grand European conferences to settle particular questions. It was also a period of development of public international law and European law. Legal rules were established in a variety of fields, e.g. the international status of rivers and the law of the sea, and international public services were developed such as the Universal Postal Union and international conventions on intellectual property. Between the two World Wars a federal movement took root in élite circles, inspired by figures such as Count Coudenhove-Kalergi who, when presiding over the Council of Europe, proposed a European federation in which states would give up part of their sovereignty and who founded a movement called the Pan-European Union, with the French statesman Aristide Briand as the Honorary President.

1.3 Developments towards integration were halted by the conflagrations of the two World Wars in the twentieth century. Even before the outbreak of the Second World War in 1939, but in particular towards the end of the war, the realisation came that European states were no longer the great powers they once were, although this took a long time to be accepted, particularly in Britain. World supremacy was shared by the United States and the Soviet Union. Thus, the contemporary European idea came to be based, first of all, on the wish permanently to prevent conflict between European states. At the beginning of the Second World War, in the face of the threat of German invasion, there had been a plan, proposed by Winston Churchill and the French Prime Minister, Paul Reynaud, for a complete union between France and Britain. This proposal was, however, rejected by the French cabinet and, under the pressure of events, it disappeared without trace. Then, in a speech to the University of Zürich on 19 December 1946, Winston Churchill relaunched the idea of European Union, a Union mainly to be founded on a Franco-German base, and at the Hague Congress in May 1948 the European Movement was founded.

1.4 The first concrete achievement was the founding in 1949 of the Council of Europe, which has its seat in Strasbourg. This organisation included most Western European countries, including the United Kingdom. Turkey also became a member. Many Central and Eastern European countries, including Russia, have now joined. It has no legislative powers but is a consultative body, with an assembly of national members of Parliament and a Committee of Ministers which discusses and adopts resolutions, recommendations and conventions in fields such as education, culture, science, penal establishments, social policy and legal affairs. Probably its greatest achievement is the European Convention for the Protection of Human Rights and Fundamental Freedoms (ECHR), which was originally administered by a Commission and a Court, now merged into a single Court, the European Court of Human Rights (ECtHR). This Convention entered into force in 1953 and has been ratified by the majority of the (now 47) Member States of the Council of Europe; the latest state to join was Montenegro in May 2007. The Treaty of Lisbon now provides in Article 6(2) of the Treaty on European Union (TEU) that the European Union 'shall accede' as a body to the Convention of Human Rights. The process of accession has been started with joint negotiations between the Member States and the two courts, the ECHR and the CJEU, but accession has not yet taken place at the time of writing.

1.5 European economic cooperation first took shape with the need to administer Marshall Plan aid from the United States to Europe. This led to the setting up of the Organisation for European Economic Cooperation (OEEC) in 1948. This soon took on a broader role in the coordination of European economic development and, after the US and Canada joined in 1960, it was renamed the Organisation for Economic Cooperation and Development (OECD). The OECD has no legislative powers but its analyses, statistics and forecasts of economic development in Europe are important, highly valued and influential. However, this was still only an inter-governmental organisation in which no member needed to give up any of its sovereign powers.

1.6 In 1950, the European idea was given an enormous advance by the inspiration of two French statesmen: Jean Monnet, who at the time held no public office, and the French Foreign Minister, Robert Schuman. The Schuman plan was formally submitted by the French Government on 9 May 1950. It consisted of three strands: political, military and economic; but only the economic strand was taken up at that stage. It set goals to be achieved by a functionalist approach, that is, by steadily transferring an ever-increasing number of '*fonctions*' or 'spheres of activity' from national to supranational control. It proposed that the whole of European coal and steel production should be placed under a supranational High Authority with far-reaching powers. Coal and steel were the industries most involved in the process of waging war, providing the raw material and the energy for the arms industry. If these industries could be pooled, it would make it very difficult and eventually impossible for the countries involved to go to war against each other. The United Kingdom's reaction to this plan was cool, and negotiations soon went ahead without it. Although initially only a Franco-German plan, enthusiastic support was received from Italy and the Benelux countries (Belgium, the Netherlands and Luxembourg). In April 1951, the European Coal and Steel Community (ECSC) was established by the Treaty of Paris. The Community consisted of six Member States: France, Germany, Italy and the Benelux countries. The Treaty came into force in July 1952. It was signed for a period of 50 years and expired in July 2002. Its relevant articles and powers were absorbed into the EC Treaty. The governing body was the High Authority under its first President, Jean Monnet. It was endowed with supranational powers and could take binding decisions without first obtaining the consent of the Member States. A Council of Ministers was created side by side with the High Authority, with the balance of power in favour of the latter, and a Common Assembly was set up for consultation, consisting of representatives of the national Parliaments. The Assembly had the power to dismiss the High Authority. There was also a Consultative Committee which advised on impending decisions. The Treaty further instituted a Court of Justice which would ensure the implementation of the Treaty and resulting secondary legislation. The ECSC's supranational powers were considerable: not only did it rationalise coal and steel production, providing major assistance to the coal industry in decline and the conversion of whole regions and their workers to other occupations, it also promoted free trade by prohibiting government subsidies, obstacles to trade, and restrictive practices, imposing fines where appropriate. In addition, it had substantive provisions which are the precursors of those in Community law such as those relating to the free movement of workers. The ECSC represented the high point of supranationality. Although ostensibly set up for a limited purpose, it was inspired by the mood of the times towards integration, federation, and political union in Europe. The preamble to the ECSC Treaty points towards this, stating that the achievement of world peace can only be achieved by creative efforts to counter impending danger.

1.7   Meanwhile, the first steps had been taken towards military cooperation. NATO, with its transatlantic dominance, was established in 1949. In 1952, a European Defence Community Treaty was proposed and signed by France, Germany, Italy and the Benelux countries, but eventually failed to be ratified by the French national assembly. Instead, an organisation with few powers, except advisory ones, was established in Brussels in 1955. This arose out of a Treaty—the Brussels Treaty—designed to continue the alliances formed in the Second World War, signed in 1948, and forming the Western European Union consisting of the six Member States of the original European Defence Community, plus the United Kingdom. Spain, Portugal and Greece then joined, as did a large number of associate members and partners throughout Eastern and Western Europe and, after languishing for many years in the shadow of NATO, it was reactivated with new tasks and a European identity. It is now absorbed into the EU, into what was, until Lisbon, the 'Second Pillar' of the Common Foreign and Security Policy, now in Title V TEU: Articles 21–46.

1.8   The failure of the European Defence Community, and the lack of any progress on the European Political Community, for which a draft statute had been proposed at the same time, led to the realisation that political integration had to be preceded by more sober economic considerations. Thus, aspirations had been scaled down by 1955, when the Messina Conference instructed the Belgian Foreign Minister, Paul-Henri Spaak, to explore possibilities for more comprehensive economic integration. The Spaak Report, presented to an inter-governmental conference in 1956, led to the establishment of the European Economic Community (EEC) and the European Atomic Energy Community (Euratom). The Treaties of Rome, setting up both Communities, were signed on 25 March 1957 and came into force on 1 January 1958. The United Kingdom had taken part in the negotiations for only a very short time and thereafter had no further involvement. Thus, the two Communities were established with the same six members as those of the ECSC. The Communities followed the institutional pattern of the ECSC, but this time, significantly, they were set up for an unlimited duration. Two new institutions were set up for each: a Commission and a Council of Ministers, with the Court of Justice and the Assembly serving all three Communities. The powers of the Commission were less than those of the High Authority. The idea of supranationality had had its day; the presence of General de Gaulle, a firm opponent of federalism, and his vision of '*l'Europe des patries*' (Europe of the nation states) continued to influence and dominate the development of the Communities and contributed to a number of crises in the 1960s, such as that which led to the Luxembourg Compromise in 1966 (see **3.17**).

1.9 After the creation of the EEC, a number of countries which did not wish to, or could not, take part, concluded various types of agreements with the European Community, which was empowered to conclude agreements with non-Member States. These agreements now come under Articles 216, 217 and 218 TFEU. There have been many such types of agreement. Association agreements have been concluded with European and non-European states, the former often as a prelude to their joining the Community. Such agreements would often contain provisions similar to those in the EC Treaty. The European Free Trade Association (EFTA) had been set up in 1960 under the leadership of the United Kingdom, after the United Kingdom had decided not to join the European Community. This consisted of Austria, Denmark, Norway, Portugal, Sweden, Switzerland and the United Kingdom. They were joined later by Finland, Iceland and Liechtenstein. In 1992, an agreement was concluded with the members of EFTA to create a European Economic Area (EEA). This agreement gave those countries access to the internal market and required the acceptance of the *acquis communautaire* (i.e. all the legislation passed and decisions taken by the Community up to the time of accession).

However, even before the Agreement was signed, a number of former EFTA states had applied to join the Community. This happened the year following the entry into force of the EEA in 1994 with Austria, Finland and Sweden. However, Norway voted against joining the Community. Switzerland, an EFTA member, voted in December 1992 against joining the EEA and there are no plans at present for it to apply to join the European Union. A special status for Switzerland has been negotiated. The EEA therefore now consists of Norway, Iceland and Liechtenstein, together with the Member States of the European Union.

1.10 It soon proved necessary to rationalise the three Communities and in 1965 the Merger Treaty, which came into force in July 1967, merged the High Authority and the two Commissions into one body, the European Commission, and provided that the Communities were to be served by one Council of Ministers. Finances were rationalised in 1971, when the financial contributions from individual Member States were replaced by the 'own resources' system. Under this system, agricultural levies, customs duties, and each Member State's share of the Value Added Tax contribution were paid directly to the Community. The Assembly, which had already called itself the European Parliament since 1958, officially became the European Parliament in 1986 in the Single European Act; the first direct elections of Members (MEPs) in the Member States took place in 1979.

1.11 Moves towards political union were never absent for long. A number of reports appeared, such as the Tindemans Report in 1975; the report of the 'Three Wise Men' in 1979; and a joint proposal for union by the German and Italian foreign ministers, Genscher and Colombo, which resulted in a Joint Declaration on European Unity, adopted by the European Council at the Stuttgart Summit in 1983. This was followed by the Spinelli Draft Treaty on European Union, adopted by the European Parliament in 1984. These initiatives, followed by the *Dooge* Report on institutional reform, and the *Adonnino* Report on a People's Europe presented by ad hoc Committees set up by the European Council in Fontainebleau in 1984, contributed to the convening of an inter-governmental conference to look at Treaty revision. The result was the proposal for the Single European Act, which was signed in 1986 and came into force on 1 July 1987. Summit meetings of heads of state or government—a term for ad hoc meetings of heads of state and government meeting not in the Council but at separate informal meetings, which later became increasingly formalised—have taken place throughout the life of the Community and became institutionalised in 1974. The European Council was formally recognised by the Single European Act in 1986 and is now the supreme political authority in the Union, which did not have formal decision-making powers until the Treaty of Lisbon (see below and **Chapter 2**) included the European Council in its list of institutions. European political cooperation, cooperation in foreign policy, grew out of these informal meetings and was first turned into the inter-governmental Pillar on the Common Foreign and Security Policy (CFSP) in the Maastricht Treaty on European Union, before becoming a separate, still largely inter-governmental, part of the Lisbon Treaty on European Union (Articles 21–46 TEU and see **Chapter 3**).

1.12 After the Community had gone through periods of stagnation in the 1970s and 1980s—known as Eurosclerosis—and the impetus towards the creation of a common market seemed to have been lost, the Single European Act (SEA) provided a step towards the revival of the single market project. This had been inspired by Lord Cockfield, the British Commissioner, who drew up a White Paper providing for moves towards a true internal market in 1992. The year 1992 became one of focus for market integration, and the efforts to comply with the deadline, although not entirely successful, nevertheless constituted considerable progress. In 1989, the European Council decided to hold two inter-governmental conferences, on proposals for Economic and Monetary Union (EMU) and on political union. As a result, the Maastricht Treaty on European Union (TEU) was adopted in 1992, and came into force in 1993. The main achievement of that Treaty was the provision for Economic and Monetary Union which entered its third stage for 11 out of the 15 Member States of the Union on 1 January 1999. Its currency, the euro, became legal tender in the 11 Member States, joined by Greece a few months later. It had a mixed reception at that time, but although it has had its ups and downs its effect on the Union has been momentous. Although Sweden held a referendum to join the euro, the vote was negative. In the United Kingdom, a referendum to join the euro was planned after the Labour Party came to power in 1997, as soon as the Chancellor of the Exchequer indicated that the time was right to do so. Having indicated several times, however, that this time had not yet come, the proposal was quietly dropped and at present it looks most unlikely that there will be entry into the EMU by the United Kingdom any time soon. Denmark, also, has stayed outside the euro. Of the new Member States, Slovenia was the first to join, followed by Cyprus, Malta and Slovakia, who fulfilled the joining criteria, and most of the others are keen to join. However, the near-collapse of the European financial system in 2008, with long-term effects for many years to come, has caused some countries to scale down their aspirations. At the time of writing (December 2011) 10 Member States of the Union are outside the Eurozone. However, in spite of many difficulties, which have led to a relaxation of some of the criteria concerning national debt ratios, no country which is a member of the Eurozone has so far been compelled to leave.

1.13   The Maastricht Treaty also officially adopted the name 'European Union' as an umbrella term governing all three Pillars. This Treaty, in its turn, provided for an inter-govern-mental conference to be held in 1996. This conference terminated in Amsterdam in June 1997 and resulted in the Treaty of Amsterdam, which was ratified in 1999 and itself provided for enlargement tied to institutional reform. This was to be achieved by the next Treaty, prepared by another inter-governmental conference (IGC). This IGC led to the adoption of the Treaty of Nice in December 2001. Its main elements concerned enlargement and a profound reform of the two inter-governmental Pillars. The ratifi-cation process was stalled for a time because of a negative referendum vote in Ireland which seemed to have been caused by Ireland's increased national contributions to the Community budget because of enlargement, and the provisions in the Second Pillar on Foreign and Security Policy concerning a European army, which were seen as a threat to Irish neutrality. After elections in Ireland which returned the government with an increased majority the decision was taken to hold a second referendum in October 2002. The Irish people this time voted 'yes' overwhelmingly, thus setting the stage for the start of the enlargement process as the last country to ratify the Treaty. The Nice Treaty duly entered into force on 1 February 2003.

As Nice could not reach agreement on institutional reform, the Treaty provided that a Convention would be called in order to prepare a Constitution for the European Union. This Convention opened in The Hague in March 2002 under the chairmanship of former French President Valérie Giscard d'Estaing. A draft constitutional Treaty was presented to the Summit Meeting of the European Council in Thessaloniki in Greece in June 2003. The intention was that the draft Constitution would then be approved by the summit meeting of heads of state or government in December 2003 in Brussels. However, no agreement could be reached there and it was only in the following June 2004 that agreement was finally reached in Rome. Initially, there were hopes that the ratification process would proceed without too many hitches. The Commission had proposed a timetable for ratification which put the most positively minded countries first, with the United Kingdom last, as it was hoped that a positive vote by all the other

Member States would have a beneficial influence on the United Kingdom's voters. This ambition was not achieved, however. After the first 'big' Member State, Spain, had predictably voted in favour, the referendum vote took place in France on 29 May 2005. The result of the vote was a resounding 'no'. This was followed by an even more astonishingly resounding 'no' in the Netherlands, on 2 June 2005, with an even larger percentage against. A period of stagnation, if not near-paralysis, followed whilst searches for another solution went on. Eventually, in June 2007, during the German Presidency, a new draft Treaty was adopted after relatively little controversy and on 13 December in Lisbon the new Treaty, which had become known as the 'Reform Treaty' was signed by all Member States and received the name 'Treaty of Lisbon'. It was hoped that this Treaty would be ratified swiftly by all Member States, especially as very few Member States proposed to have a referendum this time. This was the case in both France and the Netherlands. In the United Kingdom the government under Prime Minister Tony Blair also decided to seek approval for ratification in Parliament without resorting to a referendum—something which had been promised in its party manifesto—and this approval was duly given. However, in June 2007 Ireland, which under its constitution was obliged to hold a referendum, unexpectedly voted no again, as it had done in respect of the Nice Treaty (see this paragraph above). This was mainly due to internal problems concerning defence and the fear that strict Irish abortion laws might be compromised, but there was also concern over the proposed abolition of the principle of one European Commissioner per country, thus fuelling fears that, in the absence of an Irish Commissioner, Ireland would lose most of its influence in the European Union. This was exacerbated by a poor 'Yes' campaign by a complacent Irish government and by an energetic 'No' campaign by the opponents of the Treaty. After various meetings of the European Council had tried to meet with these objections, a Declaration was finally adopted in June 2009, in which the principle of one Commissioner per country was restored. Another referendum in Ireland, with a much better organised 'Yes' campaign, succeeded in obtaining a majority for the 'Yes' vote. Meanwhile, in June 2009, the German Federal Constitutional Court had finally given the go-ahead for Germany's ratification, deciding that the new Treaty just kept within the boundaries of acceptable transfer of competences and sovereignty. The last obstacle was raised by the Czech President, whose refusal to sign was finally overcome by the Czech Republic's joining the Protocol regarding the interpretation of the Charter of Fundamental Rights, now made binding under Article 6 Lisbon TEU (see further **Chapter 6**) which already applied to the United Kingdom and Poland. The Treaty of Lisbon thus was finally ratified in November 2009 and entered into force on 1 December 2009.

1.14 The undoubted economic success of the European Union (as it is now called) has attracted more and more members. After the accession of the United Kingdom, Ireland and Denmark in 1972, Greece, Spain and Portugal joined, partly also for political reasons. Since the collapse of the Soviet Union and Communism after 1989 and the unification of Germany in 1990, a large number of countries in Central and Eastern Europe applied to join the Union. At the Copenhagen summit in December 2002 the Member States decided that Poland, the Czech Republic, Slovakia, Hungary, the Baltic States Estonia, Latvia, and Lithuania, as well as Slovenia and the islands of Cyprus and Malta would be invited to join in the middle of 2004 and accession took place in May 2004. Bulgaria and Romania followed in 2007. A number of states have since applied for membership: agreement with Turkey and Croatia was reached late in 2005 to open negotiations, which, particularly in the case of Turkey, may last for a long time. Negotiations with Croatia have now been successfully closed and accession is expected on 1 July 2013. Iceland has also applied and negotiations are under way. The most recent applicants are Albania, Bosnia and Herzegovina, Montenegro, Serbia, Kosovo and the former Yugoslav Republic of Macedonia. However, applicants will need to overcome a number of obstacles, such as major political objections in a number of Member States and problems concerning their human rights protection. Thus, the Union may grow further, eventually to well over 30 states.

1.15 The Community, transformed into the Union, has now been in existence for nearly 60 years. It has contributed to peace, stability and prosperity in Europe, and there is no doubt that Europe might look very different today if there had not been a Union in its present form. It was born out of the wish never to have war again between major powers in Europe, coupled with the perceived need to achieve self-sufficiency in the provision of food, and these goals must be said to have been attained. War between Member States would be truly unthinkable today and the Common Agricultural Policy has certainly achieved the aim of self-sufficiency, although it has many other flaws. However, goals and objectives have changed and it is more difficult today than it was in the 1950s and 1960s to identify what stage the European idea has reached, and in which direction it should be moving. Theories of functionalism, and later of neo-functionalism, have tried to attribute different reasons and motives for the creation of the Community. Although in the early days of the Community the aspirations of many were strongly focused on 'ever closer union' it was probably never realistic to aspire to a united Europe along the model of the United States. The consensus has grown that such total unification on a federalist model is not the way forward for Europe. The failure of the Constitutional Treaty and the conscious efforts to propose a Treaty without any of the trappings of a Constitution, simply another set of amendments to the Treaties already in existence, seem to show this as well. The accession of a considerable number of small countries with economies which are behind those of the wealthier 'older' members has also contributed to the changing face of the Union. This 'widening' of the Union has undoubtedly happened at the expense of the 'deepening' desired by many of the older Member States. It is necessary to allow countries at different stages of development a much greater flexibility within the confines of the Union, whilst adhering to its basic principles. Nevertheless, the momentum of developments will inevitably lead to an 'ever closer union'. This has become more apparent recently with the advent of the crisis in the Eurozone, concerning the countries which have joined the euro, which number 17 at the time of writing. There is no consensus in the European Union as to how this crisis is to be resolved, and even the break-up of the Eurozone has been mentioned, although it is more likely that Eurozone Member States will need to move towards a much tighter fiscal Union (see further **2.41**). There is a real prospect of a 'two-tier' European Union, with countries outside the Eurozone (including the UK) moving at a different pace of progress than those within. The original idea of General de Gaulle, who spoke of '*l'Europe des patries*' (the Europe of nation states) at a press conference in May 1962, may thus be a more realistic objective.

FURTHER READING

Douglas-Scott, S., *Constitutional Law of the European Union* (Harlow: Longman, 2002) ch 1.

Duchêne, F., *Jean Monnet: The First Statesman of Interdependence* (New York and London: Norton, 1995).

Pinder, J., *The Building of the European Union* (Oxford: OUP, 1998).

Rosas, A. and Armati, L., *EU Constitutional Law: an Introduction* (Oxford: Hart Publishing, 2010) ch 2.

2 The constitutional base of the Union

SUMMARY

- ECSC Treaty (1952)
- EEC and Euratom Treaties (1957)
- Merger Treaty (1965)
- Accession of new members in 1972, 1980, 1986, 1995, 2004 and 2007
- Single European Act (1986)—progress towards the internal market and 1992
- Treaty on European Union—Treaty of Maastricht (1993)
- Treaty of Amsterdam (signed 1997, entered into force May 1999)
- Treaty of Nice (adopted December 2001, entered into force 1 February 2003)
- The Treaty of Lisbon (adopted December 2007, entered into force 1 December 2009)
- Structure and content of the Treaties

2.1 There are, in fact, several treaties which together represent the primary law of the European Union; its constitutional base. The Treaty of Paris founding the European Coal and Steel Community (ECSC) in 1952 was the very first Treaty which founded the Community. It was inspired by the ideals of Robert Schuman and Jean Monnet, and the wishes of the Member States, in particular France and Germany, to do away with the rivalries of the two industries which used the raw materials which produced the weapons of war: coal and steel. The Member States were prepared to give up their powers to a great extent to regulate those industries. This Treaty gave the Community a number of institutions, in particular a High Authority, which was charged with the task of applying the Treaty, having been endowed with supranational powers by the Treaty. It also established an Assembly, a Council of Ministers and a Court of Justice. (See also **1.6**.)

2.2 As the memory of war receded and economic concerns and states' self-interests became more pronounced, the need was felt for further European cooperation in the wider economic field. There were, even at that time, those who aspired to greater political union, but the Treaty which was eventually signed in 1957, the Treaty of Rome, established a European Economic Community (the EEC Treaty) which was built on economic objectives. At the same time a Treaty founding a European Atomic Energy Community (Euratom) provided for the pooled control of the peaceful use of nuclear power. Both these Communities were run by a Commission as their administrative body. All three Communities had one European Assembly (later the European Parliament) and one Court of Justice in common. The High Authority and the two Commissions were merged into one European Commission by the Merger Treaty in 1965.

2.3   In 1972, the first enlargement of the Communities took place through the Treaties of Accession of Denmark, Ireland and the United Kingdom. The next enlargement came in 1981, with the accession of Greece, after it had divested itself of the dictatorial regime of the colonels. This was followed in 1986 by the accession of Spain and Portugal, which had both discarded their dictatorship regimes. In 1995, there was the accession of Austria, Finland and Sweden. Norway, which had signed a Treaty of Accession in 1972 but was prevented from joining after a negative vote in a referendum, repeated the exercise in 1994, when it again signed a Treaty of Accession but was again barred from joining by a negative referendum vote.

The period up to the Single European Act 1986

2.4   Ever since the European Community's beginnings, periods of enthusiasm and frantic activity have alternated with periods of 'coasting', or even sometimes virtual stagnation. After the initial thrust in the years after 1957, disillusionment set in, together with a growth in awareness of national identity and importance. In part, this was because the initial primary aim of the Community, the prevention of war between the partners, appeared to have been achieved, and past rivalries were replaced with the common enemy of the cold war. This made countries aware of a wider global threat and of a need to maintain a close relationship with the United States.

2.5   Although the customs union had been completed ahead of the deadline in 1969, gaps existed in the Common Market because of the prevalence of so-called non-tariff barriers which acted as obstacles to trade between Member States. At this stage quotas and tariffs had been abolished, but in practice the existence of differing regulatory and fiscal regimes at national levels seriously hampered intra-Community trade. For example, there were physical barriers in the form of frontier posts, and there were technical barriers in the form of differing product standards. Although there were moves in the direction of economic and monetary union, a number of obstacles held up the move to the next stage of political union.

• *Unanimity* The first obstacle was an institutional one. In 1965 the transitional period to allow Member States gradually to move towards a customs union was coming to an end, and this entailed moves to qualified majority rather than unanimous voting in the Council. Following a disagreement on the financing of the Common Agricultural Policy, the French Government operated an 'empty chair' policy in the Community for a period, during which no French representatives attended Community meetings. In 1966 the 'Luxembourg Compromise' solved this crisis. The compromise, which did not have a definite legal status, has continued to exist and has been given legitimacy, first by the Treaty of Amsterdam and now by the Treaty of Lisbon, with a Declaration no 7 referring to arrangements for qualified majority voting (QMV) (see **3.16**). Drawn up for the benefit of France, it provided that, in cases where a vital interest of a country was involved, even if the Treaty provided for majority voting, in fact unanimous voting should be preferred. France wished any discussions to be continued until such unanimity had been achieved. This resort to unanimity led to repeated delays in progress and to stagnation in decision-making, particularly in respect of the free movement rules.

- *Oil crisis* In 1973–74 the energy crisis hit the Community hard, and triggered recession in Europe. Member States were more concerned with dealing with internal economic conditions than forging ahead with European union. A symptom of this protectionism was that many Member States used regulatory provisions, e.g. product standards, to prevent access to national markets by goods from other Member States.

- *Enlargement* With the advent of the first three new Member States (Denmark, Ireland and the United Kingdom), followed by Greece in 1981, by Spain and Portugal in 1986, by Austria, Finland and Sweden in 1995 and by 12 more states in 2004 and 2007—the Community (now the Union) has had to adapt. The accession of new members caused difficulties in terms of achieving unanimity in Council meetings. More Member States means that more diverse interests are at stake.

Internal market proposals

2.6 As a result of German/French proposals in 1985, a White Paper on completing the internal market was drawn up by Lord Cockfield, one of the two British Commissioners. It stated that to achieve the internal market, physical, technical and fiscal barriers (i.e. non-tariff barriers) would have to be abolished within the Community. It set a deadline of 1992 for the removal of a great number of different barriers. It was made clear that institutional changes were needed. The European Council stated in 1985 that 'no important economic development could be achieved unless the way the institutions functioned was changed'. The *Dooge* and *Adonnino* reports were drawn up in response to this (see **1.11**).

The Single European Act 1986

2.7 Gradually, growing dissatisfaction among Member States with the progress towards the single market, which was one of the main objectives in the Treaty of Rome, created the need for a Treaty revision. The Single European Act (SEA) 1986, which came into force on 1 July 1987, introduced more specific single market objectives, to be achieved by the increased use of qualified majority voting. A new procedure with greater involvement of the European Parliament was introduced in the form of the cooperation procedure (now abolished and replaced by the codecision procedure) and the European Parliament was given a power of veto over accession of new Member States and the conclusion of association agreements (see Articles 217 and 218 TFEU). New areas of competence for the Community were introduced or spelt out in more detail, relating to social policy, economic and monetary policy, research and technology and environmental policy. A Title on inter-governmental cooperation in foreign policy was added. The SEA also provided for the eventual creation of a Court of First Instance (CFI) to take over some of the jurisdiction of the European Court of Justice.

The internal market

2.8 The Community aimed at achieving not just a Common Market, but also an internal market. The concept of the internal market was introduced by the SEA and is described in Article 26 TFEU (ex Article 14 EC) as 'an area without internal frontiers in which the free movement of goods, persons, services and capital is ensured in accordance with the provisions of the Treaties'. The deadline for completion of the internal market was 31 December 1992.

The SEA supplemented the EEC Treaty by adding Article 100a (now Article 114 TFEU). This provided that certain measures harmonising or approximating Member States' laws affecting the functioning or establishment of the internal market could be passed in Council by a qualified majority rather than by unanimity, as was the case before.

Article 114 TFEU is a broad provision—it covers all measures which are necessary in order to achieve the 'objectives set out in Article 26'. The SEA thus considerably speeded up decision-making. However, Article 115 TFEU remains the vehicle for those measures which do not fall within the internal market definition of Article 26. The SEA began a massive programme of approximation of laws by way of harmonisation of national laws, and, increasingly, by 'mutual recognition', which constituted a less strict approach than harmonisation.

2.9 The SEA, in spite of many weaknesses which were rightly criticised, nevertheless provided a fresh push towards mainly economic integration, the primary objective being that the completion of the internal market would bring advantages to the Community in the form of increased trade. It also made some institutional reforms, such as the introduction of the cooperation procedure (now abolished), which strengthened the position of the European Parliament.

2.10 The deadline of 31 December 1992 for completion of the internal market was not met. By 1992, 95 per cent of the internal market proposals had been adopted by the Community but less than half had been transposed into the national law of the Member States. One of the thorniest problems, the abolition of border controls, was not solved until later, and even then not completely. However, the process of harmonisation continued. With the creation of the European Economic Area, the internal market experienced great expansion.

The Treaty on European Union (the Maastricht Treaty) 1993

2.11 The SEA was always intended as a step in the process towards further Treaty revision. An inter-governmental conference (IGC), which was held in Maastricht in the Netherlands, concluded with the signing of the Treaty on European Union (TEU) in February 1992. Although Denmark first rejected the Treaty in a referendum; after the meeting of the European Council of heads of state or government in Edinburgh in 1992 added protocols to the TEU containing concessions to Denmark on economic and monetary union and defence, Denmark ratified with a narrow majority in a second referendum, as did France. In the United Kingdom, the Maastricht Bill survived a number of very close votes in the House of Commons, as well as a constitutional challenge in the High Court (*R v Secretary of State for Foreign and Commonwealth Affairs, ex p Rees-Mogg* (1993)). Germany was the last country to ratify, after a constitutional challenge which was rejected, but which created a much greater awareness in Germany of the problems connected with transfer of powers from the Member State to the Community (*Brunner v European Union Treaty* (1994), see also **7.82**). The Maastricht Treaty on European Union thus entered into force in November 1993. It changed the name of the EEC Treaty to the EC Treaty (the Treaty establishing the European Community). The major achievement of the Maastricht TEU was without doubt the introduction of Economic and Monetary Union (EMU) (see further **2.41**).

2.12 The TEU (or 'Maastricht Treaty') was again intended as a stage in the process towards further integration. It provided for a further IGC 'to examine Treaty amendments'. These concerned, in particular, an institutional revision of the Treaty, of the powers of the Council, the Commission, the Parliament and the Court of Justice. France and the United Kingdom were keen to preserve or extend the Council's powers and to curb those of the Commission. Germany, in particular, wanted the Parliament to be stronger.

The Treaty of Amsterdam (signed June 1997, entered into force 1 May 1999)

2.13 After an inter-governmental conference held in Amsterdam had approved a new amendment to the Treaties the outcome was a compromise, with a number of matters not resolved.

On qualified majority voting (see **3.16**) no agreement was reached as to the distribution of votes. A Protocol to the Treaty of Amsterdam tied the questions of institutional reform, of the number of Commissioners (albeit capped at 20), and of the re-weighting of votes in qualified majority voting in the Council, to the admission of new Member States, and this had to be resolved at least a year before the admission of new members. The legislative procedures were somewhat simplified and the codecision procedure, in which the European Parliament has an equal say with the Council and may block the adoption of legislation, was extended and almost entirely replaced the cooperation procedure. (The cooperation procedure has since been abolished by the Treaty of Lisbon.) The United Kingdom had wanted a review of the jurisdiction of the European Court of Justice, but nothing was done in this respect. There was considerable reform of the 'Third Pillar' and the first steps to enlargement were announced. The United Kingdom 'opt-out' from the Social Chapter was reversed in Amsterdam and the Agreement on Social Policy attached as a Protocol to the 'Maastricht Treaty' was included in the EC Treaty.

2.14   In spite of serious endeavours to come to an agreement in Amsterdam, the question of changing the institutions and procedures was not satisfactorily resolved and had therefore to be re-examined by the post-Amsterdam inter-governmental conference preparing the Nice Treaty (see **2.17**). A major topic of discussion was to be the enlargement of the European Union to include other Member States, particularly those from Central and Eastern Europe.

2.15   Subjects which were not discussed included economic and monetary union (see **2.41**) and the Common Agricultural Policy.

2.16   The Treaty of Amsterdam was signed in June 1997. After the successive amendments of the Single European Act and the Maastricht Treaty on European Union, the Treaty texts had become unwieldy and difficult to understand. Some of the articles in the original Treaties had become spent and needed to be deleted. The Amsterdam Treaty undertook a renumbering of the articles both in the Treaty on European Union and in the EC Treaty. Thus, many Treaty Articles changed their numbering at this point. After the entry into force of the Lisbon Treaty a further renumbering had to be undertaken (see below at **2.35**).

The Nice Treaty (adopted December 2001, entered into force 1 February 2003)

2.17   In December 2001 an inter-governmental conference convened in Nice. The Treaty of Nice, agreed in December 2001, came into force in February 2003. The issue of enlargement (see **2.14**) had been tied in the Protocol to the Amsterdam Treaty to the reaching of agreement on institutional issues. First, it determined the number of votes per country under the QMV system. The total number of QMV votes was increased considerably, but efforts were made to make a better distribution of votes according to the size of population of the various states. This took account of the fact that most of the new Member States are small, or very small countries, with the exception of Poland (and, later, Romania). Secondly, the number of seats in the European Parliament would be increased to a total of 732 when all 12 Member States (the 10 in 2004, plus Bulgaria and Romania in 2007) had joined. Again, the distribution of votes was made more proportionate to the populations of the respective countries (see **Chapter 3** for more detail).

2.18 The Nice Treaty made a number of other changes. No major changes were made in the institutional balance but particularly in the case of the European Court of Justice (ECJ) and the Court of First Instance (CFI) considerable changes were made in order to streamline and speed up the functioning of the courts (see also **Chapter 4**). QMV was extended to more areas, although the more contentious ones, such as those concerning taxation and immigration, were left to unanimous voting.

At Nice, the Charter of Fundamental Rights was welcomed by Proclamation. It had been adopted in November in Biarritz by a joint Proclamation by the Council, the Parliament and the Commission. However, it had no binding force. See further **Chapter 6**.

2.19 The question of the membership of the Commission was also settled (**3.21**). However, many questions remained unsettled. This is why a Declaration on the future of the Union was annexed to the Treaty in Nice, calling for a deeper and wider debate on the future of the European Union.

2.20 Subsequent to this a European Council meeting in Laeken near Brussels decided to set up a Convention to discuss the future of the Union, to look at the status of the Charter of Fundamental Rights, proclaimed in Nice as a non-binding instrument (see also **6.58**), and to prepare a Constitutional document for the enlarged Europe to settle a 'more precise' delimitation of powers between the Union and the Member States, reflecting the principle of subsidiarity. The Convention, presided over by the former French President Valérie Giscard d'Estaing, submitted its final draft for what was now called a Constitutional Treaty to a summit in 2003. The draft dealt in particular with institutional reform, the reform of legislative instruments and the incorporation of the Charter of Fundamental Rights. The document was viewed as being too liberal by a number of Member States, although in some countries, particularly in the United Kingdom, it was considered to be too much tied to a, in its view, outdated social model. However, the ratification process stalled after negative votes in referenda held in France and the Netherlands in May and June 2005. In the period following the rejection of the draft Constitutional Treaty, further ratification moves were suspended, including in the United Kingdom and a virtual paralysis gripped the Community for a time. The Treaty of Nice remained in force. In June 2007 the European Council decided to search for a compromise which would take account of the fact that the ratification process had been completed in two-thirds of Member States, and of the reservations of the remaining one-third. As the new proposals focused on technical matters and on the solution of the institutional problems, political objections to a new Treaty (as opposed to a Constitution) and any differences of opinion of a political nature were quickly overcome. This enabled the European Council to reach unanimous agreement in October 2007.

The Treaty of Lisbon (signed December 2007, entered into force 1 December 2009)

2.21   After the rejection of the Draft Constitutional Treaty, the Treaty of Lisbon (also referred to as the Lisbon Treaty) was signed on 13 December 2007 in Lisbon. It initially received the name of 'Reform Treaty', but this was later changed to the Treaty of Lisbon or the Lisbon Treaty.

This time, a referendum was held in only one of the Member States, Ireland. This referendum was held in June 2008 and rejected the proposed Treaty by a substantial majority. This appeared to be due to various factors, a poor 'Yes' campaign by a complacent government, a fear of unwanted Irish involvement in defence matters, and a fear that strict Irish abortion laws could be affected by the new Treaty. There were also fears that the Irish voice would be lost in the Commission if Ireland no longer had its own Commissioner. Eventually, a Declaration was adopted by the European Council in December 2008 which took into account the Irish concerns and a new referendum, held in October 2009, this time voted overwhelmingly in favour of the Treaty. Ratification had proceeded in most of the other Member States, including the United Kingdom. The German Constitutional Court received a number of constitutional complaints, from individuals and from a political party. In a lengthy judgment in June 2009 it rejected some of the complaints, but ruled that the act implementing the Treaty was unconstitutional. A new bill was introduced and received a favourable vote soon after that, which enabled Germany to ratify. The last country to ratify was the Czech Republic, whose President refused to sign until the Czech Republic had been added to a Protocol limiting the effect of the Charter of Fundamental Rights, which had been made binding by the Lisbon Treaty, in respect of the United Kingdom and Poland. (See further **6.59**.)

2.22   The Treaty of Lisbon largely reproduces the Constitutional Treaty but has done away with all the elements which gave that draft treaty the character of a constitution. It is divided into the Treaty on European Union (TEU) and the Treaty on the Functioning of the European Union (TFEU).

The European Community (EC) is abolished and all references to EC are now references to the EU (European Union). The three pillar structure is abolished, the 'Third Pillar' is absorbed into the TEU and the TFEU and the 'Second Pillar' (Common Foreign and Security Policy) is a separate part of the TEU (Articles 21–46), still largely intergovernmental). The European Atomic Energy Community (Euratom) continues to exist—apart from an institutional linkage to the European Union—as an independent international organisation.

2.23   The Preamble of the Treaty of Lisbon does not make reference to the failed draft Constitutional Treaty but establishes a direct line between the Treaty of Lisbon and the Treaties of Amsterdam and Nice. Unlike the draft Constitutional Treaty, the Treaty of Lisbon expressly renounces the constitutional concept which consisted in repealing all existing treaties and replacing them by a single text called 'Constitution'. The Treaties are merely amended, and the concepts on which the amended Treaties are based reflect the renouncing of the constitutional concept. Terminology commonly used in respect of states and used in the draft Constitutional Treaty is abandoned. The term 'Constitution' is not used, the proposed 'Union Minister for Foreign Affairs' is now called 'High Representative of the Union for Foreign Affairs and Security Policy', and the proposed terms 'law' and 'framework law' are not maintained, unlike the less symbolically charged term 'decision'. The codecision procedure, however, is renamed 'ordinary legislative procedure' and is distinguished from a 'special legislative procedure'. Acts adopted according to a legislative procedure are referred to as 'legislative acts'. The symbols of the European Union—flag, anthem, motto, currency and Europe day— are not mentioned. However, 16 of the 27 Member States state in a Declaration that they will continue to use the symbols. The supremacy of Union (formerly Community) law over national law is for the first time embodied in a text, but in the form of a Declaration accompanied by explanations by the Council Legal Service. The European Union replaces and succeeds the European Community and it attains legal personality (Article 47 Lisbon TEU).

2.24   The Charter of Fundamental Rights of the European Union in its revised version of 12 December 2007 (OJ C 303/1) is given the same legal value as the Treaties (Article 6(1) Lisbon TEU), and the Union's unwritten fundamental rights, contained primarily in the Court of Justice of the European Union case law (see further **Chapter 6**), continue to apply as general principles of Union law (Article 6(3) Lisbon TEU). In addition, Article 6(2) Lisbon TEU commits the European Union to accede to the European Convention for the Protection of Human Rights and Fundamental Freedoms.

2.25   The national Parliaments 'contribute actively to the good functioning of the Union' (Article 12 Lisbon TEU). According to a Protocol on the role of national Parliaments in the European Union attached to the Lisbon Treaty, draft legislative acts of the European Union must be made available to the national Parliaments eight weeks before they are placed on the Council's agenda. Using the so-called early warning system described in the Subsidiarity Protocol, any national Parliament or any chamber of a national Parliament may, within this eight-week period, state in a reasoned opinion why it considers that the drafts in question do not comply with the principle of subsidiarity (Article 6 of the Subsidiarity Protocol). Reasoned opinions, however, only establish an obligation to review the drafts where they represent a certain proportion of all the votes allocated to the national Parliaments (Articles 7(2) and 7(3) of the Subsidiarity Protocol). Any national Parliament or a chamber thereof may bring an action under Article 263 TFEU to have an act declared void via their Member States if they deem a legislative act incompatible with the principle of subsidiarity (Article 8 of the Subsidiarity Protocol).

National Parliaments also take part in the political monitoring of Europol and Eurojust (Article 12(c) Lisbon TEU; Article 88(2), Article 85(1) TFEU), and in the so-called bridging procedure, a Treaty amendment procedure generally introduced by the Treaty of

Lisbon, they are entitled to make known their opposition to a Treaty amendment proposed by the Commission within six months after their being notified (Article 48(7); Article 81(3) TFEU). Opposition by a single national Parliament suffices to make the proposed Treaty amendment fail.

2.26 There are now seven Institutions: the European Council and the European Central Bank have been added to the institutional framework (see Article 13 TEU).

2.27 The Treaty of Lisbon also reforms institutions and procedures (see **Chapter 3** for further detail). The codecision procedure, in which the European Parliament acts in tandem with the Council, is streamlined, renamed 'ordinary legislative procedure' and becomes the normal legislative procedure. (Article 14(1) TEU; Article 289(1) TFEU). The cooperation procedure is abolished. The consultation procedure and the assent procedure are united under the term 'special legislative procedure' which only applies in specific cases provided for by the Treaties (Article 289(2) TFEU). The European Parliament also has to give consent in the conclusion of certain international agreements (Article 218(6)(a)(v) TFEU).

2.28 In addition, the European Parliament decides on the draft budget in tandem with the Council (Article 14(1) TEU; Article 314 TFEU) and exercises functions of political control. It elects the President of the Commission upon a proposal by the European Council by a majority of its component members (Article 14(1), Article 17(7) TEU).

The allocation of seats in the European Parliament (see Article 14(2)) may not exceed 750, 'plus the President', with a minimum threshold of six members per Member State, and no Member State being allocated more than 96 seats.

2.29 The Treaty of Lisbon introduces the office of the (permanent) President of the European Council, to be elected by the European Council, by a qualified majority, for a term of two-and-a-half years (Article 15(5) TEU) (see further **Chapter 3**). The Belgian Herman van Rompuy was elected to this post.

The Treaty declares qualified majority voting in the Council as the norm (Article 16(3) TEU), like the ordinary legislative procedure (see further **3.14**).

From 1 November 2014, the Commission will consist of a number of members corresponding to two-thirds of the number of Member States, unless the European Council, acting unanimously, decides to alter this number (Article 17(5) TEU; see also Article 244 TFEU). However, a decision could be taken, 'in accordance with the necessary legal procedures', to the effect that the Commission will continue to include one national of each Member State (see Presidency Conclusions of the Brussels European Council of 11 and 12 December 2008 in Brussels, EU Bulletin 12–2008, I (4), at (2)). This Declaration was adopted in order to counter Irish concerns after the loss of its first referendum, so that Ireland would not lose its own Commissioner for the time being. The Commission's delegated law-making is also given a more structured character. (See **Chapter 3**.)

The Treaty further introduces the position of the 'High Representative of the Union for Foreign Affairs and Security Policy'. This function unites membership of the Commission as its Vice-President with its function representing the Council (see further **Chapter 3**). The UK Commissioner Baroness Ashton is the first holder of this post which has a term of office of five years.

2.30   The Court of Justice of the European Communities is renamed the Court of Justice of the European Union. It still has very limited jurisdiction in the area of the common foreign and security policy. However, the Court now has in principle jurisdiction in respect of the area of freedom, security and justice, which is no longer a separate 'Pillar' but has been absorbed into the TFEU. The Court of First Instance has been renamed the General Court, and the specialised panels are now specialised courts. (See further **Chapter 4**.)

2.31   Amendment of the Treaty is now possible, not just by the previous method of an intergovernmental conference followed by full ratification according to Member States' constitutional requirements (see Article 48(4) TEU) but, for less important amendments, according to a simplified revision procedure, approved by unanimous decision of the European Council.

Amendments according to the simplified revision procedure require a unanimous decision by the European Council, which enters into force after having been approved by the Member States in accordance with their respective constitutional requirements (Article 48(6) TEU). The application of the simplified revision procedure is restricted to amendments of Part Three of the Treaty on the Functioning of the European Union relating to the internal policies and action of the European Union (Article 48(6) TEU). The amendments may not increase the competences conferred on the Union in the Treaties.

2.32   Article 50 TEU introduces the right for each Member State to withdraw from the Union.

2.33   Article 11(4) provides for a Citizens' Initiative where one million citizens may sign a petition inviting the Commission to submit a proposal on any area of EU competence.

2.34   Summary of some of the main institutional provisions of the Treaty of Lisbon:

- TEU and Part Six TFEU Institutional and Financial Provisions
- Commission: Article 17 TEU, Articles 244–250 TFEU
- European Parliament: Articles 13 and 14 TEU, Articles 223–234 TFEU
- European Council: Article 15 TEU, Articles 235 and 236 TFEU
- Council: Article 16 TEU, Articles 237–243 TFEU
- High Representative for Foreign Affairs and Security Policy, Article 18 TEU

- Court of Justice, the General Court and specialised courts: Article 19 TEU, Articles 251–281 TFEU
- Court of Auditors: Articles 285–287 TFEU
- European Central Bank: Articles 282–284 TFEU
- CFSP Title V TEU: Articles 21–41 (Foreign policy); Articles 42–46 (Security and Defence)
- Final Provisions of TEU: Articles 47–55: Article 47 (legal personality); 48 (Treaty amendment by ordinary or simplified revision procedure); 49 (application for membership); 50 (withdrawal from membership).

2.35   The Treaty of Lisbon not only did away with the three pillar structure, but also rearranged and renumbered the Treaty to a considerable extent. This book will throughout refer to the new numbering contained in the consolidated text, with the numbers of the Articles in the Nice Treaty in brackets where appropriate. A table of equivalences can be found on the Online Resource Centre at <http://www.oxfordtextbooks.co.uk/orc/horspool_humphreys7e/>. This means that Treaty articles may now have three different numbers, when referred to in the case law, depending on whether the case was decided before the Amsterdam Treaty or before the Lisbon Treaty. For example: the article prohibiting discrimination on grounds of nationality was Article 6 in the Maastricht Treaty, changed to Article 12 in the Amsterdam Treaty, and is now Article 18 (as amended) in the TFEU.

Structure and content of the Treaties

2.36   The Treaty on European Union concluded in Maastricht in its basic form, consisted of general framework articles and three so-called 'Pillars'. The First Pillar contained the European Community Treaties, i.e. the European Coal and Steel Community (ECSC) Treaty (now expired), the Euratom Treaty and the EC Treaty. The Amsterdam and Nice Treaties preserved the basic three Pillar structure of the TEU. In the main, they preserved the inter-governmental nature of, in particular, the Second Pillar, and, to a lesser extent, the Third Pillar.

2.37   The Second Pillar contained provisions on a common foreign and security policy; the Third Pillar contained provisions on cooperation in the fields of freedom, security and justice. The Third Pillar was given the name Justice and Home Affairs in Maastricht, and was later considerably amended and renamed Police and Judicial Cooperation in Criminal Matters.

2.38   The Treaty of Lisbon abolished the separate pillars, but preserved the TEU as a separate framework Treaty. Articles in the TEU are often to be considered in combination with Articles in the TFEU, which puts more detail on the outline Articles in the TEU. A number of the provisions which were included in the Nice EC Treaty are now contained in the TEU. The Common Foreign and Security Policy is included in the TEU, but as a separate Title V (Articles 21–46). The Preamble of the TEU is expanded from that of the Nice Treaty, notably by a paragraph referring to the cultural, religious and humanist inheritance 'from which have developed the universal values of the inviolable and inalienable rights of the human person ...'. As amended by the Treaties of Amsterdam, Nice and Lisbon it starts with common or framework provisions, Title I, Articles 1–8 (ex Articles 1–7), which define the principles of the Union. They speak of ever closer union among the peoples of Europe (Article 1), as did the Treaty of Rome, and adds 'in which decisions are taken as openly as possible and as closely as possible to the citizen'. A new Article 2 refers to the Union's foundation on universal values common to the Member States 'in a society in which pluralism, non-discrimination, tolerance, justice, solidarity and equality between women and men prevail'. The objectives set in Article 3 (ex Article 2 as amended) include: the promotion of peace and the well-being of the Union's peoples; more extensive development of the cooperation in justice and home affairs contained in the Maastricht TEU to make the Union 'an area of freedom, security and justice ...'; establishment of an internal market with sustainable development based on balanced economic growth and price stability; achievement of a highly competitive social market economy aiming at full employment and social progress; protection of the environment; promotion of scientific and technological advance; the combating of social exclusion and discrimination; and protecting solidarity between generations and the rights of the child. It also refers to respect for cultural and linguistic diversity and to the safeguarding of Europe's cultural heritage. Respect for the same values, adding those of fair trade, are also referred to in Europe's relations with the wider world, as is the strict observance and development of international law including respect for the principles of the United Nations Charter. The establishment of economic and monetary union, with the euro as its currency, is included. The principle of conferral, i.e. the transfer of powers (competences) from the Member States to the Union is explicitly mentioned (see further Article 5 TEU) (ex Article 5 EC Treaty). The Maastricht Treaty introduced a citizenship of the Union in the EC Treaty in Articles 17–22 EC, now Articles 18–25 TFEU (see further **Chapter 13**). The TEU now adds a Title II (Articles 9–12) with 'Provisions on Democratic Principles' setting out the rights of EU citizens, which include a Citizens' Initiative in Article 11(4) TEU and Article 24(1) TFEU, and Article 12 TEU setting out the way in which national Parliaments may be involved in the 'good functioning' of the Union. Further details are contained in Protocol no 1 on the Role of National Parliaments. All these objectives are to be achieved whilst having regard to the principle of subsidiarity.

2.39 A change made in Nice concerns Fundamental Rights. Article 7 of the TEU, inserted by the Treaty of Amsterdam, which provided for a declaration by the European Council of a 'serious and persistent breach of fundamental rights' by a Member State followed by a possible suspension of that Member State, was supplemented in Nice by a preventive clause whereby upon a proposal by one-third of the Member States, the Commission, the Parliament, or the Council, acting by a four-fifths majority and with the assent of the European Parliament may 'determine that a clear *risk* exists of a Member State committing a serious breach of fundamental rights'. Recommendations may then be addressed to such a Member State (see further **6.50** and **6.51**).

The principles of subsidiarity and proportionality

2.40 The principle of subsidiarity is given a prominent place in Article 5 TEU (ex Article 5 EC). It first refers to the limits of Union competences, which are governed by the principle of conferral (see further **Chapter 5**) and then states in Article 5(3) TEU:

> Under the principle of subsidiarity, in areas which do not fall within its exclusive competence, the Union shall act only if and in so far as the objectives of the proposed action cannot be sufficiently achieved by the Member States, either at central level or at regional and local level, but can rather, by reason of the scale or effects of the proposed action, be better achieved at Union level.

For the first time, action by Member States at central, *regional or local* level is referred to (see further **Chapter 6**). It should be noted that subsidiarity does not apply to areas which fall within the exclusive jurisdiction (or 'competence') of the Union. These areas have grown since the inception of the Treaties and concern such matters as the Common Agricultural Policy, competition rules and the common commercial policy. As more Union action is taken in fields such as a common transport policy and the environment, these matters too have and will come increasingly under the exclusive jurisdiction of the Union. Subsidiarity will only apply to areas in which there is a shared or concurrent competence between the Union and the Member States.

The Treaty includes Protocol 2 on the application of the principles of subsidiarity and proportionality which sets out to establish the principles more clearly, but does not alter the substance of Article 5 (see further **6.29**).

Economic and monetary union

2.41 Probably the most important element introduced in the EC Treaty in Maastricht, which was included unaltered in the subsequent Treaties, is the creation of an economic and monetary union (EMU). The achievement of a single currency was stated to be the ultimate aim of EMU. In an implementing decision by the Council, the single currency was named the 'euro'. A timetable was set for the achievement of EMU in three stages by 1 January 1999. Strict convergence criteria were laid down with which Member States had to comply before they could proceed to the next stage of EMU. The ratio of total government debt to gross domestic product (GDP) should not exceed 60 per cent and the ratio of annual government deficit to GDP should not exceed 3 per cent. Other criteria concern the achievement of a high degree of price stability, apparent from a low rate of inflation, avoidance of currency fluctuation within the exchange rate mechanism (ERM) for at least two years, and sustainable and durable economic convergence. The third stage was set to start on 1 January 1999 for those countries which 'fulfil the necessary conditions for the adoption of a single currency', i.e. those complying with the convergence criteria. The countries which were deemed to comply with the criteria were approved by a summit meeting of heads of state and government on 2 May 1998. Of the 15 Member States, 11 were deemed to comply with the criteria. Greece did not comply and the United Kingdom and Denmark had obtained 'opt-outs' in protocols annexed to the Treaty on European Union, which released them from the obligation to enter the third stage, although they could choose to do so. Sweden was also found not to qualify and took the decision not to proceed with its application to join EMU. Thus, on 1 January 1999, 11 Member States entered the third stage of the single currency and introduced the euro. Greece was not able to meet the entry criteria at that time, but then entered the 'eurozone' in January 2001. In January 2002 the euro was introduced as banknotes and coins in the 12 Member States which had joined the euro. The success of a smooth physical introduction, completed by the middle of February 2002, helped to fuel a short rally in the value of the euro, which had fallen steadily since its non-physical introduction in 1999. But where the euro had languished, particularly in its exchange rate to the dollar, at well below parity, it now experienced a revival and rose to parity and above. However, hopes that particularly the United Kingdom might change its negative attitude to the currency did not take hold in the UK population and in its government, too, caution ultimately prevailed. In June 2003 the British Chancellor of the Exchequer reported that the five economic tests, which he had set in October 1997 as a condition for considering a referendum on entry, had not all been achieved. Negative votes on the Draft Constitutional Treaty in May and June 2005 limited the prospect of any UK referendum on the matter yet further. Today, particularly with the advent of the crisis in the eurozone, there is a general political consensus in the UK that the country should not join. At the moment, therefore, after the accession of the new Member States there are 17 countries which are members of the 'eurozone' and 10 which are not. New Member States all intended to join the EMU, as under the Copenhagen criteria it is a condition of entry for states acceding to the EU that they be able to fulfil the requirements for monetary union within a given period of time. The timing for their entry however, has become very much more uncertain, as an ever increasing number of members of the eurozone are struggling to deal with their debts. Similarly, those countries who are currently negotiating for entry will also commit themselves to taking the euro as their currency in the years following their accession.

2.42   Article 8 EC provided for the establishment of a European System of Central Banks and of a European Central Bank (ECB). This happened after the decision on the third stage had been taken. Before that, preparations for EMU were made by the European Monetary Institute (EMI) (Article 117 EC, now repealed). Germany, after the judgment of the Federal Constitutional Court in *Brunner v European Union Treaty* (1993) (see **7.82**), needed the consent of its own Parliament before it could proceed to the third stage. The German *Bundestag* had stipulated that Germany's move to the third stage should depend on its own assessment of the attainment or failure of the conditions laid down for that stage. It gave its consent in April 1998 when the Central Bank took over from the EMI and the latter disappeared.

The sovereign debt crisis

2.43 The future of the eurozone was thrown into doubt by a sovereign debt crisis that started at the end of 2009 and worsened in 2010 and 2011. Sovereign bond market pressures brought into focus the perilous condition of the finances of several Member States. The European Financial Stability Facility (EFSF) was set up in 2010 by the 27 Member States to provide assistance to eurozone states in difficulty. Bailouts were organised by the EU in conjunction with the International Monetary Fund (IMF) for Greece (May 2010), Ireland (November 2010), and Portugal (May 2011). Greece was struggling with a budget deficit of 10.5 per cent of GDP in 2010 and a total debt of 142.8 per cent and would not be able to refinance its bonds when they became due and, therefore, a bailout was necessary. Portugal and Ireland, too, had heavy debts and deficit ratios.

Worries of contagion caused the bond yields of Italy (2010 deficit 4.6 per cent, debt 119 per cent) and Spain (deficit 9.2 per cent, debt 60.1 per cent) to approach the 7 per cent level in November 2011, considered to be the point at which the situation would become impossible without a bailout. Political upheavals caused by the economic turmoil led to Technocrats being appointed to lead both the Greek and Italian governments.

The EFSF did not have enough money to bail out all of the eurozone states in danger, and there was no agreement forthcoming on how to increase its size. Germany was steadfastly opposed to allowing the European Central Bank to use its potentially unlimited firepower to purchase the bonds of Member States in sufficient quantities to stabilise the markets.

The continuing lack of a solution caused a global stock market crisis in the second half of 2011. There was also a general crisis in confidence and the global economy appeared to be heading for another recession. After several initiatives and various meetings during 2011 that achieved very little in the way of market stabilisation, the solution found at a meeting of the European Council in December 2011 came in the form of a proposal for a Fiscal Compact whereby participating Member States would submit to a requirement for national budgets to be in balance or surplus, and to a system for surveillance with penalties for states in breach. The precise terms of the Fiscal Compact were agreed at a summit of European leaders on 30 January 2012. A new or amended EU Treaty could not be agreed on because the United Kingdom had vetoed such a proposal . The UK will not participate in the Fiscal Compact, and neither will the Czech Republic. At the time of writing financial market confidence has still not been restored and it is not clear what the outcome to the sovereign debt crisis will be. However, a new three year liquidity facility provided by the ECB to Eurozone banks seems to have resulted in lowering sovereign borrowing costs for Italy and Spain to below the crisis levels of November 2011.

Changes in legislative procedures

2.44 The Maastricht TEU introduced a number of changes in the voting system in the Council of Ministers (renamed 'the Council'). It increased the number of articles subject to QMV. It introduced a new voting procedure, the codecision procedure (Article 294 TFEU (ex Article 251 EC)). (The cooperation procedure introduced by the SEA was preserved at that time but has since been abolished.) The codecision procedure was intended to strike a more even balance of power between the institutions and, in particular, gave the European Parliament the power ultimately to reject legislation (see **5.41**). There is still, however, no opportunity for the Parliament to introduce legislation on its own or to force through a measure against the wishes of the Council. The Nice Treaty provided in a limited number of articles for the possibility of joint legislative initiative by the Parliament and the Council. In fact, quite some use has been made of this possibility (e.g. Article 225 TFEU (ex Article 192(2) EC)). The Amsterdam Treaty reduced the number of main legislative procedures involving the European Parliament to three: assent, codecision and consultation. The Lisbon Treaty has now further simplified the procedures. It has abolished the cooperation procedure. The codecision procedure has been renamed the 'ordinary legislative procedure'; and extended to a number of Treaty provisions previously subject to either the assent, cooperation or consultation procedure and introduced into a number of new Treaty provisions. Assent and consultation are now referred to as a 'special legislative procedure'. (See further **5.41-5.46**)

Fields of competence

2.45 A number of new fields of competence for the Community (now Union) were introduced by the Maastricht Treaty and further extended by the Treaties of Amsterdam, Nice and Lisbon. These include culture, public health, education, consumer protection, trans-European networks, industry and development cooperation, neighbourhood policy, services of general economic interest, energy, tourism, civil protection and administrative cooperation. Furthermore, the content of existing competences of the European Union have been extended, being incorporated from the Treaty establishing the European Community into the Treaty on the Functioning of the European Union. This concerns in particular the provisions of the common commercial policy, that extend the content of competence to foreign direct investment and the nature of competence to trade in services and the commercial aspects of intellectual property.

2.46 Articles 17–22 EC (now Articles 20–25 TFEU), introduced in Maastricht, established a citizenship of the Union. Although regulations and directives had considerably expanded the scope of the free movement articles, certain categories of persons remained excluded. In fact, the articles have been expansively interpreted by the Court of Justice and the concept of citizenship has gained ground, slowly but surely, as something above and beyond the status of an economically active person. After the Court had, as a first step, given the article a broad interpretation in Case C–85/96 *Maria Martinez Sala v Freistaat Bayern* (1998), a major step was taken in Case C–413/99 *Baumbast* (2002), where the direct effect of Article 18 (now Article 21 TFEU) was recognised by the Court of Justice. Since then both case law and Directive 2004/38 have pushed forward the development of these rights. The TEU now no longer refers to 'nationals', but always to 'citizens' and has an additional title setting out rights of citizens: Title II (Articles 9–12) with 'Provisions on Democratic Principles' (see further **Chapter 13**).

2.47 The Common Foreign and Security Policy (CFSP) (formerly the Second Pillar) grew out of a desire for more effective cooperation in foreign and defence policy. A start had been made by the Single European Act which established European political cooperation (EPC), which was no more than a loose inter-governmental agreement. The CFSP put cooperation on a more organised basis. Title V TEU, Articles 23–46 (ex Articles 11–28 TEU) sets out the provisions for this cooperation. Articles 21 and 22 of Title V contain general provisions on external action by the Union on the international scene which includes Title II of the TFEU concerning the common commercial policy. The action is to be 'guided by the principles which have inspired its own creation...' and Article 21 sets out in detail the principles and objectives of such action. Article 24 TEU and Article 2(4) TFEU reiterate the statement in previous treaties that the Union 'shall have competence...to define and implement a common foreign and security policy, including the progressive framing of a common defence policy'. Specific rules and procedures apply that 'will not affect the existing legal basis, responsibilities, and powers of each Member State in relation to the formulation and conduct of its foreign policy' (Declaration no 14 Concerning the Common Foreign and Security Policy). Decisions are taken by the European Council and the Council acting unanimously (Article 31(1) TEU) and adoption of legislative acts is excluded. The Court of Justice does not have jurisdiction except to monitor compliance under Article 40, which concerns 'restrictive measures against natural or legal persons' and the review of legality of certain decisions (see Article 275 TFEU). Via the special bridging clause in Article 31(3) TEU, however, the European Council may unanimously adopt a decision stipulating that the Council may act by a qualified majority in cases other than those referred to in Article 31(2) TEU. Decisions having military or defence implications are excluded (Article 31(4) TEU). The European Parliament is merely consulted and informed concerning essential issues and developments; it is to be ensured that its views are duly taken into consideration (Article 36 TEU).

2.48 The common security and defence policy is an integral part of the Common Foreign and Security Policy (Articles 42 to 46 TEU). The Council is granted powers to adopt decisions relating to missions 'in the course of which the Union may use civilian and military means' (Article 43(1) and 43(2) TEU). An obligation of mutual assistance is introduced for the Member States. In the case of armed aggression on the territory of a Member State, 'the other Member States shall have towards it an obligation of aid and assistance by all the means in their power, in accordance with Article 51 of the United Nations Charter' (Article 42(7) TEU). For the first time the Treaty refers to the permanent structured cooperation of Member States, which aims to contribute to making the common security and defence policy more flexible (Articles 42(6) and 46 TEU; Protocol no 10 on Permanent Structured Cooperation).

2.49 Provisions on enhanced cooperation were introduced in Nice and are now contained in Title IV Article 20 TEU, subject to the limitations laid down in this Article, and in Articles 326 to 334 TFEU which contain the detailed procedure involving the Commission and the High Representative of the Union for Foreign Affairs and Security Policy. The Council will adopt a decision only as a last resort, 'when it has established that the objectives of such cooperation cannot be attained within a reasonable period by the Union as a whole, and provided that at least nine Member States participate in it'. However, the basic inter-governmental structure of the CFSP has remained unchanged.

The area of freedom, security and justice

2.50 This was one of the areas in which change was clearly needed after the Maastricht TEU and the inter-governmental conference made considerable progress in this area. This resulted in the Treaty of Amsterdam making some major structural changes, and the pillar was renamed 'provisions on police and judicial cooperation in criminal matters'. In the Maastricht Treaty cooperation in this area had been divided between:

- Title VI of the TEU concerning inter-governmental cooperation, with minimal involvement of the EC institutions, and agreements taking the form of Conventions.

- The Schengen agreement, which was concluded outside the structure of the EC, under which Member States, as well as some non-Member States, are committed to the gradual abolition of checks at common borders.

- Some articles in the EC Treaty concerning freedom of movement, such as an internal market for the free movement of persons, and a visa regime for nationals of third countries.

2.51 The Amsterdam Treaty brought about changes affecting the systems of decision-making to be applied, the jurisdiction of the Court of Justice, the role of the European Parliament and the right of the Commission to play an active part.

Article 3(2) TEU now provides:

> *The Union shall offer its citizens an area of freedom, security and justice without internal frontiers, in which the free movement of persons is ensured in conjunction with appropriate measures with respect to external border controls, asylum, immigration and the prevention and combating of crime.*

The whole of the area is now part of the TFEU and falls under the general institutional framework.

2.52 Title V of the TFEU thus comprises Chapters 1–3 (Articles 67–81 TFEU, ex Articles 61–69 EC), which had already become part of the 'First Pillar' in the Amsterdam Treaty, and Chapters 4 and 5: Judicial cooperation in criminal matters, and Police Cooperation (Articles 82–89 TFEU, ex Articles 31 and 32 Nice TEU) which had remained within the 'Third Pillar'.

2.53 The first two chapters of Title V (Articles 67–80) concern the free movement of persons, asylum and immigration. They establish mechanisms for the establishment of an area of freedom, security and justice and are mainly governed by the normal institutional structure of the Union and the Union method. They cover policies of common interest concerning asylum, external border controls, immigration, conditions of entry and movement, as well as conditions of residence, access to employment and right to family reunion of third country nationals.

2.54   The Schengen Convention on the gradual abolition of checks at the common borders was originally concluded in 1990 between five Member States of the Union (the Benelux countries, France and Germany) and came into force on 26 March 1995 with two additional members, Spain and Portugal. Other Member States then joined, plus Iceland and Norway, so that only the United Kingdom, Ireland and Denmark were not members of the Convention. In spite of great difficulties and criticisms, it was nevertheless regarded as a useful model for the development of immigration policies under the Third Pillar and was given Treaty status. The Schengen agreement was incorporated into the Treaty, as indicated in the 'Schengen Protocol' annexed to the Treaty of Amsterdam. However, this applies only to the Schengen signatories, although the non-signatories accept the Protocol's provisions which allow the signatories to make use of the Union institutional framework. Two Protocols concerning the position of the United Kingdom and Ireland, and one concerning the position of Denmark, define and limit the impact of the provisions on those countries. As regards the United Kingdom and Ireland, these Protocols keep them out of the Schengen *acquis*, but with 'opt-in' provisions to specific initiatives, if the countries should so wish. The Convention itself therefore lost its *raison d'être* after incorporation of the Schengen *acquis*.

2.55   In the field of judicial cooperation in civil matters, the Council, on a proposal from the Commission and after consulting the European Parliament, may adopt a decision determining those aspects of family law with cross-border implications which may be the subject of acts adopted by the ordinary legislative procedure, such proposal to be notified to the national Parliaments, which can make known their opposition to the proposal within six months (Article 81(3) TFEU).

2.56   The field of police and judicial cooperation in criminal matters was the only one remaining in the former 'Third Pillar' after the Treaties of Amsterdam and Nice, and has now been absorbed into the TFEU. Title V of the TFEU now comprises the entire field of justice and home affairs, which in the Treaty of Maastricht was still entirely subject to inter-governmental cooperation.

In the context of judicial cooperation in criminal matters, the Treaty of Lisbon grants powers to the European Union to adopt 'minimum rules' in the area of the law of criminal procedure 'to the extent necessary to facilitate mutual recognition of judgments and judicial decisions and police and judicial cooperation in criminal matters having a cross-border dimension' (Article 82(2) TFEU). The European Union is granted powers to establish by means of directives 'minimum rules concerning the definition of criminal offences and sanctions in the areas of particularly serious crime with a cross-border dimension resulting from the nature or impact of such offences or from a special need to combat them on a common basis' (Article 83(1) TFEU). The list of serious crimes, which ranges from terrorism, trafficking in human beings and sexual exploitation of women and children, illicit drug trafficking, illicit arms trafficking, money laundering, corruption, counterfeiting of means of payment and computer crime to organised crime, is not exhaustive and may be extended by a decision of the Council acting unanimously after obtaining the consent of the European Parliament (Article 83(1) TFEU). The European Union may also act in all areas which have 'been subject to harmonisation measures' insofar as 'the approximation of criminal laws and regulations of the Member States proves essential to ensure the effective implementation of a Union policy' (Article 83(2) TFEU).

The Treaty allows for the extension of the competences of Eurojust, an agency of the Union with legal personality, with a view to coordinating national investigating and prosecuting authorities in cases of serious cross-border crime (see Council Decision of 28 February 2002 setting up Eurojust with a view to reinforcing the fight against serious crime, OJ 63/1). Eurojust may be given the task of initiating and coordinating criminal investigations, while formal procedural action remains reserved to the national prosecuting authorities (Article 85 TFEU). Moreover, the Council may establish a European Public Prosecutor's Office emanating from Eurojust in order to combat crimes affecting the financial interests of the Union which would be responsible for investigating and prosecuting such crimes and bringing them to judgment before the national courts (Article 86 TFEU).

In respect of police cooperation, Europol, the cross-border police office, may be given the power in an ordinary legislative procedure, in addition to the power it already had of the collection, storage, processing, analysis and exchange of information (see Article 3(1) of the Convention of 26 July 1995 on the establishment of a European Police Office, OJ C 316/2), to coordinate, organise and implement investigative and operational action jointly with the Member States' competent authorities or in the context of joint investigative teams (Article 88(2) TFEU). Any such operational action by Europol must, however, be carried out in liaison and in agreement with the authorities of the Member States whose territory is involved. The use of coercive measures remains the exclusive responsibility of the competent national authorities (Article 88 TFEU).

Special procedural provisions apply to the exercise of competences. In different fields of policy, decisions in the Council must be adopted unanimously (see Article 77(3), Article 81(3), Article 86(1), Article 87(3) and Article 89 TFEU).

2.57 Protocol no 36 on Transitional Provisions provides that in respect of police and judicial cooperation in criminal matters acts adopted before the entry into force of the Treaty of Lisbon will remain subject to the inter-governmental rules, i.e. minimal involvement of the Commission and limited jurisdiction by the Court of Justice only for those Member States who have accepted it. This period expires five years after the entry into force. The United Kingdom then has arrangements for a further 'opt-out'. (See, for detail, Article 10 (4) and (5) of Protocol no 36.)

Agreements with non-Member States

2.58 The European Union is empowered under Articles 216–218 (ex Article 300 EC) to conclude agreements with non-Member States and international organisations. There have been many such types of agreement. Association agreements have been concluded with European and non-European states, the former often as a prelude to their joining the Community. Such agreements would often contain provisions similar to those in the EC Treaty. In 1992, an agreement was concluded with the members of EFTA (the European Free Trade Association) to create a European Economic Area (EEA). This agreement gave those countries access to the internal market and required the acceptance of the *acquis communautaire*. However, even before the Agreement was signed, a number of former EFTA states had applied to join the Community. This happened the year following the entry into force of the EEA in 1994 with Austria, Finland and Sweden. However, Norway, as we have seen, voted against joining the Community. Switzerland, an EFTA member, voted in December 1992 against joining the EEA and will, consequently, not join the Union in the foreseeable future, although this remains an open question. A special status for Switzerland has been negotiated. The EEA now consists of Norway, Iceland and Liechtenstein, together with the Member States of the European Union.

Enhanced cooperation

2.59 Enhanced cooperation, which is outlined in Article 20 TFEU, allows a group of Member States within the European Union to cooperate more closely than is provided for by the rules applying to all Member States. Examples of such cooperation have existed for a long time, e.g. the Benelux agreement, the Social Protocol, EMU, and agreements such as Schengen, which were or are completely outside the Treaties. Title III, Articles 326–334 TFEU (ex Articles 11 and 11a EC) set out the conditions under which such closer cooperation may be achieved. It would only be possible in areas not subject to exclusive Union competence and should not undermine the internal market, social and territorial cohesion, nor constitute a barrier to or discrimination in trade or distort competition in respect of Member States (Article 326 TFEU).

2.60 Substantial changes to enhanced cooperation were agreed at Nice and at Lisbon. Its essential characteristics remain largely unchanged. It can only be undertaken as a last resort and must be open to all states. The minimum number of states required to establish enhanced cooperation is nine. Such a decision should only be taken by the Council, when it has become clear that the Union as a whole will not be able to achieve the objectives pursued.

2.61 Article 1 of the TEU provides that the new stage in the process towards ever closer union is one:

> *…in which decisions are taken as openly as possible and as closely as possible to the citizen.*

Several articles try to counteract the criticism that decision-making in the Union is undemocratic and lacks transparency. Article 15 TFEU (ex Article 255 EC as amended) provides for access to documents originating from Union institutions, bodies, offices and agencies, whatever their medium, for both Union citizens and other natural or legal persons residing or registered in a Member State. The public have access to meetings of the European Parliament and of the Council when considering and voting on a legislative act.

FURTHER READING

Barrett, G., '"The King is dead, long live the King": The recasting by the Treaty of Lisbon of the provisions of the Constitutional Treaty concerning national parliaments' (2008) *European Law Review* 66 et seq.

Craig, P., *The Lisbon Treaty: Law, Politics and Treaty Reform* (Oxford: OUP, 2010).

Curtin, D., 'The constitutional structure of the Union: a Europe of bits and pieces' (1993) 30 *Common Market Law Review* 17.

Dashwood, A., 'The constitution of the European Union after Nice: law-making procedures' (2001) 26 *European Law Review* 216.

Ehlermann, C. D., 'Differentiation, flexibility, closer cooperation: the new provisions of the Amsterdam Treaty' (1998) 4 *European Law Journal* 246.

Gaja, G., 'How flexible is flexibility under the Amsterdam Treaty?' (1998) 35 *Common Market Law Review* 855.

Herdegen, M., 'Maastricht and the German Constitutional Court' (1994) *Common Market Law Review* 235–249.

Lipsius, J., 'The 1996 Inter-governmental Conference' 20(3) *European Law Review* 235–249.

Nugent, N., 'The deepening and widening of the European Community: recent evolution, Maastricht and beyond' (1993) *Journal of Common Market Studies* 311.

Pescatore, P., 'Some critical remarks on the Single European Act' (1987) 24 *Common Market Law Review* 9–18.

SELF-TEST QUESTIONS

1   In what respects does the European Union come closest to being a federation and in what respects is it clearly not a federation?

2   What is meant by the statement that 'the EEC comprises a new legal order' and where was it made?

3   Discuss the reasons for the adoption of consecutive Treaty amendments and their contributions, if any, to the process of European integration.

4   To what extent is the EU legal order compatible with a 'multi-speed Europe'?

3 The institutions of the Union

SUMMARY

This chapter deals with the institutions of the Union and with associated bodies. The institutions of the Union are:

- The European Council
- The Council
- The Commission
- The European Parliament
- The Court of Justice of the European Union and the General Court
- The Court of Auditors
- The European Central Bank

We also discuss:

- The Economic and Social Committee
- The Committee of the Regions
- The European Investment Bank
- The Luxembourg Accords and the Ioannina Compromise

Introduction

3.1 According to Article 13 TEU (ex Article 7 EC) the Union has seven institutions:

- the European Council (Articles 13 and 15 TEU, Articles 235 and 236 TFEU);

- the European Parliament (Articles 13 and 14 TEU, Articles 223 and 224 TFEU (ex Articles 189–201 EC));

- the Commission (Article 17 TEU, Articles 244–250 TFEU (ex Articles 211–219 EC));

- the Council (Article 16 TEU, Articles 237–243 TFEU (ex Articles 202–210 EC));

- the Court of Justice of the European Union and the General Court (including Judicial Panels) (Article 19 TEU, Articles 251–281 TFEU (ex Articles 220–245 EC));

- the Court of Auditors (Articles 285–287 TFEU (ex Articles 246–248 EC)), elevated to a fully fledged institution by the Maastricht TEU;

- the European Central Bank (Articles 282–284 TFEU).

Each of these institutions has powers specifically assigned to it by the Treaty and 'shall act within the limits of powers conferred on it by this Treaty' and practise 'mutual sincere cooperation'.

There are a number of other bodies established:

- by the Treaties: e.g. the Economic and Social Committee (Article 13(4) TEU and Articles 301–304 TFEU (ex Articles 7(2) and 258–262 EC)) and the Committee of the Regions (Article 13(4) TEU and Articles 305–307 TFEU (ex Articles 7(2) and 263–265 EC)); the European Investment Bank, the EU's long-term lending and regional development bank (Articles 308 and 309 TFEU (ex Articles 9, 266 and 267 EC)); the Economic and Financial Committee (Article 134(2) TFEU (ex Article 114(2) EC)); the European Social Fund (Articles 162–164 TFEU (ex Article 146–148 EC)); the Committee of Permanent Representatives (Article 240(1) TFEU (ex Article 207(1) EC)); the Committee of Inquiry (Article 226 TFEU (ex Article 193 EC)); the Employment Committee (Article 150 TFEU (ex Article 130 EC)); or

- in pursuance of the Treaties: e.g. the European Environmental Agency (Regulation 1210/90).

3.2 An institution can 'act', that is take generally binding decisions. The other bodies, on the other hand, operate in specific fields and have either a purely advisory role or take decisions which are not generally binding.

3.3 The constitutive Treaties (ECSC, EEC and Euratom) provided that each of the three European Communities would be served by separate institutions. However, the Convention on Certain Institutions Common to the European Communities (1957), which came into force at the same time as the EEC and the Euratom Treaties, provided for a single Assembly and a single Court of Justice for the three Communities. A further step towards rationalisation was taken by the conclusion of the so-called 'Merger Treaty' (1965) which came into force in July 1967. The 'Merger Treaty' established the 'Council of the European Communities' which replaced the Special Council of Ministers of the ECSC, and the EEC and Euratom Councils of Ministers, and the 'Commission of the European Communities' which replaced the ECSC High Authority and the EEC and Euratom Commissions. With regard to each Community, however, the basic provisions regarding the composition, powers and jurisdiction of each of the institutions are provided for by the relevant Treaty; thus, their functions and powers differ to some extent. The ECSC Treaty expired in July 2002 and its relevant provisions were absorbed into the EC Treaty (as it then was). The Euratom Treaty continues to exist as a separate Treaty to the Treaty of Lisbon. Reference will be made below to the Articles in the Treaty of Lisbon, consisting of the Treaty on European Union, TEU, and the Treaty on the Functioning of the

European Union, TFEU, with the equivalent Articles in the Treaty of Nice in brackets where appropriate.

3.4 The unity of the institutions has been reinforced by the TEU. Article 13 TEU (ex Article 3(1) Nice TEU) provides that 'the Union shall have an institutional framework'. In other words, the EU will be served by a single set of institutions which will act to the extent that they are given the power to do so by the TEU (see Articles 4 and 5 TEU (ex Articles 3 and 5))). This is called the principle of conferral, as set out in Article 5 TEU. The single institutional framework aims at providing coherence and continuity between the EU's various activities.

3.5 After the coming into force of the Maastricht TEU (1 November 1993) the 'Council of the European Communities' renamed itself the 'Council of the European Union'. The 'Commission of the European Communities' renamed itself the 'European Commission'. Following the Lisbon Treaty, the Council of the European Union is simply referred to as 'the Council' (not to be confused with the European Council— see **3.7**) and the Court of Justice now calls itself 'the Court of Justice of the European Union' (CJEU).

3.6 The inter-governmental conferences preparing the Treaties of Amsterdam and Nice did not manage to resolve satisfactorily the question of institutional reform. However, this reform was comprehensively undertaken in the Lisbon Treaty (initially appropriately named the Reform Treaty).

The European Council

3.7 During various periods of stagnation and difficulty in the Community, heads of state and government have met at summit conferences in order to reset the political agenda. These meetings became a regular feature in 1974, when it was decided that regular summit meetings of heads of state or government and their foreign ministers would be held, although without any legal basis in the Treaty. Initially, these meetings did not include the President of the Commission, but this soon changed, and in 1986 the Single European Act enshrined the European Council in Article 2. Article 13 TEU now includes the European Council as an institution and Article 15 TEU sets out its functions. Articles 235 and 236 TFEU provide for the European Council voting system, which is by qualified majority. The European Council is now subject to the jurisdiction of the Court of Justice of the European Union, but only in respects of acts which produce legal effects vis-à-vis third parties. Article 15 TEU states that the European Council shall provide the Union with the necessary impetus for development and define general political priorities and directions. The President of the Commission is a member and one other Commissioner is entitled to attend. The High Representative of the Union for Foreign Affairs and Security Policy takes part in its work (see further **3.12**). Although previously it did not have general decision-making power, notable decisions include the decision to set up the European Monetary System (EMS) and the decision concerning Denmark taken at the 1992 Edinburgh summit (see **2.11**). Political decisions taken by the European Council were always generally followed up in the form of Community legislation. The political power of the European Council was always clearly considerable, and its meetings are widely reported and publicised. However, under the Lisbon Treaty the European Council still does not exercise legislative functions.

The President of the European Council

3.8 The Treaty of Lisbon introduces the office of the (permanent) President of the European Council, elected by the European Council, by a qualified majority, for a term of two-and-a-half years that can be renewed once only (Article 15(5) TEU). The President of the European Council prepares and chairs meetings of the European Council, to be held every six months, or special meetings if required. After each of those meetings he presents a report to the European Parliament. He also drives forward its work, and ensures the external representation of the Union on issues concerning its Common Foreign and Security Policy 'at his level' and 'without prejudice to' the powers of the High Representative of the Union for Foreign Affairs and Security Policy. The office of the President of the European Council is compatible with other European functions, but not with national office (Article 15(6) TEU). The Belgian Herman van Rompuy was elected as the first President in January 2010.

The Council

3.9 The Council is the legislative arm of the European Union. It was created in the Treaty of Rome as the Council of Ministers and is now 'the Council' of the European Union. It is important to note that it should not be confused with the 'European Council' which is a separate institution of the Union and which does not legislate. The Council, by contrast, has the task of taking the final decision on, and of carrying out, the proposals submitted to it by the Commission under the TEU and the TFEU and of acting on an inter-governmental basis under the Common Foreign and Security Policy (CFSP) where decisions are taken by the European Council and the Council acting jointly, usually by unanimity (Article 31 TEU, ex Article 23 TEU).

3.10 Although legally there is just one Council, its composition and name depend on the subject matter of its deliberations. Thus there is an Agricultural Council; a Council of Ministers of Economic Affairs and Finance, known as 'ECOFIN'; a Home Affairs Council; an Environment Council, and so on. The different configurations in which the Council meets are contained in a list adopted by the European Council by qualified majority (Article 236 TFEU). Different arrangements apply to the General Affairs Council which prepares and ensures follow-up meetings of the European Council. The Foreign Affairs Council elaborates the Union's external action (Article 16(6) TEU). The

Council consists of representatives of Member States at ministerial level, one representative per Member State, who are authorised to commit their governments (Article 16(2) TEU). This phrase was added by the Maastricht TEU amendment to the EC Treaty (as it then was) in order to make decision-making in the Council more effective and to avoid the delays which arise if representatives have to refer back to their home governments before they can take a decision. It also allows federal countries like Germany, Belgium and Spain to be represented by Ministers of the *Länder*, of the three Belgian autonomous provinces, and of the autonomous Spanish regions. In areas within their competence, the same applies to the devolved UK regions of Scotland and Wales. The meetings of the Council were generally not public, and the secrecy of the deliberations has been the subject of much criticism, viewing this as a contributing factor to the democratic deficit in the Union. Some improvement was achieved with a change in 1993 in the Rules of Procedure, which are set by the Council itself, which now provide that under certain circumstances the Council's voting record must be made public, and the Lisbon Treaty provides that the public has access to Council meetings when it votes on a draft legislative act. Thus, one part of the Council's deliberations is public, but the part dealing with non-legislative activities is not. Article 15(3) TFEU (ex Article 255 EC) provides that:

> *Any citizen of the Union, and any natural or legal person residing or having its registered office in a Member State, shall have the right of access to documents of the Union institutions, bodies, offices and agencies...*

This provision is, however, subject to limitations on grounds of public or private interest. In Case T–174/95 *Svenska Journalistförbundet v Council* (1998) the Court of First Instance (now the General Court) annulled a Council decision refusing the applicant access to certain documents. The Council put forward arguments based on public interest and on the protection of confidentiality of the Council's proceedings. On the latter argument the Court said (at paragraph 113 of the judgment) that the Council must:

> strike a genuine balance between ... the interest of the citizen in obtaining access to the documents and ... any interest of its own in maintaining the confidentiality of its deliberations.

In addition to institutions considering their own interests, they must also consider those of private persons. So where the situation is one in which 'privacy or the integrity of the individual would be infringed', the institution concerned must protect this information. However, the 'duty of openness' means that institutions should still release an expurgated version wherever possible (Case C–28/08 P *Commission v Bavarian Lager* (2010)).

Refusal to disclose should be accompanied by 'explanations as to how access to that document could specifically and effectively undermine the interest protected'. However, the Court also stated that 'it is, in principle, open to the Community institution to base its decisions in that regard on general presumptions which apply to certain categories of documents' as similar considerations would likely recur within a category (Case C–139/07 P *Commission v Technische Glaswerke Ilmenau* (2010)).

See also Case C–353/99P *Council of the European v Heidi Hautala* (2001).

Furthermore, any 'public or private interest' that might seek to restrict disclosure on grounds of confidentiality is to be interpreted narrowly; see Joined Cases C–39/05 P and C–52/05 P *Sweden and Turco v Council* (2008).

Organisation

The Presidency

3.11 The Presidency of the Council is held in turn by each Member State for a term of six months. The configurations of the presidency are decided by the European Council, except for the Foreign Affairs Council which is chaired by the High Representative (see **3.12**), on the basis of equal rotation (see Article 236 TFEU).

The Presidency was held originally in alphabetical order (based on the name of the country in its own language), but the rotation is now decided on by the European Council according to a pre-established rota. In the Draft Constitutional Treaty, now abandoned, provision was made for so-called 'Trio' presidencies, so that the Member State holding the Presidency before and after the current Presidency holder would work together with that country and provide support and assistance with their programme. These would be composed so as to consider the established order of rotation, and the size and geographical location of Member States. The Council in its Rules of Procedure in December 2009 provided as follows:

> *Every 18 months, the pre-established group of three Member States holding the Presidency of the Council for that period, in accordance with Article 1(4), shall prepare a draft programme of Council activities for that period. The draft shall be prepared with the President of the Foreign Affairs Council with regard to that configuration's activities during that period. The draft programme shall be prepared in close cooperation with the Commission and the President of the European Council, and after appropriate consultations. It shall be presented in a single document no later than one month before the relevant period, with a view to its endorsement by the General Affairs Council. This 'Troika', as it is often called, also acts when matters arise where the input of the Presidency is required, in order to prepare matters for the meetings of all the Member States.*

The Presidency has no function attributed to it in the Treaty; its original tasks were to convene and chair Council meetings and sign legislation and other acts, such as international treaties, on behalf of the Council, but it has gained far greater importance as the Union has developed and now has specific tasks under the Treaty. Any country holding the Presidency is intent on achieving special objectives which it usually announces at one of the summit meetings of the European Council before the beginning of its Presidency and presents to the European Parliament after having consulted the Commission. Particular emphasis will be laid on some aspect of Union policy and the Presidency will endeavour particularly to push through Union measures concerned with such objectives.

The High Representative

3.12   The Maastricht TEU gave recognition to the General Secretariat of the Council under the responsibility of a Secretary General. The Treaty of Amsterdam added a Deputy Secretary General, both to be appointed unanimously by the Council. The Secretary General controlled the day-to-day work of the Council, but also acted as the Council's High Representative in the common foreign and security policy. In October 1999, the first High Representative appointed to the newly restructured office was Xavier Solana, up to then Secretary General of NATO. The Treaty of Lisbon introduces a 'High Representative of the Union for Foreign Affairs and Security Policy' (Article 18 TEU) for whom provision is made as follows:

> *Article 18(1): The European Council, acting by a qualified majority, with the agreement of the President of the Commission, shall appoint the High Representative of the Union for Foreign Affairs and Security Policy. The European Council may end his term of office by the same procedure.*

> *Article 18(2): The High Representative shall conduct the Union's common foreign and security policy. He shall contribute by his proposals to the development of that policy, which he shall carry out as mandated by the Council. The same shall apply to the common security and defence policy.*

> *Article 18(3): The High Representative shall preside over the Foreign Affairs Council.*

> *Article 18(4): The High Representative shall be one of the Vice-Presidents of the Commission. He shall ensure the consistency of the Union's external action. He shall be responsible within the Commission for responsibilities incumbent on it in external relations and for coordinating other aspects of the Union's external action. In exercising these responsibilities within the Commission, and only for these responsibilities, the High Representative shall be bound by Commission procedures to the extent that this is consistent with paragraphs (2) and (3).*

Thus, the High Representative represents the Council, but is also one of the Vice-Presidents of the Commission; a 'double-hatted' function. Baroness Ashton, the British Commissioner up to that point, was appointed in January 2010 as the first High Representative. The High Representative is assisted by the European External Action Service (EEAS). This was established by the Council with the consent of the Commission and after consulting the European Parliament; and comprises a large civil service of a functionally autonomous but *sui generis* nature working in coopera-tion with the diplomatic services of the Member States. It is separate from the General Secretariat of the Council and of the Commission. It includes officials from relevant departments of the General Secretariat of the Council and of the Commission as well as staff seconded from national diplomatic services of the Member States. Taken pursuant to Article 27(3) TEU, the Council decision of 26 July 2010 established the organisation and functioning of the EEAS (2010/427/EU) and set out further details. The Service will support the High Representative 'in his/her mandate to conduct the Common Foreign and Security Policy (CFSP) of the Union, and [will] ensure the consistency of the

Union's external action' as set out in Articles 18 and 27 TEU. Council Regulation No. 1605/2002 on the financial regulation applicable to the general budget of the European Communities will now include the EEAS in Article 1. Furthermore, the annual report of the Court of the Auditors is to include the Service, and this latter must respond to the reports (Article 8).

The central administration of the EEAS is organised in the familiar EU way, in Directorates-General. While the number of these is not specified, they should include 'geographic desks covering all countries and regions of the world, as well as multilateral and thematic desks'. Directorates-General are also to be established with a view to 'administrative, staffing, budgetary, security and communication and information system matters', as well as crisis management and planning, civilian planning and conduct capability, and finally the European Union Military Staff and the European Union Situation centre, with these latter under the direct authority and responsibility of the High Representative (2010/427/EU, Article 4)) The term of office of the High Representative is five years, the same as the Commission's term of office.

The Committee of Permanent Representatives (COREPER)

3.13   The Committee of Permanent Representatives is known as COREPER, after its French acronym. The work of the representatives on the Council is prepared by this Committee. There are two levels on this Committee. COREPER I prepares the more technical questions and is composed of deputy permanent representatives. COREPER II deals with political and controversial matters on which it has to advise the Council and which may give rise to debate there. It is composed of permanent representatives who are Ambassadors to the EU. Commission officials attend COREPER meetings and participate in its work.

In urgent cases, acts of the Council may be adopted by a written vote provided all Council members agree to that procedure. If any members disagree, this procedure may not be used, as happened in Case 68/86 *United Kingdom v Council (Agricultural Hormones)* (1988). In this case the United Kingdom and Denmark opposed adoption of the directive concerned and the procedure should, therefore, not have been used.

COREPER prepares Council deliberations by drawing up two lists, the A List and the B list. The A list contains uncontroversial items which are adopted by the Council without debate. The B list contains items which do need debate within the Council before it can reach a decision.

The work of COREPER in turn is prepared by working groups of representatives of the Member States.

After COREPER had been given recognition in the TEU, an amendment by the Treaty of Amsterdam now empowers COREPER to adopt procedural decisions provided for in the Committee's Rules of Procedure, thus further easing the burden on the Council (see Article 240 TFEU (ex Article 207 EC)).

Voting procedures

3.14 Simple majority voting was, until the Treaty of Lisbon, still the default voting method. Article 16(3) TEU now provides:

> *The Council shall act by a qualified majority except where the Treaties provide otherwise.*

In the original Community of the Six, simple majority voting was sometimes used, but the Treaty often provided otherwise and the instances of simple majority voting were whittled away by provisions in the Treaties of Maastricht, Amsterdam and Nice, increasing the use of qualified majority voting (QMV). Simple majority voting is still used, e.g. for the adoption of the Council's rules of procedure (Article 240(3) TFEU (ex Article 207(3) EC)) and the adoption of the agenda and requests to the Commission to undertake studies and submit proposals (Article 241 TFEU (ex Article 208 EC)).

The Treaty of Lisbon declares QMV in the Council as the norm (Article 16(3) TEU), together with the ordinary legislative procedure (Article 16(1) TEU, Article 289(1) TFEU), in which the Council decides by qualified majority. The ordinary legislative procedure is described in detail in Article 294 TFEU. The current system of weighted votes which is carried over from the Nice Treaty is to be replaced from November 2014 by a 'double majority' system, under which a 'double majority' requires the votes of 55 per cent of the Member States, comprising at least 15 of them, and 65 per cent of the population of the Union (Article 16(4) TEU, Article 3 of Protocol no 36 on Transitional Provisions). Where the Council does not act on a proposal from the Commission or from the High Representative of the Union for Foreign Affairs and Security Policy, the qualified majority would require a 'double majority' of 72 per cent of the Member States and 65 per cent of the population of the European Union (Article 238(2) TFEU; Article 3 of Protocol no 36 on Transitional Provisions). Restrictions are imposed as a result of the 'Ioannina compromise' (see further **3.19**, the Declaration on Article 16(4) of the Treaty on European Union and Article 238(2) TFEU). A blocking minority must include at least four Council members, failing which the qualified majority shall be deemed attained. The transitional provisions relating to the definition of the qualified majority applicable until 31 October 2014 and those applicable from 1 November 2014 to 31 March 2017 are laid down in Protocol no 36 on Transitional Provisions (Article 16(5) TEU).

For the first time, deliberations and voting on draft legislative acts in the Council take place in public (Article 16(8) TEU).

Unanimous voting

3.15 Unanimous voting was used frequently until the end of 1965, when the transitional period came to an end and QMV replaced unanimity voting in many instances. In the

Europe of the Six, notwithstanding the problems described below (at **3.17**), unanimity was more easily achieved than is the case now. It is clear that it is more difficult to achieve unanimity among 27 or more Member States and that in many cases it may prove impossible to attain. If too many matters had to be decided this way, this would inevitably lead to stagnation in the progress of the Union. The Single European Act and the Treaties of Maastricht, Amsterdam, Nice and now Lisbon have extended the field of QMV very much further so that the other methods are now the rare exceptions. However, in the case of the Common Foreign and Security Policy unanimous voting is generally used. Some countries, the United Kingdom prominent among them, are reluctant to give up unanimity voting rules, or 'the veto' in matters which they consider vital and which they consider should be dealt with on an inter-governmental level. The Treaty of Amsterdam intended to introduce still more QMV, but succeeded in doing so only to a limited extent. The Nice Treaty added another 27 areas in which QMV is used. This included matters concerning free movement of citizens (Article 18 EC), industrial policy, economic, financial and technical cooperation with third countries and elements of visa, asylum and immigration policies, but it did not include taxation, social policy or the central elements of policies on asylum or immigration. The Treaty of Lisbon adds another 39 areas for QMV, but there are still subjects which are considered by different Member States as too sensitive to be subject to QMV, such as those involving direct taxation.

Qualified majority voting

3.16 In this procedure the votes are weighted per country as prescribed by Protocol 36 Article 3 on Transitional Provisions. The 1996 inter-governmental Conference (IGC) leading up to the Amsterdam Treaty was meant to reform the weighting system. It can readily be seen that the number of votes per country is not necessarily representative of its importance in terms of population. Larger countries considered themselves at a disadvantage and wanted change. They proposed a redistribution of the votes which would have given a greater weight to them and would, in their view, have constituted a more equitable distribution, proportionate to the size of their populations. However, this decision required a unanimous vote in the Council and this was blocked by the smaller countries. It was agreed that the question would be looked at again and that the problem must be solved before the first accession of any new member. This indeed happened in Nice and a redistribution of votes took place (see also **2.5**). Provision had to be made for the changing situation after enlargement in 2004 and 2007. This increased the total number of votes for QMV per Member State considerably, taking account of the fact that most of the new Member States are small or very small countries. The larger countries, in particular those with a large population, have been given more weighting. Thus, the total number of votes was increased from 87 to now 345. The qualified majority will have been achieved if two conditions have been fulfilled:

(a) the threshold for the qualified majority, a specified number of votes, must be achieved; this threshold is 255 out of 345 for the Union enlarged to 27 Member States;

(b) the decision must also be approved by a majority of Member States in cases where the Treaty requires it to be adopted on a proposal by the Commission, the usual situation. In some cases this rises to a two-thirds majority.

Furthermore, the Treaty also provides for the possibility for a member of the Council to request verification that the qualified majority is constituted by at least 62 per cent of the total population of the Union. This is a further element in favour of the larger Member States, as three of them would constitute such a majority.

The existing system is to continue until November 2014 (see Article 16 TEU and Article 238(2) TFEU). From then on, the definition of the qualified majority will be one of a double majority, so that, in order to be adopted, an act must have the support of at least 55 per cent of Member States and at least 65 per cent of the population of the EU. A blocking minority must include at least four Member States. However, between November 2014 and March 2017, any Member State may request that the current weighted voting system be applied instead of the new double majority system.

The Luxembourg Accords and the 'Ioannina Compromise'

The Luxembourg Accords

3.17 In 1966 the 'Luxembourg Accords' (also referred to as the 'Luxembourg Compromise') provided that, even where the Treaty had not provided for unanimous voting, if 'very important interests' of one or more Member States were at stake, discussions should continue until agreement was reached. France, which had been at the origin of the problem (concerning farm price proposals) which the Accords tried to solve, and which had practised an 'empty chair' policy, refusing to send its representatives to meetings, added its own view, stating that discussions should continue until unanimity had been attained.

The Accords are one of the earliest examples of a Community instrument the legal effect of which has never been comprehensively tested. It was a political compromise which was needed in order to avoid total stagnation in the Community. If one of the most important, if not *the* most important, members of a club of six decides not to cooperate, it is difficult for the club to function at all.

Circumstances have changed, however. One large country in a Community of six holds great political power, but in a Union of 27, or more, it is much more difficult, if not impossible, to make use of an instrument like the Luxembourg Accords. When the United Kingdom tried to use political means at Council level in 1996, when member-ship of the Union stood at 15, to try to force through a solution to the BSE beef crisis, it had little effect and the tactic eventually failed. Recent events again show the changed situation, where a 'veto' by the British Prime Minister in respect of the 'euro crisis' did not meet with much more success (see **2.43**).

3.18   The Accords have never been officially revoked. There were often hopes or views that they were no longer relevant, but the threat of the Accords continued to be invoked periodically, e.g. in connection with the Common Agricultural Policy (the United Kingdom in 1981) or concerning a permanent seat for the European Parliament. As the editorial comment in the August 1997 Common Market Law Review put it:

> *... predictions of demise of the Luxembourg Compromise were thus distinctly premature: it has been given a new lease of life, no longer in the demi-monde of political deals but as part of the legal machinery of the EC Treaty.*

In the Treaty of Amsterdam, the Luxembourg Compromise was also 'allowed to creep into the new Article 23 TEU (now Article 31 Lisbon TEU), second sub-paragraph'. This Article provides for action in the Common Foreign and Security Policy to be decided jointly by the European Council and the Council, by unanimity. However, the Council will act by qualified majority in certain decisions on the Union's action implementing European Council decisions (see Article 31(2) and (3) TEU). The second sub-paragraph states:

> *If a member of the Council declares that, for vital and stated reasons of national policy, it intends to oppose the adoption of a decision to be taken by qualified majority, a vote shall not be taken. The High Representative will, in close consultation with the Member State involved, search for a solution acceptable to it. If he does not succeed, the Council may, acting by a qualified majority, request that the matter be referred to the European Council for decision by unanimity.*

The 'Ioannina Compromise' on enlargement

3.19   The 1994 accession talks, held at Ioannina in Greece, proposed that upon accession of Austria, Finland, Norway and Sweden, the number of votes required for a blocking minority would rise from 23 to 27. Initially the United Kingdom and Spain objected, but Spain soon backed down, leaving the United Kingdom isolated in its opposition. The United Kingdom wanted to retain the possibility of forming a blocking minority with two large Member States and one small Member State, whereas the proposals would mean the necessary addition of another Member State to form a blocking minority. Eventually, a compromise was reached which was acceptable to them. The relevant part of the European Council's decision (paragraph c) was as follows:

> *If Members of the Council (of Ministers) representing a total of 23 to 26 votes indicate their intention to oppose the adoption by the Council of a decision by qualified majority, the Council will do all in its power to reach, within a reasonable time and without prejudice to obligatory time limits laid down by the Treaties and by secondary legislation, such as in Articles 189b and 189c [now Articles 251 and 252] of the EC*

*Treaty, a satisfactory solution which could be adopted by at least 68 votes. During
this period, and always respecting the Rules of Procedure of the Council, the President
takes, with the assistance of the Commission, any initiative necessary to facilitate a
wider basis of agreement in the Council.*

After three, rather than four, countries had joined in January 1995 (as Norway eventually
could not join because of a negative vote in its referendum) the number of 26 votes was
amended by a Council decision to 25 and the number of votes reduced from 68 to 65.

At Ioannina it had been agreed that the whole question should be re-examined by the
IGC. However, agreement could not be reached there and the Treaty of Amsterdam in
a 'Declaration to the Final Act' stated that the Compromise would stay in place until
the entry into force of the first enlargement, thus confirming the binding nature of
the agreement. Unlike the Luxembourg Accords, it is not limited to 'very important
interests', so it could be used on any matter and this makes it potentially more open
to abuse than the Luxembourg Accords. Whether the agreement was justiciable has
never been tested by the Court of Justice. The Court has held that any Community
(now Union) act which creates legal effects, irrespective of its nature, is an act *sui
generis* which is subject to the Court's jurisdiction. See Case 22/70 *Commission v
Council (ERTA)* (1971).

The Nice Treaty had been thought effectively to have repealed the Ioannina Compromise
in its Protocol and Declaration, but the Treaty of Lisbon now provides that if a group
of Member States is close to forming a 'blocking minority' discussions must continue
until a solution satisfying both parties is achieved within a reasonable period, whilst
respecting any compulsory time limits set by Union law. Declaration No 7 on Article
16(4) TEU and Article 238(2) TFEU annexed to the Treaty provides that the Council
will take a decision concerning the application of the compromise and will indicate
how it should be applied. The decision, to enter into force upon entry into force of the
Lisbon Treaty, is:

- between 1 November 2014 and 31 March 2017, a group of Member States will be
  deemed to constitute a blocking minority if it contains at least three-quarters of
  the population or three-quarters of the Member States necessary to constitute a
  blocking minority;

- as from 1 April 2017 (i.e. when a Member State can no longer request the
  application of the rules under the Nice Treaty), these percentages will go down
  to 55 per cent.

See also Protocol no 36 on Transitional Provisions, Title II Article 3. It should be noted
that the new 'Ioannina clause' remains a political compromise based on qualitative
judgments concerning a 'satisfactory solution' within a 'reasonable time' and should
not be interpreted in strict legal terms. It is rather the expression of the wish for the
Council to be able to continue its work. However, this shows again how important the
'numbers game' is in the eyes of the Member States.

The Commission

3.20 The Commission is often described as the Executive of the Union's policies. Although it is true that the Commission carries out Union decisions and policies, that is not all it does; it also proposes legislation and is, in many cases, instrumental in shaping the decision which is finally taken. Much of the Union's legislative rules are structured in such a way that the Commission has a say at the various stages when legislation is made. The Commission also has its own legislative powers under Article 106 TFEU (ex Article 86 EC) on state aid and under Articles 101 and 102 TFEU (ex Articles 81 and 82 EC) on competition. It is also given delegated legislative power by the Council (see **3.35–3.36** and **5.33–5.39**).

3.21 At present, there are 27 Commissioners, one for each Member State. Thus, after the accession of the 10 new members in 2004, the four large countries (France, Germany, Italy and the United Kingdom), lost one Commissioner. Otherwise, there simply would not have been enough worthwhile portfolios for all the Commissioners. The Nice Treaty limited membership of the Commission to one per Member State as from 2005, and imposed a ceiling of 27 once enlargement had taken place. This, therefore, meant that, if and when further enlargement occurs after the accession of Bulgaria and Romania, some countries would be without a Commissioner for a period. From 1 November 2014, when a new Commission is appointed the number of members of the Commission will correspond to two-thirds of the number of Member States, unless the European Council, acting unanimously, decides to alter this number (Article 17(5) TEU; see also Article 244 TFEU). After the entry into force of the Treaty of Lisbon, however, a decision could be taken, 'in accordance with the necessary legal procedures', to the effect that the Commission shall continue to include one national of each Member State (see Presidency Conclusions of the Brussels European Council of 11 and 12 December 2008 in Brussels, EU Bulletin 12–2008, I (4), at (2)). Thus, the number of Commissioners will continue to be one per Member State for the time being, allaying Irish fears of losing a Commissioner and with it any influence it has in the European Union. This was one of the factors which contributed to the positive Irish vote in their second referendum on the Lisbon Treaty in October 2009.

In view of the fact that Commissioners are supposed to be completely impartial and not to have any allegiance to the country from which they come it is, perhaps, surprising that this matters as much as it still clearly appears to.

Nomination and appointment procedure

3.22 According to Article 17(7) TEU the President of the Commission is to be proposed to the European Parliament by qualified majority vote of the European Council. The candidate is then elected by the European Parliament by a majority of its component members. If the Parliament does not approve the proposed Commission President, the

European Council has to propose a new President within one month, following the same procedure. The European Parliament acquired the right to approve the President under the Treaty of Amsterdam. (Under the Treaty of Maastricht, the Parliament was consulted about the Presidency and only had the right to approve or reject the Commission as a whole.) Secondly, the Council, by common accord with the nominee for President, adopts a list of the other persons it intends to appoint as Commissioners. The appointment is made from a list drawn up in accordance with suggestions made by Member States. Thus, the Council cannot appoint anyone who has not been suggested by his or her own Member State. Strict criteria for selection are contained in Article 17 TEU. The persons selected 'shall be chosen on the ground of their general competence and European commitment from persons whose independence is beyond doubt' (Article 17(3) TEU). The President, before agreeing to the list, will undertake political soundings with each Member State in order to ensure a balanced composition of the Commission. Thirdly, all the nominees, including the High Representative, are subject, as a body, to a vote of approval by the European Parliament. Finally, the new Commission is appointed by the European Council acting by a qualified majority (Article 17(7) last paragraph TEU (ex Article 214(2) EC)). The High Representative is one of the Vice-Presidents of the Commission.

According to Article 17 TEU, the members of the Commission must be chosen from among the nationals of the Member States on the basis of a system established unanimously by the European Council in accordance with Article 244 TFEU consisting of 'strictly equal rotation between the Member States, reflecting the demographic and geographical range of all the Member States'.

3.23 Commissioners are appointed for a five-year term which is renewable (Article 17(3) TEU (ex Article 214(1) EC)). Although the European Parliament now elects the President of the Commission, it still has no power to reject individual Commissioners. However, a system of hearings by the European Parliament has grown up, and in those instances where hearings of Commissioners have been highly unsatisfactory, as has happened upon the nomination of every new Commission, those candidates have always been withdrawn by their countries, showing that individual approval of Commissioners has become a *de facto* power for the Parliament. The new Commission ('Barroso II') was appointed in December 2009 for a second term until 2014 and hearings of the various Commissioners concluded in the European Parliament on 9 February 2010. Although the Parliament does not officially have to give its approval of individual Commissioners, it has become traditional to do so, and one of the potential Commissioners from Bulgaria had to be replaced as she resigned after she did not receive the approval of the European Parliament. Mr Barroso's term was extended for another five years.

Thus, this informal power for the Parliament has proved much more effective than the 'sledgehammer' power to dismiss the entire Commission.

3.24 The President of the Commission has a special position. Much depends on the President's personality. Roy Jenkins, for example, achieved the acceptance of the membership of the Commission President at the European Council sessions. Jacques Delors, President from 1985 to 1994, and one of the architects of economic and monetary union, achieved enormous prestige for the Commission and for the Community as well as a fair amount of controversy, particularly in the United Kingdom, with his vision of and dedication to Europe. Commissioners all have their own portfolio, ultimately decided upon by the President.

Status of the Commissioners

3.25 The members of the Commission have the duty and the right to perform their tasks with complete independence in the general interest of the Union. They are forbidden to seek or take instructions from any government or other body and must refrain from any action incompatible with the nature of their duties (Article 17(3) TEU). The Member States have undertaken to respect this principle and not to seek to influence the members of the Commission in the performance of their tasks. During their term of office, Commissioners may not engage in any other occupation, and even after they have ceased to hold office they are required to behave with integrity and discretion as regards the acceptance of certain appointments or benefits (Article 245 TFEU (ex Article 213(2) EC)).

3.26 Privileges and immunities ensure undisturbed performance of their duties. The Member States appoint the members of the Commission, but they cannot discharge them during their term of office. The Court of Justice, on the application of the Council or the Commission, may compulsorily retire an individual member of the Commission from office if that member no longer fulfils the conditions required for the performance of his duties or if he or she has been guilty of serious misconduct (Articles 245 and 247 TFEU (ex Articles 213(2) and 216 EC)). The Commission President may also request a Commission member to resign. Only the European Parliament can compel the Commission to resign as a body, by means of a motion of censure on its activities (Article 234 TFEU (ex Article 201 EC)).

3.27 In 1999 the 'Santer' Commission was heavily criticised by the European Parliament's 'Committee of Wise Men', which stopped short of accusing any individual Commissioner of fraud, but pointed out that it was difficult to find anyone with the slightest sense of responsibility. The Commission President, Jacques Santer, saw this as his cue to prevail upon his Commissioners to resign as a body. Thus, although the European Parliament did not actually dismiss the Commission, it was nevertheless instrumental in the Commission's eventual resignation.

The organisation of the Commission

3.28 The Commission has a President and Vice-Presidents whose number is no longer specified. The latter are appointed by the President from among its members (Article 17(6)(c) TEU), except for the 'High Representative of the Union for Foreign Affairs and Security

Policy' who is to be one of the Vice-Presidents of the Commission, but who is appointed by the European Council by qualified majority 'with the agreement of the Commission President' (Article 18(4) TEU). The Commission is required to act collectively and is generally governed by the principle of collegiate responsibility which, as the Court of Justice said in Case 5/85 *AKZO Chemie BV v Commission* (1986):

> ...is founded on the equal participation of the members of the Commission in the adoption of decisions and it follows from that principle, in particular, that decisions should be the subject of collective deliberation and that all members of the college of Commissioners bear collective responsibility on the political level for all decisions adopted.

3.29 Each member of the Commission has a personal staff—his/her *cabinet*—which assists him/her. *Cabinets* consist of a number of personally appointed political and administrative advisers whose principal functions are to tender advice and brief their Commissioner about the activities of the Commission as a whole, to speak for their Commissioner in meetings of officials and to coordinate their administrative responsibilities which may cover a number of Directorates; to provide liaison between their Commissioner and other EU institutions and the Commissioner's home Member State. The role of the *chef de cabinet* has now become institutionalised and a meeting of the *chefs de cabinet* precedes and prepares every Commission meeting.

3.30 Around 23,000 staff members work in the Commission in departments known as Directorates-General (DGs) or services. Each DG is responsible for a different portfolio (area of policy) and each is headed by a Director-General who reports directly to the President of the Commission. The Directorates-General draft laws and make recommendations which can be adopted by the college of Commissioners (the Commission) at its weekly meetings.

The administrative services of the Commission consist of DGs which are divided into Directorates which in turn are subdivided into divisions. There are four divisions, each grouping a considerable number of DGs, with changes in numbers made from time to time. The four divisions are: Policy DGs, External Relations DGs, General Services DGs and Internal Services DGs. The Secretariat General provides overall coordination and also manages the weekly Commission meetings. It is headed by the Secretary General who is answerable directly to the President of the Commission. The Commission may also delegate the implementation of specific programmes to one of its executive agencies. This can include the Commission's arrangements for planning, reporting, internal control systems, internal audit and accounts (see *Governance Statement of the European Commission*, 30 May 2007). Due to the large staff and international aspect of its operation, the Commission's administration costs ran to €3.3 billion in 2011. This represents around 2.3 per cent of the annual budget of the European Union, but includes services such as translation. In 2010 there were 550 full-time and about the same number of freelance interpreters and about 2,300 translators.

Functions and powers

3.31   The Commission's functions and powers are defined in various Treaty provisions. The main responsibilities of the Commission are provided for by Article 17(1) TEU and consist of promoting the general interest of the Union, to ensure application of the Treaties and to oversee this application under the control of the Court of Justice of the European Union. They also include the exercise of coordinating, executive and management functions and ensuring the Union's external representation insofar as this is not entrusted to others, such as the High Representative or the President of the European Council.

3.32   The first function of the Commission is as the guardian of the Treaties, ensuring that Member States, other Union institutions as well as natural and legal persons who are subject to it, apply the Treaty. Article 258 TFEU (ex Article 226 EC) provides the instrument for this supervisory task (see **Chapter 8**). The Commission has the power to take legal and administrative measures against a Member State which has violated Union law, and it can impose fines on the offending Member State (Article 260 TFEU (ex Article 228 EC)). The threat of such sanctions alone is often sufficient to make the Member State comply.

The Commission also has supervisory powers over other institutions (see Articles 263 TFEU (ex Article 230 EC) and Article 265 TFEU (ex Article 232 EC)) and **Chapter 8**) and over natural and legal persons, as for example in the field of competition law.

3.33   The second function of the Commission is to act as the executive arm of the Union. It plays a key role in the day-to-day implementation of Union law in a number of different areas such as the administration of the customs union, the Common Agricultural Policy, competition policy and state aids and the common commercial policy. It has significant powers with regard to transport, taxation and application of the various safeguard clauses. It is required to draft and implement the Union budget and to administer the special funds which finance EU regional policy. The four main funds are the European Regional Development Fund, the European Social Fund, the European Agricultural Guarantee Fund, which finances the Common Agricultural Policy, and the Cohesion Fund. There are several smaller funds to which applications can be made for financial support for a project with demonstrable cultural value. The smaller funds include JASPERS (Joint Assistance to Support Projects in European Regions) which is a technical assistance facility for the 12 countries which joined the EU in 2004 and 2007, JEREMIE (Joint European Resources for Micro to Medium Enterprises) which promotes access to finance for SMEs, JESSICA (Joint European Support for Sustainable Investment in City Areas) which supports sustainable urban regeneration, and JASMINE (Joint Action to Support Micro Finance Institutions in Europe) which provides technical and financial assistance to non-bank, micro-credit providers. Finally, the EU Solidarity Fund was set up as a response to the severe floods in Central Europe in 2002. It provides financial assistance to disaster-stricken regions within Europe. The Commission also has an important task of external representation, for example in areas where the Union has exclusive competence (see **5.57** and **5.58**).

3.34 The Commission has its own decision-making powers as well as power delegated to it by the Council. Firstly, the Commission has a decision-making power of its own under Article 105(2) TFEU (ex Article 85(2) EC) and Article 106 TFEU (ex Article 86 EC). Secondly, the Commission plays a vital role in the Union law-making process by virtue of its power to initiate legislation. Apart from a few exceptional situations where the European Parliament and the Council, or the Council and the European Parliament together, may act upon their own initiative, in most cases Article 289 TFEU provides for the 'ordinary legislative procedure' consisting of a 'joint adoption by Council and Parliament of a proposal by the Commission'. In these cases the Commission has an exclusive right of initiative, which it may have to exercise within a specified time limit. However, the Council may request the Commission to submit to it any appropriate proposals (Article 241 TFEU (ex Article 208 EC)). An important feature of the right of initiative is the right to withdraw proposals for legislation, which can have a considerable effect on legislative progress. In preparing its proposals, the Commission usually consults with representatives of the Member States. It may, and where required by the Treaty it must, also consult the Economic and Social Committee and the Committee of the Regions (Article 304 TFEU (ex Article 262 EC) and Article 307 TFEU (ex Article 307 EC)). Where the Council acts on a proposal from the Commission, it may generally amend that proposal only by unanimity (Article 293(1) TFEU (ex Article 250(1) EC)). As long as the Council has not acted, the Commission may itself alter or withdraw its proposal (Article 293(2) TFEU (ex Article 250(2) EC)).

3.35 Delegated powers: Article 290 TFEU provides that 'a legislative act may delegate to the Commission the power to adopt non-legislative acts of general application to supplement or amend certain non-essential elements of the legislative act'. The scope of such an act is explicitly defined in the Article and does not include 'essential elements which cannot be subject of delegation' (Article 290(1) TFEU). The Article also explicitly defines the conditions to which delegation is subject.

Decision-making procedure of the Commission

3.36 The decision-making powers delegated by the Council to the Commission are usually subject to the special scrutiny of committees of Council and other national representatives. This process, which is very important to decision-making, is known as '*comitology*'. Comitology involves a range of bodies attached to the Commission. Some are management committees with executive powers, as in agriculture; others are advisory, whether expert or consultative; others are regulatory committees which must concur with the proposed measure before it can be taken. The various types of committee and their procedures are further described in **5.33–5.39**.

Two Council decisions in 1987 and 1999 (87/373 and 1999/468/EC) set out detailed provisions for the use and powers of the three different types of Committee. This was inspired by the case brought by the European Parliament in 1987 (Case 302/87 *Parliament v Council* (1988)), the *Comitology* case, which, although the Parliament lost on this occasion (see further **5-35**) highlighted the need for greater transparency of the comitology system. In December 2002 the Commission proposed in a Report on European Governance, to amend the 1999 decision with the objective of 'rebalancing and strengthening the possibility for Parliament and the Council to control the Commission's exercise of its implementing powers' in the areas of codecision (see **5.41**). This was intended to be transitional in nature, pending a system of delegation of implementing powers based on the revision of the treaties (see further **5.39**).

Further powers of the Commission

3.37 The Commission has other important tasks assigned to it in the following areas:

- External relations: Article 207(3) TFEU (ex Article 133(3) EC), Articles 216 and TFEU, 218 TFEU (ex Article 300 EC) and Articles 220–222 TFEU (ex Articles 302–304 EC) provide for the Commission's involvement in opening and conducting negotiations on agreements with international organisations. Such powers are not, however, general powers: see Case C–327/91 *France v Commission* (1994). They are, however, subject to control by the Council.

- Implementation of the Union budget: see Articles 317–319 TFEU (ex Articles 274–276 and 279 EC).

- Publication of the General Annual Report (Article 249(2) TFEU (ex Article 212 EC)).

The effect on the Commission of the Maastricht, Amsterdam, Nice and Lisbon Treaties

3.38 In addition to making changes as to the appointment of the President and the members of the Commission in Amsterdam, Nice and Lisbon (see **3.20** et seq) amendments in Amsterdam and Nice such as in Articles 121 TFEU (ex Article 99 EC), 126 TFEU (ex Article 104 EC), 219 TFEU (ex Article 111(1), (3) and (5) EC) and 167–173 TFEU (ex Articles 151–157 EC) conferred new powers of investigation and initiative in a whole range of policy areas such as EMU, economic and social policy, culture, public health, trans-European networks and industry. In the Lisbon Treaty, more new areas were added: Title XX Environment (Articles 191–193 TFEU); Title XXI Energy (Article 194 TFEU); Title XXII Tourism (Article 195 TFEU); Title XXIII Civil Protection (Article 196 TFEU); and Title XXIV Administrative cooperation (Article 197 TFEU). The Common Foreign and Security Policy (see **2.47-2.49**) provides for involvement and sometimes the submission of proposals by the Commission. The codecision procedure introduced by the Maastricht Treaty, extended by the Treaty of Amsterdam and now renamed the ordinary legislative procedure by the Treaty of Lisbon (Article 294 TFEU (ex Article 251 EC)) makes the Commission less independent of the Parliament, and more involved in political management both inside the Council and the Parliament. The Commission is also subject to stricter financial controls and accountability. Detailed provisions concerning the drafting of the budget by the Commission and the presentation to the European Parliament and the Council are laid down in Chapter 3, Articles 312–316 TFEU. The Commission now operates under stricter policy guidelines which often make it clear that the primary responsibility lies with the Member States in certain areas (e.g. concerning education policy).

The European Parliament

Membership, organisation and procedure

3.39 The European Parliament (EP), previously called the 'Assembly' in the constitutive Treaties, is elected 'by direct universal suffrage in a free and secret ballot' (Article 14(3) TEU). It is composed of representatives 'of the Union's citizens' (Article 14(2) TEU) and no longer of representatives 'of the peoples of the States brought together in the Community' (Article 189(1) EC). The allocation of seats in the EP is to be determined for the first time by a unanimous decision of the European Council 'on the initiative of the European Parliament' (Article 14(2) TEU). The decision must respect the principles laid down in Article 14(2) TEU: the total number of members not to exceed 750, 'plus the President', with representation of the citizens of the Union being degressively proportional. The minimum threshold is six members per Member State, and according to Article 14(2) TEU, no Member State must be allocated more than 96 seats. The Members are referred to as Members of the European Parliament (MEPs).

Until 1979, MEPs were not directly elected but appointed from among the members of the respective national Parliaments. Direct universal elections were held for the first time in 1979. Elections are held every five years. There is still no uniform electoral procedure even though Article 223(1) TFEU (ex Article 190(4) EC) provides that the EP must draw up a proposal for elections by direct universal suffrage 'in accordance with a uniform procedure in all Member States' or, in what was originally an addition in the Treaty of Amsterdam, 'in accordance with principles common to all Member States'. The intention in the Maastricht TEU was clearly that the uniform electoral system should be some form of proportional representation. A system of proportional representation exists in a variety of forms in the vast majority of Member States, either by the use of party lists or by Single Transferable Vote. In the United Kingdom, too, the last three European elections in 1999, 2004 and 2009 were held based on proportional representation. This was not very successful as the turnout of the electorate was the lowest it has ever been. This could perhaps be blamed on the political situation but there is no doubt that the appearance of a voting system with which the electorate was totally unfamiliar was also a contributing factor.

Under the Citizenship Chapter in the Treaty (now named Non-discrimination and Citizenship of the Union, Article 22 TFEU (ex Article 19 EC)) provides that every citizen of the Union has the right to vote and stand in local and European Parliament elections in any of the Member States. In two cases, Case C–145/04 *Spain v UK* (2006) and Case C–300/04 *Eman and Sevinger v College van Burgemeester en Wethouders van Den Haag* (2006) the Court of Justice agreed that nationals of a Member State resident overseas (in Gibraltar in the first case, on the Caribbean island of Aruba in the second) should be allowed to vote in national and EP elections. In the 'Gibraltar' case the United Kingdom had made rules providing for Gibraltar UK citizens to vote after the European Court of Human Rights ruling in *Matthews v UK* (1999). In the second case the Dutch Government had attempted to exclude the Aruba residents from voting, even though Dutch nationals resident in a non-EU country had such rights.

3.40 The number of seats has been set at 751, since the elections to the EP in 2009. With the advent of the new Member States, the distribution of votes has been changed, and Germany now has 99 members, with the other 'Big Three' France, the UK and Italy, at 78 each. The main criterion for the allocation of seats is the population of the Member States concerned, but it is not mathematically precise. The distribution is at present clearly in favour of the smaller Member States and, although Germany received an additional number of seats after unification, a German MEP still represents about 10 times as many people as a Luxembourg MEP. MEPs are required to vote on an individual and personal basis and they are not bound by any instructions. During the sessions of the EP, MEPs enjoy the privileges and immunities accorded to members of national Parliaments when in their own countries, and immunity from detention and legal proceedings when in the territory of another Member State. MEPs may not concurrently be members of a national government or hold office in another Union institution but they may serve in their own national Parliaments. There are now (2012) 736 MEPs, of which over one-third are women.

3.41 Article 223(2) TFEU makes provision for regulating the performance of the duties of MEPs under a special legislative procedure by the Parliament acting on its own initiative after having sought the Commission's opinion and 'with the approval of the Council'. Rules concerning taxation of Members or former Members will require Council unanimity. Article 224 TFEU (ex Article 191 EC, second subparagraph EC) adds a legal base providing for the adoption of rules governing political parties and, in particular, their funding, to be adopted by the Parliament and the Council according to the ordinary legislative procedure.

3.42 Article 229 TFEU (ex Article 196 EC) provides that the EP will hold an annual session. The EP may also meet in extraordinary session at the request of a majority of its members or at the request of the Council or the Commission. The annual session is divided into part sessions which are convened as a rule each month, and are subdivided into daily sittings. Plenary sittings are held for one week of each month (except August), while one week a month is set aside for committee meetings and one week for meetings of political groups.

3.43 The EP does not a have a sole seat of operations. As a rule, it holds plenary sessions in Strasbourg and Brussels and its committee meetings in Brussels, while its Secretariat is based in Luxembourg. There have been disputes concerning this clearly impractical arrangement, such as in Case 108/83 *Luxembourg v European Parliament* (1984), where the Court held that a 1983 Resolution was incompatible with the Member States' decision concerning the provisional location of the EP places of work and therefore void, and in cases brought by France which jealously guards its right to have plenary sessions in Strasbourg because of its symbolic location on the border between France and Germany: Case 358/85 *France v European Parliament (Re Brussels Meetings)* (1986); Cases 358/85 and 51/86 *France v European Parliament (Re Meetings Facilities in Brussels)* (1988). This is the result of political bargaining when the Community was first established. Many members of the EP would prefer to have all its plenary sessions in Brussels, as most Committee meetings take place there and it is also the seat of the Commission and the Council. However, it has so far proved politically unacceptable to make a change and the situation is now enshrined in a special Protocol to the Treaty of Amsterdam, which provides that the seat of the Parliament will be in Strasbourg and at least 12 of its plenary sessions, including the all-important budget session, will be held in Strasbourg. Any additional plenaries may take place in Brussels; the Committees will meet in Brussels and the General Secretariat will remain in Luxembourg.

3.44 The Parliament represents nearly 500 million citizens of the European Union. MEPs sit in multinational political groups. These groups are a kaleidoscope of European politics. There are the following seven groups: the Group of the European People's Party (Christian Democrats); the Group of the Progressive Alliance of Socialists and Democrats in the European Parliament; the Group of the Alliance of Liberals and Democrats for Europe; the European Conservatives and Reformists Group; the Group of the Greens/European Free Alliance; Confederal Group of the European United Left—Nordic Green Left; and the Europe of Freedom and Democracy Group. Even these groupings fail to capture the full picture of diversity. Since it frequently takes an absolute majority of the votes cast in order to act (Article 231 TFEU (ex Article 198 EC)), a degree of consensus is essential. The detailed work of the Parliament is done in 20 standing committees, which include committees for Foreign Affairs, Human Rights, Security and Defence, Legal Affairs, Constitutional Affairs, Agriculture and Rural Development, Budgets, Economic and Monetary Affairs, Civil Liberties, Justice and Home Affairs, Employment and Social Affairs and Women's Rights and Gender Equality. Temporary committees are set up for an initial period of no longer than 12 months to deal with particular topics and issue specific reports. For example, in 2009 a Special Committee on the Financial, Economic and Social Crisis was set up. The committees prepare resolutions which are adopted by the EP in plenary sessions. Where the Parliament is involved in the legislative process (see Articles 293 and 294 TFEU (ex Articles 250 and 251 EC)) the proposal is examined by the relevant committee(s), which includes its findings and recommendations in a Report drawn up by a *Rapporteur.*

3.45 The EP elects its President (Article 14(4) TEU (ex Article 197(1) EC)) and Vice-Presidents, one per country, who together form the 'Bureau', the executive body. The

EP is assisted by a Secretary General who is appointed by the Bureau and is the head of the Secretariat. At the end of 2011 the Secretariat comprised approximately 4,600 permanent and temporary posts. Members of the Commission may (and do) attend all meetings and the European Council and the Council 'shall be heard' in accordance with conditions laid down in their Rules of Procedure (Article 230(3) TFEU (ex Article 197(3) EC)). Members of the Commission may attend all meetings and must, at their request, be heard (Article 230(1) TFEU (ex Article 197(2) EC)). Debates are public unless the EP decides otherwise. The minutes of the meetings, according to the Parliament's Rules of Procedure, are published in the Official Journal and the full debates in an annex (Article 232(2) TFEU (ex Article 199(2) EC)). Article 15 TFEU provides that the Parliament (and the Council also— Article 16(8) TEU) meet in public and that documents relating to the legislative procedure are published.

3.46 Except for the adoption of a motion of censure on the activities of the Commission (Article 234 TFEU (ex Article 201 EC; see above **3.26**)) and certain decisions within the legislative and budgetary procedures, the EP acts by an absolute majority of the votes cast (Article 231(1) TFEU (ex Article 198(1) EC)). There is a quorum when one-third of current MEPs are present in the Chamber. However, unless there is a request to do so, the number of MEPs present is not ascertained.

Powers and functions

3.47 Although the EP still has no right of legislative initiative, its participation in the legislative process has grown considerably since the original Treaties. Under the Lisbon Treaty, the codecision procedure, in which the European Parliament acts in tandem with the Council, is streamlined, renamed 'ordinary legislative procedure' and declared the norm (Article 14(1) TEU; Article 289(1) TFEU). The consultation procedure and the assent procedure are united under the term 'special legislative procedure' and are henceforth only applied in specific cases provided for by the Treaties (Article 289(2) TFEU). The stronger law-making role of the EP also affects the conclusion of international law agreements by the European Union. In areas governed by the ordinary legislative procedure, or if the approval of the EP is required by the special legislative procedure, the Council may only adopt a decision to conclude an international treaty after the EP's consent has been obtained (Article 218(6)(a)(v) TFEU).

In addition, the EP decides on the draft budget in tandem with the Council (Article 14(1) TEU, Article 314 TFEU) and exercises functions of political control. It elects the President of the Commission upon a proposal by the European Council by a majority of its component members (Articles 14(1) and 17(7) TEU). The proposal must take into account the result of the elections to the European Parliament (Article 17(7) TFEU). If the proposed candidate does not obtain the required majority, the European Council must within one month propose a new candidate to the EP (Article 17(7) TEU). Furthermore, the EP, just like the national Parliaments, scrutinises Europol's activities and takes part in the evaluation of Eurojust's activities (Articles 85(1) and 88(2) TFEU).

These procedures are described in more detail in **5.41–5.48**.

3.48 It should be pointed out that the EP, may 'request the Commission to submit any appropriate proposal on matters on which it considers that a Union act is required for the purpose of implementing the Treaty' (Article 225(2) TFEU (ex Article 192(2) EC)).

3.49 Article 15 TEU (originally inserted in the Treaty of Amsterdam) provides that, like the Commission and the Council, the EP elaborates the rules for access to its documents under its own rules of procedure. This was done to ensure greater transparency of the legislative process and make it more 'citizen friendly'.

3.50 The EP's supervisory role includes the following:

- setting up a temporary Committee of Inquiry (Article 226 TFEU (ex Article 193 EC));

- the right of petition, handled by a special Petitions Committee (Article 227 TFEU (ex Article 194 EC));

- the appointment of an Ombudsman (Article 228 TFEU (ex Article 195 EC));

- submitting oral or written questions to the Commission (Article 230(2) TFEU (ex Article 197(2) EC));

- the submission of an annual General Report by the Commission, to be discussed in open session (Article 233 TFEU (ex Article 200 EC));

- voting a motion of censure against the Commission (Article 234 TFEU (ex Article 201 EC));

- participation in proceedings before the Court of Justice of the European Union. When the Community was founded, the EP was an unelected assembly with only limited powers of consultation. It was, therefore, not considered necessary for the EP to have legal standing under the Treaty to be a party in proceedings before the Court of Justice. However, after the EP began to be directly elected and increasingly gained legislative powers under the SEA and the TEU, it needed to have *locus standi* in cases concerning its prerogatives. In a series of cases which were much criticised by those who thought the Court was going beyond its jurisdiction, the Court gradually allowed the EP increased standing. The EP may intervene in cases before the Courts: Case 138/79 *Roquette Frères SA v Council* (1980); the EP may bring an action under Article 263 TFEU (ex Article 230 EC): Case C–65/90 *European Parliament v Council* (1992); Case C–70/88 *European Parliament v Council* (1990) cf. Case 302/87 *European Parliament v Council* (1988); the EP may also bring an action under Article 265 TFEU (ex Article 232 EC): Case 13/83 *European Parliament v Council* (1985); cf. Case 377/87 *European Parliament v Council* (1988); see also Case 383/87 *Commission v Council* (1988). The changes brought about by the Court's judgments were acknowledged by the revision of Article 173 EC (now Article 263 TFEU) in the Maastricht Treaty (see **8.28–8.36**). Since the Treaty of Nice the

EP now has unlimited standing under Article 263 TFEU, paragraph 3, on a par with the other institutions;

- election of the President of the Commission (Articles 14(1) TEU and 17(7) TEU) and approval of the Members of the Commission and of the High Representative (Article 17(7) TEU third subparagraph);

- participation in the Budgetary Procedure (Articles 313–319 TFEU (ex Articles 272–276 EC)). This was first provided for in the Second Budgetary Treaty 1975. The Budgetary Procedure is further described in **5.45**.

Petitions

3.51 Any citizen of the Union or any natural or legal person residing or having its registered office in a Member State, i.e. also a non-citizen, is entitled under Article 227 TFEU (ex Article 194 EC) to address petitions on matters within the fields of activity of the Union and which concern them to the EP.

The Parliamentary Commissioner (Ombudsman)

3.52 The Maastricht Treaty introduced the power in Article 228 TFEU (ex Article 195 EC) for the EP to appoint an Ombudsman. This official may receive complaints concerning instances of maladministration by Union institutions from European citizens but also from 'any natural or legal person residing or having its registered office in a Member State', either directly or through a member of the EP on acts by the institutions. The Ombudsman may investigate such complaints if they are not or have not been the subject of legal proceedings. If the Ombudsman establishes there has been maladministration, he or she informs the institution, which has three months to reply. Thereupon the Ombudsman will forward a report to the EP and the institution concerned. The person lodging the complaint must be informed of the outcome.

Conclusion

3.53 Although, as we have seen, a number of positive changes were achieved by the Maastricht, Amsterdam and Lisbon Treaties, and its powers have been further supplemented and strengthened, the EP is still far short of being a Parliament in the proper sense of the word. It has practically no legislative initiative and a right to reject legislation, which, although much extended under the Lisbon Treaty, is still limited. In spite of being the only directly elected body in the Union, it still has difficulty in presenting itself as an effective representative of the peoples of Europe and this is reflected in the extremely low voter turn-out at European Parliament elections. Even in the most recent elections in 2009, when the Lisbon Treaty had been adopted and ratification was imminent, voter turnout was still low. In 2009, voter turnout in the EU was 43 per cent, as opposed to 45.57 per cent in 2004.

The Court of Justice of the European Union and the General Court

3.54 The judicial system of the Union was, until the Treaty of Nice, a two-tier system. It now has three tiers of courts, united under the title of the Court of Justice of the European Union (CJEU). This comprises the Court of Justice (first established by the ECSC Treaty of Paris in 1952), the General Court (created as the Court of First Instance (CFI) in 1989 in order to relieve the growing case load of the Court of Justice), and a third tier of jurisdiction now known as the specialised courts (added by the Treaty of Nice with the name 'judicial panels'). These Courts derive their fundamental task from Article 19(1) TEU (ex Article 220 EC (following Article 31 ECSC)) which provides that they 'shall ensure that in the interpretation and application of the Treaties the law is observed'. The composition, functions and how they have dealt with their functions and interpreted their tasks under Article 19(1) are discussed more extensively in **Chapter 4**.

The Court of Auditors

3.55 The Maastricht Treaty amended Article 7 EC (now Article 13 TEU) by inserting the Court of Auditors as one of the institutions of the Union. Originally, auditing of accounts was carried out within each Community. Subsequently, the Merger Treaty established a single audit board for all three Communities. The board, however, had an unhappy co-existence with the Commission. It complained that its critical comments were not heeded and it experienced delays and difficulties in obtaining information from the Commission. Its reports were not published, but sent by the Commission together with the accounts for the year, to the Council and the EP, as part of its procedure of giving discharge to the Commission.

3.56 In response to pressure from the EP which called for a European Audit Office (1973) and from the new Member States which had different traditions with respect to public sector audit, the Court of Auditors was established by the Treaty establishing a single Commission of the EC signed in 1977. The Court attained institutional status only when the Maastricht Treaty came into force. It is now governed by Articles 285–287 TFEU (ex Articles 246–248 (EC)). Article 285 TFEU provides that the Court of Auditors will consist of one national from each Member State. It sits in Luxembourg and its structure and status are in many ways similar to those of the Court of Justice. However, unlike some national courts of auditors, it does not have a disciplinary function. The Court examines the accounts and provides the European Parliament and the Council with a 'statement of assurance as to the reliability of the accounts and the legality and regularity of the underlying transactions', to be published in the Official Journal.

The present 27 members are chosen from among persons who belong, or have belonged, in their respective countries, to external audit bodies or who are specially qualified for such an office. Their function is to examine the accounts of revenue and expenditure of the Union. In order to carry out its task the Court investigates the paperwork of any organisation handling EU income or expenditure. It acts by a majority of its members. Fraud and financial mismanagement are serious problems in the Union. For years in a row the Court has refused to sign off the EU accounts. This happened for the seventeenth time in November 2011. According to the Court of Auditors errors in legality and regularity still persist in the majority of the EU's annual budget, which amounted to €147.2 billion for 2012, an increase of 3.5 per cent on 2010.

The importance of these problems was recognised by the Member States when they gave the Court the status of a Community (now Union) institution. This means, therefore, that acts of the Court of Auditors which have legal effects will be subject to the jurisdiction of the Court of Justice. In Case C–315/99 P *Ismeri Europa v Court of Auditors* (2001) the company Ismeri Europa appealed a judgment by the CFI (now General Court) in Case T–277/97 in which it had claimed damages for loss suffered as a result of criticisms of the company made by the Court of Auditors in a special report. The Court of Justice upheld the CFI's judgment dismissing the claim.

The European Economic and Social Committee (EESC)

3.57 Article 13(4) TEU (ex Article 7(2) EC) provides that the European Parliament, the Council and the Commission are to be assisted by an Economic and Social Committee. This is an advisory body intended to represent various sectional interests. According to Article 300 TFEU (ex Article 258 EC) it consists of representatives of the various economic and social components of organised civil society, among others, producers, farmers, carriers, workers, dealers, craftsmen, the professions, consumers and the general public. In practice it consists of three groups: employers, workers (largely represented by the trade unions) and 'others'. The last group includes spokesmen for farmers, consumers and the professions. Its members, are appointed by the Council for renewable five-year terms on the basis of national allocations; the largest (United Kingdom and other large countries) is 24, the smallest (Malta) is five. The number and distribution per Member State was not altered in Nice, but the ceiling may not exceed 350. This number, however, has not yet been achieved after the accession of the new Member States (344 in a Union of 27 Member States). The members, though intended to represent particular groups, may not be bound by any 'mandatory instructions' (Article 300(4) TFEU).

In certain cases the Committee has the right to be consulted by the European Parliament, the Council or the Commission. Then, however, the European Parliament, the Council or the Commission may set a time limit (of at least one month) and, if no opinion is given within that period, go ahead without it. The Treaty of Amsterdam extended the areas on which the Committee could be consulted to include guidelines and incentives in employment, legislation on social matters and application of the principle of equal opportunities and equal treatment, and public health. In the Lisbon TFEU Article 304 provides that the Committee may be consulted by the three institutions 'in all cases in which they consider it appropriate'. Failure to consult the Committee when required to do so would lead to invalidity of legislation for breach of an essential procedural requirement (Article 263 TFEU (ex Article 230 EC)).

Committee of the Regions (COR)

3.58 This Committee was established by the Maastricht Treaty in Articles 305–307 TFEU (ex Articles 263(2)–(4), 264 and 265 EC) and represents regional and local bodies within the Union. The Treaty of Nice added to this that members must hold either a regional or local authority mandate or are politically accountable to an elected assembly. Like the EESC, its role is to advise the European Parliament, the Council and the Commission, and membership is divided in very much the same way. The numbers are the same as for the EESC and the Nice Treaty again set a ceiling of 350 for membership. In 2012 the Committee of the Regions has 344 members and has the same number of alternate members from each of the 27 Member States. It was given greater autonomy by the Amsterdam amendments and no longer has a common organisational structure with the EESC. Article 305 TFEU (ex Article 263 EC) specifies that no member of the Committee may also be a member of the European Parliament. The Committee may be consulted by the three institutions 'where the Treaties so provide' and 'in all cases in which they consider it appropriate'.

The European Investment Bank

3.59 Articles 308 and 309 TFEU (ex Articles 266 and 267 EC) provide for the European Investment Bank (EIB) which is to have legal personality. Its Statute is laid down in a Protocol annexed to the Lisbon Treaty. The Articles provide for the bank's tasks, which consist of granting loans and giving guarantees on a non-profit-making basis to projects in the Union which contribute to 'a balanced and steady development of the internal market'. The bank facilitates the financing of investment programmes together with the structural funds and other Union financial instruments.

The European Central Bank

3.60 Article 13 TEU now includes the European Central Bank (ECB) as a fully fledged institution. The Bank, which together with national central banks constitutes the European System of Central Banks, was set up for when Economic and Monetary Union entered the third stage, which occurred on 1 January 2002. At the beginning of the second stage in 1994 a European Monetary Institute had been established as the precursor of the ECB (see Article 117 (ex Article 109f) EC). This has now been replaced by the ECB, which is an independent body determining policy for the single currency. The Central Bank's composition and functions are set out in Articles 282–284 TFEU.

FURTHER READING

Craig, P., *The Lisbon Treaty: Law, Politics and Treaty Reform* (Oxford: OUP, 2010) ch 3.

Douglas-Scott, S., *Constitutional Law of the European Union* (Harlow: Longman, 2002) ch 2.

Evans, A., 'European Union decision-making, third states and comitology' (1998) 47(2) *The International and Comparative Law Quarterly* 257–277.

Rosas, A. and Armati, L., *EU Constitutional Law: an Introduction* (Oxford: Hart Publishing, 2010) ch 6.

COREPER

Hayes-Renshaw, F., Lequesne, C. and Lopez, P., 'The permanent representation of the member states to the European Communities' (1989) 28(2) *Journal of Common Market Studies 119–137*.

European Council

Bulmer, S. and Wessels, W., *The European Council: Decision-Making in European Politics* (London: Macmillan, 1987).

Curtin, D., 'The constitutional structure of the Union: a Europe of bits and pieces' (1993) 30 *Common Market Law Review* 17.

Editorial Comments (1997) 34 *Common Market Law Review* 767–772.

Hartley, T., *The Foundations of European Union Law* (7th edn, Oxford: OUP, 2010) chs 1 and 2.

O'Keeffe, D. and Twomey, P., *Legal Issues of the Maastricht Treaty* (London: Chancery, 1994).

O'Keeffe, D. and Twomey, P., *Legal Issues of the Amsterdam Treaty* (Oxford: Hart Publishing, 1999).

Comitology

Craig, P., 'Delegated acts, implementing acts and the new Comitology Regulation' (2011) *European Law Review* 671.

European Parliament

Hix, S., Noury, A. and Roland, G., 'Dimensions of politics in the European Parliament' (2006) 50(2) *American Journal of Political Science* 494–511.

Hix, S. and Marsh, M., 'Punishment or protest? Understanding European Parliament elections' (2007) 69(2) *The Journal of Politics* 495–510.

SELF-TEST QUESTIONS

1   Discuss the legislative powers of the Commission under the TFEU, both original and delegated.

2   'Where Member States' vital interests are at stake, it is the Community (now Union) practice to proceed only by unanimity.' Discuss the history of this practice and its status in the light of the relevant Treaty provisions.

3   'The European Parliament has enhanced its role in the political process of the Union by intelligently exploiting the role it has been given in the judicial process.' Discuss, examining the role of the Parliament in proceedings before the European Court and the circumstances in which the Parliament can appear as a party in cases before the European Court.

4   What is meant by the expression 'institutional balance' as it has been developed in European Union law? To what extent is it useful in helping us to understand the relationships among the principal European institutions?

4 The European Courts: composition, functions, jurisdiction; preliminary rulings

SUMMARY

- The Court of Justice of the European Union
- The General Court
- Specialised courts
- Rules of Procedure
- Judicial activism
- Preliminary rulings
- Jurisdiction of national courts
- Discretionary and mandatory references
- When should a national court refer?
- Should national courts always make a reference?
- Interim measures
- Effects of preliminary rulings
- The future of preliminary rulings

4.1 The judicial system of the Union was, until the Treaty of Nice, a two-tier system. The Treaty of Nice then added a third tier and the Courts were renamed in the Treaty of Lisbon. The Court of Justice of the European Union (CJEU); established as the European Court of Justice (ECJ) by the ECSC Treaty of Paris in 1952 now consists of the Court of Justice, the General Court (formerly the Court of First Instance (CFI) created in 1989 in order to relieve the growing case load of the ECJ) and specialised courts (formerly called specialised tribunals). Article 19(1) TEU defines the fundamental task of the CJEU providing that: 'It shall ensure that in the interpretation and application of the Treaty the law is observed'.

The Court of Justice

4.2 The Court of Justice (referred to hereafter as 'the Court') is the main Court of the European Union. Article 19 TEU makes provision for the composition and activities of the Court. It consists at present of 27 judges, one from each Member State, although there is no nationality requirement. Judges are nominated on the basis of their independence and their satisfaction of conditions on suitability for high judicial office, and are appointed by common accord by Member State governments. The President of the Court is elected every three years by its judges. Judges are chosen from those with the proper qualifications for the highest judicial appointments in their home country, or who are 'jurisconsults' of recognised competence, by 'Common Accord' of the governments of the Member States after consultation with a panel—composed of former members of the Court of Justice and the General Court, members of national supreme courts and lawyers of recognised competence—which gives an opinion on candidates' suitability to perform the duties required. Their independence must be 'beyond doubt' (Articles 252 and 253 TFEU).

Articles 251–281 TFEU contain the detailed provisions for the workings of the Court of Justice, General Court and specialised courts, including the actions which the courts have jurisdiction to handle. The Court regularly sits in a 'grand chamber' of 13 judges, with the possibility of sitting in full plenary provided for by the rules in the Court's Statute (Article 251 TFEU). In the vast majority of cases, the Court sits in chambers of three, five, or (on occasion) seven judges.

4.3 The Court of Justice is assisted by eight Advocates General who are required to act 'with complete impartiality and independence' in making 'reasoned submissions on cases' with which the Court is involved (Article 252(2) TFEU). In practice, Advocates General deliver reasoned Opinions on cases in advance of the Court's final judgment, where appropriate. Such Opinions are non-binding, designed to assist the Court in its deliberations, a process in which the Advocate General plays no part. Judgments of the Court routinely refer to pronouncements made by the Advocate General's Opinion, parts of which may carry particular weight if the judgment omits to deal with an issue focused on in the Opinion.

The number of Advocates General at the Court may be increased by the Council, acting unanimously, at the request of the Court of Justice. Both judges and Advocates General are appointed by common accord of Member State governments for a period of six years, with reappointment possible. The General Court does not have any Advocates General, but may appoint a judge as an ad hoc Advocate General who does not take part in deliberations or drafting the judgment. Article 254 TFEU provides that the Statute of the CJEU may (in future) provide for Advocates General to assist the General Court.

4.4 Each member of the Court has three 'legal secretaries' (or *référendaires*) who act as their legal assistants. They undertake preliminary research and draft essential documents, including draft judgments and Opinions, but may not take part in the Court's deliberations (conducted in French) as these are secret and result in a single collegiate judgment.

4.5 The Court's procedure generally consists of a written phase, which ends in a report by the '*Juge-rapporteur*', an oral hearing, which is usually very brief, followed by the

Opinion rendered by the Advocate General. The final judgment is then given, usually after a number of months has elapsed. Over the past decade, various efforts have been made to maximise efficient working practices at the Court. For example, in the context of preliminary references, the so-called 'simplified procedure' allows the Court to dispose of references by reasoned order if: (i) the Court has already ruled on an identical question; (ii) the solution can easily be deduced from existing case law; or (iii) the solution is clear beyond reasonable doubt. Furthermore, the 'urgent' preliminary reference procedure, introduced to handle questions referred in the context of the Area of Freedom, Security and Justice (AFSJ) in 2008, fast-tracks references where the liberty of a citizen is at stake, the CJEU routinely turning around cases in a matter of weeks rather than months. The Court is increasingly dispensing with the need for an Opinion in all cases, enabling Advocates General to focus in particular on the most complex cases impacting on EU legal development.

The written procedure and the oral hearings, as well as the delivery of the Advocate General's Opinion, are translated into the official languages of the Court (there are currently 23 official languages). The Court's deliberations are subject to the principle of secrecy and are held in the absence of interpreters. Only the French language is usually used in these deliberations, although some chambers have occasionally worked in other languages such as German and English. A single collegiate judgment is delivered. This often (inevitably) represents a compromise of differing views and this may account for some of the difficulties when reading a judgment, which may sometimes appear to have an absence of reasoning on certain points.

4.6 Where an Advocate General is involved in the Court's work, his/her duty is to give reasoned Opinions on the cases brought before the Court, in open Court and with complete impartiality and independence. (S)he indicates to the Court how it should decide and gives it the arguments it needs to do so. Often the Advocate General's Opinion presents more extensive reasoning than the Court does in its collegiate decision. It may provide a pointer towards future decisions by the Court. See Slynn AG's Opinion in Joined Cases 60 and 61/84 *Cinéthèque SA v Fédération Nationale des Cinémas Français* (1985), which, although not followed by the Court on that occasion, pointed the way towards its judgment in Joined Cases C–267 and 268/91 *Criminal Proceedings against Keck and Mithouard* (1993). However, the Court is not bound to follow the Advocate General and does not always do so. Often the media in the United Kingdom reports an Advocate General's Opinion as if it were a judgment by the Court of Justice, although the judgment may well turn out to be different. This was the case, for example, in Case C–91/92 *Faccini Dori v Recreb Srl* (1994), where the Court ruled out the possibility of finding that directives could have horizontal direct effect, i.e. between individuals, something to which Lenz AG had pointed the way. Sometimes the Advocate General's Opinion is immensely influential, as was the case for Lenz AG's Opinion in Case C–415/93 *Bosman* (see **12.114** and **12.115**); Jacobs AG's Opinion in Case C–10/89 *Hag II* (changing the previous case law); Tesauro AG's Opinion in Case C–267/91 *Keck and Mithouard* (see **10.55**); and Elmer AG's Opinion in Case C–249/96 *Grant v South-West Trains Ltd* (1998), although in this case the Court also declined to follow his lead (see **6.42**).

Jurisdiction of the Court of Justice

4.7   The Lisbon Treaty's removal of the pillar structure resulted in the jurisdiction of the CJEU covering all areas of the law of the EU, unless the Treaties provide otherwise (Article 19 TFEU), with a major exception being the Common Foreign and Security Policy (CFSP) (Articles 23–46 TEU). The Court will not have jurisdiction over the CFSP, with two exceptions: (1) the Court will have jurisdiction to monitor compliance with Article 40 TEU; and (2) the Court will have jurisdiction to review the legality of decisions under Article 263(4) TFEU providing that restrictive measures against natural or legal persons have been adopted by the Council in connection, for example, with combating terrorism (freezing of assets) (Article 275 TFEU).

As a result of the abolition of the three pillar structure, which saw the field of police and judicial cooperation in criminal matters subsumed within the Area of Freedom Security and Justice (AFSJ), the Court of Justice will acquire general jurisdiction to give preliminary rulings in the AFSJ (Articles 67–89 TFEU). Consequently, any court or tribunal will be able to request a preliminary ruling from the Court of Justice in that area, rather than the highest national courts. There are, however, transitional provisions providing that full jurisdiction will not apply until five years after the entry into force of the Treaty of Lisbon (Article 10 of Protocol no 36).

As regards visas, asylum, immigration and other policies related to free movement of persons (in particular, judicial cooperation in civil matters, recognition and enforcement of judgments), the Court now has full jurisdiction, and no longer just for references from courts of last resort; the Treaty of Lisbon has repealed provisions which imposed restrictions on the jurisdiction of the Court of Justice in that context.

4.8   The Court has the following forms of jurisdiction: plenary jurisdiction and preliminary rulings.

1. Plenary jurisdiction

   (a)   Infringement actions against Member States. These actions may be brought under Article 258 TFEU, Article 259 TFEU, Article 260 TFEU, Article 268 TFEU and Article 340 TFEU (see **Chapter 8**).

   (b)   Direct actions under Articles 263 and 265 TFEU as well as under Article 268 TFEU are, since the Nice Treaty, in the competence of the General Court (see **Chapter 8**).

2. Preliminary rulings (Article 267 TFEU)

4.9   Article 267 TFEU provides for references to be made by national courts to the Court of Justice in cases concerning the *interpretation* of the Treaty as well as concerning the *validity* and *interpretation* of acts of the institutions, bodies, offices or agencies of the Union. References are different from appeals in the hierarchy of national courts. In contrast to appeals, references are always made *in the course of proceedings before a national court* and cannot be made after the case has been decided. When dealing with preliminary references, the Court of Justice does not decide the case concerned, it simply renders a decision concerning the interpretation of a point of Union law which is essential to the outcome of the case. Once this decision is given, the case returns to the national court which takes into account the Court's interpretation in order to come to its decision. This is why after each judgment in an Article 267 reference the Court of Justice will say that: 'since the proceedings are a step in the action pending before the national court, the decision on costs is a matter for that court'.

4.10   The national court will apply the Court's decision, but in doing so has discretion as to how to apply it. For example, in Case 41/74 *Van Duyn v Home Office* (1974) the Court had ruled that Directive 64/221 (now integrated into Directive 2004/38 Articles 27–29) had direct effect and that Ms van Duyn could, therefore, rely on the Directive before the English court. The English court decided that, having looked at the application of the Directive, it was justified in ruling that Ms van Duyn should be excluded from the United Kingdom (see **7.11**).

Inherent jurisdiction

4.11   Article 19 TEU provides that the CJEU 'shall ensure that in the interpretation and appli-cation of the Treaties the law is observed'. The Court has held that in order to achieve this purpose, in exceptional cases it has inherent jurisdiction which is not expressly provided for elsewhere in the Treaty. Thus, in Case C–70/88 *European Parliament v Council (Chernobyl)* (1990) it allowed the European Parliament to bring proceedings for the annulment of an act adopted by the Council, as this was necessary to protect its own prerogatives. In the Maastricht TEU, this right was incorporated in Article 230 EC (now Article 263 TFEU) and the EP's standing was made unlimited, on a par with the other Institutions, by the Treaty of Nice (see **Chapter 8**).

Interim measures

4.12   The Court of Justice of the European Union, i.e. all three component parts, has the power to award interim measures in direct actions, including infringement proceed-ings (see Articles 278 and 279 TFEU). The Court of Justice has not been called upon to decide whether it may grant interim measures in preliminary references under Article 267 TFEU. It is generally assumed there is no such power. The interlocutory powers of the national courts making references will generally be sufficient, and this now includes the power to suspend the application of a national measure based on a Community measure. See Joined Cases C–143/88 and C–92/89 *Zuckerfabrik Süderdithmarschen und Zuckerfabrik Soest* (1991), discussed further in **7.128**.

Enforcement of judgments

4.13   If a Member State fails to comply with a judgment, infringement proceedings may be brought against it by the Commission before the Court under Articles 258 TFEU (see **Chapter 8**, 'Public Enforcement of EU Law'). The burden of ensuring that a judgment is complied with seems to fall primarily on the Commission, which in most cases succeeds in persuading the Member States to comply without recourse to Court proceedings. For examples of cases in which action has been taken by the Commission against Member States for non-compliance with an earlier judgment of the court, see **8.22**.

Article 260(2) TFEU provides for the possibility of the Court imposing a financial penalty on the offending Member State if it continues to fail to comply. This has happened a few times since the provision was originally introduced in the Maastricht Treaty, but is very much the ultimate stage in persuading Member States to comply and is therefore invoked relatively rarely. The Treaty of Lisbon has speeded up the system of pecuniary sanctions. In particular, Article 260(3) TFEU, introduced by Lisbon, enables the Court of Justice to impose pecuniary sanctions at the stage of referral by the Commission under Article 258 TFEU in cases concerning a failure to notify national measures implementing a directive to the Commission.

Five years after the entry into force of the Lisbon Treaty, the Commission will be able to bring actions for failure to fulfil obligations in relation to measures concerning police cooperation and judicial cooperation in criminal matters adopted before the entry into force of the Treaty of Lisbon (Article 10(1) Protocol no 36).

Miscellaneous powers

4.14   (a) The Court may impose penalties under Article 261 TFEU in respect of Regulations adopted jointly by the European Parliament and the Council, and by the Council. This power is mainly used in competition cases.

(b) The Court of Justice has jurisdiction in disputes involving the European Investment Bank, on arbitration clauses contained in a contract concluded by or on behalf of the Community (Article 272 TFEU), in disputes submitted under special agreements (Article 273 TFEU), and may be asked for an opinion under Article 218(11) TFEU in respect of international agreements with third countries or international organisations. In case of an adverse opinion of the Court, the agreement may not enter into force unless it is amended or the Treaties are revised.

The Court of Justice acts both as a court of first instance and as an appeal court for cases from the General Court (Article 256(3) TFEU).

The General Court

4.15   The General Court (originally the Court of First Instance (CFI)) was created in 1989 as a means of relieving the former ECJ of its growing case load. This had increased from a few dozen cases in the 1960s to well over 100 in the 1970s, and to more than 400 in 1995. In 2010, the case load of the then CFI was as follows: 636 new cases (568 in 2009), 527 completed cases (555 in 2009), 1,300 pending cases (1,191 in 2009). As early as 1974 the then ECJ had already suggested the creation of a separate tribunal to hear staff cases. The SEA in 1986 finally provided for the creation of such a Court in Article 225 EC (now Article 256 TFEU). The General Court has at least one judge per Member State (at the moment 27 judges are determined by the statute). The General Court is primarily responsible for the adjudication of direct actions (actions for annulment) (Article 263 TFEU) and actions for failure to act (Article 265 TFEU); actions for damages (Article 268 TFEU and Article 340(2) TFEU); and has adjudicatory and appeal functions in respect of field-specific areas (for example, state-aid and trademarks).

There are no Advocates General, but for certain cases which may involve substantial investigations into facts, a judge may be appointed to carry out a similar function to that of an Advocate General. This judge will then not take part in the deliberations or the judgment. Although the Court of Justice itself will retain competence to give preliminary rulings, the statute may entrust such responsibility to the General Court in specific cases and such preliminary rulings may be exceptionally subject to review by the Court of Justice (Article 256(3) TFEU).

Specialised courts

4.16 The first of the specialised courts (formerly known as judicial panels), the European Civil Service Tribunal, was established in October 2005 to adjudicate in disputes between the European Union and its Civil Service (Article 270 TFEU). It is attached to the General Court and composed of seven judges appointed by a panel which seeks to ensure a geographical balance of members of the Tribunal. Since its establishment, the Tribunal has relieved the General Court of a substantial number of cases (about 25 per cent of the cases brought each year) and the Court of Justice of hearing appeals relating to those cases (about 10 per cent of cases brought each year).

This is the first of the specialised courts set up by the Council. It is possible that further specialised courts may be created in future, aiming to deal with cases in specific legal fields at first instance. Intellectual property is one such area particularly suited to the creation of a specialised tribunal, but in finding that the Council's draft agreement on the creation of a European and Community Patent Court was incompatible with EU law, Opinion 1/09 has effectively stalled efforts to establish the new tribunal. In the meantime, Article 262 TFEU allows the Council acting unanimously to attribute to the Court of Justice the responsibility of settling intellectual property disputes between private parties, particularly concerning the Union patent. An appeal from the decisions of specialised courts may be made to the General Court. Further specialised courts on competition law and trademark disputes are also being considered.

Rules of Procedure

4.17 Article 253 TFEU provides that the Court will establish its own Rules of Procedure, which require the approval of the Council.

A simplified procedure in making preliminary references enables the Court to decide by reasoned order that a matter is identical to one previously decided, thus saving a great deal of time. The Rules of Procedure further enable the *judge-rapporteur* and/ or the Advocate General to request from the parties any information they consider relevant. The Court may also issue Practice Directions for both preliminary references and for direct actions. The Court has made good use of the various procedures: making some use of the accelerated procedure, which allows it to give judgment within as little as six months of the case being brought, and frequent use of the simplified procedure.

4.18 The Treaty of Lisbon has introduced a provision requiring the Court of Justice to act with the 'minimum of delay' if a question referred for a preliminary ruling is raised in a case pending before any court or tribunal of a Member State with regard to a person in custody (Article 267(4) TFEU). This means the incorporation into the Treaty of the urgent preliminary ruling procedure (known as 'PPU', after its French acronym), which came into effect on 1 March 2008, and which applies to the AFSJ. The Rules of Procedure of the CJEU have been amended to accommodate the urgent preliminary ruling procedure, which applies only to Title V of the TFEU, the AFSJ. This new urgent procedure (Article 104b of the Rules of Procedure) provides for much more than the 'accelerated procedure' which already existed, but which could be applied only in exceptional cases. The new procedure greatly limits and simplifies the stages of the preliminary ruling procedure.

An example of a case accepted under the PPU is Case C–195/08 *Rinau* (2008) on judicial cooperation in civil matters, jurisdiction and enforcement of judgments. It concerned an application for non-recognition of a decision requiring the return of a child wrongfully retained in another Member State. In respect of the urgent procedure, the referring Lithuanian court considered that it was necessary to act urgently as this case concerned the return of a child to her parent and that any delay would be very unfavourable to the relationship between the child and the parent with whom she did not live. The damage to that relationship could be irreparable. There was also a need to protect the child against any possible harm and the need to ensure a fair balance between the interests of the child and those of her parents. The Court therefore accepted the application of the urgent procedure.

Judicial activism

4.19 When the first Community, the European Coal and Steel Community, was established in 1952, the Treaty and the institutions of the Community were to a large extent based on, and inspired by, the civil law systems of the six original founder members. The European Court of Justice, too, was probably based on the model of the French *Conseil d'Etat*, the highest French administrative court. Its jurisdiction under Articles 169, 170, 173 and 175 EEC (now Articles 258, 259, 260, 263 and 265 TFEU) was that of a supreme administrative court reviewing acts by Member States and the institutions and entertaining direct actions by individuals against the institutions only under strictly defined, limited conditions. Although the Court showed some signs of early action (for example in Case 4/73 *Nold v Commission* (1974), see **6.55**), its real development into a true, supreme court for the Community, started after the two later Communities, Euratom and the European Economic Community, had been founded in 1957.

4.20 Case 26/62 *Van Gend en Loos v Nederlandse Administratie der Belastingen* (1963) established the principle that individuals could rely on Community law before their national courts, the principle of direct effect, and Case 6/64 *Costa v ENEL* (1964) established the principle of supremacy of Community law over national law. The Court did this by interpreting the Treaty as to its 'spirit and general scheme' (for a more extensive discussion of the two cases, see **Chapter 7**). In both cases, the Court made it clear that the Treaties should be viewed as constituting a 'new legal order'. After these judgments, the Court has shown many examples of what critics might call judicial activism, but which could, on another reading, be considered a filling in of the gaps in a 'framework treaty', i.e. a text which is couched in general terms and which indicates general objectives, to be interpreted purposively, thus filling in the gaps left in the Treaty Articles. The Court, fulfilling its task in exercising its inherent jurisdiction (see **4.11**), thus proceeded to give an interpretation of Articles 173 and 175 EEC (now Articles 263 and 265 TFEU) which gave the European Parliament *locus standi* to bring cases and have cases brought against it by Member States and the other institutions (see **Chapter 8**). The invention of state liability for breaches of Union law is another example (see **Chapter 7**).

Preliminary rulings

4.21 The majority of cases decided by the Court of Justice are in response to preliminary references by national courts under Article 267 TFEU (see above **4.9**). Here the Court gives an interpretation but is not the final arbiter and does not render a definitive judgment. It gives an interpretation of Union law as a step in proceedings before the national court. In contrast to the appeals procedure where the parties to a dispute take the initiative to request an appeal, in the case of a reference the national court decides itself whether a reference to the Court of Justice is necessary. According to the Court, Article 267:

> …is essential for the preservation of the Community character of the law established by the Treaty and has the object of ensuring that in all circumstances this law is the same in all States of the Community. [See Case 166/73 *Rheinmühlen* (1974)]

4.22 The Article is 'based on cooperation which entails a division of duties between the national courts and the Court of Justice in the interest of the proper application and uniform interpretation of Community law throughout all the Member States' (Case 244/80 *Foglia v Novello (No 2)* (1981)). When a question of interpretation of Union acts is raised in a national court, the Court of Justice may, or sometimes must, be requested to give a ruling by the national court. This ruling indicates to the national court what its decision on the point should be, but it is the national court which makes the final decision. It is not an appeal procedure. It is an example of shared jurisdiction, depending for its success on mutual cooperation. The national court retains the final word in its application of the Court's interpretation. Case 41/74 *van Duyn v Home Office* (1974) is one example of how such application may differ from the intentions of the Court of Justice in giving its ruling (see **7.11**). The preliminary reference procedure has proved to be a major contributor to the development of Union law. This development began when the Court ruled in 1962 in Case 26/62 *van Gend en Loos* that individuals could also rely on Community law under certain conditions before their national courts in order to assert their Community rights. Thus, the doctrine of direct effect of Union law has opened the possibility to individuals to have access to the Court of Justice via their national court in cases where they would not have standing to have direct access to the Court of Justice. Thus, an individual may indirectly challenge action by Member States or by Union institutions before the Court and obtain a ruling from the Court which will give him/her the possibility to obtain an appropriate remedy from the national court.

4.23 The Court has jurisdiction to give preliminary rulings concerning the interpretation and the validity of Union law. Under the preliminary ruling procedure, the Court may give an interpretation of the Treaties, or rule on the interpretation or validity of acts of the institutions, bodies, offices or agencies of the Union (Article 267(1)(b) TFEU).

4.24 The phrase 'Interpretation of the Treaties' (Article 267(1)(a) TFEU) includes interpretation of provisions of both the TEU and the TFEU. However, international agreements which are not based on the Treaties do not fall within the scope of Article 267 TFEU (see Case 44/84 *Hurd v Jones* (1986), which concerned the Statute of the European School).

4.25 'Acts of the institutions' cover binding acts in the form of regulations, directives and decisions, as well as 'soft law' such as recommendations and opinions if the use of such instruments is necessary to aid the interpretation of national law adopted to implement Union law. See Case 322/88 *Grimaldi* (1989) which concerned a recommendation issued by the Commission. The Court said that, although a recommendation is not binding, it must nevertheless be taken into consideration by national courts when it is relevant to the interpretation of a national measure taken on the basis of the recommendation or where it is designed to supplement binding Community provisions.

4.26 In the same way the Court has held that an act need not be directly effective to be subject to interpretation under Article 267. See Case 111/75 *Mazzalai* (1976).

4.27 The Court has also accepted jurisdiction for the interpretation of international treaties which the Union has concluded, on the basis that these constitute 'acts of the
institutions'.

4.28 The Court of Justice cannot, in Article 267 TFEU proceedings, rule on the compatibility of a provision of national law with Union law. The Court can, however, provide national courts with all those elements, by way of interpretation of Union law,
which may enable national courts to assess that compatibility. See Case C–241/89
SARPP (1990). In Joined Cases C–143/88 and C–92/89 *Zuckerfabrik Süderdithmarschen
AG v Hauptzollamt Itzehoe* (1991) the validity of a national measure implementing
Community legislation was challenged on the basis that the Community measure itself
was invalid. The Court developed principles on the basis of which interim relief should
be granted by the national court (see also **7.127** and **7.128**). Moreover, in order to ensure
the uniform interpretation of Union law, the Court has jurisdiction to give a preliminary ruling on the interpretation of a provision of Union law in the particular case
where the national law of a Member State referred to the content of that Union provision, in order to determine the rules applicable to a purely internal situation in that
Member State. See Joined Cases C–297/88 and C–197/89 *Dzodzi v Belgian State* (1990).
In such a case the Court said that it would not look into the circumstances which had
prompted the reference, since the questions submitted by the national court concerned
the interpretation of a Community law provision. See also Case C–231/89 *Gmurzynska*
(1990) and Case C–28/95 *Leur-Bloem v Inspecteur der Belastingdienst/Ondernemingen
Amsterdam 2* (1997): the Court had jurisdiction where the situation in question was
not governed directly by Community law, but where the national legislature, in implementing a Community directive, had decided to apply the same treatment to internal
situations and to those governed by the directive, so it had aligned its domestic situation to Community legislation. In this case, the Court assumed jurisdiction in spite of
a contrary Opinion given by Jacobs AG.

4.29 Under the preliminary reference procedure, the Court will, in principle, only give an
interpretation of Union law and not advise a national court on the *application* of Union
law, nor will it order a national court to declare its national law invalid. However, it is
sometimes obvious that the Court will go beyond the mere interpretation of Union
law. Having declared in Case 106/77 *Simmenthal* (see **7.32** and **7.86**) that a national
court must apply Community law in its entirety within its jurisdiction and set aside any
national law, whether prior or subsequent, which may conflict with it, the Court held
in Joined Cases C–10–22/97 *Ministero delle Finanze v INCOGE* (1990) that this did not
mean that the incompatibility of a national rule adopted subsequently to a Community
rule had the effect of rendering that rule non-existent (see also Case 283/81 *CILFIT*, at
4.41). In Case C–206/01 *Arsenal v Reed* (2002), the Court stated in interpreting Directive
89/104/EEC that the use of the word 'Arsenal' on sports goods by a third party created
the impression that there was a connection between the goods and the proprietor of
the trademark. It therefore found an infringement. When the case returned to the
national court for a ruling, the judge, Laddie J, in *Arsenal Football Club v Reed* (2002),
held that in making findings of fact the Court had exceeded its duty of interpretation.

The national court, therefore, did not consider itself bound by the finding of the Court and decided that the goods did not indicate a trade origin and that, therefore, there was no infringement. The case was reversed on appeal. The English Court of Appeal ruled the Court's judgments are binding as to interpretation, but this does show the difficulty of finding the exact limits to the concept of interpretation and to the respective competences of the Court of Justice and the national court.

Jurisdiction of national courts

4.30 Under Article 267(2) TFEU, only a 'court or tribunal of a Member State' may refer questions to the Court. The meaning of the expression 'court or tribunal' is not confined to the central judicial arms of the state but extends also to other tribunals which are authorised to give rulings of a judicial nature. On the other hand, the expression does not cover a body which has before it a request for a declaration relating to a dispute which it is under no legal obligation to resolve.

4.31 In Case 246/80 *Broekmeulen* (1981), the Court defined the essential characteristics of a 'court or tribunal'. Dr Broekmeulen was a general practitioner (GP) who wished to register with the relevant Registration Committee in order to be entitled to practise as a GP in the Netherlands. He took his case to an Appeals Committee which, although a private body, exercised great control over medical practice in the Netherlands; it was not possible to practise without its approval. It was composed of medical practitioners, representatives of university medical faculties and government representatives. Although the Committee was not a court or tribunal under Dutch law, the Court nevertheless accepted the reference. It said that the expression 'court or tribunal' referred to:

> ...[a body which] performs its duties with the approval of the public authorities and operates with their assistance, and whose decisions are accepted following contentious proceedings and are in fact recognised as final, must be deemed to be a court of a Member State for the purpose of Article 177.

4.32 Case 61/65 *Widow Vaassen* (1966) concerned an arbitral tribunal which dealt with disputes regarding pension funds. The Court ruled this constituted a court within the meaning of Article 177 EEC (now Article 267 TFEU), as it was a permanent judicial body founded in the national law, its members were officially appointed by the government and were obliged to apply the rules of the law. The Court noted that the tribunal was bound by rules of adversarial procedure and established *inter partes* procedure as an element for a court or tribunal under Article 177. In Case 150/85 *Drake v Chief Adjudication Officer* (1986), the UK Chief Social Security Officer constituted a court or tribunal within the meaning of Article 177 EC. However, in Case 102/81 *Nordsee* (1982) an arbitration tribunal established under a contract between private individuals did not constitute a court or tribunal within the meaning of Article 177 EC; this was also applied in Case 318/85 *Criminal Proceedings Against Unterweger* (1986) where a reference was held to be inadmissible because the function of the referring body was not to resolve disputes but to submit opinions in administrative proceedings.

In Case C–24/92 *Corbiau v Administration des Contributions* (1993), the Court ruled that 'court or tribunal' could only refer to an authority which was a third party in relation to the body or person which had adopted the decision subject to the proceedings. The reference was refused on the grounds that a director of taxes acting in an administrative capacity was not a court or tribunal. It seems clear, therefore, that the criteria are that the body must be an established, permanent, compulsory jurisdiction, that it must apply rules of law and that it must also be independent of the parties in the dispute. This latter element was first suggested in Case 14/86 *Pretore di Salò* (1987). In Case C–54/96 *Dorsch Consult Ingenieursgesellschaft v Bundesbaugesellschaft Berlin* (1997) the Court took the opportunity to give a clear restatement of the criteria; the factors to be taken into account are whether the body is established by law, whether it is permanent, whether its jurisdiction is compulsory, whether its procedure is *inter partes* (see above *Vaassen*), whether it applies rules of law, and whether it is independent. In Joined Cases C–110–147/98 *Gabalfrisa* (2000) and Case C–407/98 *Abrahamsson* (2000), on the other hand, the Spanish Economic and Administrative Court held there was a separation of the judicial and the administrative function as the tribunal ruled on tax complaints against decisions by the Spanish tax administration without having received any instructions from the tax authority. The Court also rejected a reference from a regional financial authority in Vienna, on the basis that the adjudicators were appointed (although not employed) by the associated tax authority (Case C–516/99 *Walter Schmid* (2002)).

See also Case C–17/00 *de Coster* (2001) where Colomer AG criticised the *Vaassen* criteria as being vague and uncertain, but where the Court nevertheless restated the same criteria; and Court orders of 26 November 1999 in Case C–192/98 *Azienda Nazionale Autonoma delle Strade (ANAS)* (1999) and in Case C–440/98 *Radiotelevisione Italiana (RAI)* (1999) which concerned the status of the Italian Court of Audit (Corte dei Conti): a body may be considered a court or tribunal when exercising a judicial function, but cannot be treated as such when it exercises other functions, including administrative ones. Thus, the Court of Audit was not a body which could refer when exercising a function of *ex post facto* review of an administrative activity. This did not constitute a judicial function.

'Of a Member State'

4.33 The body should be in a Member State, or at least part of the judicial system of a Member State. See Case C–355/89 *Barr and Montrose Holdings Ltd* (1991), where the Court held that its jurisdiction applied to the Isle of Man, which is not covered by the entire Treaty, but to which a special Protocol annexed to the Treaty applies. Protocols have the same legal force as the Treaty itself. The Court also accepted jurisdiction in Joined Cases C–100 and 101/89 *Kaefer and Procacci* (1990), which concerned French ynesia, a French overseas territory which is part of the French judicial system. Case C–321/97 *Andersson v Svenska Staten* (1999) concerned the potential liability of an EFTA state, as Sweden then was, for damage caused to individuals by incorrect implementation of a directive referred to in the EEA Agreement (see **Chapter 7**). The Court declined jurisdiction. Although at the time of the ruling Sweden had become a Member State, the EEA Agreement had not given it jurisdiction to interpret that agreement in respect of its application to situations which did not come within the Community legal order. The Court took the same view in Case C–140/97 *Rechberger v Republic of Austria* (1999) (see further **Chapter 7**). In Case C–300/98 *Parfums Christian Dior* (1997), the Court of Justice extended the boundaries of the scope of the concept 'in a Member State' to include international courts. Its ruling confirmed that the Benelux Court of Justice (the highest court with jurisdiction to consider points of law relating to the Treaty establishing the Benelux Economic Union 1958 (Benelux Treaty)) not only had the capacity to refer under Article 234 EC (now Article 267 TFEU), but that it could be obliged to refer under Article 234(3) EC as a court of last resort, in the event that the *Hoge Raad* (Dutch Supreme Court) allowed an appeal to the Benelux Court of Justice.

Discretionary and mandatory references

4.34 Any court or tribunal may ask the Court for a preliminary ruling if it considers it necessary to enable it to give judgment (Article 267(2) TFEU). There is no obligation for the national court to make a reference to the Court ('permissive' jurisdiction) unless a question is raised before a court or tribunal 'against whose decisions there is no judicial remedy under national law' (Article 267(3) TFEU—'mandatory' jurisdiction). In the latter case a reference *must* be made to the Court provided the question will affect the outcome of the case (see Case 283/81 *CILFIT* (1982)).

4.35 The purpose of Article 267(3) TFEU must be seen in the light of the function of Article 267 TFEU as a whole, that is, to prevent a body of national case law not in accordance with the rules of Union law from coming into existence in any Member State (see Case 107/76 *Hoffmann-La Roche* (1977)).

4.36 The scope of Article 267(3) TFEU is not entirely clear. While it clearly applies to the courts or tribunals whose decisions are never subject to appeal (the 'abstract theory'), it is less clear whether it applies also to courts whose decisions in the case in question are not subject to appeal (the 'concrete theory'). It has been argued that although the wording of Article 267(3) TFEU may indicate that the abstract theory should be preferred, on the whole the case law of the Court of Justice (see Case 6/64 *Costa v ENEL* (1964)) seems to support the concrete theory. If one bears in mind the way in which the Court has interpreted Article 267(3) to give the individual the greatest possible access to the Court, the concrete theory would seem to be preferable.

When should a national court refer?

4.37 Article 267(2) TFEU provides that:

> …where such a question is raised before any court or tribunal of a Member State, that court or tribunal may, if it considers that a decision on the question is necessary to enable it to give judgment, request the Court to give a ruling thereon.

The national court, therefore, must consider that a decision on the question is necessary to enable it to give judgment. It follows that a national court may equally decide that the point of European law is not relevant to its decision, so that it is entitled not to make a reference.

4.38 In the early English case of *Bulmer and Bollinger* (1974) Lord Denning gave his interpretation of 'necessary' expressed in four guidelines. These were:

- the decision on the Community law point must be conclusive of the case;
- the national court may follow a previous Court of Justice ruling, but is free to refer the same point again if it wishes to obtain a different ruling;
- it may apply the doctrine of *acte clair* (see **4.41**);
- 'in general it is better to decide the facts first' before deciding whether a reference is necessary.

Courts should bear in mind factors such as length and extra cost of proceedings, and the importance of not unnecessarily adding to the workload of the Court. These guidelines have been cited many times by English courts, but they have also been the subject of much criticism and the courts in later cases have endeavoured to refine and qualify these arguments.

4.39 Questions as to whether a decision is necessary and whether the court has a duty to refer were considered, for example, in two cases: *Chiron Corpn v Murex Diagnostics Ltd* (1995) and *R v International Stock Exchange of the United Kingdom and the Republic of Ireland, ex p Else (1982) Ltd* (1993). In *Chiron v Murex*, which concerned proceedings for infringement of a patent, a High Court judge struck out certain paragraphs of the defendant's defence and refused leave to add others. There was an unsuccessful appeal to the Court of Appeal, after which the defendant requested the Court of Appeal to refer certain questions to the Court of Justice for interpretation and applied for leave to appeal to the House of Lords. Leave to appeal was refused and the request for a reference was adjourned until the time for petitioning the House of Lords for leave to appeal had expired, or until after the petition had been made and refused. After the petition had been refused by the House of Lords the application for a reference to the Court of Justice was renewed. Balcombe LJ, giving judgment, had pointed out in *Magnavision (SA) v General Optical Council (No 2)* (1987) that, once a domestic court has given judgment and its order has been drawn up, it is *functus officio* and has no power to make a reference under Article 177 EC (now Article 267 TFEU) 'This is so both as a matter of domestic law and as a matter of European law.' Staughton LJ, giving a concurring judgment, considered, however, that, although this is undoubtedly true in domestic law, it

> ...must yield to European law if there is a conflict. If an English court is by European law obliged to make a reference it is no answer that by our domestic law its powers are exhausted.

The reference was not made and the problem remains unresolved.

Two further cases address the problem, but do not provide a definitive answer. In Case C–99/00 *Lyckescog* (2002) the Court came to the conclusion that the court there was not a true court of last resort falling under Article 234(3) EC (now Article 267(3) TFEU) as particular circumstances made it possible to appeal to the higher court. In Case C–495/03 *Intermodal Transports* (2005) the Court said:

> Article 234 EC must be interpreted as meaning that when, in proceedings relating to the tariff classification of specific goods before a national court or tribunal, a binding tariff information relating to similar goods issued to a person not party to the dispute by the customs authorities of another Member State is submitted, and that court or tribunal takes the view that the tariff classification made in that information is wrong, those two circumstances:
>
> • cannot result, in respect of a court or tribunal against whose decisions there is a judicial remedy under national law, in the court or tribunal being under an obligation to refer to the Court questions on interpretation;
>
> • cannot, in themselves, automatically result, in respect of a court or tribunal against whose decisions there is no judicial remedy under national law, in the court or tribunal being under an obligation to refer to the Court questions on interpretation.

A court or tribunal against whose decisions there is no judicial remedy under national law is, however, required, where a question of Union law is raised before it, to comply with its obligation to make a reference, unless it has established that the question raised is irrelevant or that the Union provision in question has already been interpreted by the Court or that the correct application of Union law is so obvious as to leave no scope for any reasonable doubt. The existence of such a possibility must be assessed in the light of the specific characteristics of Union law, the particular difficulties to which its interpretation gives rise and the risk of divergences in judicial decisions within the Union.

In Case C–453/00 *Kühne & Heitz NV and Productschap voor Pluimvee en Eieren* (2004), the case concerned a 'final decision' of an administrative body which was based on a misinterpretation of Community law by a national court at last instance and that court has not referred the question to the Court of Justice for a preliminary ruling. Basing its ruling in particular on the principle of cooperation arising from Article 10 EC (now incorporated into Article 4(3) TEU), the Court stated:

The principle of cooperation arising from Article 10 EC imposes on an administrative bo[...] an obligation to review a final administrative decision, where an application for such review is made to it, in order to take account of the interpretation of the relevant provision given in the meantime by the Court where:

- under national law, it has the power to reopen that decision;

- the administrative decision in question has become final as a result of a judgment of a national court ruling at final instance;

- that judgment is, in the light of a decision given by the Court subsequent to it, based on a misinterpretation of Community law which was adopted without a question being referred to the Court for a preliminary ruling under Article 234(3) EC; and

- the person concerned complained to the administrative body immediately after becoming aware of that decision of the Court.

4.40 The problem would not arise if the Union law point, when it is decisive to the outcome, or might become so, were to be referred first to the Court. It would be in the spirit of Article 267(3) TFEU to regard that court as a court of last resort from whose decisions no appeal lies as of right. From a practical point of view, however, this would incur extra delay, and the lower court may feel it should first decide the facts, which might then make a reference unnecessary.

Should national courts always make a reference?

Acte clair and *acte éclairé*

4.41 Article 267(3) TFEU does not imply that every time a question of Union law arises the final court must refer it to the Court of Justice. A reference may not be necessary under the *CILFIT* rules (Case 283/81 *CILFIT* (1982)) which include the *acte clair* doctrine. There is no obligation to refer where the point has been decided by a previous court ruling, where:

> ... the correct application of Union law may be so obvious as to leave no scope for any reasonable doubt as to the manner in which the question raised is to be resolved.

However, before it reaches this conclusion the national court or tribunal must be convinced that the matter is equally clear to the courts of the other Member States which have different legal systems and different techniques of interpretation, and to the Court of Justice bearing in mind the peculiar characteristics of Union law, the different language versions, the Union terminology and the contextual understanding of Union law. (See also Case C–495/03 *Intermodal Transports* cited above at 4.39.)

4.42 This decision was applied by the Court of Appeal in *R v Stock Exchange, ex p Else* (1993) where Sir Thomas Bingham said:

> ...if the facts have been found and the Community law issue is critical to the court's final decision, the appropriate course is ordinarily to refer the issue to the ECJ unless the national court can with complete confidence resolve the issue itself...If the national court has any doubt it should ordinarily refer.

In this case the Court of Appeal decided it could resolve the issue itself and that it was *acte clair*, although upon a reading of the case it does not appear that the issues involved are entirely simple and straightforward.

Acte éclairé

4.43 Even if the highest court in the case considers a decision on a question raised before it necessary to enable it to settle a dispute, it need not always be obliged to refer. The Court of Justice referred to an exception to this obligation in Cases 28–30/62 *Da Costa en Schaake* (1963) where the Court said:

> ...the authority of an interpretation under Article 177 [now Article 267 TFEU] already given by the Court may deprive this obligation of its purpose and thus empty it of its substance. Such is the case especially when the question raised is materially identical with a question which has already been the subject of a preliminary ruling in a similar case.

The Court nevertheless then went on to give a ruling in the case. It should, however, be pointed out that *Da Costa* was decided on the same day as *Van Gend en Loos* and served to emphasise one of the most important and seminal judgments of the Court.

4.44 The amendments made to the Rules of Procedure of the Court in 2000 and 2001 now enable the Court to refuse a preliminary reference by reasoned order in cases where an identical point has already been decided. In Case C–256/99 *Hung* (not reported in the ECR), which was a 'test' case concerning citizenship which was identical to *Kaur*, the Court had not given a reply to questions which had been asked more than two years before, because it was waiting to give a ruling in Case C–192/99 *Kaur* (2001). The national court did not withdraw its questions after the ruling in *Kaur* had been given and the Court then made an order which had the same content as that ruling.

4.45 A number of orders have been made by the Court where it considered that the answer to the questions submitted could clearly be found in the existing case law. This was the case in Case C–307/99 *OGT Fruchthandelsgesellschaft* (2001) where the Court stated that, as it had previously found the agreement on trade-related aspects of intellectual property rights (TRIPs), annexed to the WTO Agreement, not to have direct effect, the same applied for the same reasons to the GATT Agreement which was also annexed to the WTO Agreement (see also **5.11**).

4.46 The application of the *CILFIT* rules needs to take account of the balance to be maintained between the obligation to refer which is essential for the uniform application of Union law and the need to avoid adding an unnecessary burden to the already excessive workload of the Court if a case concerns a question which is genuinely *acte clair*. The difficulty of this may be seen in the cases described above (**4.41–4.42**) as well as in others, such as the well-known refusal of the French *Conseil d'Etat*, the highest administrative court in France, to refer the *Cohn-Bendit* case to the Court of Justice (see further **7.70**).

4.47 In Case 314/85 *Foto-Frost* (1987), the Court of Justice ruled that while national courts have discretion whether or not to make a reference requesting a ruling on the validity of a Community act, they do not have power to make a finding of invalidity of an act of Community institutions. The Court ruled that national courts could reject an argument based on invalidity of a Community measure, but they could not declare a measure invalid. This decision was justified mainly on the basis that the uniform application of Community law should be safeguarded throughout the Community.

4.48 Where a judicial body has the right to make a reference under Union law, it cannot be deprived of that right by national law. See Case 166/73 *Rheinmühlen* (1974).

4.49 In Case C–415/93 *Bosman* (1996) (see **12.114**) the Court's jurisdiction to give a preliminary ruling was challenged by the Belgian Football Association on the grounds that the questions asked by the Belgian court bore no relation to the actual facts of the case or their purpose. The Court asserted (at 59) that:

> …in the context of the cooperation between the Court of Justice and the national courts provided for by Article 177 of the Treaty, it is solely for the national court before which the dispute has been brought, and which must assume responsibility for the subsequent judicial decision, to determine in the light of the particular circumstances of the case…

both the need for such a ruling and the relevance of the question which it submits to the Court.

Appeals against the order to refer

4.50 Where a lower national court makes an order for reference, the Court of Justice's long-standing view was that such orders referring questions for preliminary rulings can be appealed if national law permits an appeal from a decision of the referring court or tribunal (Case 13/61 *de Geus* (1961), Case 146/73 *Rheinmühlen II* (1974)). This question was reconsidered by the Court of Justice in Case C–210/06 *Cartesio* (2008). Whilst the main legal questions in the Hungarian reference concerned freedom of establishment, the Court made important findings focusing on the power of a domestic appellate court to vary the decision to refer made by a lower court. In respect of the reference issue, the Court found:

> Where rules of national law apply which relate to the right of appeal against a decision making a reference for a preliminary ruling, and under those rules the main proceedings remain

> pending before the referring court in their entirety, the order for reference alone being the subject of a limited appeal, the second paragraph of Article 234 EC [Article 267(2) TFEU] is to be interpreted as meaning that the jurisdiction conferred on any national court or tribunal by that provision of the Treaty to make the application of those rules, where they permit the appellate court to vary the order for reference to the Court for a preliminary ruling, cannot be called into question by the application of those rules, **where they permit the appellate court to vary the order for reference, to set aside the reference and to order the referring court to resume the domestic proceedings** (emphasis added).

Thus, whilst national procedures permitting an appeal against the making of a reference can remain in place, a national appellate court cannot ultimately override the decision of a lower national court to refer a question to the Court for a preliminary ruling. The Court's findings emphasise the authority and freedom for any national court to voluntarily make a reference under Article 267(2) TFEU, reserving the decision on the admissibility of the reference squarely with the Court of Justice.

Can a reference be stayed or withdrawn?

4.51 It is the practice of the Court to continue with the reference unless it is informed by the referring court that the reference is withdrawn or the effect of appealing in national law suspends the order for reference, or if the Court is asked by the national court to suspend the reference (see Case 13/61 *de Geus* (1962); Case 127/73 *BRT v SABAM* (1974)). In Case 31/68 *Chanel v Cepeha* (1970) the Court was informed that the case which had been referred to it had been quashed on appeal to a superior national court. It removed the case from the register and gave no ruling.

4.52 It is, however, only the Court of Justice which can make an order staying the reference once it is seised of it. It will do so where the order for reference is quashed on appeal by a superior court (see Case 106/77 *Simmenthal* (1978)). In *R v Secretary of State for the Home Department, ex p Adams* (1995) the English Court of Appeal had referred a number of questions to the Court of Justice, including one concerning the potential direct effect of Article 8a (now Article 21 TFEU) on the rights of free movement of European citizens. The case was subsequently taken off the register when political circumstances in the United Kingdom had changed and an order excluding Mr Adams from mainland Britain had been lifted. The withdrawal of that reference is to be regretted as it denied the Court the chance to rule on critically important issues raised in the reference (see further **13.52**).

Interim measures

4.53 A national court may be requested to order interim measures pending a ruling from the Court under Article 267 TFEU. Cases referred to the Court take a long time, up to two years, before judgment. In some cases, this may cause major harm to the plaintiffs.

In Case 314/85 *Foto-Frost v Hauptzollamt Lübeck-Ost* (1987), the Court suggested that a national court might grant such relief even pending a ruling on validity. In Case C–213/89 *Factortame* (1990), the Court held that the full effectiveness of Community law would be impaired if a rule of national law could prevent a court seised of a dispute governed by Community law from granting interim relief in order to ensure the full effectiveness of the judicial decision to be given on the existence of the rights claimed under Community law. The Court concluded that a court which in those circumstances considered that the only obstacle which precluded it from granting such relief was a rule of national law must set that rule aside.

Effects of preliminary rulings

4.54 The preliminary ruling is binding upon the referring court or tribunal as the interpretation or the decision on the validity of Union law by the Court is authoritative (see Case 69/85 *Wünsche* (1986)).

The ruling (on interpretation or validity) may operate as a precedent for all national courts (*erga omnes*) in subsequent cases involving the same Union provision. In exceptional cases where the interest of legal certainty so demands, the Court has been prepared to limit the general retrospective (*ex tunc*) effect of its ruling by analogy to Article 264 TFEU, despite the absence of an express provision as to the consequences of a declaration of invalidity under Article 267 TFEU.

4.55 In Case 43/75 *Defrenne* (1976) which involved the interpretation of Article 119 EEC (now Article 157 TFEU) on the principle of equal pay for men and women the Court, by analogy to Article 174 EEC (now Article 264 TFEU), restricted the temporal effect of its ruling to cases already pending before its judgment, as otherwise the judgment would have been very difficult for Member States to apply and would have entailed excessively high expenditure for them.

4.56 In Case 145/79 *Roquette* (1980), the Court, using Article 174 EEC (now Article 264 TFEU) by analogy, said that it was entitled to limit the effects in time of a judicial declaration of invalidity under Article 177 EEC (now Article 267 TFEU) despite the absence of any express provision as to the consequences of a declaration of invalidity under Article 177 EC (now Article 267 TFEU).

As a result, it can be concluded that generally the Court considers that its judgments take effect *ex tunc* except where it limits the temporal effects of its ruling.

The future of preliminary rulings

4.57 It was inevitable that the role of the Court had to change in respect of preliminary references. In the early years the Court encouraged Member States to bring preliminary references in the interest of the uniform interpretation of Community law. Gradually, the workload of the Court grew, and the questions put to it by the national courts became more complicated and sophisticated, prompting the Court to change its attitude. It started to rewrite the questions referred, irrespective of which court made the reference (see e.g. Case C–213/89 *Factortame*). Secondly, it declined jurisdiction in some references. The first case where the Court did this was in Case 104/79 *Foglia v Novello* (1980) where the parties wanted to obtain a ruling on the validity of the French tax system and on whether it violated Article 90 EC (now Article 110 TFEU) by way of a contrived use of a contractual clause to induce an Italian court to request a ruling. The contract between Foglia and Novello, a wine importer and a wine exporter, contained a clause which provided that Foglia should not bear the cost of any import duties levied by the French authorities in breach of Community law. An action was brought by Foglia before the Italian court seeking to recover the duty paid from Mrs Novello. The Italian court referred the question of the legality of the duty under Community law to the Court. The Court pointed out that it was only prepared to give a ruling on genuine disputes and refused a ruling. It said these proceedings had been brought simply to seek an answer to the question of legality of the French law. The Court again refused to give a ruling in Case 244/80 *Foglia v Novello (No 2)* (1981) which concerned the same point (see also Case C–83/91 *Meilicke*, below, at **4.61**).

The *acte clair* doctrine (see **4.41**) further qualified the unlimited acceptance of preliminary rulings by the Court.

4.58   The period leading up to, and beyond, the signing of the Maastricht Treaty on European Union saw the Court declining to accept jurisdiction in a growing number of cases. Some of these refusals were due to the fact that the Court had no jurisdiction over the Second and Third Pillars of the TEU. This situation has now been changed in the Treaty of Lisbon, with full jurisdiction over Title V TFEU, the Area of Freedom, Security and Justice (the former Third Pillar), although it has still practically no jurisdiction in the case of Chapter 2 of Title V TEU, specific provisions on the Common Foreign and Security Policy (CFSP) (the former Second Pillar).

Nevertheless, although the limits of the Court's jurisdiction are more closely defined, jurisdiction will still be generally accepted.

4.59   In Case C–130/95 *Bernd Giloy v Hauptzollamt Frankfurt am Main-Ost* (1997) the Court referred to cases in which, it said, it had:

> …repeatedly held that it has jurisdiction to give preliminary rulings on questions concerning Community provisions in situations where the facts of the cases being considered by the national courts were outside the scope of Community law but where those provisions had been rendered applicable either by domestic law or merely by virtue of terms in a contract (the Dzodzi line of cases). [See **4.28**.]

The Court said it was for the national court alone to assess the precise scope of a reference to Community law and that consideration of the limits which the national legislature may have placed on the application of Community law to internal situations is a matter for domestic law, and thus within the jurisdiction of national courts. It decided it had jurisdiction in the present case. This was confirmed by the Court in Case C–1/99 *Kofisa Italia* (2001) where Community law was not directly concerned but its application arose from an internal matter which had to be resolved under national legislation which conformed to Community law.

4.60 In Case C–33/01 *Salzmann* (2003) the Court clarified the admissibility of a reference where the circumstances of the dispute in the main proceedings were confined to one single Member State. The national court requested an interpretation of Community law for the purpose of determining the rules of national law which referred to it. The Court pointed out, as it had stated, for example in Case C–448/98 *Guimont* (2000), that it was up to the national court to determine the need for a reference and the relevance of the question (see **10.83** and **13.55**). Only in exceptional circumstances would the Court refuse a reference, where it was quite obvious that there was no relation between the facts of the case and the request for interpretation (see Case C–302/97 *Konle v Austria* (1999), and Case C–281/98 *Angonese* (2000). The Court stated as follows:

> [w]here, in relation to purely internal situations, domestic legislation adopts solutions which are consistent with those adopted in Community law in order, in particular, to avoid discrimination against foreign nationals, it is clearly in the Community interest that, in order to forestall future differences of interpretation, provisions or concepts taken from Community law should be interpreted uniformly, irrespective of the circumstances in which they are to apply [paragraph 34].

4.61 The case of *Meilicke* may well be one where the Court would have declined jurisdiction even in earlier years. In Case C–83/91 *Meilicke v ADV/ORGA* (1992) a professor of company law sued a company as a small shareholder as it refused to disclose information on 'disguised contributions' to the company and a reference was made to the Court. He had written a book about the subject, and the questions referred to the Court appeared in the book. The Court pointed out that it was essential to define the legal context in which the interpretation requested should be placed. The questions raised did not directly relate to the problem of the right of shareholders to receive information from the company's management but sought a clarification of the problem of the compatibility of a judgment of a national court with Community legislation, *in casu* a judgment of the German supreme civil court (the *Bundesgerichtshof*) and the Second Company Law Directive. The Court refused to answer the questions as it lacked the necessary basis in fact and law to do so.

4.62 Although the above case (**4.61**) may be regarded as unusual and to be judged on its peculiar facts, other cases arose where the Court again emphasised that the national court must establish the facts of the case before making the reference. In Joined Cases C–320–322/90 *Telemarsicabruzzo* (1993) two questions on the competition articles of the Treaty were referred to the Court, which the Court described as 'particularly laconic', providing so few details of law and fact as to make it impossible to identify the purpose of the questions referred. The Court declined jurisdiction and made no attempt to reformulate the questions. It sternly told the Italian court that:

> ...the need to provide an interpretation of Community law which will be of use to the national court makes it necessary that the national court define the factual and legislative content of the questions it is asking or, at the very least, explain the factual circumstances on which those questions are based.

This was particularly necessary in the complex field of competition law. In Case C–157/92 *Banchero* (1993) and Case C–387/93 *Banchero (No 2)* (1995) the Court pointed out that the Italian court had failed to define the legal or factual circumstances of the questions or at least explain the assumptions of fact on which they were based. The first case concerned the Italian tobacco monopoly and the national rules applicable to imported tobacco. The Italian court referred to the monopoly without describing any details: what was the content of the national law, what were its reasons for think-ing the national law was incompatible with Community law and making a reference? Nearly a year after the reference was made, during which time no clarification was obtained, the case was declared manifestly inadmissible by the Court in an Order. In the second case, the Court finally gave a ruling but still could not give an interpreta-tion with regard to Articles 81 and 87 (now Articles 101 and 107 TFEU). These cases undoubtedly show a tougher approach by the Court in its acceptance of jurisdiction, which has been criticised by commentators. However, in many cases it will still accept jurisdiction although not all the conditions described above have been met. This is shown for example in Case C–316/93 *Vaneetveld v le Foyer* (1994). Again, there was lit-tle information, but this case concerned a technical point and, in the view of the Court, the need was therefore less pressing and it could nevertheless give a useful reply even if the national court had not fully described the legal and factual situation. Jacobs AG emphasised that the Court had not altered its fundamental approach to Article 177 EC (now Article 267 TFEU) and the principle of cooperation and stressed that formalism should be avoided.

4.63 Probably partly as a result of this case law the Court issued a note for guidance on refer-ences by national courts (Proceedings of the Court of Justice and of the Court of First Instance of the European Communities No 34/97 (1997) 22 EL Rev 55). Such notes have been regularly re-issued to accommodate changes to Treaties, the Statute of the CJEU and to the Rules of Procedure of the CJEU. The latest Information Note on references from national courts for a preliminary ruling (2011/C 160/01) (28 May 2011) provides useful guidance for national courts on the functioning of the standard preliminary reference procedure and the urgent preliminary reference procedure (PPU). In terms of guidance for national courts drafting an order for reference, the Information Note emphasises the need for:

(a) a statement of facts;

(b) an exposition of the applicable national law;

(c) an indication of relevant EU law provisions;

(d) a statement of reasons for the reference on interpretation or validity, including specific comments on the relationship between the relevant EU law provisions and applicable national legal provisions;

(e) where appropriate, a summary of the arguments of the parties.

Submissions may be made by Member States and by the Commission. The note emphasises the need for clear and precise drafting. The national court is invited, if it wishes, to state its view on the answers to the questions referred.

FURTHER READING

Barnard, C. and Sharpston, E., 'The changing face of Article 177 references' (1997) 34 *Common Market Law Review* 1113.

Barnard, C., 'The PPU: is it worth the candle? An early assessment' (2009) 34(2) *European Law Review* 281–297.

Broberg, M.P., 'Acte clair revisited: adapting the Acte Clair criteria to the demands of the times' (2008) 45 *Common Market Law Review* 1383–1397.

Broberg M.P. and Fenger N., 'Preliminary references as a right—but for whom? The extent to which preliminary reference decisions can be subject to appeal' (2011) 36(2) *European Law Review* 276.

Craig, P., 'The Treaty of Lisbon: process, architecture and substance' (2008) 33(2) *European Law Review* 137 (note sections on the impact of the Treaty of Lisbon on the Court of Justice).

Jacobs, F.G., 'Recent and ongoing measures to Improve the efficiency of the Court of Justice' (2004) 29(6) *European Law Review* 823.

Komarek, J., 'Federal elements in the Community Judicial System: building coherence in the Community legal order' (2005) 42 *Common Market Law Review* 9–34.

Lenaerts, K.L., 'The rule of the law and the coherence of the judicial system of the European Union' (2007) 44 *Common Market Law Review* 1625.

O'Keeffe, D., 'Is the spirit of Article 177 under attack?' (1998) 23 *European Law Review* 6.

Rasmussen, H., 'The European Court's acte clair strategy in *CILFIT*' (1984) *European Law Review* 242.

Rasmussen, H., 'Present and future European judicial problems after enlargement and the post-2005 ideological revolt' (2007) 44 *Common Market Law Review* 1681.

The European Court of Justice

Stone-Sweet, A., 'The European Court of Justice' in Craig, P. and De Búrca G. (eds), *The Evolution of EU Law* (2nd edn, Oxford: OUP, 2011).

Tridimas, T., 'The Court of Justice and Judicial Activism' (1996) 21 *European Law Review* 199.

Tridimas, T., 'The role of the Advocate General in the development of Community law: some reflections' (1997) 34 *Common Market Law Review* 1349.

Vesterdorf, B., 'The Community system the years from now and beyond: challenges and possibilities' (2003) *European Law Review* 303.

Wattel, P., 'Köbler, CILFIT and Welthgrove: we can't go on meeting like this' 41 *Common Market Law Review* 177–190.

SELF-TEST QUESTIONS

1   In what circumstances will it not be proper for the Court of Justice to answer a question referred to it for a preliminary ruling?

2   What is meant by 'court or tribunal of a Member State' in Article 267 TFEU?

3   In the course of proceedings before an English court between John Brown (a private individual) and the UK Government, it is argued that certain provisions of a British statute, the Immigration Act 1971, are contrary to the European Convention on Human Rights. Brown goes on to argue as follows:

(a) the Convention is binding on the Union and therefore binding on the United Kingdom as a matter of Union law;

(b) it is directly effective;

(c) therefore, the Immigration Act should not be applied if it conflicts with the Convention.

The English court then makes a preliminary reference to the Court of Justice, requesting that it should interpret the relevant provision of the Convention and rule whether arguments (a), (b) and (c) are correct. Before the Court of Justice, the UK Government argues that the Court of Justice has no jurisdiction to interpret the Convention because it does not fall within the list of instruments in the first paragraph of Article 267 TFEU; it also rejects the arguments put forward by Brown. You have recently been appointed Advocate General at the Court of Justice. Outline your opinion.

4   'Many national courts, the British courts included, accept fairly widely the doctrine of *acte clair*. This shows an insular attitude which is incompatible with the meaning and the spirit of Article 267 TFEU and should thus be used sparingly. Even then, in order to decide whether or not the answer is obvious one should approach the matter from a thoroughly Union point of view.' Discuss.

5   To what extent is it true to say that the use made in practice of Article 267 TFEU has gone far beyond the objectives envisaged for it in the TFEU?

5

The Union legal system

SUMMARY

- Sources of law and types of acts
- Primary legislation: Treaties, Conventions, acts by Member States
- Secondary legislation: regulations, directives, decisions, recommendations, opinions
- Other sources of law
- 'Soft law'
- Legislative procedures: ordinary legislative procedure, special legislative procedure, consultation, assent
- Legislative powers: express and implied powers; exclusive and concurrent powers
- The application of the principle of subsidiarity and proportionality

5.1 The Union legal system is based on several sources of law. Union law is not universal, nor can the Union enact any legislation it pleases; its competence is limited to the powers attributed to the Union by the legal texts adopted by the Member States. The principle of this attribution of powers, or conferral, which was first described in Article 5 EC has now been spelt out much more fully in Articles 4 and 5 TEU. Both Articles emphasise that on the one hand under the principle of conferral the Union acts only within the limits of the competences conferred upon it by the Member States, but then state clearly that 'Competences not conferred upon the Union in the Treaties remain with the Member States' (Article 5(2) TEU). Article 4(1) repeats this and goes on to spell out the respect of equality of Member States before the Treaties, as well as their national identities, 'essential State functions' such as law and order, and particularly emphasising that national security remains the sole responsibility of each Member State. The competences conferred upon the Community and later the Union have grown considerably in strength and extent since the inception of the Union; the field of application of Union law has been widened by each successive Treaty and the Union institutions have received more powers through these Treaties. There is little doubt that through the interpretation of the Union powers by the Court of Justice of the European Union, further extension of their application has occurred. General principles of law which are recognised and applied by the Member States have been used by the Court to underpin the Union legal system.

The sources of Union law are:

- *primary legislation*: the Constitutive Treaties, subsidiary Conventions, acts by the Member States;

- *secondary legislation*: regulations, directives and decisions;

- *other sources of law*: international agreements, general principles of law (see **Chapter 6**), case law of the Court of Justice (see **Chapters 3** and **4**), recommendations and opinions, 'soft law': memoranda, circulars, statements and resolutions.

Primary legislation

5.2 The primary legislation of the Union may be divided into three categories: the Constitutive Treaties, subsidiary Conventions, and acts by the representatives of the Member States.

5.3 The *Constitutive Treaties* are:

- the Treaty establishing the European Coal and Steel Community (ECSC) 1952 (now expired and, insofar as necessary, absorbed into the TFEU);

- the Treaty establishing the European Economic Community (EEC) 1957;

- the Treaty establishing the European Atomic Energy Union (Euratom) 1957;

- the Convention on Certain Institutions Common to the European Communities, signed at the same time as the EEC and Euratom Treaties in 1957 and providing for a single Parliamentary Assembly and a single European Court of Justice to serve all three Communities;

- the Merger Treaty 1965, establishing a single Council of Ministers and a single Commission for the three Communities;

- the Budgetary Treaties;

- the First Treaty of Accession 1972 (Denmark, Ireland, United Kingdom); the Second Treaty of Accession 1981 (Greece); the Third Treaty of Accession 1986 (Spain and Portugal); the Fourth Treaty of Accession 1995 (Austria, Finland and Sweden); the Fifth Treaty of Accession (2004: Estonia, Latvia, Lithuania, the Czech Republic, Slovakia, Slovenia, Hungary, Poland, Cyprus and Malta); the Sixth Treaty of Accession 2005 (Bulgaria and Romania); the Seventh Treaty of Accession with Croatia was signed on 9 December 2011 and Croatia is set to join after ratification by all Member States, in July 2013.

- the Single European Act 1986;

- Treaty on European Union 1993 (TEU or Maastricht Treaty); Agreement on the European Economic Area; the Treaty of Amsterdam 1999 (TOA); the Treaty of Nice 2003; and

- the Treaty of Lisbon (2009).

The amendment procedure is now governed by Article 48 TEU (ex Article 48). There is an ordinary revision procedure as well as simplified revision procedures. In the ordinary revision procedure the initiative for a Treaty amendment which may increase or reduce Union competences may come from a Member State, the European Parliament or from the Commission. The proposal is then submitted to the Council which in its turn submits it to the European Council and to the national Parliaments. If the European Council adopts a decision to examine the proposed amendments and after consulting the European Parliament and the Commission, the President of the European Council will then convene a Convention consisting of representatives of national Parliaments, of the Heads of State or Government of the Member States, of the European Parliament and of the Commission. In the event of institutional changes in the monetary area the European Central Bank must also be consulted. The European Council may decide the amendments are not extensive enough to need a Convention. In both cases an inter-governmental conference convened by the President of the Council decides on the adoption of the amendments. Ratification then takes place by the Member States in accordance with their respective constitutional requirements. The TEU then provides for a simplified revision procedure, but only in respect of Part Three TFEU: Union Policies and Internal Actions. The European Council may then adopt the amendments unanimously and ratification takes place by Member States in accordance with their constitutional requirements. Article 48 TEU provides for further simplified procedures in other areas. The United Kingdom has adopted the European Union Act, which provides for the holding of a referendum in case of major Treaty amendment or in any cases where amendments to the Treaty are made by the simplified procedure, but involve an extension of the competence of the Union. Article 49 TEU describes the procedure to be followed when new Member States join the Union. Any European state may apply for admission if it is democratic and respects the values as contained in Article 2 TEU, e.g. human rights, equality etc. Such a Treaty of Accession must be ratified by the contracting states in accordance with their constitutional requirements: they must also accept the *acquis communautaire*. The UK European Union Act does not require a referendum in case of a pure Accession Treaty, which contains no other provisions.

5.4 Until the Treaty of Lisbon, there was no provision for a Member State to leave the Union. This is now regulated in Article 50 TEU. Any Member State may withdraw from the Union 'in accordance with its own constitutional requirements'.

5.5 There are numerous Protocols annexed to the various Treaties as well as large numbers of Declarations. The Protocols have the same legal force as the Treaties themselves, but the value of Declarations is mainly political, unless they are unanimous and referred to in the Treaty itself.

Subsidiary Conventions

5.6   Article 293 EC (now repealed) provided that Member States shall, so far as necessary, enter into negotiations with each other with a view to securing various rights for the benefit of their nationals: the protection of rights of nationals of other Member States, the abolition of double taxation, the mutual recognition of companies and the retention of their legal personality if they move to another Member State, the possibility of mergers between companies from different countries, the simplification of formalities governing the recognition and enforcement of judgments and of arbitration awards. The Brussels Convention on Jurisdiction and the Enforcement of Judgments in Civil and Commercial Matters 1968, was concluded to attain one of the objectives in the original Treaty. Another example is the Rome Convention on the law applicable to Contractual Obligations (1980), which, like the Brussels Convention, gives the Court of Justice jurisdiction to interpret its provisions. When new Member States join the Union they are expected to become parties to it.

Even if Conventions concluded between Member States do not fall within the areas covered by Article 293, they might qualify. The Schengen Agreements on the gradual abolition of checks at common borders were integrated by a Protocol to the Treaty of Amsterdam into the Treaty on European Union. Schengen consisted of two agreements which were not covered by Article 293 EC. The status of the agreements was the subject of much debate, as it was never certain to what extent they were subject to Union law, although they provided for the supremacy of Union law in case of conflict. A Protocol attached to the Treaty of Amsterdam provided that Schengen as well as related agreements and rules adopted on the basis of the agreements were to be incorporated into the framework of the European Union. The Schengen *acquis* applies to the Member States which have signed up to it. The United Kingdom and Ireland are not bound by the agreements but may elect to take part in some areas of cooperation.

In the event of conflict, the constitutive Treaties have superior status in the Union legal system. In the event of a conflict between a subsidiary Convention and a Union act such as a regulation or directive which is directly derived from the Treaty, the Union act will prevail.

Acts of representatives of Member States

5.7   The Member States sometimes act outside the scope of the institutions, for example during summit meetings of the European Council. An example is the decision taken by the Heads of State or Government meeting within the European Council in December 1992 to accommodate some of Denmark's problems which had caused a negative vote in the referendum to ratify the Maastricht Treaty. Before the existence of the European Council, such decisions or declarations were made during meetings of the Council of Ministers but were considered as acts of the Member States. Such acts sometimes have legal force, but sometimes their legal effect is not clear, as in e.g. the Luxembourg Compromise (see **3.17**), the Ioannina Compromise (see **3.19**), which was given legal force by the Amsterdam Treaty, and the Act on Direct Elections to the European Parliament.

International agreements–powers of the Union

5.8 Union law may prevent Member States from acting independently in the case of international agreements. Apart from the treaty-making powers expressly given to the Union by the Treaty provisions, essentially as regards the Common Commercial policy and Association agreements, the Union has powers to conclude agreements in areas covered by the Treaties where it has internal powers. A wide power to take action is provided by Article 352 TFEU (ex Article 308 EC), which allows the Union to take action where it should prove necessary in order to attain one of the objectives set out in the Treaties, and where the Treaties have not provided the necessary powers (see further **5.53**). How much authority the Union has to negotiate or conclude agreements instead of Member States depends on the interpretation of these powers. In a line of decisions the Court of Justice has indicated how far powers can be implied from the express powers given in the Treaties. Express powers exist in the whole field of the Common Commercial Policy, for example. Implied powers can, in the theory of parallelism until fairly recently increasingly favoured by the Court, be derived from the express, internal powers. This extends the competence of the Union to conclude agreements to any of its objectives which are concerned with internal as well as external relations.

5.9 If the Union has exclusive power to act, the Member State will be precluded from acting itself. Therefore, each time the Union adopts provisions to attain a common objective, the Member States no longer have the right, individually or collectively, to adopt measures inconsistent with those rules. There are a number of areas where the Union has exclusive power. As the Union legislates, more areas will fall under this exclusive power. The TFEU which organises the functioning of the Union now lists the categories and areas of exclusive and shared competence in specifically defined areas (see Articles 2, 3 and 4 TFEU on exclusive and 'shared' competence). In a number of cases the Court has held that existence of Union power to enter into international agreements with a non-Member State in a certain area can preclude Member States from acting independently in that area.

The common transport policy called for in Article 90 TFEU (ex Article 70 EC) provides a good example. In Case 22/70 *Commission v Council (ERTA)* (1971) the Court considered whether the Community could enter into agreements with non-Member States and stated that the authority of the Community to do so should be viewed in the light of the whole scheme of the Treaty. If such an implied power existed and had been exercised by the Community, it would be able to conclude such agreements. In the field of transport covered by Title VI TFEU (ex Title V EC) the Community had been slow in legislating. Although it was accepted that the Community had taken over from the Member States where it had legislated, the Member States were still accepted as parties to the agreement, as these powers had not yet been exercised when the new agreement was negotiated and it was a renegotiation of an existing agreement. There was a concurrent or shared power between the Community and the Member States.

In *Opinion 1/75 on an OECD local cost standard* (1975), the Court of Justice recognised that power was expressly given to the Community by Article 231 EEC (now replaced by Article 220 TFEU) which provides for the establishment of appropriate forms of cooperation with international organisations). Such express power would lead to the exclusion of concurrent powers by the Member States unless Member States had been expressly authorised by the Community to act.

In *Opinion 1/76 on a Laying-up Fund for Inland Waterway Vessels* (1977) which again concerned Title VI, as in *ERTA*, it was accepted that the Community had legislated and that the implied power which had been the subject of debate in *ERTA* was to be exercised by the Community as an exclusive power.

In *Opinion 1/91 on the Draft Agreement on a European Economic Area* (1991) the Court held that the proposed EEA Court was incompatible with the Treaty as it would have jurisdiction to decide on the competence to be attributed to the Community and to the Member States, while this was for the Court of Justice to decide under Article 219 EEC (now Article 344 TFEU).

In its Opinion on the powers of the Union in respect of the World Trade Organisation (WTO) (*Opinion 1/94 Re WTO Agreement* (1994)) the Court considered the extent of the powers of the Community. It decided that the Community had exclusive competence in the field of the Common Commercial Policy under Article 113 EEC (now see Article 207 TFEU). This applied to goods, including agricultural products. However, the Union shared authority with the Member States in the other parts of the agreement. The part of the agreement concerning services (GATS) fell partly inside, partly outside Article 113. The cross-border provision of services, where neither the provider nor the recipient of the service moves fell inside Article 113, but all other agreements concerning service provision, as well as the part of the agreement concerning intellectual property rights fell outside Article 113. The Court ruled out any application of the implied powers doctrine as given in *ERTA* and in Opinion 1/76 to either GATS or TRIPs (trade-related aspects of intellectual property). The latter agreement concerned intellectual property and was held by the Court to fall within the exclusive competence of the Member States.

5.10 There are three types of international agreements:

- agreements between the Union and one or more non-Member States;
- agreements between the Union and Member States acting jointly, and one or more non-Member States;
- agreements between Member States and non-Member States.

5.11 Agreements of the first two types are considered an integral part of Union law; agreements of the third type are generally not part of Union law. Thus, association agreements with the Union are part of Union law, as specifically provided for by Article 218 TFEU (ex Article 300 EC). This was confirmed in Case 181/73 *Haegeman v Belgium* (1974), which concerned the association agreement between the Community and Greece; in Case 12/86 *Demirel v Stadt Schwäbisch Gmünd* (1987) which concerned the association agreement between the Community and Turkey; and Case 270/80 *Polydor Ltd v Harlequin Record Shops* (1982) which concerned the agreement between the Community and Portugal. Case 87/75 *Bresciani v Amministrazione Italiana delle Finanze* (1976) concerned the Yaoundé Convention and in Joined Cases 21–24/72 *International Fruit* (1972) the Court held it was competent to review the provisions of the GATT Agreement (the General Agreement on Tariffs and Trade). Can such agreements have direct effect? In Case 104/81 *Kupferberg* (1982) the Court was asked this question concerning the association agreement with Portugal. In a lengthy ruling the Court found that they can; the provisions of such an agreement would have to be given uniform effect throughout the Community.

However, those agreements which pursue different aims from those of the Union will not be directly effective. In *International Fruit* the GATT, which was concluded before the Treaty of Rome, was held by the Court not to be capable of direct effect, even though the Community had succeeded to the obligations of the Member States within the framework of the GATT. The question arose again, after the conclusion of the World Trade Organisation agreement in 1994, of which the GATT is an integral part. The new GATT provisions contained a clear mechanism for the settlement of disputes, including a court by whose decisions Member States have undertaken to abide. In some specific cases, the Court has accepted that the GATT rules may now take precedence over Community law under certain conditions. In Case C–280/93 *Germany v Council* (1994) the Court said it is not generally possible to rely on GATT rules to challenge the legality of a Community act. There are, however, exceptions to this rule:

> … It is only if the Community intended to implement a particular obligation entered into within the framework of GATT, or if the Community act expressly refers to specific provisions of GATT that the Court must review the lawfulness of the Community act in question from the point of view of the GATT rules [see paragraph 11 of the judgment].

This last point was repeated in Case C–352/96 *Italy v Council* (1998) (paragraph 19). In Case T–256/97 *BEUC v Commission* (2000) the CFI said with reference to the GATT anti-dumping code:

> The Community legislature has signalled that where words are carried over from the GATT agreement into the Regulation, they should have the same meaning in Community law as they do in the agreement.

Public international law in EU Courts

5.12 The Court of Justice has increasingly taken account of, or sometimes deferred to, rulings by other specialised courts. It has pointed out that the Community should respect international law in the exercise of its powers (see Case C–286/90 *Poulsen* (1992) and Case C–162/96 *Racke* (1998)). In Opinion 1/91 *EEA* (1991) it pointed out that the Community's capacity to conclude international agreements:

> necessarily entails the power to submit to the decisions of a court which is created or designated by such an agreement as regards the interpretation and application of its provisions.

It has referred to rulings, for example, by the EFTA Court (in Case C–192/01 *Commission v Denmark* (2003)) citing the EFTA Court judgment of 5 April in Case E–3/00; the European Court of Human Rights (with increasing frequency, see for example in Case C–94/00 *Roquette Frères* (2002)); the Appellate Body of WTO (see Case C–245/02 *Anheuser-Busch* (2004)); and the International Court of Justice (see *Poulsen* and *Racke*).

5.13 Increasingly, the question as to how far the EU is bound by international law is raised, in particular in connection with terrorism and money laundering. Is the EU bound by public international law in the form of Security Council resolutions so that it can adopt Regulations based on them? Does the Court of Justice have jurisdiction to review provisions adopted under such Regulations on the grounds of infringement of EU human rights standards? This was the question raised in the cases in this paragraph below.

In Joined Cases C–402/05 P and C–415/05 *P Yassin Abdullah Kadi and Al Barakaat International Foundation v Council and Commission* (2008) the cases were an appeal against judgments of the CFI (now the General Court) in Case T–306/01 *Yusuf and Al Barakaat International Foundation v Council* and Case T–315/01 *Kadi v Council and Commission* which were set aside by the Court of Justice. Mr Kadi, a Saudi Arabian resident, and the Al Barakaat Foundation, situated in Sweden, had asked for the annulment of a Regulation which contained a list of designated entities drawn up by the United Nations Security Council as being associated with Osama bin Laden, Al-Qaeda or the Taleban. Those on the list were subject to orders freezing their assets in UN countries. The Council of the European Union had adopted this Regulation (No 881/2002) in 2002, replacing a previous one. The names of the complainants had been placed on the list in October 2001. The actions before the Court of First Instance (now the General Court) claimed that the Council was not competent to adopt such a Regulation and that the Regulation infringed their fundamental right to property, the right to be heard and the right to receive reasons. The CFI rejected the claims and held that the Regulation was valid. The Community had no jurisdiction, save in respect of certain overriding rules of international law, known as *jus cogens*. It held that Member States are bound to comply with Security Council resolutions under the United Nations Charter, an international treaty which prevailed over Community law. On appeal, the Court of Justice held that the CFI had erred in law in ruling that the Community courts had, in principle, no jurisdiction to review the internal lawfulness of the contested Regulation. The CFI had been right to conclude, however that the Council was competent to adopt the Regulation on its chosen legal base (Articles 60 and 301 EC jointly with Article 308 EC (now Articles 75, 215 as amended, and 352 TFEU). The Court undertook a full review of the internal validity of the Regulation in the light of the fundamental rights forming an integral part of the general principles of Community law prevailing in a Community based on the rule of law. It was the expression of a constitutional guarantee, stemming from the EC Treaty as an autonomous legal system. The Court emphasised that the review of lawfulness applied to the Regulation adopted to give effect to the international measure, not to the international instrument itself. It would not challenge the primacy in international law of the resolution on which the Regulation was based. The Court further concluded that, in the light of the actual circumstances surrounding the inclusion of the appellants' names in the list of persons and entities whose funds are to be frozen, it must be held that the rights of the defence, in particular the right to be heard, and the right to effective judicial review of those rights, had clearly not been respected. The Court did acknowledge, however, that the protection of these rights, in particular prior communication of the grounds on which the measure at issue was based, was liable to jeopardise the effectiveness of the measures freezing funds and economic resources which must, by their very nature, be a surprise and apply with immediate effect. Nor, for the same reasons, were the Community authorities required to hear the persons concerned before their names were included in the list. The Court further held that other rights, the right to defence and the right to property in the case of Mr Kadi, had also been infringed.

The Court therefore annulled the Regulation insofar as it applied to the freezing of Mr Kadi's and Al Barakaat's funds, but it did not annul the Regulation itself, maintaining its effects for a period of no more than three months in order to allow the Council to remedy the infringements found. The Court noted that in that period, on the merits of the case, it may well be that the measures taken against the applicants would prove to be justified.

This case has given rise to a great deal of discussion. Here, international law and Union law are at risk of being in conflict and Member States applying the Regulation could conceivably be in breach of international law in the form of a Security Council Resolution. It is understandable, nevertheless, that the Court sees itself as defending the Union standard of protection of fundamental rights, a higher standard than that which could be applied in international law under the UN charter. This is just as, over 30 years ago, the German Federal Constitutional Court in *Internationale Handelsgesellschaft (Solange I)* (1974) (see **7.80** and **7.81**) considered that the Community had not yet achieved the standard of protection in a human rights 'catalogue' which existed under the German Constitution, declining supremacy of Community law in this respect. Mr Kadi returned to the fray in another case brought before the General Court (Case T–85/09 '*Kadi II*' (2010)) (see also **8.37**). The General Court annulled the listing, making it clear that it was following the Court of Justice's guidance. However, it noted 'doubts' voiced in legal circles as to whether that judgment was 'consistent, on the one hand, with international law'. It then went on to list, on the other hand, the judgment's consistency with specific UN Charter provisions, the EU Treaty and even with a declaration on the Common Foreign and Security Policy annexed to the Treaty of Lisbon. The General Court concluded remarkably that 'those criticisms are not entirely without foundation' but then, expanding upon these points in six paragraphs, observed that they were not relevant as:

> ...the appellate principle itself and the hierarchical judicial structure which is its corollary generally advise against the General Court revisiting points of law which have been decided by the Court of Justice.

The General Court's judgments in both *Kadi* and *Kadi II*, where it essentially appears to retain a fondness for its former approach whilst recognising it cannot follow it, are of interest. When considered along with the Court of Justice's ruling they reflect the multiplicity of approaches available to the courts when dealing with international law and the complex judgments that have to be made, often in a sphere of much political sensitivity and academic focus. It is a potent mix, and when the above is combined also with an increasing reluctance to grant direct effect to international Agreements (see **7.8**) then questions of whether the EU, and particularly its Court of Justice, views itself as being bound by international law seem set to recur. The Court of Justice will have a chance to respond to the critics and its General Court in the appeal (Joined Cases C–584/10, C–593/10 and C–595/10 (pending)). (See also **7.9** and **8.37**.)

However, in the *FIAMM* case (Joined Cases C–120/06 P and C–121/06 P *FIAMM et FIAMM Technologies v Council and Commission* (2008)) the Court confirmed its reluctance to give direct effect to WTO rules, and underlined that a Community (now Union) measure can only be reviewed in the light of WTO rules when the measure is intended to implement a WTO obligation or when it makes explicit reference to WTO provisions (see also **7.9**).

Secondary Union legislation

5.14 Secondary Union legislation is provided for by Articles 288–294 TFEU (ex Articles 249–252 EC). The binding Union acts are regulations, directives and decisions. There are also non-binding acts: recommendations or opinions, which nevertheless are persuasive.

Regulations

5.15 Article 288 TFEU (ex Article 249 EC) provides that a regulation shall have general application and be 'directly applicable' in all Member States (see also **Chapter 7**). A regulation, therefore, will apply directly in all Member States without having to be incorporated by national legislation. The Court of Justice has stated that regulations should not be subjected to further incorporation as this could endanger the uniform application of Union law if Member States made any changes which they might argue were necessary and thus obscure the source and nature of the right. The doctrine that national measures are improper was first laid down in Case 39/72 *Commission v Italy (Re Slaughtered Cows)* (1973). A regulation provided for premiums to be paid for slaughter to counter over-production. The Italian Government passed a decree stating that the provisions of the relevant regulation were 'deemed to be included in it'. The Court said:

> By following this procedure, the Italian government has brought into doubt both the legal nature of the applicable provisions and the date of their coming into force.

According to the terms of Articles 189 and 191 of the Treaty (now Articles 288 and 297 TFEU), regulations were, as such, directly applicable in all Member States and came into force solely by virtue of their publication in the Official Journal of the Communities, and from the date specified in them, or in the absence thereof, within 20 days from publication as provided in the Treaty. Consequently, all methods of implementation were contrary to the Treaty which would have the result of creating an obstacle to the direct effect of Community law and of jeopardising their simultaneous and uniform application in the whole of the Community. The Court went on to point out that in one respect the Italian decree had departed from the terms of Community law (it set a time limit for implementation). Therefore:

> …the default of the Italian Republic has thus been established by reason not only of the delay in putting the system into effect, but also of the manner of giving effect to it provided by the decree.

5.16 Although the original Treaty of Rome provided that only regulations must be published in the Official Journal, since the Maastricht Treaty, Article 297 TFEU (ex Article 254 EC) now provides that regulations, as well as directives and decisions, must be published in the Official Journal and enter into force on the date specified in them or, in the absence thereof, on the twentieth day following that of their publication.

5.17 Regulations do not necessarily always have direct effect (see **Chapter 7**). Sometimes, it is necessary for national measures to be taken. In Case 128/78 *Commission v United Kingdom (Re Tachographs)* (1979) a regulation required implementing measures, and the United Kingdom was asked by the Court to take such measures. If the terms of a regulation are vague and further detailed provisions are advisable the Court might accept that such measures are taken, provided that they are not incompatible with the regulation (see Case 31/78 *Bussone* (1978)).

5.18 The type of act is determined, not by its form, but by its content and object (see Cases 16 and 17/62 *Confédération Nationale des Producteurs des Fruits et Légumes v Council* (1962)). If a measure is of general application, it will be considered as to its effect. In Case 92/78 *Simmenthal v Commission* (1979) the Court stated that acts, even if not in the form of a regulation, but nevertheless normative in substance, should be treated as a regulation. Joined Cases 41–44/70 *International Fruit* (1971) concerned the procedure for importing apples from non-Member States. The importers had to apply ahead of time for a licence. Each week national authorities would collate applications made during the previous week and pass the details to the Commission. The Commission would then enact the measure in the form of a regulation. However, the Court held it was really a 'bundle of decisions' concerning a 'closed category of persons', i.e. those who had made an application in the previous week (see also **8.47**).

Directives

5.19 Article 288 TFEU provides that directives are *binding* as to the *effect* to be achieved but leaves the choice as to form and method to the Member States. Directives therefore need to be incorporated into national law and are a more flexible instrument of Union law than regulations, which leave no discretion for any consideration of national differences and needs. By their very nature, however, directives may give rise to problems when they are implemented. Without doing so intentionally, a Member State may misinterpret the directive or the amount of discretion it has been given by the directive. The Member State may be of the opinion that its existing legislation already covers the provisions of the directive when this may not be the case. Examples of these difficulties will be encountered throughout this book, see in particular **Chapter 7.**

5.20 Directives are binding on those Member States to whom they are addressed. In this they also differ from regulations which are always of general application. This allows directives to be applied to some Member States and not necessarily to others. However, the large majority of directives are addressed to all Member States and, like regulations, most directives now (since the Maastricht Treaty) have to be published in the Official Journal and enter into force either on the date specified in the directive or on the twentieth day after publication (Article 297 TFEU (ex Article 254 EC)).

5.21 After the Court had found that directives could have (vertical) direct effect in Case 41/74 *van Duyn* (see further **7.11**) it was thought that the difference between regulations and directives could become blurred and perhaps disappear altogether. It has also been suggested that in order to achieve the uniform application of Union law, directives should be incorporated into national law without changing their wording. Although various proposals to establish a 'hierarchy of laws' have been made in several Treaty revisions, the Lisbon Treaty has not changed the nature of the secondary legislation and has retained the same terminology and definition of the secondary legislation.

Decisions

5.22 Decisions are specific measures issued by the Union which are binding on those to whom they are addressed. The Commission makes extensive use of such decisions, particularly in the field of competition.

Under Article 296 TFEU (ex Article 253 EC as amended), the institutions may select the type of act to be adopted on a case-by-case basis. Legal acts must state the reasons on which they are based. Failure to do this may entail annulment (see **Chapter 8**).

Recommendations and opinions

5.23 Recommendations and opinions are not legally binding. Nevertheless they are of importance and may be persuasive; recommendations must be taken into account when the achievement of Union objectives is concerned. In Case 322/88 *Grimaldi* (1989) the Court stated that national courts had to take recommendations into consideration when interpreting national law adopted in implementation of Community law.

Rulings of the Court of Justice of the European Union and general principles of law

5.24 Although there is no system of binding precedent in the Treaty, the rulings of the Court of Justice are generally considered to be a source of Union law. A number of rulings by the Court have led directly to Treaty amendments, as, for example, in Articles 263 and 265 TFEU (ex Articles 230 and 232 EC) where the changes in the European Parliament's position arising from Court rulings were embodied in the Maastricht Treaty on European Union (see **3.50**). It is also largely due to the Court's decisions granting limited standing to Parliament that since the Nice Treaty the European Parliament now has full standing, on an equal footing with the other institutions (see Article 263 TFEU, paragraphs 2 and 3 and **Chapter 8**). It was also the Court rulings in Case T–177/01 (2002) and Case 263/02 *Jégo Quéré* and Case C–50/00P (2003) *UPA*, highlighting the difficulties with the standing rules in the Treaty, which led to the amended text of Article 263, fourth paragraph (see **8.56** and **8.57**).

General principles of law originating in the Member States are considered by the Court to be an inherent part of the Treaty (see further **Chapter 6**).

Acts *sui generis*

5.25 This subject is discussed in **Chapter 8**. There are cases where it is not possible to classify an act under any of the above categories. The list of acts given has been held by the Court to be non-exhaustive. There are acts in different forms which will create legal effects and which are often referred to as being *sui generis*: they have their own particular features. Case 22/70 *Commission v Council* (the *ERTA* case, see **5.9**) dealt with a Council resolution which was held by the Court to have legal effects and could, therefore, be reviewed by the Court. Acts of the European Parliament and of the European Council are only reviewable under Article 263 TFEU (ex Article 230 EC) if they are 'intended to produce legal effects vis-à-vis third parties'. This amendment of the article in the Maastricht Treaty (further amended in the Lisbon Treaty) was the direct result of the Court's judgment in Case 294/83 *Les Verts* (1986) (see **8.31**).

5.26 The Court has also accepted in Case 34/86 *Council v European Parliament* (1986) that the act of the President of the Parliament by which he declared that the Community budget was finally adopted pursuant to the Treaty was an act susceptible to judicial review. In Joined Cases C–181/91 and C-248/91 *European Parliament v Council and Commission* (*Bangladesh* case) (1993) the Parliament sought the annulment of a decision taken by the Member States meeting in the Council to provide humanitarian aid to Bangladesh following a natural disaster. The European Parliament alleged that the contested decision was in reality an act of the Council which had budgetary implications and which should have been adopted under Article 203 EC (now Article 314 TFEU) of the Treaty. The Council's failure to do so allegedly infringed the European Parliament's prerogatives. The Council said the case was inadmissible on the ground that the contested decision was not an act of the Council but of the Member States, as described in a press release after the meeting of the Council where it was adopted, and therefore it was beyond the scope of Article 173 (now Article 263 TFEU). The Court said (judgment paragraph 922):

> ...it is true that if the Member States adopted a collective decision in breach of Community law it would be open to the Commission to initiate enforcement proceedings against the Member States under Article 169 [now Article 258 TFEU] of the Treaty.

This would not be likely in the instant case, however, as the Commission and the Member States were in agreement. But in Case C–70/88 *European Parliament v Council (Chernobyl)* (1990) the Court said (at paragraph 19):

> ...while the Commission is required to ensure that the Parliament's prerogatives are respected, that duty cannot go as far as to oblige it to adopt the Parliament's position and bring an action for annulment which the Commission itself considers unfounded.

The Court had to maintain the institutional balance and ensure the protection of Parliament's prerogatives:

> ...by means of a legal remedy which is suited to the purpose which the Parliament seeks to achieve.

5.27 What does 'legal effect' mean? In Cases 8–11/66 *Noordwijks Cement Accoord* (1967), cement-making companies received immunity from fines imposed under the competition law rules of Article 85 EC (now Article 101 TFEU) and EEC Council Regulation 17/62 from the time when the agreement was notified until the Commission reached its decision. As this was thought to be too favourable to the firms, Regulation 17 also provided that immunity shall cease to apply once the Commission had informed the firms, *after a preliminary examination*, that the agreement appeared to violate Article 81(1) (now Article 101(1) TFEU).

The Commission sent a letter to the firms stating that the Commission subjected the agreement to a provisional examination and concluded that Article 81(1) applied and that there was no exemption. Immunity would therefore cease. The firms brought cases contesting this decision. The Commission argued there was no act which could be quashed and that the letter was a mere expression of opinion. The Court rejected this. The effect of the decision was to remove immunity.

This measure deprived them of a legal situation which Regulation 17 attached to the notification of the agreement and exposed them to a grave financial risk…bringing about a distinct change in their legal position. It is unequivocally a measure which produces legal effects touching the interests of the undertakings concerned and which is binding on them. It thus constitutes not a mere opinion but a decision.

If an act only concerns the internal operation of an institution it has only internal effects. In *Les Verts* (see above **5.25**) this argument was advanced but in that case there was an effect vis-à-vis a third party.

5.28 In the absence of actions for a declaration, the Court of Justice has ruled that a statement of intention can be a reviewable act. Letters by the Commission have been so held (Case 8/55 *Fédération Charbonniere de Belgique v High Authority* (1956) and Joined Cases 7/56 and 3–7/57 *Algera v Common Assembly* (1957)). In fact, the Court has adopted a doctrine that any statement by a Union institution as to the action it intends to take in given circumstances is a reviewable act provided it is definite and unequivocal. The fact that the institution is not legally bound by such an act appears to be immaterial.

5.29 What if there are a number of steps, each being in itself a preliminary decision (by different bodies)? Case 78/63 *Huber v Commission* (1964) concerned the permanent appointment of a Commission official. The rules were that they could only be 'established' if the relevant Review Board gave a favourable report. The board's opinion was unfavourable. The Advocate General said the report was a reviewable act as the report meant that the appointing authority was legally precluded from establishing the official. The Court disagreed: the report was not separable from the final decision and it was, therefore, not reviewable on its own.

5.30 Letters, too, may be reviewable. Case 60/81 *IBM v Commission* (1981) concerned a letter written by the Commission inviting IBM to state its case and enclosing a statement of objections. IBM objected to doing this on procedural grounds claiming the statement of objections was not clear, the decision to proceed had been taken by an official, not a Commissioner; the proceedings were contrary to national law as the Commission was trying to apply EC law extraterritorially. The Court of Justice ruled that these were not reviewable acts; they were merely preliminary decisions which could be challenged only in the course of a review of the final decision. This meant, somewhat unsatisfactorily, that IBM had to bring a case on the merits first before it could raise these preliminary objections. In Case 53/85 *AKZO v Commission* (1986), confidential documents had been shown by the Commission to the complainant, ECS, so as to permit them to exercise their right to be heard during the Administrative Procedure (as was provided for in Article 19(2) of Regulation 17/62). AKZO claimed commercial secrecy and brought proceedings to annul the decision by the Commission to show documents. The Court ruled this was admissible as it directly affected AKZO's right to confidentiality, and held that by handing over documents prior to allowing AKZO to respond to its statement of reasons for doing so the Commission decision had to be declared void. However, the Court explained that it did not have jurisdiction to demand ECS return the documents. Whilst finding a breach of procedure in this case the Court also stated, on a matter of substance, that:

> It is undoubtedly for the Commission to assess whether or not a particular document contains business secrets. (at paragraph 29)

5.31 If an act is reviewable it will generally continue to have legal effect until it is annulled. However, if an act is tainted with particular serious illegality, it may be held to be void *ab initio*. In Joined Cases T–79, 84–86, 89, 91, 94, 96, 98, 102 and 104/89 *BASF v Commission* (1992) the CFI (as it then was) held Commission proceedings against a cartel to be so tainted with procedural defect that they were non-existent. The Rules of Procedure's requirements as to the signing of a decision imposing fines had not been complied with. The Court of Justice, however, took a different view and held that this defect was not so serious as to justify non-existence, but it was serious enough for the act to be annulled.

Legislative procedures

5.32 The adoption of legislation in the Union is governed by Article 288 TFEU (ex Article 249 EC). This may be done by the European Parliament acting jointly with the Council, the Council acting alone, and the Commission. The Treaty confers legislative power on the Commission only to a very limited extent, but the Council frequently delegates powers to the Commission in order to allow it to fulfil its executive function.

Decision-making procedure of the Commission (Comitology)

5.33 As is the case in most national systems, the legislative branch can delegate some implementing powers to the executive. This is also the case in the EU, whereby, some of the practical issues involved in adapting legislation are delegated to the Commission by the Council or European Parliament. Initially, this system of delegation was accompanied by the use of committees, by the Council, in order for the latter to retain some measure of control over the Commission's legislative power. This system, which was first introduced in the 1960's, became known as 'comitology'.

5.34 Under the comitology system the Commission met in closed session, often used the 'written procedure' and decided by simple majority vote. The committees were composed of representatives of the national governments and were under the chairmanship of a Commission official. Over time, however, concerns were raised regarding this delegation of power. For example, in Case 25/70 *Köster* (1970) the legality of the comitology system was challenged. The Court ruled, however, that the principle of delegation was valid and that the authorisation to the Council to delegate power to the Commission meant (1) that it was sufficient if general principles concerning the procedure were set out, and (2) that the management committee procedure did not constitute an unwarranted restriction on the decision-making power of the Commission as it did not, in fact, take decisions itself but simply obliged the Commission to communicate the measure to the Council.

5.35 Nevertheless, with the increasing role and powers of the European Parliament, it did not take long before the system of comitology was again criticised for being highly complex and lacking transparency. Of particular concern to the European Parliament was the fact that the system did not provide for any requirement to inform the Parliament of decisions taken by the committees. The consequent frustration felt by the European Parliament was evidenced by the *Comitology* case (Case 302/87 *European Parliament v Council* (1988)). In this case the European Parliament brought proceedings against the Council regarding the comitology system but was refused standing by the ECJ since the matter was not directly connected with its prerogatives and a remedy could be obtained by different means.

5.36 In an attempt to address the unequal footing of the various parties to the comitology system, the SEA made provisions for a framework decision, which would establish the principles and rules to be followed. The result was Council Decision 1999/468/EC (Comitology Decision), the legal basis of which was Article 202 EC. The Comitology Decision set out the relevant types of committee and procedures required in different instances of delegated power. To achieve this, the Decision stipulated four objectives: greater consistency in the choice of committee and in the criteria relating to this choice; simplified requirements for the exercise of implementing powers and greater involvement of the European Parliament; improved information to the European Parliament; and improved information to the public. The Decision also provided for three committee procedures: firstly, the advisory committee procedure, whereby the committee may provide non-binding recommendations; secondly the management committee procedure, in which the Commission must submit a draft to the committee, which may either approve or reject the draft by qualified majority. If it does not approve the draft, the measure may still be adopted by the Commission under certain conditions; and thirdly the regulatory committee procedure, whereby the Commission has much less input and may only adopt a measure if it is approved by a qualified majority of the committee.

5.37 Despite this development, further attempts were made to improve the comitology system. For example, in December 2002, the Commission proposed a reform, in order to clarify its executive duties and place the Parliament and Council on the same footing in exercising control over the executive function of the Commission (see also **3.36**). Then, in the White Paper on European Governance and again in the December 2002 Communication on Institutional Architecture, the Commission called for reform of the comitology procedures. It was argued that the objective of refocusing the institutions as well as increasing efficiency justified reducing, if not eliminating, the use of existing management and regulatory procedures. It also called for 'rebalancing and strengthening the possibility for Parliament and the Council to control the Commission's exercise of its implementing powers', at least in the areas subject to codecision.

5.38 Then, in 2006, a Council Decision which amended Decision 1999/468/EC created a new 'regulatory procedure with scrutiny'. This amendment gave the European Parliament better oversight and a right to veto the Commission's implementing powers which flowed from laws decided upon jointly by the European Parliament and the Council under the codecision procedure (see **5.41**). Under the amendment, should the Parliament reject a measure by an absolute majority of MEPs, the Commission must initiate a new comitology decision or use the codecision procedure to initiate a new legislative act.

5.39 Finally, however, in December 2010, the Lisbon Treaty abolished the comitology system and repealed and replaced Article 202 EC with Articles 290 and 291 TFEU. Although the comitology system will continue to apply to un-amended measures adopted before the Lisbon Treaty, all measures subsequent to Lisbon will be subject to the system of 'delegated' or 'implementing' acts.

Article 290 TFEU provides for the system of delegated acts and, in doing so, distinguishes between legislative acts and non-legislative ones. According to paragraph one of the Article, Parliament and the Council may, by means of a legislative act, delegate, to the Commission, the power to adopt 'non-legislative acts [i.e. delegated acts] of general application, to supplement or amend certain non-essential elements of the legislative act'. The legislative acts, which delegate non-legislative powers to the Commission, must explicitly state the objectives, content, scope and duration of the delegation of power and the conditions to which the delegation is subject. The legislative act can also provide that either the European Parliament or the Council may revoke the entire delegation and/or prevent the measure from coming into force. It is argued that this new system of delegated acts will permit legislation to remain simple and under the power and responsibility of the legislator, whilst being supplemented and updated by the Commission without the need to resort to repeated adoption of legislation.

Delegated acts of the Commission must also be clearly distinguished from implementing acts, the latter being those measures which are enacted on the basis of implementing powers conferred on the Commission according to the procedure stipulated in Article 291 TFEU. In February 2011, Regulation 182/2011/EU (the Comitology Regulation) was published, which repeals the 1999 Comitology Decision and lays down the rules and general principles concerning the mechanisms for control by Member States of the

Commission's exercise of implementing powers. This Comitology Regulation provides for two procedures, the advisory procedure and the examination procedure. The advisory procedure is the same as in the Comitology Decision, and the examination procedure replaces the management and regulatory procedures (see **5.36**). Therefore, under the examination procedure, the committee can approve or reject a draft implementing measure by qualified majority and, in the case where no decision is taken within the necessary time-frame, the Commission may either adopt the measure, or submit it to an appeal committee.

5.40 Lastly, the Commission also has its own decision-making power under other Treaty Articles: Article 101(3) TFEU (ex Article 81(3) EC) on exempt agreements in competition law; Article 106(3) (ex Article 86(3) EC) in relation to the application of competition policy to public undertakings; and Article 45(3)(d) TFEU (ex Article 39(3)(d) EC) whereby the Commission can draw up implementing regulations on certain workers' rights.

The ordinary legislative procedure (formerly the codecision procedure)

5.41 Most of the legislation in the Union is passed by the Council and the European Parliament (EP), acting on a proposal by the Commission, under the ordinary legislative procedure provided for under Article 289 TFEU and defined in Article 294 TFEU (ex Article 251 EC as amended). The main features of the ordinary legislative procedure are as follows:

- The Commission submits a proposal to the Parliament and the Council.
- The EP adopts a position and communicates it to the Council.

If the Council approves the position it will adopt the act concerned.

- Otherwise, the Council will adopt its common position at first reading and submit the proposal again to the EP, informing it fully of its reasons. The Commission will also inform the EP of its position.
- If within three months of such communication the EP approves the Council's position at first reading or does not take a decision, the proposed act shall be deemed to have been adopted in the wording which corresponds to the Council's position.
- If the EP rejects the common position by an absolute majority of its component members, the act shall be deemed not to have been adopted.
- If the EP proposes amendments to the Council's position at first reading within three months, the text returns to the Council, and to the Commission for an opinion.
- If the Council approves the EP amendments within three months by qualified majority, the act will be deemed to have been adopted in that form.

- If not all the amendments can be agreed by the Council, the proposal will go to a Conciliation Committee.

- This Committee, composed of an equal number of members of the Council or their representatives, and of the EP, will be convened within six weeks by the Council President in agreement with the EP President. The Commission will take part and take all necessary initiatives to try and reconcile the Council's and EP's positions.

- If a joint text is approved within six weeks, the Council and the EP each have a period of six weeks to approve the text by qualified majority in the case of the Council and by an absolute majority of the votes cast for the EP.

- If no joint text can be agreed by the Conciliation Committee or if either body fails to approve after the six-week period, the text shall be deemed not to have been adopted.

- The periods of three months and six weeks referred to may be extended by a maximum of one month and two weeks respectively at the initiative of the EP or the Council. The use of the Conciliation Committee, which could be brought in at an earlier stage under the Maastricht Treaty, is thus confined to the later stages of the procedure, and the EP has an opportunity to exercise its veto at an early stage.

The ordinary legislative procedure clearly gives the EP a real opportunity to take part in the legislative process, although legally its powers have not been greatly increased since the Treaties of Amsterdam and Nice. The 'democratic deficit' has not been greatly reduced; the EP still has mostly only a negative power and little power to propose legislation on its own. The Member States are understandably reluctant to give up too much power. Any gain in power by the EP will also have to entail a reduction in the Commission's powers. The Commission still retains most of the power of making proposals.

Other procedures where the EP adopts a regulation, directive or decision 'with the participation of the Council', or where the Council adopts these 'with the participation of the European Parliament' constitute a special legislative procedure. (Article 289(2) TFEU). There are occasions where the Council may decide alone and may consult the EP, but it does not have to. These, however, were reduced to a minimum by the Treaty of Amsterdam (e.g. Article 31 TFEU (ex Article 26 EC) on the fixing of common customs tariff duties, Article 43(3) TFEU (ex Article 37(3) EC) on the common fisheries policy, Article 121 TFEU (ex Article 99 EC) on broad guidelines of economic policy and Article 126 TFEU (ex Article 104 EC) on excessive deficits).

The special legislative procedure

5.42 Under the Lisbon Treaty the special legislative procedure has replaced the consultation, budgetary and assent procedures. However, these procedures still apply in respect of specified areas in the Lisbon Treaty.

Consultation procedure

5.43 The consultation procedure was the procedure originally provided for in most of the Treaty. It is a fairly straightforward procedure which only involves the Commission and the Council with regard to decision-making. The other institutions, the EP, as well as the Economic and Social Committee (EESC) and the Committee of the Regions, simply have to be consulted. The Commission makes the proposal, after the EP (and others) have been consulted, and the Council adopts. The procedure is as follows:

- The proposal is submitted to the Council by the Commission. A working group is usually established, made up of persons nominated by national governments, civil servants mostly, sometimes others (academics etc.). The group's powers are only advisory, but its views will be taken into account as the members will advise their governments which will vote on the measure. Sometimes, the Commission invites professional groups to agree on proposals themselves before the Commission will act. This happened for example with the Lawyer's Establishment Directive, where the European Association of Bar Councils (CCBE) was invited to agree on a draft before the Commission would proceed (see further **Chapter 12**).

- The Commission will then draft a final proposal and send it to the EP, and sometimes the EESC, for opinion. After receiving these opinions the Commission may amend the proposals in light of the opinions. The proposal is then sent to COREPER (see **3.13**). A working group of national officials is set up within COREPER to prepare a report for the Council. Commission representatives attend meetings of this group. Amendments are usually put forward by national representatives, which may or may not be accepted by the Commission.

- Finally, the proposal, together with the report of the COREPER working group, goes to the Council. If full agreement was reached in COREPER, the Council will adopt without debate. Otherwise the Council debates the issue and votes. If a technical Council cannot decide, it will go higher.

The EP's opinions have no binding force. However, when provided in the Treaty, consultation with the EP constitutes an 'essential procedural requirement' (Article 230 (ex Article 173 EC)) and, as the Court ruled in Case 138/79 *Roquette Frères SA v Council* (1980), failure to comply with it constitutes ground for annulment of the acts by the Court of Justice. On the duty of reconsultation see Case C–65/90 *European Parliament v Council* (1992). Whether reconsultation is required will depend on the type of amendments. If they are minor or in accordance with the EP's views, reconsultation may not be necessary.

In addition to mandatory consultations provided for by the Treaties, both the Commission and the Council normally seek the EP's opinion on an optional basis on a wide range of measures having a determining effect on policy. In Case 165/87 *Commission v Council* (1988) the Court recognised the validity of such optional consultations.

The use of the consultation procedure has been much reduced by subsequent Treaties. It is still present in, e.g., Article 22 TFEU (ex Article 19 EC) on conditions concerning the right of European citizens to stand and vote in municipal elections; Article 25(2) (ex Article 22(2) EC) on the strengthening of citizens' rights; Article 115 TFEU (ex Article 94 EC) concerning the establishment or functioning of the internal market; and Article 109 (ex Article 89 EC) on state aids.

Assent procedure

5.44   A second type of special legislative procedure is what was called the 'assent procedure' under the previous Treaties. This procedure was introduced by the Single European Act and extended by the TEU. It constitutes a veto right, and when assent is required the Council may act only after it has obtained the EP's agreement. It applies to important matters such as admission of new members to the Union and association agreements.

Budgetary procedure

5.45   The third type of special legislative procedure is the budgetary procedure. This procedure, which is complex, is described in Article 314 TFEU (ex Articles 272 and 273 EC as amended). The difference between compulsory and non-compulsory expenditure has been abolished and the EP has the same involvement in the entire budget. A brief, general outline of the procedure is as follows:

All the institutions, with the exception of the European Central Bank, draw up estimates of expenditure, and send them to the Commission which consolidates them into a draft budget. The draft budget is sent to the Council and the EP. The Council will adopt a position and forward it to the EP, fully informing the EP of its reasons. If, within 42 days of such communication it either adopts it or does not act, the budget is deemed to be adopted. Otherwise, the Conciliation Committee is convened and a complex procedure follows. If within 21 days of the Conciliation Committee being convened there is no agreement, a new budget must be drawn up by the Commission and the procedure followed again. Article 315 TFEU (ex Article 273 EC) provides that if no budget has been passed at the beginning of the year, a sum equal to one-twelfth of the previous year's budget may be spent each month. The monthly sums available may be increased by the Council on a proposal by the Commission, and it has to immediately forward the proposal to the EP. The latter procedure has been threatened often in the past and used from time to time and constituted a considerable power for the EP as regards non-compulsory expenditure. The Lisbon Treaty now extends the EP's powers to control over the whole of the budget.

Other special procedures

5.46   Other special procedures apply, e.g., to Articles 7 and 49 TEU and to Article 354 and 218 TFEU. However, the Lisbon Treaty has made great strides in simplifying the ordinary legislative procedure and this now applies to the majority of articles in the Treaty.

5.47 The cooperation procedure which was introduced by the Single European Act (1986) with a view to increasing the influence of the EP in the legislative process but without giving it a real power of codecision, has been abolished under the Lisbon Treaty and, where it applied, the ordinary legislative procedure now applies.

Conclusion

5.48 The balance of powers between the institutions has tended to shift in favour of the Council at the expense of the powers of the Commission. The Council Presidency has acquired real importance and tended to diminish the role of the Commission as the negotiator in the Union. The absence of the use of majority voting for many years, which led indirectly to the establishment of the European Council, has tended to strengthen the inter-governmental element. Only in the 1980s did majority voting return and the Treaties of Maastricht, Amsterdam and Nice went only some way to diminish the democratic deficit. The Lisbon Treaty further reduces the democratic deficit and makes major changes in the legislative structure.

Legislative powers

Express and implied powers of the Union

5.49 The Union has only the powers assigned to it by the Treaties (*compétence d'attribution*), while all residual powers are left with the Member States. This means the Union must act within the framework of the provisions laid down in its statutes. Article 5(2) TEU states that the Union shall act within the limits of the powers conferred upon it by the Treaties and of the objectives assigned to it by the Treaties. It has also been stated by the Court in Joined Cases 188–190/80 *France, Italy and United Kingdom v Commission* (1982) that the Union legislative power could not be described in terms of a general proposition but resulted from different Treaty provisions attributing that power for each of the areas entrusted to the Union.

5.50 With few exceptions (Articles 115 TFEU (ex Article 94 EC) and Article 352 TFEU (ex Article 308 EC) the powers held by the Union are specific. This is significant in two ways:

(1) where a measure can be validly based on one (or more) specific provision(s) of the Treaty, it may not be based on a non-specific power; and

(2) the decision-making procedure differs from one specific power to another.

The decision-making procedures involve various forms of interaction between the Commission which has near-exclusive power to make legislative proposals, the European Parliament (ordinary or special legislative procedure) and the Council (deciding with a simple majority vote, a qualified majority vote or unanimously).

5.51 There are no inherent powers: the Union only possesses the powers conferred on it, which are limited in scope. These powers are now much more fully described in Articles 3 to 6 TFEU, which spell out exclusive and shared competence and competence to carry out actions to support, coordinate or supplement actions of the Member States. However, the limitation in scope is diminished by a number of factors: the empowering provisions of the Treaty are interpreted widely, in part on the basis of the theory of implied powers. This theory, which was originally developed in the constitutional and administrative law of such countries as the United States and the United Kingdom, and which is recognised as a principle of international law, may be expressed in both a narrow and a wide formulation.

According to the narrow formulation, the existence of a given power also implies the existence of any other power which is reasonably necessary for the exercise of the former; according to the wide formulation, the existence of a given *objective* or *function* implies the existence of any power necessary to attain it. The narrow formulation was adopted by the Court of Justice as long ago as 1956 (Case 8/55 *Fédération Charbonnière de Belgique v High Authority* (1956)); the wide formulation was applied with regard to the Commission in 1987. This was in Joined Cases 281, 283–285 and 287/85 *Germany v Commission* (1987), which concerned Article 118 of the Treaty of Rome (since deleted) which gave the Commission the task of 'promoting close cooperation between member states in the social field, particularly in matters relating to…'. This gave the Commission a task, but it did not confer any legislative power. The authors of the Treaty probably thought it was not necessary. However, in 1985, the Commission, acting under Article 118, adopted a decision which obliged the Member States to consult with the Commission regarding certain matters and to inform it of draft measures and agreements concerning the topic in question. The decision was challenged by some of the Member States, but it was upheld by the Court, which held that whenever a provision of the EC Treaty conferred a specific task on the Commission, it must also be regarded as impliedly conferring on the Commission 'the powers which are indispensable in order to carry out that task'. Since the Treaty conferred many tasks on the Commission (see Article 17 TEU) this judgment is potentially very significant. Thus, wide provisions such as Article 115 TFEU (ex Article 94 EC) which empowers the Council to issue directives for the 'approximation' of such laws or other provisions of the Member States as 'directly affect the establishment or functioning of the common market' have been used to issue directives to unify the laws of Member States on a wide variety of subjects.

Article 115 TFEU might still be regarded as granting a specific power, but Article 352 TFEU (ex Article 308 EC) clearly goes beyond this: it provides for the Union to take action necessary to attain the objectives set out in the Treaties if the Treaties have not provided the necessary powers. The requirements are thus that:

- the power must be used to attain one of the objectives of the Union. There are numerous objectives, those set out, e.g., in Article 3 TEU but also in many other parts of the Treaties;

- action by the Union must be necessary for the purpose, involving a judgment of what is necessary by the Union institutions;
- the Article may only be used if the Treaty has not provided specific powers elsewhere.

The Article provides a general power, subject to the limitations described above.

5.52 An illustration of the respective roles of implied powers on the one hand and the residual powers of the institutions by Article 352 TFEU (ex Article 308 EC) on the other is provided in the Court of Justice's judgment in Case C–295/90 *European Parliament v Council (Students' Residence Rights Directive)* (1992). The Council had relied on Article 352 TFEU for the adoption of the Directive as in its view the other Treaty Articles did not provide for the necessary powers. The use of the Article was challenged by the Parliament. The Court used the doctrine of implied powers to interpret Article 6(2) (now Article 18 TFEU), concluding that the general principle of non-discrimination as to nationality could only be applied subject to special provisions of the Treaty. The object of the Article was to enable the Council:

> ...to take necessary measures...for the effective elimination of discrimination on grounds of nationality where its power has no foundation in one of the special provisions governing the different spheres of application of the Treaty. However, measures adopted under Article 6(2) of the Treaty should not necessarily be limited to regulating rights deriving from the first paragraph of the same article, but they may also deal with aspects the regulation of which appears necessary for the effective exercise of those rights.

5.53 Article 352 TFEU grants the power to act where none yet exists if it is necessary to attain one of the objectives of the Union; a new, independent power of action is created alongside the existing ones. This has been very controversial and the Court has indicated many times that the Article should only be used if no other, more specific, legal base can be found in the Treaty (see e.g. Case C–295/90 *European Parliament v Council (Student Residence Directive)* (1992) further discussed at **8.39**). Implied powers, on the other hand, are those which already exist and may be used to supplement a specific power specifically conferred on the Union if there is a need for this in order to comply with the 'principle of effectiveness' (*effet utile*) frequently referred to by the Court of Justice.

The problem of the legal base

5.54 It gradually became more and more important to determine the choice of legal base for legislation. The Single European Act and the Treaties of Maastricht and Amsterdam set up new legislative procedures and the importance of the role of one or the other of the institutions in the legislation depended on the legislative procedure which is effectively chosen by the Commission when submitting its proposal. Since the Lisbon Treaty, and the simplification of the number of legislative procedures, where the bulk of new legislation will be made jointly by the Council and the European Parliament, this problem has perhaps become less important.

The problem may be illustrated by Case C–300/89 *Commission v Council (Titanium Dioxide)* (1991). This concerned an adoption of a directive setting titanium dioxide levels. It had two objectives: to protect the environment and (because it laid down uniform standards in all Member States) to promote fair competition. The former was covered by Article 130s (now Article 192 TFEU), which then required unanimous voting in the Council and was subject to the consultation procedure with the European Parliament. The latter fell within the scope of Article 100a (now Article 114 TFEU) which was then subject to qualified majority voting and the cooperation procedure. The Commission had selected Article 100a as the base but the Council had substituted Article 130s. The Court ruled that the more general objective of Article 100a providing measures promoting the establishment of the internal market prevailed over the more specific environmental concerns of Article 130s and ruled, therefore, that 100a was the correct legal base. The concern here was undoubtedly that Parliament should be given the opportunity to use its rights under the cooperation procedure.

5.55 One of the cases where a challenge succeeded was Case C–376/98 *Germany v Parliament and Council* (2000) where the Court annulled the Tobacco Advertising Directive 1998 which was based on Articles 57(2) (now Article 53(2) TFEU), 66 (now Article 62 TFEU) and 100a (now Article 114 TFEU). The Court said that Article 100a was the wrong legal base as the objectives pursued by the directive could not be seen as genuinely aimed at the improvement of the conditions for the establishment and functioning of the internal market.

5.56 In Case C–176/03 *Commission v Council* (2005) (see **7.123** and **15.90**) the Court annulled Council Framework Decision 2003/80/JHA of 27 January 2003 on the protection of the environment through criminal law, as it had been adopted on the wrong legal base, i.e. Article 47 TEU (the Third Pillar), instead of Article 175 EC (the First Pillar) (now Article 192 TFEU) as it encroached on the powers which Article 175 conferred on the Union. Although only seven paragraphs of the decision were concerned, the decision was indivisible and, therefore, had to be annulled in its entirety. In a Communication from the Commission to the European Parliament and the Council (COM(2005) 583 final/2 of 24 November 2005), the Commission set out the implications of the judgment and listed the texts affected by it, both adopted and pending proposals under the Third Pillar (JHA), and indicated the proper legal base on which these texts should have been adopted. There were several ways in which these texts could be rectified. The simplest would be to review the instruments with the sole purpose of bringing them into line with the distribution of powers between the First and the Third Pillars. This would only work with the agreement of the Council and the Parliament, otherwise a more cumbersome procedure would have to be followed.

Exclusive and concurrent powers and the doctrine of pre-emption

5.57 Exclusive Union competence may be derived from:

(1) express provisions in the primary legislation, now detailed in Article 3 TFEU;

(2) the scope of internal measures adopted by the Union institution: at internal level within the Union this is described as pre-emption; at the external level it leads to exclusive external competence for the Union, as in some parts of the WTO;

(3) express provisions in internal Union measures; and

(4) situations where internal powers can only be effectively exercised at the same time as external powers.

Articles 4 and 5 TFEU distinguish between exclusive and shared competence. Subsidiarity can only apply to the latter. Every federal or quasi-federal system is based on a distribution of legislative and administrative powers among the federation and its members. As in the case of exclusive powers, shared powers are conferred upon the Union and upon the Union alone. The Union cannot share the exercise of such powers with the Member States. But while the powers defined as exclusive competences by the Treaty are to be exercised by the EU from their entry into force, the exercise of its concurrent powers is postponed and made subject to compliance with certain conditions. Until those conditions are satisfied, the Member States will retain the right to legislate, and will lose that right only when the EU decides to exercise its power in the area in question.

5.58 In Opinion 1/75 (1975) (see also **5.9**) the Court of Justice recognised, in the field of the common commercial policy, that the EC's powers must lead to the exclusion of concurrent powers exercisable by the Member States, other than in specific areas, as where the EC specifically authorised them to act: Case 41/76 *Donckerwolcke* (1976); or where existing obligations necessarily had to be carried out by the Member States: Case 174/84 *Bulk Oil* (1986). In Case 50/76 *Amsterdam Bulb* (1977) the Court recognised that even where EC institutions have failed to act when powers were given to them, Member States cannot act unilaterally. They must at the least cooperate with and consult the Commission since the failure to act may be a deliberate choice of economic policy in an area attributed by the Member States to the EC. See also Case 31/74 *Galli* (1975). Once the EC has used its legislative powers to set up a common agricultural market organisation, national powers to regulate the distribution stages covered by that market organisation are pre-empted. Case 14/68 *Walt Wilhelm v Bundeskartellamt* (1969) highlighted the difficulties in respecting the demarcation between national and Community competition law.

In the Treaty of Lisbon, Article 4(1) TEU expressly provides that competences not conferred upon the Union in the Treaties remain with the Member States, and Article 5(1) TEU provides that the use of Union competences is governed by the principles of subsidiarity and proportionality. Since the Treaty of Amsterdam, the use of the principles of subsidiarity and proportionality has been set out in detail in a Protocol annexed to the Treaty and a new Protocol is now annexed to the Lisbon Treaty. (See **Chapter 6** for a detailed discussion.)

FURTHER READING

Barents, R., 'The internal market unlimited: some observations on the legal basis of Union legislation' (1993) 30 *Common Market Law Review* 85.

Communication from the Commission to the European Parliament and the Council on the implications of the Court's judgment of 13 September 2005 (Case C–176/03 *Commission v Council*) (COM(2005) 583 final/2 of 24 November 2005.

Cremona, M., 'External relations and the Amsterdam Treaty' in O'Keeffe and Twomey (eds), *Legal Issues of the Amsterdam Treaty* (Oxford: Hart Publishing, 1999) 225–247.

Cremona, M., 'External relations and external competence: the emergence of an integrated policy' in Craig and de Búrca (eds), *The Evolution of EU Law* (Oxford: OUP, 1999).

Dashwood, A., 'The limits of European Community Powers' (1996) 21 *European Law Review* 113.

Douglas-Scott, S., *Constitutional Law of the European Union* (London: Longman, 2002) ch 3.

Eeckhout, P., 'EC law and UN Security Council Resolutions—in search of the right fit' in Dashwood and Maresceau (eds), *Law and Practice of EU External Relations* (Cambridge: CUP, 2008) 104–128.

Eeckhout, P., *EU External Relations Law* (2nd edn, Oxford: OUP, 2011).

Emiliou, N., 'The internal legislative powers of the European Union' in Emiliou and O'Keeffe (eds), *Legal Aspects of Integration in the European Union* (Kluwer Law International, 1997).

Emiliou, N., 'Implied powers and the legal basis of Community measures' (1993) 18 *European Law Review* 138–144.

Emiliou, N., 'Subsidiarity: an effective barrier against "the enterprises of ambition"?' (1992) 17 *European Law Review* 383.

Hervey, T., 'Up in smoke? Community (anti) tobacco law and policy' (2001) *European Law Review* 101.

London Boroughs Transport Committee v Freight Transport Association Ltd [1992] 1 *Common Market Law Reports* 5 (implicit application of the principle of subsidiarity by the House of Lords in the field of the environment).

O'Keeffe, D., 'Community and member state competence in external relations agreements of the EU' (1999) 4 *European Foreign Affairs Review*.

O'Keeffe, D., 'External, concurrent and shared competence' in Dashwood (ed.), *Foreign Policy after Amsterdam* (London: Sweet & Maxwell, 1998).

Toth, A.G., 'The principle of subsidiarity in the Maastricht Treaty' (1992) 29 *Common Market Law Review* 1079.

Van Gerven, W., *The European Union: A Polity of States and Peoples* (Oxford: Hart Publishing, 2005).

Wallace, W., Wallace, H. and Pollack, M. (eds), *Policy-making in the European Union* (5th edn, Oxford: OUP 2005).

Weatherill, S., 'Beyond pre-emption? Shared competence and constitutional change in the European Community' in O'Keeffe and Twomey (eds), *Legal Issues of the Maastricht Treaty* (London: Chancery, 1994) 13–33.

SELF-TEST QUESTIONS

1   What effects are the Treaties of Amsterdam, Nice and Lisbon likely to have on the Union legislative process?

2   How adequate, in your view, is the Union legislative process? What improvements have been made in the various treaties and what improvements do you still consider desirable?

3   What are the main types of legislative process in the European Union? What role do the different institutions play in each?

4   'Under Article 352 TFEU the Union has virtually unlimited legislative powers within the area of the Treaty.'

   Is this true and are there any restrictions on the use of this provision? What are the advantages and disadvantages of using the Article? Have the various amendments to the Treaty since the Treaty of Rome made any difference as regards its use?

5   What is meant by the legal base of a legislative measure, and why is it important?

6   'While Article 288 TFEU of the EC Treaty envisages considerable differences between regulations and directives, the practice of the Council and the Commission and the case law of the Court of Justice have substantially eliminated those differences.' Discuss.

6
General principles of law

SUMMARY

Discussion of why the Union legal order has general principles
Discussion of how the general principles work
Analysis of the following general principles:

- Overarching principles of the Union legal order
  - Subsidiarity
  - Proportionality
  - Sustainability
  - Equality

- Fundamental human rights in the Union
  - Court of Justice jurisdiction over Member State acts
  - Rights against Union institutions or agents

- Principles of administrative justice and good governance
  - Legal certainty
  - Non-retroactivity and legitimate expectations
  - Rights of process and natural justice
  - Transparency
  - Legal professional privilege

Introductory comments on general principles

6.1 In Case C–144/04 *Mangold v Helm* (2005) the Court of Justice made the following observation:

> The principle of non-discrimination on grounds of age must thus be regarded as a general principle of [Union] law. Where national rules fall within the scope of [Union] law…and reference is made to the Court for a preliminary ruling, the Court must provide all the criteria of interpretation needed by the national court to determine whether those rules are compatible with such a principle. [at paragraph 75 of the judgment]

This extract demonstrates many facets of the Court's attitude to what here are termed as 'general principles'. If a principle of law is taken to have a wider scope than a substantive legal rule, it can be understood that a 'principle' is general and may have infinite applications in a legal system, while a substantive legal rule operates only as specified. The Court of Justice, firstly, clearly views in this citation the list of what is within the category of general principles as being open and capable of addition according to legislative and other changes. Second, the Court seems to see the general principles as being a key feature of its dialogue with national courts. The Article 267 TFEU procedure for preliminary references is designed to provide such a dialogue between national courts and the Court of Justice. It enables questions on pretty much any area of law to be addressed (see **Chapter 4**). But the discussion as to general principles of Union law seems particularly appropriate to this process. The third point to be made from this short citation is that the general principles mean something important in the Union legal order. The Court of Justice indicates to national courts that Union general principles can operate to structure a reconsideration, reinterpretation and sometimes a questioning of the validity of national law. This is a consequence of the supremacy of Union law discussed in **Chapter 7**.

6.2 The Treaty of Lisbon, and the resulting Treaty on the Functioning of the European Union and the Treaty on European Union have altered the legal basis of certain rights; however general principles, having evolved over the life of the Union, have remained largely unaltered. This chapter will set out the brief history of the main general principles that inform law across the Union, and will highlight in particular the most recent changes seen in the evolution of the principles. In particular, the principle of sustainability, or sometimes 'sustainable development' is one that has increasingly come to the fore as awareness of climate change has developed.

Table 1 below (**6.3**) shows the current mention made of the principles by the two governing Treaties currently in force. These principles have all been developed by the Court of Justice and have appeared in the Treaties at different points, but have become ingrained within the Union legal system as valid points of law.

6.3 The general principles are a set of rules that overarch the Union legal order. As such these principles act as a guide to legislative enactments and as a measure against which EU law is judged. The framework directive on discrimination in employment (Directive 2000/78), the source of the age discrimination provision considered in Case C–144/04 *Mangold v Helm* (2005) (see **16.86** and **16.87**), was developed by reference to the general principle of equality as expressed in Article 19 TFEU. The Court of Justice went further in Case C–555/07 *Kücükdeveci* (2010, see **6.10**) and suggested that the general principle was 'given expression' in the framework directive, and that the general principle of non-discrimination on grounds of age, or presumably on various discrimination grounds, required a reappraisal of the way in which rights set out in directives can be enforced. That same general principle was used in Case C–13/94 *P v S and Cornwall County Council* (1996) to reinterpret Union law on sex discrimination to include a broad understanding of what was covered by sex discrimination and in particular to include discrimination against transsexuals within its scope.

Principle	TEU	TFEU	Some relevant cases
'General principles'	Article 6(3)	Article 15, Article 291(3), Article 340	
Subsidiarity	Preamble, Article 5, Article 12	Article 69, Article 352(2)	
Proportionality	Article 5, Article 12	Article 69, Article 276, Article 296	C–331/88 *Fedesa*; 181/84 *ED & F Man (Sugar) Ltd*
Sustainability and sustainable development	Preamble, Article 3, Article 21(2)(d) and (f)	Article 11, Article 119(3), Article 140(1)	C–463/01 *Commission v Germany*; C–379/98 *PreussenElektra*
Human rights and fundamental freedoms	Preamble, Article 2, Article 3(5), Article 6(2) and (3), Article 21	(Article 218)	29/69 *Stauder v City of Ulm*; 11/70 *Internationale Handelsgesellschaft*
Equality and non-discrimination	Article 2, Article 3(3), Article 4(2), Article 9, Article 21	Article 8, Article 10, Article 18, Article 19, Article 36, Article 37, Article 40(2), Article 45(2), Article 65(3), Article 95, Article 107, Article 114(6), Article 153(1)(i), Article 157, Article 200(5), Article 214(2), Article 236	C–144/04 *Mangold v Helm*; C–303/06 *Coleman v Attridge Law*
Justice	Preamble, Article 2, Article 3, Article 12	Article 67, Article 68, Article 81(2)(e), Article 276	
Legal certainty			234/04 *Kapferer v. Schlanck & Schick GmbH*; C–453/00 *Kühne & Heitz*
Non-retroactivity and legitimate expectations			63/83 *R v Kirk*; 112/77 *Töpfer*
Legal professional privilege			155/79 *AM & S Europe Ltd v Commission* (1982)
Transparency			T–105/95 *Worldwide Fund for Nature v Commission*

Table 1 Principles of law mentioned by the governing treaties.

6.4 In Case C–122/95 *Germany v Council* (1998) the general principle of equality was referred to when the Court of Justice held Community legislation invalid—it was used as a ground of annulment for a skimmed milk regime because of difference of treatment experienced by dairy farmers, who benefited from the contested rules on skimmed milk, and livestock breeders, who were disadvantaged by them. (Actions for annulment are considered in more detail in **Chapter 8**.)

6.5 This general principle has also been used to review national law, in a twin thrust application of the supremacy of Union law (see **Chapter 7**) and the obligation to interpret national law according to Union law premises, an obligation generally flowing from Article 10 TFEU but also specifically articulated in judgments such as *Marleasing* (see **Chapter 7**). There are many examples of such reviews of national law, perhaps because the boundaries between the application of Union law supremacy resulting from a specific piece of legislation and that application due to a general principle of Union law are difficult to navigate. One interesting decision of the Court of Justice on another case concerning the treatment of a person who had undertaken gender reassignment is a good example, even if the judgment needs to be handled carefully. In Case C–117/01 *KB* (2004) a couple including a transsexual were prevented from marrying in the United Kingdom because marriage is a status reserved to a man and a woman, and a transsexual's gender could not at that time be altered on the birth certificate from that recorded at birth to that acquired following the gender reassignment. The legal obstacle to marriage made the benefits attaching to marriage unobtainable to this couple, and the dispute in this case concerned pension eligibility that would be extended to the surviving partner in a married couple upon the death of the employee, but not to the surviving partner in co-habiting unmarried couples. The Court of Justice, taking account of relevant judgments from the European Court of Human Rights (ECtHR) on the right to marry, considered it fell to the English court to decide on the correct application of Union discrimination law to these rights to marry and the pension rules that were dependent upon them, but that in principle the national marriage requirement breached Union law on gender discrimination.

6.6 The Court of Justice originally took the view that there were general principles of law which, although they are not expressly referred to in the Treaties at that time, nevertheless underlined their provisions and as such bound the institutions in the performance of their duties. These derived either from principles applying in the Member States (such as those attaching to the concepts of 'justice', proportionality and the special constitutional status of human rights protection), or Union law principles as developed by the Court of Justice (for example direct effect and supremacy, discussed in **Chapter 7**) subsidiarity, although a principle with non-Union origins (see **6.15–6.23**), and even citizenship (see further **Chapter 13**), as asserted by the Court in Case C–184/99 *Grzelczyck* (2001) and Case C–192/99 *Kaur* (2001) (see **4.44** and **13.21**). Usually, the reference to 'general principles of law' is concerned with the principles which have originated in the Member States. All those stated above have now been given Treaty status (see Table 1, **6.3** above).

6.7 The references to 'any rule of law' relating to the application of the Treaty in Article 263 TFEU and to 'general principles common to the laws of the member states' in

Article 340(2) TFEU indicate clearly that it was always envisaged that the Treaty would operate in accordance with certain principles recognised by the Member States. The Court of Justice, in fulfilling its duty to ensure that 'the law is observed', has sought to structure methods of interpreting and applying Union law according to these generally accepted principles to ensure both the widest acceptance of Union law in national courts and the maximum effectiveness (*effet utile*) of the Union's objectives, sometimes to the extent of going beyond the limiting wording of a specific provision in the pursuit of a wider general aim. This method of interpretation is often termed as 'teleological' and is invariably adopted by commentators as shorthand to describe the Court's 'standard' approach, although clearly the Court also draws upon a range of other methods.

6.8 The Court of Justice has applied principles which may be common to some or all of the Member States. It appears to be sufficient that one Member State applies such a principle. In Case 155/79 *AM & S Europe Ltd v Commission* (1982), the principle of legal professional privilege was considered by the Court. Although generally the right of everyone to defend himself when charged with a criminal offence includes the right to confidentiality of documents in the hands of his lawyer, the principle is much more extensive in some countries, for example the United Kingdom, than in others. The Court drew on this experience and did not choose the lowest common denominator.

6.9 The Court of Justice now speaks in terms of the constitutional status of general principles of law within the Union. In Joined Cases C–402/05P and C–415/05P *Kadi v Council* (2008) (see also **5.13**), the Court of Justice stated at 285:

> the obligations imposed by an international agreement cannot have the effect of prejudicing the constitutional principles of the EC Treaty, which include the principle that all Community acts must respect fundamental rights, that respect constituting a condition of their lawfulness which it is for the Court to review in the framework of the complete system of legal remedies established by the Treaty.

This tentative reference to the constitutional status of general principles was confirmed in Case C–101/08 *Audiolux SA v GBL* (2009) where the Court stated unequivocally that general principles of EU law have a constitutional status and should be of general application. The issues in *Audiolux* concerned whether a general principle of equality of shareholders existed, protecting minority shareholders vis-à-vis the dominant shareholder. The Court stated, at paragraph 34, 'the mere fact that secondary Community legislation lays down certain provisions relating to the protection of minority shareholders is not sufficient in itself to establish the existence of a general principle of Community law, in particular if the scope of those provisions is limited to rights which are well-defined and certain'. It went on to state, at paragraph 63 that 'the general principles of Community law have constitutional status'. The principle in question in *Audiolux*, relating to equality between shareholders, was not found to represent a general principle of Union law, although the case is interesting as an example of the Court's willingness to consider the emergence of new general principles. Here it laid down criteria which define a rule of law as opposed to a principle.

6.10 The case of *Mangold* was quoted above (see **6.1**) as a seminal case in which the Court stated that non-discrimination on grounds of age was a general principle of law in the Union. In a later case, the Court of Justice went further. Case C–555/07 *Kücükdeveci v Swedex* (2010) (see **7.22**) concerned Ms Kücükdeveci, an employee in a German company Swedex. She had been employed at the company from the age of 18 in 1996, and was dismissed in 2007. The company calculated that she had accumulated only three years of service, because according to a German law, employment below the age of 25 need not be taken into account when calculating dismissal allowances. Ms Kücükdeveci challenged this law before the German courts claiming discrimination on grounds of age, and that the German law in question was not compatible with the Treaties or with Directive 2000/78, which includes rules on age discrimination. The Court held, firstly, that the Directive 'gives expression' to the general principle of Union law that discrimination on grounds of age is prohibited. As such, the Court echoed *Mangold* in saying that the Directive itself does not lay down the principle, which is derived from various international instruments and the constitutional traditions common to Member States. In the words of the Court:

> Directive 2000/78 merely gives expression to, but does not lay down, the principle of equal treatment in employment and occupation, and [...] the principle of non-discrimination on grounds of age is a general principle of European law in that it constitutes a specific application of the general principle of equal treatment.

The Court also refers, in paragraph 22, to the Charter of Fundamental Rights (see **6.49**), which was later given the same legal status as the founding Treaties by the Treaty of Lisbon. It is not clear whether the Court is invoking Article 21(1) of the Charter, which prohibits any discrimination based on age, or merely referring to it as evidence of a general principle. In any case to invoke the Charter would necessitate its retroactive application, which is contrary to the general principle of non-retroactivity. The Court also raised the possibility of the dominance of the doctrine of supremacy of Union law over national law, for which discussion see **Chapter 7**.

What are the general principles?

6.11 To help navigate a way through this topic, it might be helpful to consider three questions:

- Why are there general principles of EU law?
- How do they work? and
- What is included?

Some issues relevant to the reasons why the Court of Justice developed general principles can be summarised as follows. General principles of Union law are invoked to assist in the interpretation of Treaty provisions and secondary legislation, to provide

guidance for the exercise of powers granted by the founding Treaties or secondary legislation and to provide additional criteria under Article 267 TFEU for determining the
legality of acts of the Union institutions and the Member States. Where it is necessary
for the Court of Justice to fill gaps in Union law so that the existence of a loophole
will not lead to a denial of justice, it will also make use of general principles. General
principles evidence the Court's attempt to contribute to the construction of a mature
legal system based upon a combination of substantive rules and principles that aid the
understanding of those rules and the system as a whole. To that extent the principles
are like guides through the legal system.

At the same time, the Court of Justice has indicated that there is a constitutional hierarchy, with some standards prevailing over others and these principles indicating which
standard should prevail. Above all, the general principles are about the search for consistency in the creation of the Union legal order: they pull the different rules together
into something that has a shape as a whole. The difficulty is that there is not necessarily
complete agreement as to what that shape should be, and there are those who question
the activist stance of a court in such a construction project. From the Court's perspective the contribution is a consistent and mature system.

6.12 The question of how the general principles work is particularly difficult, since the most
important thing to note is that the different general principles do not all operate in the
same way. Some, such as legal certainty and proportionality (both considered below
at **6.74** and **6.24–6.29**) are clearly capable of overturning any other rule or principle
in the Union legal system, and by virtue of the application of the supremacy of Union
law, can do much the same thing to national laws too. At the other extreme, there are
general principles that seem to be not much more than aspirations for the legal order,
for example the sustainability principle (such as it is) set out in Article 11 TFEU (see
6.30–6.33) and the subsidiarity requirement of Article 5 TEU (see **6.15–6.23**). The
general principles associated with the protection of fundamental human rights form
a third category where the Court uses human rights standards to reinterpret Union
law and as a basis of actions against the institutions. There are indications that the
Court of Justice is also starting to use human rights standards in evaluating acts of
the Member States, but these principles are not applied as the same standard of review
of Union law as proportionality and legal certainty. Then there is a fourth category of
principle: the principle of equality seems to operate across the boundaries between the
other three categories, being capable of founding an annulment action (see **6.4**), being
considered subject to other general principles and at other times overlapping with the
principles relating to human rights protection.

6.13 The question of what the general principles are is more easily addressed so long as it
is remembered that there is no static list. It is perfectly possible that those principles
which are widely accepted will be reinterpreted or that others will be added in time.
The content below separates out the general principles of Union law into categories
relating to human rights standards, principles of administrative justice and governance, and principles that are specific to the EU legal order ('Union law principles').

From a certain perspective, the general rules on supremacy and direct effect and direct applicability could also be understood as general principles of Union law, although here they are considered in a separate chapter (**Chapter 7**). In any case, despite this categorisation, the general principles should not be seen as operating in separate boxes or as somehow being a discrete topic in the study of Union law, since neither approach helps with their understanding. They are generally applied and so need to be generally understood: they operate in conjunction with the specific rules of substantive law as well as being independent to such substantive rules; they are a fluid standard of review that bridge process and substance.

Overarching principles of the Union legal order

6.14 It was in the context of the protection of fundamental human rights that the Court of Justice first coined the phrase 'general principles' in Union law. It went on to create a mature legal system with the development of administrative principles and principles of good governance. However, the various drafters of Union law took the opportunity to introduce a series of other general principles which would define, expand and deepen the Union legal order. Some principles, such as the equality standard, while being common to many states' legal traditions, have become a particular benchmark for Union law and appear in many specific substantive law fields. Others, such as the subsidiarity principle, are somehow quite particular to the Union legal order even if they were clearly imported from other systems. These principles are here termed 'overarching principles' of the Union legal order. They are to be understood as principles that were adopted by the Court of Justice from legal principles already extant in legal systems of Member States. Doctrines, as discussed in **Chapter 7**, are differentiated on the basis that these were ultimately constructed by the Court of Justice, as opposed to a simple adoption.

Subsidiarity

6.15 Article 5 TEU sets out the principles of subsidiarity and proportionality. It is worth noting the provision in full:

> 1. *The limits of Union competences are governed by the principle of conferral. The use of Union competencies is governed by the principles of subsidiarity and proportionality.*
>
> 2. *Under the principle of conferral, the Union shall act only within the limits of the competences conferred upon it by the Member States in the Treaties to attain the objectives set out therein. Competences not conferred upon the Union in the Treaties remain with the Member States.*
>
> 3. *Under the principle of subsidiarity, in areas which do not fall within its exclusive competence, the Union shall act only if and insofar as the objectives of the*

proposed action cannot be sufficiently achieved by the Member States, either at central level or at regional and local level, but can rather, by reason of scale or effects of the proposed action, be better achieved at Union level.

The institutions of the Union shall apply the principle of subsidiarity as laid down in the Protocol on the application of the principles of subsidiarity and proportionality. National parliaments ensure compliance with the principle of subsidiarity in accordance with the procedures set out in that Protocol.

6.16   Subsidiarity as a principle was not new, and was familiar in many federal states such as Germany and the United States. The principle first appeared in the Community in 1975 in a report on Economic Union by the Commission. It stated that an expansion of Community powers should only occur where the Member States could not effectively accomplish the desired tasks. In 1984 the Draft Treaty establishing the European Union referred to subsidiarity in the Preamble; while this draft was adopted by the European Parliament it never progressed as it was regarded as too federalist. An awareness of subsidiarity and the environment were both brought into Community law by the Single European Act in 1986. The concept was formally introduced as a general principle of Community law in the Maastricht Treaty on European Union in 1992, where it was referred to in the Preamble, the framework articles, and most importantly, Article 3b EC (now Article 5 TEU). The principle was left unaltered by the Treaty of Amsterdam, however, shortly after the Commission issued a communication which set out its views on the application of the principle.

6.17   While the text of the principle was not altered by the Treaty of Amsterdam, a binding Protocol was added which laid out the principles of subsidiarity and proportionality more extensively. It obliged the Commission to 'consult widely before proposing legislation and, wherever appropriate, publish consultation documents'. It was also committed to justify the relevance of its proposals with regard to the principle of subsidiarity, although it is to be recalled that separate action is required for the financing of Union action in whole or in part from Union budgets. Since 1993, the Commission has also been required to submit annual reports to the European Council, the Council and the European Parliament on the application of Article 5. The Protocol also required any reasons for concluding that a Union objective could be better achieved at Union level to be substantive, or wherever possible, quantitative indicators. It also stated that the subsidiarity principle did not affect the primacy of Union law, nor did it call into question the powers conferred on the Union by the Treaty as interpreted by the Court of Justice. It stated that the principle should refer to areas in which the Union does not have exclusive competence. Unfortunately, the principle has had the effect of lengthening the legislative process as various conditions require justification and verification against the Protocol, and most Preambles to new legislation now contain a reference to the principle.

6.18   Following the changes brought about by the Treaty of Lisbon, Protocol no 2, annexed to the TFEU and TEU, now sets out the application of the principles of subsidiarity and proportionality. The Preamble sets out the wish of the parties to the Treaty to 'ensure that decisions are taken as closely as possible to citizens of the Union'. Again there is heavy emphasis on the necessity of justification of legislative acts with regard to the joint principles, and Article 5 of the Protocol states that:

> *Any draft legislative act should contain a detailed statement making it possible to appraise compliance with the principles of subsidiarity and proportionality.*

Article 8 sets out that the Court of Justice 'shall have jurisdiction in actions on grounds of infringement of the principle of subsidiarity by a legislative act, brought in accordance with the rules laid down in Article 263 TFEU'. The Commission is still required to submit an annual report on the application of Article 5 TEU, according to Article 9 of the Protocol.

6.19 Subsidiarity requires the institutions to consider the appropriateness of Union action when other action may be possible. As a principle of law it sounds very much like a standard that could be used to challenge the validity of legislation adopted either without reference to subsidiarity, or to challenge the Union legislation adopted if alternative national or regional legislation could have achieved the aim of the challenged legislation. Still, the principle is very difficult to formulate in this way and appears to have significant shortcomings as a principled standard which can be used to strike down legislation or decisions made for being a step too far on the road to centralisation. It is certainly difficult, if still possible, to imagine how the courts could come to a view on what remains essentially a political choice as to the most appropriate forum for making a decision, or the most appropriate source for the legislation once it is decided this legislation is needed. Indeed, this was the argument raised by the Council in the recent roaming charges case (Case C–58/08 *Vodafone Ltd* (2009) (see **6.23** below)). Perhaps as a general principle it is easier to see it being enforced in terms of the requirement on institutions to consider the principle and to demonstrate that subsidiarity has been thought about, rather than as a standard against which to evaluate the substance of the legislation. As such it may amount to no more than a process requirement.

6.20 The main test to see if the principle of subsidiarity has been complied with is termed the *sufficient attainment* test. Article 5(3)(a) TEU sets out the basis for this test, which is negative in formulation, and which seems to say that if the Member State cannot achieve the aim then it should be undertaken by the Union. The Commission has referred to this test as 'the comparative efficiency test', although this terminology may be misleading as the principle should not really incorporate any comparative element. A second test used is the *better attainment* test, where Union action should be preferred to Member State action if it will bring demonstrable advantages.

6.21 The Commission has improved the guidance it gives on how to analyse subsidiarity and proportionality in the revised impact assessment guidelines adopted in January 2009. These now contain two explicit sets of questions which are based on the Protocol, and which focus attention on transnational aspects which could be an indication that Member States cannot satisfactorily achieve the objectives on their own. In the course of 2008 the European Parliament adopted two resolutions which deal with subsidiarity and proportionality. In October it adopted the Commission's report on 'Better

Lawmaking 2006, on the application of the principles of subsidiarity and proportionality', which addressed the role of national parliaments in scrutiny. The European Parliament stressed the need for a common approach across the Member States of the Union towards scrutiny on grounds of subsidiarity and proportionality. The second was the Parliament's response to the Commission's Green Paper 'Towards a new culture of urban mobility'. While the responsibility of local authorities, urban mobility requires the implementation of an integrated European approach. While legislation at a Union level would not be appropriate, the Parliament noted the need for account to be taken of particular needs in the areas in which Union competence is exercised, such as budgeting policy, social and labour market policy, etc. Furthermore, impact assessments have become the main vehicle to address subsidiarity and proportionality issues within the Commission during the preparation of policy initiatives. The Impact Assessment Board plays a key role in this respect and the revised impact assessment guidelines should see further awareness and progress in this area.

6.22 The Court of Justice has given some guidance on interpreting the principle; however it has appeared reluctant to interfere with Union action. In Case C–84/94 *United Kingdom v Council* (1996), in which the United Kingdom objected to the Working Time Directive on a number of grounds, the UK argument that the subsidiarity principle had not been complied with was rejected. It was held that Community action was necessary in order to achieve the health and safety objectives set out in the Directive. Other points concerning the legal base and the requirement to give reasons (under what is now Article 296 TFEU) were also rejected by the Court. The Court of Justice also rejected similar arguments raised in Case C–377/98 *Netherlands v Parliament and Council* (2001) against the Biotechnology Patents Directive.

6.23 In the recent roaming charges regulation case, Case C–58/08 *Vodafone Ltd, Telefónica O2 Europe plc T Mobile International AG, Orange Personal Communications Services Ltd v Secretary of State for Business, Enterprise and Regulatory Reform* (2009), the Court of Justice was asked to deliberate on whether the Regulation, in setting out Union action to be taken, had breached the principle of subsidiarity. The Advocate General stated that the principle of subsidiarity requires that 'there be a reasonable justification for the proposition that there is a need for Community action'. Furthermore, while the Advocate General stated that the Court would not substitute its conclusions for those of the legislator, it would compel it to take subsidiarity seriously. However, the Court's judgment appeared to be deferential to the legislator. It held that the need for Union action was 'clear from recital 14 in the preamble to the regulation'. This may have been so in this case, but even so such reasoning is undesirable. If this is to become the standard method for applying the subsidiarity principle, by only looking at the face of the relevant legislation and its statements on the matter, then it will remain a relatively weak principle.

Proportionality

6.24 As already seen, proportionality is listed in the Treaties as a seminal principle by which legislative, judicial and other competencies must be exercised.

Article 5(4) TEU states:

> *Under the principle of proportionality, the content and form of Union action shall not exceed what is necessary to achieve the objectives of the Treaties.*
>
> *The institutions of the Union shall apply the principle of proportionality as laid down in the Protocol on the application of the principles of subsidiarity and proportionality.*

Proportionality is, therefore, a guiding principle defining how the Union should exercise its competences, both exclusive and shared. Both Article 5 TEU and the Protocol provide that the action should not go beyond what is necessary to achieve the objectives of the Treaties, however any decision must favour the least restrictive option.

6.25 In Case C–331/88 *Fedesa* (1990), the Court of Justice defined proportionality as follows:

> The principle of proportionality ... requires that measures adopted by [Union] institutions do not exceed the limits of what is appropriate and necessary in order to attain the objectives legitimately pursued by the legislation in question; when there is a choice between several appropriate measures recourse must be had to the least onerous, and the disadvantages caused are not to be disproportionate to the aims pursued.

It is clear that this definition contains the three subsidiary principles that constitute the principle of proportionality in Germany (suitability, necessity and proportionality *stricto sensu*).

6.26 The principle of proportionality has been used to challenge both Union action and Member State action in the Union sphere. The principle lays down an obligation on the part of the administration invoking a penalty or operating a policy to consider alternatives and to justify the actions chosen. The principle has been invoked in many cases, e.g. in Case 11/70 *Internationale Handelsgesellschaft* (1970) (see **6.53**). Case 181/84 *ED & F Man (Sugar) Ltd* (1985), is a good illustration of the issues. ED & F Man (Sugar) Ltd forfeited £1,670,370 when it submitted a licence application late. All sides admitted the paperwork was late but ED & F Man (Sugar) disputed it should lose the full deposit paid when it was only a few hours late with the application. The Court of Justice set out a preliminary ruling on the relevant regulations applicable to the licence and noted the different obligations in the regulations: some were concerned with sugar exports, other provisions related to the conditions attaching to licences for sugar exports. The secondary nature of the licensing obligations meant full forfeiture for breach of such obligations was disproportionate: it would be one thing to forfeit the full deposit for a breach of the export obligations itself. The licence was secondary to that obligation and therefore breach of the obligations associated with the licence should have a lesser penalty attached. A £1,670,370 penalty was therefore a disproportionate penalty compared to the aim of the regulations, and thereby unlawful.

6.27 Proportionality operates as a general principle of Union law, appearing in judgments on the whole range of Union law subjects. In Case C–390/99 *Canal Satelite Digital* (2002) a requirement that television service providers register all their equipment details was ruled disproportionate to the extent it required duplication of the registration activity either in the same state or in another Member State. In Case 302/86 *Commission v Denmark* ('Danish Bottles') (1988) (see **10.37**) the Court of Justice used the proportionality principle to mitigate the exception to free movement of goods regime allowed for in the interests of environmental protection. A deposit and return scheme on containers in Denmark was acceptable under the scope of the free movement of goods because of the environmental protection aim pursued. But a restrictive scheme which only permitted the use of certain types of containers was disproportionate to the aim pursued since the recycling of all sorts of containers achieved the same aim of environmental protection with less disruption to goods movement in the internal market. Although, the Court of Justice has held, also in the context of environmental protection and free movement of goods, that whilst a less restrictive means of protecting the environment is available Member States may still be able to adopt an alternative path. Here, in a case concerning restrictions on the use of jet-skis in Sweden, the Court considered 'particular geographic circumstances of the Member State'. But, more interestingly, the Court also accepted that such rules are 'easily managed and supervised by the national authorities' (Case C–142/05 *Mickelsson and Roos* (2009) see further **10.68**). This can be contrasted with the position in *Danish Bottles* where the Court considered whether 'all the restrictions which the contested rules impose on the free movement of goods are necessary to achieve the objectives pursued by those rules' and answered in the negative. Comparing *Danish Bottles* and *Mickelsson* provides an insight into the flexibility, in application, which the principle holds.

6.28 In the broader context Article 7 TFEU states that 'the Union shall ensure consistency between its policies and activities, taking all of its objectives into account and in accordance with the principle of conferral of powers'. Conferral can be understood by reference to Article 5 TEU, which makes conferral, on the one hand, and proportionality and subsidiarity on the other, effectively two sides of the same coin.

6.29 Article 5(4) TEU refers to the principle of proportionality.

Protocol no 2 on proportionality and subsidiarity follows another protocol on the role of national parliaments, and to some extent the two protocols can be read together. The protocol on the proportionality principle would enable parliaments to scrutinise Union legislation from the point of view of the proportionality principle prior to its adoption.

Sustainability

6.30 Union law recognises the sustainable development concept in Article 3(5) TEU, Article 21(2)(f) TEU and Article 11 TFEU, which states that environmental protection requirements must be integrated into Union policies, an exhortation that previously was found only in the Environment Title of the Treaty (at one time Article 130R EEC/EC, more latterly 174 EC). This has since been relocated to make clear the significance of the environment in the Union legal order. It is quite possible that environmental protection concepts or some other formulation of sustainable development will evolve into a general principle of Union law. Such a principle would no doubt base itself on the various environmental protection principles set out in Article 191 TFEU, such as the polluter pays principle, the precautionary principle and the principle of rectification of environmental problems at source (see **15.34–15.42**). The particular revolution of thought associated with sustainable development requires, further, that the interests of future generations be taken into account and that policy should strive towards the achievement of an equitable balance between economic, environmental and social priorities (see **15.34** and **15.40**). That too could inform a general sustainability principle.

6.31   Environmental protection has been accepted as a justification for limiting the freedom to move goods (see **7.54** and **10.27**). In Case C–463/01 *Commission v Germany* (2004) and Case C–379/98 *PreussenElektra* (2001) (see **10.79**) the Court of Justice seemed to accept that environmental protection measures could apply differently to domestic and cross-border trade with a result that the environmental protection justification operates differently to other exceptions to the general freedom to move goods. This may be seen as an expression of a general principle of sustainability although the Court did not put the matter in this way and made no reference to Article 11 TFEU or its judgments on general principles. Similarly in C–127/07 *Société Arcelor Atlantique et Lorraine v Premier Ministre* (2008) the Court was required to consider difference in treatment between companies on the basis that some were incorporated under the EU emissions trading scheme (see **15.43**) while other, competing companies, were currently excluded. Once more it did not expressly mention a sustainability principle, however, it contextualised its judgment (at paragraph 3) through reference to the United Nations Framework on Climate Change which holds the 'ultimate objective of stabilising greenhouse gas concentrations in the atmosphere at a level that would prevent dangerous anthropogenic interference with the climate system'. This, itself a clear embodiment of the sustainability principle, was combined with other environmental considerations to conclude that here 'the difference in treatment between the chemical sector and the steel sector may be regarded as justified' (see further **6.34**).

6.32   Union law then does not have much by way of case law expressions of such a sustainability principle and it seems that Article 11 TFEU, such as it is, rests more properly on the political level and is not yet a general principle that can be used to review the validity of Union law or policies. In Case C–205/98 *Commission v Austria* (2000) the Court of Justice rejected an argument made to justify differential rates of charges for the use of the Brenner Pass based upon admittedly questionable environmental considerations relating to the pollution and noise of heavy goods vehicles, insisting that the charging regime provided by Community law be applied (Directive 1999/62). The Austrian authorities had suggested that the criteria for these charges—that they should be linked to the construction and maintenance of the Pass—could be interpreted to include environmental factors in addition to those construction and maintenance costs. The Court felt it could not accept this, in a judgment that made no mention of Article 11 TFEU. Traffic transiting the Brenner Pass remains a live issue in Austria, with further cases having come before the Court of Justice on bans on vehicles operating at particular times (Case C–320/03P *Commission v Austria* (2004)), the measuring of pollution levels from traffic transiting the Alps which justified special measures limiting the flow of traffic ('eco-points') (Case 445/00 *Austria v Council* (2003)) and on Austrian rules preventing the registration of older imported vehicles on health and environmental grounds (Case C–524/07 *Commission v Austria* (2008)). An interesting case brought by Austria on the refusal of the institutions to extend the provision permitting the use of eco-points to protect the Alps from traffic pollution (Case C–161/04 *Austria v Parliament and Council*) was withdrawn before judgment. In none of these cases has the Court taken the opportunity to explain how Article 11 TFEU may resolve the disputes or be used to reinterpret Union law.

6.33 Environmental protection thus has a special status in Union law although the sustainability concept is not a general principle with the same weight and status as others—such as the proportionality principle—which have the capability of being used as a standard against which Union law can be measured by the Court of Justice. Initiatives such as the European Parliament resolution on mainstreaming sustainability in development cooperation policies (2006/2246(INI)), amongst myriad others, compound understanding of the idea as a principle of European law and policy, and along with the EU Sustainable Development Strategies of 2001 and 2006 it is likely that sustainability will receive recognition by the Court of Justice as a general principle. It is, however, difficult to understand the purpose of Article 11 TFEU in the absence of any general principle based upon it and it would be interesting should greater argument be made in the Court on the nature of the sustainability principle and how it should work as a general principle.

Equality

6.34 Equality in philosophical terms is an ancient idea, dating back to Aristotle's formulation that:

> *Equality in morals means this: things that are alike should be treated alike, while things that are unalike should be treated unalike in proportion to their unalike-ness* (Ethica Nicomachea v.3.1131a-1131b)

Many legal systems accord some version of an equality principle a special status although this is more often understood in terms of a right of those who are 'alike' to be treated alike, with less attention given its reverse, whereby the 'unalike' should be treated differently. In Case C–127/07 *Société Arcelor Atlantique et Lorraine v Premier Ministre* (2008), the Court stated:

> The general principle of equal treatment, as a general principle of Community law, requires that comparable situations must not be treated differently and different situations must not be treated in the same way unless such treatment is objectively justified.

The principle of equality in Union law means, in its broadest sense, that persons in similar situations are not to be treated differently unless that difference in treatment is objectively justified. That different treatment is discrimination, and the equality principle is sometimes understood as the principle of non-discrimination, even though the relationship between discrimination and equality is not often made clear. In Joined Cases 117/76 and 16/77 *Ruckdeschel* (1977), the Court of Justice stated, at paragraph 7:

> The prohibition of discrimination laid down…is merely a specific enunciation of the general principle of equality which is one of the fundamental principles of [Union] law.

6.35 There is a presumption that the ending of discrimination, because it is unfairly differential treatment, will produce a more equal result. The TFEU expressly prohibits discrimination on the grounds of nationality (Article 18 TFEU) and, to a limited extent, sex (Article 10 TFEU). Part Two of the TFEU, 'Non-Discrimination and Citizenship of the Union' goes some way to enhancing these standards, and lists the non-exhaustive bases of discrimination prohibited within Union law (see **Chapter 13** for further discussion on citizenship of the Union and **Chapter 16** generally on non-discrimination).

6.36 In the field of agricultural policy, Article 40 TFEU prohibits 'discrimination between producers or consumers within the Union'. Article 19 TFEU is an enabling provision which allows the Council to take measures by unanimity and 'without prejudice to the other provisions of the Treaties' in respect of discrimination based on sex, racial or ethnic origin, religion or belief, disability, age or sexual orientation. This provision cannot have direct effect although it does add to the width of the general principle of equality.

6.37 Two Directives implement the discrimination standards set out in Article 19 TFEU (Directive 2000/43 on race, and Directive 2000/78 on a general framework for equal treatment in employment). Case C–144/04 *Mangold v Helm* (2005) considered in **6.1** (above) concerned the general framework Directive on discrimination. Cases on the Directives' requirements have questioned the limits set out therein. Case C–303/06 *Coleman v Attridge Law* saw the Court state that the principle of non-discrimination on the grounds of disability is not merely limited to those who are disabled. The applicant claimed to be discriminated against on grounds of her child's disability (see also **16.93**).

6.38 In Case C–227/04P *Lindorfer v Council of the European Union* (2007), a case concerning alleged sex discrimination in employment by a woman employed by the Council where pension payments and longer-life spans for women compared to men were at issue, the Court stated: 'Article 141 EC [now Article 157 TFEU] and the various provisions of secondary legislation to which Ms Lindorfer refers, as well as Article 1a(1) of the Staff Regulations, are specific expressions of the general principle of equality of the sexes'.

6.39 In Case C–13/05 *Chacón Navas v Eurest Colectividades SA* (2006) the Court of Justice referred to a general principle of equality as a reason for standardising the interpretation of undefined terms. The case concerned an employment dispute where Ms Chacón Navas, while off work through sickness, had been dismissed. Ms Chacón Navas alleged that this amounted to discrimination on grounds of disability, and the national court that referred the matter to the Court of Justice for a preliminary ruling was uncertain the combat of discrimination on the grounds of disability included protecting a person who was sick. The Court of Justice noted that since Directive 2000/78 did not define the concept of disability, and that neither did the Directive make reference to national law interpretations of the concept, the concept required a Union level interpretation to ensure the 'uniform application of Community law and the general principle of equality'. The Court decided there was nothing in Directive 2000/78 to suggest that workers are protected by the prohibition of discrimination on grounds of disability as soon as they develop any type of sickness, basically ruling that there were important distinctions between disability and sickness. It is interesting however that the Court sees the equality concept as extending into the need for definitions of terms applied in the different legal systems.

6.40 In Case C–442/00 *Caballero* (2002) the Court of Justice ruled that workers unfairly dismissed should all be treated equally, in a case arising out of different treatment for an unfairly dismissed worker whose company then became insolvent. Spanish law did not ensure the same entitlements to an employee unfairly dismissed from a company that then went out of business. The Court considered this situation breached the equality principle and stated:

> Once discrimination contrary to [Union] law has been established and for as long as measures reinstating equal treatment have not been adopted, observance of the principle of equality can be ensured only by granting to persons within the disadvantaged category the same advantages as those enjoyed by persons within the favoured category.
>
> In such a situation, a national court must set aside any discriminatory provision of national law, without having to request or await its prior removal by the legislature, and to apply to members of the disadvantaged group the same arrangements as those enjoyed by other workers…

6.41 The combat of discrimination on grounds of nationality has been at the heart of Union law since its inception. The right of workers to move around the market has always been one of the cornerstones of the Union legal order, and that right has prompted a generalised rethink in terms of what free movement entails, and the discriminatory practices that might limit it (see **Chapter 12**). While it is easy to understand the premise behind the combat of discrimination in the context of people taking up employment, the same premise applies to all the economic freedoms protected by Union law. Indeed, much legislative and court attention has been given to the combat of discrimination in the context of the movement of goods, the provision of services and in most aspects of the building of the internal market. These matters are best approached from the perspective of the simultaneous regulation and liberalisation of the relevant freedoms or sectors (i.e. from the perspective of the law on the free movement of goods and services, for example) and are noted here simply to draw attention to the relationship with the concept of equality.

6.42 The Court of Justice took the opportunity offered by the application of sex discrimination law to set out its thinking on the general principle of equality to ensure transsexuals were protected from discrimination, defining 'sex' broadly to include discrimination related to sex, because of the general principle (in Case C–13/94 *P v S and Cornwall County Council* (1996), see **6.3**). That being so, the Court then felt it necessary to identify limits to this broad interpretation and considered that sexual discrimination could not be so broad as to include discrimination against lesbians in Case C–249/96 *Grant v SW Trains* (1998), a decision that acknowledges the step taken in *P v S* but which raises questions as to why that step could be taken and why others cannot. Discrimination against gay people is now presumably within the ambit of the general principle following the framework Directive and the decision on that Directive in *Mangold v Helm*. By including such discrimination within the bounds of the general equality principle protected by Union law this broadens its application from the specific employment sphere offered by the Directive itself.

6.43 **Chapter 16** discusses discrimination in more detail, but it should be noted that even where non-discrimination provisions exist this does not mean that discriminatory behaviour will always fall foul of the rules. Sometimes certain forms of discrimination between alike individuals can be objectively justified. Instances of indirect sex discrimination that did not fall foul of Union equal treatment law are considered in **Chapter 16**, there being certain acceptable justifications for some forms of indirect discrimination. Further, it is generally understood that justification for indirect discrimination can also arise outside the context of sex discrimination, for example with regards to indirect nationality discrimination that arises with language requirements. In Case C–379/87 *Groener* (1989) a Dutch national was able to show she had experienced indirect discrimination by an Irish language requirement imposed as a condition of work, non-Irish nationals having a clear disadvantage regarding ability in this language. However this indirect discrimination was justifiable because the Member State's objective of protecting the Irish language was acceptable. In Case 411/05 *Palacios de la Villa v Cortefiel* (2007) the Court of Justice accepted there could be objective reasons justifying compulsory retirement on grounds of age. Mr Palacios was required to retire from his job on reaching 65 by virtue of Spanish employment policy which aimed to achieve full employment by requiring employees to retire at this age. The policy had been introduced by means of a collective agreement between employers and unions. The collective agreement in question predated Directive 2000/78 and its age discrimination provisions, but Mr Palacios was required to retire after the age discrimination provisions had come into force. The Court of Justice concluded that the Spanish policy of full employment was reasonable and the implementation of it through collective agreements provided for great flexibility. Therefore it did not think the compulsory retirement of a man at 65 years of age amounted to age discrimination within the meaning of Directive 2000/78 because of the public interest being pursued by Spanish policy.

6.44 A difficult issue associated with any general equality standard, and one with which Union law has also struggled, relates to the relationship between the equality principle and various measures introduced aiming at the combat of discrimination by means that focus on discriminated against groups. The particular problem that arises relates to the positive discrimination: where advantage is accorded to the disadvantaged group to what extent does this advantage fall foul of the equality principle? In Case C–450/93 *Kalanke* (1995), measures giving priority to female applicants were designed to achieve greater equality between men and women in employment, but the means whereby this was attempted were considered by the Court of Justice to contravene equality requirements since they disadvantaged men. Similar provisions advantaging women in Case C–409/95 *Marschall* (1997) were thought compatible with the equality principle because of an additional clause which provided: 'unless reasons specific to an individual [male] candidate tilt the balance in his favour'. The Court thought this ensured the employer individually considered any man affected by the positive discrimination provisions at issue and that this saved the positive discrimination from falling foul of the equality principle. Amendments to what is now Article 157 TFEU added paragraph 4 which specifically allows for positive discrimination in Union law. That being so, the Court still ruled in Case C–407/98 *Abrahamsson* (2000) that positive discrimination provisions had to first satisfy equality standards set out in Union secondary legislation before they could be justified under Article 157(4) TFEU, in a somewhat peculiar reversal of hierarchies between the Treaty and secondary legislation that can perhaps only be understood as an expression of the significance the Court accords to the equality principle. That being so, the Court in *Abrahamsson* insisted on a further hurdle being passed before it would accept a positive discrimination measure: the measure must also satisfy and comply with the proportionality principle. This confirms the sense that there is a hierarchy within the general principles. In Case C–319/03 *Briheche* (2004) a man excluded from applying for an administrative assistant post in central government in France because of his age sought to have the age restriction set aside because women, in certain instances, were not bound by it. The exemption concerning women was motivated around encouraging widows in particular into employment. Briheche, as a widower, sought equal treatment and alleged discrimination. The Court of Justice, in a preliminary ruling that explicitly accepted 'measures which, although discriminatory in appearance, are in fact intended to eliminate or reduce actual instances of inequality which may exist in the reality of social life' (at paragraph 22) then affirmed that such measures have to satisfy proportionality requirements. The direction given to the French courts in this preliminary ruling was that this French practice was not proportionate to the aim of achieving equality although without explaining why this was so, or what criteria applied.

6.45 The result of the various judgments in this field is that positive discrimination measures are subject to the equality principle although a clause which permits individual consideration of all (male) applicants can save such initiatives. The positive discrimination judgments are interesting and worth close reading for the discussion as to different sorts of equality that there can be, or, to put the matter more precisely, discussion on what equality means in different situations.

6.46 The equality principle is more difficult than it might at first appear since its scope is to some extent unlimited in Union law but its application is more haphazard. That is not to make a criticism of the work of the institutions in trying to achieve equality—the point is that equality is both difficult to define and implement. The push towards achieving greater equality remains high on the political agenda.

6.47 Following Lisbon, the Treaty on European Union has been endowed with Title II, 'Provisions on Democratic Principles'. Article 9 TEU of this Title states '[t]he Union shall observe the principle of equality of its citizens, who shall receive equal attention from its institutions, bodies, offices and agencies'. Thus as a general principle of Union law, equality is a standard that informs legislation and against which policies, rules and particular initiatives in particular contexts are measured. It is a part of the jigsaw of the mature legal order that the Court of Justice is trying to construct, but it is a difficult piece of that jigsaw to fit with others.

Fundamental human rights in the Union

6.48 The original aims of the Communities were economic, and no mention of human or fundamental rights was envisaged. The Court of Justice nevertheless had long seen that the interests of the Union were spread so wide that it was not possible to disregard human rights and that it was necessary to develop a Union approach. Since recourse to purely national guarantees of fundamental human rights could jeopardise the existence and further development of Union law, the approach adopted by the Court of Justice was characterised by a recognition that the absence of written provisions relating to fundamental rights did not negate their existence. The position was rather that Union law needed to be supplemented by unwritten legal principles, including basic rights, which have equal status with primary Union law.

6.49 Treaty references to human rights protection were sparse. However, the Treaties, as they were amended, came to include greater reference to human rights standards. The first time that human rights were explicitly referred to was in the Maastricht Treaty on European Union (TEU), with the introduction of Article 6 TEU. Reference is also made to fundamental human rights in the preamble, in the Common Foreign and Security Policy (CFSP) chapter (in the fifth indent of Article 24 TEU), and in Article 208 TFEU on development cooperation. Article 6 TEU reflects three elements of human rights protection in te Union. The most topical is the requirement that the EU 'shall accede to the European Convention for the Protection of Human Rights'. Negotiations are ongoing, however, it is currently understood that the UK and France are blocking accession due to concerns over national sovereignty. In Article 6 TEU the Charter of Fundamental Rights of the European Union (ECHR) is also referred to, along with the statement that it 'shall have the same legal value as the Treaties'. Whilst not uncontroversial (see **6.59** below) it is generally accepted that the Charter reflects past case law of the CJEU but is desirable as it provides a higher profile for the rights contained therein, assisting both with awareness and application of them. Finally, reference is made to the classical form of fundamental rights protection in the Union, those of general principles 'as they result from the constitutional traditions common to the Member State' (see **6.54–6.47**). In that paragraph of Article 6 TEU the ECHR is also described as being a source containing rights that 'shall constitute general principles of the Union's law', this reflects the reality that even prior to accession the ECHR has had immediate effects in the Union (see particularly **6.54–6.57**).

6.50 Article 7 TEU was an addition made by the Treaty of Amsterdam which was then amended by the Treaty of Nice. It sets out a procedure for determining instances of breach of the fundamental human rights principles referred to in Article 6 TEU and allows for a suspension of certain rights, including voting rights, of a Member State, found to be in breach. If the Council determines there is a *clear risk* of a serious breach a suspension of rights may follow. There is also a corresponding article in the TFEU, which provides in Article 354 TFEU for the suspension of voting rights and certain other 'rights resulting from Union membership'.

Article 49 TEU makes the respect of the principles set out in Article 2 TEU a specific condition for membership of the European Union.

6.51 Article 7 TEU was introduced in view of the enlargement of the Union to Central and Eastern European countries, where human rights, the rule of law and democracy were often relatively new. However, the first time Articles 6 and 7 TEU were referred to was in relation to Austria in January 2000 when at the European Council summit meeting in Portugal, 14 of the then 15 Member States (all but Austria) expressed concern about the participation in the Austrian Government of the ultra-right Austrian People's Party, and its leader, Jörg Haider. The governments of the 14 Member States said that they would no longer promote any bilateral contacts with Austria, nor would they support Austrian candidates seeking positions in international organisations. Fears were expressed that there could be a violation of Article 6 TEU on the basis of the politics associated with the Austrian People's Party. Since 2004, with the first enlargement including former eastern bloc countries, the concerns relating to human rights protection standards have mainly focused around the protection of minority rights. Concerns in Latvia have focused upon the large Russian-speaking minority in that country and anti-gay discrimination. In Poland, similarly, the 2005 election of right wing parties that formed an arch-conservative coalition raised concerns about anti-gay discrimination, and the reintroduction of the death penalty in Poland. Questions were raised in the European Parliament regarding Latvian policies, while the Commission itself intervened and drew the Polish Government's attention to the Article 7 TEU provisions, threatening the suspension of voting powers. The 2007 election in Poland saw a return to centre-right Government in Poland, quietening some of the concerns. However at the end of 2007, Lithuanian authorities banned from Vilnius, the Lithuanian capital, the European Union's 'Stop Discrimination Truck', a vehicle that toured the EU promoting the Year of Equal Opportunities For All. At the same time, Lithuanian authorities blocked gay rights demonstrations and stopped a promotional campaign in Lithuania on human rights that was being funded by the EU.

The Court's case law

6.52 Despite some initial reluctance to pronounce on such matters, there was pressure on the Court of Justice from courts in Germany and Italy for Union law to pay regard to fundamental human rights and it is not that surprising that the Court of Justice acknowledged the existence and relevance of unwritten principles of law, including the protection for certain fundamental rights, as an element of the Union legal order.

In 1989 Mancini J of the Court of Justice said:

> Reading an unwritten Bill of Rights into [Union] law is indeed the most striking contribution the court made to the development of a Constitution for Europe.

The Court of Justice adopted a gradual approach. Early attempts to read fundamental rights into Union law were not successful, but in Case 29/69 *Stauder v City of Ulm* (1969) the Court of Justice took a more positive attitude. The case concerned a Commission Decision providing for cheap butter for pensioners. This was introduced to get rid of the 'butter mountain' which had been created as a result of the Common Agricultural Policy. In some, but not all, language versions of the Decision, an applicant had to present a form bearing his name and address. The applicant in this case argued this was a violation of his human rights. The Court, in reviewing the legality of the Decision, held that properly interpreted, i.e. opting for the interpretation most favourable to the recipient, and using the language version which simply required the form to be 'individualised', the contested measure contained 'nothing capable of prejudicing the fundamental human rights enshrined in the general principles of Community law and protected by the court'. Thus the Court indicated early on a recognition of fundamental rights as a general principle of Union law.

6.53 In Case 11/70 *Internationale Handelsgesellschaft* (1970) (see also **7.76**), the Court of Justice held that:

> The protection of [fundamental] rights, whilst inspired by the constitutional traditions common to the member states must be ensured within the framework of the structure and objectives of the [Union].

Thus, the Court of Justice affirmed its view that these rights, although based on national constitutions, were part of the Union general principles. The case concerned the Common Agricultural Policy, under which a maize export licensing scheme required the payment of a large deposit before the licence was granted. The German applicant forfeited part of the deposit when he failed to export all the maize before a certain date. He complained that the deposit system infringed the principle of proportionality, which is enshrined in the German Constitution (Basic Law) as a fundamental right. The German courts found a violation of such a principle but the Court of Justice did not. It stated that the validity of Union measures cannot be tested against the concepts of national law, including those of a Member State's constitution and must be judged only in the light of Union law. The Court then examined the deposit system to ascertain whether an 'analogous guarantee inherent in [Union] law' had been disregarded. It concluded, however, that this was not the case. The case was returned to the German Constitutional Court, and major problems arose when this court insisted on conducting its own examination and concluded that there had been a violation of the constitutional principle of proportionality. The potential conflict this created appeared to be laid to rest with the application of the Court of Justice's judgment in Case 345/82 *Wünsche Handelsgesellschaft v Germany* (1984) ('*Solange II*') (see, for a discussion of these cases, **7.76**).

6.54 In Case C–36/02 *Omega* (2004), considered at **11.50**, the Court of Justice stated it was 'immaterial' whether a fundamental human right had its source in a national constitution or the Union legal order as a general principle of law, since Union law would protect such a right whatever its source. Such an approach simultaneously sets out the high standard of fundamental rights protection provided for by Union law, and also demonstrates the close link between constitutionally protected norms in the different Member States and the general principles.

6.55 In Case 4/73 *Nold* (1974) the Court of Justice declared a further source of inspiration for fundamental rights, that is, 'international treaties for the protection of human rights on which member states have collaborated or of which they are signatories'. The Court of Justice observed, however, that such rights were subject to limitations 'justified by the overall objectives pursued by the Community'.

6.56 In Case 36/75 *Rutili* (1975) (see **12.21**) the Court of Justice held that various rights invoked by the applicant and contained in express provisions of Union secondary legislation were specific manifestations of more general principles enshrined in the European Convention on Human Rights (ECHR). Further references to specific provisions of the ECHR were made by the Court of Justice in Case 222/84 *Johnston v Chief Constable of the RUC* (1986) where the Court said that the requirement of judicial control reflected a general principle of law common to the Member States as laid down in Articles 6 and 13 of the ECHR. Article 6 of the Equal Treatment Directive 76/207 had to be interpreted 'in the light of the general principle'. In Case C–60/00 *Carpenter* (2002) and Case C–112/00 *Schmidberger* (2003) (see **10.18** and **10.42**) the Court of Justice concluded that Union law had to be interpreted by reference to the ECHR. In *Carpenter*, Article 8 of the ECHR on privacy and family rights was used to reformulate Union law on services (considered in **Chapter 11**). In *Schmidberger* (see **10.18** and **10.24**), Articles 10 and 11 of the ECHR on free speech and protest rights were interpreted by the Court of Justice and set against free movement internal market rights to permit road protestors' closure of the Brenner Pass inhibiting the movement of goods across Austria.

6.57 While the Court of Justice of the European Union uses the ECHR as the primary source for the fundamental human rights general principle, it also draws upon those constitutional traditions common to the Member States. In Case 44/79 *Hauer* (1979) the right to make use of one's own property was at issue, with a landowner wanting to plant vines on her land. This intention was contradicted by the Community interest which had led to a Regulation restricting the planting of vines in order to avoid over-production of wine. In this case, the Community interest prevailed but the Court of Justice considered the extent of the right to use property in its judgment and adopted a comparative approach to the establishment of this right in EU law. Reference was made by the Court of Justice to the ECHR, and to specific constitutional provisions of particular national constitutions. The Court of Justice concluded that the right to make use of one's own property had to be weighed against the Community interest which sets out a certain marker in the role of general principles in Community law, subject to the more recent judgments in *Carpenter* and *Schmidberger* (see above, **6.56**). This case also demonstrates how the Court will draw on different sources to establish the right under consideration and the approach for identifying the nature of the right where there are different sources. On occasion, the Court of Justice has also referred to the European Social Charter and a Convention of the International Labour Organisation as authority for a source of fundamental rights, for example in cases concerning discrimination in respect of employment and occupation (see Case 149/77 *Defrenne* (1978) and Case C–158/91 *Ministère Public v Levy* (1993)).

The Charter of Fundamental Rights

6.58 The original Community Treaties contained no catalogue of basic rights which could constitute a check on the exercise of power by Union institutions. At the Cologne summit in June 1999 the European Council decided to set up a body to study the drafting of a European Charter of Human Rights. This body produced a Charter that was drawn mainly from fundamental rights protection already extant in Member States, the ECHR (1950), the Declaration on Fundamental Rights drawn up by the European Parliament in 1989 and the European Union Treaties. The Charter was not intended to duplicate the ECHR, but instead to form a constitutional basis for the Union and be tailored to the specific powers of the European Union and its institutions. The Charter as agreed was proclaimed at the summit which adopted the Nice Treaty in December 2001 but it was not binding or specifically incorporated into any of the Union law Treaties. The Treaty of Lisbon saw the incorporation of the Charter into primary European law, and enabled the Court of Justice to use Charter rights in the interpretation of what is currently Union law. The Charter includes not only the rights contained in the ECHR, but also a catalogue of economic and social rights. It was not the intention that these should be new rights, but rather that the Charter should draw together existing rights within the ambit of European Union law to make them more visible and to act as a guide to the institutions.

6.59 While the Charter does not set out any new rights there was still considerable apprehension surrounding its proclamation. The United Kingdom and Poland both considered it necessary to add Protocol No 30 which concerns the specific application of the Charter in these countries. While the Protocol has been described as an 'opt-out', this status is questionable. Article 1 of the Protocol declares that 'the Charter does not extend the ability of the Court of Justice of the European Union, or any Court or tribunal of Poland or of the United Kingdom, to find that the laws, regulations or administrative provisions, practices or action of Poland or of the United Kingdom are inconsistent with the fundamental rights, freedoms and principles that it reaffirms'. It has been observed that Poland wanted a Protocol to guarantee its own vision of public morality, while the United Kingdom wanted the Protocol to guarantee its vision of social and labour rights. It was always likely that this Protocol carried more political than legal weight. This appears to have been confirmed in Case C–411/10 *N.S. v Secretary of State for Home Department* (2011) where the Court held, in answering a specific question from the UK court on the matter, (at paragraph 119) that:

> ...Protocol (No 30) does not call into question the applicability of the Charter in the United Kingdom or in Poland, a position which is confirmed by the recitals in the pre-amble to that protocol. Thus, according to the third recital in the preamble to Protocol (No 30), Article 6 TEU requires the Charter to be applied and interpreted by the courts of Poland and the United Kingdom strictly in accordance with the explanations referred to in that article.

The conclusion was that 'the obligations of the United Kingdom...do not [need] to be qualified in any respect'. In November 2009 the Czech Republic was added to the Protocol, but it clearly has limited effects. Moreover, should the Court of Justice proclaim a new fundamental right not listed in the Charter, no Protocols or Declarations will absolve Member States from legal responsibility.

6.60 Accession as set out in Article 6(2) TEU that the Union shall accede to the ECHR is likely to happen by means of an accession Treaty, and will make the European Court of Human Rights (ECtHR) the court of last instance regarding matters of human rights in the European Union, which will be a fundamental shift in the constitutional set-up of the Union. However, following the *Bosphorus* case, this accession may be the only way to close a lacuna that exempts EU Member States from liability under the ECHR when implementing EU law.

Bosphorus Airlines v Ireland (2006) concerned an Irish action to impound a Yugoslav plane that had been leased to a Turkish company. Under Regulation 990/93, Ireland had a duty to carry out sanctions against the former Yugoslavia, and had no discretion in its actions. The interpretation and application of the Regulation was contested in the light of Article 1 of the First Protocol of the ECHR which sets out a right to 'peaceful enjoyment of [one's] possessions'. The Irish Supreme Court raised preliminary questions to the Court of Justice. In reference to its own case law on property rights, the Court of Justice did not consider that Irish actions had been disproportionate.

6.61 Subsequently, Turkish lessees of the plane brought an action before the ECtHR. The ECtHR, however, determined that this was a matter solely within the jurisdiction of Ireland in the light of Article 1 ECHR. The ECtHR remarked that interference with property consisted in compliance with legal obligations flowing from

Irish membership of the EU, which it accepted as constituting a 'legitimate interest' within the meaning of Article 1 of the First Protocol. The resulting conclusion was ultimately that Member States of the EU are absolved from responsibility under the ECHR when they act in compliance with EU law. The ECtHR justified this approach by finding that '[the EU] is considered to protect fundamental rights [. . .] in a manner which can be considered at least equivalent to that for which the Convention provides'.

Court of Justice jurisdiction over Member State acts

6.62 The earlier cases concerned the application of general principles, and in particular fundamental human rights, to Union rules. It has been seen, however, that the interpretation of these principles may also apply to acts of the Member States. In Case 36/75 *Rutili* (1975) the Court of Justice said that French measures, in this case an act by French authorities carried out at their own discretion but in the implementation of a provision of Union law, restricting Mr Rutili's movement in France, had to be examined as to its compliance with the directive being implemented (Directive 64/221 which sets out the limitations on the right of free movement of workers under Article 45(3) TFEU) and also in the light of provisions of the ECHR. (See also **12.96**)

6.63 In 1989 for the first time the Court of Justice examined the validity of an act of a Member State on the basis of fundamental rights considerations. In Case 5/88 *Wachauf* (1989), the Member State was implementing a milk quota scheme and was, then, in a certain sense acting as the agent for the Community. The plaintiff was a tenant farmer. During the term of his lease he built up a dairy herd to devote his farm exclusively to dairy production. In the process he obtained a milk quota. An EC Regulation provided these quotas should be transferred on the sale, lease or inheritance of the land to the person taking over the running of the farm until the quota was surrendered. If the quota was surrendered to the state, compensation was to be paid to the milk producer. According to the German Order implementing the Community compensation scheme, the tenant farmer was unable to surrender the quota and claim compensation without the consent of the landlord. In this case such consent was withheld. The Court of Justice held that such deprivation of the fruits of his labour would be incompatible with his fundamental rights. The Court said:

> [. . .] it must be observed that Community rules which, upon the expiry of the lease, had the effect of depriving the lessee, without compensation, of the fruits of his labour and of his investments in the tenanted holding would be incompatible with the requirements of the protection of fundamental rights in the Community legal order. Since those rights are also binding on the Member States when they implement Community rules, the Member States must, as far as possible, apply those rules in accordance with those requirements.

Nevertheless, in that case, the Regulation was held to be in broad enough terms to allow for compensation to be granted, thereby allowing fundamental rights to be respected. The problem was, therefore, not with the Regulation itself, which was declared valid, but with the German implementing order. The German court was invited to look again at the implementing order so that it could be applied to award compensation.

6.64 The Court of Justice stated that Community measures which are incompatible with fundamental rights recognised by the constitutions of the Member States 'may not find acceptance in the Community'. The Court also pointed out that protection of fundamental rights in the Community is not absolute but must be considered in relation to the social function of these rights. However, any restrictions on such rights should be in accordance with the principle of proportionality (see **6.24**).

6.65 It seems that national legislative provisions which lie outside the field of application of Union law cannot at present be reviewed by the Court of Justice for compliance with Union fundamental rights and the ECHR. In Cases 60 and 61/84 *Cinéthèque* (1985), the Court of Justice held that it had 'no power to examine the compatibility with the European Convention [on Human Rights] of national law which concerns, as in this case, an area which falls within the jurisdiction of the national legislator'. The Court of Justice confirmed this approach in Case 12/86 *Demirel* (1987). Case C–168/91 *Konstantinidis v Stadt Altensteig* (1993) (see **1.2**) concerned a claim by a Greek national that the way in which his name had been transcribed from Greek (with a different alphabet) into German constituted discrimination. Advocate General Jacobs concluded that there was discrimination which could not be objectively justified. He reasoned that there was a fundamental right for any citizen of the Union to move freely anywhere in the Union and to be treated 'in accordance with a common code of fundamental values' which included the right to have the correct transcription of the spelling of his name. However, the Court of Justice did not follow its Advocate General in this and held that the transcription rules were only to be regarded as incompatible with Article 49 TFEU (then Article 52 EEC) on establishment insofar as its application would cause a Greek national such a degree of inconvenience so as to interfere with his freedom of establishment. This would only occur if the transcription would expose him to a risk of confusion with other persons.

6.66 The Court of Justice took the same approach in Case C–299/95 *Kremzow v Austria* (1997). Mr Kremzow had won a dispute in the ECtHR concerning the right to a fair trial (Article 6 of the ECHR) and his subsequent detention which had been imposed by the process that breached Article 6 ECHR. He then sought compensation in an Austrian court and made arguments concerning the effect his detention had had on his free movement rights arising from Community law under Article 21 TFEU (then Article 8a EC) and the way these rights had been infringed by the unlawful detention. A reference was made to the Court of Justice asking whether the ECHR was part of Union law and whether the Court of Justice could give preliminary rulings on its interpretation. The Court refused to be drawn on the request for a ruling on ECHR matters and said that the national (criminal) legislation in the main proceedings related to a situation which did not fall within the field of application of Community law. The Court stated at paragraph 16 of the judgment:

> [...] a purely hypothetical prospect of exercising the right of free movement for persons does not establish a sufficient connection with Community law to justify the application of Community provisions.

6.67 In Case C–144/95 *Maurin* (1996) the Court of Justice reiterated this line. The offence with which Mr Maurin was charged involved national legislation, falling outside the scope of Union law and providing the Court of Justice with an opportunity to avoid ruling on the application of the ECHR. However, in Case C–260/89 *ERT* (1991), the Court of Justice did consider national rules in the light of Union general principles and fundamental rights. The national law in question was that which set out the Greek state monopoly on broadcasting. Community law could permit such a monopoly under the public policy exception in Article 62 TFEU (then Article 66 EC) as a derogation to the general Community law freedom on services (see **Chapter 11**). The monopoly was challenged in this case by a private company. The Court of Justice, referring to its decisions in *Cinéthèque* and *Demirel* (see **6.65**), said that where national legislation fell within the field of application of Community law—as this did because the monopoly was within the derogation set out by the Article—the Court, when requested to give a preliminary ruling, must provide the national court with all the elements of interpretation which are necessary in order to enable it to assess the compatibility of that legislation with fundamental rights—as laid down in particular in the ECHR—the observance of which the Court of Justice ensures. In particular, when a Member State invoked Treaty provisions to justify a rule which restricted a basic Community freedom (here based on Articles 52 and 62 TFEU, see **Chapters 11** and **12**), this restriction should be interpreted in the light of the general principles of law and fundamental rights in particular. It was for the national court and, if necessary, the Court of Justice, to appraise the application of the provisions, and the limitations imposed on the power of Member States to apply these provisions must, therefore, be judged in the light of the ECHR. This decision demonstrates the Court of Justice's intention to ensure compliance with fundamental rights by Member States when they apply derogations from fundamental Treaty rules. The Court of Justice extended its jurisdiction in concerning itself with the protection of fundamental rights and other general principles within the Member States to include those national rules that remain clearly national rules, but which have a Union law link since the Treaty takes note of them as a derogation to the Union law freedom. Where the application of such derogation varies from one Member State to another, as will almost always be the case, the Court of Justice will define its own scope of protection of the freedom and right involved.

6.68 The Court of Justice has got into greater difficulties where the national rule at issue contradicts the Union law freedom. Such instances raise questions as to the supremacy of Union law, discussed in **Chapter 7**. Where the national rule is seen as a fundamental human or constitutional right and there is a conflict with Union law freedoms, the primacy of Union law comes into question in many courts in the European Union (see **6.53**). Case C–159/90 *SPUC v Grogan* (1991) concerned the advertising by a students' union in Ireland of legal abortion clinics in the United Kingdom (see **Chapter 11** and **7.88**). Abortion is contrary to the Irish constitution as an expression fundamental human right of the protection of the unborn. The Court of Justice did not adopt Advocate General van Gerven's formulation suggesting the following approach: that the measure represented a ban on a service which would be void but for the fact that it met an important requirement of public interest. The measure should therefore be addressed in the light of:

- whether it was compatible with the fundamental rule of the Treaty (i.e. that it was actually intended to discriminate);

- whether it was reasonably necessary to meet the requirement of public interest;

- whether it was proportionate;

- whether it was contrary to a fundamental human right;

- whether it was contrary to the ECHR.

The Advocate General's approach might have avoided difficulties. The Court of Justice contented itself with reiterating:

> In *Cinéthèque* it was stated that the Court's power of review did not extend to an area which falls within the jurisdiction of the national legislator…

yet, once a national rule is involved which has effects in an area covered by Union law and which, in order to be permissible, must be able to be justified under Union law:

> …then the appraisal of that rule falls no longer under the exclusive jurisdiction of the national legislator.

The Court of Justice said it was competent to pronounce on fundamental rights issues 'where national legislation falls within the field of application of Community law…', but the Court had no such jurisdiction with regard to national legislation outside the scope of Community law. It considered that this case did not concern an economic activity, as the information service provided by the Students Union was provided free of charge. The Court of Justice, with some relief, concluded that since the service was not economic it therefore fell outside the scope of Community law.

6.69   Case C–442/00 *Caballero* (2002), considered above at **6.40**, sets out the Court's current position. The Court stated:

> First, according to settled case-law fundamental rights form an integral part of the general principles of law whose observance the Court ensures and, second, that the requirements

flowing from the protection of fundamental rights in the [Union] legal order are also binding on Member States when they implement [Union] rules. Consequently, Member States must, as far as possible, apply those rules in accordance with those requirements.

Rights against Union institutions or agents

6.70 The measures discussed earlier in this chapter can be scrutinised for human rights compliance both in the relevant national courts and in the ECtHR in Strasbourg under the ECHR. Actions taken by Union organs can only be reviewed by the Court of Justice because the European Union is not yet a party to the ECHR even though Union law is interwoven with the ECHR. *Matthews v UK* (1999) provides a potential alternative route of action in the ECtHR against the Member States individually or jointly for a human rights review of action of Union institutions but the idea that an action can rest against all the Member States for a Union act that contravenes human rights is only an idea at this time. *Bosphorus* (see **6.60**) makes clear that the ECtHR respects the competence of the Court of Justice of the European Union to review Union law from the perspective of human rights protection. The Court of Justice has examined the action of Union organs for compliance with the rights contained in the ECHR.

6.71 Actions against Union institutions and actions for annulment or review of Union legislation are considered in **Chapter 8**). The Court of Justice has accepted, inter alia, the following rights and freedoms and enforced them against Union institutions or used them as a ground for the review of secondary Union law: freedom of religion (Case 130/75 *Prais* (1976)); respect for private life (Case C–404/92P *X v Commission* (1994)); the right to protection of personal data (Joined Cases C–92/09 and C–93/09 *Volker und Markus Scheke and Eifert* (2010)); freedom of expression (Case C–100/88 *Oyowe and Traore* (1989)); the right to a fair hearing (e.g. Case C–462/98P *Mediocurso v Commission* (2000)); the right to a fair trial (e.g. Joined Cases C–174/98P and C–189/98P *Netherlands and van der Wal v Commission* (2000)); legal professional privilege (Case 155/79 *AM & S Europe Ltd* (1982) and Case T–30/89 *Hilti v Commission* (1991)); the right to property (e.g. Case 44/79 *Hauer* (1979)); and the right to form trade unions (see e.g. Case 175/73 *Union Syndicale* (1974)).

6.72 The essence of the general principles of Union law is in origin associated with the protection of fundamental human rights. That protection has evolved out of the Court of Justice's consideration of the relationship between the rights set out in the ECHR and other 'constitutional' sources, and specific Union law rules. Fundamental human rights, as a category of general principles, operate as a measure of Union law itself, as a guide to the adoption of secondary legislation and to some extent as a means of examining national rules that come within the scope of the Union legal order. The general principle has taken on a Union-level significance in being used as a standard by which applications for Union membership are considered, and the monitoring of activities of those states who have already joined the Union.

Principles of administrative justice and good governance

6.73 The dividing line between fundamental human rights and other general principles of Union law is not always clear. There are some general principles, such as natural justice, which some might classify under the heading of fundamental human rights while others would characterise them as arising from principles of administrative law. There are, in addition, a series of general standards relating to good administration and governance that guide the institutions in the formulation of policy and secondary legislation. Such standards include transparency and openness, due process and proportionality. These standards can also be seen as general principles of Union law, although it is important to recognise that the standard envisaged by each may not be the same and may not be generally accepted by all. For example, the concept of proportionality has a strong foundation in the Union legal order, being based upon Article 5 TEU and Article 296 TFEU. Transparency on the other hand is a principle on less firm a footing. It is associated with the accession of Sweden and Finland in 1995, two countries with a tradition of openness in government, and who joined older members such as the Netherlands and Denmark, in pushing for greater transparency. There are those, however, who question the commitment to openness in the European Union and it is possible that transparency is not really a general principle at all, although it appears to be gaining some traction (see **6.83–6.85**).

Legal certainty

6.74 The principle that laws should be certain is one that is upheld in many legal systems. But the extent of this principle can vary widely. It is a principle of potentially very broad application. In Union law it has been applied in specific terms relating to the upholding of legitimate expectations and to the resistance to retroactivity or the retroactive effect of particular decisions or rules. Other limits to the scope of its application are possible. In Case 234/04 *Kapferer v Schlanck & Schick GmbH* (2006) an Austrian court, concerned that another Austrian court had misapplied a point of Community law but lacking the procedural power to amend the decision of the other court, queried whether it was required by the duty of cooperation set out in Article 6 TFEU (then Article 10 EC) to disapply Austrian court procedure rules and correct the point of Union law. The Court of Justice decided that the interests of legal certainty were not served by such action: since it is a duty on all courts to apply Union law, by virtue of the doctrine of the supremacy of Union law (see **Chapter 7**), each court should properly apply Union law up and until the final point of decision. It would actually harm the principle of legal certainty to set aside court procedure rules and amend a final decision of a different court. Having said that, national court procedure rules should ensure the effectiveness of Union law and should not operate in such a way as to treat Union law differently to domestic law, and in Case C–453/00 *Kühne & Heitz* (2004) the Court of Justice required a body reviewing a final administrative decision to take

account of Community law even if that re-opened what was otherwise a settled decision. The Court here was faced with a difficult balancing act, juggling the primacy of
Community law against the protection of legal certainty when a settled administrative decision was questioned because it did not properly comply with Community
law (see **7.35**). The Court of Justice noted the importance of both legal certainty and
the supremacy of Community law principles in a decision which saw the primacy
of Community law enforced but which was so restricted to the particular issues of
Dutch administrative law that it is unclear if any general points on legal certainty are
established as a precedent. The certainty of any legal system has to be balanced against
other norms within that system, but it seems the Court of Justice will go to some
lengths to avoid a situation where legal certainty as a principle can be used to question
foundational doctrines such as the primacy of Union law.

Non-retroactivity and legitimate expectations

6.75 Legitimate expectations are protected so that in the absence of an overriding matter
of public interest, Union measures must not violate the legitimate expectations of the
parties concerned. In Case 112/77 *Töpfer* (1978) a regulation removed the entitlement
to refunds for cancelled sugar export licences and replaced the system with one that
provided for compensation. The compensation was less than the refunds that Töpfer was
hoping for and it sought to challenge the Regulation as a breach of its legitimate expectation based on the system in place at the time it entered the market to a full refund. This
claim did not succeed, but the Court of Justice upheld the principle that a breach of a
legitimate expectation could give rise to an action in Community law. However, this
expectation must be a reasonable one. If the Union adopts a decision in order to bring
an end to a speculative situation which brings windfall profits this could not be objected
to on the principle of legitimate expectation: see Case 2/75 *EVGF v Mackprang* (1975).

6.76 The principle of non-retroactivity, applied to Union secondary legislation, precludes
a measure from taking effect before its publication. In Case 63/83 *R v Kirk* (1984) this
principle was applied to criminal proceedings arising out of the application of a regulation. Case 80/86 *Officier van Justitie v Kolpinghuis Nijmegen* (1987) concerned a criminal prosecution where the authorities sought to rely on provisions detrimental to the
defendant in a directive which was not yet implemented. The Court of Justice repeated
its often used mantra that a Member State cannot rely on an unimplemented directive
if the time for implementation has not yet elapsed. Nevertheless, there is an obligation
on the national court to interpret national law as far as possible in the light of Union
law. This obligation is, however, limited by general principles of law and, in particular,
the principles of legal certainty and non-retroactivity. Thus, as the Court of Justice
ruled in Case 14/86 *Pretore di Salò v X* (1987) that a national court's interpretation of
a directive (in this instance a directive allocating liability for environmental damage)
cannot have the effect of determining or aggravating criminal liability.

6.77 Legal certainty sometimes requires judgments of the Court of Justice to be limited in
time. The Court of Justice normally states the law as it is and this applies back to the

time the law came into force. However, in Case 43/75 *Defrenne* (1976) the Court ruled that Article 157 TFEU (then Article 119) could not be relied upon to support claims prior to the date of the judgment unless legal proceedings had already been brought; the Court of Justice concluded the same in Case C–262/88 *Barber v Guardian Royal Exchange* (1990). However, these rulings are exceptional and are perhaps inspired more by realistic considerations of not causing undue financial hardship to Member States. The normal practice has been affirmed in many cases, for example Case 811/79 *Ariete* (1980); Cases 66, 127 and 128/79 *Salumi* (1980); Case 309/85 *Barra* (1988); Case 24/86 *Blaizot* (1988); and more recently Case C–242/09 *Albron Catering* (2010) to provide protection for individuals as per the scope of the relevant measure and not to limit it, in time or otherwise, on the basis of concerns regarding the effect of the change. In the latter case the Court had clarified and defined the meaning and scope of the Acquired Rights Directive (Directive 2001/23/EC on employees' rights in the event of transfer of undertakings, businesses or parts of businesses), where a business was concerned about the volume of cases that might arise. The Court stated (at paragraph 36):

> …it is only exceptionally that the Court may, in application of the general principle of legal certainty inherent in the legal order of the Union, be moved to restrict for any person concerned the opportunity of relying on a provision which it has interpreted with a view to calling in question legal relationships established in good faith. Two essential criteria must be fulfilled before such a limitation can be imposed, namely that those concerned should have acted in good faith and that there should be a risk of serious difficulties…

Here the Court was unconvinced of such an exception existing, moreover, the additional payment of severance to the employees (potentially erroneous in light of the judgment) was also held to be irrelevant.

Rights of process and natural justice

6.78 Procedural rights are often just as important as substantive rights in safeguarding a person's interests. Union law often provides procedural safeguards. See, for example, the Citizenship Directive 2004/38/EC, Articles 8 and 9, discussed in **Chapters 12** and **13**. In Case C–175/94 *R v Secretary of State for the Home Department, ex parte John Gallagher* (1995) Mr Gallagher invoked the procedural safeguards from previous, equivalent legislation against a decision to expel him from the British mainland.

6.79 In the absence of specific procedural provisions in Union legislation, the Court of Justice may invoke general procedural principles to fill any gaps. In Case C–462/98P *Mediocurso v Commission* (2000) the Court held that respect for the rights of defence must be guaranteed even in the absence of any rules governing the proceedings in question. That principle requires that the addressees of decisions which significantly affect their interests should be placed in a position in which they may effectively make known their views. The case concerned an action for annulment of two Commission decisions reducing funding by the European Social Fund for training programmes, where the company alleged that its right to a prior hearing had not been observed. On appeal from a rejection of its claim by the General Court (at that time the Court of First Instance) of the European Union, the Court of Justice ruled that the appellant had not been asked to counter the Commission's criticisms, which had therefore not enabled it to counter the accusations made against it effectively. Taking the view that therefore rights to a fair hearing had not been observed, the Court of Justice set aside the judgment of the General Court and annulled the Commission decisions. In Case 27/88 *Solvay v Commission* (1989) a claim that there was a right not to incriminate oneself was denied by the Court of Justice, in this case in the context of a competition law regulation. Nevertheless, the Court held that national provisions which protect individuals against self-incrimination should also apply to the payment of Union law fines. However, the ruling by the ECtHR in *Funke v France* (1993) ruled that this right not to be required to incriminate oneself existed under Article 6 of the ECHR and it is therefore likely that *Solvay* is too restrictive on this point.

6.80 Natural justice is understood as a series of interlocking principles that lead to good and fair decisions. The requirements of natural justice include an individual's entitlement to a hearing before a decision is reached, to have reasons given for a decision and certain other procedural safeguards. Natural justice however rarely means exactly the same thing in each and every situation. The concept is closely linked to the operation of Articles 5 and 6 of the ECHR. Union law has recognised the importance of natural justice. In Case 17/74 *Transocean Marine Paint Association* (1974) the Court of Justice accepted that a person whose interests are perceptibly affected by a decision taken by a public authority (here a Commission Decision made under competition law powers, see **Chapter 14**) must be given the opportunity to make his views known. The entitlement to reasons for a decision also exists although this is not a generalised right. A person whose rights under Union law are adversely affected by a decision must be informed of the reasons upon which the decision was based: see Case 222/86 *UNECTEF v Heylens* (1987).

As a corollary to the right to be informed of the reasons for a decision is the right, alluded to in *UNECTEF v Heylens*, to legal redress to enable such decisions and their reasons to be challenged: see Case 222/84 *Johnston v Chief Constable of the Royal Ulster Constabulary* (1986).

6.81 The right not to be proceeded against more than once for the same act (*ne bis in idem*) was accepted as a general principle to a certain extent by the Court of Justice in Cases 18 and 35/65 *Gutmann* (1966). However, if the proceedings are by Union authorities and by national authorities, or if the proceedings are instituted by a non-member state and a Union institution (Case 45/69 *the First Boehringer Case* (1970) and Case 7/72 *the Second Boehringer Case* (1972)), the rule probably does not apply.

6.82 A penalty, even of a non-criminal nature, may not be imposed unless it has a clear and unambiguous legal basis (Case 117/83 *the Third Könecke Case* (1984)). Measures which have the effect of constituting *ex post facto* sanctions may also breach the principle (Case 14/81 *The Alpha Steel Case* (1982)) that in the absence of Union rules, national procedural rules and remedies must continue to be used. However, the use of these rules for the enforcement of Union norms must be on a comparable basis to the enforcement of equivalent national norms. Furthermore, such national procedural rules must not make the enforcement of Union rules impossible or excessively difficult: see Joined Cases C–430/93 and 431/93 *van Schijndel* (1996) and Case C–312/93 *Peterbroeck* (1996), discussed at **7.104–7.108**.

Transparency

6.83 It was noted in **6.73** above that there are many who question whether transparency and openness can constitute a general principle of the Union. Article 297 TFEU, Article 1 TEU, Article 42 of the Charter of Fundamental Rights (see **6.58–6.59**) and Regulation 1049/2001 all provide for a general right of access to documents and openness in decision making. The premise of these provisions seems to be that the European Union needs to be open to avoid being seen as bureaucratic and distant from its citizens.

6.84 The Court of Justice and the General Court of the European Union have annulled refusals by the Council and Commission to release documents requested (e.g. Case T–105/95 *Worldwide Fund for Nature v Commission* (1997)) but in Case C–353/99P *Hautala v Council* (2001) the Court of Justice, while upholding a decision of the General Court (at that time the CFI) to require the release of documents which the Council contended were politically sensitive, avoided basing this decision on any general principle of a 'right to information'.

6.85 In Joined Cases C–174/98P and C–189/98P *Netherlands and van der Wal v Commission* (2000), the Court dealt with the relationship between the right to a fair trial, the principle of access to Commission documents, and the exception to that principle based on the protection of the public interest in the context of court proceedings contained in a Decision on public access to Commission documents. Mr van der Wal asked the Commission for copies of letters replying to questions from national courts within the framework of the cooperation between the latter and the Commission in applying Articles 101 and 102 TFEU (then Articles 85 and 86 EC). The Commission took the view that disclosure could be against the public interest and hamper the sound administration of justice and adopted a decision refusing Mr van der Wal access. His action before the General Court (at that time the CFI), for annulment of that decision, was dismissed. On appeal the Court of Justice took the view that the general principle of Union law, under which every person has a right to a fair trial, inspired by Article 6 ECHR, comprises the right to a tribunal that is independent of the executive in particular, but that it is not possible to deduce from that right or from the constitutional traditions common to the Member States that the court hearing a dispute is necessarily the only body empowered to grant access to the documents in the proceedings in question. Thus, it would depend on the way in which the obligation of cooperation with national courts incumbent upon the Commission works in practice, whether there is an obligation on the Commission to refuse access to documents on the grounds of protection of the public interest. This obligation would depend on the nature of such documentation. The Commission should ensure that disclosure does not constitute an infringement of national legal procedural rules. If in doubt, it must consult the national court and refuse access only if that court objects to disclosure of the documents. In this case, the documents in question had been drafted by the Commission solely for the purpose of such court proceedings, and the Court of Justice therefore set aside the judgment of the General Court and annulled the Commission decision. In striking a more delicate balance the Court of Justice recently approved the release of a document by the Commission where, in accordance with Regulation 1049/2001/EC, the names of certain participants in a meeting had been blanked out (Case C–28/08 *P Commission v Bavarian Lager* (2010) See **3.10**). The option of redaction prior to release is clearly preferable to non-disclosure, albeit a more onerous and potentially complex option for the institutions.

Legal professional privilege

6.86 To be set against the principle of openness, protection of confidential documentation is also upheld by the Court of Justice to the extent these are expressions of due process rights or natural justice. In Case 155/79 *AM & S Europe Ltd* (1982) legal professional privilege was considered. The Court of Justice applied a principle of confidentiality of written communications between lawyers and their clients. In Case T–30/89 *Hilti v Commission* (1991), internal documents reporting the contents of legal advice obtained by a company from external lawyers was held by the Court of Justice to be entitled to the benefit of the confidentiality granted to the original information.

FURTHER READING

De Búrca, G., 'The Evolution of EU Human Rights Law' in Craig, P. and De Búrca, G. (eds), *The Evolution of EU Law* (2nd edn, Oxford: OUP, 2011) 465.

Ellis, E. (ed.), *The Principle of Proportionality in the Laws of Europe* (Oxford: Hart Publishing, 1999).

Humphreys, M., 'Free movement and roadblocks: the right to protest in the single market, case C-112/00 Schmidberger Internationale Transporte and Planzüge v Austria' (2004) 6(3) *Environmental Law Review* 190–195.

Kumm, M., 'Constitutionalising subsidiarity in integrated markets: the case of tobacco regulation in the European Union' (2006) 12(4) *European Law Journal*.

Peers, S., 'From Maastricht to Laeken: the political agenda of openness and transparency in the EU' in Deckmyn V. (ed.), *Increasing Transparency in the European Union* (Maastricht: EIPA, 2002).

Report from the European Commission on Subsidiarity and Proportionality, Brussels 2009, COM(2009) 504 final.

Rosas, A. and Armati, L., *EU Constitutional Law: an Introduction* (Oxford: Hart Publishing, 2010) chs 3 and 10.

Lord Slynn of Hadley, 'They Call it "Teleological"' (1992) 7 *Denning, LJ* 225.

Tridimas, T., *The General Principles of EC Law* (2nd edn, Oxford: OUP, 2006).

Weiler, J., 'Does the EU truly need a charter of rights?' (2000) 6 *European Law Journal* 95.

Weiler, J. and Lockhart, N., '"Taking rights seriously" seriously: The European Court and its fundamental rights jurisprudence' [1995] 32 *Common Market Law Review* 51 (part I) and 579 (part II).

SELF-TEST QUESTIONS

1   When can the general principles themselves provide a source of actionable rights of individuals? And when do the principles solely assist with interpreting Union law?

2   Identify the differences in legal effect of different general principles. Is there a hierarchy of general principles or do different principles have different roles?

3   The list of general principles is not closed. What are the criteria for developing new general principles of Union law?

4   Why does European Union law concern itself with fundamental human rights?

5   Is proportionality the most important general principle?

7
Doctrines of European Union law: direct effect, supremacy, state liability for breach of Union law and other remedies

This chapter deals with the main doctrines or principles of law: It is divided into three sections: (I) direct effect; (II) supremacy or primacy; (III) state liability for breach of Union law and other remedies.

(I) Direct applicability and direct effect

SUMMARY

Section (I) covers the following:

- Direct effect of Treaty articles
- Direct effect of international agreements
- Direct effect of regulations
- Direct effect of directives
- Horizontal and vertical direct effect
- Other ways of giving maximum effect to Union law

7.1 Article 288 TFEU (ex Article 249 EC) provides that regulations are 'directly applicable in all Member States'. Thus, regulations automatically become part of national legislation and do not require, or indeed allow, any further implementation. See Case 34/73 *Variola SpA v Amministrazione Italiana delle Finanze* (1973). The early view in the Community was that all Community legislation should apply uniformly in all Member States and, once made, should not be further interfered with by the different Member States. This was perfectly possible and acceptable to all Member States, and still is, in fields such as, for example, agriculture and customs.

7.2 Article 288 then goes on to state that directives are 'binding as to the result to be achieved', but the Member States are left to choose how they implement them. The Treaties are silent on the subject of Treaty articles. If the situation had been left at that, and the Community rules had simply been regarded as falling within orthodox international law, this would have meant that the only way in which individuals could challenge European law was where it had been incorporated into national law in the form of regulations. Regulations are automatically valid in the Member States, but not necessarily always directly effective if they need further legislation. See Case 39/72 *Commission v Italy (Slaughtered Cows)* (1973) and Case 128/78 *Commission v United Kingdom (Tachographs)* (1979).

Direct effect of Treaty articles

7.3 However, the Court of Justice changed matters. In Case 26/62 *NV Algemene Transport-en Expeditie Onderneming van Gend en Loos v Nederlandse Belastingad-ministratie* (1963) the Advocate General advised the Court to follow the orthodox line of interpretation of international law. The case concerned a reclassification for purposes of customs duties of a product (ureaformaldehyde) imported into the Netherlands. This resulted in a higher level of duty being applied to the product. Article 12 of the EEC Treaty (now Article 30 TFEU as amended) provided that existing customs duties must be dismantled and no new ones must be imposed, a so-called 'stand-still' clause. There was clearly a conflict between the national customs regulation and the Treaty article. Under Article 177 of the EEC Treaty (now Article 267 TFEU), the national court made a reference to the Court of Justice, asking:

- did Article 12 have direct application within the territory of a Member State…meaning…could nationals of such a Member State on the basis of the Article lay claim to individual rights which the court must protect?

- whether the changed duty was an unlawful increase?

We are concerned here with the answer to the first question only.

7.4 Having dismissed objections as to admissibility of the case, the Court continued by saying that the Treaty's objective was more than simply to set up an international agreement between states. The preamble referred not only to governments, but to peoples. Article 177 (now Article 267 TFEU) gave to the Court the task of securing uniform interpretation of the Treaty and confirmed that the states had acknowledged that Community law had an authority which could be invoked by nationals before their own courts. The Court went on to say:

> The conclusion to be drawn from this is that the Community constitutes a new legal order of international law for the benefit of which the states have limited their sovereign rights, albeit within limited fields, and the subjects of which comprise not only member states but also their nationals. Independently of the legislation of member states, Community law therefore not only imposes obligations on individuals but is also intended to confer upon them rights which become part of their legal heritage…

7.5 Article 12 contained clear wording and a negative objection. The prohibition was clear and unconditional and did not require a legislative implementing measure on the part of the state. The very nature of the prohibition, therefore, made it ideally adapted to produce direct effects in the legal relationships between Member States and their subjects. The Court concluded, therefore, that:

> …according to the spirit, the general scheme and the wording of the Treaty, Article 12 must be interpreted as producing direct effects and creating individual rights which national courts must protect.

This judgment set out the criteria for the direct effect of Treaty articles: they had to be clear, unconditional and not subject to further implementation. What were the limits to the doctrine? Did it only concern negative objections? Subsequently, Case 57/65 *Alfons Lütticke GmbH v Hauptzollamt Saarlouis* (1966), which concerned Article 95(1) and (3) EEC (now Article 110(1) and (3) TFEU), found that Article 95(3), which imposed a positive obligation to abolish any discriminatory taxation by the beginning of the second stage, was directly effective. Individuals could, therefore, rely on this provision before their national courts from that time.

7.6 These cases all concerned actions by individuals against official authorities, i.e. involving vertical direct effect. What of actions between one individual against another, based on a Treaty article, involving horizontal direct effect? In Case 43/75 *Defrenne v Sabena* (1976) Ms Defrenne, a Belgian air hostess, claimed she received less pay than male stewards who did the same work. This was in conflict with the 'equal pay for equal work' provision contained in Article 119 (now Article 157 TFEU). The Court dismissed arguments that Treaty articles addressed to the Member States could only be vertically effective and held that this provision, too, should be considered in the light of the principle (of equal pay), the aim of the provision and its place in the scheme of the Treaty. The Court said that:

> The fact that certain provisions of the Treaty are formally addressed to member states does not prevent rights from being conferred at the same time on any individual who has an interest in the performance of the duties thus laid down…

Despite the fact that there could be circumstances where the words 'pay' and 'equal work' needed further interpretation and, for example in cases of indirect discrimination (see **Chapter 16**), further implementing criteria, the fundamental principle still conferred a right on which individuals should be able to rely.

7.7 Many Treaty articles have since been held to have direct effect. Although the Court has held that Articles 34, 35 and 36 TFEU (ex Articles 28, 29 and 30 EC) concerning free movement of goods and Article 37(2) TFEU (ex Article 31(2) EC) on state monopolies have direct effect but may only be relied upon as against the state (see **9.7**), Articles 45, 49 and 56 TFEU (ex Articles 39, 43 and 49 EC) on the free movement of persons, as well as the 'Competition Articles' 101 and 102 TFEU (ex Articles 81 and 82 EC) have been held by the Court to be both horizontally and vertically directly effective. The article regarding discrimination as to nationality, Article 18 TFEU (ex Article 12 EC), has been held by the Court as being capable of direct effect, at first mainly used in conjunction with other Treaty articles on, for example, free movement of persons: Case 293/83 *Gravier v City of Liège* (1985) and Case 186/87 *Cowan v Trésor Public* (1989), corollary of right to receive services. Subsequently, in Case C–415/93 *Union Royale Belge des Sociétés de Football Association ASBL v Jean Marc Bosman* (1996) the direct effect of what is now Article 18 TFEU in conjunction with Articles 52 and 59 EC (now Articles 49 and 56 TFEU) on establishment and services was confirmed and professional sport was drawn more firmly into the ambit of the Treaty. See also Case 36/74 *Walrave and Koch v Association Union Cycliste Internationale* (1974) (see **12.113**). In Cases C–92/92 and C–326/92 *Phil Collins v Imtrat Handelsgesellschaft mbH* (1993) the Court ruled that what is now Article 18 TFEU could be used on its own as a basis for claiming discrimination without the need to link it to any other Treaty provision.

Direct effect of international agreements binding upon the EU

7.8 The question of direct effect of international agreements has come up many times, and more frequently recently. In Cases 21–24/72 *International Fruit Company v Produktschap voor Groenten en Fruit* (1972) the question was posed whether the GATT (General Agreement on Tariffs and Trade) provisions could have direct effect. The Court concluded that 'the spirit, the general scheme and the terms' of the provisions were different from those in the EEC Treaty. It was true that the GATT agreement intended to bind the Community but, on the other hand, the flexibility of the provisions and the fact that members to the Agreement could vary or even withdraw from it made the provisions not sufficiently precise and unconditional for direct effect to apply. Free trade agreements were also held not to be capable of creating direct effect as their aim was not to create a single market (Case 270/80 *Polydor and RSO Records Inc v Harlequin Record Shops and Simons Records Ltd* (1982)). However in Case 104/81 *Haupzollamt Mainz v Kupferberg* (1982) another provision of the same agreement was found to have direct effect, as it did fulfil the conditions and fell within the purpose of the agreement. It is true that this concerned a country, Portugal, which at the time was not yet a Member State but was a potential member. However, after the new WTO agreement had come into being in 1994, including a new GATT agreement with more binding provisions, and the existence of a court, the Court of Justice ruled in Case C–280/93 *Germany v Council* (1994) that under very limited circumstances a GATT provision could prevail over an EC provision only if the relevant EC provision expressly referred to the GATT provision.

7.9 The question of direct effect was also raised in Case C–149/96 *Portugal v Council* (1999). Portugal asked for annulment of a Council decision, arguing it was in breach of WTO rules, including GATT provisions. The Court ruled that, although the provisions of the WTO were strengthened and more effective, they were still based on the principle of mutually advantageous negotiations, there was a lack of reciprocity in applying the agreements, and the dispute settlement procedure still did not 'determine the appropriate legal means of ensuring that [the agreements] are applied in good faith in the legal order of the contracting parties'. The Court therefore declined to rule that the agreements could have direct effect in this case. In the *FIAMM* case (Joined Cases C–120/06 P and C–121/06 P *FIAMM et FIAMM Technologies v Council and Commission* (2008)) the Court confirmed its reluctance to give direct effect to WTO rules. However, it also recalled that a Community (now Union) measure can be reviewed in the light of WTO rules when the measure is intended to implement a WTO obligation or when it makes explicit reference to WTO provisions. Additionally, the Court will also interpret in the light of international law whenever possible. This is so even where the Treaty is one to which only the Member States are party and where exclusive competence remains with the Member States. This duty of interpretation is undertaken 'in view of the customary principle of good faith, which forms part of general international law, and of Article 10 EC...' (see Case C–308/06 *Intertanko*(2008)) although the practical effects of such a statement can be questioned, particularly in that case itself.

As a matter of course it has also been noted that the Court of Justice often applies Free Trade Agreements and Association Agreements without restriction, consequently many consider the EU to be eminently respectful and open to international law. However, in Case C–308/06 *Intertanko* (2008), by declining to grant direct effect to the United Nations Convention on the Law of the Sea, questions were raised in this regard, particularly due to reasoning far less robust than that in the WTO case law. Here the Court of Justice held that the Convention 'did not establish rules intended to apply directly and immediately to individuals', and thus, concluded they could not be relied upon to invalidate EU legislation. The Court held that 'doubt is not cast' on this analysis by provisions relating directly to ships and to natural and legal persons exploring the sea-bed and ocean floor. This case arguably emphasises much greater reluctance of the Court to find direct effect in respect of international agreements, beyond the previous exception of WTO law. This trend of reluctance by the Court to find direct effect probably remains, in spite of a somewhat bolder approach in Case C–366/10 *Air Transport Association v Secretary of State for Energy and Climate Change* (2011), concerning the expansion of the EU Emissions Trading Scheme to aviation (see further **15.43**). Here some provisions of the Open Skies agreement were held to be directly effective, though few would be surprised that ultimately, like in *Intertanko*, no breach of international law was found. It is worth noting that the challenged EU legislation in both *Intertanko* and *Air Transport Association* concerned environmental protection on a large scale. The issue of direct effect must also be understood in the context of EU developments in the wider context of public international law, comprising the issues of Treaties to which only the Member States are party, and customary international law. In Joined Cases C–402/05 P and C–415/05 P *Yassin Abdullah Kadi and Al Barakaat International Foundation v Council and Commission* (2008) the Court of Justice robustly held, in the context of fundamental rights, that the EU is 'an autonomous legal system which is not to be prejudiced by an international agreement'. The judgment has led to much academic discussion over the EU's current and future relationship with international law (see further **5.13**).

Direct effect of regulations

7.10 Under Article 288 TFEU regulations are directly applicable, i.e. they do not need incorporation by national legislation. They will, therefore, generally have direct effect. Sometimes, however, they need further national measures to be taken and will not immediately have direct effect. See Case 128/78 *Commission v United Kingdom (re tachographs)* (1979) and **5.17**.

Direct effect of directives

7.11 According to Article 288 TFEU, directives must be implemented by Member States, the *result* to be binding on the Member States, but leaving a choice as to *form* and *method* to the Member States. By their very nature, therefore, they are not directly applicable, as regulations are. Directives also could not have direct effect under the same conditions as Treaty articles, as they could not fulfil the condition of 'no further enactment necessary by the Member State'. However, in Case 9/70 *Grad v Finanzamt Traunstein* (1970) the Court stated that decisions could have direct effect and implied that this also applied to directives. Confirmation of this came in Case 41/74 *van Duyn v Home Office* (1974). Ms van Duyn wanted to enter the United Kingdom to take up a job with the Church of Scientology, an organisation which was considered to be socially harmful by the UK Government but which was not banned. She was refused entry and she brought an action against the Home Office. The High Court referred three questions to the Court of Justice:

- Was Article 48 directly effective? The Court said it was.
- Did Directive 64/221 have direct effect?
- How should the term 'personal conduct' be interpreted? (See **12.92**)

7.12 Article 48(3) (now Article 45(3) TFEU) permits limitations to the free movement principle of Article 48(1). The objective of Directive 64/221, adopted on the basis of Article 48 (now Article 45 TFEU), (now incorporated into Directive 2004/38, Chapter VI) is to coordinate the measures to limit movement by foreign nationals which Member States may take on grounds of public policy, public security or public health. The directive provides in Article 3(1) (now Article 27(2) Directive 2004/38) that such measures should be based exclusively on the personal conduct of the individual concerned, thus removing 'guilt by association'.

The Court said that the obligation thus imposed on Member States was 'not subject to any exception or condition' and did not require the intervention of any act by Community institutions or by Member States. As the clause derogated from the fundamental free movement principle of the Treaty, legal certainty for the persons concerned required that they should be able to rely on this obligation. The Directive did, therefore, have direct effect. Although the scope of 'personal conduct' might give rise to questions of interpretation, this is a question which the courts (national or the Court of Justice under Article 177 (now Article 267 TFEU)) could resolve and direct effect was possible as long as the wording was 'sufficiently precise'. These words were repeated in subsequent cases, most clearly for example in Case 8/81 *Becker v Finanzamt Münster-Innenstadt* (1982), where the Court said (at paragraph 25):

> Thus whenever the provisions of a Directive appear, as far as their subject matter is concerned to be unconditional and sufficiently precise, those provisions may, in the absence of implementing measures prescribed within the prescribed period, be relied upon against any national provision which is incompatible with the Directive or in so far as the provisions define rights which individuals are able to assert against the State.

See also van Gerven AG in Case C–271/91 *Marshall (No 2)* (1993) and Jacobs AG in Case C–316/93 *Vaneetveld* (1994).

7.13 As the Court indicated in *Becker*, directives have to be implemented. The date of implementation is usually contained in the directive itself but a new provision was inserted in the Maastricht TEU that otherwise implementation must take place within 20 days from publication of the directive in the Official Journal (Article 297 TFEU (ex Article 254 EC)). In Case 148/78 *Pubblico Ministero v Ratti* (1979) the Court reaffirmed that directives could have direct effect, and then went on to say (at paragraph 1642) that a Member State which had not implemented a directive within the prescribed period 'may not rely, as against individuals, on its own failure to perform the obligations which the Directive entails'. At the same time, it was clear that an individual would have to wait until the date for implementation had passed, and thus in *Ratti*, where two directives were involved, the defence was only available in respect of the one for which the implementation date had passed. In *Becker* Ms Becker could rely on the provisions of an unimplemented directive after the implementation date had passed in order to bring proceedings against the state. Thus, the argument may be used as an offensive, as well as a defensive, weapon.

7.14 In Case C–208/90 *Emmott* (1991) the Court stated that where an individual could not have initiated proceedings earlier, thus exceeding a national procedural time limit, due to the Member State's defective implementation of a directive, the national time limit should not start to run before the directive has been properly transposed. However, it seems that, although this applies to mandatory time limits for bringing proceedings, it does not apply to a rule restricting retroactivity of claims, which served to ensure sound administration.

7.15 In Case C–338/91 *Steenhorst-Neerings v Bestuur van de Bedrijfsvereniging voor Detailhandel, Ambachten en Huisvrouwen* (1993) such a rule restricting the retroactive effect of claims for benefits for incapacity for work was judged by the Court not to be affected by the non-implementation of Council Directive 79/7/EEC on the progressive implementation of the principle of equal treatment for men and women in matters of social security. This is clearly, therefore, not an absolute rule and, as always, the Court will have to strike a balance between Union interests, the interests of individuals, which often coincide with those, and the interests of Member States concerning, for example, finance and proper administration. When the Court decided that a difference in the age upon which men and women became entitled to free prescriptions was in violation of Community equal treatment principles (see Case C–137/94 *R v Secretary of State for Health ex parte Richardson* [1995]) the UK Government's action in restricting retroactive claims to six months may be seen to be justifiable on the basis of its reasoning in, e.g., *Steenhorst-Neerings.* (see further **Chapter 16**, **16.55**, **16.56**).

7.16   In Case C–188/95 *Fantask A/S v Industrieministeriet (Erhvervsministeriet)* (1997) the broad wording of *Emmott* was criticised by Jacobs AG, and the Court stated that the solution adopted in *Emmott* was justified by the special circumstances of the case, where the time limit meant that the applicant was deprived of any opportunity to rely on her right to equal treatment under a directive. It ruled that Community law did not prevent a Member State which has not properly transposed a directive from relying on a national limitation period:

> ...provided that such a period is not less favourable for actions based on Community law than for actions based on national law and does not render virtually impossible or excessively difficult the exercise of rights conferred by Community law.

7.17   In the important judgment in Case C–144/04 *Werner Mangold v Rüdiger Helm* (2005) (see also **6.1**, **16.86**, **16.87** and **7.20**) concerning the implementation of Directive 2000/78, the Court seems to say that it will not always refuse to consider cases where the date of implementation for a directive had not yet expired. There were special circumstances in that the actual date of implementation was 1 December 2003 but the Member States could choose to have recourse to an additional period of three years, subject to annual progress reports to the Commission. The Court said that this provision implied that in such a case concrete measures should be taken progressively and that 'the obligation would be rendered redundant if the member state were to be permitted, during the period allowed for implementation of the directive, to take measures incompatible with the objectives pursued by that act' (for further discussion, see **16.20**, **16.86** and **16.87**).

Horizontal and vertical direct effect

7.18   Having established that Treaty articles can have horizontal as well as vertical direct effect, i.e. they can be relied upon not only against the state, but also against an individual (see Case 43/75 *Defrenne v Sabena* (1976)) the question then arose whether the same could apply to directives. Directives, however, are addressed to the Member State, and must be implemented by them. In Case 152/84 *Marshall v Southampton Area Health*

Authority (1986), the Court pointed out that directives are only binding on the Member State to whom they are addressed and that, therefore, 'a directive may not of itself, impose obligations on an individual' and 'may not be relied upon as such against such a person'. Miss Marshall had brought a case against the Southampton Area Health Authority which had a policy of compelling women to retire earlier than men (women at 60, men at 65). This policy linked retirement to the payment of the state pension. The latter was an exception under Directive 79/7 which excludes 'the determination of old age for the purposes of granting old-age and retirement pensions' from the application of the equal treatment principle under Article 119 EEC (now Article 157 TFEU). The Court had to find, first, whether the Directive had direct effect and, if so, whether this could be horizontal as well as vertical. However, the Court found that the Area Health Authority could be regarded as 'the state' and that this applied to the state as employer, not just as a public authority. The Court confirmed that the authority was, in the words of the Court of Appeal when submitting questions for interpretation to the Court, an 'emanation of the state'. This included all organs of the administration, including authorities such as municipalities.

7.19 It is not a satisfactory situation that two individuals with exactly the same grievances should be treated differently according to whether their employer is a public authority or a private employer. One line of decisions pursued by the Court tried, therefore, to interpret the concept of public authority as widely as possible in order to minimise this difficulty, while nevertheless maintaining the principle of vertical direct effect. The high-water mark was probably in Case C–188/89 *Foster v British Gas plc* (1990). Again, this case concerned different retirement ages for men and women and the 1976 Equal Treatment Directive (Directive 76/207, now incorporated in the 'Recast' Directive 2006/54/EC). Could its provisions apply in the case of British Gas, which had been privatised by the time the case was brought, but was still a nationalised industry at the time the alleged discrimination occurred? The Court cited its previous case law where it had held that tax authorities (Case 8/81 *Becker v Finanzamt Münster Innenstadt* (1982)); local or regional authorities (Case 103/88 *Fratelli Costanzo SpA v Commune di Milano* (1989)); a constitutionally independent police authority (Case 222/84 *Johnston v Chief Constable of the RUC* (1986)) and a health authority were to be regarded as representing the state. It concluded that a body, whatever its legal form, which provided 'a public service' under the control of the state and had 'for that purpose special powers...' should be included among bodies against which (vertical) direct effect could be invoked. However, in *Doughty v Rolls-Royce plc* (1992) the Court of Appeal held that, although the company was wholly owned by the state and was, therefore, under state control, this was not sufficient, and that *Foster* indicated other criteria should also be present, in particular, the special provision of a public service and the exercise of special powers, which was not the case here. The interpretation of what is 'the state' is a matter for the national courts, but it is clear that such an interpretation should, as a matter of Union law, be as wide as possible. Are universities to be regarded as public authorities? In Continental Europe they are mainly under state control, and the answer is probably yes; with British universities there is more of a problem.

7.20 As the European Union developed, the distinction between regulations and directives became more blurred. Member States tended sometimes to incorporate directives into their legislation using the same wording, thus making them resemble regulations. It has been suggested that, after the Maastricht TEU made publication of directives in the Official Journal obligatory in Article 297 TFEU (ex Article 254 EC), the arguments for equating directives with regulations have become even stronger. In fact, directives applying to all Member States were always published in the Official Journal even before it was made obligatory. Lenz AG put forward a strong argument in favour of giving horizontal effect to directives in Case C–91/92 *Faccini Dori v Recreb Srl* (1994), repeating the above arguments. He added that the introduction of a European citizenship in Article 8(a) of the Maastricht TEU (now Article 21 TFEU) 'raises the expectation that citizens of the Union will enjoy equality, at least before Community law'. In spite of the many objections against such a route, such as those of legal certainty and legitimate expectations, he nevertheless concluded that directives adopted after the TEU should be capable of having effect *erga omnes* for the future. The Court, however, repeated the well-rehearsed arguments against horizontal direct effect and declined to follow the Advocate General. It emphasised that extending the direct effect doctrine to individuals would 'be to recognise a power in the Community to enact obligations with immediate effect', a power which at present it holds only with regard to regulations. Thus, the distinction between regulations and directives would be blurred further. This appears to be the end of that line for the time being.

However, in recent years the Court has increasingly resorted to other measures to give effect to Union law in what would, at first sight, be purely horizontal cases. For example, in Case C–144/04 *Werner Mangold v Rüdiger Helm* (2005) (see also above at **6.1**, **7.17**, **16.86** and **16.87**) the Court did not mention the question in a judgment in a case between two individuals and confined itself to dealing with the incompatibility of the national legislation with Community law where a general principle of Community law (non-discrimination) was concerned. It asserted that it was the responsibility of the national court to guarantee the full effectiveness of the general principle by setting aside the national legislation, even before the date of expiry of the implementation period. The Court seems to go further here than the Advocate General, who referred to *Marleasing* in order to come to the same conclusion.

Other means of giving maximum effect to Union law

Indirect effect

7.21 The Court of Justice is first and foremost concerned to give as much as possible useful effect (usually the term '*effet utile*' is used untranslated) to Union law. It tried, therefore, to circumvent the difficulties as to direct effect described above by pursuing another line of reasoning. This first became apparent in Case 14/83 *von Colson and Kamann v Land Nordrhein-Westfalen* (1984). Two female applicants for posts as social workers in a German prison complained about sex discrimination. The 1976 Equal Treatment Directive had been implemented in such a way that all they would receive by way of compensation was some minimal travelling expenses. They would not be able to claim appointment to the post or, in the alternative, six months' salary in lieu if the Directive could not be held to be directly effective. The Court recognised that the Directive did not include any unconditional and sufficiently precise obligation as regards sanctions for discrimination, but went on to say that Member States had a duty under Article 5 of the EEC Treaty (now Article 4(3) TEU) to '…interpret their national law in the light of the wording and the purpose of the Directive in order to achieve the result referred to in Article 189(3)' (now Article 288(3) TFEU). The national court had an obligation to interpret its own legislation in conformity with the requirements of Community law. Subsequent cases refined this principle. In Case 80/86 *Officier van Justitie v Kolpinghuis Nijmegen BV* (1987) the obligation was expressly made subject to general principles of law such as legal certainty and non-retroactivity and the effect of interpreting national legislation 'in the light of the wording and purpose of the Directive'. Criminal liability should, therefore, not be determined or aggravated as a result of the Directive. In *von Colson*, the Court said that the obligation extended only insofar as the national court is given discretion to do so under national law.

7.22 In Case C–106/89 *Marleasing SA v La Comercial Internacional de Alimentación SA* (1990), which, it must be remembered, followed the Court's ruling in *Marshall* which outlawed horizontal direct effect, the Court clarified the position. It referred to *von Colson* and repeated the national court's obligation to interpret national legislation whether adopted before or after the directive, as far as possible in the light of the wording and the purpose of the directive. This case was brought by one company against another, i.e. two non-state entities. Marleasing alleged that La Comercial's articles of association should be declared void for 'lack of cause', a ground for nullity under the Spanish Commercial Code, but not in Council Directive 68/151 (the First Company Directive) which should have been implemented by Spain. However, Spain viewed its existing Commercial Code as sufficiently implementing the Directive. The Court said that this interpretative obligation arose from the duty of Member States under Article 5 (now Article 4(3) TEU) to take all appropriate measures, whether general or particular, to fulfil their obligations under the Treaty and to 'abstain from any measure which could jeopardise the attainment…' of Treaty objectives. In two later cases: Case C–456/98 *Centrosteel v Adipol* (2000) and Joined Cases C–240–244/98 *Oceano Grupo Editorial v Rocio Murciano Quintero* (2000) the Court reiterated that a national court is obliged when applying provisions of national law predating or postdating the Community legislation (directives in both cases) to interpret those provisions, so far as possible, in the light of the wording and purpose of the Community law instrument. As in *Marleasing*, the court in *Oceano Grupo* should do so of its own motion. In Case C–555/07 *Kücükdeveci v Swedex GmbH & Co KG* (2010) (**6.10**) which concerned Council Directive 2000/78/EC establishing a general framework for equal treatment in employment and occupation, the Court found that a rule on dismissal contained a difference of treatment based on age. The rule gives less favourable treatment to employees who have entered the employer's service before the age of 25. It thus introduces a difference of treatment between persons with the same length of service, depending on the age at which they joined the undertaking. National courts, hearing proceedings between individuals, must therefore ensure that the principle of non-discrimination on grounds of age as a *general principle of European Union law* and as given expression in Directive 2000/78 is complied with, disapplying if need be any contrary provision of national legislation (in this case legislation contained in the German Civil Code), independently of whether it makes use of its entitlement to ask the Court for a preliminary ruling on the interpretation of that principle. In this case it was not possible to interpret the German Civil Code provision in conformity with the directive.

7.23 We shall see later (in **Section II**) how courts in Member States, and in particular the UK, have interpreted this obligation. It is clearly not absolute, however. In Case C–334/92 *Wagner Miret* (1993) the Court accepted that Spanish legislation could not be interpreted to give effect to the directive concerned. This case concerned the same point as the earlier case of *Francovich* (see **Section III**). The Court was looking for ways in which to solve the difficulties raised by the direct effect doctrine. It therefore accepted the suggested solution in the question raised by the Spanish court of its own motion in *Marleasing*, which concerned non-directly effective legislation. This route, as we have already seen, is not an entirely satisfactory one either. The limitations of the interpretive method were further emphasised by the Court in Case C–168/95 *Criminal Proceedings against Luciano Arcaro* (1996). The Court said (at 42), as it had done in *Kolpinghuis* (see above at **7.21**), that the interpretive obligation reached a limit when such interpretation would mean the imposition of an obligation on an individual which would determine or aggravate the individual's criminal liability as a result. In Case C–387/02 *Criminal Proceedings against Berlusconi and Others* (2005), where the Italian Prime Minister was involved in proceedings concerning allegations of fraud under Italian companies legislation pursuant to Directive 68/151/EEC, the Court stated that the Directive could not be relied upon against accused persons by the authorities of a Member State within the context of criminal proceedings, as the criminal liability of the accused could not be determined or aggravated by the Directive itself.

7.24 Case C–105/03 *Pupino* (2005) was a case brought under the former Third Pillar of the Union (see further **Chapter 2**). Under the Third Pillar the Court of Justice only had jurisdiction when a Member State chose to accept it, which Italy had done, which meant that the Court had jurisdiction in Italy. (Now the Court has full jurisdiction over Title V TFEU the Area of Freedom, Security and Justice.) In *Pupino* the Court stated that a Council Framework Decision (No 2001/220/JHA) should be interpreted in the same way as a case under the EC Treaty following a preliminary reference under Article 234 (now Article 267 TFEU), this in spite of the fact that Article 34(2) TEU in Title VI (Police and Judicial Cooperation in Criminal Matters) provided that such decisions should not entail direct effect. The Court stated (at paragraph 42):

It would be difficult for the Union to carry out its task effectively if the principle of loyal cooperation...were not also binding in the area of police and judicial cooperation in criminal matters, which is moreover entirely based on cooperation between the Member States and the institutions.

The Court concluded, therefore, that:

The national court is required to take into consideration all the rules of national law and to interpret them, so far as possible, in the light of the wording and purpose of the Framework Decision.

Incidental horizontal direct effect; triangular situations

7.25 In a number of more recent cases, the Court seems to hint at the possibility of what Craig and de Burca have termed 'incidental horizontal direct effect' where private parties were concerned on both sides, but where no particular obligation was put on the defendants. This was the case in Case C–194/94 *CIA Security International v Signalson and Securitel* (1996) where effectively a non-implementation by the state of a directive in not notifying certain technical regulations to the European Commission was pleaded by the plaintiff in horizontal proceedings to relieve him of an obligation without it imposing an obligation on the defendants under the directive (see also **Chapter 5**). In Case C–129/94 *Criminal Proceedings against Rafael Ruiz Bernáldez* (1996) compulsory motor insurance in Spain relieved the insurance company from the obligation to compensate a third party victim of a drunk driver. The Court of Justice nevertheless held that the unimplemented directive which imposed such an obligation should apply. This imposed indirectly an obligation on a private insurance company. The situation still seems to be far from clear, and the Court seems still to be taking a case-by-case approach, although not going so far as to admit horizontal direct effect of directives.

In Case 397/01–403/01 *Bernhard Pfeiffer v Deutsches Rotes Kreuz, Kreisverband Waldshut eV* (2004) the Court pointed out that the whole body of rules of national law had to be taken into account in order to achieve full effect of the directive concerned (the Working Time Directive 93/104). The Directive had direct effect, but this was a case between individuals. The Court in its answer to the third question (at paragraph 120) stated:

…when hearing a case between individuals, the national court is required, when applying the provisions of domestic law adopted for the purpose of transposing obligations laid down by a directive, to consider the whole body of rules of national law and to interpret them, so far as possible, in the light of the wording and purpose of the directive in order to achieve an outcome consistent with the objective pursued by the directive. In the main proceedings, the national court must thus do whatever lies within its jurisdiction to ensure that the maximum period of weekly working time, which is set at 48 hours by Article 6(2) of Directive 93/104, is not exceeded.

7.26 The Court turned in a different direction first indicated in Joined Cases C–6 and 9/90 *Francovich and Bonifaci v Italy* (1991). Should there be remedies available for breaches of all Community law? We will discuss this further in **Section III**.

(II) Supremacy of Union law

SUMMARY

This section discusses:

- The doctrine of supremacy (primacy) as developed by the Court of Justice
- Application of Union law in the United Kingdom and in other Member States
- Conflicts between Union law and national rules
- The relationship between national (constitutional) courts and the Court of Justice

The doctrine of supremacy

7.27 After the Court of Justice had set out the doctrine of direct effect in Case 26/62 *van Gend en Loos* (1963), giving rights to individuals to invoke Community (now Union) law in their national courts, and thus providing for Member States the possibility of making Community law as effective as possible, it next moved to the question of what happens in a situation of conflict between national law and Union law. The development of the doctrine of supremacy of Union law over national law is the reverse side of the coin and a logical sequel to the doctrine of direct effect. As with direct effect, the Treaties do not expressly provide for the supremacy of Union law, nor do they, therefore, specify how that supremacy should be applied in the Member States.

7.28 The supremacy of Union law over national law is now stated in a Declaration attached to the Treaty of Lisbon. This reiterates the doctrine as stated by the Court as follows:

> The Conference recalls that, in accordance with well settled case law of the Court of Justice of the European Union, the Treaties and the law adopted by the Union on the basis of the Treaties have primacy over the law of Member States, under the conditions laid down by the said case law.

7.29 There is also attached the Opinion of the Council Legal Service of 22 June 2007 which states:

> It results from the case-law of the Court of Justice that primacy of EC law is a cornerstone principle of Community law. According to the Court, this principle is inherent to the

*specific nature of the European Community. At the time of the first judgment of this
established case law (Costa/ENEL, 15 July 1964, Case 6/64 (footnote omitted)) there
was no mention of primacy in the treaty. It is still the case today. The fact that the
principle of primacy will not be included in the future treaty shall not in any way
change the existence of the principle and the existing case-law of the Court of Justice.*

Thus, it is clear that the supremacy of Union law is firmly established by the decisions
of the Court of Justice and the deliberations of national courts.

7.30 A first indication of what was to happen was given in *van Gend en Loos*, when the
Court spoke of the new legal order constituted by the Community for whose benefit the Member States had limited their sovereign rights. In Case 6/64 *Costa v ENEL*
(1964) the Court then spoke out far more clearly and stated:

> By creating a Community of unlimited duration, having its own institutions, its own per-
> sonality, its own legal capacity and capacity of representation on the international plane
> and, more particularly, real powers stemming from a limitation of sovereignty or transfer of
> powers from the State to the Community, the member states have limited their sovereign
> rights, albeit within limited fields, and have thus created a body of law which binds both their
> nationals and themselves.
>
> The integration into the laws of each member state of provisions which derive from the
> Community, and more generally the terms and the spirit of the Treaty, make it impossible
> for the States, as a corollary, to accord precedence to a unilateral and subsequent measure
> over a legal system accepted by them.

7.31 In order to attain the objectives of the Treaty set out in Article 5 (now Article 4(3)
TFEU) it was necessary for Community law not to vary from one state to another 'in
deference to subsequent domestic laws'.

7.32 In Case 106/77 *Simmenthal* (1978) the precedence of Community law was referred to by
the Court as a 'principle'; a national court was under a duty to give full effect to provisions of Community law:

> If necessary refusing of its own motion to apply any conflicting provision of national legisla-
> tion, even if adopted subsequently.

The national court should not wait for a national provision to be set aside by another
body before giving effect to Community law. The Court held that the legislator could
not introduce any legislation contrary to Community law.

7.33 In Case 11/70 *Internationale Handelsgesellschaft* (1970) the Court stated (at paragraph 3):

> Recourse to the legal rules or concepts of national law in order to judge the validity of
> measures adopted by the institutions of the Community would have an adverse effect on

the uniformity and efficacy of Community law. The validity of such measures can only be judged in the light of Community law. In fact, the law stemming from the Treaty, an independent source of law, cannot because of its very nature be overridden by rules of national law, however framed, without being deprived of its character as Community law.

7.34 This was true even in the face of arguments that a Community measure might run counter to a fundamental right or a constitutional principle. As we shall see below (**7.80**), this case caused difficulties in the Federal Republic of Germany. In Case C–213/89 *Factortame (No 2)* (1991) (see **7.57-7.59**) the Court replied to a question posed by the House of Lords:

> Community law must be interpreted as meaning that a national court which, in a case before it concerning Community law, considers that the sole obstacle which precludes it from granting interim relief is a rule of national law, must set aside that rule.

7.35 The supremacy principle can require the reopening of settled matters if the decision or judgment was based upon the incorrect assumption as to what the requirement of Union law might be. In Case C–453/00 *Kühne & Heitz* (2004) (see also **4.39**) Dutch authorities had made an administrative decision on the classification of poultry meat for customs tariff purposes that required Kühne & Heitz to pay more than it should if the relevant Community law provision had been correctly applied. When the Community law position was subsequently clarified, Kühne & Heitz sought a refund. From the Dutch authorities' perspective this matter had been long settled and general practice was not to reopen administrative decisions. The Court noted however that the Dutch administrative bodies are able to reopen final decisions and that the courts, when the matter came before them, had misinterpreted the Community law provision without referring the matter to the Court for a preliminary ruling. Also taking into account the promptness with which Kühne & Heitz had acted to lodge its claim, the Court indicated the supremacy principle could require this settled matter be reopened by the Dutch authorities so Kühne & Heitz could get its money back. The relationship between this expression of the requirements of the primacy of Union law over national law and legal certainty, which is itself a general principle of Union law (see **Chapter 6**), means the principle established in this case is limited: the Court's ruling in *Kühne & Heitz* closely restricted the facts of the scenario faced by Kühne & Heitz and relevant Dutch administrative law. But this application of the supremacy principle is informative as to the Court's insistence upon its scope.

7.36 The acceptance of supremacy of Community (now Union) law has resulted in difficulties in different Member States. The difficulties have concerned, in particular:

- the acceptance of primacy tested against a Member State's constitutional or 'higher' law principles; or
- the acceptance of secondary Community legislation (such as directives) as superior to a Member State's own law.

7.37 In Case C–213/89 *Factortame (No 2)* (1991) the UK courts accepted that interim relief to suspend an Act of Parliament was necessary where the Act of Parliament worked to limit Community law rights. As Lord Bridge put it, this significant step merely demonstrated the limitation on sovereignty the United Kingdom had accepted when joining the Community. German courts came to accept that Union law should not be tested against the basic rights enshrined in its own Constitution, despite the special historical, political and legal context of the protected status of human rights in German law. Italian courts recognised the need to give up the rights of its Constitutional Court to test the compatibility of Community law against the Italian Constitution. In France there were particular difficulties with accepting the supremacy of Community secondary legislation, in particular directives, over French laws. Denmark and Poland also had difficulties testing Union law against their Constitution, with the initial conclusion in Poland seeming to be that Union law is not supreme in terms of the Polish Constitution should there be clashes. We shall consider the extent to which these problems have now been resolved. Since enlargement to a membership of 27 states, with further expansion to follow, there are particular difficulties envisaged with solutions already formulated in respect of the supremacy doctrine. Many of the new Member States also have traditions and constitutional standards that to some extent conflict with a requirement of Union law, and their courts, like the courts of the older Member States, have to find a balance between the supremacy principle and the balancing of national laws with the Union legal order. To this effect, many countries have pre-empted the problems by incorporating the supremacy of Union law directly into their constitutions. There are still likely to be difficulties, however, and the doctrine of supremacy will probably adapt as part of the dialogue with these Member States' courts.

7.38 The supremacy principle as formulated by the Court of Justice can help resolve legal problems where there is a conflict between a national rule and a point of Union law by indicating to the national court that of the two rules to be applied, the court should give effect to the Union law. The response of national courts to problems arising from clashes between Union law and the particular national constitutional or culturally important issue is rarely unqualified, however. National courts may accept the principle of the supremacy of Union law but they do not always do so in exactly the way that the Court may have envisaged in its first judgments in *Costa* or *Simmenthal*.

7.39 Member States have shown diverse attitudes to the place of Union law in their legal orders. Even within a single Member State, the doctrines of direct effect and supremacy of Union law have sometimes evoked different responses from different courts. Moreover, national attitudes have changed significantly over time. This fact should be borne in mind when evaluating the acceptance of the primacy of Union law in the newer Member States.

7.40 The Treaties that constitute the basis of the Union legal order are in their origins basically international treaties and were originally seen as instruments of international law. Thus, national attitudes towards Union law depend to a considerable extent on more general understandings about the position of international law in the domestic legal systems. Member States follow one of two doctrines which govern the relationship between international and national law: monism and dualism.

7.41 Under the monist doctrine, domestic and international law constitute a single integrated legal system. As a result, in monist states international law is automatically incorporated into national law without the need for further transposition. In addition, while monism does not logically imply the precedence of international over domestic law in the event of conflict, it is commonly associated with that principle. France and Italy are examples of monist states; the Netherlands also has a monist system, albeit a qualified one. Thus, it is generally considered to be easier for monist states to accept the supremacy of Union law, although this is not necessarily always the case.

7.42 Dualism presupposes the existence of two separate systems of law: international law and national law. These two systems of law have different purposes and occupy different spheres. Under dualism, international law does not become part of national law until, and to the extent that, appropriate national measures so provide. What legislative or administrative form these measures take does not matter, provided the one selected provides for the proper transposition of the international legal measure.

A dualist Member State may still acknowledge a privileged status to Union law within its domestic legal order. Thus, both primary and secondary Union law may be entrenched in national law through an express constitutional amendment or other enactment to that effect. Depending on the instrument and language used, direct effect and supremacy of Union law may be safeguarded. Ireland, Poland and the United Kingdom are examples of dualist states.

7.43 The fact that the Court chose to assert the doctrine of supremacy in *Costa v ENEL*, a case from Italy, which is a monist country, was a matter of Community law, not of national law.

Union law in the United Kingdom

7.44 In the United Kingdom, the incorporation of Union law has presented two specific problems:

   (i) dualism is followed strictly; and

   (ii) there is the doctrine of Parliamentary supremacy. In other words, Acts of Parliament and not a constitution are the highest form of law and all Acts of Parliament have an equal weight and status, i.e. there are, in theory no Acts of Parliament that are higher than others in any legal sense, although some Acts are clearly politically more important than others.

7.45 The doctrine of Parliamentary sovereignty has come under considerable reconsideration in the light of the Human Rights Act 1998, which permits UK courts to make declarations of incompatibility where an Act of Parliament is found to violate the European Convention of Human Rights. At the same time, the Scotland Act 1998 and devolution in Northern Ireland have created a complex tapestry of legal sources in the United Kingdom with, for example, a Scottish Parliament in theory subordinate to the Westminster Parliament but still capable of introducing its own Acts. More than the actual provisions of the Human Rights Act 1998, one consequence of its operation has been to introduce a widespread understanding that there can be a hierarchy of law and that some Acts are challengeable. The UK courts have at the same time nuanced their expression of the sovereignty of Parliament with *Jackson* (2005), a case on the ban on foxhunting with hounds, indicating a willingness on the part of the courts to question Acts of Parliament from the perspective of other principles of UK law, such as the rule of law.

7.46 It should be noted that UK courts cannot disapply Acts of Parliament using the Human Rights Act 1998, in contrast to challenges to UK laws on the ground of violation of Union law.

7.47 International treaties in the United Kingdom are ratified by the government under the power known as the prerogative. Generally, the government does not need to seek prior Parliamentary approval before ratifying a treaty. Treaties entered into by the UK Government do not affect the law applied by the domestic courts and are only binding in international law. A treaty will only have effect in the domestic legal system if an Act of Parliament incorporates it. Thus, in order to incorporate the Community Treaties into domestic law, an Act of Parliament was necessary—the European Communities Act 1972. This Act enabled the United Kingdom to comply with all of the obligations of membership. The ECA 1972 has been amended to incorporate the Single European Act, and the Maastricht, Amsterdam, Nice and Lisbon Treaties, insofar as they modify the European Treaties.

7.48 The ECA 1972 section 2 provides for the application of Community (now Union) law arising from the Treaties, secondary legislation, and the case law of the Court of Justice, in the British courts. Without using the terms, section 2(1) provides for the direct applicability and the direct effect of Union law as determined by Union law. The dualist nature of the United Kingdom's relationship with international law instruments is acknowledged by section 1 of the Act, with specific provision made in this section and in section 2 to incorporate all EU law into domestic UK law using delegated legislation (Orders in Council and Statutory Instruments), where necessary, and setting out the procedure where such instruments are put before Parliament without requiring each instrument to have its own Act of Parliament. There are some matters which cannot be dealt with by means of delegated legislation set out in Schedule 2 to the ECA.

7.49 The ECA 1972 sections 1 and 2 are both backward- and forward-looking in scope, requiring the adoption of existing Union law and providing for the adoption of future Union law. The wording of section 2(1) has had the effect of making all Treaty rights, powers, liabilities, obligations and restrictions, without further enactment, legally enforceable in the United Kingdom.

7.50 The ECA 1972 section 2(1) and (4) have had extensive scrutiny in court and in academic literature. The relationship between these provisions and the constitutional premise of the sovereignty of Parliament has been much considered. The House of Lords concluded in the *Factortame* case (*Factortame (No 2)*) that all UK law, whether an Act of Parliament or any other form must always be read subject to directly enforceable EU rights (whether directly effective or not):

> The words 'is to be construed and take effect subject to directly enforceable community rights' are to be understood as having the same effect as if a section were incorporated into the [relevant statute] which enacted that the provisions...were to be 'without prejudice to the directly enforceable Community rights of nationals of any member state of the EC' (at paragraph 13 of the judgment).

(See further **7.57** on this point.) In other words, *Factortame (No 2)* secures the supremacy of EU law in accordance with *Costa v ENEL*.

Schedule 2 exceptions to the power conferred under section 2(2)

7.51 A statutory instrument cannot be used:

- when taxation is to be imposed;
- to make any provision taking effect from a date earlier than that of the making of the instrument containing the provision;
- to confer power to legislate to others (i.e. no further delegation is possible by means of a statutory instrument);
- when a new crime is being created which carries the possibility of imprisonment for more than two years or is punishable on summary conviction with imprisonment for more than three months or with a fine of more than level 5 on the standard scale.

Statutory instruments enacting EU law are made according to the positive resolution procedure; that is, they must be laid in draft and then approved by Parliament.

7.52 The ECA 1972 section 3 provides that judicial notice will be taken of Union law. It also provides, in furtherance of the aim of ensuring the uniform application of Union law, that any question as to the meaning or effect of the Treaties, or the meaning, effect or validity of Union legislation, if not referred to the Court of Justice, shall be decided by the courts in the United Kingdom in accordance with any relevant principles laid down by the Court. A statutory instrument made in 1972 under section 2(2) of the Act provided for the enforcement in the United Kingdom of judgments of the Court and fines imposed by Community (now Union) institutions.

7.53 The effect of the ECA 1972 (as amended) is to make all Union law (whether contained in primary, secondary legislation or in case law) part of UK law. This means that it can be pleaded in any relevant proceedings and does not have to be proved as a fact. There may be doubt as to whether there is an arguable Union law point. If in doubt, the matter may or must be referred to the Court of Justice depending upon the nature of the point under consideration and clarity of Union law on this point (see Article 267(2) and (3) TFEU and **Chapter 4**).

7.54 *Freight Transport Association Ltd (FTA) v London Boroughs Transport Committee(LBTC)* (1991) provides an interesting illustration of the issues. The case concerned the fitting of noise suppressors in heavy goods vehicles. Questions arose in the dispute as to the proper approach to the interpretation of directives, and the duties of a court from which there is no appeal to refer matters of Union (at that time Community) law to the Court of Justice. Two directives regulating the condition of heavy vehicles were involved: the Brakes Directive and the Sound Level Directive. In the view of the English courts, this dispute concerned environmental protection and safety measures. A different perspective, i.e. that of Community law, made vehicle control relevant. Community law occupied the field of vehicle control and vehicle control was considered an area of exclusive Community competence (see **5.57**). At this time, environmental and health and safety matters were fields where the Member States still had the power to legislate. The House of Lords decided not to refer the matter to the Court since in its view the issues fell within national competence. However, both the High Court and the Court of Appeal had interpreted the issues as also raising questions under the two directives and, therefore, being matters of Community law. The House of Lords had the option of interpreting the Community law points itself so as to take account of the directives in its decision. However, the reasoning set out by Lord Templeman denied that Community law applied at all and developed arguments on the principle of subsidiarity and shared competence between the Community and the Member States. The refusal of the House of Lords to refer the question to the Court of Justice, something it was bound to do under the provision of Article 234(3) EC (now Article 267(3) TFEU), especially in a case where its decision is a reversal of the decisions of both the High Court and the Court of Appeal, is difficult to understand. Such reference may not be necessary under the *CILFIT* rules (Case 283/81 (1982)) which include the *acte clair* doctrine (see **4.41** and **4.46**). *Acte clair* means there is no obligation to refer where the point has been decided by a previous Court ruling, and where 'the correct application of Community law may be so obvious as to leave no scope for any reasonable doubt as to the manner in which the question raised is to be resolved'. In addition: 'the matter must be equally obvious to the courts of the other Member States and to the Court of Justice'. Without taking into account the different interpretation techniques of common law and civil law countries and the difficulties inherent in comparing different language versions of the relevant source, this point of interpretation of Community law was far from clear, nor had it already been decided by the Court of Justice.

In other cases such as *Chiron Corporation v Murex Diagnostics Ltd* (1995), *R v International Stock Exchange of the United Kingdom and the Republic of Ireland, ex p Else (1982) Ltd* (1993), and *Magnavision (SA) v General Optical Council (No 2)* (1987) (see **4.39**) it would also seem that the need to make a reference is not interpreted uniformly by the British courts. The result of the *Freight Transport Association* decision was an uncertain attitude on the part of the UK courts to directives if questions arose as to the boundaries between Union law and conflicting British law on the point: in essence that is the problem with the supremacy doctrine and one of the difficulties involved in achieving a proper dialogue with the Court via the preliminary reference procedure.

7.55   One of the first pronouncements on this point came from Lord Denning in *Bulmer v Bollinger* (1974). He said: 'Parliament has decreed that the Treaty is henceforward to be part of our law. It is equal in force to any statute.' This view may not have been widely shared at this time, and even if it had been, there remained questions as to whether Community law could have greater force than a statute, by being able to prevail over any Acts of Parliament in conflict with it. (For further discussion of *Bulmer v Bollinger* and the guidelines as to whether a national court should make a reference, see **Chapter 4**.) In Case 129/79 *McCarthys Ltd v Smith* (1980) Lord Denning again considered the supremacy point:

> In construing our statute, we are entitled to look to the Treaty as an aid to its construction: and even more, not only as an aid but as an overriding force. If on close investigation it should appear that our legislation is deficient—or is inconsistent with Community law—by some oversight of our draftsmen—then it is our bounden duty to give priority to Community law. Such is the result of section 2(1) and (4) of the European Communities Act of 1972.

However, he added:

> Thus far I have assumed that our Parliament, whenever it passes legislation, intends to fulfil its obligations under the Treaty. If the time should come when our Parliament deliberately passes an Act—with the intention of repudiating the Treaty or any provision in it—or intentionally of acting inconsistently with it—and says so in express terms—then I should have thought that it would be the duty of our courts to follow the statute of our Parliament…Unless there is such an intentional repudiation of the Treaty, it is our duty to give priority to the Treaty.

7.56   The case law under the ECA 1972 and on the recognition of the supremacy of Union law is not always consistent. The overarching priority of the British courts in more recent times has been to avoid creating difficulties in the application of Union law but not necessarily to accept the absolute primacy of Union legal instruments, nor an automatic obligation to refer questions to the Court.

7.57   The supremacy of Union law and the corresponding overriding of conflicting provisions of Acts of Parliament were confirmed in the *Factortame* cases. The House of Lords, following a preliminary ruling by the Court in Case C–213/89 *Factortame (No 2)*, granted for the first time interim relief against the operation of a statute by way of an order suspending that statute. This relief was 'interim' to the extent that the validity of the statute was itself under question and the Act's suspension lasted pending the decision on its validity. This grant of interim relief affirmed the primacy of Community law in areas covered by the Treaties subsequently asserted by the Court of Justice in *Factortame (No 1)*. The *Factortame* saga had started with a complaint made by Spanish fishermen seeking to exercise a right to operate in UK fishing waters. The common fisheries policy allocated fishing quotas to different Member States with a quota thereby set for British fishing waters. Spanish nationals purchased British fishing vessels in order to fish in British waters within the British fishing quota. The Merchant Shipping Act 1988 regulated the terms under which fishing operated in UK waters, and provided that the majority (75 per cent) of shareholders of any company owning a British fishing vessel had to possess British nationality. The effect of this requirement was that Factortame, which was largely Spanish-owned, was not able to fish in the UK and the company was on the point of going out of business. Factortame therefore brought a case by way of judicial review against the British government asserting Community law rights and alleging a breach of Community law. In particular, Factortame cited Article 6 (now Article 18 TFEU as amended) concerning non-discrimination on grounds of nationality and the right of establishment (see **Chapter 12**). In interim proceedings, Factortame requested a suspension of the operation of the Merchant Shipping Act since Factortame was threatened with bankruptcy before the Court had time to rule on the main case. Under English law, it was not possible for a court to grant an interim injunction against the Crown and suspend an Act of Parliament. Parliamentary sovereignty meant that only Parliament itself could amend or repeal an Act. The House of Lords referred the case to the Court for a preliminary ruling. The Court considered that the rule preventing the application of interim relief, i.e. the suspension of an Act of Parliament, was a rule of national law and that this rule of national law should be set aside if that was the sole obstacle to the granting of interim relief (see **7.58**). When the case returned to the House of Lords, Lord Bridge accepted that it had always been clear that the duty of a British court under the ECA 1972, when delivering a final judgment, was to override any rule of national law found to be in conflict with any directly enforceable rule of Community law. He also stressed the fact that when decisions of the Court exposed areas of British statute law which failed to implement directives, Parliament had always loyally accepted the obligation to make appropriate and prompt amendments.

7.58 The political and legal ramifications of the *Factortame* judgments were significant even though the principle of supremacy, which is at the source of the disapplication of the Merchant Shipping Act 1988 by the courts, had been well understood in the United Kingdom in advance of the judgments. The contested common fisheries policy and the somewhat peculiar nature of a 'British' fishing quota being exploited by non-British Community nationals blurred the discriminatory problems within the statute in dispute. The broader issue of the manner in which the British courts had used Community law given effect in a 1972 Act (the ECA) to strike down a 1988 Act raised all sorts of questions about the continuing nature of Parliamentary sovereignty. At heart the questions which remained were twofold:

- what would be the situation if it were conclusively held that Parliament expressly contradicted a provision of Community (now Union) law in a modern statute (while still seeking to remain a member of the European Union)?

- if the supremacy of Community (now Union) law in the United Kingdom is derived from the ECA 1972, and not specifically from the Union legal system and order, would amendment or repeal of the ECA 1972 affect the operation of the supremacy principle in the United Kingdom?

7.59 The issue of Parliament acting in express contradiction of a point of Union law has yet to be definitively decided in the courts. There seems to be a presumption that the violation of Community law in the Merchant Shipping Act 1988 at issue in *Factortame* was not quite as deliberate as it might have been and express repudiation of Union law remains possible. If such a situation arose it seems quite possible the courts would respect Parliamentary sovereignty and follow the statute rather than the supremacy doctrine but it is difficult to imagine in reality how a situation could arise whereby any Parliament would deliberately contradict a provision of Union law while simultaneously seeking to keep the United Kingdom within the European Union.

7.60 The issue of the repeal or amendment of the ECA 1972 is still more complicated, since one of the generally accepted facets of the theory of Parliamentary sovereignty is no Parliament is bound by earlier legislation if it chooses not to be and that all current statutes impliedly repeal any contradicting older legislation. In *Thoburn* (2002), a case which became known as the '*Metric Martyrs* case' the question of the repeal of the ECA 1972 arose in a dispute concerning the use of metric weights and measures. The Weights and Measures Act 1985 had permitted the use of imperial (i.e. non-metric) systems, and it was argued section 1 of this Act had affected the operation of the ECA 1972 in such as way as to repeal it. This argument was rejected by the High Court in a judgment given by Laws LJ, who stated:

We should recognize a hierarchy of Acts of Parliament: as it were 'ordinary' statutes and 'constitutional' statutes. The special status of constitutional statutes follows the special status of constitutional rights…The 1972 Act is, by force of common law, a constitutional statute.

Ordinary statutes may be impliedly repealed. Constitutional statutes may not. [at paragraphs 62–63]

This judgment encourages a rethinking of the concept of Parliamentary sovereignty because of Union law supremacy. It is important to note however that the relationship between the two is, according to the British courts, a consequence of British law and the ECA 1972, not a simple expression of the primacy of Union law of its own motion.

7.61 A UK court or tribunal can deal with Union law as follows:

(i) In the application of the Union rule, the court disapplies the contradicting British rule (*Factortame*). In *R v Secretary of State for Employment, ex p EOC* (1995) a declaration was issued by the House of Lords on the Employment Protection (Consolidation) Act 1978 then in force, that the divisional court had the power to disapply those provisions in the statute relating to unfair dismissal that did not comply with Community rights arising from sex discrimination law.

(ii) In interpreting UK law in accordance with Union law, where a UK law rule is capable of different interpretations, the court should use the interpretation that best reflects the Union law aim. In *Pickstone v Freemans plc* (1988), the House of Lords held that British courts must apply a purposive construction to legislation affecting obligations under the EC Treaty, and in so doing could rely upon Parliamentary debates as recorded in Hansard, the official record of Parliamentary debate, on the relevant national legislation. Since *Pepper v Hart* (1993) reference to Parliamentary materials has been deemed permissible for questions of interpretation in law that is not Union law. *Pepper v Hart* is one example, as there are others in several fields and in several countries, of the 'spill-over' effect of Union law into national law. A similar effect can be identified in *M v Home Office* (1994) where the House of Lords awarded an injunction against the Crown in domestic proceedings, a remedy which under the Crown Proceedings Act 1947 had been previously considered to be unavailable. *Factortame* made this lack of a remedy, while it was available for Community law cases, seem ripe for rethinking.

7.62 Legislation enacted with the intention of implementing Union law, i.e. in fulfilling requirements relating to a directive, is interpreted in accordance with the relevant directive's provisions. This is the *von Colson* principle considered in **Section I** above. It was applied in *Litster v Forth Dry Dock and Engineering Co Ltd* (1990) where a claim against a private employer, which prevented any question of direct effect arising, was based on the 'Transfer of Takeovers' Directive (Directive 77/187). The statutory instrument in question had been introduced in order to implement the Directive and therefore, the House of Lords was prepared to interpret the regulation contrary to its *prima facie* meaning in order to comply with the Directive. In *Garland* (1982) Lord Diplock suggested the possibility that, unless Parliament expressly said otherwise, 'it is a principle of construction...' that the courts would always interpret a statute to comply with a Community obligation, however much this violates the language of the statute. For example, a court could 'read into' any statute the words 'except where Community law applies'.

7.63 There is something unsatisfactory in the practice of interpretation resulting in a flatly different meaning given to legislation than that which was intended at the time of enactment. The Court of Justice itself in the Spanish Case C–106/89 *Marleasing* (1990) set out a standard for purposive interpretations or the teleological approach where it held national statutes should be interpreted in the light of Community law, whether passed before or after the Community law, if possible (see **7.22**). This approach is preferable as it enables the English courts to give effect to the ECA 1972, sections 3(1) and 2(4) without the free-for-all potentially implied in *Garland*. The Court of Justice put a further gloss on this interpretative obligation in Case C–334/92 *Wagner Miret v Fondo de Garantia Salaria* (1993). The Court held that in order to interpret national law in conformity with Community law it must be presumed that the state intended to achieve the result pursued by the relevant directive. This was not possible in *Wagner Miret*. In such a circumstance, if an individual's Community law rights have not been given effect, the Court of Justice pointed courts towards considering the state's liability under the *Francovich* principles (see further **Section III**) rather than interpreting the provisions beyond what is possible.

7.64 In *Marleasing*, the Spanish law predated the Directive. *Marleasing* can itself therefore be taken as giving a broad interpretative power to the courts since the national legislation under consideration should be interpreted in the light of Union law not in force at the time the national rule was enacted. The UK courts have had difficulties extending their interpretative obligation to include UK law which had been enacted before any Union law was envisaged. In *Duke v GEC Reliance Ltd* (1988), despite Lord Templeman's undertaking that: 'the British courts will always be anxious to conclude that the UK law is consistent with Community law', the House of Lords was unwilling to interpret sex discrimination legislation in force in the United Kingdom as though it gave effect to the Equal Treatment Directive 76/207 since the legislation predated the Directive and since reading the Directive's provisions into British law in this way would 'distort' the relevant statute.

7.65 The House of Lords seemed to have concluded that the duty arising under Community (now Union) law to interpret British legislation in a manner securing consistency with Community law is confined to legislation that was passed to give effect to Community obligations. The question arose again in Case C–32/93 *Webb v EMO Cargo (UK) Ltd* (1994) (see **16.77**), where the dismissal of a woman employed to cover a period of maternity absence had been prompted when the woman providing the cover notified her employer of her own pregnancy. British courts felt that UK law on this point was clear: the situation was not a prohibited act of sex discrimination within the meaning of relevant employment legislation. Relevant points of Community law came to a different result, one which classed the treatment of Ms Webb as direct discrimination since she had been dismissed for a reason related to her pregnancy. Without overruling *Duke*, Lord Keith of Kinkel managed to construe Case C–177/88 *Dekker* (1990), which set out Community law rights on pregnancy, in accordance with the ECA 1972 section 3(1). Lord Keith noted that the Court in *Marleasing* had required national courts to construe domestic law to accord with the directive 'only if it was possible to do so'. He referred to his own remarks in *Duke* suggesting that this would only be possible if it could be done without 'distorting' the meaning of the domestic legislation, i.e. where a domestic law was 'open to an interpretation consistent with the directive, whether or not it is also open to an interpretation inconsistent with it'. The clarification on the point of pregnancy law from the Court was used to reinterpret the UK law on sex discrimination securing Ms Webb's victory in the case. Now the Employment Rights Act 1996 section 99 provides that dismissal is unlawful if the reason (or if more than one, the principal reason) for the dismissal is that an employee is pregnant or any other reason connected with her pregnancy.

7.66 The UK courts *acknowledge* the primacy of Union law and have accorded Union law a status within the different UK legal systems that ensures Union law rights supersede even well-established principles of the constitution. At the same time, the courts make efforts to ensure British laws conform to Union law points by interpreting national rules in the light of Union law. It is difficult to conclude, however, that the interpretative obligation as set out by the Court in *Marleasing* is consistently and unquestioningly applied in the United Kingdom and there is an ultimate reservation with regards to the courts' *acceptance* of the primacy of Union law: this primacy has its root in the ECA 1972, a UK statute which, as an instrument of national law in its operation remains subject to UK principles and not exclusively Union law theory. At present the dominant party in the UK coalition government (consisting of Conservatives and Liberal Democrats) is the Conservative party which has a strong euro-sceptic wing. Additionally, the European Union Act 2011 has been passed which requires a national referendum prior to any further amendments to either the TFEU or the TEU, essentially reflecting concerns over any further transfer of national powers (see further **5.3**).

The supremacy doctrine in France

7.67 There are two main separate court systems in France. The judicial courts deal with civil and criminal matters while administrative courts under a separate system review the legality of administrative action. Administrative courts may also annul legislative measures enacted by the executive. The highest court in the judicial order is the *Cour de Cassation* while the *Conseil d'Etat* is the supreme administrative court. There is also the *Conseil Constitutionnel*, which by virtue of its power of review under the French Constitution of 1958 may examine the constitutionality of legislation before it comes into force and, since an amendment which came into force in 2009, also after such legislation is in force. The role of the *Conseil Constitutionnel* came under scrutiny in Joined Cases C–188/10 and C–189/10 *Melki and Abdeli* (2010). French law required national courts 'as a matter of priority' to refer to the *Conseil Constitutionnnel* when faced with a 'question on constitutionality', and then to apply the advice given in the case before it. There was a clear risk that such an interlocutory procedure could undermine the role of the Court of Justice under Article 267 TFEU, so the Court set out some guidelines. It was ultimately concluded (at paragraph 57) that:

Article 267 TFEU does not preclude such national legislation, in so far as the other national courts or tribunals remain free:

- to refer to the Court of Justice for a preliminary ruling, at whatever stage of the proceedings they consider appropriate, even at the end of the interlocutory procedure for the review of constitutionality, any question which they consider necessary,

- to adopt any measure necessary to ensure provisional judicial protection of the rights conferred under the European Union legal order, and

- to disapply, at the end of such an interlocutory procedure, the national legislative provision at issue if they consider it to be contrary to EU law.

7.68 In France the two court systems, the judicial and the administrative, have very different traditions and the most notable feature of the French attitude towards Union law has been the different approach adopted by the judicial courts and the administrative courts, and, in particular, by the two supreme courts: the *Cour de Cassation* and the

Conseil d'Etat. While the former has sought ways of resolving the legal problems raised by French membership in the Union, the latter has, if anything, sometimes exaggerated them. Article 55 of the Constitution of 1958 provides that:

> *Treaties or agreements which have been duly ratified or approved shall, on publication, have higher authority than that of statutes, provided that the agreement or treaty in question is applied by the other party.*

This provision therefore implies that the constitutive Treaties prevail over national law without further enactment. In the judicial system, this was confirmed by the *Cour de Cassation* in *Vabre & Weigel* (1975). Vabre, a coffee importer, claimed violation of Article 95 of the EEC Treaty (now Article 110 TFEU). A customs law of 1966, i.e. legislation that was subsequent to the adoption of the relevant Community provision, conflicted with the Community law. The French court stated that:

> The EEC Treaty prevails over subsequent national statutes; it establishes a new special legal order which forms a constitutive part of the national legal orders and is directly valid for the subjects of the member states and binding for their judicial institutions.

The *Cour de Cassation* based its decision on Article 55 of the Constitution as well as on the specific nature of Community law.

7.69 The highest administrative court, the *Conseil d'Etat* (CE) avoided a clear position on the matter of supremacy of Community law for a long time, and did not refer questions to the Court of Justice under the Article 234 EC (now Article 267 TFEU) procedure, claiming that the points of Community law which were occasionally raised before it were clear. In practice, this theory offered a wide scope for subjective and controversial rulings on matters of Community law on the part of national courts in general and the CE in particular. In *Chemins de Fer Français* (1962), the CE ruled that, on the basis of Article 55 of the French Constitution, the EEC Treaty had similar status to that of French statutes (*lois*), but this did not resolve the problem of supremacy of Community law. In *Shell-Berre* (1964), the CE refused to make a reference to the Court of Justice under Article 177 (now Article 267 TFEU) on the interpretation of Article 37(1) (now Article 37(1) TFEU) and the status of state monopolies with commercial characteristics despite the fact that the meaning of that provision was subject to serious controversy. Later, in the *Semoules de France* case (1970) the CE applied a French statute despite the existence of a conflicting EEC regulation enacted before that statute. Shortly afterwards, in *Synacomex*, the CE made its first reference to the Court of Justice under Article 177 (now Article 267 TFEU).

7.70 The CE reaffirmed its negative attitude towards Community law in cases of conflict with French provisions in the celebrated case of *Cohn-Bendit* (1980). Daniel Cohn-Bendit, a German citizen born in France, was one of the leaders in the May 1968 student revolt. He had been deported after that, but when he tried to enter France in 1975 in order to take up an offer of employment, his request was refused. He challenged the decision, relying on free movement rights (see **Chapter 12**). In its decision the CE held that directives could not be invoked by individuals in national courts in order to challenge an individual administrative decision. The *Commissaire du Gouvernement*, who has a similar function to that of the Advocate General in the Court of Justice of the European Union, had cited all the relevant cases decided by the Court and had come to a directly divergent conclusion. In spite of this, the CE ignored the doctrine of the direct effect of directives which had been firmly established before *Cohn-Bendit*. Other, similar judgments followed. However, the CE recognised in *Compagnie Alitalia* (1990) that legislation adopted by the French executive, as opposed to statutes passed by the legislature, could be annulled where there was conflict with the result to be achieved under a directive.

7.71   The CE adopted a more positive attitude towards the doctrine of supremacy of Community law in its decision in *Nicolo* (1990), which concerned a challenge by two French citizens to legislation giving the right to vote and stand for European Parliament elections to non-European French citizens of the overseas departments and territories. In its judgment, the CE impliedly recognised that the EC Treaty would prevail over a French statute in case of conflict. The CE took a further step in *Boisdet* (1991) where, for the first time, it recognised the primacy of EC regulations over a French statute, even when the statute was enacted after the EC regulation concerned. Then, in cases concerning directives: *Rothmans and Philip Morris* (1993) and *Arizona Tobacco* (1992) the CE acknowledged that a directive would prevail over a subsequently adopted statute. In *Arcelor* (2007), the CE considered a question as to the validity of French legislation implementing Directive 2003/87/EC on the Kyoto Protocol and, contrary to previous practice where the CE simply ruled on the French legislation, referred a question to the Court of Justice about the validity of the Directive. The CE thereby acknowledged it could not consider the validity of French legislation that implemented a directive without at the same time questioning the validity of the directive, which the CE recognised it did not have the power to do. The CE issued a press release explaining its decision and setting out its acceptance of the supremacy of Community law, although at the same time commenting that the acceptance of the supremacy of Community law remained subject to the French Constitution.

7.72   However, the lack of any clear statement of principle in these decisions means that there are still doubts regarding the CE's attitude towards Union law in general, especially towards directives. Note, however, that CE judgments, like those of the *Cour de Cassation*, are anonymous and collegiate, and are very concise, with very little reasoning given. Therefore, indications of attitudes to Union law come from the opinions of the *Commissaire du Gouvernement* or from extra-judicial writings of the members of the CE. The CE prompted a constitutional amendment in its decision of 26 September 2002 which questioned the compatibility of the European Arrest Warrant with the French Constitution but again without expanding on the boundaries it may envisage as applying to the primacy principle in France.

7.73 The French Constitution had already been amended, in the 1990s, with the addition of Title XV (Articles 88–1 to 88–4) to make possible French ratification of the Treaty on European Union agreed at Maastricht and to make specific reference to the European Union and EC law in the French Constitution. These amendments had been required by a decision of the *Conseil Constitutionnel* (1993), which had declared the provisions of the Maastricht TEU concerning the right of EC citizens to vote in municipal elections, monetary union, and common visa policy to be incompatible with the French Constitution. There had been, prior to the Maastricht amendments, no mention of the European Community in the French Constitution. Strangely, the constitutional amendment of March 2003 prompted by the European Arrest Warrant did not refer to this new Title XV and Article 88–1 of the Constitution. The *Conseil Constitutionnel*, however, took the opportunity of a dispute concerning the French statute that transposed Directive 2000/31 on electronic commerce to comment on Article 88–1 of the Constitution and to give its view on its role regarding the scrutiny of directives and their transposition into French law. The dispute here concerned the validity of the statute in the light of alleged infringements of free expression rights and due process. In its Decision 2004–496 (of 10 June 2006) the *Conseil Constitutionnel* ruled that it would limit its review of legislation implementing Community law that was based on Article 88–1 of the Constitution, but with a proviso that the *Conseil Constitutionnel* retained the right to scrutinise Community law concerning its compatibility with 'express provisions' of the French Constitution. There is a certain lack of clarity as to what is meant by the phrase 'express Constitutional provisions', although it should be noted that the *Conseil Constitutionnel* has confirmed this line in subsequent decisions (2004–497, 2004–498 and 2004–499). What seems likely is that the *Conseil Constitutionnel* has given its authoritative stamp to the concept of the supremacy of Union law in the French legal system—even if that supremacy is based on Article 88 of the Constitution rather than emanating from the Union legal order itself—and at the same time insisted on the need for exceptional review of Union laws that may infringe Constitutional standards, i.e. fundamental rights. At the same time, the CE has similarly accepted the supremacy of Union law, but subject to the French Constitution.

7.74 The Lisbon Treaty was ratified by the French Parliament on 14 February 2008. By a decision of 20 December 2007 the *Conseil Constitutionnel* stated that an amendment to the French Constitution was necessary to implement the articles of the Lisbon Treaty affecting the exercise of national sovereignty (such as, for example, the provisions regarding the principle of subsidiarity (Article 5(3)), the ordinary legislative procedure (Article 294 TFEU), the fight against terrorism (Article 75 TFEU), judicial cooperation in civil matters (Article 81 TFEU) and judicial cooperation in criminal matters (Article 82 and 83 TFEU)).

From this perspective, the position of both the CE and the *Conseil Constitutionnel* to some extent bridges the position arrived at in the United Kingdom concerning Union law primacy and the position of the German and Italian courts, considered next.

EU law in Germany

7.75 In Germany there are five separate court systems. In addition to the ordinary courts (having jurisdiction in civil and criminal law), there are specialised courts dealing with administrative, labour, social security and fiscal matters. Each of these court systems is headed by a federal supreme court. Each system is independent of the other. On constitutional issues, however, all courts are subject to the rulings of the Federal Constitutional Court (the *Bundesverfassungsgericht—BVerfGe*) hereafter referred to as the FCC.

7.76 Germany, which has a mitigated dualist system, recognised the special position of the Union legal order as distinct from traditional international law. In *Internationale Handelsgesellschaft* (1974), which followed the Court of Justice ruling in Case 11/70 *Internationale Handelsgesellschaft* (1970) on the annulment of the Community's export licence regulations, the FCC held:

> This court—in this respect in agreement with the law developed by the European Court of Justice—adheres to its settled view that Community law is neither a component part of the national legal system nor international law, but forms an independent system of law flowing from an autonomous legal source…

In principle, the two legal spheres stand side by side and independent of one another in their validity. In particular, the competent Union organs, including the Court of Justice, have to rule on the binding force, construction and observance of Union law, and the competent national organs on the binding force, construction and observance of the constitutional law of the Federal Republic of Germany.

7.77 Article 24 of the Basic Law (the German Constitution) provides that sovereign powers may be transferred to international organisations. This provision was considered to be an insufficient basis for the ratification of Germany's accession to the Maastricht Treaty in 1993. Consequently, the Basic Law was amended in December 1992 to authorise a further transfer of powers to the European Community (as it then was). The new Article 23 of the Basic Law enabled Germany 'with a view to establishing a united Europe' to participate in the development of the European Union, which is committed to democracy, the rule of law, social and federal principles as well as the principle of subsidiarity. It ensures protection of basic rights comparable in substance to the protection afforded by the Basic Law.

7.78 The FCC's judgment in *Lütticke* (1971) made clear that in Germany, Union (at that time Community) law is applied directly and cannot be set aside by subsequent national laws and that each court is entitled not to apply national laws which are contrary to Union law.

7.79 As a rule, German courts loyally apply Union law, but there are exceptions. One branch of one of the German supreme courts (the 5th Senate of the *Bundesfinanzhof,* (the Federal Tax Court) in July 1981 wrongly applied a directive without prior request for a preliminary ruling. It referred to the French *Cohn-Bendit* case and decided on the same grounds that a directive could not be applied within the national legal order.

Following a preliminary ruling given by the Court of Justice in the *Kloppenburg* case (Case 70/83 (1984)), the 5th Senate of the Federal Tax Court took the opportunity to question the whole case law of the Court of Justice concerning the direct effect of directives. The thrust of the argument was that the Court of Justice had transgressed the proper limits of Article 189(3) (now Article 288(3) TFEU) and thereby extended the effect of directives in a way that was not covered by the German Acts of Accession to the Treaties.

On appeal, the FCC held that the ruling of the Court of Justice was binding on the Federal Tax Court and that the question of the direct effect of directives was a proper matter for the Court of Justice to decide. In its judgment, the FCC viewed the ruling by the Court of Justice as an act of judicial law-making which, however, did not transgress the proper bounds of the inherent limits on the judiciary.

7.80   One of the most difficult issues for the German legal system relates to constitutional review. The key question is whether Union law can be set aside if it violates the Basic Law, and in particular fundamental rights protected by the Basic Law. In *Internationale Handelsgesellschaft (Solange I)* (1974), the FCC noted that the protection of fundamental human rights was an essential element of the Basic Law, and that this power could not automatically be restricted by transferring sovereignty to a supranational organisation under Article 24 of the Basic Law. In the opinion of the FCC, the fundamental rights guaranteed by the Basic Law were insufficiently protected under Community law, as the Community lacked a democratically legitimated and directly elected parliament as well as a codified catalogue of human rights. The protection of fundamental rights by the Court of Justice was considered insufficient as the case law of courts could not fully guarantee legal certainty. It could be changed in any future decision. The FCC confirmed that it would not rule on the validity or invalidity of a rule of Community law, but it held that the German authorities or courts should not apply rules of Community law which infringed a rule of the Basic Law relating to basic rights as long as (in German: '*solange*') the Community did not itself provide adequate protection of fundamental rights. In cases of doubt the FCC would rule on the existence of such an infringement.

7.81   Then, in 1986 the FCC revised its position, taking into account the various developments in Community law concerning the protection of basic rights. In *Wünsche Handelsgesellschaft (Solange II)* (1987), the FCC held that the protection of fundamental rights in the Community had reached a degree where it was essentially comparable to the standard set by the Basic Law. On this basis, the FCC ruled that it would no longer exercise its jurisdiction to review secondary Community law by the standards of the fundamental rights guaranteed by the Basic Law. The FCC, however, pointed out that a transfer of sovereign rights may not impinge on the basic constitutional structure of the Federal Constitutional which encompassed the 'federal order' set up by the Basic Law.

It is clear from this judgment that the FCC had not given up its former interpretation of Article 24 of the Basic Law with regard to the implicit limitations of the transferral of rights to a supranational organisation. The judgment expressly linked the question of non-exercise of jurisdiction concerning basic rights by the FCC to the state of Community law. The FCC will be content not to exercise this jurisdiction only 'as long as' the Union, and in particular the case law of the European Court, generally ensures an effective protection of fundamental rights as against the sovereign powers of the Union (see also **Chapter 6**).

7.82 In *Brunner v European Union Treaty* (1993) the FCC used the opportunity of a constitutional challenge of the Maastricht Treaty to conduct an analysis of the Treaty and outline the limits of competence of the Community vis-à-vis the Federal Republic. The FCC judgment dealt at length with the constitutional complaint lodged by Brunner, while dismissing others as inadmissible. The FCC ruled that the transfer of powers to the Union, and in particular those concerning Economic and Monetary Union, fell within the acceptable limits of the democratic principle guaranteed by the Basic Law (Article 38 GG) which precludes such transfer if it leaves the Parliament devoid of sufficient sovereign powers. With what the newspaper *Die Zeit* called 'judicial self-restraint' (in English) the court held that the decisive factor was that the democratic foundations of the European Union should be extended in step with further integration. The Union remained a Confederation (*Staaten(ver)bund*) rather than a Federation (*Bundesstaat*), but that extensions of Community jurisdiction resulting from decisions of the Court of Justice would be 'tantamount to an extension of the Treaty', and as such, such a Court of Justice ruling could not be considered as binding. The Constitutional Court reserved the ultimate right of review in the same vein as set out in its decision in *Solange I*. The FCC, however, also stressed its 'relationship of co-operation' with the Court of Justice. A similar constitutional challenge in 1998, heard just before the decision taken by the Council as to which Member States would qualify to join EMU, was rejected by the FCC.

7.83 In its judgment after various constitutional complaints had been brought before it by private citizens as well as by a political party in respect of the ratification of the Lisbon Treaty, the FCC ruled in June 2009 that the Treaty was in accordance with the German Basic Law and simply objected to the domestic law which implemented the Treaty and annulled the law. As regards the Lisbon Treaty itself, it spelt out in a lengthy judgment the limits to which integration could go and emphasised the safeguards under the German Basic law which must be respected. It did not, however, consider that the Treaty as such exceeded the boundaries of what was acceptable under the Basic Law. A new implementing law was then passed in September 2009 and ratification duly followed.

7.84 The German Constitutional Court therefore has found an accommodation with the supremacy of Union law whereby it acknowledges that supremacy but at the same time retains a scrutiny role with regard to the fundamental doctrines of German constitutional law. In *Brunner*, the FCC implied it would resist further integration by means of Court of Justice judicial activism, because of the importance of maintaining democratic structures and popular consent for change, but at the same time committed to cooperating and working with the Court of Justice. So the FCC retains a scrutiny role but then implies it will not use this power. The so-called banana cases: Case C–280/93 *Germany v Council* (1994) and Joined Cases C–465 and 466/93 *Atlanta Fruchthandelsgesellschaft v Bundesamt für Ernährung* (1995), caused considerable contention in Germany, where German administrative and tax courts ruled on constitutional questions of proportionality and the right to private property, both fundamental rights in the Basic Law, and on whether the Banana Regulation (Council Regulation 404/93) violated the provisions of the GATT. The FCC, however, ruled in a Decision of June 2000 (2 BvL 1/97) that these heated challenges alleging human rights abuses by the Community legal order were inadmissible. The FCC stated that it had in previous cases declared itself satisfied with the standard of protection of fundamental rights in Community law, and that there was no evidence of these standards having declined. The wider power the FCC has insisted on reserving to itself to scrutinise supreme Union law from the perspective of the Basic Law has recently been clarified. The current, and most precise, definition comes from the FCC in *Honeywell* (2010). In a deferential judgment it observed (at paragraph 66):

> If the supranational integration principle is not to be endangered, *ultra vires* review must be exercised reservedly by the Federal Constitutional Court.

In the same paragraph the FCC went on to note that firstly, respect had to be had for the 'Union's own methods of justice to which the Court of Justice considers itself to be bound' and that, secondly, 'the Court of Justice has a right to a tolerance error'. Moreover, it was stated that it is not for the FCC to 'supplant the interpretation of the Court of Justice with an interpretation of its own'. Ultimately the conclusion is that:

> Interpretations [by the Court of Justice] of the bases of the Treaties are also to be tolerated which, without a considerable shift in the structure of competences, constitute a restriction to individual cases and either do not permit impacts on fundamental rights to arise which constitute a burden or do not oppose domestic compensation for such burdens.

Hence it does not look as though the FCC's much debated review function will be meaningfully exercised against the Court of Justice at any time soon.

EU law in Italy

7.85 In Italy, too, the Italian Constitutional Court has expressed reservations about the supremacy of Union law without the ultimate scrutiny of the Italian courts seeking to protect constitutional rights. In Case 6/64 *Costa v ENEL* (1964) the Court of Justice ruled that Community (now Union) law prevailed over national law, including a Member State's Constitution (see **7.30**). The Italian court had also referred the case to the Italian Constitutional Court for a ruling, as this is the only court which may declare a statute invalid. The Constitutional Court ruled that, as the then EEC Treaty had been incorporated in Italian law as an ordinary statute, the Treaty was subordinate to subsequent Italian legislation. The Court of Justice was well aware of this ruling when deciding *Costa*. The Advocate General warned of 'disastrous consequences for the future of the Common Market' and suggested that there were only two ways open to a Member State whose Constitution prevented it from giving immediate effect to Community legislation over national law: either to amend the Constitution or to amend the Treaty. As we have seen (in **7.30**), the Court of Justice ruled that Member States had given up some of their sovereign rights by joining the Community and this had made it impossible for them to give effect to a subsequent conflicting measure.

7.86 Case 106/77 *Simmenthal* (1978) ascertained that any rights or duties conferred on individuals by the Treaty must be protected, and any prior or posterior national rules, including any legislative, administrative or judicial practice which might impair the effectiveness of Community law, by withholding from the national court having jurisdiction to apply such law the power to set aside national law preventing Community rules from having full effect must be disapplied. The Court should not await a ruling from the Constitutional Court in this respect. However, in Joined Cases C–10–22/97 *Ministero delle Finanze v INCOGE '90* (1998) the Court reconsidered the judgment in *Simmenthal*, recalling that it had, essentially, held that every national court must, in a case within its jurisdiction, apply Community law in its entirety and protect rights which Community law confers on individuals, setting aside any provision of national law which may conflict with it, whether prior or subsequent to the Community rule. The Court held that it could not be inferred from that judgment that the incompatibility with Community law of a subsequently adopted rule of national law had the effect of rendering that rule of national law non-existent. Furthermore, Community law did not require that any non-application, following a judgment given by the Court, of legislation introducing a levy contrary to Community law should deprive that levy retroactively of its character as a charge and divest the legal relationship, established when the charge in question was levied between the national tax authorities and the parties liable to pay it, of its fiscal nature. Any such reclassification was a matter for national law.

7.87 In *Frontini* (1974) the Constitutional Court, while generally recognising the primacy of Community law nevertheless reserved the right to control the continuing compatibility of the Treaty with fundamental principles guaranteed by the Constitution. In *Fragd* (13 April 1989), the Constitutional Court seemed to confirm this position and questioned whether a principle of Community law as set out by the Court of Justice following a preliminary reference under Article 177 EEC (now Article 267 TFEU), could be held inapplicable in Italy if the principle infringed fundamental human rights.

A sample of other Member States' issues with the supremacy doctrine

Ireland

7.88 Early cases following the Republic of Ireland's accession accepted Community law as part of the Irish legal order and implied there were no problems with the supremacy doctrine. A constitutional amendment to join the Community ensures the primacy of Union law over Irish law, even to the extent of conflicts between Union law and the Constitution itself. However, the issue of basic rights guaranteed by the Irish Constitution has caused problems, as it has in Germany and Italy. In Case C–159/90 *Society for the Protection of the Unborn Children Ireland Ltd v Grogan* (1991) the Irish Supreme Court ruled that this constitutional right of the unborn had to be protected against any right arising from Community law as a corollary to the right to travel which may be used to carry out an abortion. Students had been publicising abortion services available in the UK and the Society for the Protection of the Unborn Children sought an injunction based on the Constitution to stop this dissemination of information. The Supreme Court referred a question on the relationship between the Irish Constitution and free movement rights to the Court of Justice. The Court of Justice avoided the essence of the supremacy dispute by finding the absence of an economic relationship between the abortion service and the information provided by the students (who did not charge for the information provision) meant it did not have to give a ruling on the point. The issue of the conflicting free movement rights in Community law and the prohibition of abortions under the Irish Constitution returned in 1992 with the particularly unhappy story of a raped pregnant 14-year-old girl whose prevention from travel to secure an abortion seemed to threaten her mental and physical health. The Supreme Court let the girl travel for an abortion as there was a real and substantial risk to her life, rather than as an expression of the supremacy of Community law.

7.89 The status of the right to life in the Irish Constitution motivated a special provision added to the Maastricht Treaty on European Union, intended to prevent such a constitutional clash in future. Protocol no 17 to the TEU on the Irish Constitution provides:

> Nothing…(in the Treaties…) shall affect the application in Ireland of Article 40.3.3 of the Constitution…(which protects the right to life of unborn children and prohibits abortions).

The legal interpretation of the Protocol on 1 May 1992 by lawyers reporting to the European Council is recorded as follows:

> It shall not limit freedom to travel between member states or, in accordance with conditions which may be laid down, in conformity with Community law, by Irish legislation, to obtain or make available in Ireland information relating to services lawfully available in member states.

Austria

7.90 Austria acceded to the European Union in 1995. In Case C–224/97 *Ciola v Land Vorarlberg* (1999) the Court of Justice firmly rejected the Austrian state's argument that national law in conflict with Community law should be obeyed until the Community law right had been established by an Austrian court. The Austrian Constitutional Court recognised in its decision of 25 June 1997 that where matters of Austrian law had been predetermined by Community law, it could not review the substance of that law by reference to the Austrian Constitution.

Spain

7.91 The Spanish Constitutional Court (the *Tribunal Constitucional*) had embraced the primacy of Community law in some of its first decisions on the matter following Spanish accession in 1985 (Judgments 252/1988 and 132/1989). The *Tribunal Constitucional* had concluded that the supremacy of Community law meant it could not review Community law, even from the perspective of a review of fundamental rights protected by the Spanish Constitution. That being so, the *Tribunal Constitucional* first decided (Judgment 64/1991) and then confirmed (Judgment 58/2004) it would scrutinise Spanish law that implemented Community law standards and directives, and also set out in its Opinion on the Maastricht Treaty (Opinion 1/1992) its view that the Spanish Constitution required reform to adopt certain provisions in the Maastricht Treaty—in particular the provisions on the eligibility of non-Spanish nationals to vote in Spanish elections. This implied an understanding that the Spanish Constitution rather than Community law retained ultimate legal authority in Spain and that the supremacy of Community law was accorded by Spanish law and not by Community law itself. This Opinion had a contested reception in Spain, and the *Tribunal Constitucional* refined its position with greater respect to the supremacy of Community law in later decisions. In Judgment 130/95 a challenge to a cooperation agreement between the Community and Morocco was rejected, and then in Judgment 13/1998 the *Tribunal Constitucional* equated Community regulations with Spanish statutes. Both these decisions demonstrated an acceptance on the part of the *Tribunal Constitucional* that it should take account of Union law in the resolution of constitutional problems.

7.92 In Judgment 58/2004 the *Tribunal Constitucional* accepted that a court's refusal to make a reference to the Court of Justice on a point of Community law could constitute a breach of Spanish Constitutional requirements on the rights to a fair hearing and effective legal protection. However, in Case C–118/08 *Transportes Urbanos y Servicios Generales* (2010) the Spanish Constitution itself was a source of discord with EU law by providing, as it did, for more efficient actions to rectify a breach of its provisions than those of EU law. In Opinion 1/2004 the *Tribunal Constitucional* sets out its most detailed statement on its view on the primacy of Community law. This Opinion was requested by the Spanish Government on the proposed Constitutional Treaty. The *Tribunal Constitucional* was clear that it considered sovereignty and fundamental human rights as being spheres where the supremacy of Community law needed to be balanced against the Spanish Constitution. This position is comparable to the view of the German Constitutional Court in that it envisages a *Tribunal Constitucional* role of ultimate review of Union law but only in the most exceptional of circumstances. As in Germany, the Spanish take on the supremacy of Union law seems to be an acceptance of it with the recognition that there are still boundaries that the Union legal system will have to respect in order to secure acknowledgement of the supremacy of Union law by the *Tribunal Constitucional*.

Poland

7.93   Poland acceded to the European Union in 2004 along with seven other central and eastern European states (in addition to Cyprus and Malta), which had only recently reasserted independence from the controlling influence of the Soviet Union (exerted, no doubt, in each to very different degrees). These eight states acceding in 2004 had particular issues with a re-emergent national identity, and indeed the special situations of the other two acceding states would suggest that national identity and the supremacy question would be contentious in all these acceding states. The Polish Constitutional Tribunal considered the relationship between the European Union Treaty and the Polish Constitution in its decision of May 2005 (K18/04). The ruling stated that Article 90(1) of the Polish Constitution permitted both the 'delegation' of competences normally carried out by organs of the Polish state, and membership of international organisations. However, in an important reservation the Polish Constitutional Tribunal made clear that Articles 90(1) and 91(3) of the Constitution did not permit acts contrary to the Constitution, and therefore made the delegation of powers to an organisation impossible if such a delegation signified the inability of the Polish Republic to continue functioning as a democratic sovereign state. This would imply that in instances where there is any clash between a requirement of Union law and a requirement of the Polish Constitution, in such circumstances the Polish Constitutional Tribunal would not accept the supremacy of Union law. That is not to say that the attitude to the supremacy of Union law in Poland is likely to be the same in the other 2004 accession states, or indeed in Bulgaria or Romania since they joined. It will be interesting to see how the Court of Justice responds to the challenges posed by enlargement.

(III) State liability and other remedies in Union law

SUMMARY

- Remedies for breach of Union law can be obtained primarily through national courts
- The Union has not harmonised remedies or procedural rules, but has over the years built up a body of case law setting out general principles which guide national courts on the

approach to the kind of remedies which should be available for breach of Union law. The most important principles are:

- that an *effective* remedy must be available,
- it must be neither *impossible* nor *too difficult* to obtain in practice, and
- it must at least be *comparable* to those available for breach of national law

- The relationship between Union and national procedural rules remains problematic, but recent cases have achieved some clarification

- Serious breaches of Union law by Member States may give rise to liability to the individual who has suffered loss

- The creation of a uniform Union remedy: state liability for breach of Union law (*Francovich*)

- The remedies which must be available include awards of damages and interim relief (injunctions)

Introduction

7.94 Most of the rules of the EU are enforced through national legal systems. Although the Court has made clear that the provisions of Union law have primacy over national law and that national rules which prevent the effective implementation of Union law must be disapplied, the principle of the autonomy of national procedural rules has been maintained. It was probably assumed when drafting the original treaties that Member States' national legal systems based on the rule of law would provide an adequate level of judicial protection through national procedural rules. Harmonisation of remedies and procedures is probably not possible because of the variety of approaches in different jurisdictions, and because procedural rules and remedies are part of a coherent whole legal system with different philosophies, histories and court systems. The consequence of this has been that the enforcement of Union law has been uneven and partial from one Member State to another. It has therefore been left to the Court of Justice to strike the balance between the autonomy of the Member States in this area and the need to ensure proper application of Union law.

7.95 Initially, therefore, and until the 1980s, the Court of Justice contented itself with laying down guidelines for national courts to follow when they were considering what would constitute a suitable remedy for breach of EC rules. Drawing on Article 10 EC (wording now included in Article 4(3) TEU), the Court has obliged national courts to take into account two principles or guidelines laid down by the Court of Justice to ensure the proper application of Community law. These guidelines are contained in two cases:

- Case 33/76 *Rewe-Zentralfinanz v Landwirtschaftskammer* (1976);
- Case 45/76 *Comet BV v Produktschap voor Siergewassen* (1976).

In *Comet* the Court stated:

> It is for the domestic law of each member state to designate the courts having jurisdiction and the procedural conditions governing actions at law intended to ensure the protection of the rights which subjects derive from the direct effects of Community law, it being understood that such conditions cannot be less favourable than those relating to similar actions of a domestic nature…(non-discrimination principle).

The position would be different only if these rules made it impossible in practice to exercise rights which the national courts have a duty to protect.

In *Rewe* the Court said:

> Although the Treaty has made it possible…for private persons to bring a direct action [before national courts based on EC law], it was not intended to create new remedies in the national courts to ensure the observance of Community law…On the other hand…it must be possible for every kind of action provided for by national law to be available for the purpose of ensuring observance of Community provisions having direct effect, on the same conditions as would apply were it a question of observing national law.

Thus, to sum up, as long as national law provided a remedy similar to that provided for breach of a similar national rule, and did not make it impossible in practice to exercise Community law rights, i.e. complied with the principles of equivalence and non-discrimination, Community law was satisfied.

7.96 This was illustrated by Case 199/82 *Amministrazione delle Finanze dello Stato v San Giorgio* (1984). Fixed charges on cattle health inspections had been declared unconstitutional by the Italian court. On the basis of that order, San Giorgio brought an action to recover the charges paid and a reference was made to the Court. The Court referred to its judgment in Case 68/79 *Hans Just v Danish Ministry for Fiscal Affairs* (1980) where it had ruled that it was for the Member States to ensure that repayment of charges in accordance with the rules of their internal law was not subject to less favourable conditions than those in domestic law and must not make it impossible in practice to exercise the rights conferred by the Community legal system. In *San Giorgio* the Court said that Community law did not prevent a national legal system from disallowing the repayment of charges which have been unduly levied where to do so would entail unjust enrichment of the recipients. National law could, therefore, take account of the fact that such charges had been passed on to others by incorporating them in the price of the goods. However, the Court's answer to the Italian court's question was that a Member State cannot make repayment of national charges levied contrary to the requirements of Community law conditional upon the production of proof that those charges have not been passed on to other persons if the repayment is subject to rules of evidence which render the exercise of that right virtually impossible, even where the repayment of other charges levied in breach of national law was subject to the same restrictive conditions. *San Giorgio* reinforced the principle that national law must not make the remedy for breach of Community law extremely difficult. In fact, therefore, under *San Giorgio* there could be a better remedy for breach of Community law than for breach of national law. The question of how *effective* the remedy was, or the question of what was to happen when national law provided no remedy, remained unclear for some time.

The principle of effective remedies

7.97 In Case 14/83 *von Colson v Land Nordrhein-Westfalen* (1984) two German nationals claimed that the provisions of German law implementing Directive 76/207 (the Equal Treatment Directive) were inadequate to ensure that their EC rights were protected. The German law only enabled those wronged by breach of the rights contained in the Directive to recover the actual amount lost. The case is significant because the Court pronounced on the nature of the remedy that the national court must provide and ruled that sanctions must be *effective, adequate and act as a deterrent and must be such as to guarantee real and effective protection*. This started a new stage in the development of remedies. *Von Colson* drew on Article 5 of the Treaty (now included and expanded in Article 4(3) TEU): the duty of the Member States to take all appropriate measures to ensure the fulfilment of obligations arising under the Treaty, *and* to facilitate the achievement of the Community's tasks. It should also be noted that here, as throughout the whole corpus of Union law, the principle of proportionality applies and lies at the heart of the *von Colson* judgment, i.e. the means chosen to provide the remedy must be appropriate to the infringement and it must be adequate, *and* act as a deterrent (see Article 5(4) TEU).

7.98 In Case 222/84 *Johnston v Royal Ulster Constabulary* (1986) the Court enlarged upon the general principle of effective judicial protection. In that case the RUC had submitted a ministerial certificate stating that national security required that the issue of arming women police officers in Northern Ireland was one that the Court could not consider. Article 6 of the Equal Treatment Directive (76/207) required that those who consider themselves wronged within the scope of the Directive, must be able 'to pursue their claims by judicial process'. There was no previous indication what 'judicial process' meant and it was assumed that it meant being able to bring the matter before a court. However the Court laid down that Community law required that the principle of *effective judicial protection*, first raised in *von Colson*, meant that the Member State must take measures which are sufficiently effective to achieve the aims of the directive. This principle precluded a minister from relying totally on the certificate, because it would disable the claimant from having her case properly considered.

7.99 In the light of *von Colson* and *Johnston* it could now be said that the concept of effective judicial protection includes a proper hearing and an effective remedy for the applicant and is an aspect of the general effectiveness principle laid down in *Simmenthal* and reinforced in *Factortame* (see **7.57–7.59**). The general effectiveness principle referred to in those cases means that national courts are required to disapply any national measures which would prevent the effective application of Union law.

7.100 Effectiveness was taken a stage further in Case C–271/91 *Marshall v Southampton and South West Hampshire Area Health Authority (No 2)* (1993) (*Marshall (No 2)*) where the Court considered Article 6 of Directive 76/207 again. The Court held that Article 6 was directly effective *and* that the requirement of effective judicial protection meant that the claimant who has suffered loss as the result of a breach of Community law (in this case because there was an upper limit for compensation under the Employment Protection Act 1975) must receive full compensation for her loss. Where damages are chosen as the main remedy by the Member State, all the financial loss including interest on the award between the date of the breach and the judgment must be made good; the Court said that this was prevented by the application of the upper limit.

Thus the rule laid down in *Rewe* and *Comet* (see **7.95**) that the remedy must be comparable to remedies for breach of national law, i.e. non-discriminatory, and possible in practice to be relied upon, has been extended. If no remedy or an inadequate remedy exists in national law, it inevitably follows (although the Court did not actually say this), that the national system would have to improve on the remedy that was available or invent a new one.

7.101 In later cases, such as Case C–338/91 *Steenhorst-Neerings* (see further **7.15** and **16.55**) and Case C–66/95 *R v Secretary of State for Social Security, ex p Eunice Sutton* (1997) the Court showed a greater amount of caution in deciding what constitutes an effective remedy. In *Steenhorst-Neerings*, it considered the retroactive limitation of a benefit to be compatible with Community law; in *Eunice Sutton* non-payment of interest on a claim for social security benefit was contrasted with *Marshall (No 2)* and distinguished from the finding there on the basis that such benefits did not constitute compensation for loss as suffered in *Marshall*.

The principle of equivalence

7.102 The principle of equivalence, i.e. that rules for protecting Union rights must not be less favourable than those governing domestic actions, was established in *Rewe* and *Comet* explained more fully later, especially in Case C–261/95 *Palmisani v INPS* (1997) and Case C–326/96 *Levez v Jennings (Harlow Pools) Ltd* (1998). Both cases involved the existence of time limits in national law. The Court of Justice in *Palmisani* explained that to establish that there is no discrimination between domestic and Community remedies in particular cases, it must be shown that the claims must be similar, the procedural rules on which the comparison is based must not be considered in isolation, but in their procedural context, and those procedures must not be chosen at random but must be of a similar kind.

In *Levez* the Court (at paragraph 41) stated that the principle of equivalence requires that the rule at issue be applied without distinction, whether the infringement alleged is of Community law or national law, where the purpose and cause of action are similar. Here the evidence showed that other discrimination claims in UK law were not subject to the same limitation.

In Case C–78/98 *Preston v Wolverhampton Healthcare NHS Trust* (2000), when asked by the House of Lords to provide further explanation, the Court emphasised that the equivalence of national procedural rules should be ascertained by an objective and abstract assessment, taking into account the role, operation and any special features of those rules.

At this point in the developing case law it is clear that national remedies and national procedure available for enforcing or protecting Union rights must comply with the principles of equivalence and effectiveness. It will be seen that the latter principle is often less important than the former.

Procedure

7.103   As with remedies, Union law has adhered to what has been called the principle of procedural autonomy. This means that the procedure followed by national systems for the enforcement of Union law was a matter for each national legal system subject to the principles in *Rewe* and *Comet* (above). It is for the domestic system of each Member State to designate the courts having jurisdiction and to determine the procedural conditions for the recovery of damages, *provided that any conditions may not be so framed as to render the recovery of damages impossible in practice or excessively difficult.* However, the implication of this is that national procedural rules can still make a remedy difficult to obtain. For example, in many cases time limits are short, whether the matter is one of purely national law or of Union law, and can lead to making the right in effect impossible to achieve. This is what occurred in *Rewe* and *Comet*. Guidelines in those cases tried to find a balance in demarcating the extent of national autonomy in matters of procedure and the effective enforcement of Community law. In Case C–208/90 *Emmott v Minister for Social Welfare* (1991) (see **16.55**) the three-month limitation to bring an application for judicial review had led the Court of Justice to rule that, while reasonable time limits satisfied the principle of procedural autonomy, 'account must nevertheless be taken of the particular nature of directives'. The consequence could be that for wrongly transposed directives, time cannot begin to run until the directive is properly transposed. This has given rise to many criticisms, especially as the *Francovich* principle may expose the state to massive claims. A number of subsequent similar cases have distinguished *Emmott* and it may now be said that the *Emmott* principle will only be applied when the state is seriously in default in failing to implement a directive and obstructing the claimant from relying on it. The issue now appears to have been settled by Case C–188/95 *Fantask* (see **7.16**). Time limits appear to be acceptable to the Court provided that the principle of equivalence is upheld and despite the fact that they may threaten the effectiveness of the protection offered by Union law. But many other procedural rules can prevent or inhibit the application of Union law and can also threaten the principle of effectiveness. The following cases illustrate this.

7.104 In Joined Cases C–430 and 431/93 *van Schijndel and van Veen v Stichting Pensioenfonds voor Fysiotherapeuten* (1996) and Case C–312/93 *Peterbroeck, van Campenhout SCS & Cie v Belgian State* (1996) a more fundamental change to the general principle of procedural autonomy occurred. The issues here involved national courts whose procedural rules disabled Community law points from being argued when the parties had not argued EC law themselves. In most legal systems, it is the parties themselves who decide which facts and law will be presented to the court, leaving the judge to decide the outcome on the facts and law as presented. But in order to secure the effective implementation of Community law, must the national judge raise EC law of his own motion, despite the principles of procedural autonomy, the passivity of the judge, and even where national law precluded the judge from taking the initiative?

7.105 In *van Schijndel*, the applicants challenged a national law imposing compulsory membership of an occupational pension scheme. They lost at first instance where their arguments were based solely on national law, but then appealed to the *Hoge Raad*, the Dutch Supreme Court, raising Community law points, on the grounds that the Appeal Court should have considered 'if necessary of its own motion' the question of the compatibility of compulsory Fund membership with EC law, for example, Articles 3(f), 5, 52–58, 59–66, 85, 86 and/or 90 EC (now Articles 4(2)(g) TFEU, 4(3) TEU, 49–54, 56–62, 101, 102 and/or 106 TFEU). This would mean raising new points and procedural rules in the Netherlands provided that parties could only raise new points of law and then only if they did not involve new considerations of fact. The claimants were not able to comply with this rule as raising Community law meant a new investigation of fact. The *Hoge Raad* referred questions to the Court as to whether the relevant Dutch procedural rules were compatible with Community law and whether the national court is required to raise points of EC law of its own motion, even where the parties to the proceedings had not relied upon them. In Dutch law there is a limited right for the judge to do this.

This raised the fundamental question of whether the procedural rule under consideration made it excessively difficult or even impossible to rely on Community law, something which is prohibited. The Court held that while Community law does not *require* national courts to abandon the passive role generally assigned to them, nor were national judges required to go beyond the ambit of the dispute defined by the parties, these being fundamental principles of the legal systems of most Member States, nonetheless, in considering the compatibility with Community law of national procedural rules, the national court should consider the role and purpose of the provision in question in the legal system. This can be described as permitting a purposive approach to the rule in question.

7.106 In *Peterbroeck*, compatibility of Belgian (tax) law with Community law was considered. Here the claimant only raised the EC law point at the Court of Appeal level (after its claim had been rejected by the Regional Director of taxes) and this new point of law was *time-barred* under the relevant national law (60 days from the certified decision of the tax director). The question here was whether EC law must be interpreted as meaning that a national court hearing a dispute concerning Community law must set aside a provision of national law (here time limits) which it considers makes the power of a national court to apply Community law, which it is bound to safeguard, subject to the making of an express application by the claimant *within a short time limit*, which is not always applied to national law.

7.107   Both cases were really concerned, inter alia, with the question of whether a national rule which presumptively precluded a national court from considering EC law of its own motion was itself compatible with EC law. Again drawing on Article 5 of the Treaty (now Article 4(3) TEU) and the principle of loyal (now sincere) cooperation the Court ruled:

> Each case which raises the question whether a national procedural provision renders application of Community law impossible or excessively difficult must be analysed by reference to the role of that provision in the procedure, its progress and its special features, viewed as a whole, before the various national instances. In the light of that analysis the basic principles of the domestic judicial system, such as protection of the rights of the defence, the principle of legal certainty and the proper conduct of procedure, must, where appropriate, be taken into consideration. (*Peterbroeck* at paragraphs 12–14)

In *Peterbroeck* the Court held that the Belgian rule had to be disapplied because it made the application of EC law *impossible*. Therefore, pursuant to the obligation of cooperation under Article 5 EC (now Article 4(3) TEU), and the principles of non-discrimination and equality and *effectiveness*, a national court must, if necessary, apply directly effective Community law *of its own motion if necessary* provided national law permits or obliges the court to do this for national rules. Thus if a rule of national law prevented the application of Community law, then this must be set aside (paragraph 18).

However, in *van Schijndel* the Court, while reaffirming this principle, took the view that in this case the raising of the new EC point would force the national court to give up its passive role and go beyond what the parties had decided was the dispute, the Belgian rule so disenabled the party from raising the EC point (due to the short time scale) that the rule that made it impossible for the national court to raise the EC point of its own motion could not be justified.

7.108   These cases may seem difficult to reconcile. Jacobs AG (whose views had not been followed in *Peterbroeck* but had been followed in *van Schijndel*) writes

> *The Court was perhaps influenced by the fact that in Peterbroeck the Belgian rule was rather restrictive by comparison with equivalent rules in other member states and should be thought of as a 'hard case' and rather exceptional.*

What do these cases tell us in relation to the autonomy of procedure principle? The two cases do not seem substantially different but it may be that in a case where the national court would really have to abandon its passive role in relation to the parties, too many important justifications for passivity would have to be jettisoned. On the other hand, where the national rule did not have the same scope, but it would nevertheless make the exercise of Union rights impossible, procedural autonomy must give way to supremacy of EU law. Thus:

> *in order to determine whether a given national rule renders the exercise of a Union right excessively difficult, the reasons for the application of that general rule in the context of the case should be examined to see whether it is justified. Thus the question of excessive restrictiveness would seem to depend on the precise details and circumstances of the individual case.*

This complicates the role of the national court and makes prediction difficult because each time the national court will be involved in applying a type of proportionality test whereby the rule in question will have to be analysed in order to ascertain its objective, and whether the means adopted can be justified by some fundamental principle of the domestic legal system. The test is vague and can result in an easy justification for any rule. It may be that this shows that a balance is being struck between procedural autonomy and the principle of effectiveness.

7.109 The following cases seem to show a confirmation of the Court's concern to strike such a balance.

Case C–126/97 *Eco Swiss China Time v Benetton International* (1999); the Court held that if a national court was required by its domestic rules of procedure to grant an application for the annulment of an arbitration award as national rules of public policy had not been observed, it was also obliged to grant such annulment if there had been failure to comply with the prohibition under Article 85(1) EC (now Article 101(1) TFEU). The national rules were subject to strict limits of public policy. Although the Court acknowledged that such strict national limits were necessary in order to safeguard the effectiveness of arbitration proceedings, it was in the interest of uniform interpretation of Community law that an application based on Community law should be granted, as the arbitration body, according to the Court's own case law, was not a court or tribunal within the meaning of Article 177 EC (now Article 267 TFEU), and therefore could not make a preliminary reference itself.

In Case C–302/97 *Konle v Austria* (1999) the Court ruled that any public body which is responsible for causing a breach should make reparation. There is no need in a federal state like Austria to make changes in the distribution of powers of such bodies, but simply to ensure that national procedural rules do not make it more difficult to protect the rights of individuals derived from the Community legal system.

Conclusion

7.110   It is still for the national court to decide the remedy and to follow its own procedures, but clearer guidance now exists on what that remedy should be as well as the validity of national procedure. The principle of effectiveness is paramount. What 'effectiveness' amounts to will vary from case to case, but it must be appropriate (this may be the same as proportionate), adequate (i.e. compensate the victim for actual loss) and readily available, i.e. in practice not excessively difficult. If it is excessively difficult because of procedural rules (as in *Peterbroeck* and in *Eco Swiss China Time*) then the national court is required to raise Union law of its own motion so as to ensure the effective application of EU law. Nevertheless, each case must be considered within its own context and the context includes the procedural rule in question (see above *Peterbroeck* at paragraphs 12–14, set out in **7.107**).

The creation of a uniform Union remedy

7.111   One of the difficulties which those seeking to rely on Union rights may face is that Union law itself inhibits the possibility of a remedy, for example, where as a consequence of the doctrine of horizontal direct effect (see **Section I** above) the claimant cannot enforce a Union right against a private party and hence the wronged claimant can get no remedy at all. But usually this occurs because of the failure of the Member State to implement the directive in question. Until Joined Cases C–6 and 9/90 *Francovich and Bonifaci v Italy* (1991), as has been seen, the Court of Justice had left remedies in the hands of national legal systems, but since that case the Court has departed from this position and laid down a new Union rule of state liability. In *Francovich* Italy had failed to implement Directive 80/987 on the protection of employees in the event of the insolvency of their employer. Although the Directive was held not to be directly effective, the Court held that the protection of Community rights would be weakened if individuals were unable to obtain any effective remedy when their rights were infringed by a breach of Community law for which a Member State can be held responsible. The Court, again drawing on Article 5 of the Treaty (now Article 4(3) TEU), i.e. the obligation of the Member State to ensure fulfilment of the obligations arising out of the Treaty, introduced the principle of state liability to the individual, stating that this created a right to a Community remedy, not a national remedy, which derives from the Treaty and is inherent in its system. Provided that the claimant could show that the right being relied upon was one which could be identified from the Community measure and that a causal link existed between the state's breach of its obligation and the harm suffered by the individual, the state would be liable in damages even if the measure was not directly effective. Thus a successful claimant must in principle be able to recover his loss from the state.

7.112 The principle of state liability is known in most of the Member States which have a civil law system and this was, therefore, not considered to be as major a development by most states as it was by the common law members of the Community.

Although very important, the case left open a number of questions, principally as to the conditions under which liability would arise.

Conditions for liability

7.113 In the long running Joined Cases C–46 and 48/93 *Brasserie du Pêcheur v Germany*, and *R v Secretary of State for Transport, ex p Factortame (Factortame No 3)* (1996) answers to these questions were given by the Court. In those cases Germany and the United Kingdom had respectively been in breach of the Treaty by enacting laws which breached Treaty provisions. The Court ruled that liability would not arise for all breaches; but in those cases where the breach was sufficiently serious in that the state had manifestly and gravely disregarded the limits of its discretion, liability would arise. Where there was no discretion (as in *Francovich*) and the state had simply failed in its obligation under Article 189 EC (now Article 288 TFEU), for example to implement a directive, then, provided that the other *Francovich* conditions were present, that is identifiable individual rights and a causal link, liability would arise. But when the breach occurred in cases where the state had had a wide discretion to make legislative choices, the right to reparation depended not only upon the breach having been sufficiently serious but on a number of other factors. The factors to be considered, with respect to the definition of a serious breach, include: (a) the clarity and precision of the rule breached; (b) the measure of discretion left to the national authorities; (c) the question whether the infringement and damage caused was intentional or involuntary; (d) whether any error of law was excusable; and (e) whether the position of the Community institutions may have contributed towards the Member State's breach of Community law.

7.114 A breach of Union law will be sufficiently serious if it has persisted despite a judgment that has established the infringement, or a preliminary ruling or settled case law of the Court has made it clear that the conduct constituted an infringement. What was not relevant was whether the measure in question creates direct effect, or whether an Article 169 or 170 EC (now Articles 258 and 259 TFEU) action had established the breach.

Case C–140/97 *Rechberger v Austria* (1999) concerned incorrect implementation of the Package Travel Directive 90/314 EEC in two points. Only trips with a departure date of 1 May 1995 or later were protected by the Directive, and instead of providing for full refunds and repatriation costs in the case of insolvency of the travel company, Austria had only provided for insurance cover or bank guarantee. Austria had acceded to the Union on 1 January 1995, and had no discretion in the duty of full implementation. Such incorrect implementation constituted a sufficiently serious breach. Austria's argument was that there was no direct causal link, only the result of a chain of 'wholly exceptional and unforeseeable events'. The Court answered that even such events would not have presented an obstacle to the refund of money or the repatriation of travellers if the Directive had been correctly implemented and found, therefore, that there was a causal link.

The question of damages in relation to state liability under *Francovich*

7.115 When the Court finds that there has been a serious breach as discussed above (**7.114**), and that the measure in question (whether a directive or regulation or Treaty article) creates identifiable rights for the individual seeking to rely on it, and that there is a causal link, the national court must provide a remedy. Where the *right* to damages exists, then it is national law which will determine the nature and extent of damages. The right to full compensation has already been established in *Marshall (No 2)*; exemplary damages for unconstitutional or oppressive conduct must also be available where this is provided for in national law and the total exclusion of profit in the context of economic and commercial litigation is not acceptable, as this would make reparation practically impossible in these circumstances. The Court of Justice has in effect harmonised the conditions for state liability with that of the conditions for liability of the Union institutions under Article 340 TFEU (ex Article 288 EC). (See **8.77**)

The application of state liability

7.116 There have been other cases where the breach has consisted of either non-implementation of directives (as in *Francovich*) or improper implementation of them (*BT* case, below) or improper application of them (*Hedley Lomas*, see below (**7.117**)). The Court has, in applying the principles laid down in *Francovich* and the *Factortame* and *Brasserie du Pêcheur* cases, provided additional qualifications, for example where the state had a wide discretion as in Case C–392/93 *R v HM Treasury, ex p British Telecommunications plc* (1996) (*BT* case) where the issue was concerned with incorrect implementation of a directive. In the *BT* case it was claimed that the Member State could determine which services were to be excluded from its scope, but the United Kingdom had chosen (wrongly as it turned out) to exclude certain services from the operation of the directive. This was held to be improper implementation. The important question was whether the United Kingdom had to pay compensation to the injured party. It was urged that a distinction ought to be drawn between non-implementation as in *Francovich* and improper implementation as here. The Court refused to draw this distinction, but reiterated that the only question was whether the breach was sufficiently serious—i.e. had there been a manifest and grave disregard on the limits on the exercise of its powers? In the instant case the Court found that no such breach had occurred because the wording of Article 8(1) of Directive 90/351 was imprecise and ambiguous and the construction placed on it by the United Kingdom was not manifestly incorrect; furthermore no guidance from the Court existed and the Commission had not raised the matter with the United Kingdom when that country had implemented the Directive in question. This appears to imply that an element of fault has to be present in order for liability to be established.

7.117 On the other hand in Case C–5/94 *R v Ministry of Agriculture, Fisheries and Food, ex p Hedley Lomas (Ireland) Ltd* (1996) the issue of non-compliance with the requirements of Directive 74/577 led to the claimant suing the UK government for loss of profit it had suffered. Hedley Lomas was an exporter of live animals destined for slaughter in Spain; the UK government had systematically refused to grant export licences for this purpose on the grounds that the Spanish slaughterhouses did not observe the provisions of the relevant Directive ensuring a minimum standard of humane treatment for animals sent to slaughter. In the action brought by Hedley Lomas claiming damages for its loss during the period of the ban, the Court declared that the export ban was a quantitative restriction on exports within the meaning of Article 34 EC (now Article 35 TFEU), and was not covered by Article 36 EC (now Article 36 TFEU). The lack of monitoring of slaughterhouses could not excuse the UK from non-compliance with the law:

> In this regard the Member States must rely on trust in each other to carry out inspections in their respective territories.

Where the state has completely failed to implement a directive, that will constitute a serious breach per se. In Joined Cases C–178, 179, 189 and 190/94 *Dillenkofer v Germany* (1996) the Court stated that if the Member State fails to take any measures to achieve the objectives of the directive, that Member State has manifestly and gravely disregarded the limits of its discretion. That gives rise to a right of reparation on the part of the individual, provided that the rights can be identified and a causal link exists as required by *Francovich*.

7.118 In Case C–352/98P *Laboratoires Pharmaceutiques Bergaderm and Goupil v Commission* (2000) the Court said that the concept of a 'sufficiently serious breach' of Community law by an institution must be interpreted in the same way with regard to an institution as it is for a Member State. This concerned an action by a pharmaceutical company and its chief executive, seeking compensation for damage allegedly suffered as a result of the preparation and the adoption of a Commission directive relating to cosmetic products. The Court dismissed the appeal against the judgment of the Court of First Instance and recalled the principle laid down in Joined Cases C–46 and 48/93 *Brasserie du Pêcheur* and *Factortame* (1996) that the conditions under which the Member States may incur liability for damage caused to individuals by a breach of Community law cannot, in the absence of particular justification, differ from those governing the liability of the Community in like circumstances. The protection of the rights which individuals derive from Community law cannot vary depending on whether a national authority or a Community authority is responsible for the damage. As regards non-contractual liability of the Community as well as that of the Member States, the decisive test for finding that a breach of Community law is sufficiently serious is whether the Member State or the Community institution concerned manifestly and gravely disregarded the limits on its discretion. Where the Member State or the institution has only considerably reduced, or even no, discretion, the mere infringement of Community law may be sufficient to establish the existence of a sufficiently serious breach. Moreover, the general or individual nature of a measure taken by an institution is not a decisive criterion for identifying the limits of such discretion.

7.119 In Case C–424/97 *Haim* (2000), the question as to discretion was also raised. Mr Haim, a dentist, brought an action to obtain compensation for the loss of earnings which he claimed to have suffered as a result of the refusal of an association of dental practitioners, a public body, to register him, in breach of Community law. The Court was asked whether, where a national official had no discretion in applying national law conflicting with or in a manner not conforming with Community law the mere fact that he did not have any discretion in taking his decision gives rise to a serious breach of Community law. The Court replied that the existence and scope of the discretion which should be taken into account when establishing whether or not a Member State has committed a sufficiently serious breach of Community law must be determined by reference to Community law and not by reference to national law. The question of discretion was, therefore, not relevant. Liability for reparation for loss and damage caused by non-compliance with Community law lies with any public body which caused the damage.

7.120 There is little doubt that Case C–224/01 *Köbler v Austria* (2003) is one of the most important cases in this respect to come before the Court. Up to that judgment, the question of whether a last instance court in a Member State could be considered as an organ of the state such that would cause the state's liability in the case of an erroneous judgment had not been addressed. Herr Köbler, a university professor, had applied for a special length of service increment related to his pension under the Austrian 1956 Salary Law. This was refused on the basis that his service had not been completed entirely at Austrian universities, but at universities in other Member States. Herr Köbler alleged that this constituted indirect discrimination contrary to Article 39 of the Treaty and Council Regulation 1612/68 on the freedom of movement of workers in the Community. An original reference to the European Court by the supreme Administrative Court had been withdrawn following an inquiry by the EC as to whether the Court wished to maintain its request for a reference in the light of the Court's ruling in Case C–15/96 *Schöning-Kougebetopoulou v Freie und Hansestadt Hamburg* (1998) which gave strong support to Herr Köbler's case as it had held that promotion on grounds of length of service with a public body without taking account of comparable employment in other Member States constituted indirect discrimination. Nevertheless, the Austrian Court then dismissed his claim on the basis that it considered the special increment as a loyalty bonus, which constituted an objective justification for a derogation from the freedom of movement provisions.

On a second reference the fundamental question was raised whether the decision of a national supreme court could give rise to state liability, in the light of the fact that Austrian law expressly precluded state liability in respect of loss and damage caused by decisions of its supreme courts. Not surprisingly, a number of Member States intervened: Germany, France, the Netherlands and the United Kingdom, and the case was heard by the full Court. Many objections were raised, ranging from *res judicata*, the principle of legal certainty and the independence of the judiciary to the judiciary's place in the Community legal order and the comparison with procedures available before the Court to render the Community liable under Article 288 EC (now Article 340 TFEU). The Court held, however, that the principle of state liability must apply even where the infringement is attributable to a supreme court. This was consistent with the decisions in *Francovich* and *Factortame* and with the principle of international law where the state is viewed as a single entity. The principle of state liability for judicial decisions was accepted, albeit subject to restrictive and varying conditions as Advocate General Léger had pointed out in his Opinion at paragraphs 77–82. The European Court of Human Rights also provided for compensation where the Convention was infringed by a court of last instance (see ECtHR *Dulaurans v France*, judgment of 21 March 2000). National courts played an essential role in the protection of the rights of individuals which they derive from Community law. The effective protection of those rights would be weakened if individuals were unable to obtain redress for damage caused by a decision of a supreme court which was in infringement of Community law. This extension of state liability was not incompatible with the principle of *res judicata*: a claim for compensation need not involve the invalidation of the decision giving rise to the damage. In line with settled case law, the Member States themselves would have to designate which courts would determine issues of liability arising from supreme court decisions.

The Court also confirmed that the *Factortame* conditions still applied and considered whether the breach could be seen as being sufficiently serious. However, it then gave a very restrictive interpretation: regard must be had to the special nature of the judicial function and to the legitimate requirements of legal certainty. It stated (in paragraph 53):

> State liability for an infringement of Community law can be incurred only in the exceptional case where the court has manifestly infringed the applicable law.

There was a clear discrimination on the facts and the Austrian Court's decision was incorrect. It then applied the 'sufficiently serious' condition in a very restrictive way, in contrast to the Advocate General's Opinion, and concluded that the court's withdrawal of its reference had simply been based on a misreading of *Schöning* and that, therefore, the infringement could not be regarded as manifest in nature and sufficiently serious. Thus, although the principle of a potential liability of the Member State for breach of Community (now Union) law through an incorrect judgment of a supreme court was acknowledged, the requirements for such a breach to be established appear to be so stringent that the possibility of such a breach, at least at the present time, seems small.

7.121   The *Köbler* judgment was further refined in two cases. In Case C–173/03 *Traghetti del Mediterraneo v Repubblica Italiana* (2006) the Italian court (*Tribunale di Genova*) asked whether state liability of a Member State towards an individual for harm caused by violation of Community law by a supreme court would be excluded if the violation arose from an interpretation of the national law, or an assessment of the facts and the evidence, and whether state liability therefore should only be incurred in case of fault or serious negligence. The Court stated that:

> Community law precludes national legislation which excludes state liability...for damage caused to individuals by an infringement of Community law attributable to a court

adjudicating at last instance by reason of the fact that the infringement in question results from an interpretation of provisions of law or an assessment of facts or evidence carried out by that court.

Community law also precluded legislation which limited such liability solely to cases of intentional fault and serious misconduct on the part of the court 'if such a limitation were to lead to exclusion of the liability of the Member State concerned in other cases where a manifest infringement of the law was committed'.

In Case C–511/03 *Staat der Nederlanden (Ministerie van Landbouw, Natuurbeheer en Visserij) v Ten Kate Holding Musselkanaal BV* (2005) the claimants alleged that they had suffered loss as a result of a failure by the Commission to give an authorisation under Commission Decision 94/381/EC of 27 June 1994 concerning certain protection measures with regard to bovine spongiform encephalopathy and the feeding of mammalian-derived protein, and sought compensation from the Netherlands on the ground that the state had erred in not having brought proceedings against the Commission under Article 232 EC (now Article 265 TFEU). The Court ruled under a preliminary reference by the *Hoge Raad*, the Dutch Supreme Civil Court, that Community law did not impose any obligation on a Member State to bring, for the benefit of one of its citizens, an action against an EC institution under Article 230 EC (now Article 263 TFEU) for annulment of an act adopted by the institution, or under Article 232 EC (now Article 265 TFEU) for failure to act, although it did not in principle preclude national law from providing for such an obligation.

Liability of banks

7.122 There have been a growing number of cases against banking supervisors for alleged negligence or improper conduct. Supervisory action has been made increasingly more accountable by means of legislation (mainly the implementation of European directives). However, up to the present time, EU legislation has avoided putting any provisions on liability for supervisory authorities in its banking directives. It might have been expected that this may be considered not to be necessary if the rules under *Francovich* liability could be applied to supervisory authorities, thus creating a uniform remedy without the need for specific regulation. However, in Case C–222/02 *Peter Paul, Cornelia Sonnen-Lütte and Christian Mörkens v Bundesrepublik Deutschland* (2004) it was made clear by the Court that EU banking directives could not be interpreted in such a way as to give rise to *Francovich* liability of a Member State for deficient prudential supervision of credit institutions.

Depositors with a bank which went bankrupt had lost their deposits. The question was whether Directive 94/19 or the other directives in the field of credit institutions which confer on depositors the right to have the competent authorities take supervisory measures in their interest meant that German legislation which provided for banking supervisory authority to be exercised 'only in the public interest' would be contrary to Community law. The Court answered that the Directive intended to introduce cover for depositors in the event of unavailability of deposits made with a credit institution which was a member of a deposit guarantee scheme. If such compensation, therefore, was guaranteed by the scheme, the Directive could not be interpreted as precluding a national rule to the effect that:

> ...the functions of the national authority responsible for supervising credit institutions are to be fulfilled only in the public interest, which under national law precludes individuals from claiming compensation for damage resulting from defective supervision on the part of that authority.

Commentators have argued that the Court's approach is narrow and that it seems to interpret *Francovich* liability as only arising when a measure confers rights on individuals, whereas this is a condition applying to direct effect, and that it was precisely the difficulties with that condition which the *Francovich* judgment intended to remedy. The Court also seems to have taken a very strict approach in only referring to 'legally enforceable' rights, whereas a more flexible approach might open up a right to compensation if there were more emphasis on the protection of the rights of depositors. This might be more in line with the Court's general approach to state liability and to Article 340 TFEU (ex Article 288 EC) liability, where liability is assessed in accordance with the 'general principles common to the Member States'. It may well be that the *Peter Paul* judgment is a peculiar one on the facts and should not necessarily be seen as a backward step in respect of state liability in general. It may not even be applicable in other areas of prudential supervision, particularly where the interests of investors are regarded as being important.

Environmental criminal liability

7.123 Legislative attempts at adopting a European Union level framework for environmental criminal liability have run into difficulties, as is discussed in **Chapter 15**. The primary motivation for proposals for Union environmental criminal liability rules is that despite the number of Union environmental law provisions there are many cases of major non-compliance and the sanctions currently established by the Member States are generally not sufficient to achieve full implementation of Union law. An institutional dispute between the Council and the Commission, supported by the European Parliament, arose with the Council deciding to act under Third Pillar powers and adopting a limited Framework Decision on Environmental Criminal Liability in the face of Commission insistence that there should be Community (i.e. First Pillar) legislation in this field, and that the legislation needed to be stronger than the Council's Framework Decision. The matter ended up before the Court of Justice. The Court decided in Case C–176/03 *Commission v Council* (2005) (see **15.90**) that the framework decision should be annulled because it encroached upon the powers conferred on the First Pillar—the Community—by the Environment Title of the Treaty and the legislative competence of Article 175 EC (now Article 192 TFEU). The possibility of encroachment on the powers of the Member States in respect of criminal law with directives, and all their potential for supranational effect caused concern in some Member States, but the Commission remained convinced of the need for some Community law measure on environmental criminal liability. The Commission published a Communication on 24 November 2005 which pointed out that the judgment had clarified the distribution of powers between the First and Third Pillars as regards provisions of criminal law. The Court had found (at paragraph 47 of the judgment) that:

> As a general rule, neither the criminal law nor the rules of criminal procedure fall within the Community's competence. However the last-mentioned finding does not prevent the Community legislature, when the application of effective, proportionate and dissuasive criminal penalties by the competent national authorities is an essential measure for combating serious environmental offences, from taking measures which relate to the criminal law of the Member States which it considers necessary in order to ensure that the rules which it lays down on environmental protection are fully effective.

The Commission suggested this reasoning applied generally to all Community policies and freedoms which involve binding legislation with which criminal penalties should be associated in order to ensure their effectiveness. The Commission would have to determine on a case-by-case basis where such criminal law measures were required to ensure the full effectiveness of Community law. This would presumably now apply to all binding legislation, but excepting the CFSP. The Commission made it clear that it does have a 'criminal law policy'.

Application of these principles in the United Kingdom

7.124 In the national law of some Member States, however, state liability for an unlawful act is limited and difficult to establish, and the absence of any judicial remedy is in principle manifestly a breach of the principle of effective protection of EU law. This has created a particular problem for the United Kingdom. In the United Kingdom the right to damages is a private law action and it is not enough to prove a breach by the defendant of his or her Union law rights. Damages will only be available if the defendant's action constitutes a tort, a breach of contract or a breach of a statutory right entitling the defendant to damages. This approach does not fulfil British Union law obligations.

To meet the problem involving enforcement of Community law in the United Kingdom, Lord Denning had, years ago, suggested that we needed a new tort which he suggested should be called 'Breach of Community law', but this was not pursued at the time, and it remained problematic as to how the United Kingdom was to meet its obligations to provide an effective judicial remedy for breach of EC law when no cause of action existed in English law. This is especially true in the case of public authorities, who are given considerable latitude by statute and case law as to how they carry out their obligations. The normal action against a public authority is an application for judicial review, and liability of the Crown when exercising its sovereign powers is not possible unless a tort can be proved. In *Bourgoin SA v Ministry of Agriculture, Fisheries and*

Food (1986) the Court of Appeal had to face this problem when a French exporter of turkeys who had been excluded from the United Kingdom market by an (unlawful) statutory instrument sought compensation for their loss of trade during the period of the ban. As explained above, in English law it is not possible to obtain damages against the Crown unless it can be shown that some tort has been committed. It was suggested there that the tort of misfeasance in public office might be available (as, in an earlier case, the tort of breach of a statutory duty was suggested), but the Crown settled the case and left the matter undecided. In the final stage of the *Factortame* litigation, the House of Lords accepted that there had been a serious breach of Community law by the United Kingdom but rejected the tort of misfeasance in public office, at least for this case, and instead ruled that this had been the tort of breach of statutory duty. This had already been promoted in an earlier case, *Garden Cottage Foods Ltd v Milk Marketing Board* (1982), this despite the fact that in non-EC cases this tort has been applied inconsistently by the Court. However, breach of Union law when based on the *Factortame* criteria, is now the normal right of action in the United Kingdom in actions against public bodies including the Crown.

Although there have been a number of cases since *Köbler*, the Court has generally left it up to the national court to decide whether a breach of Community law has been sufficiently serious. For example, in Case C–278/05 *Robins* (2007) the Court drew the attention of the national court to a number of elements which might have been thought to have shown conclusively that there had not been a sufficiently serious breach. No one knew exactly what the directive in question meant (this concerned Article 8 of Directive 80/987 EEC on the Protection of Employees' rights in case of Insolvency of the Employer, the same Directive as the one involved in the *Francovich* case) and the Commission had never suggested that there was anything wrong with the United Kingdom's implementation of the Directive. The Advocate General thought this should have been sufficient, but the Court sent the matter back to the national court for consideration.

Twenty Years after *Francovich*

7.125 Taking stock 20 years after *Francovich* a number of elements have become apparent. The number of cases post-*Francovich* is small. The highest number of references has been by UK courts, but even that number was only 11 cases. There have been no references from any of the more recent Member States. Commentators suggest that as an enforcement mechanism the value of *Francovich* lies in its deterrent effect, which is only a collateral function of the remedy.

Recent cases have generally indicated that the three *Factortame* requirements: the existence of a rule intended to grant rights to individuals, sufficiently serious breach and a direct causal link, are sufficient to give rise to a right to reparation for individuals. A requirement of fault is not necessary. This is illustrated in Case C–429/09 *Guenter Fuß v Stadt Halle* (2010).

Mr Fuß was a firefighter who worked an average weekly number of hours in excess of the maximum period provided by Directive 2003/88 concerning certain aspects of working time, OJ 2003 L 299/9. Article 6(b) of the Directive lays down a maximum average weekly working time of 48 hours. There is a possibility of derogation in Article 22(1) which, however, requires, inter alia, the agreement of the worker concerned. No worker should suffer detriment by his employer if he is not willing to do so. This derogation option had not been transposed into national law during the relevant period. Mr Fuß claimed reparation for the damage suffered. The Court held that, although the Directive did not expressly provide for sanctions, the principle of state liability was inherent in the system of the EU Treaties. It held that Article 6(b) is a rule of social law of particular importance which is intended to confer rights on individuals and has direct effect. As in previous case law concerning public sector workers in civil protection the Court had already ruled it considered the breach of requirements under Article 6(b) of the Directive a sufficiently serious breach.

The requirement of fault was not held by the Court to be necessary. In *Fuß* German law made a public sector worker's right to reparation subject to the condition of fault by the employer. The Court referred to *Factortame* and held that the three conditions are sufficient to give rise to an individual's right to reparation and that national law was precluded from requiring additional conditions.

7.126   Case C–118/08 *Transportes Urbanos y Servicios Generales* (2010) showed a problem in respect of equivalence. Difference in treatment arose because of the existence of a national system of constitutionality review which, in fact, barred the damages claim of the applicant because of time limits and a requirement of exhaustion of all domestic remedies. The Court found that the principle of equivalence had been breached. If Transportes Urbanos had been able to base its action for damages on a judgment of the Spanish Constitutional Court declaring legislation to be unconstitutional, its action might have succeeded. In fact, the only difference between the two actions was the fact that the breach of the law on which they were based was established on the one hand, by the ECJ based on Article 258 TFEU and , on the other hand, by the Spanish Constitutional Court judgment. (See further **7.92**).

Interim measures as a remedy

7.127   Interim measures are important because the validity of EU law (and sometimes national law) has to be decided by the Court and the time lag requires that rights be preserved pending the decision.

In Case C–213/89 *R v Secretary of State for Transport, ex p Factortame* (1990), for example, the claimant sought an injunction to have the operation of section 14 of the Merchant Shipping Act 1988 disapplied pending the final determination of the legality of that provision by the Court of Justice. An injunction is a temporary order of the Court to maintain a current state of affairs or to prevent the other party doing something which would prejudice the outcome of the case. The application of the effectiveness principle might require an interim measure to be available to the party seeking to rely on EU law. It is for national courts to uphold rights guaranteed by Union law; thus in the United Kingdom, where an injunction could not be granted against the Crown, the Court ruled that such a national legal rule must be set aside. The law now is that the national courts are required to grant injunctive relief according to criteria established for national law but taking into account the need to protect Union law rights. Thus the urgency of the matter, the balance of probabilities of success, and the impact on the outcome are the major factors, i.e. whether there is a substantial risk of irreparable harm if the injunction is not granted.

7.128 When, however, the issue depends either on the validity of a national measure based on the Union regulation, or the validity of the Union measure itself, a different approach to the grant of interim relief has been followed (Joined Cases C–143/88 and C–92/89 *Zuckerfabrik Süderdithmarschen AG v Hauptzollamt Itzehoe and Zuckerfabrik Soest GmbH v Hauptzollamt Paderborn* (1991)). Here the stress has been on upholding the validity of the Community measure; it is presumed to be valid so long as a competent court has not made a finding of invalidity. Serious doubt as to validity must exist, the national court must make a reference to the Court, and, pending that, the suspension of enforcement must retain the character of an interim measure. All national courts must take a uniform approach to this because otherwise the uniform application of Community law would be jeopardised. In Joined Cases C–465 and 466/93 *Atlanta Fruchthandelsgesellschaft mbH v Bundesamt für Ernährung und Forstwirtschaft* (1995) an application for positive interim relief was requested; the applicants wanted the supply of bananas to be continued pending a challenge to the Community measure concerned. The Court upheld its approach in *Zuckerfabrik* (above) stating that the:

> …interim protection which national courts must afford to individuals must be the same, whether they seek suspension or enforcement of national administrative measures adopted on the basis of a Community regulation or the grant of interim measures settling or regulating the disputed legal position or relationships for their benefit (at paragraph 28).

The Court also considered the criteria for interim relief in this kind of case. For the urgency test to be satisfied the damage relied upon must materialise before the Court of Justice can give a ruling on the contested measure, and the national court must take account of the damage which will be caused to the legal regime which the contested measure establishes, including the cumulative effect if other courts adopted similar measures. In particular the national court must respect the balance struck by the Court between the Community interest and the interest of the economic sector concerned.

FURTHER READING

Section I

Bronckers, M., 'From "Direct effect" to "Muted Dialogue": recent developments in the European Courts' case law on the WTO and beyond' (2008) 11 (4) *Journal of International Economic Law* 885–898.

'Case C–188/89 *Foster and Others v British Gas plc*', annotation by E Szyszczak (1990) 27 *Common Market Law Review* 859.

'Case C-194/94, *CIA International SA v Signalson SA and Securitel SPRL*', annotation by P.J. Slot (1996) 33 *Common Market Law Review* 1035.

Coppel, J., 'Horizontal direct effect of Directives?' (1997) 26 *International Law Journal* 69.

de Búrca, G., 'Giving effect to European Community Directives' (1992) 55 *Modern Law Review* 215.

Eeckhout, P., *EU External Relations Law* (2nd edn, Oxford: OUP, 2011).

Jacobs, F., 'Direct effect and interpretation of international agreements in the recent case law of the European Court of Justice' in Dashwood, A. and Maresceau, M. (eds), *Law and Practice of EU External Relations* (Cambridge: CUP, 2008) 13–33.

Mendez, M., (2010) 'The legal effect of Community agreements: maximalist Treaty enforcement and judicial avoidance techniques' 21(1) *European Journal of International Law* 83–104.

Pescatore, P., 'The doctrine of Direct Effect: an infant disease of Community Law' (1983) 8 *European Law Review* 155.

Schermers, H., 'No direct effect for Directives' (1997) 4 *EPL* 529.

Winter, J., 'Direct applicability and direct effect: two distinct and different concepts in Community law' (1972) *Common Market Law Review* 425.

Section II

Aziz, M., 'Sovereignty lost, sovereignty regained? Some reflections on the Bundesverfassungsgericht's Bananas Judgement' (2002–3) 9 *Columbia Journal of European Law* 109–40.

Bradley, A., 'The sovereignty of Parliament: form or substance?' in Jowell and Oliver (eds), *The Changing Constitution* (7th edn, Oxford: OUP, 2011) ch 2.

Craig, P., 'Britain in the European Union', in Jowell and Oliver (eds), *The Changing Constitution* (7th edn, Oxford: OUP, 2011) ch 4.

Dutheil de la Rochère, J., 'Conseil Constitutionnel (French Constitutional Court) Decision No 2004–496' (2005) 42 *Common Market Law Review* 859–869.

van Gerven, W., 'Bridging the gap between Community and national laws' (1995) 32 *Common Market Law Review* 679–702.

Hoffmeister, F., 'Constitutional Implications of EU Membership: a view from the Commission' (2007) 3 *Croatian Yearbook of European Law and Policy* 59–97.

Jacobs, F., 'The evolution of the European Legal Order' (2004) 41 *Common Market Law Review* 303–316.

Kumm, M., 'The Jurisprudence of Constitutional Conflict: Constitutional Supremacy in Europe before and after the Constitutional Treaty' (2005) 11 *European Law Journal* 262–307

Pliakos, A. and Anagnostaras, G., 'Who is the ultimate arbiter? The battle over judicial supremacy in EU law' 36(1) *European Law Review* (2011) 109–123.

Slaughter, A., Stone Sweet, A. and Weiler J.H.H., (eds), *The European Court and National Courts— Doctrine and Jurisprudence: Legal Change in its Social Context* (Oxford: Hart, 1998).

Walker, N., (ed.) *Sovereignty in Transition* (Oxford: Hart Publishing, 2003).

Walker, N., 'The idea of constitutional pluralism' (2002) 65 *Modern Law Review* 317.

de Witte, B., 'Direct effect, supremacy, and the nature of the legal order' in Craig and de Búrca (eds), *The Evolution of EU Law* (Oxford: OUP, 1999) 177–213.

Section III

Biondi, A., 'The European Court of Justice and certain national procedural limits: not such a tough relationship' (1999) 36 *Common Market Law Review* 1271.

de Búrca, G., 'National procedural rules and remedies' in Lonbay and Biondi (eds), *Remedies for Breach of EC Law* (Chichester: Wiley, 1997).

Communication from the Commission to the European Parliament and the Council on the Implications of the Court's Judgment of 13 September 2005 (Case C-176/03 *Commission v Council*) of 24 November 2005 COM(2005) 583 final/2.

Craig, P., 'Once more unto the breach: the Community, the state and damages liability' (1997) 109 *Law Quarterly Review* 67.

Hilson, C., 'The role of discretion in EC law on non-contractual liability' (2005) 42 *Common Market Law Review* 677–695.

Jacobs, F., 'Enforcing Community Rights and Obligations in National Courts: Striking the Balance' in Lonbay and Biondi (eds), *Remedies for Breach of EC Law* (Chichester: Wiley, 1997).

'Joined Cases C-94 and 95/95, *Daniela Bonifaci and Others & Wanda Berto and Others v INPS*; Case C-373/95, *Federico Maso and Others, Graziana Gazzeta and Others v INPS*; and Case C-261/95, *Palmisani v INPS*', annotation by A Odman (1999) 35 *Common Market Law Review* 1395.

Kakouris, C., 'Do the member states possess judicial procedural "autonomy"? ' (1998) 34 *Common Market Law Review* 1389.

Ross, M., 'Beyond *Francovich*' (1993) 56 *Modern Law Review* 55.

Steiner, J., 'From direct effect to *Francovich*' (1993) 18 *European Law Review* 3.

Tison, M., 'Do not attack the Watchdog! Banking Supervisor's liability after *PETER PAUL*' (2005) 42 *Common Market Law Review* 639–675.

Tridimas, T., 'Liability for breach of Community law: growing up and mellowing down?' (2001) 38 *Common Market Law Review* 301.

SELF-TEST QUESTIONS

Section I

1   Do you agree that direct effect is one of the greatest achievements of the European Court of Justice?

2   To what extent is it possible to distinguish between direct applicability and direct effect?

3   Was the European Court of Justice right in not accepting the horizontal direct effect of directives in *Faccini Dori*? Do you agree that the recognition by the European Court of the horizontal direct effect of directives would blur irretrievably the distinction between directives and regulations?

4   Consider the purpose of the doctrine of indirect effect in relation to *Marleasing*. What are the difficulties with this doctrine?

Section II

1   What does the statement that the Community constitutes a new legal order mean? Is this legal order additional to or part of any English legal order?

2   How and why was the doctrine of supremacy developed by the Court of Justice?

3   Compare the attitudes of the German Federal Constitutional Court and the French *Conseil d'Etat* to the European Court of Justice's concept of the primacy of Community law. Are the European Court's views accepted unreservedly? If not, are there similar difficulties in both national jurisdictions?

4   'There are now few remaining obstacles to the acceptance by national courts of the primacy and direct effect of Union law.' Discuss, and consider by what means the remaining obstacles could best be removed.

5   'It is unhelpful to focus the relationship between national and Union law upon constitutional conflicts, creating rules that make up hierarchies. Constitutional clashes are infrequent, and where they arise they require specific solutions with a recognition of the difference giving rise to the clash. Rather, a focus on courts' everyday management of the relationship between national and Union law permits an understanding of common constitutional ground.' Discuss.

Section III

1   What principles does the Court of Justice apply in its assessment of legal remedies?

2   Why was it necessary for the Court to develop case law concerning remedies for Member State breach of Union law?

3   What were the Court's conditions for state liability in *Francovich*? Did the case assist in creating a solution for shortcomings in Union law?

4   What key questions were left unanswered in *Francovich*? Have some answers been found in subsequent cases?

8

Public enforcement of Union law (Articles 258–260 TFEU); review of legality and damages (Articles 263, 265, 268, 277 and 340(2) TFEU)

This chapter focuses on direct actions before the Court of Justice, and is divided into two sections. Section I deals with direct actions relating to public enforcement of EU law between the Commission and Member States (Article 258 TFEU) and between Member States (Article 259 TFEU). The financial consequences of failure to remedy infringements are also covered (Article 260 TFEU). Section II deals with actions challenging the legality of binding institutional acts (action for annulment, Article 263 TFEU; action for failure to act (Article 265 TFEU); plea of illegality (Article 277 TFEU), and briefly examines the action for damages against EU institutions (Articles 268 and 340(2) TFEU)—a Treaty-based action from which parallels can be drawn to the evolution of state liability, through the Court's case law (see **Chapter 7**, in particular **7.111**).

Please note that in general the Lisbon Treaty Articles under the TFEU are referred to. From time to time, it was necessary to refer to the previous Treaty numbers, either as the original numbers under the EEC Treaty and later the EC Treaty after the Maastricht Treaty, or as the updated numbers after the re-numbering in the Amsterdam Treaty.

TFEU 258–260 were Articles 169–171 EEC or EC and Articles 226–228 EC post-Amsterdam. Articles 263, 265, 268, 277 and 340 TFEU were Articles 173, 175, 178, 184 and 215 EEC or EC and Articles 230, 232, 235, 241 and 288 post-Amsterdam.

(I) Public Enforcement of Union law

SUMMARY

The efficacy and uniformity of Union law cannot be guaranteed without effective enforcement mechanisms. In the EU legal system, enforcement is achieved in a 'centralised' manner through the public enforcement powers under Articles 258–259 TFEU, and in a 'decentralised' manner, with private enforcement possible through preliminary references, invoking the doctrines of primacy and direct effect, and ultimately through state liability, as developed by the Court. Section I of this chapter examines the first of these enforcement mechanisms: public enforcement procedures which can be taken by the Commission under

Article 258 TFEU in its role as guardian of the Treaties and, secondly, by the Member States themselves under Article 259 TFEU. Section I covers the following:

• the Article 258 TFEU procedure

• the administrative stage

• the judicial stage

• consequences of the judicial stage (financial penalties, Article 260 TFEU)

• the Commission's discretion

• the Article 259 TFEU procedure

Article 258 TFEU

Introduction

8.1 The Commission has an essential duty under Article 17 TFEU to 'ensure the application of the Treaties and of the measures adopted by the institutions pursuant to them'. In exercising this role as 'Guardian of the Treaties', the public enforcement mechanism under Article 258 TFEU is the most significant and wide-ranging of the weapons available to the Commission to maximise Member States' compliance with Union law. In addition to Article 258, the TFEU grants further specific enforcement procedures to the Commission in particular areas of Union law (for example, supervision of breaches of state aid rules, under Article 108 TFEU). Under Article 271 TFEU (ex Article 237 EC) the Board of Directors of the European Investment Bank and the Governing Council of the European Central Bank are given equivalent powers to those granted to the Commission under Article 258 TFEU.

In entrusting the general Article 258 TFEU procedure to the Commission, the Treaty places the supervision of breaches of Union law by Member States in the hands of a supranational, independent and neutral arbiter and so seeks to secure even-handed enforcement across the Union. This enforcement power is enthusiastically wielded by the Commission. The Commission issues an annual report on the monitoring of the application of Community law which provides details of Member States' infringements, trends of infringement proceedings in areas of law, and provides valuable statistical information on the operation of Articles 258–260 TFEU in the relevant year (The European Commission's 28th Annual Report on Monitoring the Application of EU Law ((COM(2011) 588), available from the Commission's website).

8.2 The Article 258 TFEU enforcement action is now so widely used that the Commission has stated that Article 258 TFEU is not simply a legal device for enforcing Union law, but is also an instrument for achieving policy goals. By choosing to pursue certain breaches of Union law (the Commission has a discretion as to when to take enforcement action (see **Chapter 3**)), the Commission has significant power to influence the development of Union law and policy. The Commission, may, for example, bring an Article 258 TFEU action where there is a genuine difference of opinion between the Commission and the Member State as to the interpretation of the relevant Union law obligation in order to clarify the nature of that obligation. It may, of course, also commence proceedings with the specific intention of condemning the Member State or delivering a warning about the existence of a violation.

A particularly important feature of Article 258 TFEU, however, is the communication channel it establishes between the Commission and the Member States during the pre-litigation phase (see this paragraph below). The Commission has stressed the importance of establishing cooperation and dialogue with national authorities so that recourse to the full Article 258 TFEU procedure, culminating in an action before the Court of Justice, can be avoided. To that end, Commission officials regularly visit Member State authorities in order to encourage cooperation and communication on the application of Union law and resolve possible infringements. During these so-called 'package meetings' Commission officials will consider a set of possible infringements and attempt to achieve non-contentious solutions as far as possible. The Commission views these bilateral meetings as equal in importance to the actions taken in the context of the formal Article 258 TFEU enforcement procedure in dealing with infringements of Union law (*Twelfth Annual Report* on Commission Monitoring and Application of Community Law (1995)) and, indeed, this informal stage may be responsible for the high volume of complaints (approximately 70 per cent) which are closed before a letter of formal notice needs to be sent to a Member State (*Twenty-Fifth Annual Report*, 2008). The increased use of bilateral meetings has been used by the Commission with foresight in order to prevent possible transposition difficulties (and hence, avoid future infringements): for example, some 20 bilateral meetings with Member State authorities were held to facilitate the implementation of the Services Directive (*Twenty-Seventh Annual Report* (2010). The more systematic approach to handling alleged infringements (through initiatives such as 'A Europe of Results' (COM(2007) 502), the EU Pilot scheme and a greater variety of informal tools to promote compliance) has enabled the Commission to continue to negotiate settlements without recourse to litigation in the vast majority of instances.

The communication between the Commission and the Member State during the pre-litigation phase of Article 258 TFEU procedure can therefore serve as a very effective form of alternative dispute resolution. Ultimately, Article 258 TFEU operates at the controversial interface between Member States' Union obligations and independent supranational enforcement. Consequently, the Union exercises political sensitivity when employing Article 258 TFEU.

The application of Article 258 TFEU

8.3 The enforcement mechanism may be triggered when a Member State allegedly fails to comply with an obligation under the Treaties. The range of actions (or omissions) by a Member State that may provoke an enforcement action under Article 258 TFEU include: violating a Treaty provision, or violating Union legislation (for example, through enacting national legislation which expressly violates EU law); administrative acts or judicial decisions which violate or are otherwise contrary to EU law; breaching agreements con-cluded by the Union with a third country or non-compliance with a judgment of the Court of Justice. The most common omission which triggers enforcement action relate to the transposition of Directives: for example, incorrect transposition of a Directive (C–383/92 *Commission v UK* (1994)), delayed transposition, a complete failure to trans-pose a Directive (Case 29/84 *Commission v Germany* (1985)), or failure to communicate details of transposition by the Member State to the Commission. So-called 'non-commu-nication' cases comprise around 22 per cent of the Commission's infringement caseload (*Twenty-Fifth Annual Report* (2010)). Liability can also attach to Member States where the conduct of state agencies causes the Treaty infringement, even where such institu-tions are constitutionally independent (Case 77/69 *Commission v Belgium* (1970)).

8.4 Certain breaches are more prevalent than others. A typical and increasingly popular ground for action by the Commission is breach by the Member State of the Article 4(3) TEU duty of sincere cooperation. Inadequate implementation of Union law, in particu-lar, is vigorously pursued by the Commission. In a majority of cases, the Member State has failed to implement a directive, but failure to bring into force the necessary measures to implement fully a regulation, where implementing measures are necessary, will also be pursued, as in Case 128/78 *Commission v United Kingdom (Re Tachographs)* (1979). In an effort to improve the record of Member States in the transposition of directives and to avoid enforcement action, the Commission organises meetings in the Member States (called directive missions) to consider how the Member State is approaching the imple-mentation of directives and to address any potential problems. Member States appear to be improving with respect to the implementation of directives, however. In its *Eighteenth Annual Report* (COM(2001) 309), the Commission reported a sharp improvement in the transposition rate, with Member States achieving the highest rate since 1992. The Commission was particularly encouraged by the fact that the transposition rate was up across all the Member States. This improvement continued and, by 2004, the situation had further improved even with enlargement. Even the 10 new Member States achieved high percentages of their transposition rates, and by 31 December the average was 97.95 per cent for the 15 'old' Member States, 97.30 per cent for the 10 new members, achiev-ing an EU-wide average of 97.69 per cent. According to European Commission data on the progress of the respective Member States in notifying the transposition of EU direc-tives, Bulgaria and Romania have improved steadily. While in March 2007 Romania was the weakest country of the EU-27 with only 91.4 per cent transposition rate, it was able to gradually improve its performance. In January 2009, it reached 99.30 per cent transposition rate, which made the country rank in ninth place of all Member States. Bulgaria reached a better transposition rate right from the start, so that its improvement in notifying the transposition of EU directives has been less considerable. The country improved its transposition rate from 98.46 per cent in March 2007 to 99.39 per cent in January 2009, putting it in sixth place of the EU-27.

An integrated system for electronic notification of national measures for the transposi-tion of directives came into operation in May 2004 and all 27 Member States now vol-untarily notify national measures for transposition of directives through the Electronic Notification database.

8.5 Alleged violations come to the attention of the Commission either through its own monitoring activities or investigations, or more often, through complaints from individuals or undertakings. In its *Eighteenth Annual Report*, for example, the Commission referred to the importance of complaints from the public in detecting infringements. It is a matter of some controversy that individuals and lobbying groups who complain to the Commission, and who are in fact encouraged to do so by the Commission, do not, as discussed below, have standing before the Union courts to challenge a subsequent refusal to act by the Commission, and that complainants are, in general, peripheral to the enforcement procedure.

The public enforcement mechanism is essentially bilateral action between the Commission and the relevant Member State. Notwithstanding the value of citizens' complaints in highlighting possible violations, efforts have had to be made to manage complainants' expectations of the Article 258 TFEU procedure. Measures to streamline the process for alerting the Commission to possible infringements (e.g. 'CHAP' discussed at **8.24** below) have decreased the proportion of active infringement proceedings originating from citizens' complaints. According to its *Twenty-Fifth Annual Report*, the proportion stood at 53 per cent in 2009, and decreased to slightly over 40 per cent in 2010. This builds on a downward trend evident since the mid-1990s, owing much to the introduction of new working methods at the pre-contentious stage, and corresponding with the Commission's long-standing view that, while it has sought to 'construct a people's Europe whose doors are always open to complainants', the objective of the Article 258 TFEU procedure is to bring an erring Member State back into line and not to provide individual solutions to individual problems (*Fourteenth Annual Report* (1997)). The main purpose of the Article 258 TFEU procedure is thus to induce Member States to comply with their Union obligations and not to protect individuals. The Commission's view is that specific redress for complainants for harm caused by a Member State is generally a matter for the national courts.

The Article 258 TFEU procedure

8.6 The enforcement procedure as set out in Article 258 TFEU involves a number of distinct stages. First, at the pre-contentious stage where an alleged infringement is found by or notified to the Commission, there is a phase of dialogue between the Commission and Member State authorities to ascertain whether a violation is present, and to allow the Member State time to explain the situation and/or reach an agreed solution with the Commission. Where appropriate, much of the pre-contentious phase can be done via the CHAP or EU Pilot methods (see **8.24**). Second, where concerns persist after this dialogue, the formal administrative phase begins with the issue of a letter of formal notice. A second administrative step involves the issue of a reasoned opinion. The standard time limit for Member State responses to the letter of formal notice and reasoned opinion is two months. Where a settlement is not reached at the administrative phase, a minority of infringement proceedings will be referred to the Court of Justice. Following the Court's declaratory judgment, further action to impose financial penalties under Article 260 TFEU is possible, in the event of non-compliance with the Court's judgment on the part of the Member State. The remainder of this section examines the administrative and judicial stages, and the imposition of financial penalties in more detail.

The administrative stage

8.7 The administrative procedure is characterised by dialogue between the Commission and the Member State as resolution of the difficulty is sought—it provides an important channel for communication between Member States and the Commission. The Court of Justice stated in Case 85/85 *Commission v Belgium* (1986) that the purpose of the administrative phase is to give the Member State an opportunity to justify its position or comply with the Treaty requirements of its own accord. It is only when that process fails that the Commission proceeds to demanding compliance.

8.8 The TFEU provides for two stages in the administrative phase; the issuing of a formal letter and, if there is no resolution, the subsequent delivery of a reasoned opinion. Before initiating the formal administrative procedure, however, the Commission will first advise the Member State informally of the alleged breach and request an explanation. Resolution will often arise at this point. If this is not the case, a letter of formal notice which defines the subject matter of the dispute is sent to the Member State. This letter, which will request the Member State to submit its observations within a period of time, usually two months, allows the Member State to prepare its defence. The letter must set out the complaint in general terms, but it is not subject to the strict requirements of precision which apply to the reasoned opinion (see below) as, as the Court of Justice has found, it cannot, by necessity, contain anything other than an initial brief summary of the complaint (Case C–191/95 *Commission v Germany* (1998)). As part of the Commission's drive to improve its working practices in relation to Article 258 TFEU, it is now enforcing the time limit set out in formal letters for responding to the complaint more rigorously. The Commission has also set about, in its own terms, 'dedramatising' the letter of formal notice in order to restore its primary function of seeking observations from the Member State in question. In its *Seventeenth Annual Report* it noted that the letter of formal notice must be used for its true purpose and only request information from the Member State. It must not express the Commission's legal position. The ability of the Member State to respond to the Commission's allegations and submit observations on the complaint as set out in the formal letter is seen as an essential procedural guarantee, adherence to which is an essential formal requirement of the Article 258 TFEU procedure.

Reasoned opinion

8.9 If the issue remains unresolved and the Commission considers that the Member State has failed to fulfil a Treaty obligation, the Commission may then move to the second stage of the administrative phase and deliver a reasoned opinion. Delivery of the reasoned opinion forms a very important part of the Article 258 TFEU procedure and ensures that the Member State is formally and fully informed of the nature of the charges laid against it. The reasoned opinion will state why, in law and fact, the Commission believes that the Member State has violated its Treaty obligations and must be based on the same complaints as are set out in the letter of formal notice. It will give the Member State a reasonable period of time, again, often two months, within which to remedy the alleged breach, failing which the Commission may refer the matter to the Court of Justice. The reasons for the Commission's action must be set out. In Case 274/83 *Commission v Italy* (1985) the Court of Justice interpreted this requirement as an obligation on the Commission to provide a coherent and detailed statement of the reasons leading the Commission to believe that there has been a breach of a Treaty obligation (see also Case 7/61 *Commission v Italy* (1961)). It appears that the reasoned opinion does not have to counter all the arguments made by the Member State in response to the formal letter and, as confirmed by the Court of Justice in Case C–247/89 *Commission v Portugal* (1991), that it need not set out the steps necessary to remedy the breach. The Court of Justice has also consistently held that the content of the legal arguments ultimately made by the Commission before the Court of Justice (if the action proceeds to the judicial phase) must be largely the same as the content of the reasoned opinion (Case C–52/90 *Commission v Denmark* (1992) and Case C–217/88 *Commission v Germany* (1990)). As a result, the Commission may not raise complaints in its application before the Court of Justice which have not been covered in the reasoned opinion. It is clear, however, that although the reasoned opinion and the proceedings must be broadly based on the same complaints as are set out in the letter of formal notice, it is not necessary that in every case they are exactly the same as long as the subject matter of the proceedings has not been extended or altered, just limited.

Weaknesses in the reasoned opinion may, in certain circumstances, be remedied by the Commission's conduct during the informal procedure. This was the case in Case 23/84 *Commission v United Kingdom* (1986), where certain UK milk pricing rules were at issue. During the informal negotiations, the Commission had highlighted the fact that the compatibility of price differentiation criteria in the milk products market with Community rules could be assessed independently of any effects such criteria had on the functioning of the common organisation of the milk market. Neither the letter of formal notice nor the reasoned opinion had explicitly raised this point. Nevertheless, the Court of Justice allowed such an argument to be made as it had been flagged during the informal stage. The application to the Court of Justice must state the specific grounds for the action. It is not sufficient simply to refer to the reasoned opinion (Case C–347/88 *Commission v Greece* (1990)). It is clear from Case 48/65 *Lütticke v Commission* (1966) that the reasoned opinion cannot be challenged as an act of the Commission under Article 263 TFEU as it is not a binding act. The Court of Justice found in that case that no measure taken by the Commission during the administrative stage has any binding force, and that as a result annulment actions by third parties were, in principle, inadmissible. The Member State may, however, challenge the legality of the reasoned opinion at the judicial phase of the Article 258 TFEU action.

8.10 The nature and purpose of the reasoned opinion was examined by the Court of Justice in Case C–191/95 *Commission v Germany* (1998) in the context of the application of the principle of collegiality and collective responsibility to members of the Commission. Germany challenged the issue of a reasoned opinion to it in respect of its alleged failure to implement correctly certain company law directives concerning the disclosure of annual accounts, on the grounds that the members of the Commission did not have sufficient information made available to them when making the decision to issue the reasoned opinion. The Commissioners had not seen the draft reasoned opinion. The Court confirmed that a decision to issue a reasoned opinion (or to commence judicial proceedings) was subject to collegiality and that, accordingly, the information necessary to reach that decision should be available to each Commissioner, although it was not necessary for the Commission to decide on the exact wording. The Court described the decision to issue a reasoned opinion as neither an administrative nor managerial decision but, as the reasoned opinion formally stated the infringement and concluded the pre-litigation procedure, one which was part of the supervisory function entrusted to the Commission under Article 155 of the Treaty (now set out in Article 11(1) TEU) and which could not be delegated. The Court also noted that the issue of a reasoned opinion was a preliminary procedure without binding legal effect for its addressees and was merely a stage which might lead to judicial proceedings. If settlement was not forthcoming after its issue, the reasoned opinion then served to define the subject matter of the dispute.

8.11   If the Member State fails to comply with the reasoned opinion, the Commission may then, using the reasoned opinion as the basis for the action, initiate legal proceedings before the Court of Justice. It is under no obligation to bring an action. It is clear from *Lütticke* that the decision to initiate proceedings is a matter entirely for the Commission's discretion.

8.12   The conduct of the Commission during the administrative phase is subject to review. At the judicial stage, the Court of Justice may examine the Commission's actions during the administrative phase for procedural irregularities and declare the action void for infringement of an essential procedural requirement if the Commission does not comply with the procedural guarantees under Article 258 TFEU. One essential element of the administrative stage is that the Member State be given the opportunity to respond to the allegations. In Case 51/83 *Commission v Italy* (1984), where the Commission took an Article 258 TFEU action against an alleged violation by Italy of Article 30 EC (now Article 34 TFEU), the Court explained that the opportunity for the Member State to submit its observations was an essential guarantee required by the Treaty and an essential formal requirement of the Article 258 TFEU procedure. In that case, the reasoned opinion raised issues which had not been covered in the letter of formal notice, and so Italy had not been in a position to offer its observations fully. The Member State is not, however, required to offer observations. The Member State must also be granted a reasonable time within which to respond to the letter of formal notice and to remedy the breach following the issue of the reasoned opinion. The Court of Justice uses a reasonableness standard in assessing the appropriateness of the time period granted to the defaulting Member State. In Case 293/85 *Commission v Belgium* (1988), an Article 258 TFEU action by the Commission against Belgium, for not implementing a decision of the Court of Justice in an earlier case, was dismissed as the Belgian authorities had not been given adequate time to respond to the letter of formal notice or comply with the reasoned opinion. The Court of Justice held that in assessing whether the time period granted was reasonable, it would examine all the factors in the case, including whether the action was urgent, although it would take into account whether the urgency arose from a failure by the Commission to take action earlier and whether the Member State had been aware of the Commission's position prior to the commencement of the Article 258 TFEU procedure. The Commission had been aware of the alleged violation for several months before sending the letter of formal notice, which gave Belgium a mere eight days to respond, and issuing the reasoned opinion, which gave the Member State 15 days to respond. The Court of Justice made clear that the Commission could not rely on urgency which had developed through its own failure to take action earlier. In Case 85/85 *Commission v Belgium* (1986), by contrast, the Court of Justice found that allowing less than two months to elapse between the issue of the letter of formal notice and the ultimate issuance of proceedings was, in the circumstances, reasonable. An important factor in that case was that significant communication took place with Belgium during the informal stage. Further, Belgium had not challenged the Commission view at any point during the informal procedure, nor had it in any way attempted to comply with the wishes of the Commission. Conversely, in general the pre-litigation procedure must not be of such excessive duration that the Member State's right to a defence is infringed in that the delay makes it more difficult for the Member State to rebut the Commission's arguments (Case C–207/97 *Commission v Belgium* (1999)).

8.13 The Commission's actions are also subject to scrutiny by the European Ombudsman (see Article 228 TFEU). The European Ombudsman is charged with dealing with instances of maladministration by Union institutions and bodies and so may conduct investigations into the conduct of Article 258 TFEU proceedings by the Commission. In one instance, the issuing of a press release announcing a decision to terminate infringement proceedings before the complainant was informed was criticised, and the Commission modified its procedures accordingly.

The judicial stage; interim measures

8.14 Once the judicial stage has commenced, but not before, the Commission may apply for interim measures under Article 279 TFEU. Article 279 TFEU, curiously, gives the Court of Justice wider powers at the interim stage of the judicial procedure than during the full action. The Court of Justice may, under Article 279 TFEU, suspend the application of any contested act or grant any necessary interim measures. The main action, by contrast, may only result in a declaration that the Member State has failed to fulfil a Union law obligation. It is clear, however, from Article 83(2) of the Rules of Procedure of the Court of Justice that such measures may not be granted unless there are circumstances giving rise to urgency, and factual and legal grounds establishing a *prima facie* case for the measures to be granted. The grant of interim measures must not prejudge the points of fact or law at issue. In Case C–180/96 *United Kingdom v Commission* (1996) the Court, in the context of an application by the United Kingdom to suspend a Commission decision banning the export of British beef to the EC, reiterated that showing the requisite urgency involves establishing that the Article 186 EC (now Article 279 TFEU) measure sought must be granted to avoid serious and irreparable harm, and that the interests at stake must also be balanced. In Case C–246/89R *Commission v United Kingdom* (1989) the Commission took action against the United Kingdom under Article 169 EEC (now Article 258 TFEU) on the basis that the Merchant Shipping Act 1988, which required that vessels registered in the United Kingdom be under British ownership, was contrary to the Treaty. The Commission requested that an interim order be made suspending the nationality requirements of the Act. After an examination of the UK interests at stake, the Court of Justice found that the Commission had made out a *prima facie* case based on the putative directly effective rights of the Spanish fishermen who were prohibited from fishing as a result of the nationality requirement. The issue was also seen as sufficiently urgent, as Spanish firms were suffering serious economic loss as a result of the contested Act (see further **Chapter 7, Section II**).

The main action

8.15 It is clear from Case 240/86 *Commission v Greece* (1988) that the Commission may proceed with the legal action even if the Member State remedies the breach after expiry of the time limit set in the reasoned opinion (although it may not if the Member State acts within the time limit). In that case Greece claimed that the action by the Commission before the Court of Justice was inadmissible as it had lifted the requirement that cereal importers hold a foreign currency permit approved by the Bank of Greece, which the Commission alleged was in breach of Treaty obligations, before the judicial action commenced. The Court of Justice found that Greece had not complied with the reasoned opinion within the stated time limit and so the action by the Commission was admissible. The Court confirmed this point in Case C–355/98 *Commission v Belgium* (2000) where it stated that the question of whether a Member State had fulfilled its obligations was to be determined by the situation prevailing in the Member State at the end of the period set out in the reasoned opinion. Member States will often request that judicial proceedings be stayed in order that the Commission can assess new developments, but the Court of Justice usually looks unkindly on such applications on the ground that it is for the Commission, on expiry of the time limit, to decide whether or not to bring an action and that, accordingly, once it has decided to proceed, it would be inappropriate for the Court to stay the proceedings (Case C–212/98 *Commission v Ireland* (1999)). The Member State may concede the action before judgment but after the action has commenced, in which case the Commission may ask that the case be removed from the register. Alternatively, it may continue to pursue the action as the Commission may consider it important to secure a determination that a breach had actually occurred to affirm or clarify the relevant principles of EU law. It may also, as the Court confirmed in *Commission v Greece* (1988), be important to establish a basis for the liability of a defaulting Member State, as such a determination may be significant in establishing rights which might accrue to third parties, particularly in the light of *Francovich* liability (see **Chapter 7, Section III**).

The Court of Justice then examines the merits of the case (together with any breaches of procedural requirements as already outlined) and determines whether a breach of Union law has occurred. An objective finding of failure to comply with Union obligations is sufficient for a successful Article 258 TFEU application by the Commission. Further proof of inertia or opposition by the Member State is not required (Case 301/81 *Commission v Belgium* (1983)). Equally, the fact that the failure had no adverse effects is not relevant to the finding of an infringement (Case C–150/95 *Portugal v Commission* (1997)).

Defences

8.16   As a general rule, the Court will not look on the various excuses offered by Member States in respect of their failure to comply with EU obligations with a kindly eye. In 128/78 *Tachographs*, the excuse offered by the United Kingdom that practical difficulties (there was significant resistance to the introduction of the tachograph or 'spy in the cab' among transport trade unions) were behind the failure to implement fully the Tachograph Regulation was given short shrift. The Court held that unilateral breaches of EEC law, driven by a Member State's own conception of its national interest, brought into doubt the principle of the equality of Member States and would not be tolerated. In a similar vein, the defence of necessity has not found favour with the Court. In Case 7/61 *Commission v Italy* (1961) Italy, in breach of the Treaty, suspended the importation of certain pig-meat products claiming that such action was necessary due to a serious crisis in the pig-meat market. The Court rejected the argument as to necessity and urgency, finding that the Treaty itself contained appropriate procedures, at that time, for dealing with emergencies. Similarly, internal legal, constitutional or administrative difficulties will not avail a Member State.

8.17   Predictably, the Court of Justice has dispatched in robust terms any contention, based on the public international law principle of reciprocity, that breach by other Member States or by a Union institution allows the defaulting Member State to withdraw from its Union obligations. In Joined Cases 90 and 91/63 *Commission v Luxembourg and Belgium* (1964) Luxembourg and Belgium maintained duties on import licences for milk in violation of the Treaty. They claimed in their defence that the Council had failed to put in place Community measures on the common organisation of the milk market, as it was required to do. The Court rejected this contention stating that the new Treaty legal order, which included the procedures for the identification and supervision of breaches of EEC law, was not limited to reciprocal obligations. Failure by a Community institution to carry out its obligations did not release a Member State from its EC obligations. The same analysis applies to excuses based on non-compliance by other Member States. In Case C–146/89 *Commission v United Kingdom* (1991) the United Kingdom had extended its baseline for fishing purposes in breach of EEC rules. In the course of the judicial proceedings the United Kingdom pointed out that other Member States had made similar adjustments but the Court simply referred to what it termed the well-established principle that implementation of EEC law by Member States could not be made subject to a condition of reciprocity.

8.18   While it accepts the possibility of *force majeure*, the Court is not usually sympathetic to such claims. In Case 101/84 *Commission v Italy (Transport Statistics)* (1985) Italy had breached a Community directive by not submitting certain statistical information on road transport, but raised *force majeure* as the relevant data-processing centre had been bombed. The subsequent delay of four and a half years, however, was found to be unacceptable, with the Court finding that while *force majeure* might have applied at the time, it only applied for the length of time that an administration exercising a normal degree of diligence would require to replace the equipment and provide the data.

8.19 Finally, another defence raised at times by Member States is that while Union law may not be applied as a matter of law, administrative practices are such that, in fact, Union law is actually applied. The Court has rejected this contention on the grounds that the very existence of national law which breaches Union obligations gives rise to uncertainty. In Case C–381/92 *Commission v Ireland* (1994) the administrative practices followed by Ireland (it had informally notified the relevant inspectors in the beef industry as to what actions were required to comply with the directives in question, which had not been officially implemented) did not absolve Ireland from its breach of EC law.

8.20 While in the judicial proceedings the Commission may not extend the complaint beyond the scope of the formal letter and reasoned opinion, the Member State is not similarly barred from raising defences which it had not previously referred to during the pre-litigation procedure. In Case C–414/97 *Commission v Spain* (1999), in an action concerning an infringement of the Community VAT rules, the Commission sought to prevent Spain from raising pleas which had not been raised during the pre-litigation period. The Court found that any requirement to raise all defences in advance during the pre-litigation period would be contrary to the general principle of respect for the rights of the defence. Proper conduct of the pre-litigation procedure was an essential guarantee required by the Treaty, not only to protect the Member State, but to clearly define the subject matter. Once the subject matter was defined, however, the Member State had the right to raise all pleas available to it.

Consequences of the judicial phase: financial penalties under Article 260 TFEU

8.21 The result of the legal proceedings, should the Court of Justice find that there has been a violation, is a declaration that the Member State has failed to fulfil an obligation under the Treaty. Article 260(1) TFEU provides that the Member State must then act to rectify the situation by taking 'the necessary measures to comply with the judgment of the Court of Justice'.

This declaratory remedy is not, however, completely satisfactory. The Court has often repeated (see for example Case C–291/93 *Commission v Italy* (1994)) that while Article 260 TFEU does not itself state a time limit for compliance, on interpretation it does require that the necessary action be undertaken immediately. Member States have, however, on occasion, taken a very long time to comply with the judgment. This behaviour can undermine the uniformity and efficacy of Union law. In such cases, the only course of action available to the Commission prior to the Maastricht TEU was a second Article 175 EEC action for breach of Article 173 EEC (now Articles 260 and 258 TFEU).

8.22 This inherent weakness in the infringement procedure was addressed, to a certain extent, through the introduction of a further procedure to impose financial penalties by the Maastricht TEU. Prior to the Treaty of Lisbon, if the Member State defied the

Court's declaratory judgment following infringement proceedings, the Commission had the option of taking a further administrative procedure involving similar stages as the infringement procedure (a fresh pre-contentious stage giving the erring Member State the opportunity to submit observations, a fresh letter of formal notice and a new reasoned opinion) to bring an action under Article 228 EC (now Article 260 TFEU) for the imposition by the Court of Justice of a 'lump sum or penalty payment' if the Member State failed to comply with the second reasoned opinion. Changes made by the Treaty of Lisbon amended this process in two ways. Firstly, Article 260(2) TFEU was amended, dropping the requirement for a new reasoned opinion to be issued to the erring Member State. However, the Member State still has the opportunity to defend its position at the initial informal stage and in response to the new letter of formal notice. Second, Article 260(3) TFEU was added, providing that even where the Commission brings a case before the Court for the first time against a Member State which has not notified measures transposing a directive, it may specify the amount of the lump sum or penalty payment to be paid by the Member State in question as that 'which it considers appropriate in the circumstances'. However, if the Court finds an infringement, the amount of the penalty payment or lump sum it imposes may *not* exceed the amount specified by the Commission and the payment obligation takes effect on the date set by the Court in its judgment. In assessing the level of the daily fine, the Commission takes account of the gravity of the breach, the duration of the breach and the ability of the Member State to pay, with a view to the need for a dissuasive effect (see further, Commission Communications (SEC(2005) 1658), (SEC(2010) 923), (SEC(2010) 1371) and (SEC(2011) 1024)). The decision as to whether to impose a periodic penalty payment or lump-sum penalty lies squarely with the Court (Case C–121/07 *Commission v France* (2008)).

The penalty provisions appear to be proving effective, and the Statistical Annexes to the Commission's Annual Reports consistently show that the vast majority of Member States respond to penalty decisions by rapidly coming into line with Union law, either before the case is referred to the Court or shortly afterwards. In 2000, the first fine was imposed on a Member State under Article 228 EC (now Article 260 TFEU). The Court ordered Greece to pay a penalty payment in respect of its failure to comply with an earlier judgment of the Court concerning environmental obligations (Case C–387/97 *Commission v Greece* (2000)). In its ruling, the Court emphasised that the Commission's guidelines on the levying of penalties do not bind the Court, but are a useful point of reference. It found that the penalty must be appropriate to the circumstances and proportionate to the breach and the Member State's ability to pay. The Court also found that the degree of urgency that the Member State in question should fulfil its obligations could vary, depending on the breach. The basic criteria which should be taken into account in setting the penalty were, therefore, the duration of the infringement, its degree of seriousness and the ability of the Member State to pay. The Court imposed a penalty of €20,000 per day (from the date on which the judgment was originally served), down from the Commission's proposal of €24,600 per day. In Case C–278/01 *Commission v Spain* (2003) the Court was more severe with Spain in imposing a penalty payment of €624,150 per day and per 1 per cent of bathing areas in Spanish inshore waters for not complying with the Court's judgment in Case C–92/96 *Commission v Spain* (1998) which declared the failure of Spain in its obligation to implement Bathing Water Directive 76/160.

In Case C–304/02 *Commission v France* (2005) the Court imposed for the first time both a penalty payment and a lump sum fine. France had failed to comply with the Court's judgment in Case C–64/88 *Commission v France* (1991) requiring it to stop selling undersize fish and was 'maintaining a lax attitude in respect of infringements'. Although the Commission only asked for a periodic penalty the Court ordered France to pay a lump sum fine of €20 million and a penalty payment of €56,761,250 for each additional six-month period during which it failed to comply. The Court pointed out that the Commission's suggestions do not bind the Court and that the Court may exercise its discretion to set a penalty payment appropriate to the circumstances and proportionate to the breach that has been established and to the relevant Member State's ability to pay.

In Case C–77/04 *Commission v France* (2006) the Court had to decide another relatively rare action for failure to fulfil obligations under Article 228 EC (now Article 260 TFEU). France argued that the fact that the Commission had reformulated the complaints against it during the proceedings had rendered the action inadmissible. The Court held that the requirement that the subject matter of the proceedings is circumscribed by the pre-litigation procedure cannot go so far as to mean that in every case, the operative part of the reasoned opinion and the form of order sought in the application must be exactly the same, provided that the subject matter of the proceedings had not been extended or altered but simply limited. This allowed the Commission to mitigate its complaint because it could take account of partial measures to comply, adopted during the course of the proceedings. Nevertheless, the Court established that the breach still subsisted at the date of the Court's examination of the facts, and therefore decided to impose a lump sum penalty as well as a periodic penalty payment. The Court recalled the purpose of such a fine: both penalties are intended to place the Member State concerned under economic pressure, inducing it to put an end to the infringement. Both payments are decided upon according to the degree of persuasion needed for the Member State to alter its conduct. The Court has discretion to set a penalty payment in the light of the basic criteria. Regard is also to be paid to the effects of failure to comply with private and public interests and to the urgency of inducing the Member State concerned to fulfil its obligations.

The Court repeated that the guidelines for this—as set by the Commission—while helpful, did not bind the Court and it ordered the Member State to pay a penalty higher than that proposed by the Commission.

A recent example of a Member State citing the financial crisis affecting the Eurozone as a basis for challenging the level of penalty imposed was decided in Case C–407/09 *Commission v Greece* (2011). The case concerned Greece's failure to comply with an earlier judgment of the Court which had found that Greece failed to transpose Directive

2004/80/EC relating to compensation to crime victims, on time. The Greek authorities had argued in defence that the financial and political difficulties (including calling early elections) had prevented compliance. In particular, the Greek authorities were unable to guarantee that the funds were available to comply with the compensation scheme envisaged by the Directive, and the early election necessitated the domestic process of transposing the Directive to re-start. In its judgment, the Court reiterated its long-standing position that a Member State cannot rely on issues affecting its domestic legal order to justify non-compliance. The Court emphasised that all relevant factors should be taken into account when determining the level of financial penalty; the penalty should remain appropriate and proportionate to the breach. So whilst the long duration of the breach (29 months—albeit resolved by the time the Court set the penalty), and the fact that the breach affected fundamental rights and freedoms in the context of free movement of persons weighed heavily in favour of a severe penalty, the Court also took account of Greece's compromised ability to pay, on the basis of economic data provided to the Court. On that basis, an arguably modest lump-sum penalty of €3million was imposed.

8.23 Individuals who suffer harm as a result of a breach of Union law by a Member State can bring an action for damages against the Member State under the *Francovich* principle (see **7.115**). Significantly, in Case C–46/93 *Brasserie du Pêcheur SA v Germany* (1996) the Court confirmed that a breach of Community law would be considered sufficiently serious (as required by the tests for establishing state liability) if it has persisted despite a ruling finding that an infringement of Community law had been established (see **7.114**). In some respects this is, perhaps, the most effective deterrent of all.

Commission discretion

8.24 The Commission will not pursue every infringement of EU law by a Member State under Article 258 TFEU. While the Commission has a duty under Article 17 TEU to ensure that the Treaty is applied, it is not under a parallel obligation to take proceedings against a Member State at any stage of the Article 258 TFEU process. The Commission alone is competent to decide whether it is appropriate to issue the letter of formal notice, issue the reasoned opinion, or take the Member State before the Court of Justice (Case C–207/97 *Commission v Belgium* (1999)). Workload pressures and political considerations each play a part in deciding which infringements to pursue. The Commission is not, therefore, as relentlessly even-handed as one would expect from a neutral enforcer of Union law. Article 258 TFEU operates at the level of inter-institutional relations, with the Commission fulfilling a politically sensitive role in policing the application and implementation of EU law by the Member States and it is not mechanically applied to all violations.

Recent Annual Reports have suggested that the Commission is becoming increasingly strategic in exercising its discretion, its *Twenty-Fifth Annual Report* stressing that to maximise the benefit to citizens and business, 'the Commission must prioritise work on infringements having the greatest impact on the general good'. There is clear evidence that the Commission's enforcement role must be more targeted in an enlarged Union. Its Annual Reports identify the legal fields in which the highest numbers of alleged infringements take place (the 2010 Annual Report showing that environment, internal market and taxation are the most infringement-prone policy areas, accounting for 52 per cent of all infringement cases), and the legal fields which are responsible for the most new infringements (in 2010, health and consumer protection accounted for the highest number of *new* infringement cases (the vast majority being non-communication cases; followed by environment and internal market)). These statistics may help the Commission in its use of resources in monitoring and managing the infringement process.

Two areas where the Commission is becoming particularly proactive relate to management (pre-infringement) tools and to preventative measures. Focus on improving management of the Commission's enforcement role has developed in the context of the 'Europe of Results' initiative (COM(2007) 502). 'CHAP' (registry of complaints and enquiries, operational since September 2009) and 'EU Pilot' (problem-solving with Member States, operational since April 2008) are two recent innovations which aim to create a more streamlined and efficient management of complaints and enquiries, promoting their investigation and negotiated resolution as early as possible. In 2010, 4035 cases were registered via the CHAP database; 52.5 per cent were closed following the Commission's initial response, and a further 14 per cent were closed due to lack of competence. Of the remaining 17 per cent of complaints which were investigated further via EU Pilot, 9 per cent led to the initiation of formal infringement proceedings. The EU Pilot project serves a similar function vis-á-vis citizens' complaints, but the initiative also promotes inter-institutional engagement on complaints and enquiries. Member States have gradually become involved with EU Pilot, with all Member States except Luxembourg and Malta currently involved. Complaints lodged in CHAP which cannot be automatically addressed by the Commission are transferred to EU Pilot, at which point further factual or legal information can be sought, and the relevant Member State given an opportunity to suggest a solution to the alleged infringement. Where negotiated solutions to complaints are not reached, they are transferred to the Commission's infringement database (NIF) for activation of the formal infringement procedure. The Commission's own-initiative cases begin in EU Pilot, where Member States are participating in the scheme. In the first two years of the EU Pilot scheme, some 160 cases triggered the administrative phase of infringement proceedings under Article 258 TFEU, with some 81 per cent of complaints resolved at the earliest stages.

Use of these initiatives is enabling the Commission to approach its enforcement role in a more systematised manner, maximising opportunities to negotiate solutions with Member States at early stages in the process. The initiatives involve citizens in a more transparent complaints process, and should ultimately enable the Commission to target its resources on the most serious infringements.

An added benefit for Member States has been the Commission's increased focus on prevention of infringements. The Commission is seeking to pre-empt problems with transposition and application of new legislation by emphasising prospective application of EU law in impact assessments, and promotes implementation plans to support transposition of new directives. The Commission sees implementation plans as an opportunity to do what is essentially an implementation 'risk assessment'—to identify obstacles to achieving timely and correct implementation of the relevant legislation in Member States, and to identify actions which can counter such risks. Whilst implementation plans are not routinely produced in tandem with all draft directives, efforts are being made to draw up implementation plans in the sectors where infringements are particularly prevalent (environment, internal market, and more recently health and consumer protection). These tools aiming to prevent problems with implementation—and avoid future infringement proceedings—are supplemented with other mechanisms such as the SOLVIT internal market network, operational since 2003 and aimed at tackling conduct complained of by the general public through closer cooperation between national authorities and the exchange of good practice; written materials (such as guidelines, handbooks); and specific events (seminars, bilateral meetings) also feature in some areas.

The Article 259 TFEU procedure

8.25 The procedure in Article 259 TFEU largely tracks Article 258 TFEU. Under Article 259 TFEU, a Member State may take enforcement action against another Member State where it considers that the Member State has failed to fulfil an EU law obligation. While Article 4(3) TEU provides that Member States have a duty to take all appropriate measures to ensure the fulfilment of obligations under the Treaty, enforcement action by Member States is, inevitably, much rarer due to the likely political ramifications.

8.26 The Member State wishing to bring an Article 259 TFEU action against another Member State before the Court must first bring the matter before the Commission. The Commission then plays a vital role in easing tension between the Member States. The Commission is required to deliver a reasoned opinion after each Member State involved has been given the opportunity to present its case and submit observations both orally and in writing. If the Commission does not issue a reasoned opinion within three months, the Member State may still proceed with a legal action before the Court. The result of such an action, if the case is made out, will be a declaration that the Member State failed to fulfil an obligation under EU law. The Member State will then be required to take remedial action under Article 260 TFEU and may be subject to fines if it does not comply.

8.27 Article 259 TFEU actions are extremely rare as, for political reasons, Member States are very reluctant to tackle each other directly and usually rely on the Commission to take action where necessary. In one infamous example, France claimed that UK fish conservation measures were contrary to Community law and initiated an Article 172 (now Article 259 TFEU) action (Case 141/78 *France v United Kingdom* (1979)). The Court ultimately found in favour of France. A more recent example can be found in Case C–388/95 *Belgium v Spain* (2000): Belgium commenced infringement proceedings against Spain before the European Court of Justice for alleged breach of the provisions of the Treaty relating to free movement of goods. Belgium argued that the Spanish rules which require Rioja wine to be bottled in cellars in the region of production in order to qualify for the 'controlled designation of origin' (*denominacion de origen calificada*) were detrimental to the free movement of goods. The Court of Justice held that the Spanish rules where to be regarded as compatible with Community law despite their restrictive effect on trade as they constituted a necessary and proportionate means of upholding the great reputation of the Rioja controlled designation of origin. In a recent example, an Article 227 EC (now Article 259 TFEU) action reached the Court despite the Commission's decision not to issue a reasoned opinion due to the political sensitivities involved (Case C–145/04 *Spain v UK* (2006)). The Spanish claim against the manner in which the UK provided European Parliamentary voting rights to the citizens of Gibraltar was dismissed.

(II) Review of Legality and Damages

SUMMARY

This section examines how the legality of acts of Union institutions are reviewed by the Union Courts. It discusses:

- Actions for annulment: Article 263 TFEU
- Reviewable acts
- *Locus standi*
- Privileged, semi-privileged and non-privileged applicants
- Time limitations
- Grounds for annulment
- Effects of an annulment
- Actions for failure to act: Article 265 TFEU
- *Locus standi* under Article 265 TFEU
- Indirect challenge and the plea of illegality: Article 277 TFEU
- Contractual and tortious liability: Articles 268 and Article 340(2) TFEU
- Jurisdiction of the Court under Article 7 TEU

Action for annulment: Article 263 TFEU

8.28 Article 263 TFEU empowers the Court of Justice of the European Union to review the legality of binding institutional acts. Reflected in some form in almost all Member States' legal systems, but largely modelled on French administrative law, Article 263 TFEU is an important safeguard against abuses of authority by Union institutions and is a key element of the Union system of judicial review.

Reviewable acts

8.29 The range of acts subject to review under Article 263 TFEU has been interpreted broadly by the Court of Justice and covers institutional acts which have binding effects. Article 288 TFEU lists the binding acts which may be adopted by the Union institutions (regulations, directives and decisions), but in determining whether the contested measure is reviewable, and in the light of its oft-repeated view that Article 263 TFEU not be interpreted restrictively (as expressed in the *ERTA* case discussed below, see **8.30**), the Court of Justice looks to the nature and effect of the measure and does not simply consider its form.

8.30 As long ago as Case 22/70 *Commission v Council (ERTA)* (1971) the Court of Justice ruled that a Council resolution which set out the position to be taken by the Council in the preparation of a European road transport agreement could be challenged under Article 263 TFEU (at this time Article 173 EEC), despite the Council's argument that the measure was simply a coordination of policies among Member States. The Court considered that the contested resolution was binding and was designed to have legal effects on relations between the Commission and the Member States and on inter-institutional relationships. The Court stated that Article 173:

> [t]reats as open to review by the Court all measures adopted by the institutions which are intended to have legal force. An action for annulment must therefore be available in the case of all measures adopted by the institutions, whatever their nature or form, which are intended to have legal effects.

The *ERTA* approach is echoed in Case C–316/91 *European Parliament v Council* (1994), where the Court of Justice found that a development aid regulation adopted by the Council under the Fourth ACP-EEC Convention was subject to review despite its adoption pursuant to an internal Convention agreement rather than pursuant to the Treaty, as:

> [a]nnulment must be available in the case of all measures adopted by the institutions, whatever their nature or form, intended to have legal effects. It follows that an action...is admissible irrespective of whether the act was adopted by the institution pursuant to the Treaty provisions.

8.31 In a similar vein, the Court of Justice, while considering whether acts of the European Parliament that were not at this time included in the list of reviewable acts, concluded if the acts created legal effects vis-à-vis third parties, the Court could exercise judicial review. In Case 294/83 *Les Verts v European Parliament* (1986) the Court stated:

> Article 173 [now Article 263 TFEU] referred only to acts of the Council and Commission. However, the general scheme of the Treaty was to make a direct action available against all measures adopted by the institutions which are intended to have legal effects.

In this case, the allocation by the Parliament of campaign funds for the 1984 elections, which had been based on the existing membership of the Parliament, was challenged by the Greens as discriminating against those seeking election for the first time. The Court of Justice reasoned that in a Community based on the rule of law, all institutions of the Community must be subject to review and pointed to the fact that Parliament could now adopt binding acts. The contested allocation decision governed the rights and obligation of political groups, produced legal effects vis-à-vis third parties, and so was reviewable. Then Case 34/86 *Council v European Parliament* (1986) established that a declaration by the President of the Parliament as to the final adoption of the general budget of the EC was reviewable as the budget was an act capable of producing legal effects vis-à-vis private parties. And then, in Case 190/84 *Les Verts v European Parliament* (1988) the Court ruled that measures adopted by Parliament which have purely internal effects within the administration of Parliament and which do not produce legal effects for third parties are not reviewable under Article 173 EEC (now Article 263 TFEU). Equally, a decision by Parliament to set up a committee of enquiry was found by the Court of Justice not to produce legal effects vis-à-vis third parties, and so fell outside the scope of Article 173: Case 78/85 *Group of the European Right v European Parliament* (1986).

8.32 On occasion, the Commission has attempted to prevent review of certain 'soft law' measures. In Case C–325/91 *France v Commission* (1993) a Commission communication which imposed detailed reporting obligations on Member States with respect to public funding of public undertakings was held to be reviewable despite the Commission's argument that it was not intended to have legal effects. The Commission argued the communication simply explained the nature of obligations already established in an earlier directive. The Court found that the communication had added new obligations to those imposed by the directive and so 'was intended to have legal effects of its own distinct from [the directive]', and was therefore a reviewable act. Given the increasing tendency of Union acts to take the form of what might appear to be 'soft law', it is interesting that the Court of Justice has for many years now taken an expansive and vigilant approach to their review.

8.33 Administrative acts taken by the Commission in the area of competition policy are frequently challenged. **Chapter 14** sets out the Commission's policing role in Competition law enforcement, and the operation of Competition law by the Commission therefore gives rise to various calls for the scrutiny of Commission acts. In Joined Cases 8–11/66 *SA Cimenteries CBR Cementbedrijven NV v Commission* (1967) the administrative act challenged was a registered letter sent by the Commission. The letter was not called a decision, but it produced legal effects for the companies concerned in that it stated that a group of companies no longer had immunity from fines, brought about a distinct change in their legal position and so was open to challenge under Article 173 EEC (now Article 263 TFEU). That the form of the contested measure is of limited importance is clearly seen in Case T–3/93 *Air France v Commission* (1994) where an oral statement by a Commission official, reported by a press agency, to the effect that a proposed acquisition by British Airways of Dan Air fell outside the scope of the Merger Regulation 4064/89 as it did not have a Community dimension, was found to be reviewable. Despite what it termed the unusual form of the measure, the Court of First Instance (now General Court) found that the statement produced legal effects for the Member States, for the parties concerned and for their competitors. The Commission measure must, however, be definitive. In Case 60/81 *IBM v Commission* (1981) a Commission letter notifying IBM of certain alleged abuses of Treaty competition rules was challenged by IBM. The Court found that Article 173 EEC was designed for measures which have binding legal effects and affect the interests of the applicant by causing a distinct change to the applicant's legal position. Here, the act challenged was adopted through a specific procedure and so was only open to review if it definitively set out the final position of the Commission or Council and was not a provisional measure (see also Case T–37/92 *BEUC and NCC v Commission* (1994)). In this case, review of the contested measure might have prejudiced the substance of the final decision of the Commission on the alleged violation of the competition rules. Where the preliminary decision concerns the disclosure of confidential documents, however, it will often be subject to review. In Case 53/85 *AKZO Chemie BV v Commission* (1986) the Court found that a decision of the Commission, taken while infringement proceedings were still in progress, to disclose confidential information to the party who had originally complained of AKZO's behaviour, could be subject to review even though a final resolution of the proceedings had not been reached. Finally, where appropriate, the Court will sever an initial Commission measure which has legal effects from a larger contractual procedure at national level in order to subject the Commission measure to review. In Case C–395/95P *Geotronics SA v Commission* (1997) a Commission decision rejecting a bid by the applicant to be included in a Phare programme tender was found to be reviewable by the Court of Justice as it produced legal effects for the applicant (overruling the Court of First Instance), even though the Commission decision was simply part of a larger contractual procedure where the ultimate tender decision would be made at national level.

8.34 Certain acts will not be reviewable. In Joined Cases C–181 and 248/91 *European Parliament v Council and Commission* (1993) the European Parliament challenged both a decision by the Member States in Council granting special aid to Bangladesh and the Commission measures taken to implement that decision. The Court of Justice ruled that although the contested decision was called an act of the Council, it was in fact an act of the Member States acting collectively. Equally, the Commission action was the result of a special delegation to it by the Member States and was not the result of a Council delegation, so it was not reviewable. In Case T–584/93 *Roujansky v Council* (1994) the Court of First Instance (now General Court) found that a declaration by the European Council that the Maastricht Treaty was to enter into force on a certain date was not subject to review as the European Council was not listed as an institution subject to the annulment action and was not subject to the jurisdiction of the Community Courts. (This situation has now changed since the European Council has become an institution under the Lisbon Treaty and thus it is included in Article 263 TFEU in the list of institutions whose acts are reviewable, like the European Parliament, insofar as these acts are intended to produce legal effects vis-à-vis third parties.) The Court of First Instance also found that the Maastricht Treaty was not subject to review under Article 230 EC (now Article 263 TFEU) as it was not an act of a Community institution. Further, Acts of Accession whereby the Union enlarges will not be reviewed (Joined Cases 31 and 35/86 *LAISA v Council* (1988)).

8.35 The requirement that a challenged act must be an act of a Union institution, does not mean that agreements between the Union and other international bodies or non-Member States are exempt from review. It does not mean it has to be a *unilateral* act of a Union institution. In Case C–327/91 *France v Commission* (1994) the Court of Justice rejected the Commission's argument that Article 173 was restricted to unilateral Community acts and that an agreement entered into between the Commission and the US was not, as a result, subject to Article 173:

> The exercise of powers delegated to the Community institutions in international matters cannot escape judicial review under Article 173 [Article 263 TFEU]....

8.36 Finally, Case 48/65 *Lütticke v Commission* (1966) established that a reasoned opinion delivered by the Commission in the course of Article 169 EEC (now Article 258 TFEU) proceedings may not be reviewed under Article 173 EEC (now Article 263 TFEU) as it is not a binding act.

Reviewable acts and the Common and Security Policy (Title V TFEU)

8.37 Union acts implementing international agreements, in particular UN Security Council resolutions raise difficult questions regarding the proper role of judicial review. The Common Foreign and Security Policy (CFSP) produces legal instruments in that the European Council and the Council can make important policy and specific decisions. However the nature of the decisions adopted under the CFSP is quite different to the legislative acts of the rest of the Lisbon Treaty, and there is little scope for judicial review of such decisions. And then, where the CFSP initiative results in binding Union legislation, even that is difficult to subject to judicial review because of hierarchies that apply in international law that make the European Union Courts unwilling to question policies agreed across the international political plane.

In Case T–315/01 *Kadi* (2005) the Court of First Instance (now the General Court) reviewed a Community regulation adopted in furtherance of a CFSP Common Position itself passed pursuant to other provisions, namely Security Council Resolutions. Common Position 2001/154/CFSP set out the Council's policy on measures to be taken against the Taliban in Afghanistan, and the freezing of 'funds and other financial assets of Usama bin Laden and individuals and entities associated with him'. Kadi unsuccessfully challenged a Community regulation that froze assets following the CFSP Common Position. The Court of First Instance ruled that since the Community regulation and the CFSP Common Position were descended from UN Security Council Resolutions the Court had no authority to call into question, even indirectly, their lawfulness in the light of Community law and that it was bound, insofar as possible, to interpret and apply that law in a manner compatible with the obligations of the Member States under the Charter of the United Nations. However, on appeal to the Court of Justice the Court reversed this ruling and ruled, in a judgment reminiscent of the '*Solange*' cases, (see **7.80–7.81**) that the Court considered that the review of the validity of any Community measure in the light of fundamental rights must be considered to be the expression, in a community based on the rule of law, of a constitutional guarantee stemming from the EC Treaty as an autonomous legal system which may not be prejudiced by an international agreement. The Court emphasised that the review of lawfulness ensured by the Community courts applies to the Community act intended to give effect to the international agreement at issue, and not to the international agreement itself. On 26 February 2009, Mr Kadi brought another action before the Court of Justice to annul Regulation no 1190/2008, insofar as he is concerned by it (Case T–85/09, pending). He submits that the contested Regulation lacks a sufficient legal basis because it appears to amend Regulation 881/2002 without relevant determination by United Nations which, in the applicant's opinion, is a precondition for the amendment of that Regulation. He also argues that Commission failed to undertake an assessment of all relevant facts and circumstances in deciding whether to enact the contested Regulation and therefore manifestly erred in its assessments; it also failed to provide compelling reasons for maintaining the asset freeze against him (see also **5.13** for a detailed discussion).

Privileged applicants

8.38 Article 263(2) TFEU provides that the Commission, the Council, the European Council, the European Parliament, the European Central Bank and the Member States all have standing by right as they are considered to have a direct interest in any of the acts under review. These privileged applicants do not have to establish a particular interest in the action. In Case 230/81 *Luxembourg v European Parliament* (1983), Luxembourg brought the equivalent of an Article 263 TFEU action under the ECSC Treaty to annul a resolution by the Parliament to hold committee meetings and other plenary sessions outside Luxembourg. Arguably, Luxembourg did have a strong interest to protect, but, in any event, it was not required to demonstrate a particular interest because, as a privileged applicant, it had *locus standi* as of right.

Semi-privileged applicants

8.39 The European Central Bank, the Court of Auditors and the Committee of the Regions are semi-privileged applicants, insofar as their right to seek review is more limited. They may take an action only 'for the purpose of protecting their prerogatives'. Until the Nice Treaty, the Parliament, too, was a semi-privileged applicant. Even that position was acquired only after a long, hard fight by the Parliament since it had not had any sort of standing rights in the original versions of the Treaties. In a creative series of judgments the Court of Justice, concerned to redress what it saw as an institutional imbalance, acted as a dynamic agent for change by introducing Parliament as an applicant under Article 173 EEC (now Article 263 TFEU) to produce a result now provided for in the Treaty itself. Case 138/79 *Roquette Frères v Council* (1980) and Case 139/79 *Maizena v Council* (1980) (the *isoglucose* cases) established that the Parliament did, under Article 37 of the Statute of the Court of Justice, have the right to intervene voluntarily in cases before the Court of Justice. Parliament used this facility to great effect to protect its right to be consulted in decision-making. Then, in Case 294/83 *Les Verts v Parliament* (1986) the Court ruled that all measures of Parliament having legal effect were subject to review under Article 263 TFEU (then Article 173) and in Case C–70/88 *European Parliament v Council (Re Chernobyl)* (1990), the Court ruled that Parliament had the right to bring an Article 173 action when its own prerogatives (such as its right to participate in the legislative process as laid down in the Treaty) were directly affected. Employing a classic form of constitutional rhetoric, the Court found that these (unenumerated) prerogative powers of Parliament were part of the institutional balance created by the Treaty and the omission of Parliament from Article 173 was a procedural gap which could not prevail over the fundamental interest in maintaining this institutional balance. The Parliament was vigorous in asserting its rights. For example, in Case C–295/90 *European Parliament v Council (Student Residence Directive)* (1992) the Court accepted that Parliament's prerogatives to participate in decision-making were at stake when Parliament sought to annul Directive 90/366 on vocational training on the basis that it had been erroneously adopted under Article 235 (now Article 352 TFEU) which merely provided for consultation of Parliament (see further **3.39**).

Since the Nice Treaty, the Parliament is no longer in the category of semi-privileged applicants because it is now a privileged applicant, with the entitlement of automatic access to the Court for Article 263 TFEU actions, but the history of the development of Parliament's access to the Court demonstrates that the Court will pay regard to the needs of institutional balance rather than the precise list of institutions who can bring court actions set out in the Treaty Article.

Non-privileged applicants

8.40 Natural and legal persons may bring an annulment action under Article 263(4) TFEU, but they are non-privileged applicants and have difficult hurdles to clear to gain access to the Court. The General Court has jurisdiction in these actions, and appeal is to the Court of Justice. Article 263(4) has been interpreted strictly and restrictively by the Court in a line of cases which inevitably raise questions as to the nature of the protection of the individual in the Union legal order. The Court of Justice has on occasion, however, lowered the hurdles presented by Article 263 TFEU when the specific facts of the case seemed to call for judicial review. This was the case in Case C–309/89 *Codorníu*, discussed further below at **8.49**. Treaty amendments up to this time had not relaxed these standing rules; however the Lisbon Treaty liberalises the terms under which individuals can make use of Article 263 TFEU to some extent.

The provisions of the fourth paragraph of ex-Article 230 EC have been amended in Article 263(4) TFEU. If we juxtapose the two articles we shall see the changes made and how they may be intended to affect future cases. Article 230(4) reads as follows, (those words which have been amended in italics):

> Any natural or legal person may, *under the same conditions, institute proceedings against a decision addressed to that person or against a decision which, although in the form of a regulation or a decision addressed to another person, is of direct and individual concern to the former.*

Article 263(4) TFEU reads as follows (amendments in italics):

> Any natural or legal person may, *under the conditions laid down in the first and second paragraphs, institute proceedings against an act addressed to that person or which is of direct and individual concern to them and against a regulatory act which is of direct concern to them and does not entail implementing measures.*

In Article 263(4) TFEU, the word 'Decision' has been replaced by the word 'Act', thus widening the field of instruments, although it still has to have legal effect; the words '*against a decision which, although in the form of a Regulation or a Decision addressed to another person*' have been replaced by the simpler formula '*or which is of direct and individual concern to them*'. On the whole there have been few problems with the requirement in the first part: an act addressed to a person. It was under the second part, where the individual had to show under Article 230 EC (now Article 263 TFEU) that an act called a Regulation was in fact a Decision or a 'bundle of Decisions' of direct and individual concern to them, where problems have arisen. Although the word 'Decision' has been replaced by the wider term 'Act' the requirement of direct and individual concern remains for acts not addressed to the applicant.

The new second limb of Article 263(4) TFEU refers to a regulatory act which does not entail implementing measures (see further **8.57**). Moreover, the individual only has to show *direct concern* and no longer individual concern. Much of the case law decided under Article 230 EC will still apply but other cases have been overtaken by the new wording.

Finally, Article 263 TFEU has added a paragraph providing that acts setting up bodies, offices and agencies of the Union may lay down specific conditions and arrangements concerning actions brought by individuals (natural or legal persons) against acts of such bodies, offices or agencies of the European Union which are intended to produce legal effects in relation to them.

These changes were made as a direct result of the extensive case law of the Court of Justice concerning this part of Article 263 TFEU. Some of the case law may therefore have been taken account of in the new wording. Below we discuss a number of cases which have constituted the main thrust of the reasoning of the Court of Justice and which the Court may well return to in future judgments. Much of the case law discussed below should still apply after the coming into force of the Lisbon Treaty.

Decision addressed to the applicant

8.41   A decision, which under Article 288 TFEU is 'binding in its entirety upon those to whom it is addressed', may be challenged by the natural or legal person to whom it is addressed. Commission decisions addressed to companies in the area of competition law are frequently challenged. If the addressee of the contested decision brings the action within the two-month time limit which is set for all Article 263 TFEU actions (see below), the claim will be admissible.

Acts not addressed to the applicant, but of direct and individual concern to them

8.42   The admissibility criteria of Article 230 EC (now Article 263 TFEU) posed formidable challenges where the contested decision was not addressed to the applicant. A natural or legal person was able to bring an annulment action under Article 230 EC (now Article 263 TFEU) where the contested measure was a decision addressed to another person (and so outside the first category) but was, nonetheless, a decision of direct and individual concern to the applicant. Direct concern and individual concern should be seen as separate elements of the test. The application of this deceptively simple test has been problematic. The approach of the Court of Justice was to interpret the concept of individual concern, in particular, restrictively so that, in practice, the applicant challenging a decision addressed to another person faced a formidable obstacle before an action could be brought. It is in the second part of the test that the Lisbon Treaty finally provides for the prospect of change. Individual concern will not have to be shown for regulatory acts which directly concern a person.

Individual concern

8.43   In Case 25/62 *Plaumann & Co v Commission* (1963), the Court of Justice established the test for determining whether a contested decision, addressed to another person, was of individual concern to the applicant. The Commission had issued a decision, addressed to the German Government, refusing to suspend the import duty imposed on importers of clementines to Germany. One of the importers concerned, Plaumann, challenged this decision on the grounds that, as a large scale importer of clementines, it was individually concerned. The Court stated the test for individual concern as follows:

> Persons other than those to whom a decision is addressed may only claim to be individually concerned if that decision affects them by reason of certain attributes which are peculiar to them or by reason of circumstances in which they are differentiated from all other persons, and by virtue of these factors distinguishes them individually just as in the case of the person addressed.

In applying this test the Court examined whether Plaumann was a member of an open or closed class and so distinguished from all other persons. The Court found that Plaumann was affected by the decision simply by reason of engaging in a commercial activity (importing clementines) covered by the decision, which could have been practised at any time by any person. This was not enough to create a closed class and thereby distinguish the applicant in relation to the decision as in the case of the addressee. So, as a member of a general and open class, Plaumann was not individually concerned.

8.44 Subsequent case law has shown that establishing the circumstances or attributes which differentiate the applicant from all other persons presents a troublesome task for the applicant. In Case 11/82 *Piraiki-Patraiki v Commission* (1985), the Court found that certain cotton traders had entered into contracts which were to be carried out during the months to which the contracts applied and that this constituted a circumstance which distinguished them from any other person concerned by the decision, insofar as the execution of their contracts was wholly or partly prevented by the adoption of the decision.

8.45 The Court found in a number of other cases that individual concern could be shown, for example in Case 169/84 *COFAZ v Commission* (1986), where the Court granted *locus standi* to the applicant to challenge a Commission decision, taken under Article 88(2) (now Article 108(2) TFEU) and addressed to the Netherlands, on the lawfulness of a state aid. The then Court of First Instance found in Case T–32/93 *Ladbroke Racing Ltd v Commission* (1994) that individuals would not be in a position to establish individual concern simply by virtue of having requested, in that case, the Commission to adopt remedial measures under Article 86(3) EC (now Article 106(3) TFEU). It would seem that the changes in Article 263(4) TFEU do not affect the above case law.

Decision by way of a regulation, where the applicant is directly and individually concerned

8.46 Before the amendment of Article 230(4) EC by Article 263(4) TFEU, generally speaking, individuals could not challenge regulations due to their abstract and general nature, the question of the appropriateness of such general legislative acts being one for the legislators rather than the Court. Only where a regulation dropped its general character and, in deciding a specific issue, became in practice a disguised decision, standing might be granted to review the regulation-cum-decision if direct and individual concern could also be established.

8.47 Initially, the Court of Justice focused on whether the contested regulation applied to a closed category of persons. In Cases 16 and 17/62 *Confédération Nationale des Producteurs de Fruits et Légumes v Council* (1962) the Court found that the essential characteristics of a decision included the need to ascertain whether the measure in question was of individual concern to specific individuals.

Similarly, in Joined Cases 41–44/70 *International Fruit Co v Commission* (1971) the Court found that if the 'Regulation' applied to a closed group of people and reflected past events it would not have the character of a true regulation but was actually a bundle of disguised decisions.

Sometimes, however, the Court adopted a more flexible approach, as in Case C–152/88 *Sofrimport v Commission* (1990), where the Court looked for individual concern without examining whether the Regulation was in fact a Decision.

8.48 In some cases the Court of Justice also permitted individual challenges to regulations even where the measures did exhibit legislative characteristics and did not seem to apply to a closed and fixed group. This was the case in Case C–309/89 *Codorníu SA v Commission* (1994) where the Court accepted that a measure was of general legislative character but still allowed a challenge by an individual.

8.49 Despite the *Codorníu* decision on standing, the Court of Justice remained reluctant to grant standing for challenges to regulations which had a legislative character. In particular, it has been slow to find that applicants challenging regulations which have general legislative effects are, in some way, differentiated from all other persons by reason of certain attributes or circumstances, as in *Codorníu*. In Case C–209/94P *Buralux v Council* (1996) the Court found that the measure produced legal effects on categories of persons in a general and abstract manner and so could not be challenged even though the number and identity of those affected could be determined. Buralux was affected in the same way as every other operator in the waste transfer business. The Court did not follow the Advocate General's view that since Buralux was the largest importer of waste in France and Germany, it would be particularly seriously affected by the import prohibition envisaged by the Regulation.

8.50 The Court of First Instance (now the General Court) adopted a similarly restrictive approach to challenges to regulations. In Case T–472/93 *Campo Ebro Industrial SA v Commission* (1995) isoglucose producers attempted to challenge a regulation aligning the price of sugar in Spain, arguing that they were individually concerned as they were the only producers of sugar in Spain at the time the Regulation was adopted, and the only producers to have been adversely affected by the reduction in the price of sugar. Stating that the general application and legislative nature of a measure could not be called into question simply because it was possible to define the number of persons to whom it applied, the Court of First Instance found that even if the applicants were the only producers affected by the Regulation, they were affected in their objective capacity as isoglucose producers in the same way as any other traders in the sugar sector who actually or potentially were in an identical situation. The same reasoning was applied by the Court of First Instance in Case T–47/95 *Terres Rouges Consultant SA v Commission* (1997) where banana importers into the Community who were responsible for 70 per cent of all bananas exported from the Ivory Coast challenged a regulation which restricted the quantity of bananas which could be exported into the Community from the Ivory Coast. The CFI characterised the measure as a general legislative act drafted in abstract and general terms and found that the applicants were not individually concerned.

8.51 The cases have not, however, all been in one direction. In Joined Cases T–125 and 152/96 *Boehringer v Commission* (1999), the applicant was successful in challenging a regulation. The Court ruled that the applicant was individually concerned as the Regulation was adopted after a formal request from the applicant that limits be set, the earlier foundation Regulation on which the contested Regulation was based provided that the applicant be involved in the process of setting limits, and the draft Regulation had been notified to the applicant. Nonetheless, it appears that the Courts remained concerned to protect general legislative measures from individual challenge. Although the cases described in **8.46–8.50** above may now fall under the heading of 'Regulatory act' and therefore would not need to show individual concern, they would still have to show direct concern (see **8.58**) and the absence of a need for implementing measures.

Decision by way of a directive

8.52 Cases concerning challenges to Directives by individuals under Article 230 EC were generally not successful. In Case T–135/96 *UEAPME v Council* (1998), where a European Association representing the interests of small and medium-sized enterprises challenged Directive 96/34 on parental leave, the CFI (now General Court) found the Directive was a legislative measure and could not be characterised as a Decision. As in *Codorníu*, however, the CFI went on to address whether, notwithstanding its general legislative character, the association was individually concerned. It found that it was not. The CFI did point out, however, that the mere fact that the contested measure was in the form of a directive was not sufficient, of itself, to render the action inadmissible as Community institutions could not be allowed, through their choice of instrument, to deprive individuals of judicial protection.

Anti-dumping regulations

8.53 The Court of Justice took a less stringent approach to standing and has been quicker to find that a true regulation could be open to challenge (where it could be shown to be of direct and individual concern to the applicant) where the regulation was an anti-dumping measure. See also Case C–358/89 *Extramet Industrie SA v Council* (1991)).

The difficulties raised by individual concern for natural and legal persons: interest groups

8.54 Thus, the formulation of the standing rules served, in effect, to exclude individuals from judicial review of Community acts in all but a few cases. Further, it made the position of lobbying groups and collective associations particularly difficult. The Court held in a number of cases that associations which protect the collective interests of a group of persons would not be considered directly and individually concerned by measures affecting the general interests of the group and so could not take an annulment action where the members could not do so on an individual basis: Joined Cases T–447, 448 and 449/93 *AITEC v Commission* (1995). In Case C–321/95 P *Stichting Greenpeace Council (Greenpeace International) v Commission* (1998), Greenpeace claimed to have *locus standi* to challenge a decision on financing, the finance to be used for the construction of a power station, on the grounds that the persons they represented were individually concerned by the measure. Greenpeace sought to argue that some environmental rights needed to be represented by organisations since otherwise no natural or legal person would have the direct and individual concern necessary to be able to exercise them in court. The Court confirmed a ruling of the Court of First Instance and found that Greenpeace was not individually concerned by the financing decision and that therefore no Article 230 EC (now Article 263 TFEU) action would be heard.

Exceptions or reinterpretation of the rigidities of the *Plaumann* criteria for individual concern before the Lisbon Treaty

8.55 The cases cited above show that the Court of Justice has sometimes tried to be flexible with respect to its test for individual concern, and it is possible to see the rigidities of the *Plaumann* criteria as having been reviewed and to some extent loosened by subsequent judgments. The cases where the Court appeared to take a more relaxed approach to standing can, however, largely be explained by the particular and exceptional factors present in those cases. In *Piraiki-Patraiki* (see 8.44) the Greek Act of Accession required the Commission to take particular account of those undertakings likely to be affected by protective measures. In *Sofrimport* (see 8.47), the particular situation of goods in transit when the contested Regulation was adopted was at issue. In *Codorníu* (see 8.48), the applicant was in a particularly distinctive situation as it held a very large market share in the product affected by the Regulation and, further, its legal rights under a prior trademark were extinguished by the Regulation. Thus, although the term 'Decision' has now been replaced with the more general term 'Acts' the requirement of direct and individual concern subsists and *Plaumann* still would seem to present significant difficulties to many applicants.

The rigidities of the standing rules and human rights arguments

8.56 The Court of First Instance (now the General Court) in 2002 appeared to offer greater scope for the review of Community acts and decisions in Case T–177/01 *Jégo-Quére et*

Cie v Commission (2002), taking notice of human rights arguments. Jégo-Quére was a fishing company which used nets with a mesh of 80mm, which were banned by a Community regulation. It applied to the CFI for an annulment of two provisions of the Regulation. The Commission argued that the action was inadmissible as, based on the previous case law, Jégo-Quére was not individually concerned. While the provisions in question were of direct concern to Jégo-Quére, it was not individually concerned in that the net mesh size rules applied equally to all fishing operators subject to the Regulation. In deciding that the action was admissible, and that Jégo-Quére was individually concerned, even though the Regulation was of general application, the CFI took a radically different approach to the question of individual concern. It noted that the previous case law prevented a number of individuals from challenging measures of direct application which directly affected their legal position, and that none of the other procedural routes available under the Treaty provided an appropriate vehicle for challenging the legality of a Community measure. However, in Case C–50/00 P *Unión de Pequeños Agricultores v Council (UPA)*, concerning a challenge by a trade association to a regulation of general application, the Court of Justice found that while the condition that individual concern must be shown was to be interpreted in light of the principle of effective judicial protection (the human rights issue considered by the CFI in *Jégo-Quére*), by taking into account the various circumstances which may distinguish an applicant individually, 'such an interpretation cannot have the effect of setting aside the condition in question, expressly laid down in the Treaty, without going beyond the jurisdiction conferred by the Treaty and the Community courts'. It concluded that it was for the Member States, if necessary, in accordance with Article 48 TEU to reform the system and rules on standing currently in force. This was no doubt in response to the Court of Justice's position, but also to concerns that were subsequently expressed in the European Court of Human Rights about access to courts, Article 6 of the Convention and in particular the particular problems with Article 230 EC (now Article 263 TFEU) and the review of Community law, noted in European Court of Human Rights case Application Number 45036/98 *Bosphorus Hava Yollari Turizm Ve Ticaret Anonim Sirketi v Ireland* (2006). However, in its judgment on the appeal in the *Jégo-Quére* case, Case C–263/02 P, the Court of Justice repeated much of the argument in *UPA* in allowing the appeal. The Court indicated an applicant who found the standing rules restrictive should explore alternative avenues, for example the preliminary reference procedure in Article 234 EC (now Article 267 TFEU) (considered in **Chapter 4**), and that it did not then think that human rights arguments altered the terms of debate, or the restrictive stance it had previously taken, on the standing entitlement provided by Article 230 EC (now Article 263 TFEU). The Court stated that the Treaty had:

> Established a complete system of legal remedies and procedures designed to ensure review of the legality of acts of the institutions, and had entrusted such review to the Community Courts. (paragraph 30)

In terms of the specific human rights issues under consideration, the Court stated it was for the Member State to establish a system of legal remedies and procedures which ensured respect for the right to effective judicial protection.

Effect of Lisbon Treaty

8.57 The Lisbon Treaty appears to have taken precisely some of those steps to reform the criteria for standing. The requirement of individual concern is still present in the first limb of Article 263(4) TFEU, in respect of 'an act', no longer just a decision, but has now been removed from the second limb of Article 263(4) TFEU in respect of a 'regulatory act' which needs no further implementation and is of direct concern. This might mean, therefore, that some of the cases described above, and, in particular, the cases of Case T–177/01 *Jégo-Quére et Cie v Commission* (2002) and Case C–50/00P *Unión de Pequeños Agricultores v Council*, could now have been decided in favour of the aggrieved parties.

The word 'act' in the first limb of Article 263(4) TFEU clearly widens the type of act beyond that of a mere decision. However, there is doubt as to the interpretation of the word 'regulatory act…which entails no implementing measures' and its exact meaning. Although it appears to widen the interpretation beyond that of the original wording in Article 230 EC 'decision addressed to another person or decision in the form of a regulation' the exact scope is unclear. The removal of the requirement of individual concern here also widens the category of parties which could bring an action under this heading. As it is the concern of the Court to give the maximum possible effect to Union law, it could be expected to give a positive interpretation to these terms, looking beyond actual words, and giving a teleological interpretation, looking for the purpose behind the text as drafted.

Direct concern

8.58 The contested measure must also be of direct concern to the applicant. Direct concern will be established where there is a direct causal link between the challenged Community measure and its ultimate impact on the applicant. In Case 69/69 *Alcan v Commission* (1970) the Belgian and Luxembourg governments lobbied the Commission to increase the Belgian allocation of low tariff aluminium. The Commission refused to increase the quota and the decision was challenged by the applicant. The Court found that the decision was not of direct concern as, even if the Commission had agreed that the quota could be increased, the decision would not have required the Member States to increase the quota. This always seemed an unsatisfactory ruling and the Court of Justice has since accepted that where the implementation of the Community decision is a foregone conclusion, as would be expected where the Member State has sought permission or authorisation for the action, the measure will be of direct concern to the applicant. In *Piraiki-Patraiki* (see 8.44) a Commission decision authorised the French Government to impose a quota system on the import of Greek yarn. The Court of Justice decided that any possibility that the French Government would not impose the quota was purely theoretical, and therefore the decision was of direct concern to the Greek applicant. Direct concern will also be established if the Member State indicates in advance how it will exercise the discretion it enjoys under the contested Union measure (Case 62/70 *Bock v Commission* (1971)). The question seems to be also how much discretion is left to the Member State in implementing a Union decision. In Case C–403/96P *Glencore Grain Ltd v Commission* (1998) the Court stated that for a measure to be of direct concern the measure must directly affect the legal situation of the individual and leave no discretion to the addressees of the measure who are entrusted with the task of implementing it. This would seem to have been confirmed in the addition to the 4th paragraph of Article 263(4) TFEU of 'a regulatory act which…does not entail implementing measures'.

Time limitations

8.59   An annulment action must be brought within two months of the publication of the measure or its notification to the applicant or, in the absence thereof, within two months of the day on which the contested measure came to the notice of the applicant (Article 263(5) TFEU). Notification involves communication of a detailed account of the measure's content and the reasons for its adoption. The time period runs from notification of the full text of the decision and not from when a brief summary of the decision's content was notified to the applicant (see Case C–143/95P *Commission v Socurte* (1997)). This time bar is strictly enforced and filters out a number of actions (for example, see Case C–178/95 *Wiljo NV v Belgium* (1997)). The Rules of Procedure of the Court do provide for short extensions of the two-month period in certain limited circumstances. The party alleging the existence of a time bar has the responsibility of showing on what date the decision was notified: Joined Cases T–70 and 71/92 *Florimex BV v Commission* (1997) and Case T–94/92 *X v Commission* (1994).

Grounds for annulment

8.60   Once an applicant has been given access to the Court to make an argument based on Article 263 TFEU the request for annulment of a decision must be based on certain grounds. The grounds for annulment are set out in Article 263(2) TFEU. A measure may be annulled for lack of competence on the part of the Union institution(s) which has adopted the measure. This is a difficult ground to establish considering the broad powers held by the Community. Infringement of an essential procedural requirement is another ground for annulment. For a classic example of failure to adopt the correct legislative procedure, see Case 138/79 *Roquette Frères v Council* (above at 8.39). Compliance with the duty to give reasons is another key procedural requirement. In Case T–105/95 *WWF UK v Commission* (1997) a Commission decision refusing access to Commission documents was annulled for breach of the duty to give reasons. This duty is assuming an ever-greater importance in the Union order. A measure may also be annulled for infringement of the Treaty or any law relating to its application and this ground is very often raised in annulment proceedings. Infringements under this ground include infringements of general principles of Union law, discussed in detail in **Chapter 6**. Case C–152/88 *Sofrimport*, noted above at 8.47, concerned a breach of the principles of legal certainty and legitimate expectations, and a number of annulment actions have attempted to raise breach of the fundamental human rights which form a part of the general principles as grounds for review. The Court of Justice has not often found that there has been a breach of these rights. Finally, a measure may be annulled for misuse of powers. In Case 105/75 *Giuffrida v Council* (1976) an unsuccessful applicant for a position in the Commission brought an action alleging that the competition was, in reality, a smokescreen as the position in question had already been reserved for another Commission official. The Court found that the competition had been held for the sole purpose of appointing a particular Commission official to a higher grade and so was contrary to the aims of the recruitment procedure and a misuse of powers. In addition to recognising the need to review abuses of authority by covering misuses of power and breaches of Treaty rules, the grounds for annulment also reflect the fact that the Union legal order is a formal one, where institutional acts must have a legal basis and follow the relevant procedural requirements.

8.61 If the action is well founded, the measure will be declared void under Article 264 TFEU. A declaration of nullity will be retroactive and will be of general application.

8.62 Article 266(1) TFEU provides that: 'The institution whose act has been declared void will be required to take the necessary measures to comply with the judgment of the Court of Justice of the European Union.' Accordingly, the institution concerned is required to ensure that any act intended to replace the annulled measure is not affected by the irregularities identified in the annulling judgment.

8.63 The Court of Justice is permitted by Article 264(1) TFEU to rule that certain or all parts of a measure which has been declared void will, nonetheless, continue in force for certain periods of time if it considers such an action necessary. In Case C–295/90 *European Parliament v Council* (1992), although the Court annulled Directive 90/366 which concerned the elimination of discrimination with respect to vocational training, it found that outright annulment would undermine the exercise by students of the right of residence for vocational training reasons and, further, that the date for the implementation of the contested Directive had passed. As a result, reasons of legal certainty justified a declaration that the Directive would continue to have legal effects until such time as the Council replaced it with a directive which had been correctly adopted. As well as providing an illustration of when the Court will limit the temporal effects of an annulment, the case also shows that the Court will not restrict this power to regulations, as seems to be suggested by the strict wording of Article 264(2) TFEU. Similarly, in Case C–21/94 *European Parliament v Council* (1995) the Court annulled a regulation on transport policy for breach of an essential procedural requirement, but declared that the measure would remain in effect until the Council had passed a replacement measure in order to avoid any discontinuity in the transport harmonisation programme and to ensure legal certainty. See also Case C–388/92 *European Parliament v Council* (1994) and Case 81/72 *Commission v Council* (1973). In these cases it is worth noting that the Court often refers to the fact that the party seeking annulment does not object to the measure remaining in force until a replacement act is passed, or that there is no serious dispute with respect to the content of the measure. An interim order may, of course, suspend the operation of the contested measure until a final ruling is made if the Court finds this is necessary. It is also clear from Case C–137/92 P *Commission v*

BASF (PVC) (1994) that, in certain extreme cases, a measure may be so defective that it will be declared void *ab initio*, or non-existent.

Article 263 TFEU and Article 267 TFEU

8.64 Article 267(1)(b) TFEU, which allows preliminary references to be made by national courts on the 'validity and interpretation of acts of the institutions, bodies, offices or agencies of the Union', may, in certain circumstances, provide an indirect alternative for individuals who wish to challenge Union acts. Article 267 TFEU is considered in more detail in **Chapter 4**. A national court may, in the course of an action by an individual for judicial review of a Union measure and its application to him, or, during an action taken against an individual for non-compliance with a Union act and its national implementing measure, where the validity of the Union act is raised, refer a question to the Court of Justice of the European Union on the validity of the Union act in question. This route may be particularly useful with respect to regulations because, as we have seen, individual applicants faced particular obstacles in establishing standing to challenge regulations under Article 230 EC, although this situation may now have improved under the different wording of Article 263(4) TFEU.

8.65 In Joined Cases 133–136/85 *Rau v BALM* (1987), the Court held that the possibility of bringing an annulment action under Article 175 EEC (now Article 265 TFEU) did not prevent the validity of the Community decision being raised in an action in a national court against a national measure implementing that Community decision. The Court then placed limitations on when the national courts and the preliminary reference procedure may be used to challenge Union measures. In Case C–188/92 *TWD (Textilwerke Deggendorf) v Germany* (1994), a company tried to raise the legality of a Commission decision (addressed to the German Government and finding that aid granted to the company by the German Government was unlawful and had to be repaid) in the German national courts. The Court held that the invalidity of the Commission decision could not be raised in proceedings against the German authorities' implementing decision before the national courts where the company had not applied under Article 173 EEC (now Article 263 TFEU) for annulment of the contested Commission decision within the prescribed period, and where the company could undoubtedly have done so. The Court found that the company:

> Was fully aware of the Commission decision and of the fact that it could without any doubt have challenged it under Article 173 EC [now Article 263 TFEU].

The Court referred to the fact that the company had been informed in writing of the Commission decision by the German authorities and had also been informed of the possibility of taking an annulment action. The Court took a similar line in Case C–178/95 *Wiljo NV v Belgium* (1997) where the plaintiff sought to challenge the validity of a Commission decision (which stated that a vessel owned by Wiljo did not come within the terms of a particular exemption from certain Community scrapping requirements) in proceedings before the national courts concerning the national measure implementing the Commission's decision. It found that where the Commission decision was addressed to an owner of a vessel and that owner had not brought an action under Article 173 EC (now Article 263 TFEU) within the time limits, the Commission decision was binding on the national courts and its invalidity could not be raised under Article 177 EC (now Article 267 TFEU). The Court found that the time period within which annulment proceedings could be brought was designed to ensure legal certainty and, as a result, a decision which had not been challenged by its addressee within the time period became final and definitive against him. The Court rejected any arguments based on the *Rau* principle, pointing out that in *Rau* the plaintiffs had brought an action for annulment of the decision in question and that the Court of Justice had not, therefore, dealt with the effect of a time bar to an annulment action on subsequently raising the validity of the Community measure in national proceedings. The Court noted the *TWD* principle applied where there was a failure to bring an Article 173 EC action in circumstances where the action could 'undoubtedly' have been brought. As the addressee of the decision, Wiljo was in such a position. It appears from Case C–241/95 *R v Intervention Board for Agricultural Produce, ex p Accrington Beef Co Ltd* (1997), however, that, where it is not clear that the individual would have standing to challenge the contested Community act under Article 263 TFEU the validity of the act may be raised in national proceedings and so through a preliminary reference, despite the fact that an annulment action is time-barred. The Court found that in *TWD* the company was, without doubt, entitled to bring an action and had been notified to that effect, but that here:

> Since the contested provisions are contained in a Community regulation and are addressed in general terms to categories of persons defined in the abstract and to situations determined objectively, it is not obvious that an action…under Article 173 EC [now Article 263 TFEU]…would have been admissible.

As a result, the reference was admissible despite the fact that the companies in question had failed to bring an annulment action within the time limit. The Court took a similar position in Case C–408/95 *Eurotunnel SA v SeaFrance* (1997) finding that the *TWD* principle did not apply where the contested provisions were contained in a directive and where, as a result, it was not obvious that an annulment action would have been admissible.

Actions for failure to act: Article 265 TFEU

Introduction

8.66 Article 265 TFEU provides for judicial review of failures to act by Union institutions and so serves to compel an institution to act when it has a legal duty to take a particular action. The Article also applies to bodies, offices and agencies of the Union which similarly fail to act. The Article acts as a complement, and is similar in structure, to Article 263 TFEU. The Court of Justice examined the relationship between the two remedies as long ago as Case 15/70 *Chevalley v Commission* (1970) finding that the two Articles 'merely prescribe one and the same method of recourse'.

8.67 Before an omission by one of the institutions, bodies, offices or agencies is treated as reviewable, the failure to act must amount to a breach of a Treaty obligation. Article 265 TFEU therefore covers all failures to act where there is legal duty under Union law to take action. In Case 13/83 *European Parliament v Council* (1985), the Parliament brought an action with respect to the alleged failure by the Council to establish a framework for a common transport policy as required under Article 74 of the Treaty (now Article 90 TFEU). The Court of Justice found that the obligation to introduce a common transport policy in the Article was not sufficiently precise that a failure to pursue a common transport policy amounted to a breach of the Treaty. The Court found that an applicant under Article 175 EEC (now Article 265 TFEU) must specify the measures which the erring institution has failed to take and so allow for remedial action. The Parliament had not specified the measures necessary in order to achieve a common transport policy and so the claim could not succeed under Article 175. The Parliament was successful in one respect, however. It had requested the Council to take specific action under the then Article 75(1)(a) and (b) (now Article 91(1)(a) and (b)TFEU) with respect to international transport and non-resident carriers. This failure to act was a breach of a specific obligation under the Treaty.

Article 265 TFEU and standing

8.68 Article 265 TFEU provides that 'the Member States and the other institutions of the Union' have standing to bring an action and they are all privileged applicants under Article 265 TFEU. In Case 13/83 *European Parliament v Council* (see **8.67**) the Court of Justice confirmed that Parliament was 'an institution of the Community' and so did have standing.

8.69 Mirroring the position under Article 263 TFEU, natural and legal persons have limited access to the Court. Such a person can only bring an action in connection with a binding act which the institution in question had an obligation to address to him. Despite this apparently restrictive formula, it is clear from the case law of the Court that Article 265 TFEU is not limited to review of a failure to take a decision actually addressed to the applicant. It also covers measures which, had they been taken, could have been challenged by the applicant under Article 263 TFEU. In Case 246/81 *Bethell v Commission* (1982) the Court held that the omitted act must be an act which the applicant was legally entitled to claim. The applicant had requested the Commission to take action against price fixing between airlines and, unhappy with the Commission's response to his request, took action under Article 175 EEC (now Article 265 TFEU). The Court of Justice found that while the applicant had, as a frequent user of airlines, an indirect interest in the proceedings, since he was not 'the actual addressee' of a decision that could be declared void or of a duty to act imposed on the Commission, the application was held to be inadmissible.

8.70   Further evidence of the difficulties faced by individuals is provided by Case 247/87 *Star Fruit v Commission* (1989) where the applicant sought to challenge a refusal by the Commission to take Article 258 TFEU enforcement proceedings. The Court simply found that:

> The Commission is not bound to commence the proceedings…but in this regard has a dis-cretion which excludes the right for individuals to require that institution to adopt a specific position.

8.71   Under Article 266(1) TFEU, if the Article 265 TFEU action succeeds, the institution is required to take the necessary measures to comply with the judgment of the Court of Justice.

The plea of illegality: Article 277 TFEU

8.72   Like Articles 263 and 265 TFEU, Article 277 TFEU (ex-Article 241 EC) permits chal-lenges to certain acts of Union institutions, bodies, offices or agencies but it differs in that it only allows such acts to be challenged indirectly. Article 277 TFEU claims are not separate forms of action. The plea of illegality may only be raised in the context of proceedings which have already been initiated on other grounds (Joined Cases 31 and 33/62 *Wöhrmann v Commission* (1962)).

8.73   The use of Article 277 TFEU to challenge Union measures indirectly can perhaps be best illustrated by its incidental application in Article 263 TFEU (ex Article 230 EC) proceedings. As we have seen, legal and natural persons faced significant difficulties in bringing an action under what is now Article 263 TFEU against a regulation owing to its general nature. Article 277 TFEU now no longer refers to a regulation but to 'an act of general application', words with a wider meaning which, however, include a regulation. An individual may, however, challenge a specific decision addressed to him under Article 263 TFEU on the grounds that the act of general application on which the decision is based is illegal, provided that the conditions of Article 263 TFEU are met. The individual may challenge the act of general application from which the decision is derived or which the decision is implementing by raising a plea under Article 277 TFEU of illegality of the act. The challenge to the act is therefore made under Article 277 TFEU in an incidental manner to the main annulment proceedings concerning the contested decision. The challenge to the act may be taken on this indirect basis under Article 277 TFEU in the course of the larger Article 263 TFEU proceedings, even where a direct challenge to the act under Article 263 TFEU is time-barred so long as the deci-sion subject to the Article 263 TFEU action is being challenged within the time limits.

8.74   Before the Lisbon Treaty the action appeared only to cover regulations and to be limited in scope. Case 92/78 *Simmenthal v Commission* (1979), however, made it clear that the action also covered acts of the institutions which produce similar effects to regulations but which do not take the form of regulations. Already at that time the Court found in *Simmenthal* that what is now Article 277 TFEU must be given a wide interpretation in order to:

> Provide those persons who are precluded by Article 173 [now Article 263(2) TFEU] from instituting proceedings directly in respect of general acts with the benefit of judicial review of them at the time when they are affected by implementing decisions which are of direct and individual concern to them.

Here is another example where the Court showed its desire to give the greatest possible effect to Union law and the amended wording of Article 277 will no doubt also receive a wide interpretation by the Court.

8.75 If the Article 277 TFEU plea succeeds, the act is 'inapplicable' and may not stand as the basis for the contested decision which will, as a result, be void. The act itself will not be annulled.

Contractual and tortious liability of the Union

Contractual liability of the Union and Article 340(1) TFEU

8.76 The first paragraph of Article 340 TFEU (ex Article 288(1) EC) deals with the contractual liability of Union institutions and compensation actions. It provides that liability shall be governed by the law applicable to the contract. The Union's contracts will normally contain a choice of law clause. There is no specific procedure for compensation. The jurisdiction of the Court over contractual arbitration clauses is governed by Article 272 TFEU.

Damages against Union institutions (non-contractual liability): Articles 268 and 340(2) TFEU

8.77 Union liability in tort, described as 'non-contractual liability', is governed by Articles 268 and 340(2) TFEU. Article 340(2) TFEU provides that liability arises 'in accordance with the general principles common to the laws of the Member States'. The liability here covered is not specified and it has been a matter for the Court to interpret its ambit. The Union may be liable for both the wrongful acts on the part of one of its institutions, and the wrongful acts on the part of its servants. As long as the wrongful acts are committed in the performance of a Union official's duties, the institution concerned may be sued. These concepts are derived from French law, but are applied by the Court of Justice in its own way. The Court has drawn on the common elements governing tortious liability in the Member States in order to develop its own specific principles of Union law.

The parties

8.78 There is no requirement applicable to the party bringing the action. However, there is a question as to against whom such an action should be brought: Article 340(2) TFEU states that 'the Union' shall make good any damage. In Cases 63–69/72 *Werhahn v Council and Commission* (1973) the Court ruled that such action should be brought against the institution which is responsible. If two institutions are involved, it is quite correct to bring the action against both. Where Union liability is involved because of one of its institutions' actions, the Union should be represented before the Court by the institution(s) against which the matter giving rise to liability is alleged.

Time limit

8.79 Article 43 of the Statute of the Court of Justice sets a time limit of five years, running from the occurrence of the event giving rise to liability for a claim to be brought: see Case 51/81 *de Franceschi* (1982). The limitation period only begins to run from the moment when the damage becomes known. In Cases 145/83 and 53/84 *Adams v Commission* (1985) (see **8.84**), the applicant became aware of the event giving rise to the damage he suffered after the time limit had expired and the Court ruled that the limitation period does not begin to run until the injured party becomes aware of the event giving rise to his claim. In Joined Cases 256, 257, 265, 267/80 and 5/81 *Birra Wührer v Council and Commission* (1982) confirmed that for the purposes of Article 43 of the Statute of the Court, the five-year limitation period runs from the time of actual damage, and not from the earliest time the action could have commenced.

Wrongful act

8.80 The Court of Justice requires proof of fault on the part of the Union, an institution or an employee acting in an official capacity, and damage suffered by the applicant with a causal link between the fault committed and the damage. Failures that could give rise to damage include civil wrongs; abusive application of powers; non-performance of obligations; breach of a superior rule of law (pursuant to Case 5/71 *Aktien-Zuckerfabrik Schöppenstedt* (1971), see **8.85**); and breaches of the duty of confidentiality and the duty to warn the applicant (pursuant to Joined Cases 145/83 and 53/84 *Adams* (1985), see **8.84**).

Damage

8.81 Damage must be actual. In Joined Cases 5, 7 and 13–24/66 *Kampffmeyer* (1967) the Court of Justice admitted claims for loss of profit. In Case 74/74 *CNTA* (1975) (see **8.87**) the Court admitted claims for losses due to currency fluctuations. In staff cases, damages may be claimed for anxiety and injured feelings by a Union employee wrongfully dismissed or unfairly treated: Joined Cases 7/56 and 3–7/57 *Algera* (1957–58). Actual damage must be proved, or at least imminent damage which is foreseeable with sufficient certainty: Joined Cases 56–60/74 *Kampffmeyer* (1967).

8.82 The damage must not be too remote: Case 4/69 *Lütticke* (1971), and where the applicant is able to pass on the loss sustained to his customers the damage may be adjudged to be non-existent: Joined Cases 64, 113/76, 167, 239/78, 27, 28 and 45/79 *Dumortier (Quellmehl & Gritz)* (1979) (see **8.83** and **8.87**).

Causal link

8.83 The Court has accepted the notion of a causal link on a number of occasions without any further elaboration. In Joined Cases 64, 113/76, 167, 239/78, 27, 28 and 45/79 *Dumortier (Quellmehl & Gritz)* (1979) (see **8.87**), the Court ruled that there is no obligation for the Community to make good: 'Every harmful consequence, even a remote one, of unlawful legislation.' Further, the Court stated the damage alleged must be '...a sufficiently direct consequence of the unlawful conduct of the institution concerned'.

The burden to prove the causal link between the harmful behaviour of Union institutions and the alleged damage falls on the applicant: Case 40/75 *Bertrand* (1976).

8.84 Other criteria applicable to the causal link can be summarised as follows:

- The required causal link will be established in a claim on misleading information only if the information would have caused an error in the mind of a reasonable person: Case 169/73 *Compagnie Continentale* (1975).
- The causal link may be severed by contributory negligence on behalf of the applicant: C–308/87 *Grifoni* (1990).

Joined Cases 145/83 and 53/84 *Adams v Commission* (1985) illustrate the requirements in an unusual and regrettable set of facts. This case is one of the few where an individual has been awarded substantial damages, but it is a remarkable and tragic one. Mr Adams was employed by the Swiss pharmaceutical company Hoffmann-La Roche and had passed certain confidential documents on to the Commission which contained evidence of violation of the competition law Article 86 EC (now Article 106 TFEU). He had left Switzerland but returned there for a visit and was arrested and imprisoned for having violated Swiss law on commercial secrecy. While he was in prison his wife committed suicide. After his release he sued the Community for damages. The Court held that the Commission had violated its duty of confidentiality by not taking steps to prevent Hoffmann-La Roche from learning the name of the informant. However, Mr Adams's damages were reduced by 50 per cent to take into account his own contribution in failing to protect his own interests.

Distinctive nature of the remedy

8.85 Non-contractual liability under Article 340(2) TFEU exists as a separate remedy from the remedies for judicial review under Articles 263 and 265 TFEU. Case 5/71 *Aktien-Zuckerfabrik Schöppenstedt v Council* (1971) concerned a regulation under which no compensation was payable in case of loss. Schöppenstedt sued for damages and the Council contested admissibility on the grounds that such compensation would nullify the legal effect of the regulation. The Court stated damages claims and judicial review claims were two separate types of action, while finding that no compensation was payable. *Schöppenstedt* is an important judgment because it set out for the first time the principles governing Union liability for acts of the institutions (see **Chapter 7, Section III**). The language it used in setting out these principles has been echoed in the later judgments of the Court concerning liability of Member States for violation of Union law (see **Chapter 7, Section III**).

8.86 Article 340 TFEU may be used to obtain damages for the effects of an unlawful regulation as a separate remedy from the remedies under Articles 263 and 265 TFEU for judicial review, even though the regulation at issue is of a general legislative nature and cannot be the subject of an action by a private party under Article 263 TFEU (Joined Cases 9 and 11/71 *Compagnie d'approvisionnement (No 2)* (1972); Case 4/69 *Lütticke* (1971)).

Liability for legislative acts

8.87 Liability extends to acts of a legislative or normative character, such as regulations, provided that there is a 'sufficiently flagrant violation of a superior rule of law for the protection of the individual' (the '*Schöppenstedt* formula'): Case 5/71 *Schöppenstedt*, see **8.85**).

The *Schöppenstedt* formula contains three requirements:

- *First requirement*: breach of a superior rule of law. In Case 74/74 *CNTA* (1975), the Commission was held liable to pay compensation for losses incurred as a result of regulation which abolished with immediate effect and without warning the application of agricultural export subsidies: this was a serious breach of the principle of legitimate expectation;

- *Second requirement*: the breach must be sufficiently serious. In Joined Cases 83, 94/76, 4, 15 and 40/77 *HNL* (1978) a legislative act that had been found invalid was at issue. The Court ruled that the Community did not incur responsibility for damage caused by a legislative act solely because that act had been found illegal or invalid. In a legislative field involving wide discretion, the Community will not be liable unless the institution concerned has 'manifestly and gravely disregarded the limits on the exercise of its powers'. In Joined Cases 64, 113/76, 167, 239/78, 27, 28 and 45/79 *Dumortier* (1979) (see also **8.82** and **8.83**) a breach of the principle of non-discrimination was held to be sufficiently serious, and therefore giving rise to a damages claim. Producers of quellmehl and gritz, used in the brewing industry, were a small, clearly-defined group, and their losses went beyond the risks normally inherent in their business. In Case C–220/91 P *Commission v Stahlwerke Peine-Salzgitter AG* (1993) the Court of Justice held that arbitrariness in decision-making was not required to show that there had been a sufficiently serious breach. *Dumortier* should not be understood as stating that damages are only to be awarded where there is a small number of potential claimants. In Joined Cases C–104/89 and C–37/90 *Mulder No 2* (1992) a damages claim was successful even where there was a large number of potential claimants.

• *Third requirement*: the rule of law infringed must be one for the protection of the individual. In Joined Cases 9 and 12/60 *Vloeberghs* (1961): the principle of free movement of goods was not intended for the benefit of coal importers and so therefore damages were not payable, while in Joined Cases 5, 7 and 13–24/66 *Kampffmeyer* (1967), where a provision in an EC regulation intended at ensuring 'appropriate support for agricultural markets' intended to benefit, inter alia, the interests of individual undertakings such as importers, could give rise to damages.

8.88 From the case law it seems that as long as a legislative measure can be construed as designed in part to benefit a particular group of people then the third requirement is met. Moreover, the fact that an individual would not have standing to challenge the measure under what was Article 230 EC due to lack of direct and individual concern did not necessarily mean that the provision was not intended to protect his interests. Standing should now be easier to show as only direct concern is required. In Case C–352/98P *Bergaderm* (2000) the Court defined a 'sufficiently flagrant violation of a superior rule of law for the protection of the individual' in the same terms as a 'sufficiently serious breach' for the purposes of Member State liability for breaches of Community law rights (see **Chapter 7** and **8.85**, above). Bergaderm unsuccessfully sought damages because of the effect of a directive which prohibited the use of certain substances in cosmetics, arguing that the directive should be considered an administrative act rather than a general legislative measure because Bergaderm was the only entity affected by the measure. The Court ruled in *Bergaderm* that under Article 288(2) EC (now Article 340(2) TFEU) the 'sufficiently flagrant violation' threshold depends upon the clarity of the rule breached, the extent of discretion left to the relevant authorities, whether the error of law was excusable and whether the breach was intentional.

Limits of Union liability

8.89 Where the acts of servants or employees acting in an official capacity are at issue, the Union's vicarious liability extends only to those acts of its servants which, by virtue of an internal relationship, are the necessary extension of the tasks entrusted to the institutions (Case 9/69 *Sayag v Leduc* (1969)). This is a very restrictive interpretation of the Union's vicarious liability. *In casu*, the use of a private car by a Community servant could only be considered as constituting performance of his duties in the case of *force majeure* or exceptional circumstances of such compelling nature that the Community could not otherwise perform its functions. This, therefore, did not cover the use of a servant's private car during the performance of his duties.

8.90 The Court of Justice also considers the concurrent fault on the part of the Member States in the assessment of Union liability. The Court has proceeded by way of the following analysis: (a) is there joint liability on the part both of the Union and the Member State? If there is, then (b) is the Member State to be considered primarily liable so that it would be reasonable for it rather than the Union to pay compensation? If so, then (c) the applicant must pursue his remedy in the national courts before the Court of Justice can further entertain his claim: see Joined Cases 5, 7 and 13–24/66 *Kampffmeyer* (1967) (see 8.87); Case 96/71 *Haegeman* (1972). But where the real complaint is about the conduct of Union institutions, or where it is clear that national law can provide no remedy, an action under Article 340(2) TFEU may be admissible: see Case 281/82 *Unifrex* (1984); Case 175/84 *Krohn* (1986).

The parallel between the principles of state and Union liability

8.91 State liability is considered in **Chapter 7, Section III**, and there are important parallels between actions for damages arising against Member States for breaches of Union law rights, and non-contractual liability claims arising against the Union. The Court of Justice stated in Joined Cases C–46 and 48/93 *Brasserie du Pêcheur; Factortame III* (1996) that the test for state liability should not be different from that of the Community itself under Article 288(2) EC (now Article 340(2) TFEU). In Case C–352/98P *Bergaderm* (2000) (see 8.88) the Court then drew on the factors listed in *Brasserie du Pêcheur* for the purposes of establishing the 'sufficiently flagrant violation of a superior rule of law for the protection of the individual' (as per the *Schöppenstedt* formula, see 8.85 and 8.87) and the Community's liability under Article 288(2) EC. There is, however, a question with both Member State and Union liability claims as to the requirement of a 'superior rule of law' and its breach. According to the *Schöppenstedt* formula, liability only arose if there was a flagrant violation of a superior rule of law. In Case 224/01 *Köbler* (2003) (see 7.120) the argument was that such a condition should apply to infringements by national courts, if liability were to be extended to actions by national courts. However, in *Bergaderm* the Court did not consider the superior rule of law condition and held that the general or individual nature of a measure was not a decisive criterion for identifying the limits of an institution's discretion. This would indicate that the difference between legislative and administrative measures was no longer considered to be of major importance, and that the Court is likely to make further links between Member State liability and Union liability in future decisions.

FURTHER READING

Section I: Public Enforcement

European Commission's Twenty-Eighth Annual Report on Monitoring the Application of EU Law (COM(2011) 588). Earlier reports should be considered where appropriate.

Kilbey, I., 'The interpretation of Article 260 TFEU (ex Art 228 EC)' (2010) 35 *European Law Review* 370–386.

Prete, L. and Smulders, B., 'The coming of age of infringement proceedings' (2010) 47(1) *Common Market Law Review* 9–61.

Smith, M., 'Enforcement, monitoring, verification, outsourcing: the decline and decline of the infringement process' (2008) 33(6) *European Law Review* 777–802.

Wennerås, P., 'Sanctions against Member States under Article 260 TFEU: alive but not kicking?' (2012) 49(1) *Common Market Law Review* 145.

Section II: Judicial Review

Arnull, A., 'Private applicants and the action for annulment under Article 173 of the EC Treaty' (1995) 32 *Common Market Law Review* 7.

Berry E. and Boyes S., 'Access to justice in the Community Courts, A limited right' (2005) 24 *CJQ* 224.

Craig, P., 'Standing, rights and the structure of legal argument' (2003) 9 *European Public Law* 493.

Gutman, K., 'The evolution of the action for damages against the European Union and its place in the system of judicial protection' (2011) 48(3) *Common Market Law Review* 695.

Hilson, C., 'The role of discretion in EC law on non-contractual liability' (2005) 42 *Common Market Law Review* 677.

Tridimas, T., 'Liability for breach of Community law: growing up and mellowing down?' (2001) 38 *Common Market Law Review* 301.

Usher, J.A., 'Direct and individual Concern – an effective remedy or a conventional solution' (2003) 28 (5) *European Law Review* 575.

Ward, A., *Judicial Review and the Rights of Private Parties in EU Law* (2nd edn, Oxford: OUP, 2007).

Wyatt, D., 'The relationship between actions for annulment and references on validity after *TWD Deggendorf*' in Lonbay and Biondi (eds), *Remedies for Breach of EC Law* (Chichester: Wiley, 1997).

SELF-TEST QUESTIONS

Section I: Public Enforcement

1   Discuss how the Treaty allows the Commission to ensure that Member States fulfil their Treaty obligations.

2   Examine the extent to which the power given to the Commission to bring an action under Article 258 TFEU is a discretionary power. Why is the Commission given such a wide discretion?

3   Does a private party have standing to challenge a refusal by the Commission to bring an enforcement action against a Member State which is in breach of EU law?

4   Has the Court of Justice placed any limits on how the Commission manages the Article 258 TFEU action in order to protect the Member States?

5   What are the consequences of a declaration by the Court of Justice that a Member State has failed to fulfil an obligation under the Treaty? How was the position improved by subsequent Treaties?

6   Why is the Article 259 TFEU power rarely used by Member States?

Section II: Judicial Review

1   How can the European Court of Justice review actions of the Union institutions?

2   What types of Union acts may be reviewed by the Union Courts under Article 263 and Article 265 TFEU?

3   'Natural and legal persons face formidable obstacles in challenging an act of a Union institution before the Union Courts. The Lisbon changes may have eased some, but not all, of these obstacles.' Discuss.

4   What is meant by 'direct concern'?

5   Compare the position of privileged and non-privileged applicants in bringing a direct action against a Union institution.

6   (a) Assume that Samson is the sole importer of Indonesian typewriters in the United Kingdom and that such typewriters are not imported into any other Member State. In 2004 the United Kingdom Government accuses him of falsely labelling the typewriters as British products but has insufficient evidence to take action. In 2010 the United Kingdom learns that Samson intends to import a further large quota which it suspects he will market under the brand name of a German manufacturer. It requests the Commission to adopt a regulation banning the importation of typewriters from Indonesia for the year 2010. This is done. Can Samson bring proceedings against the Commission under Article 263 TFEU?

     (b) Assume that in 1998 the Council adopts a regulation giving Union nationals with a law degree from a Member State the right to practise in any other Member State. Article 7, however, provides that if the degree was obtained before the Member State where it was obtained had joined the Union, a special examination in Union law (set by the Commission) must be passed. Justinian is a Greek who obtained his degree in Greece in 1969. Does he have standing to bring annulment proceedings (against Article 7 only) under Article 263 TFEU? Would the position be any different if the measure was adopted in the form of a decision addressed to each of the Member States?

7   'There are certain circumstances where neither an action for failure nor an action for annulment are available, and a party may be left without any judicial remedy whatsoever against the conduct of the institutions.' Is this a true description of the situation? Discuss.

9

Free movement of goods (I): the abolition of customs duties and internal taxation

SUMMARY

- Basic concepts
- The customs union—common customs tariff
- Free movement of goods provisions in the Treaty
- Customs duties and charges having equivalent effect
- Internal taxation: discriminatory and/or protective
- VAT issues
- Excise duties and duty-free

Introduction

9.1 The European Union combines elements of a customs union, an internal market, common economic policies and provisions for economic and monetary union for all Member States, including the operational rules for the euro and the euro area. The premise of all these rules is that the European Union strives towards economic integration: see Articles 2, 3 and 4 TFEU. The Union was intended from its inception to be more than a free trade area, i.e. an arrangement between states in which they agree to remove customs duties and quotas in trade between them, but where they remain free individually to determine the duties on imports from third countries.

9.2 A *customs union* is a customs area involving various states cordoned off by a single external tariff and within whose boundaries no customs duties or quotas apply to all goods regardless of their origin. Once goods originating in a third country have been admitted anywhere in the customs union, they may circulate freely throughout the Member States. The customs union thus presents itself as a single trading block to the outside world.

9.3 An *internal market* entails yet closer integration among the participating states. The objective of the internal market is to achieve not just free movement of goods, but also free movement of services and of the means of production (labour and capital).

It comprises common external regulation for both goods and services as well as for production factors. Thus, the internal market encompasses a customs union and in addition needs free movement of labour, i.e. persons, as labour is a factor of production and a major element in the production of goods.

The customs union

9.4 The free movement of goods is a central feature of the European Union and a foundational freedom of the internal market. The 'four freedoms' in the Treaty on the Functioning of the European Union are the free movement of goods, persons, services and capital. The next two chapters are concerned with the free movement of goods. In order for goods to move without obstacle within the Union, it was necessary, first of all, to abolish customs duties and similar charges between the Member States (Article 31 TFEU (ex Article 26 EC)), to deal with internal taxation (Article 110 TFEU (ex Article 90 EC)), and to see to it that non-pecuniary obstacles, such as quantitative restrictions and similar barriers, should not exist without good reasons (Articles 34, 35 and 36 TFEU (ex Articles 28, 29 and 30 EC)).

9.5 The Treaty on the Functioning of the European Union includes two chapters dealing with free movement of goods entitled 'Chapter 2—Customs Cooperation' (Article 33 TFEU) and 'Chapter 3—Prohibition of Quantitative Restrictions Between Member States' (Articles 34–37 TFEU). Chapter 2 in Title VII, which lays down common rules on competition, taxation and approximation of laws, deals with tax provisions and internal taxation in Articles 110–113 TFEU. Previous versions of the Treaties provided for the abolition of existing duties within a transitional period, and Article 30 TFEU prohibits the imposition of *new* duties. Article 28 TFEU provides that the Union will 'comprise a customs union which will cover all trade in goods, and which shall involve the prohibition between Member States of customs duties on imports and exports and of all charges having equivalent effect and the adoption of a common customs tariff in their relations with third countries'.

9.6 In addition to the removal of barriers to trade within the EU itself, a customs union includes the harmonisation of customs regulations on trade with third countries. To this effect, the EU has established, and operates, a common customs tariff (CCT), i.e. a single external tariff applied by all EU Member States to imports originating in third countries, the level of which is fixed by the Council on a proposal from the Commission (Article 31 TFEU). In addition, Union customs rules must be considered in a wider international context, especially in the light of the arrangements under the World Trade Organisation (WTO) which include the General Agreement on Tariffs and Trade (GATT).

The necessary uniformity of regulation of the external commercial relations of the Member States is ensured through the Customs Code, as updated by Regulation

No 450/08/EC. This codifies all the provisions of customs legislation governing the Union's trade with third countries.

Free movement of goods provisions in the Treaty on the Functioning of the European Union

9.7 The Treaty on the Functioning of the European Union lists the following main obstacles to the free movement of goods in the EU:

- customs duties on imports (and exports): Articles 28 and 30 TFEU;
- charges having equivalent effect to customs duties: Articles 28 and 30 TFEU;
- discriminatory internal taxation on imported goods: Article 110 TFEU;
- quantitative restrictions on imports: Article 34 TFEU and exports; Article 35 TFEU;
- state monopolies of a commercial character: Article 37 TFEU.

9.8 No definition is given in the EU Treaty of the term 'goods', which is used interchangeably with the term 'products'. See for example the difference in terminology between Article 28(1) and (2) TFEU. However, the Court of Justice stated in Case 7/68 *Commission v Italy* (1968) that:

> By goods within the meaning of [Article 28 TFEU], there must be understood products which can be valued in money and which are capable, as such, of forming the subject of commercial transactions.

Obviously, this definition is very wide and has been held to cover, inter alia, articles of an artistic, historic, archaeological or ethnographic nature. Case 7/68 *Commission v Italy* (1968); gold and silver collectors' coins, provided the coins were not in circulation as legal tender: Case 7/78 *Thompson* (1978); all forms of waste: Case C–2/90 *Commission v Belgium* (1992); as well as electricity: Case C–393/92 *Almelo* (1994).

9.9 This chapter deals with *pecuniary* charges imposed on goods which may constitute an obstacle to the free movement of goods across borders within the Union.

In the original Treaties, fiscal policy and taxation were mainly deemed to fall within the competence of the Member States. The Treaty is generally only concerned with problems of *indirect* taxation such as customs duties, internal taxation and VAT, whereas direct taxation is not, generally speaking, within the competence of the Union.

It should be noted that, once goods enter the Union at any point of entry, they are in free circulation therein and no further obstacles can be put in their way unless they are justified by one of the exceptions provided for by the Treaty.

Customs duties and common customs tariff

9.10 In the original EC Treaty, Article 12, which became the first article to be found to be directly effective by the Court in Case 26/62 *van Gend en Loos* (see above **Chapter 7**), prohibited the raising of customs duties or the introduction of new ones. It was known as the 'standstill' provision. Article 30 TFEU, which has replaced Article 12, now simply states that:

> *Customs duties on imports and exports and charges having equivalent effect shall be prohibited between Member States. This prohibition shall also apply to customs duties of a fiscal nature.*

Article 28 TFEU provides for the prohibition of all customs duties on imports and exports and of charges having equivalent effect and for the establishment of the common customs tariff in relation to third countries, i.e. those which are not Member States. The CCT makes goods from within the EU more competitive than those from third world countries because third world country goods attract duty on entering the EU. In the early years of the EEC, attention was concentrated on the CCT and as a result the tariff was established ahead of schedule. In addition, all customs duties such as those at issue in Case 26/62 *van Gend en Loos*, i.e. between Member States, were removed in advance of the 1969 deadline for the end of the transitional period. When the Court of Justice found that Article 12 (now Article 30 TFEU) had direct effect, this meant that the abolition of customs duties was made more effective, as individuals and companies could turn directly to their national courts in case of difficulties. In time, the articles in the EEC Treaty relating to the abolition of the duties as well as to the establishment of the CCT were therefore removed from the Treaty. Thus, the original European Economic Community and its precursor to the current internal market law was remarkably successful at achieving the customs union, but other barriers to the free movement of goods, i.e. charges having equivalent effect to customs duties, still remained.

9.11 A customs duty is a charge, determined on the basis of a tariff, specifying the rate of duty to be paid by the importer of the host state. Customs duties are prohibited because they are protectionist: they make the imported good more expensive than the rival domestic product.

Charges having equivalent effect to a customs duty

9.12 The abolition of customs duties does not necessarily mean that goods will remain free from other charges. There are numerous charges and other compulsory payments that can have the same effect as customs duties, that is, rendering the imported goods more expensive in comparison to domestically produced goods. In practice, the effect of such charges is no different from that of import or export duties. Consequently, such charges are referred to as 'charges having equivalent effect' (CEEs) or 'equivalent charges to customs duties'. The prohibition was introduced to prevent Member States from circumventing the prohibition on customs duties by dressing them up or being creative with them in such a way that they manifest themselves as something else. It is not always easy in practice to determine whether a specific charge amounts to a 'charge having equivalent effect'. In Joined Cases 2 and 3/62 *Commission v Luxembourg and Belgium* (1962), the Court defined equivalent charges as:

> Duties whatever their description or technique, imposed unilaterally, which apply specifically to a product imported by a Member State but not to a similar national product and which by altering the price, have the same effect upon the free movement of goods as a customs duty.

The Court of Justice gave a fuller definition of a CEE in Case 24/68 *Commission v Italy* (the 'statistical levy' cases 1969) where it said:

> Any pecuniary charge, however small and whatever its designation and mode of application, which is imposed unilaterally on domestic or foreign goods by reason of the fact that they cross a frontier…constitutes a charge having equivalent effect…even if it is not imposed for the benefit of the State, it is not discriminatory or protective in effect and if the product on which the charge is imposed is not in competition with the domestic product.

The relevant criterion is always the discrepancy in the treatment of imported goods in comparison with domestically produced goods, to the extent that the discrepancy is disadvantageous to imports. See Case 132/78 *Denkavit* (1979).

9.13 There are many examples of charges imposed on imported products by reason of the fact that they cross a frontier. The key feature of the term is the reference to 'any pecuniary charge' which means that this concept relates only to fiscal measures and the reference to 'however small' indicates that there is no *de minimis* rule. Therefore, any charge, irrespective of the amount, even 10 lire as in the statistical levy case, will breach Article 30 TFEU. The mode or designation of the rule is also immaterial: irrespective of the way in which a Member State describes the charge it will breach Article 30 TFEU. For example, Case 24/68 *Commission v Italy* (1969), charges made on the pretext of collecting statistics; Case 132/80 *United Foods and Abele v Belgium* (1981), charges made for health inspections on products from other Member States; and Case 132/82 *Commission v Belgium* (1983), charges for storage prior to the completion of customs formalities.

9.14 The absolute prohibition on CEEs applies even where the money is not used for a protectionist purpose. In Joined Cases 2 and 3/69 *Sociaal Fonds voor de Diamantarbeiders v Brachfeld* (1969), Belgian law required all importers of uncut diamonds to pay a levy into a workers' social benefit fund. The Court of Justice ruled that the nature of the prohibition on customs duties was general and absolute. The purpose for which any levy was made was of no importance. The prohibition was based, therefore, on the fact that:

> Any pecuniary charge—however small—imposed on goods by reason of the fact that they cross a frontier constitutes an obstacle to the movement of such goods.

The Court said that customs duties were prohibited independently of any consideration of the purpose for which they were introduced and the destination of the revenue obtained. The Court is seemingly only interested in the effect of the charge on the free movement of the goods, by the subsequent imposition of a charge.

Therefore, in this case the Belgian law was contrary to Article 30 TFEU (then Article 12). The Court has intimated that if a state wishes to pursue other objectives, such as welfare, etc., then the internal taxation system should be used, deriving tax from all goods irrespective of origin of production.

9.15 The Court of Justice considered levies in the electricity market in the Netherlands. In Case C–206/06 *Essent Netwerk Noord* (2008), the Court of Justice ruled that Article 30 TFEU (ex Article 25 EC) precluded any statutory rule under which domestic purchasers of electricity were required to pay their net operator a price surcharge on the amounts of domestic and imported electricity which were transmitted to them. That surcharge was then passed on to a statutory body which also happened to be joint subsidiary of the four domestic generating undertakings which had also previously managed the costs of all electricity generated and imported. In fact the surcharge was used to offset costs borne by domestic electricity generators, thereby forming the equivalent of a charge having equivalent effect to an import tariff.

9.16 One of the charges most frequently imposed on products entering and leaving a country are those for health inspection. Animal products and plants may still be subjected to such inspections if these are necessary to protect public health. Article 36 TFEU provides for exemptions from the free movement of goods, inter alia, on grounds of public health and the protection of national treasures. Inspections of imports of slaughtered meat, fruits and vegetables, living animals and plants may, therefore, be necessary, but could the inspection fee charged violate Article 28 TFEU? This question has given rise to a complex body of case law. The Court has held that inspection fees levied only on imported products violated Article 28 TFEU (then Article 9), even though some other inspection fee was levied on similar domestic products: Case 29/72 *SpA Marimex v Italian Finance Administration* (1972). Later, the Court held that a state could not justify a fee on the ground that the inspection is necessary to protect general health, stating that the public should bear the cost and not the importer: Case 87/75 *Bresciani* (1976). However, the Court added that if the same fee is charged for the inspection of imported products and of domestic products, 'applied according to the same criteria and at the same stage of production', then the fee is not a charge equivalent to a duty, but rather a systematically applied internal tax, which is to be analysed under Article 110 TFEU (then Article 95).

9.17 In many sectors, a system of Union-wide health and safety inspections has been set up. In Case 46/76 *Bauhuis v Netherlands* (1977), the Court held that a fee for the health inspection of bovine animals, required by a Community agricultural regulation before export to another state, did not constitute an illegal charge equivalent to an export duty, provided the fee covered only the actual cost of the inspection. In Case 77/72 *Capolongo v Maya* (1973), Italy had introduced a charge on imported egg boxes as part of an overall charge on cellulose products, the aim being to finance the production of paper and cardboard in Italy. The charge was imposed on all egg boxes, imported and domestic, but the Court said there was breach of Article 13 (now repealed) which provided for the progressive abolition of customs duties. It was discriminatory if it was intended exclusively to support activities which specifically benefited the domestic product.

9.18 Case 77/76 *Fratelli Cucchi v Avez SpA* (1977) concerned the legality of a levy on imported sugar; domestic sugar was subject to the same levy. The proceeds were to finance the sugar industry, both beet producers and sugar refiners. The Court held that:

- if the charge had the *sole* purpose of financing activities for the specific advantage of the domestic product;
- if the taxed domestic product and the domestic product to benefit are the same; and
- the charges imposed on the domestic product are made up in full by the benefit

this would be a charge equivalent to customs duty.

Even if the charge gave only partial benefit to the domestic product, it may still breach Article 110 TFEU (see Case 73/79 *Commission v Italy* (1980)).

9.19 The above cases show that it is not always easy to distinguish between acceptable and unacceptable charges. If the UK Government imposes conditions on imported beef which reflect the same rigorous animal health conditions and inspections which British beef undergoes and the same charges are made for such inspections for British as for imported beef, this may be justifiable on health grounds, but it would not be acceptable if the intention was to make it more difficult for non-British beef to be sold in the United Kingdom than for domestic beef.

Defences/justification

9.20 The Treaty does not provide any defences to a breach of Article 30 TFEU. The Court has rejected attempts by the Member States to parallel the derogations that exist in the other free movement areas. This said, the Court has recognised three instances where a charge may be lawful:

(1) payments for a genuine administrative service rendered to the importer/exporter;

(2) charges for inspections required by European Union law: Case 18/87 *Commission v Germany* (1988); or international law: Case C–111/89 *Bakker Hillegom*(1990);

(3) charges falling within the scope of internal taxation: Case 78/76 *Steinike und Weinlig* (1977).

Charges for services rendered

9.21 Although the Court of Justice has stated in a number of cases that charges for services rendered *are* lawful, this is as long as the payment is in consideration for a genuine service of direct benefit to the importer or exporter. It has imposed a number of conditions to limit the scope of such charges. Article 30 TFEU will not apply if the national court considers that the charge in question is the consideration for a service actually rendered to the importer and is of an amount commensurate with that service. It is however, difficult to convince the Court that any charge is a service, and it is wary about the abuse of this rule. In Case 63/74 *Cadsky v Istituto Nazionale per il Commercio Estero* (1975), an inspection charge was levied by the Italian state for quality control of exported vegetables. Italy argued that such quality controls improved the reputation of Italian produce abroad and were, therefore, of benefit to all exporters. The Court of Justice considered that such a benefit was too remote from individual exporters and that the charge could not be regarded as an individual service to an exporter. In Case 170/88 *Ford España v Spain* (1989) a flat rate charge was made for customs formalities carried out at the place of destination. Spain argued that this was of benefit to the importer who thus did not to have to carry out these formalities at the border. However, the charge was made on a flat-rate basis and the Court again considered this could not be a specific service to an individual importer. In Case 340/87 *Commission v Italy* (1989) certain formalities were carried out for importers outside defined hours and this *was* considered to be a specific service for which an additional charge could be made. However, it was found that the customs posts should have been open anyway during those hours under EC regulations and, therefore, the charge could not be considered to have been imposed for a specific service. In Case 24/68 *Commission v Italy* (statistical levy) (1969) (see above at **9.12** and **9.13**) the Italian Government argued that the 10 lire levy constituted consideration for a service (as the information supplied afforded importers a better competitive position on the Italian market and exporters enjoyed a similar advantage abroad); the Court disagreed. It stated that because the statistical information was beneficial to the economy as a whole it should have been paid for by the general public, and not by the individual importer.

There are inevitably borderline cases, the foremost of which is Case 132/82 *Commission v Belgium* (1983). Belgium charged for the use of a special warehouse within the country where customs formalities could be completed instead of at the frontier. The Commission argued that this constituted a breach of Article 30 TFEU (then Article 25 EC). The Advocate General in the case made a compelling argument that this facility provided a specific benefit for the importer. The Court disagreed and found that when payments of storage charges are demanded solely in connection with the completion of customs formalities, it could not be regarded as the consideration for a service actually rendered to the importer.

Charges arising under a provision of EU law

9.22 If charges are imposed under Union rules they will not be considered to be charges having an equivalent effect to a customs duty and as such the costs can be passed on to the importer provided they satisfy the following four conditions:

(1) they do not exceed the actual costs of the inspections in connection with which they are charged;

(2) the inspections in question are obligatory and uniform for all the products concerned in the Union;

(3) they are prescribed by EU law in the general interest of the Union;

(4) they promote the free movement of goods and, in particular, if they avoid obstacles which may have been raised by unilateral inspection measures instituted under Article 36 TFEU (see further **Chapter 10**).

9.23 In Case C–18/87 *Commission v Germany* (1988), where the above criteria (**9.22**) were laid down, the German *Länder* were entitled to charge a fee to cover the costs of veterinary inspections on imported live animals carried out under Directive 81/389 which concerned the protection of animals during international transport. In Case 46/76 *Bauhuis v Netherlands* (1977) some of the fees paid for animal health inspections were related to national law requirements, and some to Community law requirements under a directive. The Court held that the Community law charges promoted the free movement of goods, as they removed obstacles to free movement which national measures under Article 36 TFEU (ex Article 30) would have created. The national inspection charges, however, did constitute an obstacle to free movement and were, therefore, considered to be an equivalent charge.

The same reasoning would also apply to charges for inspections carried out under international agreements, as long as the need for unilateral inspection is again removed.

Charges falling within the scope of internal taxation

9.24 Where a charge 'relates to a general system of internal dues applied rationally and systematically, in accordance with the same criteria to domestic products and imported products alike' then the legality and charge falls to be considered under Article 110 TFEU.

Discriminatory or protective taxation: Articles 110–113 TFEU

9.25 Articles 110–113 TFEU (ex Articles 90–93 EC) are to be found within the 'Tax Provisions' under Title VII, Chapter 2 of the Treaty on the Functioning of the European Union. The intention of these articles is to prevent Member States from replacing the customs duties they had been obliged to abolish with discriminatory internal taxes. Article 110 TFEU has been directly effective since Case 57/65 *Alfons Lütticke GmbH v Hauptzollamt Saarlouis* (1966). This case confirmed that the doctrine of direct effect did not just apply to Treaty articles containing a prohibition or 'stand-still' clause, as was the case in Case 26/62 *van Gend en Loos* (see **Chapter 7**).

9.26 Articles 28–30 and 110–113 TFEU are complementary but mutually exclusive. The distinction is logical and easily discernable: the first set of Articles (28–30) deals with goods arriving at the frontier, while Articles 110–113 deal with taxes imposed internally by the Member State. The distinction has its importance. Whereas charges at the border are seldom justified and do not have to be protectionist, internal taxation may be justified as long as it does not discriminate against imported products. Such discrimination may take the form of direct or indirect discrimination. The first paragraph of Article 110 TFEU deals with direct or indirect taxation imposed on similar products; the second paragraph deals with taxation which would afford indirect protection to other products. It is pivotal to the understanding of Article 110 TFEU, that Member States are accorded considerable discretion to determine the content of their own taxation policy. This discretion still exists because the Member States have been extremely reluctant to accord the European Union the ability to set tax policy, for a number of reasons. The ability to tax and spend is one of the key elements of any Member State's domestic government's arsenal, when it comes to electing parties in general elections. Votes are seemingly often won by promises of tax cuts and tax rebates, and these are also tools by which aspects of Member State competences are funded. The ability for a Member State to independently fund a war would be seriously hampered if tax levels were set in Brussels. It is therefore unlikely that the EU will have competence in this area for many years, if ever. The current concern, therefore, is that any scheme of taxation making a distinction between products does so only on the basis of objective criteria which is unrelated to the place of origin.

9.27 Even if there is little or no domestic production, the tax levied on imported products will still be regarded as internal taxation if the tax is part of a general system of internal taxation applying equally to whole classes of domestic or foreign products (see Case 78/76 *Steinike & Weinlig v Germany* (1977)). In Case 90/79 *Commission v France* (the French *Reprography* case) (1981) a levy was imposed on reprographic equipment, most of which was imported. The Court of Justice said that the fact that most of the goods on which the tax was imposed were imported was not in itself sufficient to fall foul of Article 110 TFEU (then Article 95). If the levy related to:

> [a] general system of internal dues applied systematically to categories of products in accordance with objective criteria irrespective of the origin of the products [at paragraph 14]

then it would not be caught by Article 110 TFEU.

9.28 Since Article 110 TFEU is contained in Title VII of the Treaty dealing with tax provisions, on the face of it this Article would, therefore, not apply to products originating in third countries. According to Article 28(2) only provisions within the first two chapters apply to products originating in third countries. Article 110 TFEU only refers to products 'of other Member States'.

However, in Case 193/85 *Co-operativa Co-Frutta* (1987) Article 110 TFEU (then Article 95) was interpreted by the Court in parallel to the other rules on the free movement of goods. This case concerned taxation of non-EEC bananas imported into Italy through other Member States. The Court referred to the principles of the common customs tariff and the common commercial policy which meant that products, once imported into the Community and in free circulation, should not be subject to discriminatory or protective internal taxation. Article 110 TFEU would not be infringed, however, if the goods are imported directly from a third country into the Member State.

9.29 In contrast to Articles 30 and 34 TFEU, internal taxation only constitutes a breach of Union law under Article 110 TFEU if it is discriminatory or has protective effect. Furthermore, it only applies to products imported from other Member States. Nevertheless, in Case 142/77 *Statens Kontrol v Larsen* (1978) the Court said the aim of the Treaty was to guarantee generally the neutrality of systems of internal taxation. If this meant, therefore, that discriminatory taxation imposed on a product to be *exported* constituted an obstacle to the free movement of goods, such a tax was also incompatible with the Treaty. As *Larsen* and *Co-Fruita* show, the Court again showed its readiness to 'fill the gap' in the terms of a particular Treaty provision in order to attain the objectives of the Treaty.

Discriminatory taxation

9.30 Discriminatory taxation is dealt with under two heads of Article 110 TFEU. The first head relates to products that are similar. The second relates to products that are deemed to be in a competing relationship.

Similar products

9.31 Article 110(1) stipulates that:

> No Member State shall impose, directly or indirectly, on the products of other Member States any internal taxation of any kind in excess of that imposed directly or indirectly on similar domestic products.

Determining whether products are similar

9.32 Since the inception of Article 110 TFEU the Court of Justice has applied two tests to determine whether goods are similar or not. It may seem obvious when goods are similar; however, trying to discern between dark and light tobacco or wine made from grapes and wine made from fruit is not always an easy exercise. The Court of Justice commenced deliberations in this field by applying a formal test which examined whether the product fell within the same fiscal, customs or statistical classification system. This was not always satisfactory, primarily as in some instances little thought had actually gone into this initial classification, with the tangible end result that some goods that were quite obviously similar were in fact deemed not to be. The second approach adopted by the Court centred on a factual comparison of the products, taking into account an economic analysis of their use. The scope of Article 110(1) TFEU is determined on the basis of similar and comparable use not necessarily on the basis of strict similarity. The Court has variously considered methods of manufacture, properties, origin, meeting the same needs of consumers (both current and future), process of creation, organoleptic properties and objective characteristics in trying to determine similarity.

9.33 By way of illustration the following cases demonstrate the approach that the Court has taken in assessing similarity. In Case 106/84 *Commission v Denmark* (1986) and Case 243/84 *John Walker & Sons Ltd v Minister for Skatterog Afgifter* (1986) the Court accepted that wine made from grapes and wine made from other fruit were similar, although the alcohol content was achieved in different ways. Both came from the same basic product and both were fermented. Thus, they could satisfy the same needs of consumers, although this was to be assessed by the potential development of consumer habits rather than by the existing situation. However, Scotch whisky and liqueur made from fruit were not similar: they were made from different basic products, cereal as against fruit, and obtained by different methods, distillation as against fermentation. Moreover, their respective alcohol content differed significantly. Different spirits are not necessarily always similar if they have sufficiently pronounced different characteristics. Some spirits have relatively specific uses, whereas others are used more widely and may be consumed neat, mixed or diluted (see Joined Cases 168, 169 and 171/78 *Commission v France, Italy and Denmark* (1980)).

Direct discrimination

9.34 Under the heading of discriminatory taxation, the discrimination can be manifest in one of two ways: first, direct discrimination and, secondly, indirect discrimination.

Direct discrimination involves less favourable treatment of the imported product on the ground of its origin; the most obvious example of this is where only the imported product is subject to the tax: Case 57/65 *Lütticke v Hauptzollamt Saarlouis*(1966). In this case powdered milk from Luxembourg was imported into Germany but was subject to a tax which did not apply to domestically produced products. Direct discrimination may also manifest itself in less obvious ways. For instance, where an imported product is taxed at a much higher rate than the domestic product or the Member State uses different methods for calculating tax for the domestic product and the imported product. The conditions by which the tax is paid or tax relief calculated and disseminated may also constitute direct discrimination. In the instance where the same products are charged the same amount of tax, but the method of collection favours the domestic product, this would constitute discrimination (see Case 55/79 *Commission v Ireland* (1980), where importers were required to pay the charge immediately, whereas domestic producers were allowed a longer time to pay). Again it is crucial to note that there are no express defences to Article 110 TFEU. Directly discriminatory taxes breach Article 110 TFEU and cannot be saved. The action that the Member State has to take in this situation is to remove the discriminatory element of the taxation policy and so equalise the tax.

Indirect discrimination

9.35 Indirect discrimination, although more difficult to determine, is also outlawed. Indirect measures on their face (in law) make no reference to the origin of the product, but in reality (in fact) it imposes a practical and particular burden on the imported goods. The concept is best illustrated by the following cases: in Case 112/84 *Humblot v Directeur des Services Fiscaux* (1985) cars with a power rating of below 16 CV were taxed on a progressive, gradual scale. Above this rating, all more powerful cars were taxed at a much higher, and at a flat rate. Traditionally, French cars are smaller than, for example, German cars and there was no French car produced which had a power rating of more than 16 CV. Humblot successfully challenged the much higher tax. The Court said that this tax was liable to cancel out any advantages imported cars might have in terms of maintenance, comfort etc. It offended against the principle of neutrality with which domestic taxation must comply. The French subsequently amended the system of taxation. However, this too was declared by the Court to be incompatible with the Treaty in Case 433/85 *Feldain v Directeur des Services Fiscaux* (1987), because the amended system modified the discrimination, but did not eliminate it and still favoured the smaller French cars.

9.36 In Case C–290/05 *Nádasdi* (2006) and Case C–333/05 *Németh* (2006), the applicant had purchased a car in Germany, and had applied, on return to Hungary, to register the vehicle in that Member State. A tax levied on the import of the car, which was determined on the technical and environmental aspects of the vehicle, was contested by both applicants. The Hungarian court referred the cases to the Court of Justice. As the tax was levied by virtue of the characteristics of the car, and not solely due to the fact that the vehicle had crossed a frontier, the measures should be considered under Article 110 TFEU (ex Article 90 EC). The Court examined the nature of registration of vehicles within Hungary, and that of vehicles imported into the country. In the former category, registration charges were based on the value of the car, which would diminish with the age of the vehicle. By contrast, a car imported into Hungary of any age would attract a registration fee based on characteristics of the car, and could cost substantially more to register. The fact that depreciation of the car was not taken into account caused the tax to be caught by Article 110 TFEU.

9.37 In Case C–313/05 *Maciej Brzeziński v Dyrektor Izby Celnej w Warszawie* (2007), the claimant had purchased a car in Germany, and on return to Poland had paid excise duty on the car. He requested the reimbursement of this sum on the grounds that it was contrary to Community law. Upon reference to the Court of Justice, the Court stated that the measure was a matter of internal taxation and therefore did not fall under Articles 28 and 30 TFEU (ex Articles 23 and 25 EC). The Court then turned to Article 110 TFEU (ex Article 90 EC), reiterating established case law that Article 110 TFEU is infringed where the tax charged on the imported product and that charged on a similar domestic product are calculated on different criteria which may have the effect of attracting a higher excise duty on imported goods. The Court stated that a charge would be incompatible if it exceeded the residual amount of the same duty incorporated into the market value of similar vehicles previously registered in the Member State, thus raising the charge.

Following on from this, the Court reiterated its findings in the similar case, Case C-426/07 *Krawczyński* (2008). It stated that the first paragraph of Article 110 TFEU (ex Article 90 EC) should be interpreted as precluding an excise duty imposed on the sale of vehicles in Poland following their import into the country but prior to their registration there, where the amount of the duty exceeds the residual amount of the same duty incorporated into the market value of similar vehicles previously registered in that Member State. In other words, a duty levied on imported vehicles that did not take into account the age, and market value of the vehicle, in comparison to levies on domestic vehicles that did, was incompatible with Article 110(1) TFEU.

9.38 In Case 127/75 *Bobie v Hauptzollamt Aachen-Nord* (1976) the German system of taxation of beer was scrutinised. The system was designed to benefit small producers by imposing lower taxes on lower volumes of production. For imported products, however, a uniform rate applied which was mid-way between the two rates imposed on German beer producers. This, therefore, had an adverse effect on Bobie, a small Belgian brewery which would have paid less if it had been a small German brewery. The Court ruled that this was discriminatory. If it was not possible administratively to apply different rates to imports as it was difficult to obtain production figures from foreign breweries, the lowest rate should be applied to imports. This may well result in reverse discrimination by treating importers more favourably, but reverse discrimination is not outlawed by the Treaty.

9.39 Distinguishing direct and indirect discrimination under Article 110(1) TFEU is important; whilst direct discrimination on the grounds of nationality cannot be justified, tax rules of a Member State which tend nonetheless to favour the national producers may be saved if there is some objective justification for the conduct complained of. The Court will allow the defence that there was some objective policy reason, which is acceptable to the Union, to justify the state's action. The philosophy behind this is to prevent the Treaty articles from becoming too harsh or draconian in their application. Provided therefore that the national interest is unconnected with the origin of the product, that it pursues an objective recognised by the EU as legitimate, and that the steps taken to protect that interest are proportionate, then there is no breach of Article 110 TFEU. Environmental protection in Case 132/88 *Commission v Greece* (1990); consumer protection/morality in Case 252/86 *Bergandi* (1988); regional development in Case 196/85 *Commission v France* (1987); and public security in Case 140/79 *Chemial*

Farmaceutici (1981) are all successful instances where potential justifications put forward by the Member State have been recognised by the Court, allowing the Member States to justify tax arrangements which differentiated between certain products on the basis of objective criteria.

Goods in competition

9.40   Where goods are not deemed to be similar for the purposes of Article 110(1) TFEU then paragraph 2 of Article 110 will be examined to ascertain whether the goods are in competition with each other. Competition extends to satisfy paragraph 2 in instances where it may only be partial, indirect or potential. If any such competition is found the Court will then go on to analyse whether the domestic goods benefit from 'indirect fiscal protectionism'. The second paragraph of Article 110 TFEU applies if taxation on imported products is set so that it affords protection to domestic products. Such protection does not have to be proved in reality; it is sufficient if the tax mechanism is likely to achieve such a result. The protective effect has to be assessed by looking at the overall position. Protection may exist even where the domestic product is similarly subjected to unfavourable treatment, if the proportion of domestic product so treated is minimal. The reverse also applies if only a small percentage of the imported product is given favourable treatment. As long as imports are treated unfavourably in comparison to domestic products, protection probably exists.

Article 110(2) TFEU stipulates 'Furthermore, no Member State shall impose on the products of other Member States any internal taxation of such a nature so as to afford indirect protection to other products'.

Determining competing products

9.41   How does the Court determine whether products are in competition with each other? Would wine and beer, for example, be in competition so that they should not receive different internal tax treatment? The Court has adopted a number of tests to determine whether goods are in competition. It has applied an economic test based on cross-elasticity of demand. The Court considers whether, if the price of one product goes up, sales of the other increase. The Court has also taken into account the nature of manufacturing, the composition of the product and consumer preferences (present and future). The overriding objective of the Court is subjectively to analyse all the inherent characteristics and ask the question whether the tax system is likely to bring about the protective effect which Article 110 TFEU is seeking to prevent.

9.42   The seminal case with respect to goods in a competing relationship is Case 170/78 *Commission v United Kingdom* (1980). Here the Commission maintained that wine and beer were competing products as there was some actual, and also potential, substitution of one product for another. The UK Government pointed to the differences in manufacture, basic product, price structure and alcohol content. Consumers would consume beer in pubs and in connection with work, whereas wine consumption was more unusual and special and part of a different social custom. The Court rejected the view that the degree of substitutability should be tested against one country or one region as consumer habits could not be considered as fixed. It accepted the Commission's argument that both drinks are capable of meeting identical needs: they may be used as thirst-quenching drinks or to accompany meals. Consumer habits should not be crystallised by giving advantages to one drink over another. Nevertheless, the Court qualified this by finding a competitive relationship only between beer and the cheaper wines with lower alcoholic strength. Twenty years later, it would seem that the Commission's view has been vindicated. It is quite clear that consumer habits in the United Kingdom *have* changed and that much more wine is consumed, both in pubs and privately, than was the case 30 years ago.

9.43 In Case 184/85 *Commission v Italy* (1987) and in Case 193/85 *Co-operativa Co-Frutta v Amministrazione delle Finanze dello Stato* (1987) the Court regarded bananas and table fruit typically produced in Italy as being in partial competition because they were alternative choices for the consumer. The banana production in Italy was so small as to be negligible and a tax imposed on both domestic and imported bananas was therefore regarded as giving indirect protection to Italian table fruit. Even if this case concerned a charge on a product from another Member State when there is little or no similar or identical domestic production, it does not constitute a charge equivalent to a customs duty, but an internal tax under Article 110 TFEU if it relates to a general system of internal dues applied systematically to categories of products in accordance with objective criteria irrespective of the origin of the product. If we contrast this case with Case 27/76 *United Brands Co v Commission* (1978) we see a different approach by the Court in a slightly different context. Although in the Article 110 TFEU cases the Court considered the degree of substitutability sufficient to constitute partial competition which could justify a finding of fiscal protection, in an Article 102 TFEU case (then Article 86) such substitutability was not sufficient to conclude that bananas did not form a market distinct from other fruit markets (see further **14.100**).

9.44 The result of a finding that the goods are in a competing relationship and that there has been an element of protectionism means that only the protective effect need be removed. This may mean a small percentage increase or decrease in the level of tax; *prima facie* it does not require equalisation of the tax rates. Moreover, in Case C–167/05 *Commission v Sweden* (2008) the Court of Justice appeared to establish a *de minimis* principle regarding the removal of the competitive disadvantage, where 'the difference in the tax treatment of those two products is not liable to influence consumer behaviour'. Such a principle indicates a less intense review of Member State internal taxation. This case can be compared with the more intensive, and less presumptive, approach regarding consumer behaviour in Case 170/78 *Commission v United Kingdom* (1980); see **9.42**. However, the exact parameters of any newly established margin for Member States remain unclear, questionable and possibly dependent on subject matter.

A globalised approach to Article 110 TFEU?

9.45 The Court has taken a variety of approaches in this field, and it has been difficult to discern whether it has used limb 1 or 2 of Article 110 TFEU; it has sometimes instead adopted a globalised approach. There is merit in such an approach as in some cases inevitably the products are both similar and also in a competing relationship, as evidenced by the wine and beer litigation. As outlined above the remedies to be derived from the two approaches differ, and this may lead to interesting conclusions: do you tax the products at the same level—by equalising the tax regime; or do you simply remove the protective effect; or is it possible that the tax can be justified? To remove the inevitable confusion, the Court has adopted a far more rigorous approach to deciding between the two paragraphs. It is clear now that the two approaches will be dealt with in a mutually exclusive way. The importance of discerning the difference is also highlighted by the tangible result that an individual may receive from an action in this area. Article 110 TFEU is directly effective and as such it can be invoked by individuals in the national courts. Individuals will ultimately be seeking repayment of any unlawful charges. The availability of damages was established in Case C–68/79 *Hans Just I/S* (1980) where the Court said that Member States had to ensure the repayment of charges levied contrary to Article 110 TFEU (ex Article 90 EC) subject to the principle of national procedural autonomy and unjust enrichment (see also **7.96**). Moving under limb 1 or 2 will have an obvious effect on the damages payment that an individual may receive.

Excise duties and duty-free

9.46 Market integration can never be complete and distortions continue to be caused by the absence of harmonisation of excise duties, such as those imposed in the United Kingdom on petrol, alcohol and cigarettes. These duties are much lower or absent in other Member States, such as France, and this continues to cause distortions in the market.

9.47 These duties were at first regarded very much as within the competence of the Member States. In Case C–296/95 *R v Customs and Excise Comr, ex p EMU Tabac* (1998), a company, acting as agent on behalf of individuals in the United Kingdom, acquired cigarettes and tobacco in Luxembourg from another company for consumption by those individuals. The first company also arranged for the goods to be transported. It was paid for its services. The Court of Justice ruled that the United Kingdom was entitled to charge excise duty on these products.

Until July 1999 it had been possible to buy certain products 'duty-free', i.e. not subject to tax and duty, on ships travelling between Member States and in airports and on aircraft travelling between Member States. This then came to an end and 'duty-free' is now confined to travel beyond the external borders of the Union. The situation since has highlighted the different policies of Member States in respect of the raising of excise duties, as large cross-border movements of shoppers are to be noted, for example from France to Italy and from the United Kingdom to France, to purchase goods such as alcoholic drink and tobacco products.

9.48 With the accession of new Member States in 2004 and 2007, a number of cases concerning excise duty have been brought before the Court of Justice. There had already been a case before the Court in 1999 (Case C–166/98 *Socridis v Receveur Principal des Douanes*) (1999) where the applicant argued that Directives 92/83 and 92/84 on the harmonisation of excise duties were incompatible with Article 110 TFEU (ex Article 90 EC) because they introduced a system of taxation authorising discriminatory and anti-competitive practices which indirectly favoured wine production over beer production. However, the Court found that the Directives left the Member States sufficient discretion in the choice of implementation of the rules, and that they were, therefore, not contrary to Union law.

Harmonisation of taxation

9.49 The European Union has power to harmonise laws relating to indirect taxation to the extent that it is necessary to ensure the establishment and functioning of the internal market (Articles 113 and 115 TFEU). Progress has been made in the fields of VAT, excise duties and corporation tax. However, it is no surprise that tax harmonisation remains a difficult and sensitive issue in the EU. National sovereignty remains the prerogative of the Member States, yet this is seemingly at odds with the need to avoid distortions to trade and investment in an increasingly integrated single market. Ultimately, reform of Member States' tax systems would benefit the domestic economy, as well as reduce cross-border distortions. The need for adjustments and for tax harmonisation arises in relation to taxes on consumption and on capital. Proposals to approximate rates of indirect taxation with broad tax bands, introduced under the internal market programme have not so far met with any degree of success.

Value added tax

9.50 When the Treaty of Rome was first signed, all Member States, with the exception of France, applied cumulative taxes on firms' turnovers. Their disadvantage was that they were cumulative from one stage to the next, making it impossible to determine the amount of tax included in the price of a product. The amount of tax depended on the number of stages in the production chain. Articles 110 and 111 TFEU stipulate, on the one hand, that imported products may not be taxed more highly than similar domestic products and, on the other, that any repayment of tax on export may not exceed the taxes actually paid on the product concerned. Under the system of Value Added Tax (VAT), which is being progressively harmonised in the Union, the export of goods from one Member State to another is exempt from VAT, whereas the importation of goods into a Member State is subject to the payment of VAT in that Member State. The Sixth VAT Directive (Council Directive 77/388) established a uniform VAT base, but there is not yet a uniform VAT rate in the EU; there is a band with lower and upper limits, but the upper limit is not fixed whereas a lower limit is only permitted under special, limited exceptions (see Directives 92/77 and 92/111). Zero rating (e.g. for books and children's clothes in the United Kingdom) still remains permissible.

9.51 The reason for the adoption of a uniform VAT base was, in fact, unrelated to tax. The reason was the adoption by the Council of Ministers of a decision to finance the Community (now Union) budget through its own resources, part of which was to be made up of a given percentage of the common VAT base. Own resources are not calculated on the basis of national VAT receipts, but on the VAT base which, therefore, had to be the same in all Member States if each were to make an equitable contribution to the Union budget.

9.52 The eventual goal is to switch VAT payments from the state of destination to the state of origin. This means that the seller in the state of origin, selling to someone from another Member State, would charge VAT on the purchase which the buyer would then claim back in his own home state. This is proving difficult to achieve and, meanwhile, a transitional system stays in place. An example of difficulties which arise under the present system is given below (**9.54**).

9.53 As importation is always a chargeable event, irrespective of whether the importer is commercial or a private person, VAT may be levied where goods were not originally intended for export or when the goods were acquired second-hand. This was the subject of the dispute in Case 15/81 *Schul v Inspecteur der Invoerrechten* (1982), which involved a boat imported into the Netherlands, thus attracting VAT, which was purchased second-hand in France. The value of the boat was higher than its original value, on which VAT had been paid in France. No VAT would have been payable in the Netherlands on such a second-hand sale.

9.54 This may appear to be a breach of Article 110 TFEU, but was correct under the VAT Directive. The Court's approach was as follows: the second-hand price of a boat sold within the Netherlands would reflect the fact that VAT had been paid on the boat when new, and Community law should, therefore, be interpreted in such a way that the sale of a boat purchased in another Member State would also reflect such an element. In calculating the value of the boat for tax purposes on importation, the French VAT element in the original price should be taken into account and deducted. It was suggested that this should be the same proportion of the second-hand price as the original VAT had been of the new price, but could not exceed the VAT actually paid. Dutch VAT on importation should then be calculated on the second-hand price minus the French VAT. The residual French VAT (not exceeding the amount actually paid) should then be deducted from the Dutch VAT due. The overall effect should be that the same tax would be payable on the boat as on one bought in the Netherlands. Thus, Article 110 TFEU (ex Article 90 EC) would have been complied with as there was no discrimination against the imported product. Taxation in the country of origin, the ultimate objective, would do away with the need for such complex considerations.

FURTHER READING

Danusso, M. and Denton, R., 'Does the European Court of Justice look for a protectionist motive under Article 95?' [1990] *Legal Issues of European Integration* 67.

Easson, A., 'Fiscal discrimination: new perspectives on Article 95' (1981) *Common Market Law Review* 521.

Hedemann-Robinson, M., 'Indirect discrimination; Article 95(1) EC back to front and inside out' (1995) 1 *EPL* 439.

Molle, W., *The Economics of European Integration: Theory, Practice, Policy* (5th edn, Aldershot: Ashgate, 2006) pt I.

Oliver, P., *Free Movement of Goods in the European Community* (4th edn, London: Sweet and Maxwell, 2003) chs 1–4.

Oliver, P. and Henning Roth, W., 'The internal market and the Four Freedoms' (2004) 41 *Common Market Law Review* 407.

Vanistendael, F., 'The limits to the new Community tax order' (1994) 31 *Common Market Law Review* 293.

SELF-TEST QUESTIONS

1 What are the differences between a duty, a charge and internal taxation?

2 Can any charges imposed on goods by reason of crossing a frontier be justified?

3 Can a charge be both a customs charge and internal taxation?

4 Gaston, a French farmer, sells a lorryload of beef to Kevin, a retail butcher in Folkestone. When the consignment arrives in Dover, Customs stop the load and inform Kevin there have been recent outbreaks of BSE in France and it is, therefore, necessary to subject the meat to a thorough health check. This will cost a considerable amount as the check has to be carried out by qualified BSE experts, of whom there are only a few in the United Kingdom. Under EU law, are the authorities entitled to do this? If so, who should pay for such a check?

10 Free movement of goods (II): quantitative restrictions and measures having equivalent effect

SUMMARY

- Prohibition of quantitative restrictions and measures having equivalent effect: Articles 34 and 35 TFEU
- Distinctly and indistinctly applicable measures
- Derogation (Article 36 TFEU)
- The rule of reason
- The principles of mutual recognition and equivalence
- The ruling in *Keck* and its continuing aftermath
- Reverse discrimination

Prohibition of quantitative restrictions and measures having equivalent effect

10.1 The abolition of customs duties and charges having equivalent effect alone (see **Chapter 9**) would not have been sufficient to guarantee the free movement of goods within the single market. In addition to pecuniary restrictions there are other barriers to trade of a non-pecuniary nature, usually in the form of administrative rules and practices, protectionist or otherwise, which are equally capable of hindering the free flow of goods from one Member State to another. Articles 34 and 35 TFEU (formerly Articles 28 and 29 EC, and originally Articles 30 and 34 EEC) are designed to eliminate these barriers and cover a much wider range of measures than Articles 28 and 30 TFEU, but unlike for these latter Articles, provision is made for derogation under Article 36 TFEU (formerly Article 30 EC, and originally Article 36 EEC, again). To avoid repetition, these Articles will be referred to using their TFEU Article numbers only in this chapter.

The relevant Treaty Articles for this chapter are therefore:

- Article 34 'Quantitative restrictions on imports and all measures having equivalent effect shall be prohibited between Member States.'

- Article 35 'Quantitative restrictions on exports, and all measures having equivalent effect, shall be prohibited between Member States.'

- Article 36, the derogation from the free movement provisions set out in Articles 34 and 35 TFEU, set out in full below at **10.16**.

The term 'measure' in Articles 34 and 35 TFEU

10.2 All of the above Treaty (**10.1**)provisions are addressed to, and relate to, measures taken by Member States. However, 'measures taken by Member States' has been interpreted in the widest sense to include the activities of any public body, legislative, executive or judicial, or even a semi-public body, such as a quango, exercising powers derived from public law. In Case 222/82 *Apple and Pear Development Council v K J Lewis Ltd* (1983) a body set up under a statutory instrument and funded by levies paid by private individuals under a statutory obligation was held by the Court of Justice to be subject to Article 34 TFEU.

The term 'measures' is not necessarily concerned with binding measures: Case 249/81 *Commission v Ireland ('Buy Irish Campaign'*, 1982). In 1978 Ireland launched a programme to promote Irish products. An action was brought by the European Commission under Article 258 TFEU (then Article 169) to put a stop to this. Certain activities of the Irish Goods Council—a government-sponsored body charged with the promotion of Irish goods, principally through advertising and the use of a 'Guaranteed Irish' symbol—were held to be in breach of Article 34 TFEU. Even though no binding measures were involved, the Council's actions were capable of influencing the behaviour of traders and thereby frustrating the aims of the then Community in relation to the free movement of goods. The campaign was a reflection of the Irish Government's considered intention to substitute domestic products for imported products on the Irish market and thereby to check the flow of imports from other Member States. Therefore, although the Irish Government was not setting a limit on the number of imported goods—indeed the proportion of sales of Irish goods in relation to all goods fell—and although the advertising campaign was a non-binding measure (i.e. it was not adopted formally by the Irish Government), the campaign still fell within the ambit of Article 34 TFEU. The Court indicated the potential effect of the campaign on imports from other Member States was comparable to that resulting from government measures of a binding nature.

The scope of 'Member States'

10.3 Although Articles 34 and 35 TFEU are addressed to Member States, this does not mean that Union institutions or individuals are free to act in breach of these provisions. However, Union institutions may derogate from them where they are expressly authorised to do so by other provisions of the Treaty; for example, in implementing the Common Agricultural Policy as contained in Articles 38–44 TFEU (ex Articles 32–38 EC): Case 37/83 *Rewe-Zentral* (1984).

Defining quantitative restrictions

10.4 The prohibition, as between Member States, covers quantitative restrictions which usually relate specifically to quotas and bans. In Case 2/73 *Geddo* (1973), the Court defined quantitative restrictions as 'measures which amount to a total or partial restraint of, according to the circumstances, imports, exports or goods in transit'. Quantitative restrictions are quotas limiting the quantity of goods coming into a state as well as bans on imports, which was noted by the Court of Justice in Case 34/79 *Henn and Darby* (considered at **10.17**) as being the most extreme form of prohibition. It is usually positive actions which infringe Article 34 TFEU; however, a Member State can infringe Article 34 TFEU by omission, i.e. failing to take action where it is under a duty to act. In Case C–265/95 *Spanish Strawberries* (see **10.18**) the French authorities failed to take action to prevent striking French farmers from blockading ports and in Case C–112/00 *Schmidberger* (see **10.18** and **10.42**), the Austrian authorities decided to allow a demonstration by an environmental group to proceed which had the effect of blocking a major motorway. In both instances the inaction by the Member States constituted a restriction on the free movement of goods and were found in principle to have breached Article 34 TFEU.

Measures equivalent to a quantitative restriction (MEQR)

10.5 Whilst quantitative restrictions concern quotas or a total ban on imports into a Member State, there is another prohibition under Article 34 TFEU which covers 'measures equivalent to a quantitative restriction' (MEQR). MEQRs cover a range of measures, which can be seen to have as detrimental an effect on the free movement of goods as bans or quotas. Common examples have related to national rules on the shape, packaging and content of goods.

To offer Member States some guidance as to the meaning and scope of these prohibited measures, the Commission issued Directive 70/50. Although the Directive was issued under Article 33(7) EEC (now repealed) and therefore applicable only to measures to be abolished during the transitional period, it serves to provide non-binding guidelines to the interpretation of Article 34 TFEU. The Directive provides a non-exhaustive list of measures capable of having equivalent effect to a quantitative restriction. The guidelines fell into two parts. Article 2 of Directive 70/50 covers 'measures, other than those applicable equally to domestic or imported products'. This category of measures is known as '*distinctly applicable measures*', meaning that imports are identified specifically in them and placed at a disadvantage. Article 3 relates to measures which cover equally domestic and imported goods of particular types: '*indistinctly applicable*' measures. It also covers measures affecting the marketing of goods. The reason for prohibiting this kind of measure was that goods which complied with what was acceptable in one Member State might not comply in another. This would mean for example that manufacturers would need to operate two or more lines of production or accept that the second Member State's market was closed to them. As the following illustrates, the judicial interpretation of Article 34 TFEU has gone well beyond this Directive.

Dassonville

10.6 The Court, in Case 8/74 *Procureur du Roi v Dassonville* (1974) introduced its own definition of 'measures having equivalent effect to quantitative restrictions'. The definition is now taken as the classic formulation of the concept. A dealer in Belgium had bought Scotch whisky in France. This had been imported from the United Kingdom which, at the relevant time, was not a Member of the EEC—the precursor of what is now the European Union. The whisky was, therefore, in free circulation in what was then the European Common market. Belgian law required that this product had to be accompanied by a certificate of origin, in order to prevent fraud, but there was no certificate and it would have been very difficult to obtain one as the whisky had long since left Scotland. Dassonville made up his own certificate. As a result, he was prosecuted for forgery. On a reference from the Belgian court to the Court of Justice under Article 267 TFEU (then Article 177 EC), the Court held that the requirement of a certificate constituted a MEQR, as it would be more difficult for the importer to obtain a certificate for a product already in free circulation in another Member State than for a product coming directly from the country of origin. The Court gave its definition of a MEQR, now known as the '*Dassonville* formula':

> All trading rules enacted by Member States which are capable of hindering, directly or indirectly, actually or potentially, intra-Community trade are to be considered as measures having an effect equivalent to quantitative restrictions.

10.7 The range of restrictions that this seminal definition incorporates is huge and as such, much time and effort has been expended in trying to work out the exact parameters. As will be shown later, some limits have been placed on the extent to which it can be used. At this point it can be noted that the scope includes rules which have an actual effect on goods trade as well as those that have the possibility of having an effect at some time in the future.

Distinctly applicable MEQRs

10.8 In *Dassonville*, the Court of Justice did not distinguish between national rules which only apply to imports (now commonly known as distinctly applicable MEQRs), and those national rules which apply both to imports and domestic products alike (known as indistinctly applicable MEQRs). The two situations are different as later case law well demonstrates.

Distinctly applicable measures are roughly similar to directly discriminatory measures. The key feature is that imported goods are treated less favourably than the domestic product—when under the provisions of Article 34 TFEU they should be treated in the same way. The tangible result of a distinctly applicable rule is that the national measure results in the imported product sustaining a different burden in law as well as in fact. Distinctly applicable rules can only be saved or justified by recourse to the specific exceptions set out in Article 36 TFEU.

10.9 Many instances of distinctly applicable MEQRs have come before the Court of Justice. In Case 249/81 *The Buy Irish Campaign* (noted at **10.2**), the government-sponsored campaign which encouraged consumers to buy Irish products on the basis of their nationality clearly infringed Article 34 TFEU. A requirement for importers to be licensed has also been held to breach Article 34 TFEU. In Case C–324/93 *Evans Medical & Macfarlane Smith* (1995), the British Government insisted that importers be licensed. Even in instances where the granting of a licence is automatic and a mere formality, this again will be regarded as a MEQR and breach Article 34 TFEU, as in Joined Cases 51 and 54/71 *International Fruit Co v Produktschap voor Groenten en Fruit* (1971). The logic behind this is that the importer would have to waste time and spend money applying for a licence, which the domestic producer would not have to do, and this therefore would be the barrier to the trade and also act as a deterrent to potential importers. Hygiene inspections carried out on imported goods may also infringe Article 34 TFEU because they involve delay and expense. Case 4/75 *Rewe-Zentralfinanz* (1975) involved German legislation which required that imported apples were to be subject to inspections. Case 124/81 *Commission v UK* ('*UHT Milk*', 1983) involved the requirement that imported UHT milk be subjected to rigorous inspection. Both these cases were again found in principle to breach Article 34 TFEU on account of the deterrent effect that the delay and expense would have had on the free movement of goods.

Indistinctly applicable MEQRs

10.10 Distinctly applicable rules, considered above (**10.8**), are overtly discriminatory and ultimately the discrimination is clear on the face of the measure at issue. However, discrimination is not always so obvious, and can be hidden or disguised. Indistinctly applicable measures are those rules and practices which in law apply to both national and domestic products alike, but place a heavier burden on the imported goods. Again, the objective is to remove the hindrance to trade that these seemingly non-discriminatory rules impose. Instances of indistinctly applicable measures manifest themselves in a number of scenarios. The key example is where a national producer has to satisfy only one regulator in the home state whereas an importer of goods must satisfy the system in the state of origin and a second regulatory system in the host state. The concomitant cost in satisfying the second regulatory system is the key hindrance to trade, and it is the objective of Article 34 TFEU to remove or minimise this effect to cross-border trade.

10.11 The case law on indistinctly applicable measures can be grouped under four commonly arising situation headings, namely; origin-marking requirements; packaging requirements; contents and ingredients restrictions; and name restrictions.

Origin-marking requirements

10.12 The Court of Justice found in Case 207/83 *Commission v United Kingdom* ('*Origin Marking*', 1985) that a requirement that all goods designate their origin made it possible for the British consumer to exercise a prejudice against imported goods. Even though the rule treated all goods in the same way, a discriminatory effect was found. Although such origin-marking may be acceptable for a regional or local product such as Parma ham or Devon clotted cream, associated with the named location, the Court has interpreted the practice restrictively. In Case 113/80 *Commission v Ireland* ('*Irish Souvenirs*', 1981) souvenirs depicting typically Irish symbols such as shamrock or wolfhounds were marked as Irish origin. The measure fell foul of Article 34 TFEU as the place of manufacture of the product was not relevant. The measure was discriminatory without justification.

Origin-marking requirements infringe Article 34 TFEU because they impose an extra burden on importers, many of whom find difficulties in complying with the law because they will commonly only find out about it when they try and import goods into a host country. Secondly, origin-marking encourages seemingly latent nationalistic prejudice in shoppers, who may consciously or subconsciously select domestically produced goods in preference to imports, primarily on the basis of their nationality.

Packaging requirements

10.13   National laws which dictate how a product is to be packaged often infringe Article 34 TFEU. Whilst such rules seemingly place all goods traders under the same burden, the tangible result is that those who wish to import into the Member State will have to adapt their manufacturing processes. If all the 27 Member States dictated that margarine should be packaged in different ways, the costs of meeting these requirements would be prohibitive to anyone seeking to trade in margarine. The prime example of a packaging requirement breaching Article 34 TFEU is Case 261/81 *Walter Rau v De Smedt PvbA* (1982) where Belgian legislation required margarine to be packaged in cubes (see **10.35** and **10.47**). Similar effects can be seen in Case C–470/93 *Mars* (1995, see **10.73**) and Case C–220/98 *Estée Lauder Cosmetics v Lancaster* (2000) (see **10.35**) which both involved German legislation on packaging which breached Article 34 TFEU.

Contents and ingredients restrictions

10.14   A series of cases have been held to contravene Article 34 TFEU where the national legislation prescribed or restricted the contents or ingredients of products. In Case 120/78 '*Cassis de Dijon*' (1979), German legislation which laid down the minimum alcohol level of 25 per cent for certain spirits was in breach of Article 34 TFEU (see **10.29**), as in Case 788/79 *Gilli and Andres* (1980), where Italian legislation required all vinegar to be made from wine. In Case 407/85 *Drei Glocken* (1988), the Court held that an Italian rule requiring dried pasta to be made only from durum wheat and not common wheat or a mix of the two, was an indistinctly applicable MEQR. Subsequently, Case C–123/00 *Bellamy* (2001), which involved Belgian legislation dictating that bread could not be sold with a salt content greater than 2 per cent; Case C–95/01 *Greenham* *and Abel* (2004, see further **10.22** and **10.48**) where French legislation prohibited the sale of any food and drink containing a particular chemical substitute; and Case C–420/01 *Commission v Italy* ('*Red Bull*', 2003), where the Italian legislation banned beverages with a more than 125mg of caffeine, all breached Article 34 TFEU in principle as indistinctly applicable MEQRs. As illustrated later, some of these national rules have been saved by being justified by the Member States on account of public health derogations.

Name restrictions

10.15 In respect of designation, the Court has ruled that Member States cannot reserve a generic name for products that are manufactured out of a specific raw ingredient or contain only a given proportion of raw ingredients. In Case 286/86 *Deserbais* (1988) the Court said that a French rule restricting the name Edam to cheese with a minimum fat content of 40 per cent breached Article 34 TFEU because it had the effect of excluding German cheese which had lawfully been produced with a fat content of 34 per cent. In Case C–14/00 *Commission v Italy* (2003) the Court said that an Italian rule limiting the name chocolate to products made without vegetable fats and requiring chocolate with vegetable fats to be described as 'chocolate substitute' contravened the Article. The same conclusion was arrived at in Case C–12/00 *Commission v Spain* (2003), which dealt with very similar facts. In addition to this, where national authorities in one Member State ban or restrict the use of a name which is commonly used elsewhere, this may also constitute a breach of Article 34 TFEU. In Case C–315/92 *Clinique Laboratories* (1994), when German authorities refused to allow the use of the term 'clinique' for cosmetics on account of the medical connotations of the name, the Court of Justice held that the Article had been infringed.

Grounds of derogation under Article 36 TFEU

10.16 Article 36 TFEU contains an exhaustive list (i.e. the list cannot be added to unless the Treaty is amended) of derogations which allow national measures to take precedence over the free movement of goods where they serve important interests recognised by the Union as valuable. This means that in some instances the Member State's restriction will be found not to breach Article 34 TFEU. The rationale behind this is that there is some overriding consideration that takes precedence over the freedom to move goods. All such measures reflecting considerations taking priority over goods trade, under Article 36 TFEU and the exceptions to be considered below, must be proportionate. Any measure that is taken must be the most appropriate and least restrictive option open to take. Similarly, the measure must not constitute a means of arbitrary discrimination or a disguised restriction on trade between Member States. The burden of proving that an Article 36 TFEU derogation has been made out rests with the Member State seeking to rely on it.

Article 36 TFEU sets out the grounds on which a Member State can argue that a measure is justified as follows:

> The provisions of Articles 34 and 35 shall not preclude prohibitions or restrictions on imports, exports or goods in transit justified on grounds of public morality, public policy or public security; the protection of health and life of humans, animals or plants; the protection of national treasures possessing artistic, historic or archaeological value; or the protection of industrial and commercial property. Such prohibitions or restrictions shall not, however, constitute a means of arbitrary discrimination or a disguised restriction on trade between Member States.

Public morality

10.17 Each Member State is allowed to determine what constitutes public morality for itself. This was set out at a relatively early stage in Case 34/79 *R v Henn and Darby* (1979) where the Court indicated that 'in principle, it is for each Member State to determine in accordance with its own scale of values and in the form selected by it the requirements of public morality in its territory'. The case involved the importation into the United Kingdom of obscene films and magazines from the Netherlands; the United Kingdom sought to justify a ban on such imports on the grounds of public morality. A *prima facie* breach of Article 34 TFEU, the ban on pornography, was justified under Article 36 TFEU.

The margin in which this justification can be used was explored in Case 121/85 *Conegate* (1986), which involved the importation of life-sized inflatable dolls into the United Kingdom from Germany. It was argued by the defendants that the dolls would be used in window displays; however reading the descriptions that accompanied the dolls suggested that the dolls were destined for more vigorous uses. The UK authorities seized the dolls, preventing their trade, and justifying this action under the public morality heading of Article 36 TFEU. The Court was more suspicious of the United Kingdom's justification based on public morality than in *Henn and Darby*, as it was common knowledge that the same sort of dolls could be manufactured in the United Kingdom. In instances where goods could cause offence, to restrict the free movement of goods, when it is apparent that within the Member State seeking to rely on the particular justification, that Member State condones domestic manufacture—is untenable. The United Kingdom in this case was therefore unable to rely on the public morality defence.

Public policy

10.18 This derogation is narrowly construed and the Court of Justice has been very reluctant to expand the parameters of what might appear to be a wide justification. As early as 1961 in Case 7/61 *Commission v Italy* (1961) the Court indicated that this heading would not provide Member States with broad and general fallback provisions for legitimising trade limiting measures. In Case 177/83 *Kohl v Ringelhan & Rennett SA* (1984) the Court stated: 'whatever interpretation is to be given to the term "public policy" it cannot be extended so as to include considerations of consumer protection'.

The public policy derogation has been successfully invoked just once before the Court of Justice, in Case 7/78 *R v Thompson, Johnson and Woodiwiss* (1978). In this case there was a British ban on the export of silver coins, which extended to those that were not in circulation or legal tender. The aim was to prevent them from being melted down or destroyed. As it was a criminal offence in the United Kingdom to melt down coins, the Court said that 'a ban on exporting such coins with a view to preventing their being melted down or destroyed in another Member State is justified on grounds of public policy within the meaning of [Article 36 TFEU] because it stems from the need to protect the right to mint coinage which is traditionally regarded as involving the fundamental interests of the state'.

The derogation has been increasingly invoked in a number of cases that have involved protests which have interfered with the free movement of goods. In Case 231/83 *Cullett v Centre Leclerc Toulouse* (1985) the Court was unsympathetic to these arguments. Subsequently in Cases C–265/95 *Commission v France* ('Spanish Strawberries', 1997); *International Trader's Ferry Ltd* (1998) and Case C–112/00 *Schmidberger* (2003) the Court of Justice and the House of Lords in the United Kingdom all wrestled with the interplay between the 'public policy' exception to the free movement of goods under Article 36 TFEU and the respect for fundamental human rights. Human rights would appear to be a corollary to the Article 36 TFEU 'policy' exception. In *Schmidberger* the Court of Justice accepted the right to protest as being able to disrupt goods movement legitimately, while the obligations of the state were to balance the right to move goods against the right to protest (see further **10.42**).

Public security

10.19 The Court of Justice has traditionally been sympathetic to arguments based on public security even with the presence of an economic element in the national legislation at issue. Case 72/83 *Campus Oil* (1984) illustrated that where a country is dependent almost exclusively on imports for its supplies of petroleum the public security exception can be invoked. This case concerned a requirement on petrol companies operating in Ireland to buy a certain proportion of their needs from a state-owned installation at a price fixed by the Irish Government. The Court of Justice accepted the public security justification for this requirement. As the law was regarded as serving the public security needs, the Court said that the importance of ensuring a supply of petroleum based products transcended and surpassed purely economic considerations.

In Case C–398/98 *Commission v Greece* (2001) the Court of Justice reinforced the decision that it had made in *Campus Oil*, noting that the 'maintenance on national territory of petroleum products allowing a continuity of supplies to be guaranteed constitutes a public security objective'. However, in this case, the Court rejected the justification under Article 36 TFEU on account of the fact that the Greek legislation was preoccupied with protecting the economic status of oil refineries rather than the requisite public security of Greece.

The broad approach to public security was reinforced in Case C–367/89 *Richardt and Les Accessoires Scientifiques* (1991) which involved a Luxembourg law that required a special transit licence for the import and export of goods of a special strategic nature. A transit company was prosecuted under Luxembourg law for failing to have acquired requisite clearance for moving prescribed goods. The Luxembourg law was challenged during the prosecution and the Court of Justice stated that the 'concept of public security within the meaning of [Article 36 TFEU] covers both a Member State's internal security and external security'. The importation, exportation and transit of strategic goods could affect the public security of a Member State—and as such the rule was justified.

The protection of the health and life of humans, animals and plants

10.20 The protection of health and life of humans, animals, or plants is the derogation to the free trade right that is most frequently invoked, and the Court of Justice has stated, in Case C–170/04 *Rosengren* (2007) (considered further below at **10.22**) that the protection of human health 'ranks foremost' among the list of derogations in Article 36 TFEU. In *Rosengren*, the Court also made it clear that it is for Member States to decide upon the degree of protection they wished to ensure for their citizens under this heading. However, as recently reiterated by the Court, it is possible to exceed this discretion, most obviously where a measure goes beyond what is necessary to attain the objective the Member State claims to pursue, and therefore breaches the proportionality principle (see for example Case C–108/09 *Ker-Optika* (2010) (**10.63**)). As will be shown, the Court is often suspicious of attempts by the Member States to use health as a method of restricting trade. As such the science must be sound and the policy used by a Member State proportionate.

10.21 In spite of this the justification has been successful on a number of occasions. In Case 174/82 *Sandoz* (1983), the Dutch authorities refused to grant authorisation for the importation of muesli bars which contained added vitamins, from Germany where they were lawfully sold. Given, however, the uncertainty pertaining to scientific research into the effects of the chemicals such as these added vitamins the Court said the rules were justified. In Case C–366/04 *Schwarz* (2005) the Court of Justice accepted a requirement that chewing gum sold in vending machines be wrapped in packaging, since in the past 'non-packaged goods were impaired by moisture or insects…within vending machine containers'. The Court accepted the public health justification for the packaging requirement, after carefully considering its proportionality. There does not need to be a shared consensus of concern about health risks and a Member State can use this justification to ban products on health grounds where other states continue to permit their sale. A French ban on 'Red Bull', a drink widely available in other states, in Case C–24/00 *Commission v France* (2004), whilst found *prima facie* to violate Article 34

TFEU, could be justified on the grounds of public health. The Court of Justice also seems particularly sympathetic to the health justification for trade limiting measures when they are directly related to the functioning of the national health system. In Case C–324/93 *Evans Medical* (see **10.9**), the British Government refused to grant a licence to an importer of narcotic drugs on the ground that the imports might undermine the sole licensed manufacturer in the United Kingdom, which could have the effect of jeopardising the reliability of the supply of a particular drug in the United Kingdom. The Court indicated that, provided the action taken was proportionate and it was not based on economic grounds, such a licensing system, and the refusal to grant a licence, were within this heading.

10.22 The protection of health ground can fail to justify measures in two common scenarios: first, a lack of scientific or empirical research to suggest that there is a real health risk makes the use of this heading untenable and, secondly, a failure to comply with the principle of proportionality will make health measures affecting trade unjustified. In Case C–270/02 *Commission v Italy* (2004), the Court of Justice stated that the Italian Government had failed to produce evidence to explain any risk to public health. In Case C–95/01 *Greenham and Abel* (2004, see further **10.14** and **10.48**), the Court of Justice was minded to point out that it would be far more willing to allow the justification if the Member State could point to reputable international scientific research to back up its claims. In its judgment a restriction to the free movement of goods can only be brought about if the alleged risk appears to be sufficiently established on the basis of the latest scientific data available at the date of adoption of such a decision. Ultimately the Court pointed out that risk assessments, juggling the risk to health with the free movement of goods, cannot be based on purely hypothetical considerations. Finally in Case C–170/04 *Rosengren* (2007) the Court concluded that a Swedish ban on the importation of alcoholic drinks by private individuals was disproportionate despite the Court's ready acceptance of Member States' health concerns about alcohol abuse, and the linked concern of the desire to protect young people from excessive alcohol consumption. The ban affected everyone and so manifestly went beyond the aim of protecting young people, while the broader health aims of limiting alcohol consumption among the rest of the population were thought to be somewhat unrealistic in the context of a ban on private import when alcohol continued to be available through the monopoly, approved suppliers.

10.23 Article 36 TFEU protects not only human health but also animal health. In Case C–67/97 *Bluhme* (1998), which involved the prohibition of the import of any bee onto the Danish Island of Laeso, in the interest of protecting the indigenous animal population, the ban could be justified. Following this case it became questionable whether the protection of health derogation includes environmental protection. In Case C–28/09 *Commission v Austria* (2011) the Court confirmed the interchangeability of wealth and environmental protection arguments, accepting where one is raised the other does not need to be. This also confirms the position reached in Case 142/05 *Mickelsson and Roos* (2009, see **10.78** and **10.79**) where environmental protection was included in the Article 36 TFEU public health derogation. Measuring aiming at environmental protection are within the health exception included in Article 36 TFEU, and such measures can inhibit quite legitimately the free movement of goods.

Protection of national treasures possessing artistic, historical or archaeological value

10.24   To date, the Court of Justice has not decided any cases based on this derogation. It was invoked in Case 7/68 *Commission v Italy* (1968), but the matter at issue was dealt with under Article 30 TFEU, and as such Article 36 TFEU could not be applied. A raft of secondary legislation exists in this field, which may account for the lack of litigation with respect to this derogation.

Protection of industrial and commercial property

10.25   This derogation covers the protection of patents, trademarks, copyright and design rights in general. The intention behind it is to protect private, as distinct from public, interests. The Court of Justice has been engaged in lengthy and often complicated analysis of this derogation, often trying to balance the free movement of goods with the prevailing interests that are to be found in the exploitation of intellectual property rights.

10.26   The different headings above (**10.17–10.25**) set out the justifications to measures limiting goods movement included in Article 36 TFEU. The question whether a measure can be justified is separate from the question as to whether the measure amounts to arbitrary discrimination against trade within the Union. The justification must be established under the first sentence of Article 36 TFEU, while the second sentence is concerned with the use and effects of the measure under consideration to ensure that the justification is not misused: Case 97/83 *Melkunie* (1984). Measures which Member States seek to justify under Article 36 TFEU must not only fit within the justification headings in the first sentence of Article 36 TFEU, they must also satisfy the general proportionality requirement which is the second sentence of the Article: Case 7/68 *Commission v Italy* ('*Art Treasures*', 1968); Case 124/81 *UHT Milk* (see **10.9**).

10.27   Although the grounds listed in Article 36 TFEU appear extensive, they have been narrowly construed. Case 40/82 *Commission v United Kingdom* (1982) shows the reluctance of the Court to exceed a narrow interpretation of the Article. A UK ban on the importation of poultry meat and eggs allegedly because of an outbreak of the highly contagious 'Newcastle disease', particularly in France, was held by the Court not to be justified. The motives for the ban were suspect; little or no consultation with either Community (as then) institutions or Member States had taken place; and the ban was imposed just before Christmas to prevent the importation of turkeys into the United Kingdom. The Court of Justice held that the health justification for the ban was not made out, and that the ban was a fairly clear example of the 'arbitrary discrimination' and 'disguised restriction on trade' expressly provided for in the second sentence of the Article. French turkey producers subsequently brought a damages claim against the UK Government, which was struck out in the Court of Appeal as no tort could be identified. Nevertheless, the UK Government paid compensation: see *Bourgoin v MAFF* (1986).

0.28 The provisions set out in the second sentence of Article 36 TFEU must be observed. If a measure is in principle justified on any grounds enumerated in Article 36 TFEU it will cease to be so if it falls within the second sentence of this provision and is a means of arbitrary discrimination or a disguised restriction on trade between Member States. The Court has indicated that the principle of proportionality constitutes the basis of the second sentence of the Article: Case 227/82 *Van Bennekom* (1983). It is for the national court to establish, for example, that a risk to health exists and that the national rules are necessary to give effective health protection. Thus, the second sentence is designed to ensure that the justifications permitted in the first sentence of the Article are not abused: in Case 53/80 *Officier van Justitie v Koninklijke Kaasfabriek Eyssen* (1981) a Dutch ban on the use of nisin, a preservative considered harmful by the Dutch authorities, was acceptable as a Member State is entitled to protect the public from substances where there is genuine scientific doubt as to their safety. In relation to the first sentence of the Article, the second sentence operates as a further 'notwithstanding' provision, and an overriding requirement: Case 102/77 *Hoffmann-La Roche* (1978).

Confining *Dassonville*: developing the rule of reason

10.29 In view of the very wide definition of measures having equivalent effect to quantitative restrictions given in *Dassonville* and to a large extent repeated in subsequent cases, it is not surprising that the Court subsequently accepted the need to restrict the effect of that definition. In 1979 the Court in *Cassis de Dijon* took decisive action. The Court of Justice created a parallel set of derogations that Member States could plead as an alternative to Article 36 TFEU. This is sometimes referred to as 'the rule of reason'.

In Case 120/78 *Rewe-Zentral AG v Bundesmonopolverwaltung für Branntwein* ('*Cassis de Dijon*', 1979), the German authorities refused the importation of a French liqueur, Cassis de Dijon, which had a lower alcohol content (between 15 per cent and 20 per cent) than the equivalent German products (25 per cent alcohol minimum). The claimants attacked the alcohol content rule as a MEQR. The German authorities advanced arguments of public health and consumer protection, arguing that: (a) the marketing of drinks with a lower alcohol content might more easily induce a tolerance towards alcohol than drinks with a higher alcohol content; and (b) the fixing of a lower limit for the alcohol content of certain liqueurs was designed to protect the consumer against unfair practices on the part of producers and distributors of alcoholic beverages. Liqueurs with a lower alcohol content would have an unfair competitive advantage as alcohol was by far the most expensive ingredient in the drink. The Court ruled that the measure did fall within Article 34 TFEU and thus the fixing of minimum alcohol levels for beverages imported from another Member State was prohibited. The Court specifically stated, however:

> Obstacles to movement within the Community resulting from disparities between the national laws relating to the marketing of the products in question must be accepted in so far as those provisions may be recognized as being necessary in order to satisfy mandatory requirements relating in particular to the effectiveness of fiscal supervision, the protection of public health, the fairness of commercial transactions and the defence of the consumer.

10.30 The Court made plain that such a 'rule of reason' is subject to the condition of the second sentence of Article 36 TFEU, i.e. that the prohibition or restriction may not constitute a means of arbitrary discrimination or a disguised restriction on trade between Member States. In any event it is now established that the rule of reason will only be available to justify measures except perhaps environmental measures, see **10.37**, which apply equally to domestic as well as imported products, i.e. only to indistinctly applicable measures: Case 113/80 *Irish Souvenirs* (see **10.12**). Thus, the rule cannot save a distinctly applicable measure such as the one in *Dassonville*, although this is subject to what appears to be a single exception, considered below at **10.77**. In an attempt to remove confusion surrounding the term 'mandatory requirements' the Court of Justice has used other synonymous terms such as 'objectives of general interest', 'overriding interests', 'overriding requirements', and 'overriding reason in the general interest'. The *Cassis* case gave a list of four 'mandatory requirements', but it is clear from the language used in the judgment that there is no limit to the number of mandatory requirements that can be created, i.e. it is an inexhaustible list. The list, as illustrated below (**10.33–10.42**), extends to a range of interests.

10.31 Prior to *Cassis*, it was assumed that any measure falling within the *Dassonville* formula would breach Article 34 TFEU and could only be justified on the grounds provided for by Article 36 TFEU. Since *Cassis*, at least where indistinctly applicable measures are concerned, courts may apply the rule of reason to Article 34 TFEU. If the measure is necessary to protect mandatory requirements, its breach of Article 34 TFEU will be justifiable. Distinctly applicable measures on the other hand, will normally breach Article 34 TFEU but may only be justified under Article 36 TFEU. The distinction is significant, since the mandatory requirements permitted under *Cassis* are wider than the grounds provided under Article 36 TFEU and, unlike the latter, are non-exhaustive. This use of the rule of reason is recognition by the Court of the need, pending action at Union level, to allow Member States to act in order to ensure that certain interests or values are guaranteed in the general interest. Measures coming under the rule of reason must be applicable to domestic and imported products alike, and be reasonable and proportionate.

Developing the list of mandatory requirements

0.32 The list of mandatory requirements has not remained static, and paragraphs **10.33–10.42** set out the evolving headings of mandatory requirements justifying measures limiting goods trade in addition to the exceptions listed in Article 36 TFEU. It should be noted that the law on mandatory requirements is not a simple extension of Article 36 TFEU grounds of exception, even if, as noted at **10.23**, *Micklesson and Roos* blurs the distinction. There are two options for a Member State seeking to restrict the freedom to move goods because of an important public interest: firstly, Article 36 TFEU grounds, and secondly, the mandatory requirements, following *Cassis*. It is easier to treat each option separately.

Protection of public health

0.33 Whilst this is usually covered by Article 36 TFEU, Case 120/78 *Cassis de Dijon* recognised it as a mandatory requirement.

Fairness of commercial transactions

0.34 In Case 286/81 *Oosthoek's Uitgeversmaatschappij BV* (1982, see further **10.65**) national rules prohibiting the offer of free gifts to buyers of encyclopaedias fell within the scope of Article 34 TFEU. Legislation restricting certain forms of advertising and sales promotion might limit trade within the Union; even if the scheme was indistinctly applicable it might force a producer to adopt different schemes or to discontinue a scheme which was thought to be particularly effective. However, the Court accepted that the system of offering free gifts might mislead consumers as to the real prices of certain products, thus distorting competition. Therefore, legislation restricting or even prohibiting such practices was capable of contributing to the mandatory requirement of consumer protection and fair trading. Fair trading was also claimed, but rejected, in Case 16/83 *Prantl* (1984).

Defence of the consumer

0.35 This defence has been successfully invoked in Case 220/81 *Robertson and Others* (1982), which concerned Belgian legislation requiring the hallmarking of silver-plated goods. The defence of the consumer has on the whole proven to be difficult to argue successfully in court. In Case C–315/92 *Clinique Laboratories* (1994, see **10.15** and **10.47**), Case C–470/93 *Mars* (see **10.73**) and Case C–220/98 *Estée Lauder v Lancaster* (2000) each time it was raised it failed. In Case 94/82 *De Kikvorsch Groothandel-Import-Export BV* (1983), Dutch legislation prevented the importation of German beer because of rules concerning the level of acidity and because of alleged confusion from information contained on the label concerning the strength of the original wort used in the production of beer, creating confusion in respect of the indication of alcoholic strength. A particularly striking example is Case 178/84 *Commission v Germany* ('*German Beer Purity*', 1987), where the German beer purity laws prevented importation of other beers which had additives. In both cases the Court denied that the mandatory requirement of consumer protection justified such a prohibition on imported beer. It is clear that the presumed expectations of an average consumer are of one who is reasonably well informed, observant and circumspect. Arguments primarily fail in this area because the contested national legislation is not in line with the principle of proportionality, i.e. the measures have gone beyond what is reasonably necessary to achieve the objectives in the circumstances: see Case 261/81 *Rau* (see **10.13**).

Improvement of working conditions

10.36 Case 155/80 *Oebel* (1981) dealt with a series of German rules relating to the opening times of bakeries, the tangible effect of which was that bakeries were prohibited from making bread to export to nearby Luxembourg and Belgium in time for the early morning breakfast market. The Court stated the restriction entailed in the opening time rules was justified, indicating that 'the prohibition on working before 4am constituted a legitimate element of economic and social policy…within the objectives of the public interest pursued by the European Community'.

Protection of the environment

10.37 In Case 302/86 *Commission v Denmark* ('*Danish Bottles*', 1988) the Court of Justice stated:

> The protection of the environment is one of the [Union's] essential objectives, which may justify certain limitations of the principle of the free movement of goods…it must therefore be stated that the protection of the environment is a mandatory requirement which may limit the application [of Article 34 TFEU].

The justification was subsequently used in Case C–2/90 *Commission v Belgium* ('*Walloon Waste*' (1992), see also **15.40**); Case C–284/95 *Safety Hi-Tech Srl v S & T Srl* (1998); Case C–389/96 *Aher-Waggon* (see **10.48**); and most significantly in Case 379/98 *PreussenElektra*, considered more fully at **10.79** and further at **10.23**.

Protection of culture

10.38 This was added to the list by Cases 60 and 61/84 *Cinéthèque* (1985) which dealt with the prohibition of sale or rental of films on video until 12 months after a film's debut at a cinema. The Court of Justice held that a national system which, in order to encourage the creation of cinematographic works irrespective of their origin, gives priority, for a limited period, to the distribution of such works through cinema, is justified. The factual situation giving rise to the *Cinéthèque* judgment would probably be treated differently today, in the light of the Court of Justice's development of additional criteria for consideration before triggering the application of Article 34 TFEU in the *Keck* decision, set out at **10.55** below. However, *Cinéthèque* is still authority that protection of culture can be a legitimate interest limiting the free movement of goods under the *Cassis de Dijon* rule of reason.

Diversity of the press

0.39 In Case C–368/95 *Familiapress v Bauer Verlag* (1997) Austrian legislation directed against sales promotion which prohibited publishers from including prize crossword puzzles in their papers was held by the Court to be caught by Article 34 TFEU. The Court accepted, however, that there could be a justification, stating the 'maintenance of press diversity may constitute an overriding requirement justifying a restriction on free movement of goods, based on the need for diversity in the media'. Rules aiming at achieving media diversity would be justifiable so long as the rules were proportionate.

The effectiveness of fiscal supervision

0.40 This was established in *Cassis de Dijon* and Case 823/79 *Carciatti* (1980).

Maintenance of social security system

0.41 Case C–120/95 *Decker* (1998) added this justification to the list. The case involved a Luxembourg national, who used a prescription obtained in Luxembourg to purchase a pair of spectacles from an optician in Belgium. He tried to reclaim the cost from the Luxembourg social security authorities; this was refused. He argued that this was contrary to Article 34 TFEU. The rule requiring the prescription be used in Luxembourg was found to be justified on the ground that there could be a risk of seriously undermining the financial balance of the social security system.

Protection of fundamental rights

0.42 In Case C–112/00 *Schmidberger* (considered at **10.18**), the Austrian authorities permitted an environmental group to stage a demonstration designed to raise awareness of traffic pollution. The knock-on effect of the demonstration was that the Austrian motorway linking German and Italy was blocked to traffic for 30 hours at the Brenner Pass. Schmidberger alleged this constituted a breach of Article 34 TFEU. The Court of Justice agreed that in principle this breached the Article, however it was justified by the overriding consideration linked to the respect of fundamental rights of the individual protesters. In this case it is clear that there was a tricky balancing act between traders' right to free movement and protestors' right to free expression. In this case the fundamental rights prevailed, thus creating a new justification. The case is of seminal importance as it brings fundamental rights into the arena of justifications for what would otherwise be breaches of Article 34 TFEU.

Proportionality and acceptable public interest limitations on free movement

10.43   Any justifications under the mandatory requirements, as with Article 36 TFEU derogations, must be used proportionally. In Case C–24/00 *Commission v France* (2004), the Court of Justice indicated that:

> The Member States must comply with the principle of proportionality. The means which they choose must therefore be confined to what is actually necessary to ensure the safeguarding of public health or to satisfy overriding requirements regarding, for example, consumer protection, and they must be proportional to the objective thus pursued, which could not have been attained by measures less restrictive of intra-Community trade.

In Case 320/03 *Commission v Austria* (2005, see also 10.80) the Court of Justice found that Austria had failed to meet its obligations to ensure the free movement of goods by permitting a ban on lorries above a certain weight carrying certain specified goods from travelling on a motorway across the Tyrol between Germany and Italy. The Court acknowledged the environmental protection motivation for the vehicle ban, which in other circumstances could have justified the initiative, but considered both the way in which the ban was introduced and the lack of time for adjustment permitted by the Austrian action made it disproportionate to the environmental protection aim pursued. This approach was reiterated in Case 524/07 *Commission v Austria* (2008, also at 10.80).

Principles of mutual recognition and equivalence

10.44   In *Cassis* the Court also set out the connected principles of mutual recognition and equivalence. It said (at paragraph 14):

> There is therefore no valid reason why, provided that they have been lawfully produced and marketed in one of the Member States, alcoholic beverages should not be introduced into any other Member State; the sale of such products may not be subject to a legal prohibition on the marketing of beverages with an alcohol content lower than the limit set by the national rules.

While the basic principle in *Dassonville* has a very wide scope, it proceeds from a negative standpoint, that is, a prohibition. In *Cassis* the Court attempted to force the Member States to adopt a more positive approach to the principle of the free movement of goods, that of the mutual acceptance of goods. The Communication gave the

Commission's interpretation of the *Cassis* judgment. The 1985 White Paper on completing the internal market followed, and in the Court's case law in the field of the free movement of goods and, more recently, services the principle of equivalence has been established. The Communication, the White Paper and Court of Justice case law have set in place a presumption that, once goods have been lawfully produced and marketed in one of the Member States, they may be imported into any other state. The presumption may only be rebutted by evidence that the goods in question pose a threat to one of the headings of important interest in Article 36 TFEU or to one of the mandatory requirements. The tangible result is to place the burden of proof on the authorities of the Member States seeking to justify their domestic legislation.

10.45 The Commission took action against France in Case C–184/96 *Commission v France* (1998). France had issued a decree regulating trade descriptions for *foie gras* and other, similar, products. The decree specified a minimum base content of *foie gras* to permit the use of the name. However, the decree failed to include a mutual recognition clause allowing similar products which did not entirely conform to these minimum requirements to be marketed in France. France claimed justification on the grounds of consumer protection and the prevention of false descriptions. The Court ruled that the absence of a mutual recognition clause was disproportionate. Although France was entitled to ensure that goods from other Member States which were markedly different should not be sold under the name *foie gras*, this should not apply to products which were very close, but not wholly in conformity with the product. Generally, as in *Cassis*, the Court has expressed the idea of equivalence in terms of a Member State being obliged to accept goods lawfully produced and/or marketed in another Member State.

10.46 This was also declared expressly in Case 27/80 *Fietje* (1980). In that case the Court held that the obligation to use a certain name on a label could make it more difficult to market goods from another Member State and the rule would therefore have to be justified on grounds of consumer protection. If the label was such that it provided information on the nature of the product, that could be justified, unless the same information could be read from the original label on the product from the other Member State. It was for the national court to decide whether this was so.

10.47 The presumption will, however, be hard to rebut; the Court has applied the principle of proportionality rigorously excluding all measures that go beyond what is strictly necessary to achieve the desired end. In Case 261/81 *Rau* (1982, noted at **10.13** and **10.35**), Belgian legislation required margarine to be packaged in square packets to distinguish it from butter. Thus, the importation of margarine packaged in any other form was prohibited. The Court held that, although the measure was aimed at the protection of consumers, the measure was disproportionate and was, therefore, prohibited by Article 34 TFEU. In Case 178/84 *German Beer Purity* (noted at **10.35**), involving German legislation on the additives permitted in beer, the German Government tried to argue that it needed stricter laws on beer purity than other Member States on account of the fact that the average German drank more beer than the average citizen of other Member States. The Court of Justice did not accept this assertion which made it practically impossible for France and other Member States' beer to be sold in Germany. The additives in question were used in beers lawfully produced in the exporting Member States, and hence the mutual recognition principle applied. In Case 470/93 *Mars*, and Case 315/92 *Clinique Laboratories* (see **10.15** and **10.35**), German consumer protection law arguments were rejected, and the Court held in each case that the German legislation was in breach of Article 34 TFEU. Principally, as the goods concerned were lawfully manufactured and marketed in France, the mutual recognition principle applied, and the German Government failed to show why it needed stricter laws than in France.

10.48 From the case law it would appear that the best way to rebut the presumption favouring free trade without restrictions is to identify specific national characteristics which would justify different national legislative provisions. Case 188/84 *Commission v France* (1986) concerned woodworking machines imported from Germany, which did not afford the same level of protection to their users as machines manufactured under French legislation. This was designed to protect users of the machines against their own mistakes, and this legislative difference in standards was accepted, with the effect of restricting the import of German machines. In Case C–42/90 *Bellon* (1990), French legislation that banned certain Italian patisserie products due to the fact that they contained sorbic acid, managed to rebut the mutual recognition free trade presumption on health grounds by taking into account different national dietary habits. In Case C–389/96 *Aher-Waggon* (1998), German legislation which set aircraft noise emission levels more restrictively than that permitted in other Member States, was found to be justified as Germany is a very densely populated state, and therefore the mutual recognition free trade presumption could be rebutted on the ground that the state attached special importance to ensuring that its population is protected from excessive noise emissions. Case C–95/01 *Greenham and Abel* (see further **10.14** and **10.22**) dealt with French legislation that banned an ingredient in fruit drinks. The Court of Justice held that the ban would only be permissible if the French authorities could show that the rules were necessary and proportionate in the light of national nutritional habits and reputable international scientific evidence, thereby rebutting the presumption requiring mutual recognition of standards applicable in other Member States.

Reaching the limits of Article 34 TFEU?

10.49 The wide definition accorded to MEQRs in *Dassonville* meant that a whole variety of national provisions which might have an effect on the free movement of goods could fall within its scope. The result was that importers, retailers and anyone else concerned with the trading of goods had the ability to challenge a broad range of rules that affect goods trade. Even rules with only a marginal effect on trade came to be challenged. The Court of Justice encountered difficulties in a series of cases in which the Court had not specifically stated that the contested measure fell within or beyond the scope of Article 34 TFEU, but left it up to the national courts to assess the measure in the light of its objective and the necessity and proportionality of that objective: see Cases 60 and

61/84 *Cinéthèque* (**10.38** and **10.50**), and cases on Sunday shop trading hours noted at **10.51–10.54**.

10.50 In a series of other cases the Court found that the national provisions in question had no impact on trade within the Union, were not MEQRs and as such fell outside Article 34 TFEU. In Case 155/80 *Oebel* (see **10.36**) the Court considered a rule relating to a prohibition on baking and selling bread at night; Case 75/81 *Belgium v Blesgen* (1982) concerned a limitation on selling spirits in public places; and Case C–23/89 *Quietlynn & Richards v Southend Borough Council* (1990) related to a limitation on pornographic material. It was also suggested by Slynn AG in *Cinéthèque* that a French rule banning the sale or hire of videotapes of films during the first year after their release should fall outside the ambit of the Article. He said:

> In an area in which there are no common Community standards or rules, where a national measure is not specifically directed at imports, does not discriminate against imports, does not make it any more difficult for an importer to sell his products than it is for a domestic producer, and gives no protection to domestic producers, then in my view *prima facie*, the measure does not fall within [Article 34 TFEU], even if it does in fact lead to a restriction or reduction in imports.

However, the Court of Justice did not follow the Advocate General, ruling that the measure did fall within the Article, but could be objectively justified as long as it was proportionate.

10.51 It is against this background that one should view the Sunday trading cases which ultimately led the Court to reconsider its case law on Article 34 TFEU in Case C–267, 268/91 *Keck and Mithouard* (1993, see **10.55**). The following cases deal with the problem of national rules regulating when goods can be sold. In Case 145/88 *Torfaen Borough Council v B&Q plc* (1989) in the United Kingdom, the sale of certain goods was banned on a Sunday. The law was challenged throughout the United Kingdom by, amongst others, B&Q, a large DIY chain. B&Q became involved in various county court actions in the United Kingdom. In a bid to justify opening on Sundays, in contravention of these rules, B&Q alleged that the ban on Sunday trading infringed the Article in the sense that it was a measure that could actually or potentially, directly or indirectly, hinder trade within the Union. Surprisingly, the Court found that the ban fell within the ambit of the Article and it was thus for the UK Government to justify the measure. Some statistical evidence on the effects of the opening hours rule on trade was offered in this case, but, as many commentators noted, the Article had become a *carte blanche* for traders to trade rather than a means of ensuring market access to non-domestic goods in the context of the internal market. The Court concluded its remarkably brief judgment by ruling that the Article:

> Does not apply to national rules prohibiting retailers from opening their premises on Sunday where the restrictive effects on Community trade which may result therefrom do not exceed the effects intrinsic to rules of that kind.

10.52 In Case C–312/89 *Conforama* (1991) and Case C–332/89 *Marchandise* (1991), the Court simply stated—without seeking to support its statement by any reasoning—that the restrictive effects on imports of legislation banning employment in shops on Sundays were proportionate to the end pursued. Accordingly, it held quite generally that legislation prohibiting the employment of staff on Sunday was compatible with Article 34 TFEU, without in any way limiting this ruling to employment in shops.

10.53 In the United Kingdom it was not clear that the Sunday opening hours were anything to do with protecting employees. In Case C–169/91 *Stoke-on-Trent and Norwich City Council v B&Q plc* (1992), the Court said that nevertheless account had to be taken of whether the restrictive effects of the opening hours rules on trade within the then Community were 'direct, indirect or purely speculative and whether those effects do not impede the marketing of imported products more than the marketing of national products'. If this were so, although the measure could be caught by Article 34 TFEU, so long as it was proportionate there would be no breach of the Article.

10.54 This ruling prompted suggestions that the Court was developing a new category of measure in addition to the categories of distinctly and indistinctly applicable measures: measures which apply equally in law and in fact to all traders. The premise of the case law up to this time was that Article 34 TFEU dealt with unequal burdens, either distinctly or indistinctly applied. The Court of Justice seemed to be suggesting a new line of thinking relating to measures applying equally to domestic and imported goods both in fact and in law and producing an equal burden on domestic and imported products.

Eventually, the prospect that such national rules, with no real link to market penetration, would fall so easily inside Article 34 TFEU was reconsidered in the Court and the *Keck* judgment amended the framework.

Keck and certain selling arrangements

10.55 Case C–267, 268/91 *Keck and Mithouard* (1993) concerned the criminal prosecution in France of the applicants for selling (French) coffee and beer at a loss contrary to French law. The applicants invoked Article 34 TFEU as a defence arguing that the French rule hindered the free movement of goods within the scope of the *Dassonville* formula. The Court first noted that the aim of the national legislation was not to regulate trade in goods between Member States and that although the measure might have an effect on the volume of trade, that was not determinative as to whether a national rule should be caught by the Article. The Court then stated that the increasing tendency of traders to invoke the Article where the rules were not aimed at products from other Member States led it to 're-examine and clarify its case law'. The Court said that the mutual recognition principle and the mandatory requirements principle, as laid down by *Cassis*, continued to apply to requirements to be met by goods 'such as requirements as to designation, form, size, weight, packaging, labelling and presentation'.

The Court then declared:

> However, contrary to what has previously been decided [Article 34 TFEU] will not be infringed by national rules relating to certain selling arrangements that apply in the same manner, both in law and in fact, to all traders within the national territory.

So, the choice was between 'rules that lay down requirements as to designation, form, size, weight, packaging, labelling and presentation' to be met by goods where one continued to apply *Cassis*; and 'certain selling arrangements'. In *Keck* the Court held that these 'selling arrangements' fell outside Article 34 TFEU altogether and thus did not need to be justified.

10.56 The distinction can be summarised as follows:

Marketing requirements: these are rules that regulate the goods themselves, which are still governed by Article 34 TFEU and the *Dassonville* formula, and are prohibited. These rules are *prima facie* contrary to Article 34 TFEU and require justification, under either Article 36 TFEU or the *Cassis de Dijon* mandatory requirements.

Selling arrangements: these are rules concerning not the goods themselves, but rather how, when and where they are marketed. These rules fall outside of the scope of Article 34 TFEU altogether. In *Keck*, the Court of Justice said that these rules were *prima facie* lawful, although they are subject to two preconditions:

(1) The national rules alleged to constitute a selling arrangement 'apply to all relevant traders operating within the national territory'.

(2) That the provisions must 'affect in the same manner, in law and in fact, the marketing of domestic products and of those from other Member States'.

Keck, even at first sight, narrows the scope of Article 34 TFEU. The Court's failure to list the cases it overruled and the ambiguity of 'certain selling arrangements' did not, however, make for absolute clarity.

Post-*Keck* case law

10.57 It has been through the preliminary reference procedure under Article 267 TFEU that the concept of a selling arrangement has been clarified—at least to an appreciable extent. However, in some cases the distinction between a 'marketing' or product 'requirement' and a 'selling arrangement' is not easily drawn. In Case C–368/95 *Familiapress* (noted at **10.39**) a prohibition in Austria on the sale of periodicals containing prize competitions, although a rule about sales promotions and looking like a selling arrangement within the meaning of *Keck*, was held to fall within Article 34 TFEU as it had a bearing on the actual content of the product. However, the measure could be justified by the mandatory requirement of press diversity because by falling within Article 34 TFEU it still benefited from the *Cassis de Dijon* rule of reason.

Restrictions on advertising

10.58 Prior to the ruling in *Keck*, in Case 362/88 *GB-INNO-BM* (1990) the Court of Justice ruled on a piece of Luxembourg legislation preventing advertising campaigns that made reference to the pre-sale price of a product. The Court found this to be incompatible with Article 34 TFEU as it was capable of hindering trade. In Joined Cases C–1 and 176/90 *Aragonesa and Publivia* (1991) the Court of Justice found that legislation which prohibited the advertising of alcohol over a certain strength in the mass media and other public places was found to fall within the parameters of *Dassonville*. Post-*Keck* it is now clear that national rules imposing partial restrictions on advertising will not fall within the Article since they are 'selling arrangements'. In Case C–292/92 *Hünermund* (1993), decided a month after *Keck*, the Court ruled that the German regulation in question fulfilled the test in *Keck* and thus fell outside the Article. The rule related to a prohibition on excessive advertising for non-medical products sold legally in pharmacies. In Case C–412/93 *Leclerc-Siplec v TFI Publicité and M6 Publicité* (1995), the Court of Justice ruled to the same effect as regards a French ban on advertising certain products on TV. The rationale for this rule was to maintain the income of newspapers (especially local papers) from advertising. It thus had no link with market access. In instances where there are rules that place total restrictions on advertising these will not be deemed to be 'selling arrangements'.

10.59 In Joined Cases C–34, 35 and 36/95 *KO v De Agostini and TV-Shop* (1997) measures against a TV advertiser broadcasting from another Member State did not fall within Article 34 TFEU as long as they affected product marketing in the same way. It was a selling arrangement (televised advertising) which applied to all traders within the national territory. Whether the ban affected in the same manner the marketing of domestic products and of those from other Member States, which, it will be remembered, is the proviso for 'selling arrangements' falling outside the scope of Article 34 TFEU, was a matter for the national court to determine. However, the Court did point out that a total ban on advertising would deprive the applicant of its most effective (or, as the applicant put it, its only) weapon to penetrate the Swedish market and that national courts should look at the question of proportionality. The Court interpreted the rules concerning the freedom to provide services (see **Chapter 11**) in much the same way, saying there was also an obstacle to that freedom, when taking account of the international nature of the advertising market.

Sunday trading rules and opening hours

10.60 In Cases C–69 and 258/93 *Punto Casa SpA v Sindaco del Commune di Capena* (1994) an Italian law regulating business opening hours for retail sales provided for the total closure of shops on Sundays and public holidays. The claimants operated shops that frequently opened on Sundays. The Court concluded that such regulations fell within the definition of selling arrangements and that Article 34 TFEU did not apply:

> To national legislation on the closure of shops which applies to all traders operating within the national territory and which affects in the same manner, in law and in fact, the marketing of domestic products and of those from other Member States.

10.61 In Joined Cases C–401 and 402/92 *Tankstation't Heukske* (1994) rules relating to restrictions on Sunday trading were also held to pass the test in *Keck* and thus fall outside the scope of the Article, thereby drawing a line under the unsatisfactory and at the time still unresolved problem of Sunday opening hours discussed above at **10.52-10.54**.

Sale of goods through designated methods

10.62 The Court in Case C–391/92 *Commission v Greece* (1995) ('*Processed Milk*') indicated that a rule requiring a good to be sold through designated methods was a mere limitation on the means of distribution of a good without affecting its composition, and as such was a 'selling arrangement'. The requirement here was that processed milk for infants could only be sold in pharmacies. The rule applied equally to all products irrespective of origin and to all traders. This case clearly demonstrated the purpose of the *Keck* judgment, preventing the Union system from being clogged up with issues not relating to market access: the Court did not want to extend Article 34 TFEU in such a way as to become embroiled in what are essentially questions of domestic policy. Such cases also reveal that selling arrangements relate to measures determining *when* or *how* goods may be sold. Furthermore, the *Processed Milk* case shows that selling arrangements include by whom and where products are sold.

10.63 Regulating designated methods of sale was also considered in Case C–108/09 *Ker-Optikabt* (2010), where contact lenses were required by Hungarian law to be sold only in certain specialised shops or 'by home delivery for final consumption'. The claimant company operated online with delivery through mail order. The Court noted that the limitation on the mailing of the products to which the 'electronic contract' had pertained 'deprives traders from other Member States of a particularly effective means of selling those products and thus significantly impedes [market] access' and therefore did not fulfil the *Keck* criteria of applying equally in fact as well as law.

The Court then undertook a particularly intense proportionality analysis of the Hungarian state's public health defence, and accepted that the restriction was associated with an acceptable need, as recognised in Hungary, of qualified staff for eye examinations, advice on the wearing of contact lenses and advice on the relevant types, however:

> It should be observed that those services are required, as a general rule, only when contact lenses are first supplied. At the time of subsequent supplies, there is, as a general rule, no need to provide the customer with such services. It is sufficient that the customer advise the seller of the type of lenses which were provided when lenses were first supplied the specifications of those lenses having been adjusted, where necessary, by

an ophthalmologist who has issued a new prescription which takes into account any change in the customer's vision.

10.64 The potential for e-commerce to provide wide choice and good value to the consumer in many ways epitomises, and then exceeds, the initial concept of the EU internal market itself. The Commission itself aims to double e-commerce by 2015. It can be expected that generally, and with few excluded sectors some of which are services (such as gambling, see, generally, **Chapter 11**), the Court too will seek to promote the virtues of e-commerce wherever possible. In this case that aim of promotion of e-commerce was supported through detailed analysis, and subsequent rejection, of a Member State restriction, followed by specific advice for reform; namely the division of eye examinations from the act of purchase wherever possible.

Restrictions on certain forms of sale promotions

10.65 In Case 286/81 *Oosthoek* (see **10.34**), decided prior to *Keck*, the Court of Justice ruled that Dutch legislation that prohibited free gifts being offered as part of a sales promotion was prohibited under Article 34 TFEU. This was followed in Case 382/87 *Buet* (1989). However, applying the *Keck* principle it is probable that these cases would now have been deemed to have involved selling arrangements and as such fallen outside the reach of the Article.

Presentation requirements

10.66 In Case C–416/00 *Morellato* (2003) the Court of Justice decided that a requirement prescribed by Italian law that bread had to be sold wrapped constituted a selling arrangement. The case differs from *Walter Rau* (see **10.13** and **10.35**) which would still fall foul of Article 34 TFEU because of the direct packaging requirement imposed in *Rau*. In *Morellato*, bread could be imported unwrapped and then sold wrapped. The distinction being that it was the retailer who was carrying out the wrapping task. The simple wrapping process was incapable of restricting the free movement of goods.

Rules on the use of products

10.67 Case C–110/05 *Commission v Italy* (2009) concerned an Article 258 TFEU (ex Article 226 EC) action against the Italian state following the introduction of Italian legislation that prohibited motorcycles and quadricycles from towing a trailer. The Commission claimed that the prohibition regulating the use of these bikes and trailers was a restriction on the free movement of goods contrary to Article 34 TFEU. It was argued in the case that rules on the use of products were effectively equivalent to the *Keck* rules stating that selling arrangements were in principle outside the scope of the Article. The Court of Justice did not agree and ruled that regulations on the use of products were within the scope of the Article. The Court held that the restriction on the use of motorcycle trailers in principle breached the Article but could be justified. The breach of the Article was found because consumers unable to lawfully use a motorcycle with a trailer would be unlikely to purchase one, thereby hindering trade within the internal market. The restriction on trade was however justified on grounds of road safety.

10.68 The position that rules on product use falling within the scope of Article 34 TFEU but being justifiable has been confirmed in Case C–142/05 *Mickelsson and Roos* (2009). The Court of Justice held that Swedish rules on the use of personalised watercraft (the term 'jet-ski' is generally used to describe the vehicles, although a jet-ski is a particular product which has been trademarked) on navigable waterways were caught by the prohibition of measures hindering free movement of goods under Article 34 TFEU. Sweden had restrictions on jet-skis that limited their use to certain waterways, many of which were used for high volumes of commercial traffic and which were therefore unappealing to jet-ski users. The effect overall was that there were very few waterways were jet-skis could or would want to be used, and this therefore meant consumers logically had limited interest in buying jet-skis in Sweden. This impact on the market of the product, while not self-evidently imposing greater burdens on importers, thus had considerable effect because of the scope of the impact on consumers. However, the fact that the rules on product use were reviewable under the Article did not mean these rules were unacceptable so long as the national courts considered the justifications on the product use rules complied with European Union law. The rules here were justifiable in terms of their environmental protection objectives, and in terms of the Article 36 TFEU ground relating to the protection of health and life of humans, animals and plants, two related grounds that the Court here considered together (see further **10.79**, below).

10.69 The Court's clear reluctance to extend *Keck* to rules on the use of products is replaced instead by the application of a softer proportionality test, thereby achieving the central aim of *Keck* via other means. Whereas the Court has traditionally demanded that Member States take the least restrictive measure necessary to achieve the ends sought (see **10.43**), the margin afforded in both these cases appears greater. In Case C–110/05 *Commission v Italy* (2009) the Court noted that:

> Although it is possible, in the present case, to envisage that measures other than the prohibition laid down [by Italy]…could guarantee a certain level of road safety… Member States cannot be denied the possibility of attaining an objective such as road safety by the introduction of general and simple rules which will be easily understood and applied by drivers and easily managed and supervised by the competent authorities.

Similarly, in *Mickelsson and Roos*, the Court applied this rule by analogy (citing the above paragraph) to environmental protection mentioning also the 'particular geographical circumstances' of Sweden in combination. It appears then that this rule headlines greater deference from the Court to Member State authorities, and is also flexible enough in its application to be influenced by the specific facts of each case. It will be interesting to monitor both its frequency of deployment and development in future cases (Case C–137/09 *Josemans* (2010), a services case, see **11.53**)); and Case C–400/08 *Commission v Spain* (2011), an establishment case).

The conditions in *Keck* and the difficulties in finding a consistent rule

10.70 The condition before a 'selling arrangement' can fall outside the scope of Article 34 TFEU in *Keck* is that 'the provision affect in the same manner, in law and in fact the marketing of domestic products and those from other Member States'. There have been a number of cases which have examined this condition. In *De Agostini*, mentioned at **10.59**, the Court of Justice questioned whether the Swedish legislation would satisfy this condition. The Court left the final determination to the national referring court. In Case C–405/98 *Gourmet International Products* (see **10.74**) the Court of Justice clearly stated that this condition was definitely satisfied. The absolute prohibition by the Swedish legislation on advertising was regarded as affecting the marketing of products from other Member States more heavily than the marketing of domestic products and therefore constituted an obstacle to trade between Member States. As such the rule had to be considered within Article 34 TFEU. Case C–254/98 *TK-Heimdienst* (see **10.75**) involved Austrian legislation that required purveyors of food, who wished to sell their goods on rounds in Austria to have a place of fixed establishment in the Member State itself. The Court of Justice indicated that the condition in *Keck* of application in the same manner to domestic and foreign goods was not satisfied. Purveyors, who wanted to sell goods from mobile premises on the rounds in Austria would have to invest in fixed establishment premises before they could sell their goods. The Court indicated that 'in order for goods from other Member States to enjoy the same access to the market of Austria as domestic goods, they have to bear additional costs'.

10.71 Case C–322/01 *Deutscher Apothekerverband* (2003) involved German legislation prohibiting the internet sale of most medicines which meant that only pharmacists based in Germany could sell medicine. The Court stated that although pharmacists in Germany could not use internet sales either, they were still free to sell the same products over-the-counter in their dispensaries. For pharmacists not established in Germany, that option was not available. For out-of-state providers the internet provided 'a more significant way to gain access to the German market'. The Court concluded that 'a prohibition which has a greater impact on pharmacist established outside German territory could impede access to the market for products from other Member States more than it impedes access for domestic products'. The German legislation was therefore not a 'selling arrangement' but was an indistinctly applicable MEQR and was *prima facie* in breach of Article 34 TFEU. It was, however, subject to justification under Article 36 TFEU.

Clarifying the clarification

10.72 There are still problems with *Keck*. Although most of the cases so far cited fit in well with the formula of certain 'selling arrangements' that do not discriminate in law or in fact, some situations do not fit well in any interpretation of the current law. First, the criterion of selling arrangements ignores the fact that products are often distributed in a marketing mix where appearance and content (governed by *Cassis*) are inseparable from its advertising (a 'selling arrangement': *how* a product is sold). Moreover, as Jacobs AG observed in his Opinion in the *Leclerc-Siplec* case (see **10.58**), advertising is crucial for market access—without doubt the ability to launch and sustain a Union-wide advertising campaign of the producers' choice (subject to Article 36 TFEU or the mandatory requirements) is one way of aiding the free movement of goods. Secondly, Jacobs AG in the same Opinion criticised the requirement of discrimination in law or in fact:

If an obstacle to free movement exists, it does not cease to exist simply because an identical obstacle affects domestic trade.

10.73 Case C–470/93 *Mars* (1995) is an example of the sort of problems which may arise in spite of *Keck*. This case is very much on the borderline between *Keck* and *Cassis* and could have been decided either way. It has therefore been subject to a fair amount of controversy. As part of a Europe-wide publicity campaign, ice-cream bars were offered in wrappers marked '+10 per cent' while the quantity of each product had in fact been increased by 10 per cent exactly. The German unfair competition watchdog brought proceedings against Mars GmbH under German unfair competition law arguing that consumers could be misled in two ways. First, one could assume that the 10 per cent increase in quantity was granted without any price increase; and second, the actual increase in quantity was considerably smaller than the coloured marking on the wrapping suggested: the coloured marking itself occupying much more than 10 per cent of the surface of the wrapper. The German court referred the case to the Court of Justice asking whether the prohibition in question was compatible with the principles of the free movement of goods. The problem in this case is that advertising measures such as the one Mars introduced are of a dual nature. On the one hand, they act as a sales promotion tool; on the other hand, they affect the product itself—here, its packaging. Had Mars started a similar campaign without changing the product packaging, e.g. by using posters with the same message, this campaign would have been regarded as being a mere 'selling arrangement', and thus outside the scope of Article 34 TFEU. However, both the Court and the Advocate General concluded in this case that the Article was applicable because:

A prohibition…which relates to the marketing in a Member State of products bearing the same publicity markings as those lawfully used in other Member States, is by nature such as to hinder intra-Community trade. [para 13 of the judgment]

Once it was established that the actions of the watchdog did not benefit from the 'selling arrangement' categorisation they were considered from the perspective of the mandatory requirements. Consumer protection was not accepted as a justification for the prohibition, as the price had not been increased and a 'reasonably circumspect consumer' is aware of the fact that there is not necessarily a link between the size of markings and the size of the increase in the product. Article 34 TFEU therefore precluded the German action in this case and permitted Mars's promotional ploys.

10.74   In Case C–405/98 *Konsumentenombudsmannen v Gourmet International Products* (noted in **10.70**), the Court ruled that the reasoning laid down in *Keck* was not applicable here. Free movement of goods and services provisions did not preclude a prohibition, imposed by Swedish legislation, on the advertising of alcoholic beverages in periodicals, unless it is apparent that the protection of public health against the harmful effects of alcohol could be ensured by measures having less effect on trade within the Union. The Court held that, in the case of products like alcoholic beverages, the consumption of which is linked to traditional social practices and to local habits and customs, a prohibition of all advertising directed at consumers in the form of advertisements in the press is liable to impede access to the market by products from other Member States more than it impedes access by domestic products. Such a ban would not have that much effect on the sales of domestically produced alcohol which already had an established market, but it would make it much more difficult for imported alcohol to enter the market.

10.75   In Case C–254/98 *TK Heimdienst* (2000) only local Austrians were given licences to sell groceries from vans in the administrative district where they were based. This could have been justified as it intended to promote sales by local shopkeepers. However, this disadvantaged a German shopkeeper, based no more than five miles away, just across the border, who could not obtain a licence, whereas an Austrian shopkeeper, based no nearer, could. Although the rule did not intend to discriminate as to nationality, in fact the effect on goods of different origin was different. The problem as to whether this Austrian rule was a 'selling arrangement' (and covered by *Keck*) or a rule relating to the products (only justifiable under Article 36 TFEU or the mandatory requirements) was avoided by the discriminatory effect of the rule. The problem remains, however, and could still arise in other areas, less near state borders.

10.76   On the whole it can be said that the Court has been consistent in its post-*Keck* case law. There are a number of straightforward *Keck* cases such as *Hünermund* and *Leclerc-Siplec* (**10.58**). By consistently following the approach set out in *Keck* the Court has restored legal certainty after a period of incoherent case law. And by introducing a fairly straightforward criterion of 'selling arrangement' without many details, conditions or exceptions, the Court has made sure that there is room for a later refinement of the term. Not all post-*Keck* cases, however, are entirely predictable, as seen in the case of *Mars*.

10.77   On the back of the complex solutions found in *Gourmet* and *De Agostini* (see **10.70** and **10.59**), Case C–20/03 *Burmanjer* (2005) and Case C–441/04 *A-Punkt Schmuckhandel* (2006) have again shown the usefulness of the *Keck* approach to escape the rigidity of the *Dassonville* rule. In *Burmanjer* the issue was whether Belgian legislation which makes it a criminal offence to carry on itinerant sales activities (i.e. doorstep selling) involving the offer and conclusion for subscriptions to periodicals, without prior authorisation, is contrary to Article 34 TFEU. With respect to the application of the Article, Leger AG considered that although the legislation was indeed applicable to everyone wishing to exercise itinerant activity of the kind at issue, it was 'not inconceivable that it may affect the marketing of periodicals from other Member States more than the marketing of national periodicals'. The Court disagreed, and considered the Belgian legislation a 'selling arrangement'. The Court added from the information that it had in its possession, the rule would be too insignificant and uncertain to be regarded as being such as to hinder or otherwise interfere with trade between Member States. The Court of Justice left it to the national court to decide whether the *Keck* conditions were satisfied. *A-Punkt Schmuckhandel* dealt with a rule of a Member State which prohibited the door-to-door sale of silver jewellery. While stating that in principle rules on the sale of jewellery in people's homes did not in principle breach the Article, the Court of Justice again left it to the national court to decide whether the *Keck* conditions were satisfied by consideration of the specific Austrian rules at issue. The Court of Justice set out some guidance that should be considered by national courts in assessing whether the rules on jewellery sales should fall within the Article. The Court noted the rules applied to all traders operating in Austria and to all goods; the Court also stated that evidence submitted showing the rules affected the volume of goods traded was not in itself sufficient to trigger the application of the Article.

10.78 The *Keck* decision, and the introduction of the 'selling arrangement' question into the consideration of whether Article 34 TFEU applies to a rule affecting trade in goods, has difficulties. The distinction between 'selling arrangements' and the composition of products is not always workable, and there are many who question whether the 'selling arrangements' exemption sits comfortably with the overall objectives of the internal market. There seems little likelihood the Court of Justice will rethink its approach to these questions soon however, even if the recent decisions on the approach to rules on product use suggests the Court decided against including product use rules within a *Keck*-type carte blanche exception to Article 34 TFEU and instead decided to consider such scenarios in a *Cassis*-type approach. So while the 'selling arrangements' criteria limiting the scope of Article 34 TFEU is being retained, it does not look like it is to be extended to other areas in this dynamic area of market law.

The blurred distinction between Article 36 TFEU and 'mandatory requirements'

10.79 Both Article 36 TFEU and the *Cassis de Dijon* line of cases' concept of mandatory requirements set out exceptions to the application of Article 34 TFEU's prohibition on rules affecting the volume of trade. There are, as is noted at **10.30**, important distinctions in the approach and operation of Article 36 TFEU grounds and the mandatory requirements, but in Case 142/05 *Mickelsson and Roos* (2009, see **10.68**) the Court of

Justice stated that the protection of health and life of humans, animals and plants, and the mandatory requirement of environmental protection were 'closely related objectives', and that they should be 'examined together' in this case. Since the judgment in Case C–379/98 *PreussenElektra* (2001) (see also **10.23**) the question of the status of the environmental protection mandatory requirement had been at issue, because the normal rules applicable to the operation of the environmental justification for trade limiting rules did not seem to apply. In *PreussenElektra*, German legislation obliged electricity supply undertakings to purchase the electricity produced in their area of supply from renewable energy sources and to pay for it in accordance with a statutory minimum price. Although the Court ruled that the German legislation constituted, at least potentially, an obstacle to intra-Union trade, it then stated that account should be taken of the aim of the provision and of the particular features of the electricity market (at paragraph 72 of the judgment). The provision was designed to protect the environment and the health and life of humans, animals and plants. The Court observed that the nature of electricity makes it difficult to determine its origin and in particular the source of energy from which it was produced. Furthermore, there was a proposed directive in which the Commission had taken the view that the implementation in each Member State of a system of certificates of origin for electricity produced from renewable sources capable of being the subject of mutual recognition was essential in order to make trade in that type of electricity both reliable and possible in practice. Therefore, the Court concluded that 'in the current state of Community law concerning the electricity market' the German legislation was not incompatible with Article 34 TFEU (at paragraph 81). Jacobs AG questioned whether this was a case for relaxation of the rule that the list of exceptions in Article 36 TFEU was exhaustive, and that environmental protection should be a justification of a rule even if it were discriminatory. However, the Court allowed the justification on the grounds of environmental protection, a *Cassis* type justification, but stated the legislation was not incompatible with Article 36 TFEU. The possibility that measures with discriminatory impact can be justified on grounds of environmental protection suggests a special position for obstacles to the free movement of goods justified on environmental protection grounds.

10.80 While the *PreussenElektra* judgment may be specific to the context of the features of the electricity market, the Court had confirmed this treatment of environmental obstacles by reference to Article 34 TEU in Case 320/03 *Commission v Austria* (2005, see also **10.43**, above) before the decision in *Mickelsson and Roos* and in Case C–28/09 *Commission v Austria*. Here an Austrian ban on vehicles over 7.5 tonnes carrying certain goods was held to breach Article 34 TFEU since the ban was disproportionate to the end pursued. The Court recognised nevertheless the air quality aim being pursued as environmental protection, even if it was not being pursued proportionately, and did not seem to question the legitimacy of pursuing this environmental protection objective despite the discriminatory effect of the measure. The Austrian ban on these vehicles had a heavy effect upon non-Austrian traders, either importing goods into Austria, or whose trade was in transit across Austria, compared to Austrian traders. There was little obvious discriminatory impact on importers with the Swedish rules on jet-ski use in Case 142/05 *Mickelsson and Roos* and so the question of the relationship between the health exception under Article 36 TFEU and environmental protection as a mandatory requirement was less significant. It still may be that the Court will be open to accepting a national rule that has a discriminatory effect on imports if that rule is justified on grounds of environmental protection, as per the *PreussenElektra* precedent, and at the very least the relationship between environmental protection and the health exception under Article 36 TFEU seems close, even if health protection and environmental protection seem to be different aims. There are limits, however. In Case 524/07 *Commission v Austria* (2008) an Austrian ban on the registration of imported second-hand vehicles that did not comply with environmental standards did not apply to registrations for vehicles already in Austria. Both the environmental objective and discriminatory effect of the measure here were self-evident but the fact that the measure had environmental protection objectives did not save it. The Court ruled that proportionality should also be considered, and decided the Austrian vehicle registration rules breached Article 34 TFEU, and could not be justified under Article 36 TFEU or an environmental protection mandatory requirement because measures with less discriminatory effect were possible.

Reverse discrimination, or the 'wholly internal situation'

10.81 Reverse discrimination is the much rarer situation where a national rule overtly discriminates against domestically produced goods. A Member State may well continue to impose stricter rules on its domestic product than on the foreign product. Article 34 TFEU does not apply to the wholly internal situation, and as such reverse discrimination is compatible with Article 34 TFEU. The philosophy behind the permission of reverse discrimination is that it theoretically encourages national rules to improve quality of domestic production and make the products more attractive to customers, whilst not influencing imported products. In Case 98/86 *Mathot* (1987) the Court of Justice said that a Belgian law requiring butter produced in Belgium have certain details listed on its packaging, that was not imposed on imported butter, did not breach the Article.

There was no cross-border element to the complaint and therefore Community law was not triggered.

10.82 Case C–298/87 *Smanor* (1988) concerned the labelling of yoghurt, a title reserved in France only to fresh yoghurt. A seller of deep frozen yoghurt, having spent several years locked in litigation with the French authorities over use of the name, finally referred the question of compatibility with Article 28 (now Article 34 TFEU) to the Court for a preliminary ruling. While admitting that the facts in question were of a wholly internal situation, the Court still found it necessary to provide an answer, stating that the provision in question, if encountered by sellers of frozen yoghurt in other Member States, could hinder the free movement of goods. The Court did stress that its verdict on the legislation in question was, however, not applicable in the case before it. Yet in the somewhat confusing judgment of *Pistre*, the Court appeared to venture even further into Member State competence.

10.83 Three years later, in the case of *Guimont*, the Court had the opportunity to clarify the position on preliminary rulings and wholly internal situations. Indeed, the Court chose to return to its position under *Smanor*, stating that 'such a rule falls under Article 28 [now Article 34 TFEU] only in so far as it applies to...the importation of goods'.

10.84 In Joined Cases C–321–324/94 *Pistre* (1997) the designation of French *jambon de montagne* ('mountain ham') was reserved for ham from pigs living on particular high mountain slopes in France. This meant that ham from other pigs, even if living the same type of life, could not bear that designation. In fact, foreign producers did call their products 'mountain ham' without encountering problems. A French producer who used the designation without being entitled to do so was prosecuted. The producer claimed the prosecution was a breach of Article 34 TFEU. The French Government argued it was a purely internal situation and that the Article did not apply. The Court held that just because the situation was confined to one Member State, it did not mean the Article could not apply. If the effect of the measure was to facilitate the marketing of domestic goods to the detriment of foreign goods this meant there could be at least a potential hindrance to trade within the Union. In Case C–448/98 *Guimont* (2000) a French rule allowing only cheese with a rind to be sold as *Emmental* again did not hinder imports in practice. The Court said this rule was potentially an obstacle to trade, but there was no Community law reason why the rule could not be applied to French producers. This is different to *Pistre*, where no foreign product could ever achieve the standard set by the French rule, whereas in the simpler *Guimont*, as in *Cassis*, there was no reason why a foreign producer could not reach that standard. In the Case C–72/03 *Carbonati Apuani* (2004), the 'Carrara Marble' case, a tax on marble exported from an Italian town was duly held to be an infringement of the Union provisions on free movement of goods, and contrary to Article 25 EC (now Article 30 TFEU). This restored case law to the same line as followed in *Guimont*, giving rise to a distinction between intrastate and wholly internal situations.

Article 35 TFEU

10.85 Article 35 TFEU states:

> *Quantitative restrictions on exports, and all measures having equivalent effect, shall be prohibited between Member States.*

The case law relating to Article 35 TFEU is much less extensive than that relating to Article 34 TFEU, as it is usually in the Member States' interest to encourage exports. The Article does however, have a role to play in respect of economically sensitive exports such as essential raw materials and politically sensitive exports. Article 35 TFEU, in the same vein as Article 34 TFEU, prohibits both quantitative restrictions and measures equivalent to quantitative restrictions. As with Article 34 TFEU, Article 35 TFEU is directly effective. Measures which clearly discriminate against exports will usually be found to be in breach of Article 35 TFEU, the most obvious of which are export bans and quotas.

Quantitative restrictions under Article 35 TFEU

10.86 The prohibition of quantitative restrictions was at issue in Case C–47/90 *Établissements Delhaize frères et Compagnie Le Lion SA v Promalvin SA and AGE Bodegas Unidas SA* (1992), where a Belgian company ordered 3,000 hectolitres of Rioja wine from Spain. Spanish rules imposed a quota on the amount of wine available for export in bulk to other Member States, but did not impose any restriction on domestic sales. The Court stated that the rules clearly breached Article 35 TFEU. Many breaches of Article 35 TFEU by the Member States can be justified under Article 36 TFEU which applies here in the same way as to Article 34 TFEU. In Case C–5/94 *Hedley Lomas* (1996), the Ministry for Agriculture, Fisheries and Food in the United Kingdom banned live animal exports to Spain. The United Kingdom sought to justify this ban on exports, *prima facie* contrary to Article 35 TFEU, on the grounds of the defence of protection of animal health. This argument was rejected for lack of evidence. The United Kingdom's refusal to issue an export licence for a quantity of live sheep intended for slaughter in a Spanish slaughterhouse was contrary to the Article. In Case C–203/96 *Dusseldorp* (1998), a Dutch prohibition on the exportation of waste oil filters, which was sought to be justified by virtue of the mandatory requirement relating to environmental protection was held to be a breach of the Article. The Dutch justification was not accepted as the ban was motivated by purely economic considerations. However, as noted in **10.18**, the position was different in Case 7/78 *Thompson* where a UK law which prohibited the exportation of old coins from the United Kingdom was held again to be a *prima facie* breach of the Article, but was justifiable on the grounds of public policy under Article 36 TFEU.

Measures having equivalent effect to a quantitative restriction under Article 35 TFEU

10.87 Article 35 TFEU also prohibits MEQRs and there is a direct parallel with the case law under Article 34 TFEU. In Case 53/76 *Bouhelier* (1977), concerning a quality inspection of watches exported from France, the rule had the aim of ensuring that quality standards were maintained; however no such inspection was required for domestic watches. This was held by the Court to be a MEQR and the Article was infringed. In Case 237/82 *Jongeneel Kaas* (1984), a Dutch law requiring cheese exporters to possess an export licence was held to be in breach of the Article. In a rare example of Treaty infringement proceedings brought under Article 259 TFEU (ex Article 227 EC) by one Member State against another, Belgium brought proceedings against Spain in Case C–388/95 *Belgium v Spain* (2000) for maintaining in force national legislation providing that, in order for wine to be able to use its designation of origin as Rioja it had to be bottled in that region. In the earlier case, C–47/90 *Delhaize* (1992) (see **10.86**) the Court had held that measures limiting the quantity of wine which could be exported in bulk whilst allowing such sales in bulk within the region were in breach of Article 35 TFEU. In the *Belgium v Spain* judgment, however, the Court said that new evidence had since been gathered demonstrating an underlying justification of such measures and that the obligation of bottling wine in the region was compatible with Community law as a necessary and proportionate means of protecting the quality of such products in the absence of any less restrictive alternative measures. The Court therefore dismissed the action as the rule could be justified on the grounds of protection of commercial property under Article 36 TFEU, Rioja being recognised as a brand that merited protection of its name.

Indistinctly applicable rules under Article 35 TFEU

10.88 In contrast to Article 34 TFEU, Article 35 TFEU will only apply if there is discrimination and thus indistinctly applicable measures will not fall within its scope. In Case 15/79 *Groenveld* (1979) domestic producers of meat products were prohibited from stocking or processing horsemeat. Horsemeat cannot be easily detected in meat products and this rule was intended to avoid the risk of horsemeat being present in products being sold to countries where the consumption of such meat is forbidden. The Court said that this was not a discriminatory measure as it applied equally to domestic products and exports, and it was therefore permitted.

10.89 In Case C–412/97 *ED Srl v Italo Fenocchio* (1999) the suggestion was made that not all directly discriminatory measures would be caught by Article 35 TFEU, leading to the suggestion that there is a *de minimis* rule. The case related to a domestic law which permitted a summary order for payment to be made where the defendant resided in the host Member State. These orders could not be made against defendants living in other Member States. The complainant argued that this rule had the effect of discouraging exports. The Court of Justice disagreed and made reference to the limited, uncertain and indirect effect that the provision was likely to have on the free movement of goods. They thus found that the rule did not breach the Article.

Article 35 TFEU and the purely internal situation

10.90 In Case C–293/02 *Jersey Produce Marketing Organisation* (2005) the question arose as to whether rules in Jersey which made exportation to the United Kingdom of potatoes produced in Jersey subject to the completion of various formalities were contrary to Article 35 TFEU. The Court of Justice affirmed that Jersey and the United Kingdom are one and the same Member State. On this basis the assumption could be made that this left the rules to be a matter for domestic law, and was to be regarded as a purely internal matter. It is well established that the argument that a purely internal matter avoids falling within Union law is no longer a sustainable argument in customs duties cases: regional barriers are obstacles to be removed exactly as intra-Union ones. The Court then looked at the potential for the potatoes to be re-exported, and came to the conclusion that re-exportation was a distinct possibility. The possible re-exportation of potatoes from the United Kingdom to another Member State was used as the basis to establish a breach of the Article. As the re-exportation could not have been excluded, the Court of Justice then considered the imposed requirements. It held the requirement that growers should be registered with a local public organisation and the requirement that marketing organisations could only export potatoes if they concluded a marketing agreement with a local public organisation were contrary to the Article. This case increases the parameters of the application of Article 35 TFEU. The approach adopted by the Court signals that a pragmatic approach will be taken: the primary aim of Article 35 TFEU is to facilitate the free movement of goods, and internal rules on exports can fall within its scope.

Directive 98/34 on the provision of information in the field of technical standards and regulations

10.91 Directive 98/34/EC requires Member States to notify the Commission of any draft technical regulations before they can be checked for their compatibility with Union law. This Directive has assumed considerable significance in the light of the Court's rulings in various cases. In Case C–226/97 *Lemmens* (1998) the Court explained the scope of its judgment in Case C–194/94 *CIA Security International v Signalson and Securitel* (1996) concerning Directive 83/189/EEC (now consolidated in Directive 98/34), which provides for preventive checks, at Community (now Union) level, of national technical standards and regulations. The Court had held in that judgment that breach by a Member State of its obligation to notify the Commission in advance of the introduction of technical standards constituted a substantive procedural defect such as to render the technical regulations in question inapplicable, and thus unenforceable against individuals. In *Lemmens*, the Court stated however that, while failure to notify the Commission renders technical regulations inapplicable inasmuch as they hinder the use and marketing of a product which is not in conformity with them, failure to notify does not have the effect of rendering unlawful any use of a product which is in conformity with the un-notified regulations. The requirement of notification of such standards exists in order to avoid the creation of new obstacles to trade in goods between Member States.

FURTHER READING

Barnard, C., *The Substantive Law of the EU: The Four Fundamental Freedoms* (Oxford: OUP, 3rd edn, 2010).

Commission, Communication to the European Parliament, the Council, the Economic and Social Committee and the Committee of the Regions: A coherent framework for building trust in the Digital Single Market for e-commerce and online services (COM(2011) 942).

Davies, G., 'Can selling arrangements be harmonised?' (2005) 30(3) *European Law Review* 370–385.

Gormley, L., 'Reasoning renounced? The remarkable judgment in *Keck v Mithouard*' [1994] *European Business Law Review* 63.

Hilson, C., 'Discrimination in Community free movement law' (1999) 24 *European Law Review* 445.

Kaczorowska, A., 'Gourmet can have his Keck and eat it!' (2004) 10 *European Law Journal* 479–94.

Koutrakos, P., 'On Mortelmans, "The Common Market, the internal market and the Single Market": What's in a market?' (1998) 35 *Common Market Law Review* 101.

Kraft, D., 'Advertising restrictions and the free movement of goods—the case law of the ECJ' (2007) 18(3) *European Business Law Review* 517.

Maduro, M., *We the Court: the European Court of Justice and the European Constitution: A critical reading of Article 30 of the EC Treaty* (Oxford: Hart Publishing, 1998).

Oliver, P. and Roth, W., 'The internal market and the Four Freedoms' (2004) 41 *Common Market Law Review* 407.

Oliver, P. and Enchelmaier, S., 'Free movement of goods: recent developments in the case law' (2007) 43(3) *Common Market Law Review* 649.

Shuibhne, N., 'The free movement of goods and Article 28 EC: an evolving framework' (2002) 27 *European Law Journal* 408.

Reich, N., 'How proportionate is the proportionality principle?' (paper presented at the Oslo conference on 'The Reach of Free Movement', 18–19 May 2011. (available at <http://www.jus.uio.no/ifp/forskning/prosjekter/markedsstaten/arrangementer/2011/free-movement-oslo/speakers-papers/norbert-reich.pdf>).

Weatherill, S., 'After *Keck*: some thoughts on how to clarify the clarification' (1996) *Common Market Law Review* 885–906.

Weatherill, S., 'Recent developments in the law governing the free movement of goods in the EC's internal market' (2006) 2 *European Review of Contract Law* 90.

Weiler, J.H.H., 'From Dassonville to Keck and beyond: an evolutionary reflection on the text and context of free movement of goods' in P Craig and G de Burca (eds), *The Evolution of EU Law* (Oxford: OUP, 1999).

SELF-TEST QUESTIONS

1   What are measures having an equivalent effect to a quantitative restriction (MEQR)?

2   Do the cases of *Keck* and those following it represent a change in the attitude of the ECJ towards defining what is a MEQR?

3   Do the judgments on product use suggest a rethinking of the approach developed in *Keck*?

4   Are the mandatory requirements recognised in *Cassis de Dijon* to be understood as exceptions to Article 34 TFEU (thus extending Article 36 TFEU) or as taking measures out of the ambit of Article 34 TFEU altogether?

5   The UK currently bans two wheel, self-balancing personal transport devices (some sold as 'Segways') from both pavements (as they are classified as motor vehicles) and roads (as they do not comply with UK road traffic law). The Segway is a two-wheeled device with a top speed of 12mph. Advise the UK of possible justifications for this ban considering particularly proportionality issues.

11

Free movement of services: the freedom to provide and receive services

SUMMARY

This chapter reviews the law on the free movement of services in the European Union, considering its relationship to the law on the free movement of goods and persons. It covers:

- The push to develop the service economy
- Definitions of services and the requirement of remuneration
- Non-economic services
- Services, non-discrimination and the direct effect of Article 56 TFEU
- The freedom to provide a service
- The freedom to receive a service
- Services provided across borders where neither the recipient nor the provider move across borders
- Public interest grounds and limitations on service provision
- Illegal services
- The move to a focus on market access and the facilitation of service provision
- The Lisbon Strategy and the Services Directive

The service economy and the law on services

11.1 Services are omnipresent in the European Union economy, generating almost 70 per cent of GNP and jobs and offering considerable potential for growth and job creation. Services provided in the EU economy encompass a broad range of activity from professional services providing legal or financial advice, through education, music, sport, building, plumbing and news, to hairdressing or service in a restaurant. Recognising the range of services provided in the EU and the potential for growth underpinning service provision, the Lisbon European Council in March 2000 launched a process of economic reform, the overriding aim being to make the EU the most competitive and dynamic knowledge-based economy in the world by 2010. Directive 2006/123/EC on Services in the Internal Market sets out a clear focus for the EU economy upon services. The Directive's objectives relate to strengthening the positions of both service providers and of recipients of services, promoting the quality of services and establishing effective cooperation among the Member States relating to the management of services.

11.2   Services sit with goods as tradable items in the internal market, and the regulation of services can be compared with the law and regulation providing for the free movement of goods. There are many parallel approaches and similar regulatory results. However, services and goods are different in the respect that goods are tangible items and services are not. The law on services also has a close relationship with the internal market law on persons, since often the question relating to the rights of service providers is really a question about the rights of economically active people in the European economic area. Situations at the intersection between the Union law provisions on service and persons relate to:

- professionals, such as lawyers, established and subject to the professional rules of conduct in one state but operating an office across the border in another state from which occasional services are provided;

- persons or undertakings operating a permanent base of operations in more than one state; and

- undertakings established in one Member State that post their employees temporarily to another Member State to provide services.

The Court of Justice's approach to such scenarios is to apply the freedom set out in Article 56 TFEU (ex Article 49 EC) on services wherever the provisions on free movement for workers or the right of establishment do not fit.

11.3   However, the law on services must still be separated from the freedoms associated with goods and people movement because of the nature of the Union legal system, dependent as it is upon the operation of national jurisdiction. Article 57 TFEU itself states that Article 50 TFEU protects services 'insofar as they are not governed by the provisions relating to the freedom of movement of goods, capital and persons'. In Case C–36/02 *Omega* (2004), considered below (**11.50**) the Court of Justice ruled that in a dispute raising issues relating both to goods and services, where a national measure prevented trade in both, the Court would examine the trade limiting rule in relation to just one of these two fundamental freedoms (i.e. goods or services) 'if it is clear that, in the circumstances of the case, one of those freedoms is entirely secondary in relation to the other and may be attached to it'. In this case, the Court concluded the freedom to provide services prevailed over the free movement of goods and therefore considered the matter by reference to Article 56 TFEU rather than Article 34 TFEU (ex Article 28 EC).

11.4   The principle of non-discrimination on grounds of nationality underpins the law on workers, establishment and services alike, and the rules on services apply to persons where there are gaps in the coverage provided by the rules on workers and establishment.

11.5   Services law then is related both to the law on the movement of goods and the law on the movement of people. The right to move goods around the internal market was considered in **Chapters 9** and **10**, and consideration of the law on services follows on from this because the services and goods are both traded. The law on services therefore sits at the intersection between goods and people and encompasses both Union law on the market and the evolution of rights associated with European citizenship.

11.6 Exceptions to the right provided to service providers and recipients, as people, are permitted by virtue of Article 62 TFEU, which cross references service provision exceptions with the exceptions applicable to establishment rights, and permits 'special treatment for foreign nationals on grounds of public policy, public security or public health', a provision that mirrors a similar exception to the rights of workers. This category of exception is considered in **Chapter 13** on citizenship.

11.7 From a Union law perspective, the provision of services is primarily a temporary cross-border activity. This is so because, should the provision of services take on a permanent basis in a Member State, the service provider or recipient must have established or moved (as a worker or a self-employed person) to the host state. And if the service provider moves to a new state for the purposes of the business, then the law on establishment, rather than services, will apply to the situation.

11.8 The distinction between service provision and establishment is necessitated in practice by the different Treaty provisions that apply to the different situations. The boundary between service provision and establishment can be seen in Case C–55/94 *Gebhard* (1995) which emphasised that the key distinguishing feature is duration. Establishment conveys a permanency, while services, as construed by the Treaty, are provided on a temporary basis across borders. The temporary nature of services has to be determined 'in the light, not only of the duration of the provision of the service but also of its regularity, periodicity or continuity'. As a caveat to this, it is clear from Case C–215/01 *Bruno Schnitzer* (2003) that service providers can equip themselves with the relevant infrastructure in the host Member State, provided it is necessary to perform the service, without this meaning they become automatically regarded as established in the second Member State. The reason for this is that in some instances establishment may require registration or some other administrative requirements, and such requirements should not generally inhibit the freedom to provide a cross-border service.

11.9 Provisions on services are possibly the most dynamic in the Treaty because of the wide conception of what constitutes a service. The breadth of what the Treaty articles seek to allow and the extent to which they seek to facilitate the service economy has led to this becoming a hotly debated area in terms of both the case law developments and legislative output. With respect to the 'restrictions on freedom to provide (cross-border) services', the Court has held that the rights protected by Article 56 TFEU are wider than protection from discrimination on grounds of nationality or residence (Case 33/74 *van Binsbergen v Bestuur van de Bedrijfsvereniging voor de Metaalnijverheid* (1974) (see further **11.11**)). Further, Article 56 TFEU is not just confined to obviously economic activities, such as those of craftsmen and the professions, but has been seen to extend to the fields of literature, arts, music, sport, education, ecommerce, the press and broadcasting.

Non-discrimination and the direct effect of Article 56 TFEU

11.10 The rights created by Article 56 TFEU were originally understood in terms of the right of non-discrimination. The discrimination combated by Article 56 TFEU could take many forms; it may be direct or indirect, and much of the case law, in fact, involves indirect discrimination. This is well illustrated in Case 33/74 *van Binsbergen v Bestuur van de Bedrijfsvereniging voor de Metaalnijverheid* (1974). A Dutch national, Mr Kortmann, who practised in his own country as a legal adviser and representative in social security matters, was engaged by Mr van Binsbergen in the Netherlands as his legal representative. His client had then moved his home to Belgium and corresponded from there with the Dutch court, so it seemed as if he was 'established' in Belgium. The court registrar told him he could no longer act for van Binsbergen, as under Dutch social security procedures legal representation of persons in social security matters could only be furnished by persons established in the Netherlands.

The Court ruled that Article 56 TFEU specifically applied to a situation where a service provider (here, a lawyer, Mr Kortmann) was prevented from providing a service because of residence in another Member State. The Court stated:

> A requirement that the person providing the service must be habitually resident within the territory of the state where the service is to be provided may, according to the circumstances, have the result of depriving [Article 59 EEC (now Article 56 TFEU)] of all useful effect.

The Court concluded that cross-border activity did not necessarily mean that the two persons involved in the service relationship should be of different nationalities. Since Article 56 TFEU was relevant, the Court considered the questions that had been referred to it.

The questions referred to the Court of Justice were:

(1) did Article 56 TFEU have direct effect?

(2) could a state require residence as a condition to perform the services in issue?

Most of the submissions from the Member State governments had accepted that Articles 56 and 57 TFEU could have direct effect at least as regards discrimination on grounds of nationality. The significance of the case was that the legal adviser was obviously not suffering from that sort of discrimination. Mr Kortmann, his client, the social security court, and the domestic law in question, were all Dutch. The Dutch law did not mention nationality, but simply disqualified any legal adviser of any country who was not established in the Netherlands. The rule requiring the lawyers to be habitually resident in the Netherlands, was held to discriminate against foreign nationals who were less likely to be living in the Netherlands. It was an indirectly discriminatory rule. The extension of Article 56 TFEU to non-discriminatory rules was further developed in the Cases C–76/90 *Säger* and Case 279/80 *Webb* (**11.34** below).

1.11 However, the general right provided in Article 56 TFEU can be derogated from in certain situations (**11.29-11.43** below—the part on limitations).

The Court in *van Binsbergen* developed the possibility of objective justification, separate from Article 62 TFEU (ex Article 55 EC), in this case, where the national law in breach of Article 56 TFEU is non-discriminatory. Such a line of reasoning has a close relationship with the approach to the free movement of goods, and the line of cases on mandatory requirements (see **10.29**). This is explored further below (**11.34-11.43** and **11.54–11.56**).

The meaning of services

11.12 Article 56 TFEU provides a general right to provide services across the Member State borders in the internal market. Article 56 states:

> *Restrictions on freedom to provide services…shall be prohibited in respect of nationals of Member States who are established in a Member State other than that of the person for whom the services are intended.*

11.13 The concept of services is defined in Article 57 TFEU by means of a non-exhaustive list of examples:

> *'Services' shall in particular include; (a) activities of an industrial character; (b) activities of a commercial character; (c) activities of craftsmen; (d) activities of the professions. Without prejudice to the provisions…relating to the right of establishment, the person providing a service may, in order to do so, temporarily pursue his activity in the Member State where the service is provided, under the same conditions as are imposed by that State on its own nationals.*

The case law, in line with the wider aims of developing the service economy, has expanded on the list of services covered in Article 56 TFEU. Tourism, medical treatment, financial services, business and education services, television signals, cable television signals, debt collection work, lotteries, insurance and prostitution have all been found to be services for the purposes of Article 56 TFEU. Given this diverse list, it would appear that there is little subject matter that would fall outside the Treaty provisions, the corollary to which is that there are very few individuals seeking to supply services on a temporary basis who are denied the benefits of Article 56 TFEU.

Remuneration

11.14 Whether the provision of remuneration in return for an activity is key to that activity being classed as a service is contested. Article 57 TFEU states services protected by Article 56 TFEU are 'normally provided for remuneration', a requirement that expressly removes gifts and unsolicited activity from the scope of the Treaty articles. This has clear links with the Court's reasoning whereby activities that do not demonstrate an economic link between the provider and the recipient are excluded from the scope of services and Article 56 TFEU. However, remuneration does not usually present a problem, and it is unclear whether payment for an activity is crucial to that activity falling within the definition of what constitutes a service. In a series of cases the Court of Justice has held that it is not essential that the person who receives the service be the person who provides the remuneration (see in particular Case 352/85 *Bond van Adverteerders v Netherlands* (1988), at paragraph 16). In Cases C–51/96 and C–191/97 *Deliège* (2000), an athlete's participation in a judo competition was regarded as the provision of services for remuneration even though she was unpaid for her time in the competition itself. Successful sports stars gained income from the publicity associated with the sport and their celebrity status. The Court stated:

> Sporting activities and, in particular, a high-ranking athlete's participation in an international competition are capable of involving the provision of a number of separate, but closely related, services even if some of those services are not paid for by those for whom they are performed.

11.15 However, the absence of remuneration can result in an activity not being considered a service and thereby not being protected by Article 56 TFEU from interference in its provision or delivery. In Case C–159/90 *SPUC v Grogan* (1991) (see also **6.68**) a dispute arose when an Irish students union sought to provide information on services that were classed as illegal in Ireland but were legal elsewhere in the Union. Abortion services were legalised in the United Kingdom in the late 1960s, however abortions were illegal in neighbouring Ireland by virtue of the constitutional right to life and protection of the unborn child. The student union sought to provide information in Ireland to women on clinics that carried out abortions in the UK. When Irish authorities sought to enforce the constitutional prohibition on abortions by banning the information distribution activity, the students union sought to rely upon Article 56 TFEU and the right to provide a service in order to continue. However, the Court concluded that since remuneration was not provided by the recipients of the information on clinics, the student union's activity could not amount to a service within the scope of Article 56 TFEU.

Economic services and other activities

11.16 Activities at the margins of the scope of Article 56 TFEU should be considered in terms of their objectives. For example, state education is provided to a state's citizens for a range of purposes most closely related to the state's interest in providing for the welfare of citizens. In Case 263/86 *Humbel* (1988) the Court of Justice concluded that where a state provided public education to its (young) citizens, the state was not engaging in 'gainful' activity, and, as such, state education should not be considered as a service within the meaning of Article 56 TFEU. Therefore, a state activity that seeks to fulfil a social, cultural or educational duty should not be understood as a service for remuneration for the purposes of Article 56 TFEU.

The Court has considered whether rules of sporting bodies could interfere with the provision of a service and inhibit service providers' rights. In Case C–519/04P *Meca Medina v Commission* (2006) the Court considered the question of whether sport is a service and whether participants in sporting events are service providers. Two long distance swimmers had fallen foul of anti-doping rules when tested positive for nandrolone at the World Cup in Salvador de Bahia in Brazil. Their first and second place finishes in the competition had been revoked and both swimmers were suspended from participating in competitive swimming events for four years (reduced to two on appeal). The swimmers wanted to participate in a swimming competition in an EU Member State during the period of their ban. They claimed that the doping rules and the ban they were subjected to were not compatible with EU competition and services law, in particular because the rules restricted their possibility of providing a (sporting or entertainment) service in a Member State. The Court of Justice therefore considered whether sporting events were services protected by Article 56 TFEU and noted that it had previously ruled that sport is subject to Union law insofar as it constitutes an economic activity (see Cases C–415/93 *Bosman* at **12.114**, and C–191/97 *Deliège* noted above at **11.14**). As such, the activities of semi-professional or professional sportsmen were either 'work' or the provision of services for remuneration. The Court decided that Article 45 TFEU (ex Article 39 EC) on workers' rights and Article 56 TFEU on services do not only apply to the action of public authorities but also extend to rules of any other nature aimed at regulating gainful employment and the provision of services in a collective manner. So the rules applied to sporting bodies were capable of review by reference to Article 56 TFEU. However, the Court ruled in *Meca-Medina* that Articles 45 and 56 TFEU do not affect rules of purely sporting interest which have nothing to do with economic activity. The anti-doping rules concerned were considered to be of purely sporting interest and as such enforceable despite their effect of restricting participation in the event. Sports therefore fall within the definition of services to the extent they are economic and most clearly straddle the boundary of what constitutes a service and what does not.

Services and cross-border activity

11.17 Article 56 TFEU as illustrated is very broad. At its core is the prohibition of national laws that discriminate against service providers from other Member States.

Three broad categories of cross-border activity are covered by Article 56 TFEU:

- cross-border activity with the service provider moving temporarily from state A to state B;

- cross-border activity with recipient of the service moving temporarily from state A to state B;

- cross-border activity with no person moving; the service itself moves (e.g. tele-communications, television).

11.18 The Court of Justice has noted on many occasions that an economic event or relationship could entail a range of services triggering Article 56 TFEU (*Bond* and *Deliège*, above at **11.14**). For example, broadcasting can entail services involving the production of a programme, the transmission of the programme on a television channel, the relationship between the company transmitting the programme and its customers, and the relationship between the company transmitting programmes and advertisers. The combination of activities could be seen as a single service, or each component of this business could be understood as a separate service. So long as remuneration forms part of the process at some stage, and if there is a cross-border component, then Article 56 TFEU will apply creating rights for the service providers and recipients alike. However, where a service is provided without cross-border activity the activity could still be considered from the point of view of the law on establishment rights.

The freedom to provide a service

11.19 Article 56 TFEU clearly sets out a freedom to provide services, and the scope of this right was demonstrated in *van Binsbergen* (**11.10**). In Case C–224/97 *Ciola* (1999), an Austrian company which provides moorings for boats on Lake Constance was limited in its line of business by an Austrian rule that restricted the number of moorings held by boat owners resident in other Members States. The Court held this breached the Article since it interfered with the company's attempts to provide a service.

The freedom to receive services

11.20 Article 56 TFEU does not mention recipients of services, but even before the Court had ruled that recipients of services, too, fell under the Article, Directive 64/221 on public policy, public security and public health exceptions (in Article 1) and Directive 73/148 on rights of movement and residence (in Article 1(c)) expressly covered recipients as well as providers of services. In Joined Cases 286/82 and 26/83 *Luisi and Carbone* (1984), two Italians had been fined for taking more money out of Italy than the (then) currency regulations permitted in order to go to other Member States as tourists and to receive medical treatment. The Court of Justice ruled that the ability to travel to receive a service, here both tourism and medical services, was a 'necessary corollary' of the right to provide a service, and was therefore also covered by Article 56 TFEU. In Case 186/87 *Cowan v Trésor Public* (1989), a French law provided for compensation for injuries to French nationals and residents who are victims of crimes. Mr Cowan was on a visit to Paris and was robbed and injured. The Court answered the question posed by stating that Article 18 TFEU (then Article 6), prohibiting discrimination as to nationality, must be interpreted as meaning that in respect of those who travel within the Community (as it then was) as recipients of service, the award of compensation to a victim of crime could not be made dependent on a residence qualification. Individuals should therefore be protected from harm on the same basis as nationals and persons residing there, even when compensation is financed by the state's treasury.

1.21 In Case C–348/96 *Calfa* (1999) Mrs Calfa, an Italian national who had been charged with possession and use of prohibited drugs while staying as a tourist in Crete, appealed on a point of law against the decision of the criminal court ordering her to be expelled for life from Greece. The Court of Justice, when asked for a preliminary ruling, examined whether such a penalty was compatible with the internal market rules on the freedom to provide services, Mrs Calfa being regarded as a recipient of tourist services. The Court concluded that there was clearly an obstacle to that freedom and that this obstacle to receiving services could not be justified by the public policy exception relied on by Greece. The national legislation provided for automatic expulsion following a criminal conviction, without any account being taken of the personal conduct of the offender or of the danger which that person represented for the requirements of public policy, contrary to Directive 64/221/EEC (now repealed and replaced and included in Directive 2004/38, but see **7.11**). In the same vein, in Case C–45/93 *Commission v Spain* (1994), the Court of Justice condemned a Spanish law which provided for free admission to state museums for Spanish nationals and non-Spaniards resident in Spain but not to tourists. The Commission considered that as museums were a reason why tourists from other Member States visited other Member States, there was a close link between freedom of movement and museum admission. The Court found that the Spanish rule breached both Articles 18 and 56 TFEU.

Service recipients who travel, including tourists, therefore have a general right to equal treatment compared to nationals and long-term residents in the host state.

Health care provision and the receipt of services

11.22 A growing number of cases have concerned the receipt of services that fall under social security schemes. Specifically in relation to health care, a common question arises relating to eligibility for service provision in different Member States where the service recipient travels to other countries to receive health care and then bills their own health service provider for the treatment received. Health care has traditionally been provided by each Member State for its citizens funded by either premiums or direct taxation. In Case C–158/96 *Kohll v Union des Caisses de Maladie* (1998), the Court asserted that such treatment amounts to economic services and as such should create an entitlement protected by Community law.

11.23 Prior authorisation to travel to another Member State may be required to receive health care, and can be justified if proportionate. In Case C–157/99 *Geraets-Smits v Stichting Ziekenfonds VGZ and Peerbooms v Stichting CZ Groep Zorgverzekeringen* (2001), persons registered with social security sickness insurance in the Netherlands were subject to a requirement of authorisation to receive medical treatment in another Member State. The Court said such authorisation could be subject to (i) the condition that the treatment must be 'normal in the professional circles concerned' and (ii) the condition that the medical treatment must be necessary.

The Court stated that authorisation to travel to receive treatment that would be funded by the home state health system can be refused on the grounds of lack of medical necessity only if the same or equally effective treatment can be obtained 'without undue delay' in a hospital having a contractual arrangement with the insured person's sickness fund.

The Court also ruled that the requirement that the treatment should be 'normal in the professional circles concerned' meant that treatment cannot be refused where the treatment concerned 'is sufficiently tried and tested by international medical science'. This ensured that the treatment concerned is assessed according to international and not just national criteria.

11.24 In Case C–372/04 *Watts* (2006)the Court of Justice confirmed that the provisions of the freedom to receive services apply regardless of the different way medical services are provided in the United Kingdom, where they are free at the point of delivery and funded from taxation, and in France, where services are provided under insurance arrangements and thereby technically paid for at each occasion. The Court also held that the system of prior authorisation which governs the reimbursement by the NHS of the cost of hospital treatment provided in another Member State deters or even prevents patients from applying to providers of hospital services established in another Member State and thus constitutes an obstacle to the exercise of the freedom to receive services.

The Court did find that there were circumstances in which the prior authorisation system could be justified, but authorisation could not be refused on the simple ground that while the waiting lists seemed very long, the treatment was provided free of charge. As a result, the British NHS was required to provide mechanisms for the refund of the cost of hospital care in another Member State to patients to whom that service is unable to provide adequate treatment within a reasonable period.

11.25 In Case C–512/08 *Commission v France* (2010), the Court upheld a national requirement for prior authorisation in order for the competent institution to be responsible for payment for treatment planned in another Member State involving the use of major medical equipment outside a hospital setting. According to the Court, with due regard to the organisation of public health policy and the financial balance of the social security system, such a requirement is justified by the need to maintain adequate planning policy for major medical equipment in order to ensure a geographically stable, balanced and accessible supply of state-of-the-art treatment and to avoid as far as possible any waste of resources.

1.26 That being so, in Case C–173/09 *Elchinov* (2010) the Court held that national legislation which excludes in all cases reimbursement for hospital treatment in another Member State without prior authorisation is not consistent with Article 49 EC (now Article 56 TFEU) and Article 22 of Regulation 1408/71/EEC, as amended. Although EU law does not preclude, in principle, a system of prior authorisation, it is nevertheless necessary that the conditions attached to the grant of such authorisation be justified. According to the Court, that was not so in the case of the legislation at issue, in that it deprived an insured person who was prevented from applying for such authorisation or was not able to wait for the answer of the competent institution, of reimbursement from that institution in respect of such treatment, even though all other conditions for such reimbursement to be made were met. Reimbursement in respect of such treatment is not likely to compromise achievement of the objectives of hospital planning, nor seriously undermine the financial balance of the social security system. Therefore, the Court concluded that the legislation constituted an unjustified restriction on the freedom to provide services.

Services that move, where the provider and recipient do not

11.27 Businesses providing services such as telephone, email, internet, cable services could be established in one Member State, service customers in another Member State, and neither party could ever move across the borders since the service itself is capable of movement. Such activity is also protected by Article 56 TFEU.

11.28 In Case C–384/93 *Alpine Investments* (1995, see further **11.40**), a Dutch company wanted to telephone individuals in the Netherlands and in other Member States, in particular Belgium, France and the United Kingdom, with a view to offering various financial services. The offer of financial services was prohibited in the Netherlands by the Dutch Ministry of Finance unless the service provider had the prior written consent of clients, in a rule that effectively banned cold calling. The Court of Justice held that the prohibition on telephoning potential clients in another Member State without their prior consent can constitute a restriction on freedom to provide services since it deprives the operators concerned of a rapid and direct technique for marketing and contacting clients. In Case 352/85 *Bond* (1988), Dutch law prohibited the distribution by cable of radio and television programmes transmitted from other Member States which contained advertising aimed at the Dutch public. The Court of Justice also considered this measure breached Article 56 TFEU.

Limitations on services freedom

11.29 The tension between the general right to provide and receive services and state regulation of certain activities is similar to the developed case law on the free movement of goods, where a general right to trade is set against limits imposed on the movement of goods because of important national interests. The state may have determined that certain activities are illegal, or that consumers need protection in certain service sectors.

11.30 Various services, legal in one state, but illegal in another, have come for consideration in the Court of Justice. In Case C–159/90 *SPUC v Grogan* (1991) (see **11.15**), the Court focused on the definition of what constituted a service and found the information provided in this case was not a service because its provision had not been for remuneration. A number of cases concerning activities such as betting and lotteries have come before the Court of Justice when they have been legal in one Member State, but banned in the state where the service provider seeks to sell the service. These are considered below at **11.47–11.48**.

11.31 The Court's approach is to set out the general right to provide or receive a service, but to acknowledge that certain obstacles to service provision can be acceptable. As with the law on the free movement of goods, discriminatory measures can only be justified under the specific Treaty provisions setting out derogation from the general right, whereas measures applying in a non-discriminatory way, indistinctly applicable measures or measures with an effect on trade can fall foul of Article 56 TFEU but can be objectively justified, if proportionate.

In Case 76/90 *Säger v Dennemeyer & Co* (1991) (see **11.55**), the Court of Justice stated:

> The freedom to provide services may be limited only by rules which are justified by imperative reasons relating to the public interest and which apply to all persons and undertakings pursuing an activity in the State of destination in so far as that interest is not protected by rules to which the person providing the service is subject in the State in which he is established. In particular, these requirements must be objectively necessary in order to ensure compliance with professional rules and must not exceed what is necessary to attain these objectives.

11.32 A national rule restricting the freedom to provide services must be compatible with the requirements of Article 56 TFEU. The rule can demonstrate compatibility with the Treaty by satisfying a four-part test, as follows:

- the rule must be non-discriminatory;
- the rule must be justified by imperative requirements in the general interest;
- the rule must be suitable for the attainment of the objective it pursues; and
- the rule must not go beyond what is necessary in order to attain its objective.

11.33 The requirement of the general good is comparable to the 'rule of reason' and the mandatory requirements in the area of the free movement of goods. In Case C–288/89 *Gouda* (1991) the Court listed the public interest grounds that it recognised (see **11.34** below).

Public interest grounds limiting the Article 56 TFEU freedom

11.34 Restrictions on the freedom to provide services may be justified by the general good. In Case 279/80 *Criminal Proceedings against Webb* (1981), the Court held that a British-registered agency for the supply of temporary workers could not place people in the Netherlands without the agency also being registered there, because registration fulfilled different functions in the two countries. In the Netherlands rules on the registration of employment agencies were intended to promote good labour relations and protect the interests of employees: it was apparently thought that permanent workers in an industry might resent the presence of temporary workers. For this reason the use of temporary workers was severely restricted. In certain industries it was entirely forbidden and, even where it was permitted, they could not be paid more than permanent employees. In the United Kingdom, on the other hand, registration was simply intended to ensure the suitability of the persons operating the agency. The Court also noted the sensitive nature of temporary employment agencies which are even banned in some countries. Although the freedom of provision of services was one of the fundamental principles of the Treaty and may be restricted only by provisions justified by the general good, here the court held that such justification existed and that, therefore, Webb could not place workers in the Netherlands without being registered there.

11.35 On the other hand, in Case C–113/89 *Rush Portuguesa v Office National d'Immigration* (1990) Portuguese workers employed by a company providing services in Belgium were required to be in the possession of work permits at a time when Portuguese citizens did not have full free movement rights in Community law because of transitional arrangements associated with Portugal's accession to the Community. The workers were subject to the rules of employment and social security in their own country. The Court ruled that such a rule was incompatible with Article 56 TFEU.

11.36 In Joined Cases C–369/96 and C–376/96 *Arblade and Leloup* (1999) the Court was asked about the limits imposed by Community law on the freedom of the Member States to regulate the social protection of persons working on their territory. One issue was whether social obligations imposed by Belgian law were applicable in respect of workers of an undertaking set up in another Member State who were temporarily deployed in Belgium in order to perform a contract. The Court stated first that national rules categorised as public-order legislation were not exempt from compliance with the provisions of the Treaty, as otherwise the primacy and uniform application of Union legal system would be undermined. Another issue was whether the requirements imposed by the Belgian legislation could be justified by overriding reasons relating to the public interest. If so, the Court then considered whether the interest was already protected by the rules of the Member State in which the service provider was established or whether the same result could be achieved by less restrictive rules. Provisions guaranteeing a minimum wage were justified but, in order for their infringement to justify the criminal prosecution of an employer established in another Member State, they had to be sufficiently precise and accessible for them not to render it impossible or excessively difficult in practice for such an employer to determine the obligations with which they were required to comply. On the other hand, the obligation to pay employer's contributions to the '*timbres-intempéries*' (bad weather stamps) and '*timbres-fidélité*' (loyalty stamps) schemes could be justified only if, first, the contributions payable gave rise to a social advantage for the workers concerned and, second, those workers did not enjoy in the state of establishment, by virtue of the contributions already paid by the employer in that state, protection which was essentially similar to that afforded by the rules of the Member State in which the services were provided. Obligations to draw up certain documents and keep them in certain places and for certain times would only be compatible with the Treaty if they were necessary in order to enable effective review of compliance with the national legislation and if no comparable obligations existed in the state in which the undertaking was established.

11.37 However, the issue of employee protection when considered as a cross-border service rather than as a free movement of workers issue under Union law creates contentious problems. In Case 341/05 *Laval* (2007) Swedish construction workers and their unions sought to take action against the use of temporary workers, not treated according to the same standards as Swedish workers, by a Latvian company. Because of the temporary nature of the Latvian company's operations, Article 56 TFEU was at issue rather than other Treaty provisions on persons or employment. The Swedish unions sought to impose a blockade against the Latvian company, intending to force the company to sign a collective agreement respecting Swedish wage conditions and employment terms. The Court of Justice ruled that since the Latvian company protected its employees to the standards at the time required by Community law, an attempt to force it to comply with further standards common in Sweden breached the company's rights to provide a cross-border service, protected by Article 56 TFEU. Collective employment agreements cannot be imposed on companies providing services even where the provision of the service entails workers moving to a state where different employment conditions prevail.

11.38 In Case C–346/06 *Rüffert* (2008), a Polish provider of building services was contracted in Germany. The German contract contained a declaration regarding compliance with collective agreements, more specifically, regarding payment to employees of at least the minimum wage in force at the place where those services were to be performed. This was consequently higher than the Polish statutory minimum wage. The company, using workers from Poland who were paid at the Polish minimum wage rate, was fined for breach of contract. The Court was asked whether the contractual clause was a restriction on the freedom to provide services under Article 56 TFEU. The Court concurred with the Advocate General, who stated that by requiring undertakings performing public works contracts to apply the minimum wage laid down by the 'Buildings and public works' collective agreement, the law may impose on service providers established in another Member States where minimum rates of pay are lower, an additional economic burden that may prohibit, impede or render less attractive the provision of their services in the host Member State. The Court also determined that such a measure could not be considered to be justified by the objective of ensuring the protection of workers. The German Government also argued that the measure at issue was necessary to avoid the risk of seriously undermining the financial balance of the social security system. While the Court had ruled in *Watts* that this cannot be ruled out as a potential overriding reason of public interest, the argument was rejected by the Court, leaving Rüffert free to supply labour below the locally agreed minimum wage.

11.39 In addition to the protection of workers, the Court has recognised the following public interest grounds:

(1) professional rules intended to protect the recipients of services (Joined Cases 110 & 111/78 *Ministère Public v Willy van Wesemael and others* (1979), and more specifically in Case C–3/95 *Reisebüro Broede v Sandker* (1996) where the Court developed this justification specifically with relation to the practice of law in light of the sound administration of justice);

(2) protection of intellectual property (Case 62/79 *Coditel* (1980));

(3) consumer protection (Case C–180/89 *Commission v Italy* (1991, tourist guides); Case 205/84 *Commission v Germany* (1986, on insurance policies); consumer protection and the fight against crime, Case C–42/07, *Liga Portuguesa de Futebol Proffissional* (2009);

(4) conservation of the national historic and artistic heritage (Case C–180/89 *Commission v Italy* (1991));

(5) dissemination of knowledge of the artistic and cultural heritage of a country (Case C–154/89 *Commission v France* and Case C–198/89 *Commission v Greece*);

(6) cultural policy (Case C–288/89 *Gouda* (1991) and Case C–353/89 *Commission v Netherlands*).

As with the free movement of goods derogations under the *Cassis de Dijon* mandatory requirements, the list is not exhaustive, and, as such, other justifications have been recognised and are discussed below.

11.40 In Case C–384/93 *Alpine Investments* (1995) the Court recognised the interest in safeguarding the reputation of the Dutch financial markets. The Court has further recognised road safety; the coherence of a scheme of taxation; the effectiveness of fiscal supervision; preserving the financial balance of a social security system; ensuring the adequacy of regular maritime services to, from and between islands; maintaining the standard of skilled work; protection of the environment; and ensuring a balance between sporting clubs, all as grounds upon which the public interest will pervade over the freedom to provide services under Article 56 TFEU.

11.41 Case C–519/04P *Meca-Medina v Commission* (2006), referred to above (see **11.16**) showed that sporting rules can legitimately restrict participants in a competition even where the sport and its competitions can be classed as services for the purposes of Article 56 TFEU.

11.42 Therefore, a legitimate public interest can give rise to a limitation on services. This is considered further, below, where the Court's approach to facilitating access to the market for service providers and recipients is considered (11.54). It should be noted that any limitation on services arising because of a public interest must be applied proportionately (see 11.43 below), and must be applied equally and without discrimination. Since such limitations affect individuals' ability to fulfil economic or other objectives as service providers or recipients, the Court required in Case C–60/00 *Carpenter* (2002) that the limitation concerned fundamental human rights, and in particular, in the context of this case, rights associated with a family life. The relationship between economic rights and individual entitlement is considered in more detail in **Chapter 13** on citizenship.

Proportionality and limitations on services

11.43 The right to provide a service, and the right to receive services, are fundamental to the Union legal order. They are part of the basis upon which the market is constructed. So any restriction of this freedom will be scrutinised carefully. In any case where a Member State has invoked a public interest requirement which has been accepted by the Court, any steps taken to guard this interest will be assessed in light of the principle of proportionality (see 6.24). This principle raises questions as to whether the measures are suitable for securing the attainment of the objective and, secondly, whether they go beyond what is necessary in order to attain it. Case C–17/00 *De Coster* (2001) illustrates the application of this principle. The case involved a tax on satellite dishes. The result was that satellite services were taxed, but cable services were not. The tax was seen to interfere with the provision of services because broadcasters in the home state had unlimited access to the cable distribution system. The Belgian authorities argued that this tax could be justified on the grounds of 'the uncontrolled proliferation of satellite dishes in the municipality and thereby preserving the quality of the environment'. The Court doubted whether the measure was suitable to attain this objective and decided that the tax exceeded what was necessary to achieve the objective of protecting the urban environment; there were a number of other less restrictive measures by which the aims could be achieved. Similarly, in Case 451/03 *Servizi Ausiliari Dottori Commercialisti Srl v Calafiori* (2006), Italian rules on tax advice and assistance reserved such services to Tax Advice Centres. ADC Servizi wanted to provide tax advice and assistance in addition to the financial services it already offered. The Court of Justice recognised the sensitivity of tax advice and the need to provide a proper service to citizens, however, it concluded that the Italian legislation went too far by requiring the range of tax advice services it provided for to be carried out by Tax Advice Centres exclusively, and thus breached Article 56 TFEU.

Illegal services

11.44 Illegal services, such as betting or the lottery, do not escape the application of Article 56. Consequently, any restrictions on the provision of illegal services must be justified. It is often the case that restriction of national legislation is aimed at protecting the consumer; however, such restrictions must still pass the test of proportionality, despite the margin of discretion given to states with regard to the regulation of illegal services.

11.45 In Case C–275/92 *Customs and Excise v Schindler* (1994), the promotion and sale of lottery tickets by agents of a German company was at issue since, at this time, lotteries were prohibited in the United Kingdom. Member States intervening in the case argued that lotteries are mostly subject to strict control and, indeed, generally run by public authorities. Schindler were agents of SKL, a public body responsible for organising lotteries on behalf of four *Länder* in Germany. They sent advertisements and application forms to the UK inviting people to participate in the German Lottery and, subsequently, were prosecuted for breaching the (then) national law banning lotteries. Nonetheless the Court said that the legislation prohibiting lotteries was a non-discriminatory obstacle to the freedom to provide services contrary to Article 56 TFEU. The Court accepted that the rules could be justified on social and cultural grounds and the concern to prevent fraud. This was in addition to the protection of players and maintenance of order in society.

11.46 In Case C–67/98 *Questore di Verona v Zenatti* (1999), Italian legislation reserving to certain bodies the right to take bets on sporting events was also seen as fulfilling a public interest. In *Zenatti* the Court said that it was for the national court to verify whether, having regard to the specific rules governing its application, the Italian legislation concerned was genuinely intended to realise the objectives justifying it and whether the restrictions it imposed were proportionate in the light of those objectives.

11.47 In Case C–42/07 *Liga Portugesa de Futebol Profissional* (2009), the Court was asked to rule on justifications to breaches of Article 56 TFEU. Regulation of betting on games of chance in Portugal had been reserved to a single company, Santa Casa, for more than 500 years. However Bwin, a company registered in Gibraltar, offered the chance to bet on games of chance over the internet. Bwin was fined in Portugal for breaching the national law on regulation of betting. The Court began by stating that:

> [Article 56 TFEU] requires the abolition of all restrictions on the freedom to provide services, even if those restrictions apply without distinction to national providers of services and to those from other Member States, when they are liable to prohibit, impede or render less advantageous the activities of a service provider established in another Member State where it lawfully provides similar services.

It was not seriously contended that the Portuguese law did not contravene Article 56 TFEU, however the Portuguese government argued that the rule could be justified by reference to overriding reasons of public interest such as the objectives of consumer protection and the prevention of both fraud and incitement to squander money on gambling. The Court noted that the fact that a Member State had opted for a different level of protection to another Member State 'cannot affect the assessment of the need for, and proportionality of, the provisions enacted', and these must be assessed in the light of the objectives pursued by the relevant authorities. It further stated that 'national legislation is appropriate for ensuring attainment of the objective pursued only if it genuinely reflects a concern to attain it in a consistent and systematic manner'. As such the Court concluded that the fight against crime 'may constitute an overriding reason of public interest' that was capable of justifying such restrictions in the games-of-chance sector.

11.48   In Case C–6/01 *Associação National de Operadores de Máquinas Recreativas and Others* (2003) Portuguese legislation restricted the running of games of chance to casinos within gaming zones created by decree. ANOMAR, an association of gaming machine operators in Portugal, challenged the restriction on the grounds that it breached the freedom to provide services. Yet the Court held that the Portuguese legislation was capable of restricting the freedom to provide services, as it prevented operators from providing gambling machines outside the gaming zones. The Court then concluded that the Portuguese policy was justified on grounds of consumer protection and the maintenance of order in society. However, in Case C–243/01 *Gambelli and Others* (2003) the Court refused to apply the usual justifications. *Gambelli* concerned Italian rules restricting the provision of internet gambling services to state-run or state-licensed organisations. The Court stated:

> In so far as the authorities of a Member State incite and encourage consumers to participate in lotteries, games of chance and betting to the financial benefit of the public purse, the authorities of that state cannot invoke public order concerns relating to the need to reduce opportunities for betting in order to justify measures such as those at issue in the main proceedings.

11.49   Case C–268/99 *Jany v Staatssecretaris van Justitie* (2001) concerned the provisions of one of the 'Europe agreements' for a candidate country which had applied to join the European Union. The Court said these provisions should apply in the same way as the Treaty provisions. The Court referred to *Schindler* and *Grogan* in ruling that Polish prostitutes' services in the Netherlands were to be regarded as services provided for remuneration. Prostitution was tolerated or even regulated in most Member States. It would appear that services which are not illegal in all Member States would be capable of constituting a service within the meaning of the Treaty.

11.50   In Case C–36/02 *Omega* (2004) the Court of Justice accepted that constitutional values protecting fundamental human rights could give rise to a limitation on service opportunities. Here, combat games provided participants with the opportunity to fight and fire weapons in simulated scenarios using lasers. German authorities considered simulated violence, and in particular a 'killing game', to contravene provisions in the German Basic (Constitutional) Law protecting human dignity. The Court of Justice ruled:

> Since both the Community and its Member States are required to respect fundamental rights, the protection of those rights is a legitimate interest which, in principle, justifies a restriction of the obligations imposed by Community law, even under a fundamental freedom guaranteed by the Treaty such as the freedom to provide services.

11.51 In Joined Cases C–447/08 and C–448/08 *Sjöberg and Gerdin* (2010), the Court considered whether Swedish legislation prohibiting the promotion of gambling without a licence was in breach of Article 56. It was found that the penalties laid down for infringement of this prohibition were found to be different for those operating abroad. Those who were organised outside of Sweden and who were found to have promoted gambling without a licence could receive criminal penalties of a fine and imprisonment for up to six months. In contrast, those who were organised in Sweden and who promoted gambling without a licence could only receive administrative penalties. Consequently, the legislation concerned treated comparable situations differently, to the detriment of companies established in other Member States.

11.52 It was found that internet gaming organised by a company established in another Member State did not pose greater risks of fraud and crime to the detriment of consumers than gaming organised clandestinely by a company established within the national territory. However, the court held that considerations of a cultural, moral or religious nature can justify restrictions on the freedom of gambling operators to provide services, in particular 'when it might be considered unacceptable to allow private profit to be drawn from the exploitation of a social evil or the weakness of players and their misfortune'. A Member State may therefore use its discretion to restrict the operation of gambling by entrusting it to public or charitable bodies. In this case, the gaming operators concerned were private, profitable undertakings that could never have obtained licences under Swedish law. Therefore, although the legislation did breach EU law, the restriction reflected the objective of the exclusion of private profit-making interests from the gambling sector and may moreover be regarded as necessary in order to meet such an objective.

11.53 Case C–137/09 *Marc Michael Josemans v Burgemeester van Maastricht* (2010) questioned whether national rules restricting access to Dutch coffee-shops to residents fell within the scope of the Treaty. In particular, the referring court asked whether the prohibition was justifiable based on the aim of reducing drug tourism and public nuisance. The Court held that the general prohibition of illegal drugs in the EU and the particular status of cannabis in the Netherlands, where use is tolerated rather than actually legal, meant that a coffee-shop owner could not rely on the principles of free movement and non-discrimination regarding the marketing of cannabis. However, the Court found that the owner could rely on Article 56 and the freedom to provide services in relation to the food and non-alcoholic beverages that are also sold. In that regard, the Court found that the national rules at issue did constitute indirect discrimination, as non-residents were more likely to be foreigners. However, the Court ruled that the measure was justifiable in light of the legitimate aim of combating drug tourism. Moreover, the Court ruled that the measures were suitable and proportionate, as they did not prevent non-residents from entering establishments that do not sell cannabis, and particularly in light of the fact that other measures to prevent drug tourism had proven ineffective.

The focus on market access and the facilitation of services

11.54 The dynamism of this area of law, and the development of the public interest exceptions to the general right to provide a service, demonstrate a move away from basic rules grounded in the combat of nationality discrimination to attempts to facilitate service provision more generally, and to use the legal structures to enable service providers and recipients to access the market. In Cases C–369 and 376/96 *Arblade* (1999) the Court of Justice stated:

> It is settled case law that Article 59 of the Treaty [now Article 56 TFEU] requires not only the elimination of all discrimination on grounds of nationality against providers of services … but also the abolition of any restriction, even if it applies without distinction to national providers of services and to those of other Member States, which is liable to prohibit, impede or render less advantageous the activities of a provider of services established in another Member State where he lawfully provides similar services.

11.55 This approach was first evident in Case C–76/90 *Säger*, noted above (see **11.31**), where a dispute arose on services attaching to patents. A German law required those monitoring patents to have a licence. This licence was granted on condition that those seeking to monitor patents held certain professional qualifications, for example as a lawyer or patent agent. Dennemeyer, a British company, monitored patents on behalf of clients, particularly in Germany, and informed them when the fees were due for renewing the patents. The commission charged by Dennemeyer was lower than that charged by German patent agents. German patent agents complained that Dennemeyer were trading without a licence. The Court of Justice, when questioned on the operation of Article 56 TFEU were referred to it, decided that the German rules prevented undertakings established abroad from providing services to patent holders established in Germany and prevented patent holders from freely choosing the manner in which their patents were to be monitored. Therefore the German rules breached the Article, subject to any justification. The Court concluded that there was a right of access to markets to provide or receive services, and that this right can only be limited by imperative public interests.

11.56 In Case C–94/04 *Cipolla-Macrino* (2006) the Court made clear it is for national courts to determine whether the legislation achieves the requirements. Here a dispute over property involving lawyers (some providing services across the border) gave rise to fees that did not fit with the fixed scale of fees for lawyers applicable in Italy. National measures prohibited agreement outside of these scales. This clearly fell within the scope of Article 56 TFEU because the scale 'deprives lawyers established in a Member State other than the Italian Republic of the possibility, by requesting fees lower than those set by the scale, of competing more effectively with lawyers established on a stable basis in the Member State concerned and who therefore have greater opportunities for winning clients than lawyers established abroad'. In other words, the scale had the effect of limiting access to the market for providers, limiting choice for consumers and limiting access to a service recipient. In light of the fact that individuals need quality advice in court proceedings, the Italian authorities justified the lawyer fee scales out of a desire to limit excessive competition between lawyers which would result in a deterioration in the quality of the services provided to the detriment of consumers.

The Court of Justice accepted that both the protection of consumers, in particular recipients of the legal services, provided by persons concerned in the administration of justice and, secondly, the safeguarding of the proper administration of justice, were both imperative public interests. The Court therefore concluded it was a matter for national courts to decide whether national legislation fulfils objectives associated with protecting these public interests, taking account of: the level of fees; the quality of the services provided; the practicalities of minimum fees for such services; specific features of the market in lawyers' services with its asymmetry of information between 'client-consumers' and lawyers; and the effect of professional status rules; and proportionality.

Services Directive

11.57 Directive 2006/123/EC on services entered into force at the end of 2009. The Directive correlates with Directive 2005/36/EC on the recognition of qualifications in that both cover temporary service provision and the freedom of establishment. The Services Directive required detailed discussion and protracted negotiation before it was agreed, and was contentious at the time of adoption because of concerns associated with further threats to the public-service ethos of some Member States.

11.58 The Services Directive fits within the 'Lisbon Strategy', the strategy agreed at the Lisbon European Council summit in 2000 ('Towards a Europe of Innovation and Knowledge') which pushed the Union towards focusing on the services economy. However, agreeing the detail of the services strategy took some doing, as is shown by the gap between the summit and the agreement of the Services Directive. Broadly speaking the Directive is aimed at facilitating the free movement of services by removing legal and administrative barriers to trade in the services sector. Its objectives relate to easing freedom of establishment and the freedom to provide services; strengthening the rights of service recipients; promoting the quality of services and enabling administrative cooperation between the Member States. The Directive is fairly general in its application and questions remain as to the point and purpose of legislation seeking to regulate such a broad range of activities in such a general way. Many types of services are excluded from its coverage (e.g. non-economic services of general interest, social services, private security services) and a series of derogations is provided for.

11.59 The Commission is planning to publish in 2012 the results of a performance check of the Single Market for services conducted in 2011. In addition to the publication of these results, the Commission will also conduct inquiries into three specific issues, namely the link between services and professional qualifications, the manner in which restrictions on capital ownership and legal form affect certain services sectors and the difficulties for cross-border services providers resulting from insurance requirements. These studies are intended to assist the Commission in the development of specific initiatives by the end of 2012.

FURTHER READING

Art, J.Y., 'Legislative lacunae, the Court of Justice and freedom to provide services' in Curtin and O'Keeffe (eds) *Constitutitonal Adjudication in European Community Law and National Law* (Ireland: Butterworths, 1992).

Barnard, C., *The Substantive Law of the EU: The Four Freedoms* (Oxford: OUP, 2010).

Biondi, A., 'In and out of the Internal market; recent developments on the principle of free movement' [1999/2000] 19 *Yearbook of European Law* 469.

Cabral, P., 'Cross-border medical care in the EU—bringing down a first wall' [1999] 24 *European Law Review* 387.

Cabral, P., 'The internal market and the right to cross-border medical care' (2004) 29 *European Law Review* 673.

Davies, G., 'Welfare as a service' (2002) 29 *LIEL* 27.

Fuchs, M., 'Free movement of services and social security—Quo vadis? (2002) *European Law Journal* 536.

Hatzopoulos, V., 'Recent developments of the case law of the ECJ in the field of services' (2000) 37 *Common Market Law Review* 43.

Martinsen, D.S., 'Towards an internal health market with the European Court of Justice' (2005) 28 *West European Politics* 1035.

Sieveking, K., 'ECJ rulings on health care services and their effects on the freedom of cross-border patient mobility in the EU', (2007) 9 *European Journal of Migration and Law* 25–51.

Snell, J., *Goods and Services in EC Law* (Oxford: OUP, 2002).

Van Nuffel, P., 'Patients' free movement rights and cross-border access to healthcare' 12 *Maastricht Journal of European and Comparative Law* 3 (2005) 253.

SELF-TEST QUESTIONS

1   What are services for the purposes of the Treaty on the Functioning of the European Union?

2   How has the Court of Justice broadened or changed focus on non-discrimination in protecting service providers/recipients?

3   Should the same criteria apply to restrictions on the right to provide services as apply to limits to the freedom to move goods?

4   Are there 'special services' which should not be subjected to general rights under Article 56 TFEU?

5   The move to liberalise services in the European Union has tended to be focused upon freeing up market access. To what extent does this approach differ from the Court's stance towards public interest grounds limiting service provision?

12 Citizenship and free movement of persons: workers and establishment

SUMMARY

This chapter looks at the free movement of workers and freedom of establishment, and places this within the framework of Citizenship of the European Union.

- Introduction
- Free movement of workers
  - Who is a worker?
  - Right to reside
  - Access to social advantages and other benefits
  - Rights for workers' families
  - Rights of the unemployed
- Freedom of establishment
  - Services v establishment
  - Non-discrimination and equal treatment
  - Freedom of establishment and people
  - Freedom of establishment and companies
- Exceptions to the free movement of persons
  - Public policy
  - Public security
  - Public health
  - The public service exception
  - The wholly internal situation
- Special cases
  - Sport
  - Lawyers
  - Education

Introduction

12.1 The free movement of workers is one of the original four freedoms in the Treaty of Rome establishing the European Economic Community. Free movement of workers was essential for the construction of an internal market, and for several decades the freedom to move within the Community maintained its strict link with economic activity.

12.2 To achieve the objectives of an increased standard of living and economic expansion, and to be able to achieve one market where goods could move freely, it was necessary to attain the fullest possible mobility of the economically active part of the population. These aspirations are embodied in the original Treaty in the articles concerning free movement of workers (now Articles 45–48 TFEU), self-employed persons (now Articles 49–55 TFEU) and the provision of services (now Articles 56–62 TFEU), dealt with in **Chapter 11**). Regulation 1612/68 was one of the first to be adopted. It describes in greater detail the rights of migrant workers. Articles 10 and 11 of the Regulation were repealed and replaced by the Citizenship Directive 2004/38 (see below at **12.5**) but the remainder of the Regulation remains in force.

12.3 However, as the Union developed into much more than just an economic unit, and there was a growing realisation that there should be an integration of all the peoples of Europe, the free movement articles were interpreted expansively by the Court of Justice and in secondary legislation. This trend reached its first high point in the adoption of directives on the rights of residence for employees and self-employed persons who had 'ceased their occupational activity'. Three directives concerning the right of residence for retired people, for students and for those who have sufficient resources for themselves and for family members were adopted in 1993 just before the entry into force of the Maastricht Treaty.

12.4 Citizenship of the Union was added to the Treaties as part of the changes agreed at Maastricht. Although there was initially doubt as to what, if anything, this concept added to the existing free movement of persons provisions, it was always in principle a dynamic set of entitlements which recognized that a union should involve all of the people. This marked the beginnings of a truly meaningful European citizenship. (See further **Chapter 13**.)

12.5 Council Directive 2004/38/EC on the right of citizens of the Union and their family members to move and reside freely within the territory of the Member States marked another milestone in the development of Union citizenship. Entered into force on 30 April 2006, the Citizenship Directive covers all the areas previously covered by legislation and repeals and replaces most of the older directives. In several instances, the Directive goes beyond what was provided in prior-existing legislation and case law, but in other instances, it is more restrictive. It should be noted that the Directive repeals Articles 10 and 11 only of Regulation 1612/68 (as further amended by Regulation 2434/930) on Freedom of Movement of workers within the Community.

12.6 The Court has emphasised many times that the three Treaty chapters on Workers, Establishment and Services should be treated equally in respect of entry, stay and non-discrimination, and has interpreted them in parallel. Articles 45, 49 and 56 TFEU (ex Articles 39, 43 and 49 EC) all have direct effect and do not depend on subsequent implementation by the Union. The rights guaranteed under the three chapters have been further detailed in directives, many of which also have direct effect. These rights cannot be applied without restriction and Member States retain the possibility to limit the rights for reasons of public policy, public security or public health, or because the activity is connected with the exercise of public authority. Such restrictions must, however, be proportionate to the aim pursued.

12.7   As was the case with the Treaty articles relating to the freedom to provide a service, the rights created by Articles 45 and 49 TFEU were originally understood in terms of the right of non-discrimination, i.e., the principle of equal treatment as reflected above in **Chapter 6**. This discrimination could take several forms: it could be direct, e.g., consisting of restrictions or exclusions based on nationality; or it could be indirect, e.g., requiring a minimum residence period for access to social benefits.

12.8   The primary rights granted in the Treaty to workers and the self-employed have given way to a whole host of secondary, and even tertiary, derived rights enjoyed by people such as workers' non-EU spouses and partners, children and jobseekers.

12.9   Moreover, these rights extend not only to workers, but also to employers. The Court stated in Case C–350/96 *Clean Car Autoservice GmbH v Landeshauptmann von Wien* (1998) that the right of workers to be engaged and employed without discrimination necessarily entails as a corollary the employer's entitlement to engage them in accordance with the rules governing freedom of movement for workers. Thus, an employer can rely on these rules as much as the workers themselves; and a rule providing that at least one manager of an undertaking has to be an Austrian resident constituted indirect discrimination.

Free movement of workers

2.10   Treaty Articles 45–49 TFEU are the provisions for the free movement of workers. Article 45 TFEU lays down the principles and Article 46 TFEU provides details of implementation. Case law has interpreted these provisions to mean that there shall be no discrimination as to nationality, that those in search of employment are to be entitled to do so, that those who have moved to another Member State for the purpose of employment should be allowed to remain there when they fall ill or retire, and that they should be allowed to take their families with them and have the same social security benefits as a Member State's nationals. These provisions are subject to exceptions, narrowly interpreted by the Court, in respect of public policy, public security and public health (Article 45(3) TFEU), and in respect of employment in the public service (Article 45(4) TFEU).

2.11   The first and largest group of the economically active are the employed. The Treaty refers to this group as 'workers' and, over the years, with the help of the Court of Justice, a Union definition of 'worker' has been established.

Who is a worker?

12.12   The definition of the concept of 'worker' is not given in primary or secondary legislation. Rather, the concept of 'worker' is an autonomous EU concept, gradually established by the Court of Justice. As such, its meaning is not dependent on the laws of Member States. In that regard, the Court explained in Case 75/63 *Hoekstra (née Unger)* (1964) that Articles 48–51 of the Treaty (now Articles 45–49 TFEU) would be deprived of all effect if the meaning could be modified by national law. The Court went on to specify that a 'worker' is not exclusively someone who is currently employed, but that it may also cover those persons 'likely to remain in the territory of a Member State after having been employed in that state'.

12.13   The concept of 'workers' covers those engaged in part-time work for less than the minimum wage. In Case 53/81 *Levin v Staatssecretaris van Justitie* (1982), Mrs Levin was a British national residing in the Netherlands, married to a non-Union national. She had part-time employment as a chambermaid, and earned a wage which was below the minimum considered necessary for subsistence in the Netherlands. The Court rejected the Dutch interpretation of 'workers' in favour of a Union concept. In deciding so, the Court provided a contextual interpretation and referred to the objective of the improvement of standards of living and a harmonious development of economic activities. Part-time work, although it may provide an income lower than the minimum subsistence wage in the country concerned, constituted for a large number of people an effective means of improving their living conditions. The effectiveness of Union law would be impaired and the achievement of the objectives of the Treaty would be jeopardised, if only those who worked full-time and attained at least the minimum wage for subsistence were considered to be workers.

12.14   The work engaged in by a 'worker' must be provided for remuneration and be effective and genuine, not marginal or ancillary. In Case 139/85 *Kempf v Staatssecretaris van Justitie* (1986), the Court of Justice held that a worker is an individual who performs services for and under the direction of another, for remuneration. Remuneration was deemed to include the situation of trainee teachers working under supervision and receiving remuneration for giving lessons to pupils in Case 66/85 *Lawrie-Blum v Land Baden-Württemberg* (1986). While part-time employment is not excluded from the field of application of the rules, the work must, however, be effective and genuine and not purely 'marginal and ancillary'. It includes, as in *Levin*, those who receive less than the minimum wage, and those who receive supplementary benefits, as in *Kempf*. Mr Kempf was a part-time music teacher who gave lessons for 12 hours a week. The Court made it clear that, as long as the aforementioned criteria are satisfied, the motives which may have prompted the worker to seek employment in another Member State are of no account and must not be taken into consideration.

12.15   The work itself must be an economic activity. In Case 196/87 *Steymann v Staatssecretaris van Justitie* (1988), although Mr Steymann received no remuneration for his work in a religious community, he was looked after by the community in return for his work.

According to the Court, this was sufficient to constitute an economic activity. However, in Case 344/87 *Bettray v Staatssecretaris van Justitie* (1989) the work of someone under a compulsory social rehabilitation scheme to help him overcome his drug addiction was not considered to be an economic activity. This was because the scheme had as its primary purpose the reintegration of potential workers into the labour market. Its objectives were social, not economic.

2.16 In more recent cases, the Court has clarified the concept further, applying objective criteria to the test of 'effective and genuine' work. This could include someone in occupational training if there was proof that the trainee had worked long enough to become fully acquainted with the job performed (see Case C–3/90 *Bernini v Minister van Onderwijs en Wetenschappen* (1992). Here, as in Case C–357/89 *Raulin v Minister van Onderwijs en Wetenschappen* (1992) which concerned someone working under a contract with no fixed hours, the Court emphasised that it was ultimately a matter for the national court to decide if such a person has the status of worker). In a case very reminiscent of *Bettray*, Case C–456/02 *Trojani* (2004) involved a destitute French national who had been given accommodation in a Salvation Army hostel in Brussels where (as part of a personal socio-occupational reintegration programme) he performed a variety of jobs for about 30 hours a week and received free board and lodging in return. The national court raised the issue of residence in its reference to the Court of Justice. The Court left it to the national court to determine whether Mr Trojani's services performed under the direction of the hostel were real and genuine or marginal and ancillary. It did, however, provide some guidelines: the national court should ascertain whether the services performed were capable of being treated as being part of the labour market; regard must be made to the status and practices of the hostel, the content of the social reintegration programme and the nature and details of the services performed. Mr Trojani was in possession of a residence permit and could invoke Article 18 TFEU (ex Article 12 EC) in order to secure treatment equal to that accorded to Belgian nationals.

12.17 An allowance for a former prisoner of war did not fall within the scope of the legislation (see Case C–386/02 *Baldinger* (2004)), but a French resident who worked for the French armed forces stationed in Germany and who was entitled to 'interim assistance' paid to workers whose employment contract had been terminated did suffer indirect discrimination as he had to pay tax twice on this (once in Germany and once in France; see Case C–400/02 *Merida* (2004)). Students on courses which require practical experience in another Member State may also be regarded as workers (see Case C–27/91 *URSAFF v Hostellerie le Manoir* (1991)). In Case 197/86 *Brown v Secretary of State for Scotland* (1988) (see **12.33** for more on this case) a student who undertakes casual work in a country in which (s)he intends to study may be regarded as a worker. Classification as a worker will depend on the person's intention as evidenced by the duration of the work and the extent to which the person has acquired the necessary skills. Thus, Mr Brown could not claim the full status of worker as he had acquired the status as a worker solely on the basis of having been admitted to university. Whereas in Case 39/86 *Lair v Universität Hannover* (1988) Lair could claim to be a worker as her work was connected with her wish to enter university, but not undertaken solely in preparation for her course.

12.18 In its judgment in Case C–138/02 *Collins* (2004) the Court drew a distinction between Member State nationals who have not yet entered into an employment relationship in the host Member State and those who are already working in that Member State. Mr Collins possessed dual Irish and American nationality. After studying for one semester in the United Kingdom in 1978, he returned to the United Kingdom for a stay of approximately 10 months in 1980 and 1981, during which time he did part-time and casual work. In 1998 he returned to the United Kingdom in order to find work in the social services sector. He claimed jobseeker's allowance which was refused on the ground that he was not habitually resident in the United Kingdom. The Court stated (in paragraph 28) that Mr Collins could not be regarded as a worker for the purpose of Title II part I of Regulation 1612/68 as amended by Regulation 2434/92 because no link could be established between his stay in the United Kingdom in 1981 and his search for another job more than 17 years later. His position in 1998 must therefore be compared with that of any national of a Member State looking for his first job in another Member State (paragraph 29). Member State nationals who move in search of work benefit from the principle of equal treatment only as regards access to employment (paragraph 31). Only those who have already entered the employment market may claim the same social and tax advantages as national workers based on Article 7(2) of Regulation 1612/68 (paragraph 31).

12.19 The Court's judgment in *Collins* should be contrasted with its judgment in Case C–413/01 *Ninni-Orasche* (2003) where the Court held that the fact that a national of a Member State has worked for a temporary period of two-and-a-half months in the territory of another Member State, of which she is not a national, can confer on her the status of a worker within the meaning of Article 39 EC (now Article 45 TFEU), provided that the activity performed as an employed person is not purely marginal and ancillary.

12.20 Professional training may also qualify as employment. In Case C–10/05 *Cynthia Mattern and Hajrudin Cikotic v Ministre du Travail et de l'Emploi* (2006) Ms Mattern had completed a professional training period as a care assistant in a host Member State. The Court found that the training fulfilled the conditions to qualify it as employment. The amount of remuneration or the origin of the funds from which the training is paid did not have any consequence in regard to whether or not the person is a worker for the purposes of Union law. Referring to Article 11 of Regulation 1612/68 (now replaced by Directive 2004/38), which granted the right of family members of employed or self-employed Union workers to join their family within the Union, the Court noted that Ms Mattern was to be classed as a worker for the purposes of Union law.

Right to reside

12.21 Article 45 TFEU provides workers with the right to reside in another Member State for the purpose of employment. One of the first cases to affirm the right of residence granted in the Treaty was Case C–48/75 *Jean Noël Royer* (1976). Mr Royer, a French national, had several convictions in France. He joined his French wife in Belgium where she worked, but, when entering Belgium, did not comply with the administrative formalities of entry. He was then ordered to leave Belgian territory. Although he left, he returned a few months later and again failed to comply with entry formalities. Eventually, Belgium issued an expulsion decree based on Royer's personal conduct being a danger to public policy and the fact that he failed to observe the conditions attached to the residence of aliens in Belgium, i.e., that he did not possess a residence permit. Among other questions (see paragraph 18 of the judgment) the Court held that the right of a worker to enter a Member State and reside there is conferred directly from the Treaty and is not the result of a Member State's conferral of a residence permit. See also Cases C–36/75 *Roland Rutili v Ministre de l'Intérieur* (1975) (see **6.62** and **13.52**) and C–100/01 *Ministre de l'Intérieur v Aitor Oteiza Olazabal* (2002) (see **13.53**).

2.22 Directive 2004/38 lays down rules for residence permits, including detailed provisions for the acquisition of a residence card for both the Union citizen himself and for his family members. However, like the judgment in *Royer*, a residence permit is simply evidence of the Union right of residence and failure to obtain one is not sufficient reason to expel a Union national. Although there is reference in the Directive to the fact that a valid residence permit may not be withdrawn from those who are involuntarily unemployed, this would not seem to cover the case e.g. of Mr Vitale (see **13.20**). The simple production of a passport or identity card upon entry suffices and visas may not be required. Article 10 of Directive 2004/38 specifies other documents which are necessary for proof of connection with the primary mover for family members who are not nationals of a Member State. In Case 157/79 *R v Pieck* (1980) the Court stated that failure to comply with the national requirements for obtaining a residence permit should not lead to disproportionate penalties, such as imprisonment or deportation. Article 9(3) of Directive 2004/38 confirms this and states that failure to comply with the requirement to obtain a residence card may make the person liable (only) to proportionate and non-discriminatory sanctions. See also Case 118/75 *Watson and Belmann* (1976).

12.23 In Case C–325/09 *Secretary of State for Work and Pensions v Maria Dias* (2011), the Court held that possession of a valid residence permit does not in itself confer a right of permanent residence. Ms Dias, a Portuguese national, had previously acquired a residence permit in the UK under Directive 68/360 (now replaced by Directive 2004/38) and lived there according to its conditions for a period of five consecutive years. However, this period ended before the transposition of the Citizenship Directive in the UK in 2006. Subsequently, for a period in 2003–4, Ms Dias became voluntarily unemployed and not self-sufficient, thereby breaking the conditions of her residence. The question referred was whether Ms Dias could still acquire a permanent right of residence. The Court first held that periods of residence based on a permit issued before the transposition of Directive 2004/38 and which do not satisfy the conditions for entitlement to a right of residence cannot be considered sufficient so as to acquire permanent residence under Directive 2004/38. However, the Court also held that a right of permanent residence could be acquired if a person has legally resided in another Member State for five years prior to the transposition of the Directive, provided that any periods during which the person no longer met the requirements for the acquisition of a right of residence were less than two consecutive years. The Court has also held that, even in cases brought before the adoption of the Directive, the periods of residence could not be disregarded. For example, in Case 162/09 *Secretary of State for Work and Pensions v Taous Lassal* (2010) the Court held that periods of residence completed before the date of implementation of the Directive could not be ignored because, to do so, would be contrary to the objectives and effectiveness of the Treaty.

Access to social advantages and other benefits

Definition of 'social advantages'

12.24 'Social advantages' for the migrant worker are, as the Court explained in Case 207/78 *Even* (1979):

> Advantages, linked to a contract of employment or not, generally granted to migrant workers primarily because of their objective status as workers or by virtue of the mere fact of their residence on the national territory

12.25 In Case 152/73 *Sotgiu v Deutsche Bundespost* (1974) Mr Sotgiu, a migrant worker from Italy, received a lower separation allowance for working in Germany than those whose place of residence when they were first employed was in Germany. The Court held that this was an indistinctly applicable measure which was nevertheless discriminatory as it affected migrant workers more. In Case 15/69 *Württembergische Milchverwertung-Südmilch AG v Salvatore Ugliola* (1970), Mr Ugliola was held to be entitled to have his period of military service in Italy taken into account in Germany when calculating the length of his employment. The rule that only military service in the German Army (the *Bundeswehr*) counted was, again, an indistinctly applicable measure which nevertheless was discriminatory.

12.26 Social advantages also include an entitlement to railcards for discounted rail travel for large families in France (see Case 32/75 *Cristini v SNCF* (1975)), and the right to speak German in proceedings conducted in Belgium where such a right is available to Belgian nationals, (see Case 137/84 *Mutsch* (1985)).

12.27 At first, financial advantages were not held by the Court of Justice to be 'social advantages'. However, in *Collins* (see **12.18**) the Court considered that the fundamental principle of equal treatment in Union law which also applies to jobseekers from another Member State under Article 39(2) EC (now Article 45(2) TFEU) extends to benefits of a financial nature such as a jobseeker's allowance. The Court considered here that, in view of the recent establishment of Union citizenship and the interpretation of the case law of the right to equal treatment enjoyed by citizens of the Union, it was no longer possible to exclude such a financial benefit from the scope of Article 45(2).

.28   Social advantages should be distinguished from social security benefits. Social advantages cannot be exported, whereas social security benefits may be exported in many, but not all, cases. In Case 65/81 *Reina v Landeskreditbank Baden-Württemberg* (1982) an interest-free 'childbirth loan' granted under German law to German nationals in order to stimulate the birth rate was held to be a social advantage. Therefore, an Italian couple in Germany was also entitled to the loan, despite the argument the loan had little to do with encouraging free movement of workers, as it was a political right linked to nationality. The Court viewed it as a measure to ease the financial burden on low-income families and did not address the demographic point. However in *Cristini* (above at **12.26**), the Court clarified its stance with regard to demographic social benefits and held that an Italian widow was nevertheless entitled to French benefits, despite their being part of French demographic policy.

Residence requirements

2.29   Access to social and other benefits by workers may be conditional on the satisfaction of a residence requirement. The original Social Security Regulation (EEC) 1408/71 intended to coordinate social security schemes existing in the various Member States. The Court has generally sought to remove unjustified obstacles to freedom of movement resulting from different laws on social security. In Case C–18/95 *Terhoeve v Inspecteur van de Belastingdienst Particulieren/Ondernemingen Buitenland* (1999) the Court held that the obligation on a worker who had moved from one Member State to another to pay higher social security contributions, without benefiting from higher benefits in return, was an obstacle to free movement.

2.30   In Case C–406/04 *De Cuyper* (2006) the Court came to the conclusion that a residence requirement could be justified. Mr De Cuyper, a Belgian national, was granted unemployment allowance in Belgium. In receiving the allowance he declared that he was living alone, and living in Belgium. During a routine check, the applicant admitted that he had been living in France and returning to Belgium every three months. When the allowance was suspended, Mr De Cuyper appealed. The Court found that the benefit in question was an unemployment allowance, even though the recipient was not required to sign on or be available for work. Under Article 21 TFEU, the right to free movement and residence of Union citizens within the territory of the Member States of Union citizens is guaranteed. The residence requirement placed on the unemployment benefit by the Belgian authorities clearly infringed this right.

However, the Court noted that such a restriction can be justified if it is based on objective considerations of public interest independent of the nationality of the persons concerned and proportionate to the legitimate objectives of the national provisions (these justifications will be discussed further below). Furthermore, the Court stated that 'a measure is proportionate when, while appropriate for securing the attainment of the objective pursued, it does not go beyond what is necessary in order to attain it'. The Belgian authorities argued that the residence requirement was necessary in order for inspectors to monitor the status of benefit claimants, and that this would be impossible if claimants lived in other Member States. The Court agreed that less restrictive monitoring practices would not have been capable of achieving the objective pursued and that the residence requirement was therefore justified.

Education and vocational training

12.31 In Case C–40/05 *Kaj Lyyski v Umeå universitet* (2007) the Court confirmed that conditions of access to vocational training fall within the scope of the Treaty. Mr Lyyski, in applying for a teacher training course in Sweden, indicated on his application form that he intended to carry out the practical training part of the course in a Swedish-speaking school in Finland. His application was rejected on the grounds that, as he was not employed in a Swedish school, he could not prove that he was eligible for the scheme. Citing *Gravier* (see **12.141**), the Court stated that the conditions of access to vocational training fell within the scope of the Treaty, and that both higher education and university education fall under the category of 'vocational training'. The Court found that the provisions of the training scheme constituted an infringement of the freedom of movement under what is now Article 45 TFEU, and could be justified only by reference to legitimate aims and pressing issues of public interest. The Court agreed with Sweden that assessment of the teaching skills of a trainee teacher is manifestly more difficult when the teacher is undertaking training in another Member State and that the objective of preserving and improving the Swedish education system could be a legitimate interest, provided it was applied proportionately. Therefore, such an exclusion was justifiable, as long as this was not evidence of exclusion 'as a matter of principle', or a 'blanket ban'.

12.32 In *Lair* (see **12.17**) the Court ruled that a person does not cease to be an immigrant Union worker just because (s)he gives up work in order to become a full-time student. Nevertheless, in order to retain worker status there must be a connection between the course of study and the immigrant's previous work. The vocational training, therefore, must be relevant to the worker's previous occupation. This would not apply, however, if the worker became involuntarily unemployed and had to retrain in another occupational activity in order to obtain another job. Vocational training was narrowly defined by the Court and had to be alternate, or closely linked, to an occupational activity, particularly during apprenticeship. This interpretation would not, therefore, cover universities. Despite this, a maintenance grant, with which this case was concerned, could be considered a social advantage under Article 7(2) of Regulation 1612/68 and could, therefore, be claimed.

12.33 However, in Case 197/86 *Brown v Secretary of State for Scotland* (1988), the work placement was only available to students who had been offered a university place (see **12.17** for facts of the case.) Although the Court had decided in *Lair* that Article 7(2) of Regulation 1612/68 could apply to maintenance grants, in this case it ruled that if the immigrant obtained the employment solely by virtue of the fact that he had already been offered a university place, he would not be entitled to the grant as a worker. This is because the employment was merely incidental to the university course (see **12.58**).

Tax advantages

2.34 An increasing number of cases concerning direct taxation have come before the Court. In Case C–279/93 *Schumacker* (1995) and Case C–80/94 *Wielockx* (1995) the Court interpreted Article 48 of the Treaty (now Article 45 TFEU) as meaning that a Union national who gained his main income and almost all of his family income in a Member State other than his state of residence was discriminated against if his personal and family circumstances were not taken into account for income tax purposes in the home state. Following these judgments German legislation provided that a couple could, under certain circumstances, be subject to tax in Germany even when they did not permanently reside there, so that they would also be entitled to the tax concessions accorded to residents which took account of their personal and family circumstances.

2.35 Case C–152/03 *Hans-Jürgen Ritter-Coulais and Monique Ritter-Coulais v Finanzamt Germersheim* (2006) confirms that all forms of direct tax discrimination, which impede the exercise of a fundamental freedom (in this case the free movement of workers) is precluded by EU law. The case concerned a couple, both of whom were teachers working in Germany. When addressing their income tax liability, they unsuccessfully applied for the negative income deriving from their house in France to be taken into account. According to German legislation, the couple were not allowed to deduct, for the purposes of computation of their taxable income in Germany, the income losses relating to their use of a private dwelling, simply because it is situated in another Member State. The Court held that:

> all of the Treaty provisions relating to the freedom of movement for persons are intended to facilitate the pursuit by Community national of occupational activities of all kinds throughout the Community, and preclude measures which might place Community nationals at a disadvantage when they wish to pursue an economic activity in the territory of another Member State [paragraph 33].

Therefore, the German legislation at issue was precluded by Article 45 TFEU.

2.36 Case C–527/06 *R.H.H. Renneberg v Staatssecretaris van Financiën* (2008) concerned a Dutch national who transferred his residence to Belgium, although continued to work in the Netherlands. When addressing the taxation of his income, Mr Renneberg applied, unsuccessfully, for deduction of the negative income relating to his Belgian dwelling. This negative income consisted of the difference between its rentable value and the interest paid on the mortgage. The Supreme Court of the Netherlands asked the Court of Justice whether EU law precludes national legislation which imposes a residence condition in order to be able to deduct negative income relating to a house used as a dwelling. The Court first held that Article 45 TFEU is applicable in the case, since Mr Renneberg was employed in a Member State other than that in which his residence is located. It then went on to state that the taking into account of the relevant negative income, or the refusal to do so, depended on whether or not the taxpayer was resident in the Netherlands, and this difference in treatment was disadvantageous to non-resident taxpayers. Such a difference in treatment could not be justified when there was no objective difference between the situations of the resident and non-resident and, therefore, constitutes a discriminatory measure, inconsistent with EU law. The Court said that Mr Renneberg, who:

> derives most of his taxable income from salaried employment in a Member State ... is, for the purposes of taking into account his ability to pay tax, in a situation objectively comparable, with regard to his Member State of employment, to that of a resident of that Member State who is also in salaried employment there [paragraph 66].

As a consequence, Article 45 requires that, in such circumstances,

> negative income related to a dwelling in the Member State of residence is to be taken into account by the tax authorities of the Member State of employment for the purposes of determining the basis of assessment of taxable income [see paragraph 68].

Rights for workers' families

12.37 As briefly indicated above, the rights granted in the Treaty regarding the free movement of workers has given birth to a variety of derived rights enjoyed by various groups of people such as the spouses, partners and children of workers. These derived rights will be explored below.

Right of residence

12.38 Regulations 1612/68 (later amended by Regulation 2434/92 and in part (Articles 10 and 11) replaced by Directive 2004/38) and 1408/71 were interpreted widely by the Court in relation to rights for workers' families. This extended the material scope of the regulations to include elements such as income support, old-age benefits and disability allowances as regards migrant workers themselves (see Case C–326/90 *Commission v Belgium* (1992)). The personal scope of the regulations was also extended, as the aim of the legislation was the full integration of the migrant workers into the host state which, therefore, had to include his/her family and any dependents. Members of a migrant worker's family have the right to install themselves with the migrant. This does not imply that the family must live under the same roof permanently.

12.39 Article 13(2)(a) of Directive 2004/38 states that annulment of a marriage or partnership will not entail the loss of the right of residence of an EU citizen's family—who are not nationals of an EU Member State—as long as the registered partnership not only lasted for at least three years prior to annulment, but also spent at least one of these years in the host Member State. In Case 267/83 *Diatta v Land Berlin* (1985), a separated, albeit not divorced, wife of a worker living separately could not, therefore, be denied a right of residence. This right of residence is not an independent right, but is derived from that of the worker. However, as *R v Secretary of State for the Home Department, ex p*

Sandhu (1982) shows, this matter is not entirely clear-cut. Mr Sandhu was an Indian national whose German wife had returned to Germany with their child when the marriage had broken down. After a visit to Germany Mr Sandhu was refused entry into the United Kingdom and the Court of Appeal and House of Lords considered his rights had come to an end when his wife returned to Germany. As the situation was different from that of *Diatta* it is not immediately obvious that this should have been considered as 'acte clair' (see **4.41**). In Case C–466/00 *Kaba* (2003) UK law differentiated between spouse of a migrant (non-British) worker and the spouse of a person who is present and settled in the United Kingdom for purposes of determining of a period of prior residence in order to qualify for indefinite leave to remain. In view of the fact that the situations were not comparable under Union law, the question of whether the law at issue was discriminatory was irrelevant.

2.40   The interpretation of the term 'spouse' in Article 10 of Regulation 1612/68 (now replaced by Directive 2004/38) was clarified by the Court in Case 59/85 *Netherlands v Reed* (1986) where a British national who went to the Netherlands to live in an unmarried relationship with her British partner, who was working there, was denied right of residence by the Dutch authorities. The Court ruled that the term 'spouse' could only refer to a married person and that a general widening of the term would be unjustifiable in view of the lack of 'general social development' in all the Member States towards treating unmarried couples in the same way as married ones. However, in this case, the Dutch Government treated an unmarried companion in a stable relationship with a Dutch national as a spouse. Therefore:

> It must be recognized that the possibility for a migrant worker of obtaining permission for his unmarried companion to reside with him, where that companion is not a national of the host member state, can assist his integration in the host State and thus contribute to the freedom of movement of workers. Consequently, that possibility must also be regarded as falling within the concept of a social advantage for the purpose of Article 7(2) of Regulation 1612/68.

2.41   The original term 'spouse' in Regulation 1612/68 was subsequently extended in Article 2 of Directive 2004/38 to include registered partners, if such partnership is considered by the host country to be equivalent to marriage. In addition, Article 3(2)(a) of the Directive also extends derived free movement rights to other 'members of the household' in the country from which the primary resident comes, or 'where serious health grounds strictly require the personal care of the family member by the Union citizen'. In Article 3(2)(b) these rights are also extended to 'the partner with whom the Union citizen has a durable relationship, duly attested'. In interpreting this latter provision the Member States should thoroughly examine the circumstances and justify any denial of entry.

2.42   Case C–109/01 *Akrich* (2003) concerned a Moroccan national who was twice deported from the United Kingdom, returned there illegally and married a British citizen. He was deported to Ireland at his request, where his spouse had been established since 1997.

He then applied for revocation of this order and for entry clearance into the United Kingdom. The applicant relied on the Court's judgment in Case C–370/90 *Singh* (see **12.109**) whereby the 'Union element' had been triggered by the fact that the applicant's spouse had gone to another Member State to work and had then returned. Mr and Mrs Akrich were perfectly open in stating that their move to Ireland was temporary as 'they had heard about EU rights' (para 36) and that they intended staying for six months and then returning to the United Kingdom. Aspects of the judgment in Akrich were overruled in Case 127/08 *Metock* (2008) (see **13.37**) but the Court's observations relating to the motives of persons exercising free movement entitlements remain applicable today. The Court stated that the motives of a citizen seeking work in a Member State are not relevant in assessing the legal situation of the couple at the time of their return. The conduct at issue here could not constitute an abuse of entitlements even if, at the time the couple went to another Member State, the applicant did not have the right to stay in the United Kingdom. It would be an abuse, however, if these Union rights were invoked in the context of marriages of convenience and in that case Regulation 1612/68, Article 10, would not apply. If the marriage was genuine, even if the spouse upon his return was not legally resident, regard should nevertheless be had to Article 8 of the ECHR which expresses the right to respect for family life and which is one of the fundamental Union rights. See also the case of *Chen* (at **13.41**).

Education for members of workers' families

12.43   The most extensive educational rights are enjoyed by children of workers. These rights are based on Article 12 of Regulation 1612/68 (see **12.2** and **12.5**). Children residing in the same host Member State as their parents enjoy the same educational rights as nationals of that state, including connected rights such as grants. Workers themselves have rights under Article 7(3) of Regulation 1612/68 which provides for equal access to vocational training.

12.44   Children of nationals of one Member State who fulfil the worker criteria have access to courses of general education, apprenticeship and vocational training under the same conditions as children of nationals. In Case 76/72 *Michel S v Fonds National de Reclassement des Handicapés* (1973), the disabled son of an Italian worker in Belgium was entitled to Belgian disability benefit following the death of his father. The Court held that his rights did not just cover access to courses; as Article 12 of Regulation 1612/68 called upon Member States to encourage children of migrant workers to attend courses 'under the best possible conditions' and this meant that the list of educational arrangements in the Regulation should also include disability benefit (see also the Opinion of Mayras AG). Case 9/74 *Casagrande v Landeshauptstadt München* (1974) continued the reasoning in *Michel S* and held that access for workers' children to education in Article 12 of the Regulation ('admitted to courses…under the best possible conditions') also included any 'general measures intended to facilitate educational attendance' such as an educational grant for a secondary school in Germany. The provision has also been held to cover grants to migrant workers' children to study abroad, even if this is in the country of origin of the parent and child (Case C–308/89 *Di Leo v Land Berlin* (1990)).

2.45 Case C–413/99 *Baumbast and R v Secretary of State for the Home Department* (2002) appears to have moved the goalposts to a considerable extent. The Court stated that children of migrant workers should be allowed to continue their education in the host Member State under any circumstances, even if their primary carer parent was in danger of losing residence either due to divorce or because the migrant worker had ceased to work there. The Court went on to hold that the child's primary carer should be allowed to reside in the Member State as the child's primary carer. The Court cited Article 12 of Regulation 1612/68, but also Article 8 of the European Convention on Human Rights, which contains the requirement of respect for family life (see **13.40–13.41** and *Zambrano* at **13.42**).

2.46 Bearing in mind the foregoing, it is becoming apparent that, although the rights of dependants of workers are not yet as extensive as those for workers themselves, *Baumbast* and *Zambrano* have extended those rights considerably since, for example, Case 316/85 *Centre public d'aide sociale de Courcelles v Lebon* (1987). In this case the adult child of a worker was no longer entitled to benefits which were of no advantage to the worker himself. This restricted interpretation also applies to jobseekers, as in the case of *Antonissen* where the Court said that the rights of jobseekers would not necessarily be the same as those for workers (discussed below).

Rights of the unemployed

Jobseekers

2.47 The corollary of the right to enter and to work is the right to remain for a reasonable time while looking for a job. Article 45(3) TFEU provides for this right, but refers to the right of free movement only 'to accept offers of employment actually made' (Article 45(3)(a) TFEU). The Court has interpreted this provision expansively, as in Case C–292/89 *R v Immigration Appeal Tribunal, ex p Antonissen* (1991), pointing out that 'a strict interpretation of [Article 45(3) TFEU] would jeopardise the actual chances that a national of a Member State who is seeking employment will find it in another Member State and would, as a result, make that provision ineffective'. The Article therefore had to be interpreted as giving a non-exhaustive list of rights for nationals of Member States in the context of free movement, including the right to move and stay within the territory of the Member State for the purposes of seeking employment.

2.48 Why and for how long will someone be considered to be a jobseeker? In *Antonissen* (see **12.47**) the Court said that it was not contrary to Union law to require an individual to leave a Member State's territory if he had not found work for six months, unless he could show that he was continuing to seek work and had a genuine chance of finding it. Therefore the six-month limit which applied to a jobseeker in the United Kingdom was acceptable, but both Advocate General Darmon and the Court refused to state a clear time limit. The time granted must be reasonable and a further extension is acceptable if evidence of a genuine chance of employment could be shown after expiry of the six-month period.

Rights of residence for jobseekers

12.49 The right of residence is a Union right which should be distinguished from social rights which do not always extend as far. In the case of Mr Collins (see **12.18**) the second question posed to the Court concerned the problem whether Directive 68/360 granted a right of residence to a person seeking work. In line with *Antonissen* (see **12.47**), the Court held that the right of residence derived from Article 45 TFEU may be limited in time but if after expiry of that period the person concerned provides evidence that he is continuing to seek employment and that he has genuine chances of being engaged, he cannot be required to leave the territory of the host Member State.

12.50 The residence condition imposed by UK legislation was more easily satisfied by UK nationals and this could be justified only if based on objective considerations independent of the nationality of the persons concerned and proportionate to the legitimate aim of the national law. It was legitimate to ensure that there was a genuine link between the application for an allowance and the employment market by establishing that the person concerned was genuinely seeking work for a reasonable period. However, for it to be proportionate, the period of residence required for that purpose may not exceed what is necessary. As a consequence, the Court held:

(1) Mr Collins could not be regarded as a worker. It was, however, for the national court or tribunal to establish whether the term 'worker', as referred to by the national legislation at issue is to be understood in that sense.

(2) A person in the circumstances of Mr Collins does not have a right to reside in the United Kingdom solely on the basis of Council Directive 68/360/EEC (now replaced by Directive 2004/38).

(3) The right to equal treatment laid down in Article 39(2) EC (now Article 45(2) TFEU), read in conjunction with Articles 12 and 17 EC (now Articles 18 and 20 TFEU), does not preclude national legislation which makes entitlement to a jobseeker's allowance conditional on a residence requirement, insofar as that requirement may be justified on the basis of objective considerations, independent of the nationality of the persons concerned and proportionate to the legitimate aim of the national provisions.

12.51 Article 6 of Directive 2004/38 appears to be less generous in providing for a right of residence of up to three months, only without formalities other than the requirement to hold a valid identity card or passport. Chapter IV of the Directive also provides for a right of permanent residence after five years of continuous residence for Union citizens and their family members who are not Union citizens. This applies to both workers and the self-employed.

12.52 Article 7 of Directive 2004/38 lays down the conditions for a right of residence for more than three months for primary movers and family members. If they are not workers or self-employed they must have sufficient resources not to become a burden on the financial system of the host state and must have comprehensive sickness insurance. This includes students (Article 7(1)(b)). The status may be retained in case of sickness, involuntary unemployment or taking up vocational training connected with the previous employment.

Equal treatment for jobseekers

2.53 In Collins the Court also extended the fundamental principle of equal treatment in Union law to benefits of a financial nature such as jobseekers' allowance. The Court considered that, in view of the establishment of citizenship of the Union and the interpretation of the case law of the right to equal treatment enjoyed by citizens of the Union, it was no longer possible to exclude such a benefit of a financial nature from the scope of Article 45(2) TFEU.

2.54 In a case that followed on from *Collins*, the Court interpreted Regulation 1408/71, which provides that a Member State can require Union citizens to complete a certain period of work within the host Member State before allowing them to claim unemployment benefit. It is interesting to compare the conclusion in this case with the legislative line taken in Directive 2004/38. Article 24(2) of the Directive states that by way of derogation to the equal treatment principle the host Member State 'shall not be obliged to confer entitlement to social assistance for the first three months of residence...' or even longer for jobseekers.

2.55 In Case C–346/05 *Monique Chateignier v Office national de l'emploi (ONEM)* (2006) Mrs Chateignier, a French national, married a Belgian national and went to live in Belgium. After declaring to the Belgian authorities that she had Belgian nationality, the applicant received unemployment benefit. Following a subsequent declaration of French nationality by the applicant, and an investigation by Belgian authorities which confirmed she did not hold Belgian nationality, unemployment benefits were withdrawn on the basis that she had not completed even one day's work in Belgium. The applicant then completed one day of work, and reapplied for unemployment benefits, which were regranted. The Court noted that implicit in the applicant's claim for benefits was a declaration that she was seeking employment, and that the benefits at issue were unemployment benefits within the scope of Regulation 1408/71. As a national of a Member State seeking employment in another Member State, the applicant fell under Article 39 EC (now Article 45 TFEU) and was therefore entitled to equal treatment with nationals of the host Member State. The inclusion of the applicant's nationality meant that she was placed in a disadvantageous position, and this was precluded by Article 45 TFEU. Interestingly, the Court noted that Article 67(2) and (3) of Regulation 1408/71 permitted Member States to make the acquisition, retention or recovery of the right to unemployment benefits subject to the completion of periods of employment in accordance with the relevant legislative provisions under which benefits are claimed. However, no such requirement had been incorporated into Belgian legislation, meaning that no such period could be required by the state authorities.

Voluntary unemployment

12.56 Voluntary unemployment is only mentioned in Article 7(1) of Regulation 1612/68, in Article 7 of Directive 68/360 and now in Article 7(3) of Directive 2004/38. In Case

C–413/01 *Ninni-Orasche* (see **12.19**) the Court held that she was not necessarily voluntarily unemployed (within the meaning established by the relevant case law of the Court) solely because her fixed-term contract of employment had expired.

12.57 Article 7(2) of Regulation 1612/68 provided that there should be no discrimination in respect of 'social advantages' and this was interpreted by the Court as including access to education. Someone leaving employment in order to become a student on a vocational course may still retain his/her status as a worker, even if (s)he left employment voluntarily, provided there was an evident link between the employment and the course of study (see Case C–357/89 *Raulin v Minister van Onderwijs & Wetenschappen* (1992) and Case C–3/90 *Bernini v Minister van Onderwijs en Wetenschappen* (1992); also see **12.16**).

12.58 However, a difficulty arose in *Brown* (see **12.17**). Mr Brown was a student with dual British and French nationality who had gone to school in France. He had been accepted by the University of Cambridge for a course in electrical engineering, and decided to gain some work experience by taking up a position in Scotland for eight months. The job he had been offered was only available to students who had been offered a university place. The Court had previously decided in *Lair* (see **12.17**) that Article 7(2) of Regulation 1612/68 could apply to maintenance grants. However, it also ruled that if the immigrant obtained the employment solely by virtue of the fact that he had already been offered a university place, he would not be entitled to the grant as the employment was merely incidental to the university course. Mr Brown was engaged on a full-time occupational activity in order to prepare for his university studies. Nonetheless, the Court ruled that although the work he did was clearly of a genuine and non-ancillary nature—and thus fulfilled all the 'worker' criteria as set out in *Levin* (see **12.13**)—he could not benefit from all the social advantages granted to Union workers, as the work had been undertaken after he had been accepted for his electrical engineering degree and was not a preparation for further employment. This meant, therefore, that he could not claim a full maintenance grant. The Court clearly valued the purpose of the work in its determination of the extent to which benefits would be granted even though it had said in *Levin* that the purpose of the work was immaterial. Subsequent to this case law, it appears that EU legislation has become more restrictive. In the light of the more restrictive provisions in the Citizenship Directive regarding those who are not workers or self-employed, it could be asked whether case law pre-dating the Directive would be decided the same way today.

Freedom of establishment

Services v establishment

12.59 People who move to work in another Member State are likely to be employees. The greatest movement of persons is, therefore, likely to be that of 'workers'. Nevertheless, there was a clear need to provide for similar rules for others: the self-employed, those who wish to move in order to carry out certain activities on a temporary basis, to set up in business or to exercise an independent profession in one of the Member States. Many of the rules are similar, but there are also special requirements for the self-employed. What happens if a Dutch plumber wants to repair someone's central heating in Belgium? Should a French qualified medical specialist be allowed to go to Germany temporarily to exercise his/her profession, or to set up practice there? Should a lawyer from one Member State be allowed to appear before the court of another or to put up his/her business plaque and practise in that country? What happens if someone conducts an activity in another Member State without going there and, therefore, does not cross a border?

12.60 The right of establishment and the freedom to provide services share many common features and provisions. Articles 49–55 TFEU (ex Articles 43–48 and 294 EC) are the provisions covering freedom of establishment for the self-employed. This includes not just individuals, as in the case of workers, but also legal persons, companies or firms, and any profit-making undertakings (Article 54 TFEU); see also Case 197/84 *Steinhauser v City of Biarritz* (1985), concerning a restriction on the renting of trading premises. The right to provide services is covered by Articles 56–62 TFEU (ex Articles 49–55 EC) and is dealt with in **Chapter 11,** although parallel cases involving the service freedom will be considered in the remainder of this chapter.

12.61 It is not always possible to determine exactly whether an activity falls within Article 49 TFEU or Article 56 TFEU, i.e. whether an activity should be treated as raising questions relating to establishment or services law. An engineering business with its headquarters in the Netherlands could either set up a branch in Belgium to service its Belgian customers or offer its services to Belgian clients from its office in the Netherlands. The first case would constitute establishment; the second would refer to the provision of services. The Court interprets these provisions to provide for the fullest possible freedom of movement for self-employed persons wishing to engage in economic activities, regardless of the exact nature and extent of the provision of the service involved. This is ultimately based on the wider concept of citizenship and the facilitation of free trade ideals within the EU.

12.62 Léger AG stated in Case C–55/94 *Gebhard* (1995) (see **11.8** and **12.131**) that the right of establishment and the provision of services constituted two separate branches of Union law, dealt with by two separate chapters of the Treaty which do not overlap. He pointed out that establishment means integration into a national economy, whereas the freedom to provide services merely enables a self-employed person established in a Member State in which he is integrated to exercise his activity in another Member State. He added that establishment and the provision of services are mutually *exclusive*, therefore distinguishing the rules governing the two types of activity.

In other words, someone intending to settle in another Member State for economic ends and be integrated permanently in the host state's economy would be regarded as claiming the right of establishment. Services, on the other hand, are of a temporary nature (see in particular *Gebhard,* which reinforced this, and outlined that the key distinguishing feature is duration). The temporary nature of services must be determined 'in the light, not only of the duration of the provision of the service but also of its regularity, periodicity or continuity'. As a caveat to this, service providers can use the relevant infrastructure in the host Member State, provided it is necessary to perform the service, and not become automatically regarded as established in the second Member State (Case C–215/01 *Bruno Schnitzer* (2003)). Such arrangements have the added benefit of escaping any instances where establishment would require registration or some other administrative formality, whereas provision of services may not.

Non-discrimination and equal treatment

12.63 The freedom to exercise a trade or profession is fundamental to the objectives of the Union. The economy cannot develop as it is intended to if there are obstacles to some of the principal production factors such as labour and the transfer of skills.

12.64 Both the right of establishment and the freedom to provide services rest first of all on the prohibition of discrimination, i.e., the right to equal treatment with nationals of the host Member State. This has occurred despite the absence of a provision equivalent to Article 7(1) and (2) of Regulation 1612/68 on workers. In the case of the freedom to provide services, the Court has read Article 49 EC (now Article 56 TFEU) so as to require equal treatment in respect of the terms and conditions on which a service is provided or received, and equal treatment in respect of social and tax advantages (see Case 186/87 *Cowan* (1989) and Case C–45/93 *Commission v Spain* (1994), below (see also **11.21**)).

12.65 With regard to the freedom of establishment, the original Article 54 EEC (now Article 50 TFEU) provided for a general programme for the abolition of restrictions. This is now no longer included in Article 50 TFEU, but the article retains the detailed instructions to the Member States to act in order to facilitate establishment. The original programme stated that obstacles to the right of establishment included not only laws prohibiting non-nationals from exercising professional activities, but also, for example, work permits, merchant or professional cards, and more costly measures, such as deposits and bonds, or provisions subjecting non-nationals to double supervision, or requiring them to establish themselves in order to provide services. The programme also provided for an end to the restrictions on movement and residence, which was achieved in Directive 73/148 (a directive that paralleled Directive 68/360 for workers). Directive 2004/38 on Citizenship now covers these provisions.

Freedom of establishment and people

12.66 The Citizenship Directive 2004/38 sets out rights of residence for the self-employed of more than three months in Article 7. The provisions largely follow in line with the case law discussed thus far. A right of residence of more than three months is granted to all Union citizens if they (a) are workers or self-employed in the host Member State; or (b) have sufficient resources for themselves and their families, so as not to become a burden on the host Member State (including comprehensive sickness cover); or (c) are enrolled at a private or public establishment for the principal purpose of study. Other relevant provisions include: Article 10 (on issuance of residence cards) and Articles 16 and 17 (on the right of permanent residence).

2.67 The ancillary rights to those set out in the primary legislation by Article 49 TFEU dealing with the self-employed are also to be found in the Citizenship Directive, e.g., Article 7(1)(d) provides that the family members accompanying Union citizens who satisfy the conditions in Article 7(1)(a) through (c) shall also have the right of residence in the territory of another Member State.

Professional qualifications and work experience

2.68 Although Article 49 has been found to have direct effect, the Commission nevertheless embarked on a programme, drafting a number of specific directives in order to give further substance to the Article, primarily to provide for an equivalence of professional standards between Member State nationals. In the 1960s and 1970s more than 50 directives were issued in such diverse fields as the medical and para-medical professions, agriculture, architecture, crafts, hotel and restaurant businesses, commercial agents and the film industry. Many of these directives took a long time to draft and adopt; for example, a directive for architects took approximately 15 years. However, even these 'sectoral' directives did not eliminate all the problems which arose in respect of recognition of professional training and qualifications, as the standards they laid down were minimum standards expressed in general terms.

12.69 The Commission subsequently changed its approach to directives towards a preference for a more general directive recognising professional qualifications. The result was Directive 89/48 (now replaced by Directive 2005/36), which provided for a general system of equivalence for university diplomas for courses lasting at least three years. In addition, there must be completion of professional training, where appropriate, in addition to the university diploma. The Directive was based on two principles: (1) mutual trust between Member States; (2) mutual recognition, i.e. the assumption that certificates awarded in the Member States should be accepted in good faith. The education must, however, be comparable: if there are significant differences between training periods, for example, additional evidence of professional experience or additional examinations may be required. This directive was followed by Directive 92/51 (now replaced by Directive 2005/36) on the mutual recognition of post-secondary training of shorter duration, such as vocational training courses. Directive 1999/42 (also replaced by Directive 2005/36) of the European Parliament and Council provided for a third general system for the recognition of professional qualifications which extended the mutual recognition approach to the sectoral directives, based on experience and skills in addition to the possession of qualifications or diplomas.

12.70 In Case 2/74 *Reyners v Belgium* (1974) (see **12.107**) Mr Reyners, a Dutch national, fulfilled all the requirements to become an *'avocat'* in Belgium. However, Belgian law at that time required *avocats* to have Belgian nationality and when Mr Reyners applied to be admitted to the Belgian Bar and to be qualified as an *'avocat'* his application was turned down. The Belgian *Conseil d'Etat*, the highest administrative court, referred the case to the Court, asking whether Article 52 EEC (now Article 49 TFEU) had direct effect. The Court replied:

> In laying down that the freedom of establishment shall be attained at the end of the transitional period, Article 52 EEC thus imposed an obligation to attain a precise result, the fulfilment of which had to be made easier by, but not made dependent on, the implementation of a programme of progressive measures.

It did not matter that the Council had so far failed to issue all the directives necessary for implementation under Article 54 EEC (now Article 50 TFEU). Individuals could rely directly on the Article. However, the directives had not lost all interest since they would contribute towards defining the scope of the exercise of freedom of establishment (see *van Binsbergen* **11.10** for a parallel case involving services).

12.71   Thus, the pressure for the drawing up of directives had been taken off, but it still proved necessary to have the directives, as will be seen, in particular, in the case of lawyers (see **12.124**). The aim of the directives arising from the establishment Article was to facilitate matters, not to make implementation depend on it.

12.72   In Case 71/76 *Thieffry v Conseil de l'Ordre des Avocats à la Cour de Paris* (1977) a Belgian national, who had obtained a law degree at a Belgian university, which was recognised as equivalent by the University of Paris, proposed to train for the Paris Bar. He was refused on the grounds that he did not possess a French law degree. The Court ruled that this was indirect discrimination, prohibited by Article 52 EEC (now Article 49 TFEU). In Case 11/77 *Patrick v Ministère des Affaires Culturelles* (1977) a British architect had obtained a degree in the United Kingdom which was recognised by France on the basis of a ministerial decree. Although there was no directive, such a qualification, recognised by authorities of the host Member State as equivalent, should be accepted by the Member State concerned. The Court held that, even in the absence of a directive, it is possible to take advantage of the right of establishment, provided some state authority has recognised the diploma as equivalent. Subsequently, Case C–61/89 *Bouchoucha* (1990) concerned a French national who had obtained a diploma in osteopathy in the United Kingdom. Under French law only qualified doctors were allowed to practise as osteopaths and he was prosecuted when he attempted to practise in France. Although Directives 75/362 and 75/363 (now absorbed by Directive 2005/36; see **12.81**) concerned harmonisation and mutual recognition of medical qualifications, they did not define the activities of a 'doctor'. The Court said:

> In the absence of Community legislation...each Member State is free to regulate the exercise of that activity within its territory without discriminating between its own nationals and those of the other Member States.

2.73 Case 115/78 *Knoors v Secretary of State for Economic Affairs* (1979) concerned a plumber of Dutch nationality, who had trained in Belgium. The ECJ considered a specific Directive in this area (which was the first of its kind) and which provided that where the exercise of the activity in a Member State depended on the possession of certain qualifications:

> That Member State shall accept as sufficient evidence of such knowledge and ability the fact that the activity in question has been pursued in another Member State.

The Court held that the Directive excluded any possibility of a national abusing the free movement rules so as to gain easier qualifications in another Member State and, therefore, Knoors could benefit from the protection of the Directive. This decision indicated that reverse discrimination is not a problem if there is a directive in existence, however, if there is no directive, a national of a Member State cannot rely simply on Article 49 TFEU. This was illustrated in the two cases both of which concerned Mr Auer, a French citizen who had acquired a veterinary qualification in Italy and tried to practise in France. (Cases 136/78 *Ministère Public v Auer* (1979) and 271/82 *Auer v Ministère Public (No 2)* (1983)). In the first case, the Court agreed that Mr Auer could not rely on Article 43 EC (now Article 49 TFEU) alone. However, in the second case, by which time directives covering veterinary qualifications had been passed, the Court accepted that he could rely on the directives.

12.74 In Case 222/86 *UNECTEF v Heylens* (1987) Mr Heylens was a Belgian football trainer who was prosecuted by the French football trainers' union. He was practising as a trainer in France but without qualifications which the French authorities recognised as equivalent. The Court held that in the absence of Community legislation the French system of recognising diplomas nevertheless had to look objectively at the qualifications held by a national of another Member State, recognising the level of knowledge and qualifications which its holder can be assumed to possess in the light of that diploma, [and] having regard to the nature and duration of the studies and practical training which the diploma certifies that he has carried out.

12.75 Similarly, in Case C–340/89 *Vlassopoulou v Ministerium für Justiz, Bundes-und Europeaangelegenheiten Baden-Württemberg* (1991) Mrs Vlassopoulou was a Greek national with a Greek law degree who had practised German law in Germany for a number of years. Her application for admission to the German Bar was rejected. The Court stated that Member States had an obligation under Article 49 TFEU (then Article 43 EC) to take into consideration a person's qualifications acquired in another Member State and make a comparison between those and the national rules.

12.76 Whether a Member State must recognise qualifications obtained outside the European Union varies. Case C–154/93 *Tawil-Albertini* (1994) concerned a dental qualification obtained in the Lebanon by a French national. Belgium, the UK and Ireland had recognised the qualification as equivalent but France refused. The Court ruled that the sectoral dental Directive did not provide for qualifications obtained outside of what was then the area of the European Community. The Directive only contained provisions concerning minimum qualifications and therefore other Member States could not be bound by an agreement between another Member State and a non-Member State. However, in Case C–319/92 *Haim v Kassenzahnaertzliche Vereinigung Nordrhein* (1994) the applicant had a non-Member State (Turkish) qualification. He had practised in Belgium and was authorised to practise in Germany. However, when he applied to be allowed to practise within the German social security system, he was told he had to undergo two years of training. The Court referred to *Vlassopolou*: the period spent practising under a social security scheme in another Member State should be taken into account by the German authorities.

12.77 Case C–238/98 *Hocsman v Ministre de l'Emploi* (2000) is particularly important. The applicant's basic medical diploma was obtained outside the EU, in Argentina. However, his specialisation (urology) was obtained in Spain, and he had practised lawfully as a specialist in a Member State. He also worked in France as a specialist in French hospitals. He then applied to be admitted to the French professional medical association, but was refused. The Court applied *Vlassopolou* and *Heylens* and stated that the medical association should consider his application taking into account all the qualifications obtained and the relevant experience, and comparing the specialised knowledge thus acquired with the national requirements.

12.78 The more recent adoption of Council Directive 2009/50/EC on the conditions of entry and stay of third country nationals for the purposes of highly qualified employment (the 'Blue Card' Directive) goes some way toward providing highly-qualified third-country nationals with an efficient method for the portability of their qualifications among EU Member States. The Blue Card enables highly qualified third country nationals to enter, re-enter and stay in the issuing Member State and pass through other Member States, work in a specific sector of employment and enjoy equal treatment with nationals regarding, among other things, recognition of diplomas. After they have resided legally in a Member State for 18 months, they may move to another Member State to work in highly qualified employment. Some restrictions apply, such as national limits on the number of non-nationals accepted under the Blue Card programme. It is important to note, however, that according to Protocols annexed to the TEU and the EC Treaty, the United Kingdom, Ireland and Denmark do not take part in the Directive and, as such, are not bound by it or subject to its application.

12.79 A recent series of cases at the Court highlights the definition of 'work experience' under Directive 89/48 (which has been replaced by Directive 2005/36). In Joined Cases C–422/09, C–425/09 and C–426/09 *Vasiliki Stylianou Vandorou, Vasilios Alexandrou Giankoulis and Ioannis Georgiou Askoxilakis v Ipourgos Ethnikis Pedias kai Thriskevmaton* (2010) each queried what experience could be taken into account when assessing 'professional experience' in the context of a regulated profession. In response, the Court stated that the term refers to the pursuit of a regulated activity that is typically subject to the possession of a diploma. Any experience gained prior to obtaining the diploma is therefore not to be counted as 'professional experience'. The Court went on to hold that even where a diploma is held in one Member State, any experience in another Member State prior to authorisation to pursue the profession cannot be regarded as 'work experience' under the Directive. However, any measures for authorisation, including the imposition of supplementary requirements to cover any substantive differences between qualifications and experience, cannot be applied disproportionately so as to prejudice the freedom of movement of workers and establishment.

2.80 A difficulty may also arise in the case of professions which are recognised in one Member State but not in another. Case C–234/97 *Fernandez de Bobadilla v Museo Nacional del Prado* (1999) concerned a Spanish national seeking to practise her profession as an art restorer in Spain. She was a holder of a postgraduate degree in the United Kingdom but was rejected for a post at the Prado as the collective agreement there did not recognise this qualification. The Court held that a profession regulated by collective agreement—if it is the result of a single national policy or even if it resembles other agreements entered into on an individual basis by other public bodies—will fall under the directives for the recognition of diplomas and professional education and training. Even if there is non-regulation, i.e. no general procedure for recognition, it is up to the public body itself to investigate and ascertain equivalence. (See also Case C–164/94 *Arantis v Land Berlin* (1996) concerning the profession of geologist and Case C–424/09 *Christina Ioanni Taki v Ipourgos Ehtnikis Pedias kai Thriskevmaton* (2011) concerning the profession of an environmental engineer).

12.81 The Commission built upon the rules laid out in Directive 93/16/EEC (free movement of doctors) and Directive 1999/42/EC (recognition of professional qualifications) in two stages. During the first stage, it integrated the sectoral directives into a consolidated framework. Then, during the second stage, it adopted Directive 2005/36 relating to the mutual recognition of professional qualifications. This consolidated and replaced the above directives as well as the sectoral directives (Articles 21–49 of the Directive). The Directive follows the same principle of mutual recognition that inspired the original directives. Directives 77/249 (Lawyers' Services) and 98/5 (Lawyers' Establishment) were untouched, although the Commission is currently reviewing the Establishment Directive and investigating whether separate regulation is necessary in the light of Directive 2005/36. The principal effect on lawyers is that they are covered by the part of the Directive that relates to the general system for the recognition of evidence of qualifications in cases of establishment, which replaces the Diplomas Directive 89/48. In respect of the specific professions covered in Title III, Articles 21–49, where the applicant has the minimum qualifications required, (s)he is entitled to automatic recognition of those qualifications and may, therefore, take up the same profession in the host Member State. However, in Title III Chapter 1, which deals with mutual recognition generally, the applicant only has a right to have the authorities of the host state consider his/her qualifications and it is then up to the Member State to decide on any additional training or experience the applicant needs. See *Vlassopoulou* (above, at **12.75**).

12.82 Directive 2005/36 is currently being reviewed by the European Commission, with a view towards its modernisation. In its Green Paper (COM(2011) 367 final), the

Commission designates the recognition of professional qualifications as 'a fundamental building block of the Single Market'. However, there are concerns regarding the continuing low rate of mobility of professionals, which is, in part, due to complicated national procedures. As part of this modernisation, the Commission is considering the introduction of a European Professional Card, which would take advantage of the latest technology to enhance communication between Member States. It seems, therefore, that progress is being made. In December 2011, the Commission adopted a legislative proposal for amending Directive 2005/36 and the Regulation on administrative cooperation through the Internal Market Information System (COM(2011) 883 final).

Freedom of establishment and companies

12.83   The right of establishment is described in Article 49 TFEU as the right of a natural person or a company to settle in a Member State and to pursue an economic activity there. This includes the right to set up and run a company and the right to pursue an occupation in a self-employed capacity. The exceptions to this right contained in Articles 51 and 52 TFEU therefore also apply to companies. Article 49 covers the right for individuals as well as 'companies and firms', which are defined in Article 54 TFEU as those 'constituted under civil or commercial law', including cooperative societies and other 'legal persons...'. It excludes, however, non-profit-making organisations. Article 54 TFEU provides that 'companies or firms' are treated in the same way as natural persons. For example, in Case C–213/89 *Factortame (No 2)* (1991) it was determined that the principle of non-discrimination as to nationality in Article 12 EC (now Article 18 TFEU) also applies to companies (see **7.57-7.59**).

12.84   A more complex example of broader economic scope may be found in Case 270/83 *Commission v France* (1986). In this case the Court found France in breach of its Treaty obligations. France refused to grant on the same terms, the benefit of shareholders' tax credits in respect of dividends paid to branches or agencies of French companies. In other words, the conditions for the granting of these tax credits differed between branches and agencies of insurance companies in France whose registered office is located in another Member State, and those insurance companies whose registered office was in France. In its judgment, the Court rejected the French argument relating to the avoidance of double taxation through corporation tax and dividend tax.

12.85   In Case C–254/97 *Baxter v Premier Ministre* (1999) the Court held that Articles 43 and 48 EC (now Articles 49 and 54 TFEU) precluded legislation giving tax allowances to companies established in France exploiting proprietary medicinal products, which meant they could deduct from a special levy on their pre-tax turnover only the expenditure which was incurred on research carried out in France. Although there were French-based undertakings which incurred expenditure outside the country and foreign undertakings which incurred such expenditure within France, the tax allowance seemed likely to have a more detrimental effect on undertakings having their principal place of business in other Member States.

2.86   In Case 81/87 *R v HM Treasury and IRC, ex p Daily Mail and General Trust plc* (1988) the *Daily Mail* claimed that the UK statutory requirement that companies transferring their central management abroad must obtain Treasury permission first, was an obstacle to their freedom of establishment. The statutory provision also enabled the Treasury to ask the company to liquidate some of its assets, thus making it liable for capital gains tax, whereas companies resident abroad had no such liability. The Court pointed out that Article 43 EC (now Article 49 TFEU) provided for the setting up of agencies, branches or subsidiaries. However, since wide variations in company law still existed in the Community, the Treaty could not confer the right on a company to transfer its central management to another Member State:

> While retaining their status as companies incorporated under the legislation of the first Member State.

2.87   Case C–264/96 *ICI v Kenneth Hall Colmer (Her Majesty's Inspector of Taxes)* (1998) concerned discriminatory fiscal treatment in respect of corporation tax. Under UK law, companies belonging to a consortium through which they control a holding company were only entitled to tax relief if the holding company's business consisted wholly or mainly in the holding of shares in subsidiaries established in the United Kingdom. This constituted an obstacle to the freedom of establishment in one Member State of a company incorporated in another Member State. The reasons justifying the discrimination submitted by the UK government were rejected by the court; namely that the measure was based on the risk of tax avoidance and the diminution of tax revenue (resulting from the fact that revenue lost through the granting of tax relief on losses incurred by resident subsidiaries could not be offset by tax on the profits on non-resident subsidiaries). The discrimination was not necessary to protect the cohesion of the tax system at issue. A similar decision may be seen in Case C–307/97 *Saint-Gobain v Finanzamt Aachen-Innenstadt* (1999). See also Case C–200/98 *X AB and Y AB v Riksskatteverket* (1999).

12.88   In Case 107/83 *Ordre des Avocats au Barreau de Paris v Klopp* (1984) the Court ruled that the right to set up branches in other Member States included the right for a lawyer to set up more than one place of work, subject to professional rules of conduct. At that time, there was no directive coordinating national provisions governing access to and the exercise of the legal profession. The French rules restricted French lawyers to membership in only one local Bar. Nevertheless, there was the possibility for a foreign lawyer to have an office in another country. Therefore, even if national rules provide that someone may only have one professional location, this does not preclude a lawyer from another Member State from setting up an office in another Member State. For more on lawyers generally, see below **12.124** and, in particular, *Gebhard* (**11.8** and **12.131**).

12.89   In Case 39/75 *Coenen v Sociaal Economische Raad* (1975) the Court stated, however, that although the requirement of business residence in the country where a profession is exercised may be justified, the individual could not be required to have his private residence there as well.

Exceptions to the free movement of persons

12.90 The right to free movement of workers, as interpreted by the Court of Justice, is an extensive right, limited only by the provisions contained in Article 45(3) and (4) TFEU. These exceptions (some of which were discussed in the case law cited in **Chapter 11**), also apply to establishment and services. These exceptions have been construed narrowly by the Court from the very beginning. Of course, a state must be able to protect itself from having to admit individuals who can cause real harm to its own citizens, such as those who are a threat to national security, those who are likely to cause real disruption to the order of the state or those who threaten the health or well-being of its citizens. Despite this, a state should not use these exceptions to keep out, or discriminate against, those who are genuinely seeking to move for their own benefit and that of their family and who do not, upon objective examination, constitute a real risk. It is often the role of the Court to balance these two groups of (sometimes divergent) interests. The use of the exceptions, if invoked successfully, means the exclusion of a person from the state, either by non-admission or by deportation. As a consequence, such measures should only be taken if absolutely necessary.

Limitations on grounds of public policy, public security and public health

12.91 Articles 27–33 of Directive 2004/38 provide detail to the exceptions contained in Article 45(3) TFEU with regard to workers and in Article 52(1) TFEU for the self-employed and those providing or receiving services. The exceptions may not be invoked to serve economic ends. However, as we have seen in previous chapters, the Court does sometimes allow non-economic exceptions of the 'Cassis de Dijon' type (i.e. indistinctly applicable measures) (see in particular 10.29). The interpretation of the concepts of public policy and, to a lesser extent, public security, has not been straightforward and has evolved over the years.

12.92 In the early case of van Duyn (Case 41/74 van Duyn v Home Office (1974)) the Court held that the Member State, in this case the United Kingdom, had the ultimate say in whether an individual's conduct was contrary to public policy. The Court referred to Article 3(1) of Directive 64/221 (later absorbed by Directive 2004/38) which provided that:

> Measures taken on grounds of public policy shall be based exclusively on the personal conduct of the individual concerned.

The Court considered that van Duyn's ongoing association with a body or an organisation—namely the Church of Scientology in this case—could in itself constitute personal conduct which may be considered as a voluntary act by that person. The fact that the Scientology organisation was not prohibited, and thus British nationals could work for it, was then considered by the Court. The concept of public policy had to be strictly interpreted and was, moreover, subject to control by Community institutions. Nevertheless, circumstances justifying recourse to the concept of public policy may vary, and thus it was necessary to allow the competent national authorities a certain amount of discretion. Therefore, the English court still had the discretion to refuse entry to Miss van Duyn on the basis that her conduct was 'socially harmful', although the Scientology movement by which she was to have been employed was not prohibited in the United Kingdom. The Court pointed out that the right of residence may be refused to nationals of other Member States who wish to take up employment, even when it could not refuse its own nationals. This was the first UK case brought before the Court and the first case to indicate clearly that a directive may have direct effect. It appears that the Court was keen to establish the principle of direct effect, however, it may have exercised caution in interpreting the public policy concept, so as not to give it a Community dimension.

2.93   However, in Cases 115 and 116/81 *Adoui and Cornuaille v Belgium* (1982) the Court did not accept that a Member State could deport those who were working in a non-prohibited job (in this case, prostitution) in Belgium. The judgment in this case would indicate that *van Duyn* would not be decided in the same way today. In fact, Advocate General Mancini wrote extra-judicially that it was overruled by *Adoui*. If such cases were now to be decided by a national court, without making a reference, the decision would likely follow *Adoui*. See for comparison the *Schindler* line of cases (**11.45**).

12.94   How much discretion does a Member State have in restricting a EU citizen's right of free movement; can it penalise or expel those it considers as undesirable? In Case 30/77 *R v Pierre Bouchereau* (1977), a French national who was employed in the United Kingdom was found guilty for possession of illegal drugs. The national court, before imposing a deportation order, asked the Court of Justice whether deportation would infringe Bouchereau's right to freedom of movement under Article 45 TFEU (then Article 48 EEC) and Article 3(2) of Directive 64/221/EEC. The Court found that

> in so far as it may justify certain restrictions on the free movement of persons subject to Community law, recourse by a national authority to the concept of public policy presupposes, in any event, the existence, in addition to the perturbation to the social order which any infringement of the law involves, of a genuine and sufficiently serious threat affecting one of the fundamental interests of society.

12.95   Joined Cases C–482 and 493/01 *Orfanopoulos and Oliveri* (2004) concerned Greek and Italian nationals who were long-term residents in Germany. They had committed various offences for which they had served prison sentences. They were served with deportation orders, together with their families. As is increasingly the case, the Court considered the free movement articles as well as Article 21 TFEU (ex Article 18 EC) and the general principles, in particular fundamental rights and respect for family life. The Court stated that Directive 64/221 (now absorbed by Directive 2004/38) precluded national legislation which provided for expulsion of foreign nationals without taking into account factual matters which may have contributed to the 'substantial diminution of the present threat which the conduct of the person concerned constitutes to the requirements of public policy', for example, if considerable time had elapsed between the expulsion order and the review of that order. Article 45 TFEU (then Article 39) and Article 3 of Directive 64/221 also precluded national legislation or practices which, even if taking into account family circumstances, were based on the presumption that the person must be expelled without proper account being taken of his personal conduct and the danger he represented for the requirements of public policy. However, the national authorities should instead balance the threat and the fact that the person had received a particular sentence for specific offences against the fact that he had resided for many years in the host Member State and could plead family circumstances against the expulsion. The Court held that assessment must be made 'on a case-by-case basis by the national authorities of where the fair balance lies between the legitimate interests at issue ... in compliance with the general principles of Community law and, in particular, by taking proper account of respect for fundamental rights, such as the protection of family life'. See also Cases 131/79 *R v Secretary of State for Home Affairs, ex p Mario Santillo* (1980), 157/79 *R v Pieck* (1980) (see **12.22**), 348/96 *Calfa* (1999). See also, in Case C–215/03 *Oulane* (2005) where the Court interpreted the right of residence in another Member State under Directive 73/148/EC as meaning that this right may not be made, under certain conditions, subject to the production of a valid identity card or passport.

12.96 In Case 36/75 *Rutili v Ministre de l'Intérieur* (1975) Mr Rutili, an Italian citizen had been prohibited from entering certain regions of France because of his known political activities. The Court said that this could only be accepted if such a prohibition could also have been imposed on French citizens under the same conditions. However, internal provisions in France were much less restrictive than the conditions the French authorities wanted to apply to Mr Rutili and, therefore, Mr Rutili's right to free movement could not be impeded. (See *Olazabal* at **13.53**)

12.97 In Case C–531/06 *Commission v Italian Republic* (2009) and Joined Cases C–171/07 and C–172/07 *Apothekerkammer des Saarlandes and Others v Saarland and Ministerium für Justiz, Gesundheit und Soziales* (2010), the Court reconfirmed that whilst the national legislation in question did constitute restrictions of the freedom of establishment these were, in fact, justified on grounds of the protection of human health. These cases concerned medicinal products which the Court held as distinguishable from other goods because of their therapeutic value. As a result, Member States can legitimately seek ways to ensure the proper and correct consumption of medicines and can therefore require that medicinal products be supplied by pharmacists enjoying genuine professional independence. Since non-pharmacists by definition lack the training, experience and responsibility equivalent to those of pharmacists and, consequently, do not provide the same safeguards, it follows that a Member State may take the view that the operation of a pharmacy by a non-pharmacist may represent a risk to public health.

12.98 Could limits be imposed on an undertaking on the ground that it would use the right of establishment to circumvent the law of a Member State? In Case C–212/97 *Centros v Erhvervs- og Selskabsstyrelsen* (1999) Danish nationals resident in Denmark formed a company in the United Kingdom which did not trade there. The Danish authorities opposed the registration of a branch of that company in Denmark as they considered that the undertaking was in fact seeking to circumvent national rules concerning, in particular, the paying up of a minimum capital. The Court held that such a practice constituted an obstacle to freedom of establishment and that the fact that a national of a Member State who wished to set up a company chose to form it in the Member State whose rules of company law seemed to him the least restrictive could not, in itself, constitute an abuse of the right of establishment. Also, the practice could not be justified as an imperative requirement in the public interest for the protection of creditors. Furthermore, the principle of proportionality meant that the Member State should have adopted the available measures which were less restrictive or which interfered less with fundamental freedoms. The Court observed that nothing precluded the Member State concerned from adopting any appropriate measure for preventing or penalising fraud, in relation to the company or its members, when it had been established that they were in fact attempting to evade their obligations towards creditors established on state territory. The refusal to register the company was thus contrary to the Treaty.

2.99 Articles 27–33 of Citizenship Directive 2004/38 repealed and replaced Directive 64/221 which, as illustrated above, concerns the Member States' rights to restrict the free movement of workers and individuals on the ground of public policy, security and health. In addition to the codification of the above case law, the Citizenship Directive provides protection against expulsion. Article 28(3)(a) provides what is often referred to as 'enhanced protection' by preventing a Member State from taking an expulsion decision against a Union citizen who has resided in the host state for the previous 10 years, unless such decision is based on imperative grounds of public security, as defined by Member States. Any Union citizens excluded in this manner may apply to have the exclusion order lifted after a reasonable period, or in any event, after three years from enforcement of the final exclusion order which has been validly adopted in accordance with Union law. In order to succeed, the Union citizen must demonstrate that there has been a material change in the circumstances which justified the exclusion decision (Article 32(1)).

Article 27(2) indicates that measures taken on grounds of public policy or public security must be proportionate and must be based exclusively on the personal conduct of the individual concerned. Such conduct 'must present a genuine, present and sufficiently serious threat affecting one of the fundamental interests of society. Justifications that are isolated from the particulars of the case or that rely on considerations of general prevention shall not be accepted.' See Case 30/77 *R v Bouchereau*, at **12.94**.

12.100 Case C–145/09 *Land Baden-Württemberg v Panagiotis Tsakouridis* (2010) concerned a Greek national, who had spent most of his life in Germany. After being sentenced to a term of imprisonment of more than five years, he was subject to an expulsion order from Germany. The ECJ was asked under what conditions the right to enhanced protection could be lost, and whether Article 16(4) of the Citizenship Directive should be applied (whereby permanent residence will be lost if the individual is absent from the host Member State for a period exceeding two consecutive years). The Court held that, when making such an expulsion order, the national authorities should look to all relevant factors, in particular, the length and frequency of individual absences from the host Member State and the reasons for the absences. The Court also held that, in order for the expulsion to be proportionate where the individual has spent most of his life in the host state, the reason for expulsion must be very good. Despite this the Court reiterated that the threshold in Article 28(3), stating that a threat to public security that is of a particularly high degree of seriousness, is sufficient for expulsion. According to the Court, trafficking in narcotics as part of an organised group could attain this threshold. See also *Dias* at **12.33.**

The public service exception

12.101 The second restriction on the free movement of workers is contained in Article 45(4) TFEU: employment in the public service. It is echoed in respect of the self-employed in Article 51 TFEU, and also in Article 62 TFEU which refers to Article 51, which speaks of the exercise of official authority.

12.102 This exception, like the previous, has also been interpreted narrowly by the Court. The articles themselves do not define the concept of public service or of official authority, instead the Court has held that there should be a Union interpretation of the concepts. In Case 152/73 *Sotgiu v Deutsche Bundespost* (1974) the Court stated that the exception only applied to certain activities connected with the exercise of official authority. Mr Sotgiu, an Italian working for the German post office, had been discriminated against. A separation allowance paid to workers living away from home was increased for those living in Germany but not for those who lived abroad at the time of recruitment. Although this applied without distinction to all nationals, it clearly affected foreign workers more than German nationals. The German post office pleaded the public service derogation, but the Court pointed out (at paragraph 4) that this exception should not 'have a scope going beyond the aim in view of which the derogation was included'. The aim was the protection by Member States of rights to exercise state sovereignty by restricting access to certain parts of the public service. The provision could not, however, 'justify discriminatory measures with regard to remuneration or other conditions of employment against workers once they have been admitted to the public service'. The position might change, however, if the non-national were promoted to a job where Article 48(4) EEC (now Article 45(4) TFEU) did apply.

12.103 In Cases 149/79 *Commission v Belgium* (1980) and 149/79 *Commission v Belgium (No 2)* (1982), the Commission brought proceedings against Belgium for violation of Article 48(4) EEC by a Constitutional requirement that all those working for local authorities or public enterprises in Belgium should possess Belgian nationality. This included nurses, gardeners, railway workers and night watchmen. The Court stated (at paragraph 10):

That provision removes from the ambit of [Article 45(1) to (3)] a series of posts which involve direct or indirect participation in the exercise of powers conferred by public law and duties designed to safeguard the general interests of the State or other public authorities. Such posts in fact presume on the part of those occupying them the existence of a special relationship of allegiance to the State and reciprocity of rights and duties which form the foundation of the bond of nationality.

The Court focused on the aim of the Article and looked at the two requirements, which appear to be cumulative rather than alternative. However, other posts such as those of garden hands, cleaners, hospital nurses etc. clearly did not fall within that definition. Posts which might be within the scope of the Article were those of technical office supervisors, stock controllers, and possibly night watchmen as they may have easy access to the secrets of the public authority concerned.

2.104   The public service exception in respect of the self-employed contained in Article 51 TFEU was analysed by the Court in Case 2/74 *Reyners v Belgium* (1974) (see **12.70**). The case established that Article 51 TFEU (ex Article 52 EC) had direct effect. Also, the Court of Justice was asked to consider whether the exercise of the profession of 'avocat' constituted the exercise of public authority and could, thus, be restricted to Belgian nationals. The Court considered that a wholesale restriction of the profession was not necessary and would be disproportionate. It was sufficient if the exclusion of non-nationals was limited to 'those activities which, taken on their own, constitute *a direct and specific connection with the exercise of official authority*' [emphasis added]. If in a profession the, even occasional, exercise of functions pertaining to public authority could not be severed from the other activities of the profession, the exception would apply. If on the other hand, the exercise of official authority is separable from the professional activity, such an extension of the exception would not be possible. The Advocate General in *Reyners* described the exercise of official authority as 'that which arises from the sovereignty and the majesty of the powers of the state'.

2.105   The application of Article 45(4) TFEU cannot depend solely on the legal nature of the relationship between the employee and the administration. The Court's case law concerning nurses and teachers clarifies this view, although problems remain. In Case 66/85 *Lawrie-Blum v Land Baden-Württemberg* (1986) (see **12.14**) the Court stated that the concept of public service has to be interpreted narrowly, as directly involving the exercise of powers conferred by public law and contributing to safeguarding the general interests of the state. The activities of a teacher and *a fortiori* of a trainee teacher do not, however, involve the exercise of powers conferred by public law. If the application of Article 45(4) TFEU were made dependent on the legal nature of the relationship between the employee and the administration this would enable the Member State to determine at will what posts should be covered by the exception. As the Court had pointed out in Case 149/79 *Commission v Belgium* (see **12.103**) 'employment in the public service' must be understood as meaning those posts which involve: (1) direct or indirect participation in the exercise of powers conferred by public law; (2) the discharge of functions the purpose of which is to safeguard the general interests of the state and of other public authorities which require a special relationship of allegiance to the state on the part of persons occupying them; and (3) reciprocity of rights and duties which form the foundation of the bond of nationality. The posts excluded are confined to those which, having regard to the tasks and responsibilities involved, do not display the characteristics of activities of the public service. Those very strict conditions were not fulfilled in the case of a trainee teacher and, therefore, his/her employment could not be described as employment in the public service within the meaning of Article 45 TFEU.

12.106 In Case C–15/96 *Schöning-Kougebetopoulou v Freie und Hansestadt Hamburg* (1998) the Court held that a clause contained in a collective agreement which ignored previous periods of employment in the public service of another Member State for the purpose of determining promotion was incompatible with Union law. Such a clause clearly disadvantaged migrant workers who had spent part of their careers in the public service of another Member State and thus breached the principle of non-discrimination.

12.107 Several recent cases have discussed the application of the public service exception in the context of nationality requirements for entry into the notary profession (Cases C–47/08 *Commission v Belgium*; C–50/08 *Commission v France*; C–51/08 *Commission v Luxembourg*; C–52/08 *Commission v Portugal*; C–53/08 *Commission v Austria*; C–54/08 *Commission v Germany*; and C-61/08 *Commission v Greece*). Rules in force in the Member States concerned restricted entry to the notary profession to persons possessing home nationality. This restriction was, according to the Member States, justified by Article 51 TFEU (ex Article 45 EC) because the activities carried out by notaries were connected with the exercise of official authority. The Court disagreed, and held that the Member States were in breach of Article 49 TFEU (ex Article 43 EC). It stated that the activities of a notary were not directly and specifically connected with the exercise of official authority, as the notary cannot unilaterally alter a document agreed by two parties, can only undertake certain activities and may only collect taxes on behalf of a third party. The requirement by law of authentication by a notary did not change this, nor did the fact that a notary's activities provided legal certainty and so are carried out in the public interest.

The wholly internal situation

12.108 The provisions for the free movement of persons do not ensure complete free movement within the Union for all citizens. Apart from the limitations contained in the Treaty itself in Article 45(3) and (4) and Articles 51 and 62 TFEU, other restrictions exist as well. In order to avail oneself of the free movement provisions in the Treaty, there has to be a 'Union element'. A wholly internal situation does not, therefore, fall under the application of Union law, at least not under that of the provisions we have discussed. In Case 175/78 *R v Saunders* (1979), Mrs Saunders had been prosecuted in the United Kingdom for disobeying a court order to move to Northern Ireland and not to return for three years. The Court of Justice refused to rule as this concerned a 'wholly domestic situation'. The same applied in Cases 35/82 and 36/82 *Morson and Jhanjan v Netherlands* (1982), where the Surinamese parents of Dutch nationals were refused entry to the Netherlands. They sought to enter relying on Article 10 of Regulation 1612/68 (now replaced by Directive 2004/38) which allows relatives in the ascending line of the worker to join him. They had never worked in any other Member State and the Court considered, therefore, that this also concerned a 'wholly internal situation'. This was confirmed in Cases C–64 and 65/96 *Land Nordrhein-Westfalen v Uecker* and *Jacquet* (1997) when two non-EU nationals with two German spouses residing and working in Germany sought to invoke Article 7 of Regulation 1612/68. The Court declined to allow the claim.

.109 However, in Case C–370/90 *R v Immigration Appeal Tribunal and Surinder Singh, ex p Secretary of State for the Home Department* (1992) the Union element was held to be present, despite the Member State claiming that the matter concerned a wholly internal situation. An Indian husband and his British wife had worked in Germany. When they returned to the UK, the government considered that the Indian husband's right of residence depended on the British wife's right of residence as a national, not as an EU worker. However, the Court ruled that the matter was not wholly internal because the fact that the spouses had both worked in Germany triggered the Union element. Mrs Singh's husband was therefore entitled to enter as the spouse of a Union national.

2.110 The citizenship articles (20–25 TFEU) introduced by the Maastricht TEU have introduced a new element. Article 21 TFEU provides that 'every citizen of the Union shall have the right to move and reside freely within the territory of the Member States, subject to the limitations laid down in the Treaties and by the measures adopted to give them effect'. It could therefore be argued that the situation in *Saunders* and *Adams* (see **Chapter 13**) might be viewed differently by the Court today, as the citizenship provisions might be considered by the Court to have an impact and provide a remedy. However, in *Morson and Jhanjan* this might be more difficult.

Special cases of free movement

2.111 A number of issues span the law on free movement of persons, freedom of establishment and the freedom to provide and receive services in relation to specific areas of EU law and policy. These areas are treated separately here in order to demonstrate how the lines between free movement of workers, establishment and services may be blurred when it comes to professional sport, the practice of law and education.

Free movement in the field of professional sport

2.112 Until Article 165 TFEU, the EU did not have competence in the field of sport. This meant that the Court of Justice was often forced to fit cases involving sport into one of the four freedoms. However, professional sport did not often lend itself to regulation in the traditional sense, especially as regards competition rules. Article 165(2) TFEU states that Union action shall be aimed at 'developing the European dimension in sport'. Although sport is associated with public health, education, employment, environment, media and culture, this section will focus on its relationship with the free movement of workers, establishment and services and examine how these provisions have been specially applied to deal with the nuances of professional sport.

12.113 Sport is subject to the Treaty insofar as it concerns an economic activity. In Case 13/76 *Donà v Mantero* (1976), the Court held that Italian football teams could not be prevented from hiring non-Italian players. Nevertheless, selection rules concerning national teams playing in international competitions could be limited to those of a particular nationality (see also Case C–36/74 *Walrave and Koch v Association Union Cycliste Internationale* (1974)). This 'national exception' is one of many exceptions created by the Court in order to deal with the special case of sport.

12.114 Case C–415/93 *Union Royale Belge des Sociétés de Football Association ASBL v Jean Marc Bosman* (1996) made a considerable contribution towards clarifying the situation concerning professional sport. Mr Bosman, a player with the Belgian club RC Liège, had been transfer-listed but was refused the certificate necessary for any foreign transfer. Mr Bosman was suspended and unable to play for the whole season. Mr Bosman and UEFA issued proceedings against RC Liège. The former argued breach of Article 48 EEC on free movement of workers, as well as Articles 85 and 86 EEC on competition (now Articles 45, 101 and 102 TFEU). UEFA claimed their rules regarding transfer and nationality had received Commission approval. The transfer rules of FIFA, UEFA and URSBSFA (Belgian football association) required that when a player's contract had expired, any new club signing him must pay the old club a fee. Regarding nationality under the rules of UEFA (and most European Associations), in official matches, a club could not field more than three players who were nationals of other Member States, plus two other 'assimilated' players (the so-called 3+2 rule).

In his Opinion, Lenz AG said that the rules are subject to Article 45 TFEU insofar as they regulated the employment of professional footballers. He found that the Belgian rules on foreign players were discriminatory. He accepted that the previous rulings meant that selection for national or perhaps regional representative teams might be limited to those of a particular nationality without involving discrimination within the scope of the Treaty (see *Donà* and *Walrave*, **12.113**). This should not, however, be extended to matches where player choice was based on economic considerations and not sporting representation.

12.115 Lenz AG went on to say that Article 45 TFEU (ex Article 48 EEC) read together with Article 49 TFEU (ex Article 52 EEC) goes beyond a discrimination rule towards a broader principle which governs restrictions on free movement if they relate to *access* to the employment market rather than the *exercise* of an occupational activity (paragraph 205 of the Opinion). The transfer rules fell within the scope of Article 48 and may only be justified by imperative reasons in the general interest and may not go further than is necessary to attain those objectives (the proportionality principle). In this case, the objective was to preserve a balance between financial and sporting interests of clubs, but the Advocate General doubted that the system fulfilled that objective. Other less restrictive systems could also fulfil the objective, e.g. a collective wage agreement could limit the salaries paid by the clubs to the players or a system of distribution of the club's receipts, such as receipts at the gate and fees received for televised matches among the clubs. The argument that the money was necessary to compensate for the cost of training young players was acceptable in principle, but the same aims could be achieved at least as efficiently by other means which did not impede the free movement of workers. The Advocate General also discussed the application of Article 101 TFEU (ex Article 85 EC): the transfer system and restrictions on foreign players were horizontal agreements. This aspect was not dealt with by the Court. It is, however, of crucial importance in the implementation of the judgment, as the *Bosman* case shows, that the Article 45 TFEU structure is insufficient and Article 258 TFEU actions cannot be used. Thus, the enforcement relies each time on the individual's actions, unless the Commission takes the view that collective dominance is involved.

2.116 The Court agreed that Article 45 TFEU (ex Article 48 EC) applied and answered the first two questions posed as follows:

> (1) Article 48 of the EC Treaty precludes the application of the rules laid down by sporting associations, under which a professional footballer who is a national of one Member State may not, on the expiry of his contract with a club, be employed by a club of another Member State unless the latter club has paid to the former club a transfer, training or development fee.
>
> (2) Article 48 of the EC Treaty precludes the application of rules laid down by sporting associations under which, in matches in competitions which they organise, football clubs may field only a limited number of professional players who are nationals of other Member States.

The Court was aware, however, that this would have a major impact on the football transfer system, and consequently limited the temporal effect of the judgment (as in the *Defrenne* and *Barber* cases, see **Chapter 16, 16.31, 16.50** on discrimination). It declared that the direct effect of Article 48 could not be relied upon in respect of transfer and other fees already paid or payable under an obligation which arose before the date of the judgment, except for those individuals who had already brought proceedings before their national courts.

2.117 The real significance of the judgment lies in the general principles set out by the Court, moving away from the narrower confines of the football industry. The Court referred to Case 81/87 *R v HM Treasury and IRC, ex p Daily Mail and General Trust plc* (1988) (see **12.86**) where it had linked Article 45 TFEU (ex Article 48 EC) with Article 49 TFEU (ex Article 52 EEC) in its concern to establish coherent principles of free movement. This judgment applies only to cases with a 'Union element'. The Court confirmed that Article 45 TFEU did not apply to a wholly internal situation. A better basis for analysis would have been Article 101 TFEU (ex Article 85 EEC), as the problems concern private agreements irrespective of nationality. However, the Court stated (at paragraph 103):

> It is sufficient to note that, although the rules in issue in the main proceedings apply also to transfers between clubs belonging to different national associations within the same

> Member State and are similar to those governing transfers between clubs belonging to the same national association, they still directly affect players' access to the employment market in other Member States and are thus capable of impeding freedom of movement of workers.

12.118 The Court referred to Joined Cases C–267/91 and C–268/91 *Keck and Mithouard* (1993) (see **10.55**) (contrasted with Case C–384/93 *Alpine Investments v Minister van Financiën* (1995), which concerned a challenge under Article 59 EC (now Article 56 TFEU) to a Dutch prohibition on 'cold calling' as a technique to offer services in the territory of other Member States). The Court rejected an analogy with *Keck* and highlighted the material distinction between the two situations (see also **10.55**, **11.28** and **11.40**). *Bosman* could not be considered comparable to the rules on selling arrangements for goods which in *Keck* had been held to fall outside the ambit of Article 34 TFEU (ex Article 30 EC).

The Court made reference to Case C–19/92 *Dieter Kraus v Land Baden-Württemberg* (1993) and Case C–55/94 *Reinhard Gebhard v Consiglio dell'ordine degli Avvocati e Procuratori di Milano* (1995) (see **12.131**) which elaborate principles governing the lawfulness of national measures that restrict the exercise of fundamental Treaty provisions. Such rules should not, however, breach the principle of proportionality. They should ensure achievement of the aim pursued and not go beyond what is necessary for that purpose.

12.119 The ruling establishes a clear link between the rules concerning free movement of goods in Article 34 TFEU (ex Article 30 EC) and the exemptions under Article 36 TFEU (ex Article 36 EC) and *Cassis* (see **10.29**) and those governing free movement of persons in Articles 45, 49 and 56 TFEU (see **12.10**). However, there are clearly differences in the way in which the Court applies the rules in regard to the various Treaty Articles.

12.120 The *Bosman* case provoked a revolution in the world of professional football, causing an explosion in the use of foreign players. Nevertheless, generally clubs appear to have coped well with the change and the fear that it would be detrimental to young players and their training does not seem to have materialised.

12.121 In Joined Cases C–51/96 and C–191/97 *Deliège v Ligue Francophone de Judo et Disciplines Associées ASBL* (2000) Judokas needed permission from their federation to take part in an international sports competition which did not involve national teams. The Court said that participation in a high-level international competition did fall within the concept of services, even if they are not paid for by those for whom they are intended. However, the rules did not involve nationality questions or those governing access to the market (as in *Bosman*) but simply were necessary selection rules which, by their nature, did limit the number of participants. Such rules could not be regarded as constituting a restriction on the freedom to provide services. (See **Chapter 11**.) See also Case C–519/04P *Meca Medina v Commission* (2006) where the Court considered the question of whether sport is a service and whether participants in sporting events are service providers (see further **11.16**). The Court had previously decided (see *Bosman*) that Article 45 TFEU on workers' rights and Article 56 TFEU on services not only apply to the action of public authorities but also extend to rules of any other nature aimed at regulating gainful employment and the provision of services in a collective manner. However, this did not affect rules of purely sporting interest (such as the anti-doping rules concerned here) which have nothing to do with economic activity.

2.122 Case C–176/96 *Lehtonen* (2000) concerned rules establishing transfer deadlines in the Belgian basketball federation. The deadlines were different for players from within the European Union and for players from outside the European Union. The Court found that Mr Lehtonen was a worker (as in *Bosman*) and that the rules did constitute an obstacle to free movement. They might be justified by the fact that late transfers could change the sporting strength of a team and affect the competitive element in achieving a championship and, in this case, it was up to the national court to look at the rules from the perspective of proportionality.

2.123 Recently in case C–325/08 *Olympique Lyonnais SASP v Olivier Bernard, Newcastle United FC* (2010), the Court was called on to give a preliminary ruling on whether Article 45 TFEU precludes national provisions requiring a 'joueur espoir' (trainee athlete) to pay damages if he/she signs a professional contract with another club at the end of his training period, and, if so, whether such a provision might be justified by the need to encourage the recruitment and training of young professionals. The Court answered the first question in the affirmative, holding that the prospect of being sued for damages for signing elsewhere is likely to discourage the player from exercising free movement. In consideration of the second question, the Court highlighted the importance of sport and its social and educational function in the EU, stating that such a restriction may be justified as suggested, providing the restriction is proportionate and actually capable of achieving the stated objective. However, in this instance, the Court found that the damages were not calculated according to the actual training costs incurred by the training club, and therefore 'went beyond what was necessary to encourage recruitment and training' (paragraph 48). See also Cases 438/00 *Deutscher Handballbund eV v Maros Kolpak* (2003) and 265/03 *Simutenkov* (2005).

Free movement and lawyers

2.124 It will have become apparent from reading the preceding chapters that one of the areas that has been the subject of much litigation is the ability for lawyers to either provide services or establish themselves in other jurisdictions and, more specifically, the ability to have their qualifications recognised in the host state (see **12.129**). The legal profession is one in which administration of the national interest has been particularly prominent, and this is due to the complexity of the various professions that disseminate legal services, and the varying cultural and social priorities that exist in the Member States.

Lawyers wishing to practise under their own professional title in other Member States of the EU may do so in two mutually exclusive ways: they may either provide their services temporarily in another Member State, or seek to establish themselves permanently there. The 1977 Services Directive (77/249) governs the pursuit of professional activities by lawyers on a temporary basis. Lawyers can essentially provide any legal service which members of the local legal profession may legitimately provide, with the exception of probate and conveyancing. If representation of others in legal proceedings is reserved to a nominated profession in a Member State, that state may require a visiting lawyer to be accompanied by a local lawyer when appearing before its courts or tribunals.

12.125 The parameters of the Services Directive were made clear in Case 427/85 *Commission v Germany Re Lawyers' Services* (1988) where the Court held that a German directive could require a visiting lawyer to act in conjunction with a German lawyer where there is a mandatory requirement of representation, but only in defined circumstances. Exceptionally, a 'conjunction rule' can apply in all criminal proceedings, even where it is not necessary to be represented by a lawyer and the 'conjunction' arrangements are best worked out between the visiting and the host lawyers themselves. So, although there was no objection to a statute laying down a general framework, the detailed rules contained in the German implementing act were seen to be too restrictive and consequently contrary to Articles 56 (ex Article 59 EC) and 57 TFEU (ex Article 60 EC) and Directive 77/249. The Court indicated that the monopoly rights of members of specialised (but not local) Bars, such as that attached to the Supreme Court in the United Kingdom, could validly be maintained against visiting lawyers from another Member State.

12.126 The Services Directive does have limitations, and was found not applicable in Case 292/86 *Gullung v Conseils de l'Ordre des Avocats du Barreau de Colmar et de Saverne* (1988). Gullung was of French and German nationality, and a *Rechtsanwalt* in Offenburg. He was denied membership of the French Bar for reasons of character. He had previously been a *notaire* in France for 20 years, before he resigned following disciplinary measures taken against him by the relevant disciplinary body (*Chambre disciplinaire des notaires du Haut-Rhin*). He then attempted to be registered on the list of *conseils juridiques* of Marseille and to be admitted as an *avocat* to the Mulhouse Bar. Both were refused on grounds of character. Appeals were turned down on the grounds that he did not offer the safeguards of dignity, integrity and repute necessary to practise as an *avocat*. Mr Gullung tried to rely on the Lawyers' Services Directive (77/249). One of the questions before the Court was whether the scope of the Directive was subject to the requirements of public policy. The Court indicated that someone who had been barred from access to the profession for reasons relating to dignity, good repute and integrity could not rely on the Directive. The Court said that in view of this, it was unnecessary to consider the possibility of relying on the public policy concept. It ruled that a person who is a national of two Member States and who has been admitted to the legal profession in one of them, may rely upon the Directive in the other Member State. Furthermore, Article 49 TFEU (ex Article 52 EC) must be interpreted as meaning that a Member State whose legislation requires *avocats* to be registered at a Bar may impose the same requirement on *avocats* from other Member States who take advantage of the right of establishment.

.127 The Court shaped the law relating to the permanent establishment in another Member State prior to the development of a directive on establishment. The scope of Article 49 TFEU was demonstrated in Case C–107/83 *Ordre des Avocats au Barreau de Paris v Klopp*, where the Court ruled on the compatibility of a French rule whereby lawyers 'should practise in such a way as to maintain sufficient contact with their clients, the judicial authorities and abide by the rules of the profession'. Klopp was a German national, a qualified *Rechtsanwalt* and a member of the Düsseldorf Bar. In 1981 he applied to be registered as an *avocat* at the Paris Bar. He planned to set up chambers there, as well as retaining his chambers in Germany. He was refused permission by the Paris Bar Council, as their rules required *avocats* to establish chambers in one place only. The Court held that this rule imposed an unjustifiable restriction on the freedom of lawyers to establish themselves in other EU Member States. The Court said that:

> in the absence of specific Community rules in the matter, each Member State is free to regulate the exercise of the legal profession in its territory. Nevertheless that rule does not mean that the legislation of a Member State may require a lawyer to have only one establishment throughout the Union. Such a restrictive interpretation would mean that a lawyer once established in a particular Member State would be able to enjoy the freedom of the Treaty to establish himself in another Member State only at the price of abandoning the establishment he already had.

The reality of the Member State's argument would have been to prevent the many forms of multi-jurisdictional practice that are now evident across the EU and very important to the economy in the Member States.

2.128 Council Directive 98/5, commonly known as the Establishment Directive, now serves to facilitate the permanent practice of law in a Member State other than that of an individual's professional qualification, without the need to re-qualify in the 'host state'. In reality this means that a lawyer qualified in one Member State is entitled to give legal professional advice and pursue legal professional activities in another Member State using his/her home state title. In the host state, the lawyer may advise on the law of his/her home state, International Law, Union Law as well as the law of the host state. It is mandatory to register with the host bar association or law society. Lawyers will also have to observe the host profession's code of professional conduct in addition to their own professional rules. In instances of direct conflict between the two sets of rules, the host state's rules will prevail.

The legal profession, training and the mutual recognition framework

2.129 Union law also facilitates the integration of lawyers into another state's profession in two ways. First, lawyers, who have practised the law of another Member State and/or EU law for three years under their home title whilst being established in the chosen Member State, may obtain the title of the host legal profession by submitting proof of such practice to the host Bar association. The onus is on the migrant lawyer to establish to the satisfaction of the admitting authority that they have been effectively and regularly engaged in host state law and/or EU law issues for the minimum period. Second, once dually or multiply qualified, the lawyer is entitled to use both or all of his legal professional titles. Directive 2005/36 on the recognition of professional qualifications applies to those lawyers seeking recognition of professional qualifications 'for the purpose of immediate establishment under the professional title of the host Member State' (at preamble 42). Directive 2005/46 specifically refers to the continued operation of Directive 77/249 on the exercise by lawyers of the freedom to provide services, and the Lawyers Establishment Directive 98/5, so, as a consequence, all three directives operate in tandem.

12.130 The reach of Article 49 TFEU is evident from Case C–107/83 *Ordre des Avocats au Barreau de Paris v Klopp* (1984). This case concerned a German lawyer who applied to be registered as an *avocat* at the Paris Bar. However, because he intended to set up chambers in Paris, as well as retaining his chambers in Germany, his application was refused. The Paris Bar Council argued that this decision was in line with the French rule whereby lawyers 'should practise in such a way as to maintain sufficient contact with their clients, the judicial authorities and abide by the rules of the profession'. However, although the Court held that in the absence of specific Community rules on the matter, each Member State is free to regulate the exercise of the legal profession in its territory, it decided that, in this case, the rule imposed an unjustifiable restriction on the freedom of lawyers to establish themselves in other EU Member States. According to the Court, the effect of such a rule was to mean that a lawyer, once established in a particular Member State, would only be able to enjoy the freedom of the Treaty to establish himself in another Member State if he abandoned the establishment he already had. To hold otherwise would prevent the many forms of multi-jurisdictional practice that are now evident across the EU and which are very important to the economy in the Member States.

12.131 Of seminal importance in this field is Case C–55/94 *Reinhard Gebhard v Consiglio dell'ordine degli Avvocati e Procuratori di Milano* (1995). In this case, the Court acknowledged that the regulatory bodies in the Member States have rules governing the dissemination of legal activities which are often embodied in client care, confidentiality and professional ethics regulations. These rules often impose restrictions on the free movement of lawyers. However, in the interest of protecting the professions, the rule of law and the users of legal services, they are on the whole justifiable. The Court addressed a number of issues in this case, particularly elucidating on the distinction between establishment and services.

Mr Gebhard was a German national, qualified in Germany. He first joined a partnership in Milan and then established his own practice there 10 years later. Mr Gebhard did not himself practise Italian law, he assisted Italian lawyers whose clients were faced with problems of German law. Following a number of complaints by Italian practitioners the Milan Bar Council prohibited Mr Gebhard from using the title '*avvocato*' and started proceedings against him for breach of the Italian law implementing the Lawyers' Services Directive (Directive 77/249). Mr Gebhard appealed to the National Bar Council which referred questions concerning the interpretation of the Directive to the Court. The ECJ was asked to interpret Directive 77/249 and Articles 52 and 59 EC (now Articles 49 and 59 TFEU) and, in particular, was asked: (a) whether an Italian law which prohibited the establishment either of chambers or of a principal or branch office was compatible with the Directive; and (b) what were the criteria to assess whether a lawyer's activities were of a temporary nature. In answer to written questions by the court Mr Gebhard stated that although he did not have his own chambers in Germany he was a member of a *Bürogemeinschaft*—an office from which several independent lawyers practise—in Stuttgart, where he spent 20 per cent of his time in Germany.

2.132 Léger AG stated that the right of establishment and the provision of services constituted two separate branches of Union law which are dealt with by two separate chapters of the Treaty and do not overlap. He pointed out that establishment means integration into a national economy, whereas the principle of freedom to provide services merely enables a self-employed person established in a Member State in which he is integrated to exercise his activity in another Member State. He added that establishment and the provision of services are mutually *exclusive*. He therefore distinguished the rules governing the two types of activity. Services are covered by the Lawyers' Services Directive which provides for lawyers to be able to practise under their original professional qualification, whereas the establishment of lawyers was still governed by Article 49 TFEU. This would now be different with the coming into force of the Lawyers' Establishment Directive (Directive 98/5).

2.133 The conditions imposed on establishment are much stricter than those imposed on the mere provision of services. The two criteria to distinguish the two situations were: (a) the temporal criterion—services were 'episodic' or irregular; (b) the geographic criterion—an established person in a Member State is principally dealing with the market of that state where he concentrates his activity, whereas the provider of a service would only exercise his activity in that place on an ancillary basis. In Case 33/74 *van Binsbergen v Bestuur van de Bedrijfsvereniging voor de Metaalnijverheid* (1974) the Court had held that if a person provided services almost entirely in the other Member State for the purposes of avoiding the professional rules of conduct which would apply to him if he were established there:

> Such a situation may be subject to judicial control under the provisions of the chapter relating to the right of establishment and not of that on the provision of services.

The lawyer who establishes himself in a Member State must conform to local rules as long as they are not discriminatory. The Advocate General's conclusion was that the host Member State could prohibit a lawyer providing services from opening chambers in that state. This does not mean, however, that a rule absolutely prohibiting the opening of an office in the host Member State is acceptable.

The location of the lawyer's principal centre of activity and the duration and frequency of the services provided in the host Member State are appropriate criteria for establishing a clear demarcation between the activity of a lawyer which comes under the provision of services and that which comes under the heading of establishment. The Court agreed with the Advocate General that Gebhard's situation was such that he was established. It reaffirmed the right of professionals to establish a second professional base. The exercise of the right and the conditions for its exercise depended on what activities the migrant intended to pursue. It is also clear now that providers of services can maintain an office or other 'local infrastructure' as long as they can show its necessity for the provision of their service. The rule in Case 205/84 *Commission v Germany* (1986) where the Court indicated that a 'permanent presence' would of necessity indicate establishment, is thus modified. The following parts of the *Gebhard* judgment, act as a guide to the parameters, which can incidentally be taken in the wider light and applied generally to the freedom to provide services and establishment.

- the temporary nature of the provision of services is to be determined in the light of its duration, periodicity and continuity;

- the provider of services may 'equip himself with the infrastructure necessary' for the performance of the service, i.e. he may open an office;

- if someone practises on a stable and continuous basis and holds himself out from an established professional base, this is establishment;

- the possibility of establishment and the conditions for the exercise of the right must be determined in the light of the activities he intends to pursue;

- if there are no rules, the person is free to establish himself and pursue his activity in the host Member State. If there are rules and conditions, the national of another Member State should in principle comply with them;

- national measures which constitute an obstacle to the exercise of the fundamental freedoms guaranteed by the Treaty must comply with the principles of non-discrimination and proportionality; they must be justified by imperative requirements in the general interest and be suitable for securing the attainment of the objective they pursue;

- Member States must take account of the equivalence of diplomas, as had been done in Case 71/76 *Thieffry v Conseil de l'Ordre des Avocats à la Cour de Paris* (1977) and, if necessary, proceed to a comparison of the knowledge and qualifications required by their national rules and those of the person concerned.

12.134 In Case C–313/01 *Christine Morgenbesser v Consiglio dell'Ordine degli Avvocati di Genova*, the Court dismissed the notion that a traineeship could be a regulated profession and therefore neither Directive 2005/36 (at this time the mutual recognition provisions were covered by Directive 89/48) nor Directive 98/5 applied. Ms Morgenbesser was not a fully qualified professional in her home state. Morgenbesser was a French national, with a French qualifying law degree awarded in 1996. She briefly worked as a trainee lawyer in France before joining an Italian firm of *avvocati* in Genoa. Her application to the Genoa Bar for admission as a *praticante* (trainee lawyer) was rejected on the grounds that she did not have the necessary qualifications for admission, namely, a legal qualification recognised by an Italian University. The Court ruled that, although the qualifications did not need to be identical, the competent national authorities must take into consideration all the qualifications of the migrant in the assessment of his/ her whole training in order to make an objective assessment. Where there was only a partial equivalent, the host state could require the applicant to show the acquisition of knowledge, skills and qualifications that were lacking. Thus the judgment extended the right of free movement to lawyers who were still in training.

Fees

.135 Case C–289/02 *AMOK Verlags GmbH v A&R Gastronomie GmbH* (2003) concerned the reimbursement of legal costs further to proceedings before a German court, between an Austrian company (A&R) and a German company (AMOK). A&R, who won the initial case, asked for its lawyers' fees to be reimbursed by AMOK. However, it requested the reimbursement of the fees of their Austrian lawyer, in accordance with the Austrian scale, which was more expensive than the German scale. Additionally, A&R sought reimbursement of the fees of the German local lawyer with whom the Austrian lawyer worked in conjunction. The Court held that Articles 49 and 50 EC (now Articles 56 and 57 TFEU) and Directive 77/249 are to be interpreted as not precluding a judicial rule which limits the level of fees to those which would have resulted from representation by a lawyer established in Germany. Nonetheless, Article 56 TFEU and the Directive are to be construed as precluding a judicial rule which provides that the successful party to a dispute, in which that party has been represented by a lawyer established in another Member State, cannot recover from the unsuccessful party, in addition to the fees of that lawyer, the fees of a lawyer who, under the national legislation in question, was required to work in conjunction with a local lawyer. Consequently, although Member States are free to set the thresholds for costs awards, they must take into account fore-seeability of the parties, and cannot use rules to prevent recovery of costs incurred from using a local lawyer where they are compelled to do so. Therefore, A&R could claim reimbursement of the fees for the services of the German lawyer with whom the Austrian lawyer worked in conjunction, as well as the fees for the Austrian lawyer.

2.136 In Case C–309/99 *JCJ Wouters, JW Savelbergh and Price Waterhouse Belastingadviseurs BV v Algemene Raad van de Nederlandse Orde van Advocaten* (2002), the Court was asked to consider whether a regulation brought in by the Netherlands Bar was contrary to Article 85(1) EC (now Article 105(1) TFEU) which prohibited joint ventures between lawyers and other professionals, in this case, accountants. Two issues were raised. The first was whether the prohibition restricted competition by disallowing lawyers and accountants to enjoy economies of scale. The second was whether such a restriction infringed intra-Union trade in the form of freedom of establishment and the freedom to provide services. Other Member States allowed lawyers and accountants to practise as partners, and such a restraint by the Netherlands Bar might have the effect of dis-suading lawyers and accountants from other Member States from carrying on business in the Netherlands. The Netherlands Bar argued that while lawyers were subject to certain professional requirements such as client confidentiality, accountants and other such professionals were not. It argued that the restriction was necessary in order to ensure the proper practice of professional conduct of lawyers within the Netherlands. The Court, agreeing with the Netherlands Bar, found this to be an adequate justification for the restriction, regardless of the fact that such inter-professional joint ventures were recognised in other Member States.

12.137 Joined Cases C–94/04 *Federico Cipolla v Rosaria Fazari, née Portolese* and C–202/04 *Stefano Macrino and Claudia Capoparte v Roberto Meloni* (**11.56**), concerned lawyers' fees in Italy. The lawyers' clients refused to pay the legal fees on the grounds that the rates were illegal. According to them, the fees breached Italian law, which states that any agreement which derogates from the minimum and maximum fees set by the Italian scale is void. The ECJ was asked to interpret Articles 10 (now replaced in substance by Articles 4(3) TEU, and 81 and 82 EC (now Articles 101, 102 TFEU)). The Court held the prohibition of derogation (by agreement) from the minimum fees set by the Italian profession's scale was a restriction within the scope of Article 49. According to the Court, the rules in question were liable to render access to the Italian legal services more difficult for lawyers established in another Member State than for those established in Italy. This prohibition deprived such lawyers of the possibility—by requesting fees lower than the minimum set by the scale—of competing more effectively with lawyers established in Italy. With regard to the argument that the scale was justified by overriding requirements of public interest (namely the protection of the consumers receiving the legal services and the proper administration of justice) the Court left this to the national courts to decide. However, it provided some guidelines for the substantive evaluation of such an argument: (1) Is there a correlation between the level of fees and the quality of the legal services provided and is the setting of minimum fees an appropriate way of attaining the public interest objectives pursued? (2) Is there an asymmetry of information between 'client-consumers' and lawyers? (3) Could the public interest objectives be achieved by other means?

12.138 It is worthwhile to highlight here the potential impact of the Services Directive (Directive 2006/123), which entered into force in December 2009 (see **Chapter 11**). Its provisions on professional civil liability insurance, multidisciplinary partnerships, commercial communications and quality policy are likely to affect the way in which lawyers' services can be provided. Also of importance is Directive 2005/36 relating to the mutual recognition of professional qualifications. The Directive consolidated and replaced Directives 89/48 and 92/51, but, as noted in **12.81**, it is currently under review. Lawyers are covered by the part of the Directive relating to the general system for the recognition of 'evidence' in cases of establishment, which replaces the Diplomas Directive 89/48. More generally, the Commission is reviewing the impact of all free movement legislation on the legal profession, to coincide with its mandatory review of the Lawyers Establishment Directive. Following the *Wouters* case (**12.136**), it will be interesting to see the direction taken by the Court in this area. While mutual recognition of qualifications may be encouraged throughout the Union, this case in particular raises the question of whether *Cassis de Dijon*-style mandatory requirements may be employed by the Court in order to allow Member States a degree of leeway when regulating professions.

Free movement and equal treatment in education

.139 In the original Treaty of Rome there was no reference to non-vocational education. Article 128 EC (now repealed) only referred to the drawing up of general principles for vocational training. The Maastricht TEU introduced a new Title on Social Policy, Education, Vocational Training and Youth. Chapter 3 of this Title set out the provisions for education, vocational training and youth. Title XII of the TFEU sets out provisions on education, vocational training, youth and sport. Article 6 TFEU refers to Union competence in these areas, however Article 165 TFEU sets out the detailed provisions allowing the Union to exercise competence. Educational programmes had been established earlier, such as Erasmus (Dec 87/327), Commett (Dec 86/365 and 89/27), and Lingua (Dec 89/489). The European Commission, in 2006, established the Lifelong Learning Programme (2007–2013). The Programme consists of four sub-programmes: the Comenius programme for schools; the Erasmus programme for higher education; the Leonardo da Vinci programme for vocational training and education; and the Grundtvig programme for adult education. The most commonly known, the Erasmus programme on educational exchanges, was introduced on the basis of Article 128 of the 1957 Treaty of Rome (now deleted) and of Article 235 EC (now Article 352 TFEU).

.140 At the beginning, educational rights mainly arose from the connection of the recipient with a worker, the most extensive of which were enjoyed by children of workers. This is based on the understanding that, in order to achieve freedom of movement for workers and, therefore, allow them to bring their family, their children obviously must enjoy full educational rights. Educational rights for workers and for children and dependants of workers, are established by the secondary legislation. A third category of rights has been developed by the Court for students in general.

Tuition fees loans and maintenance grants

2.141 More restricted, but more widely available now, are rights of free movement for students which include rights to equal treatment and thus the right not to have to pay additional fees. In Case 152/82 *Forcheri v Belgium* (1983) the wife of a Commission official wanted to attend a non-university course in Belgium. She was required to pay an enrolment fee, a '*minerval*', which did not have to be paid by Belgian students. The Court based its arguments on Article 7 EEC (now Article 18 TFEU) read in conjunction with Article 128 EEC (now repealed) and ruled that Mrs Forcheri could not be discriminated against under the nationality rule. Case 293/83 *Gravier v Liège* (1985) concerned a French national whose parents lived in France and who came to Belgium to do a four-year course on strip cartoons. She was required to pay the '*minerval*' payable by all non-nationals. This enrolment fee was not based on residence, since, although resident non-nationals were excused the fee, no Belgian citizen, wherever resident, was required to pay it. The legal issues were: did Article 7 EEC (now Article 18 TFEU) have direct effect? The Treaty was concerned with an 'economic' Union. Does this cover education in general? The Court distinguished educational policy (what subjects are to be taught etc.), which is outside the Treaty, from questions of access to the educational system. Therefore, the general principles drawn up for vocational training under Article 128, which facilitate free movement and conditions for access to such training, fell within the scope of the Treaty. The imposition of the '*minerval*' in this context constituted discrimination on grounds of nationality.

12.142 General rights for students thus include rights in respect of tuition fees, but the right to maintenance grants will depend on the individual's status as economically active, most generally as a worker. The Citizenship Directive includes those rights previously set out in Directive 93/96 relating to students. Article 7(1)(c) of this Directive provides for a right of residence in any Member State for any Union citizen enrolled at a private or public establishment for the principal purpose of following a course of study.

12.143 In the UK, students who are British nationals are now entitled to three forms of financial support: tuition fee loans, which cover the costs of tuition fees and which are paid directly to the University in question; maintenance loans, which are paid directly to all students who request them to help cover living costs; and maintenance grants, which are means-tested and paid in addition to maintenance loans in order to cover additional living costs. In Case C–209/03 *Bidar* (2005) the Court of Justice ruled that Union citizens resident in Member States other than their own are protected by the Article 18 TFEU (ex Article 12 EC) prohibition on discrimination against nationals of other Member States in the context of applications for student assistance by means of loans or grants to cover maintenance costs.

The case followed a line of cases concerning citizenship rights of students including Case C–184–99 *Rudy Grzelczyk v Centre Public d'aide sociale d'Offignies-Louvain-La Neuve* (2001) (see **12.148**) and Case C–224/98 *D'Hoop v Office national de l'emploi* (2002), and concerned a French citizen who enrolled on a course at University College London. He applied for a student loan to finance living expenses but was rejected because he did not have his permanent residence in the United Kingdom. Bidar claimed that this was discrimination because of his nationality. The Court agreed. It stated that such requirements risk placing nationals of other Member States at a disadvantage. Such a difference in treatment could be justified only if it was based on objective considerations, independent of the nationality of the persons concerned, and was proportionate to the legitimate aim of the national provisions. It was permissible for a Member State to ensure that a grant to cover maintenance for students from other Member States did not become an unreasonable burden (paragraph 56) and it was, therefore, legitimate to grant such assistance only to students who had demonstrated a certain degree of integration into the society of that state (paragraph 57). The Court ruled as follows:

> The first paragraph of [Article 18 TFEU] must be interpreted as precluding national legislation which grants students the right to assistance covering their maintenance costs only if they are settled in the host Member State, while precluding a national from another Member State from obtaining the status of settled person as a student even if that national is lawfully

resident and has received a substantial part of his education in the host Member State and has consequently established a genuine link with the society of that state. [paragraph 63]

Finally, the Court refused to limit the temporal effects of the judgment. This case did not apply to EU nationals who come to the United Kingdom to study at a university after having had their initial schooling in another Member State. These individuals were entitled only to tuition grants, but not to maintenance. Nevertheless, those citizens who can demonstrate their integration into the host state are entitled to equal treatment in terms of access to support for their studies in terms of student loans. Note that, from 2012, universities in England and Wales will be allowed to increase the cost of tuition fees by almost three times the previous amount. This tuition fee increase was introduced by the British Government in December 2010, but has been criticised for the obvious impact it will have on the number of foreign students coming from other EU Member States to study at English and Welsh universities. Scottish universities charge no tuition fees to Scottish or EU students.

.144 However, in Case C–158/07 *Förster v Hoofddirectie van de Informatie Beheer Groep* (2008) the Court accepted a Member State can specify a time period during which Union citizens studying in a Member State other than their own should reside in that State before being considered as fully integrated. Ms Förster, a German national, settled in the Netherlands where she enrolled for training as a primary school teacher and for a course in educational theory learning throughout which she worked. She applied for a maintenance grant which she was granted by the IB-Groep. The IB-Groep took the view that Ms Förster was to be regarded as a 'worker' within the meaning of Article 45 TFEU (then Article 39 EC), and consequently should be treated in the same way as a student of Dutch nationality as regards maintenance grants under Article 7(2) of Regulation 1612/68. However, when the IB-Groep discovered that Ms Förster had not been working for part of 2003 (therefore could not be regarded as a worker) they made a claim for the repayment of the maintenance grant for that period.

The Court was asked whether, and in what conditions, a student who is a national of a Member State, and travels to another Member State in order to study there, can rely on the first paragraph of Article 18 TFEU in order to obtain a maintenance grant. It was also asked whether the application to nationals of other Member States of a prior residence requirement of five years may be regarded as compatible with the first paragraph of Article 18 TFEU. If so, is it necessary, in individual cases, to take into account other criteria pointing to a substantial degree of integration into the society of the host Member State.

The Court held that Ms Förster could rely on Article 18 to obtain a maintenance grant provided that she had resided for a certain duration in the host Member State. It also held that the first paragraph of Article 18 does not preclude the application to nationals of other Member States of a requirement of five years' prior residence, as this is designed to ensure that students from other Member States are integrated into the host Member State.

12.145 Case C–73/08 *Nicholas Bressol and Others and Céline Chaverot and Others v Gouvernement de la Communauté française* (2010) concerned higher education and admission policies in Belgium. A national Decree included a residence requirement as one of the eligibility criteria for admission to certain programmes for the first two years of undergraduate studies that were financed primarily out of public funds. The residence requirement was based on the fact that the region in question had received a large influx of students from a neighbouring state that had recently implemented restrictive policies in their education system. This influx was said to have placed an excessive burden on public finances and to have placed the quality of education at risk. The Court disagreed and stated that the residence requirement constituted indirect discrimination on the grounds of nationality. However, such a restriction could be justified if the basis for the residence requirement was to secure a high level of health protection. The national court must assess whether the Decree went beyond what was necessary to meet the objective and whether it could be met by less restrictive means.

Vocational training

12.146 Vocational training is considered by the Court to be any form of education which prepares for a particular profession or trade. Case 24/86 *Blaizot v University of Liège* (1988) extended the concept further. Blaizot and the other plaintiffs were all French veterinary students who had paid the '*minerval*' in Belgium. The Court considered that veterinary studies fell within the meaning of the term 'vocational training' even though they were pursued at a university. Neither the provisions of the Treaty nor its objectives gave any indication that the term should be restricted so as to exclude all university education. There were significant variations across the Member States in the availability of different studies and the way they are treated. An exclusion of university education from the definition of the term 'vocational training' would thus result in unequal application of the Treaty in different Member States. University courses which prepare for a career rather than just increase general knowledge were covered, even if the acquisition of that knowledge is not required by law, regulation or administrative provision. The second part of the veterinary course was vocational, the first part was not, but as, according to the Court, access to the second part presupposed the successful conclusion of the first, they must be considered as a whole. However, the Court refused to allow retrospective application of the judgment.

Right of residence derived from education

12.147 The right to education can itself result in derived rights. In Case C–408/08 *Teixeria* (2010) and Case C–310/08 *Ibrahim* (2010) the Court of Justice ruled that the children of a Union citizen who works or has worked in the host Member State have independent rights of residence in the host state. Moreover, the parent caring for them, if that person does not otherwise have an entitlement to remain in that state, can continue to live there while the children remain in education without having to demonstrate sufficient resources not to be a burden on that state's social security systems. The children's rights to continue their education in the state, and to have a parent present as carer, arise from Article 12 of Regulation 1612/68. Ms Teixeira, a Portuguese national, who had previously worked in the United Kingdom, but was not currently in work, applied for housing assistance for homeless persons but was refused on the basis she was not legally resident in the United Kingdom. Ms Teixeira accepted that she had no right of residence in the United Kingdom under Article 7(1) of Citizenship Directive 2004/38 in that she did not satisfy the conditions of being a worker or being self-sufficient. However, she successfully claimed a right of residence in the United Kingdom on the grounds that her daughter was in education there. In *Ibrahim*, a Somali national, previously married to a Danish national, applied for housing assistance in the United Kingdom as the carer of her four children who held Danish nationality and were in school in the United Kingdom. The Court of Justice maintained that the right of residence in the host Member State of the parent who is the primary carer of a child exercising the right to pursue his/her education in accordance with Article 12 of Regulation 1612/68 is not conditional on that parent having the status of migrant worker, or having sufficient resources for support and comprehensive sickness cover. It also held that the right of residence in the host Member State of the parent who is the primary carer for a child of a migrant worker, where that child is in education in that state, ends when the child reaches the age of majority, unless the child continues to need the presence and care of that parent in order to be able to pursue and complete his/her education.

2.148 It therefore seems to be clear that, although students can claim certain advantages, these advantages are not as extensive as those which are available for workers. However, this statement may be contrasted with the Court's decision in Case C–184/99 *Rudy Grzelczyk v Centre public d'aide sociale d'Ottignies-Louvain-la-Neuve* (2001), which centred on education rights on the basis of EU citizenship alone. *Grzelczyk* concerned a French national who was studying in Belgium and had obtained entitlement to the '*minimex*' (a minimum subsistence allowance paid by the Belgian state). Payment of that allowance to him was stopped because, under Belgian legislation, this grant was only paid to those nationals of other Member states who came within the scope of Regulation 1612/68. This condition, however, did not apply to Belgian nationals and the Belgian tribunal therefore asked the Court whether Articles 18 and 21 TFEU (ex Articles 12 and 18 EC), relating to the principles of non-discrimination and of citizenship of the Union respectively, precluded such disparity in treatment. The Court found first of all that the treatment accorded to Mr Grzelczyk constituted discrimination solely on the ground of nationality because the only bar to grant of the *minimex* was that he was not a Belgian national. The Court then continued as follows:

> Within the sphere of application of the Treaty, such discrimination is, in principle, prohibited by Article 12 EC. In the present case, Article 12 EC must be read in conjunction with the provisions of the Treaty concerning citizenship of the Union in order to determine its sphere of application....[paragraph 30].

Restrictions to free movement of persons after accession of new Member States in 2004 and 2007

12.149 The Treaty of Accession for the 10 new Member States which came into force on 1 May 2004 contained provisions for the temporary limitation of free movement of persons, and, in particular, workers, by way of derogation from Regulation 1612/68, during a transitional period. This was commonly referred to as the '2+3+2' year arrangement, designed progressively to reduce the older Member States' power to adopt restrictive measures. These provisions mainly applied to the eight states of Central and Eastern Europe, as there was a widespread view that there would be a particularly important migration flow from those countries to the 'old' Member States, and not to Cyprus and Malta, as the situation in those two states is quite different. Similar, albeit stricter, limitations were imposed upon Bulgaria and Romania upon their accession on 1 January 2007. The United Kingdom, which had imposed few restrictions in 2004, did impose such restrictions in 2007. It had been the case with other accessions, for example those of Spain and Portugal, that the fears of mass-migration were not necessarily always borne out. The expected volume of migration this time was, however, severely underestimated, particularly in the case of the United Kingdom, but also elsewhere in the European Union. Although the labour market, particularly in the United Kingdom, benefited greatly from an influx of skilled labour, willing to work at low wages, into an expanding labour market, problems have arisen in respect of housing, health, schooling and so on. Nevertheless, the Accession Treaties contain a detailed schedule of transitional measures. The Member States were free to decide whether to derogate from the free movement principles, subject to two limitations:

(a) a standstill clause: more restrictive measures could not be applied later; and

(b) Member States must give preference to workers who are of the nationality of the new Member States over third country workers.

12.150 As the Accession Treaties do not refer to association agreements (such as the 'Europe agreements' concluded with a view to accession) a situation could arise where a family member is treated less favourably after accession than before. The transitional measures are due to end five years after accession. In cases where there is serious disturbance of a state's labour market 'or threat thereof and after notifying the Commission', a Member State may continue to apply the measures for another two years. Furthermore, any Member State may at any time ('in case of serious disturbances of the labour market') apply to the Commission for a suspension of the application of Articles 1–6 of Regulation 1612/68. For example, in August 2011, the Commission authorised Spain to suspend the application of Articles 1–6 of Regulation 1612/68 with regard to Romanian workers. The Treaties of Accession also contain a reciprocity clause, so that new Member States are allowed 'to maintain in force equivalent measures' with regard to nationals of other Member States. All restrictions on the 2004 entrants ended on 30 April 2011, and most Member States have lifted them wholly, partially or are on the way to doing so. For Bulgaria and Romania the end date is 31 December 2013. Similar restrictions will apply to Croatia which, in December 2011, signed a Treaty of Accession to the European Union. The country will become the 28th Member State in July 2013.

FURTHER READING

Adinolfi, A., 'Free movement and access to work of citizens of the new Member States: the transitional measures' (2005) 42 *Common Market Law Review* 469.

Commission Green Paper on Modernising the Professional Qualifications Directive, (COM/2011/0367 final).

Communication from the Commission to the European Parliament, the Council, the European Economic and Social Committee and the Committee of the Regions on the impact of free movement of workers in the context of EU enlargement reports on the first phase (1 January 2007–31 December 2008) (COM/2008/0765 final).

Ellis, E., 'Social advantages: a new lease of life' (2003) 40 *Common Market Law Review* 639.

Kostakopoulou, T., 'European Union citizenship: writing the future', (2007) 13(5) *European Law Journal* 623.

Lee, R.G., 'Liberalisation of legal service in Europe: progress and prospects' (2010) 30(2) *Legal Studies* 186–207.

Lonbay, J., 'The regulation of legal practice in the UK and beyond' in Bridge (ed.), *UK Law for the Millennium* (2nd edn, London: BIICL, 2000) 594.

Moore, M., 'Freedom of movement and migrant workers' social security: an overview of the Court's jurisprudence 1992–1997' (1998) 35 *Common Market Law Review* 409.

O'Keeffe, D., 'Judicial interpretation of the public service exception to the Free Movement of workers' in Curtin and O'Keeffe (eds), *Constitutional Adjudication in European Community and National Law* (Ireland: Butterworths, 1992) 89.

O'Keeffe, D., 'Equal rights for migrants: the concept of social advantages in Article 7(2) Regulation 1612/68' (1985) *Yearbook of European Law* 93.

Shaw, J., Hunt J. and Wallace, C., *The Economic and Social Law of the European Union* (Palgrave, 2007).

Treaties of Accession [2003] OJ L236 and [2005] OJ L157.

Weatherill, S., 'Bosman changed everything: the rise of EC sports law' in Azoulai, L. and Maduro, M.P., (eds), *The Past and Future of EU Law: The Classics of EU Law Revisited on the 50th Anniversary of the Rome Treaty* (Oxford: Hart Publishing, 2010).

White, R., *Workers, Establishment and Services in the European Union* (Oxford: OUP, 2004).

SELF-TEST QUESTIONS

1 How does an individual qualify as a 'worker'?

2 What rights and social advantages do workers enjoy? Are the rights enjoyed by their families equally extensive?

3   Why are directives needed if Articles 45 and 49 TFEU have been held to have direct effect by the European Court of Justice?

4   How otherwise than through economic activity as a worker can a Union citizen living in a Member State other than his or her own demonstrate integration into the host state? Is it only when a citizen is economically active that full protection from discrimination arises from the Treaty?

5   Should the same criteria be applied to the free movement of persons and to the free movement of goods in respect of restrictions?

13 Citizenship and free movement rights: beyond economic links

SUMMARY

- Introduction
  - Charter of Fundamental Rights
  - The European Convention on Human Rights
  - The Citizenship Directive
  - Equal treatment and direct effect
- Facets of citizenship
  - Citizenship v free movement rights
  - Who is a citizen?
  - The right to move and reside freely
  - Spouses and partners
  - Primary carers
  - Right to education
  - Citizenship and names
- European Citizens' Initiative
- Problems with citizenship
  - Reverse discrimination
  - Third country nationals

Introduction

13.1 Although the concept of citizenship of the European Union is not a new idea, it was not until 1993 that it was represented in the Treaties. While there is a separate chapter devoted to citizenship rights in the Treaty on the Functioning of the European Union (Part Two, Articles 18–25 TFEU, ex Articles 12–22 EC) it must be noted that the Union is not a nation state, cannot confer nationality, and cannot, therefore, subsume the role played by Member States. Indeed, citizenship of the European Union is dependent upon nationality of a Member State. Union citizenship, on the other hand, is a different concept.

13.2 Concrete steps were first taken towards the establishment of a European citizenship at the Paris Summit in 1974, during which a working group was established in order to study the conditions under which 'citizens of the Member States could be given special rights as members of the [Union]'. Subsequently, the Tindemans Report advocated the grant of certain civil and political rights to nationals of Member States, including the right to vote and stand for public office. In addition, reports such as the European Parliament's Scelba Report, and the Addonino Reports on 'A People's Europe' discussed rights of citizens. However, although the term 'citizenship' was much used, it was seldom defined. The importance of the free movement of citizens for the enhancement of the Union's economic development was recognised early, and the Commission's guidelines for a Union Policy on Migration suggested that freedom of movement for citizens should go beyond that extended to workers for the purposes of employment. The first traceable reference, in the European context, to the concept of citizenship is to be found in a letter of the Prime Minister of Spain to the President in Office of the Council, prior to the Dublin summit in June 1990. The summit endorsed Spain's proposal and submitted to the Council for consideration the following question:

> How will the Union include and extend the notion of [Union] citizenship carrying with it specific rights (human, political, social, the right of complete free movement and residence etc) for the citizens of the Member States by virtue of these States belonging to the Union?

The Spanish Government further submitted a Memorandum on European Citizenship, designed to address the problem of Member State nationals being treated as no more than 'privileged foreigners'. The proposals included the granting to all Union citizens the rights to full freedom of movement and residence: incorporating political participation in the host Member State; specific rights in the areas of health, social affairs, education, culture, the environment and consumer protection; rights to assistance and diplomatic protection by other Member States; rights to petition the European Parliament; and other rights to be agreed in the future. The Commission Opinion of 21 October 1990 made clear its agreement with Spain's proposals, stating that it saw the creation of Union citizenship as a way of strengthening democracy. This was seconded by the Danish Government's proposal of the right of Union nationals to vote in local elections in the Member State in which they were resident.

13.3 The issue of the protection of citizens' rights eventually resulted in the creation of the European Ombudsman's Office. While the Council did not consider human rights to be part of the provisions on citizenship, the Commission and Parliament argued both for the inherent inclusion of fundamental rights within the Treaty to be invoked by citizens, and the need for the Union to accede to the European Convention on Human Rights. The citizenship provisions that were finally approved were then included in the Maastricht Treaty (in Articles 8, 8a–8e EC, now Part II, Articles 18–25 TFEU).

13.4 At the time, the preamble to the TEU set out that the High Contracting Parties 'resolved to establish a citizenship common to the nationals of their countries'. This was followed up in Article B of the Common Provisions, which included as one of the objectives of the Union, strengthening 'the protection of the rights and interests of the nationals of its Member States through the introduction of a citizenship of the Union'. The fact that provisions on citizenship are contained in a separate part of the Treaty was interpreted by some commentators at the time as significant, indicating the relative importance of the measures and their implementation.

13.5 In the Maastricht Treaty, the original citizenship provisions set out in Article 8 EC, stated that 'Citizens of the Union shall enjoy the rights conferred by this Treaty and shall be subject to the duties imposed thereby'. The Treaty of Amsterdam, at the behest of Denmark, qualified this in the subsequent sentence so as to avoid misunderstanding by adding that 'Citizenship of the Union shall complement and not replace national citizenship'. While this latter clause has been included within the provisions of the TFEU, the reference to duties imposed upon persons by reason of their citizenship of the Union has been removed. Article 9 of the TEU states that

> *... the Union shall observe the principle of the equality of its citizens*

and adds

> *Every national of a Member State shall be a citizen of the Union. Citizenship of the Union shall be additional to national citizenship and shall not replace it.*

Part Two of the TFEU, entitled 'Non-Discrimination and Citizenship of the Union', gives a definition of citizenship and sets out the rights protected (Article 20 TFEU).

13.6 Other hallmarks of citizenship are laid down in the Treaties such as: the right to diplomatic or consular protection by authorities of any Member State on the same conditions as the nationals of that Member State (Article 23 TFEU); and the right to petition the European Parliament, to apply to the European Ombudsman and to write to any of the institutions, bodies, offices or agencies in any of the official European languages and receive an answer in that language (Article 24 TFEU).

Charter of Fundamental Rights

13.7 The Charter was drawn up by a study group, set up at the Cologne summit in 1999 with the intention of cataloguing the various fundamental rights spread around the EU Treaties, the case law of the Court of Justice, the European Convention on Human Rights and the Declaration on Fundamental Rights of the European Parliament 1989. As such, the aim of the Charter was not only to collect together existing rights, but also to codify new rights. For an example see Article 3 of the Charter, which prohibits the use of eugenics, the use of body parts for financial gain and cloning. It sets out a list of rights to be upheld within the Union, categorising them under the subheadings of Dignity, Freedoms, Equality, Solidarity, Citizens' Rights, Justice, and General Provisions of Interpretation and Application. Article 6(1) TEU states that 'the Union recognises the rights, freedoms and principles set out in the Charter of Fundamental Rights of the European Union of 7th December 2000 ... which shall have the same legal value as the Treaties'. Article 6(2) TEU goes on to say that the 'provisions of the Charter shall not extend in any way the competences of the Union as defined in the Treaties'.

Yet, despite this latter provision, the United Kingdom, the Czech Republic and Poland still thought it prudent to repeat the statement on the definition of competence in an additional Protocol to the Treaties.

13.8   Rights additional to those set out in the Treaties can also be found under the fifth subheading on citizens' rights. Article 41 provides for the 'Right to Good Administration'. This appears to mirror other provisions of the Charter falling mainly under the subheading of Justice, but entails the right to have one's affairs handled 'impartially, fairly and within a reasonable time by the institutions, bodies, offices and agencies of the Union'. Article 42 provides for the right of access to documents of institutions of the Union. Finally, Article 45 sets out the rights of freedom of movement and residence. Paragraph (2) of this Article is of particular interest. It deals with the granting of residence rights to nationals of third countries legally resident in the territory of a Member State.

13.9   As will be seen below (**13.57**), this freedom of movement has been implemented in what is known as the Long-Term Residents Directive (Council Directive 2003/109 of 25 November 2003 concerning the status of third country nationals who are long-term residents).

13.10   The Charter now has primary legal status within the Union, although for the rights to be actionable a Union element must still be invoked. Of interest is the promise, set out in Article 6(2) TEU of Union accession to the European Convention on Human Rights. Negotiations, in particular between the CJEU and the ECtHR, have been taking place since early 2010 and, while undoubtedly a complex process, accession would have the effect of making the body of Union law subject to Convention rights, and of making the ECtHR the court of final appeal in the Union. However, even though the Court of Justice currently accounts for Convention rights in its reasoning, and even though the ECtHR has equally taken Union case law into consideration in its reasoning, (see *Bosphorus*, discussed at **6.60** and **8.56**), it remains to be seen whether a dual system of rights protection will result from accession.

The European Convention on Human Rights

13.11   The European Convention on Human Rights (ECHR) and its interpretation and enforcement mechanism, the European Court of Human Rights are under the auspices of the Council of Europe, and therefore institutionally and constitutionally separate from the European Union. However as noted, ECtHR case law has generally paralleled that of the Court of Justice and has increasingly been seen as a point of reference by the latter.

13.12   Because the ECHR required transposition into national law in order to become fully justiciable within that state, the resulting legislation incorporated into national laws the rights set out in the original Convention. As such, the application of the rights therein depend on the willingness of the Member States to transpose the ECHR. The ECHR sets out a list of rights, including the right to life (Article 2), the right to liberty and security (Article 5), the right to respect for private and family life (Article 8), freedom of thought, conscience and religion (Article 9), freedom of expression (Article 10), freedom of assembly and association (Article 11) and the prohibition of discrimination (Article 14).

The Citizenship Directive

3.13 Directive 2004/38, the 'Citizenship' Directive, sets out the rights of freedom of movement, both extensively in the Preamble, and in Chapter III of the body of the Directive. This Directive applies to all EU citizens and their families. However, the pre-existing differences between the rights of the economically active and the non-economically active have been incorporated into the Directive and will continue to apply, but only for the first five years of residence. After that time a citizen and his or her family will acquire an unconditional right to live permanently in the host state on equal terms with the nationals of that state.

3.14 In all cases, Member States can refuse entry or terminate the right to reside on grounds of public policy, public security and public health in a manner similar to that discussed in **Chapter 12**. The provisions of Directive 2004/38 are discussed in this chapter with an explanation of the changes they introduce to existing law. The Directive replaces the previous 'piecemeal' approach to rules on free movement with a single Directive applicable to all EU citizens and their families. However, due to the preservation of distinctions between the economically active and non-economically active, it remains important to understand existing case law in relation to the two separate categories.

13.15 Directive 2004/38 repeals and replaces the following Directives:

- Council Directive 68/360 on rights of entry and residence for workers and their families

- Council Directive 74/148 in relation to establishment and service-providers

- Council Directive 90/364 on the general right of residence

- Council Directive 90/365 on residence rights of retired persons

- Council Directive 93/96 on residence rights of students

- Council Directive 64/221 on the refusal of entry or residence on the grounds of public policy, public security and public health.

Directive 2004/38 also replaces Articles 10 and 11 of Council Regulation 1612/68 on rights of family members of workers.

Equal treatment and direct effect

13.16 As is the case regarding the free movement of services, workers and establishment, the principle of equal treatment fundamentally underpins the concept and reasoning of EU citizenship. The general right of equality is discussed in detail in **Chapter 6**, however it suffices here to note that the principle of equal treatment is set out in Article 19 TFEU and Articles 2 and 9 TEU, the latter of which expressly states 'the Union shall observe the principle of the equality of its citizens'. Furthermore, Articles 20 and 21 of the Charter of Fundamental Rights, and Article 24 of Directive 2004/38, also set out the principle.

13.17 Moreover, *Baumbast* (**12.45**) established that the provisions of the Treaty granting citizens the right to move and reside freely are capable of having direct effect, similar to the provisions on workers, services and establishment.

Facets of citizenship

13.18 Directive 2004/38 establishes citizenship of the EU as the 'fundamental status' of those exercising their right of free movement (Preamble, paragraph 3). This approach is founded on the status of citizenship (Articles 20–21 TFEU, ex Articles 17–18 EC) and the principle of non-discrimination (Article 18 TFEU, ex Article 12 EC).

Citizenship v free movement rights

13.19 The distinction between citizenship rights and those covered by the other free movement provisions was discussed in Case C–318/05 *Commission v Germany* (2007), where the Court stated that Article 18 EC (now Article 21 TFEU) rights are supplementary to the economic free movement rights contained in Articles 39, 43 and 49 EC (now 45, 49 and 56 TFEU), and that the latter are to be determined in priority to citizenship rights. This was echoed in the discussion in Case C–522/04 *Commission v Belgium* (2004), where the Court found Belgium to be in breach of its obligations under Article 18 EC (now Article 21 TFEU), even though the discussion throughout the case related to the freedom to provide services.

13.20 The case of Mr Vitale in *R v Secretary of State for the Home Department, ex p Vittorio Vitale and Do Amaral* (1996) was one of the first cases which explored citizenship just after the entry into force of the Maastricht Treaty containing the Citizenship articles. Mr Vitale, an Italian citizen, was a reluctant jobseeker who found no work, as he was looking for part-time work only in a very limited area of London and only between 10.00 am and 4.00 pm as a part-time chef or guitar player. He challenged the decision by the Home Office withdrawing his benefit and asking him to leave.

The Court of Appeal considered the question of the possible direct effect of Article 8a (now Article 18 EC), but came to the conclusion that there was none. The court was asked to refer the question to the ECJ. Although the *CILFIT* rules (Case 283/81 *CILFIT v Ministry of Health* (1982); see **4.41**) permitted the court to refer the matter even if the case was clear, it declined to do so and instead dismissed the appeal. Even at the time, there seemed to be good arguments for reference. This was later confirmed when the Court found Article 18 to have direct effect in *Baumbast* (see **13.17** and **13.40** below). It must be remembered, however, that the Court of Appeal's analysis of Article 8a (now Article 18 EC) was supported by the view of the Commission and of most academic writers. Although Mr Vitale was informed by the Home Office that he should make arrangements to leave the United Kingdom, it was also made clear that there was no intention to deport him.

The arguments in the cases highlighted the growing awareness in the English courts of the increasing contrast between the EC as an 'economic' entity, and the political and constitutional developments represented by the EU. The Court of Appeal emphasised, however, that it was the responsibility of UK Parliament, not the court, to determine the consistency of EU developments with the national interests of the UK.

3.21   The Court took a similarly restrictive view in Case C–192/99 *R v Secretary of State for the Home Department, ex p Kaur* (2001), which involved an interpretation of the concept of 'nationals' in the UK Treaty of Accession 1972. The Court ruled that a state Declaration on the definition of 'nationals' did not have the effect of depriving people who did not satisfy the definition of any rights under Community law from the benefits of EU citizenship. Rather, such failure prevented EU citizen rights from arising in the first place (paragraph 25 of the judgment). It is an indication of how far the Court has moved in matters of citizenship. See also the judgment in Case C–148/02 *Garcia Avello* (see **13.45**).

13.22   Case C–274/96 *Bickel and Franz* (1998), although mainly concerned with the application of Article 6 EC (now Article 18 TFEU), mentioned Article 18 EC (now Article 21 TFEU) without discussing the issue further. The question referred was whether it was compatible with Community law to refuse to allow the application of rules on the equal use of German with Italian, in particular in criminal proceedings involving German-speaking Community nationals travelling and staying in Bolzano. The Court replied that Article 6 (now Article 18 TFEU) of the Treaty precludes any such refusal, since it would constitute, at least, indirect discrimination on the grounds of nationality against recipients or potential recipients of services (see Case 186/87 *Cowan v Trésor Public* (1989) at **11.20**).

13.23   In Case C–378/97 *Criminal Proceedings against Wijsenbeek* (1999) criminal proceedings had been instituted against Mr Wijsenbeek, a Dutch MEP, who had refused to show his passport and establish his nationality when requested to do so upon re-entering the Netherlands. The Court referred the question of whether Articles 7a and 8a EC (now Articles 26 and 21 TFEU) had direct effect. The Court of Justice did not answer, but simply stated that:

> even if, under Article 7a or 8a of the Treaty, nationals have the unconditional right to move freely within the territory of the member states, the member states retain the right to carry out identity checks at the internal frontiers of the Community …

Penalties could be imposed as long as they were proportionate and comparable to those imposed for similar domestic offences.

13.24   Case C–520/04 *Pirkko Marjatta Turpeinen* (2006), referred by the Finnish Supreme Court, concerned questions of residence and citizenship more directly. Mrs Turpeinen, a Finnish national who had retired to Spain, claimed that she should be taxed progressively on her pension, as would have been the case were she resident in Finland. Instead, she paid a fixed rate of tax far exceeding the level under progressive taxation, due to her Spanish residence. While pointing out that direct taxation remained within the competence of Member States, the Court stated that such competence must be exercised so as to comply with Community law. Having found that the case did not fall under Article 39 EC (now Article 45 TFEU) due to the appellant's retired status, the Court turned to Article 18 EC (now Article 21 TFEU). The Court held that national legislation which places at a disadvantage citizens who have exercised free movement runs counter to the principle of equality that underpinned the development of Union Citizenship, and that where the pension constituted all or most of the appellant's income, legislation leading to unequal taxation based on residence was unlawful.

13.25   The question of residence was raised once again in a preliminary reference in Case C–192/05 *TasHagen v R.A. Tas* (2009) where the applicants, who had an entitlement to a Dutch war pension, were denied this because they lived in Spain. The Court found that the requirement of residence in the country where the pension originated was in breach of Article 18(1) EC (now Article 21(1) TFEU).

13.26   This case should be contrasted with Case C–406/04 *De Cuyper v Office national de l'emploi* (2006) (see **12.30**). This case concerned a residence requirement for access to unemployment benefit when the applicant did not have to show availability for work because of her age. Furthermore, Article 10 of Regulation 1408/71 did not include access to unemployment benefit to be made available to nationals resident in other Member States. However, a residence requirement would limit the right of Union citizens to move and reside freely within the Union and could only be justified by reference to 'objective considerations of public interest independent of the nationality of the persons concerned, and proportionate to the legitimate objective of the national provisions'. Belgium imposed the requirements in order for the state to closely monitor the applicant's situation. This was deemed reasonable by the Court.

Who is a citizen?

13.27   As noted in **13.1**, to be a citizen of the European Union, it is necessary to hold the nationality of a Member State. This can be resolved by recourse to the laws of that Member State alone. The EU cannot grant, or remove, nationality and, therefore, cannot grant or remove citizenship of the Union. This was laid down by a Declaration on nationality of a Member State which was attached to the TEU at Maastricht. It is the exclusive competence of Member States to determine who can and cannot access rights as a citizen of the Union and this position was upheld by the Court of Justice in Case C–369/90 *Micheletti* (1992). The Court found that the conditions governing the acquisition and loss of nationality were matters which, under international law, fell within the exclusive competence of the Member State concerned.

13.28   The Court has stressed that when exercising competence with regard to the acquisition and loss of nationality, Member States must have due regard to EU law. Case 135/08 *Janko Rottmann v Freistaat Bayern* concerned Dr Rottmann, an Austrian national by birth, who moved to Germany in 1995. Prior to his move he was being investigated by Austrian authorities under suspicion of having committed a serious fraud. In 1997 Austrian authorities issued a warrant for his arrest; however, the following year Dr Rottmann applied to become a German national. During his application he made no mention of the proceedings against him, and he became a national of Germany in 1999, thus losing his Austrian nationality under Austrian law. When the proceedings against Rottmann came to light in Germany, the German authorities withdrew his naturalisation retroactively on the grounds that he had obtained it by deception. He was therefore left without a nationality. Rottmann challenged the decision before a German court, which referred questions to the Court of Justice for a preliminary ruling.

3.29 Since Rottmann was effectively stateless, the question at issue was whether Rottmann consequently also lost Union citizenship and its associated fundamental freedoms. The Court of Justice ruled that there was no breach of Union law arising when Member State authorities withdrew nationality from an individual who had obtained that nationality by deception, so long as the principle of proportionality was respected. This meant that EU law (in particular by reference to Article 20 TFEU) does not prevent the loss of Union citizenship as a result of the revocation of nationality by one Member State and does not require an individual's original nationality to resume automatically. The decision on whether the stateless Dr Rottmann could re-acquire Austrian nationality remained a question for Austrian authorities, although the process whereby this decision was made would be subject to Union law principles.

The right to move and reside freely

13.30 Article 21 TFEU (ex Article 18 EC) sets out the right of all citizens to move and reside freely within the territory of the Union.

13.31 The rest of the Article sets out powers pertaining to the Parliament and Council under both the ordinary legislative procedures (Article 21(2)), and the special legislative procedure (Article 21(3)), although this latter applies only to measures concerning social security or social protection (see **Chapter 3**). In earlier versions of this Article, powers of the Parliament and Council to give effect to the provision in Article 21(1) TFEU were not to 'apply to provisions on passports, identity cards, residence permits or any other such document or to provisions on social security or social protection'. Case law of the Court since the insertion of this provision at Nice 2002 required its removal and the insertion of Article 21(3) TFEU. Relevant case law on the necessity of residence permits and visas is discussed in **Chapter 12**, see **12.21**.

Article 21 functions in tandem with Article 45 TFEU on the free movement of workers. It simply extends the freedom of movement to the non-economically active. However, limitations still remain on the provision of social security.

13.32 Case C–85/96 *Martinez Sala* (1998) was the first case in which the Court of Justice deliberated on the scope and rationale of citizenship of the Union. Here, a Spanish national residing in Germany with only a certificate stating that she had applied for a residence permit, contested the refusal of social security as discriminatory under Article 12 EC (now Article 18 TFEU). However, Germany argued that since the appellant was neither a worker nor a jobseeker, and was therefore not *ratione personae* under the Treaty, she could not rely on Article 12. The Court, by contrast, held that as a national of a Member State lawfully residing in another Member State, the appellant came within the scope *ratione personae* of the Treaty provisions on EU citizenship, in particular Article 17(2) (now Article 20(2) TFEU). She was therefore entitled to social security.

13.33   In Case C–162/09 *Taous Lassal* (2010), the Court considered whether the right of permanent residence derived from Article 16 of the Citizenship Directive could be applied to an applicant who completed her five years' residence before the Directive's transposition date. The applicant in this case was a French national who had lived and worked in the UK for over five years. She had returned to France for 10 months before returning to the UK and attempting to collect income support which she was refused on the grounds that she had no right to reside in the UK. In holding that the applicant should indeed be granted a right of permanent residence, the Court relied on the aim and purpose of the Citizenship Directive, i.e., to 'facilitate the exercise of the primary and individual right to move and reside freely' (paragraph 30). Moreover, it noted the important role of permanent residency as a means of 'promoting social cohesion' and strengthening Union citizenship (paragraph 32). The Court did not consider that temporary absences after five years, even prior to the date of transposition, should have any effect on a citizen's right to permanent residence under the Directive. According to the Court, an absence of less than two consecutive years in that time would not negate the right granted in Article 16.

Spouses and partners

13.34   The Citizenship Directive also applies to family members of Union citizens but only if they 'move or reside in a Member State other than their own' (Article 3(1)). Therefore, the rights of EU nationals and their family members under free movement law are only activated once they have exercised the right of free movement. This would still exclude the case of *Morson* (Case 35, 36/82 *Morson and Jhanjan v Netherlands* (1982), see **12.108**) which involved a wholly internal situation and was therefore outside the scope of EU law.

13.35   Article 2(2) defines family members covered by the Directive. For example, spouses are included under Article 2(2)(a). The concept of 'spouse', as provided under Regulation 1612/68, was generally interpreted by the Court of Justice to mean a husband or wife and not a cohabiting partner. However, in Case 59/85 *Netherlands v Reed* (1986), Ms Reed, who was not married to her partner, contested the denial of her right of residence in the Netherlands. The Court said that, although the term 'spouse' could only refer to a married person, the Dutch treated an unmarried companion in a stable relationship as a spouse. Consequently, the Court deemed her a 'social advantage' under Article 7(2) of Regulation 1612/68.

3.36 Directive 2004/38 recognises registered partnerships and marriage for residence purposes, but only where legislation in the host Member State provides for registered
partnerships, and only on the terms of the relevant national legislation (Article 2(2)
(b)). Article 3(2)(b) of the Directive refers to cohabitees and states that Member States
should 'facilitate' the entry of a 'partner with whom the Union citizen has a durable
relationship, duly attested'. No definition is provided of 'durable', nor are details given
of how the relationship may be attested, but Member States must carry out an extensive
examination of the personal circumstances and justify any refusal of entry or residence
to the partner. Consequently, the right of residence applies solely to the spouse or partner of the citizen and any family member whose 'serious health grounds strictly require
the personal care by the Union citizen' should have entry to the Union 'facilitated' (see
13.39 et seq). If a person has worked in another Member State and then returned home,
his family members keep their European Union law rights even after returning to the
home state (see Case C–370/90 *Surinder Singh* discussed at **12.109**). See also the Court's
clarification in *Akrich*, discussed at **12.42**) whereby the requirement was very narrowly
interpreted. However, a third country national spouse of a Union citizen must have
been lawfully resident within the territory in order to take advantage of Union rights of
residence.

3.37 The issue of a third country national spouse's prior lawful residence in a Member State
and the effects of Case C–109/01 *Akrich* (see **12.42**) were discussed in Case C–1/05
Yungying Jia (2007). Here the Court stated that Community law does not require
Member States to make the grant of a residence permit to nationals of a non-Member
State, who are family members of an EU national who has exercised his/her right of
free movement, *subject to the condition that those family members have previously been
residing lawfully in another Member State*. Despite this decision, the Court expressly
overruled *Akrich* in the more recent case of C–127/08 *Metock and Others v Minister for
Justice, Equality and Law Reform* (2008). This case concerned a reference from the Irish
High Court relating to four cases before it. Each concerned a non-Irish EU Member
State national who had arrived in Ireland and who had applied for asylum there. In
each case asylum had been refused, however, each had married a non-Irish national
who was resident in Ireland. None of the marriages were marriages of convenience.
Following marriage, each of the non-EU spouses applied for a residence permit as a
spouse of an EU citizen. The applications were refused by the Minister for Justice on
the grounds that the spouse did not satisfy the condition in Ireland's legislation implementing Directive 2004/38, whereby a citizen of an EU country who is a family member of an EU citizen may reside with or join that citizen in Ireland only if he is lawfully
resident in another Member State. The Court of Justice was asked to rule on whether
such a condition of prior lawful residence was compatible with the Directive and held
that it was not, and that the application of the Directive is not conditional on family
members having previously resided in another Member State, expressly overruling the
judgment in *Akrich* and *Yungying Jia*.

13.38 The issue also arose in Case C–459/99 *MRAX* (2002), where the Court was asked for
a preliminary ruling on the right of residence of third country nationals married to

Member State nationals who had either entered the Member State unlawfully, or who had entered lawfully but had failed to renew their residence permit. Emphasising the importance of proportionality, the Court found that expulsion from the territory of a Member State on the sole ground that a visa had expired would be 'manifestly disproportionate' to the breach of the sanctions concerned. Once again, unless the third country national poses a threat to public policy, security or health, proof of identity and marriage to a Member State national should suffice to preclude expulsion.

Primary carers

13.39   The provision in the Citizenship Directive relating to children (Article 2(2)(c)) covers 'direct descendants who are under the age of 21 or dependants' and, (according to Article 2(2)(d)), 'dependent direct relatives in the ascending line of the EU national and his spouse or partner'. Other family members such as siblings or cousins still have no automatic rights to accompany the worker, but under Article 3(2)(a) Member States should 'facilitate' the entry of other family members not covered by Article 2(2) who are dependent on the EU national or members of his household, or 'where serious health grounds strictly require the personal care by the Union citizen'. Again the Member State must carry out a detailed investigation and must justify any refusal of entry or residence.

13.40   In Case 413/99 *Baumbast and R* (2002) (see **12.45**) two scenarios were considered. In the first, the Court held that it was not relevant that one of the children held Union nationality or that the other did not. Both had arrived with their Union citizen father. As a consequence, the mother was entitled to remain in the United Kingdom as the carer of these children, while they completed their education. In the second scenario, the children of a French national and US citizen residing in the UK had the right to continue their education in the UK, even after their parents' divorce. Accordingly, the American mother, whose rights of residence would have lapsed upon her divorce from her French husband, was entitled to remain in the UK as carer of the children.

13.41   Subsequently, in Case 200/02 *Zhu and Chen* (2004), Mr and Mrs Chen travelled to Ireland to give birth to their second baby, in order to avoid the one child policy in China and also to gain Irish nationality for the child. Such nationality meant that the child acquired an automatic right of residence within the EU. While a right of residence for dependent relatives was recognised under Directive 90/364 (now Directive 2004/38) for dependent relatives in the ascending line, Mrs Chen's case was the exact opposite. The Court found that, regardless of the motives of the individuals concerned in travelling to Ireland, to deprive the mother of residence would be to effectively deprive the child of its right to residence as provided under Article 21(1) TFEU.

13.42   In Case C–34/09 *Ruiz Zambrano,* the Court granted a right of residence to the Colombian parent of an EU citizen in order to prevent the deprivation of the child's enjoyment of the benefits of citizenship, despite their not having exercised any of the four freedoms. A husband and wife, both Colombian nationals, applied for asylum in

Belgium and were refused. They remained in Belgium and had two children there, who consequently obtained Belgian nationality. Mr Zambrano worked without a work permit for quite some time before his contract became temporarily suspended. He subsequently claimed unemployment benefit and was refused on the grounds that he did not possess a work permit. A reference was made to the Court of Justice by the Brussels Employment Tribunal, asking the following questions: whether Articles 18, 20 and 21 TFEU confer a right of residence in Belgium on a relative in the ascending line who is a third country national and upon whom his minor children (who are EU citizens) are dependent; and whether these articles exempt him from having to obtain a work permit in that Member State. After acknowledging that the case involved a wholly internal situation, Advocate General Sharpston's opinion highlighted the fact that case law has confirmed that the exercise of EU citizenship rights has not strictly been dependent upon physical movement between Member States. Indeed, she wrote that premising citizenship rights on physical movement to another Member State yields a result that is 'both strange and illogical' (paragraph 86) and concluded that Articles 20 and 21 TFEU must be interpreted as granting a right of residence based on citizenship and independent of the right to move between Member States. However, she also stated that national provisions refusing to grant a derived right of residence to an ascendant relative of an EU citizen may be tolerated, providing they respect the principle of proportionality. The Court of Justice agreed with the Advocate General's opinion, but held that Article 20 TFEU would only preclude a Member State from refusing to grant a right of residence to an individual, whose children are EU citizens with nationality and residence in the Member State concerned, if such a refusal would deprive the children of the 'genuine enjoyment of the substance of the rights' attached to their status as EU citizens (paragraph 45). In this case, to deny residence would result in a situation where the children would be forced to leave the EU with their parents and, therefore, unable to exercise the substance of their EU citizenship rights. (Contrast this case with *McCarthy* at **13.56**).

Right to education

13.43   As discussed in **Chapter 12**, the Court has increasingly demonstrated a desire to create a single market for education within the Union. In Case C–209/03 *Bidar* (2005) the Court ruled that a provision requiring students to be 'settled' in the host Member State for the purposes of obtaining a student loan was incompatible with Article 12 EC (now Article 18 TFEU). Instead, the Court stated that the Member State could require that the student had 'established a genuine link with the society of that Member State'. (See **12.143**). In Case C–158/07 *Jacqueline Förster* (2008) (considered at **12.144**) the Court confirmed that Member States can interpret the requirement of a 'genuine link with the society of that Member State' as necessitating residence for five years before a grant is paid to assist with studies.

13.44   Joined Cases C–11/06 and 12/06 *Morgan and Bucher*, Ms Morgan was a German national who worked as an *au pair* in the United Kingdom before applying to study there. She applied to the German authorities for a grant, but her application was rejected because, under German law, the grant was subject to the condition that the course of study should constitute a continuation of education or training pursued for at least one year at a German establishment. Ms Bucher, also of German nationality, moved to a town on the German border with the Netherlands in order to study in the latter country. She applied for a grant but this was rejected on the grounds that she was not 'permanently resident' in that town. The German legislation therefore imposed a two-fold obligation on the receipt of a grant for study abroad. Firstly the applicant must have attended an educational establishment in Germany for at least one year, and second, the applicant must continue that same education in the host Member State. The Court found this to be a restriction on free movement of Union citizens as set out in Article 18 EC (now Article 21 TFEU).

Citizenship and names

13.45 The Court of Justice has also had to consider whether national measures regulating the translation, recognition or alteration of Union citizens' names, are discriminatory and/or create a barrier to a Union citizens' right to free movement. Case 168/91 *Konstantinidis* (1993) concerned the incorrect translation of the applicant's name into German, and the resulting barrier to their recognition by the state. Agreeing with Advocate General Jacobs' interpretation, whereby the incorrect translation of an individuals' name could constitute a barrier to the free movement of workers within the Union, the Court relied on Article 18 TFEU (then Article 12 EC) to uphold the applicant's right not to be discriminated against, by the Member State, when translating his given name (see **1.2**). Similarly, in Case C–148/02 *Garcia Avello* (2003), an application was made to the Belgian State, on the behalf of two minors, to change their family name. The purpose of the change was to allow the children to bear the same surname in both Belgium and Spain (of which they have dual nationality). The Court considered that Articles 18 and 20 TFEU prohibited the refusal of the application, as such a measure could potentially give rise to huge confusion and pose a barrier to the exercise of their rights to free movement.

13.46 In Case C–353/06 *Grunkin and Paul* (2008), the family name of a German child was brought into question. According to German law, the name of a person is determined by the law of the state of his/her nationality and, furthermore the use of a double-barrelled surname (such as a combination of both the mother's and father's names) is prohibited. However, in this case, the child concerned was born and registered with a double-barrelled surname in Denmark, where this is permissible. When the registered office in Germany refused to acknowledge the name of the child, the national court referred to the Court of Justice, asking specifically whether the judgment in Case C–96/04 *Standesamt Stadt Niebüll* (2006) applied. In *Niebüll*, the Court held that a name valid under Danish law must be recognised by German law. Answering in the affirmative, the Court held that it was contrary to Article 18 EC (now Article 21 TFEU) to require a person to have different names in different Member States, as this was likely to hamper the right to move and reside freely within the territory of the Member States.

3.47   Finally, a national restriction on the use of titles of nobility was upheld by the Court of Justice in Case C–208/09 *Ilonka Sayn-Wittgenstein v Landeshauptmann von Wien* (2010). The case concerned an Austrian citizen who was adopted by a German national whose surname had ties to nobility. Under Austrian law a title of nobility, as part of a surname, is prohibited, and therefore, when the applicant's new name was registered in Austria it was subsequently corrected to remove the part indicating nobility. The Austrian court asked whether the legislation concerned restricted the right of free movement and residence for EU citizens. The Court answered in the affirmative, stating that the law in question did restrict the right to free movement under Article 21 TFEU. However, the restriction was permissible as it was proportionate.

European Citizens' Initiative

3.48   The European Citizens' Initiative ('ECI') was introduced by the Lisbon Treaty through the addition of Article 11(4) TEU under Title II, Provisions on Democratic Principles. The Article provides that not less than one million citizens may take the initiative of inviting the European Commission to make a proposal on matters where citizens consider that a legal act of the Union is required for the purpose of implementing the Treaties.

The initiative is designed to complement the citizenship rights contained in Articles 20–25 TFEU (ex Articles 17–22 EC). But, quite how this new initiative will operate in practice is yet to be determined.

13.49   The benefits and reach of the ECI should however, not be overstated. Regulation 211/2011 on the Citizen's Initiative provides further details on the procedure which consists of several stages designed to ensure the legitimacy and 'European character' of the initiative. However, whether, in practice, they will present a series of complex and possibly insurmountable administrative and logistical barriers, remains to be seen.

13.50   Once a citizens' committee has been established to liaise with the European institutions, the proposed citizens' initiative must be registered with the Commission who will verify that the proposal fulfils certain conditions: namely that it has been submitted by a properly formed support committee; that the subject matter of the proposal falls within EU competences; that it is not frivolous, abusive or vexatious; and that it is not contrary to the values outlined in Article 2 of the TEU (Article 4(2)).

13.51   The citizens' committee then has 12 months to collect statements of support, have them verified by the responsible Member State authorities and submit them to the Commission. Once submitted, Articles 10 and 11 of the Regulation provide that the citizens' committee can be received by the Commission to allow them to elaborate on the issues raised in the initiative, and can be entitled to a public hearing before the European Parliament. The Commission must then, 'within three months, set out in a communication its legal and political conclusions on the citizens' initiative, the action it intends to take, if any, and its reasons for taking or not taking that action'. The Regulation applies from 1 April 2012. Only from this date has it been possible to launch a Citizens' Initiative.

Problems with citizenship

Reverse discrimination

13.52 Described by some as 'a necessary evil', the idea of the wholly internal situation concerns the applicability of a national measure to the nationals of that Member State, while nationals of another Member State are exempt. This issue has long been contentious. Joined Cases C–29/94 and C–35/94 *Aubertin* (1995) saw the Court rule that Union measures do not preclude national provisions requiring nationals of the Member State concerned to possess a qualification not required of nationals of another Member State. This is the case, even though such a ruling clearly results in discrimination. In other words, measures contrary to Union law, contested in a factual situation that does not include a cross-border element, or invoke other Union freedoms, will remain lawful. This approach has been explained by reference to the original aim of the Union—that of *access* to markets, not the right of unfettered commerce within those markets. The citizenship articles have not had the same impact with regard to 'internal exile' which the ECJ prohibited under *Rutili* (see **6.62** and **12.21**). In that case the Court said that Mr Rutili could not be prevented from moving freely anywhere in France as he could rely on his Union right to free movement as an Italian citizen in another Member State. Previously, this right could not be claimed by Union citizens in respect of their own state. However, this rule appears to have changed. In the British case *R v Secretary of State for the Home Department, ex p Adams* (1995) an exclusion order was made against Mr Adams under the Prevention of Terrorism (Temporary Provisions) Act 1989, prohibiting his entry into the UK for three years because of his alleged terrorist activities in Northern Ireland. Mr Adams argued that the internal nature of the case should not prevent the application of EU free movement principles. Upon appeal, the UK Court of Appeal disagreed and stated that it would be 'astonishing' if there were no national security derogation. Due to changing circumstances (Mr Adams was no longer excluded from mainland UK) the case was withdrawn from the ECJ.

13.53 However a subsequent case continued the debate. Case 100/01 *Oteiza Olazabal* (2002) (see **12.21**) concerned a Spanish national of Basque origin with links to ETA, an organisation accused of terrorist activity. He was refused a residence card in France but was allowed provisional residence subject to a prohibition on residence in certain parts of France including those close to the Spanish border. He was also prohibited from leaving his locale in France without authorisation. Lower courts were of the opinion that *Rutili* prevented this sort of measure. However, the Court of Justice stated that there was nothing in the Treaty or secondary legislation implementing the free movement provisions which precludes a state from imposing administrative police measures, limiting that worker's right of residence to a part of the national territory. According to the Court, this is only possible if:

- the measure is justified by reasons of public order or public security based on his individual conduct,

- the measure is the least onerous option, i.e. that the only other option would be to ban the worker from the entirety of the national territory, and

- the activities giving rise to the measure attract, in the case of nationals of that Member State, punitive measures or other genuine and effective measures designed to prevent it.

3.54 The Court appears to have taken notice of the problem of reverse discrimination in its case law. *Martinez Sala* and *Baumbast* (see **13.32** and **13.40**) saw the Court find a cross-border element in facts where the applicant was no longer exercising one of the four freedoms. Instead, the Court was satisfied that the applicant could rely on Union citizenship or a link to a person who did exercise one of the five freedoms, even if that link was no longer in existence. Moreover, in Case 60/00 *Carpenter* (2002) although the applicant, Mrs Carpenter, a third country national, was unemployed and did not possess a residence permit, the fact that her entrepreneur husband sold a 'significant proportion' of his services to buyers in other Member States was sufficient for the Court to grant her a right of residence. Invoking the provisions on free movement of services, the Court concluded that the deportation of Mrs Carpenter would affect the ability of Mr Carpenter to conduct his business. Allowing such a tenuous link to one of the economic freedoms to trigger citizenship rights reduces the problem of the wholly internal situation. Moreover, such a generous approach to finding a link with economic activity, if it were applied to those who *receive* services from another Member State such as television programmes, could see the scope of persons who then fall within Union law increase exponentially.

13.55 Additionally, the Court has shown an increasing willingness to give preliminary rulings on matters wholly internal to the Member State, with a view toward providing guidance to national courts. This development can also be seen in the following free movement of goods cases: Case C–298/87 *Smanor* (1988), Case C–321/94 *Pistre* (1997) and Case C–448/98 *Guimont* (2000) (see **Chapter 10**).

13.56 See also the decision in *Ruiz Zambrano* (2011) (see **13.42**) which relied on the citizenship provisions to grant a right of residence to the third country national parent of an EU citizen in a wholly internal situation. This judgment contrasts with that in Case C–434/09 *McCarthy* (2011). McCarthy had dual UK and Irish nationality and was born and lived in the UK. In November 2002 she married a Jamaican national who did not have leave to remain in the UK. In 2004, she and her husband applied to the Secretary of State for a residence permit under EU law as, respectively, a Union citizen and the spouse of a Union citizen. The application was refused on the ground that McCarthy was not a 'qualified person' (i.e. a worker, self-employed person, or self-sufficient person) and that consequently, her husband was not the spouse of a 'qualified person'. The Supreme Court of the United Kingdom referred two questions for a preliminary ruling, the first of which was whether a person of dual Irish and British nationality who has resided in the UK for her entire life was a 'beneficiary' within the meaning of Article 3 of Directive 2004/38. In response, the Court pointed out that the facts of the case involved a wholly internal situation and thus Directive 2004/38 was deemed inapplicable. The second question was whether Article 21 TFEU was applicable on the facts. The Court held that Article 21 is not applicable so long as the national measure at issue does not have the effect of depriving the individual of the genuine enjoyment of the substance of the rights conferred by EU citizenship, or of impeding the exercise of his right of free movement and residence within the territory of the Member States. The Court specifically distinguished this case from *Zambrano* since the national measure at issue does not have the effect of requiring Mrs McCarthy to leave the territory of the EU in the way the children of Mr Zambrano would have been required to leave, were he denied a right of residence. See also the recent case C– 256/11 *Dereci* where the Court limits the principle in *Zambrano* to apply only where the removal of a parent or parents would result in the EU national being deprived of the opportunity to exercise the substance of their rights as citizens.

Third country nationals

13.57 It must first of all be noted that third country nationals, i.e. those not holding the nationality of a Member State of the European Union, have no Union rights. Differences occur not only between Union citizens and third country nationals with regard to rights of movement, family reunion, and social security, but also the treatment afforded to third country nationals in different Member States. Third country nationals may acquire rights in the EU based on cooperation agreements between their country of origin and the EU, such as those concluded with Turkey, and with the Maghreb countries. Furthermore, third country nationals working for an EU-based company, and undertaking employment in another Member State, may also acquire rights, although these can be few and far between.

13.58 Access to justice by third country nationals can also be contrasted with that of Union citizens, who have the opportunity of recourse to supranational mechanisms of adjudication once domestic legal resources have been exhausted. Third country nationals have no such recourse and, as such, are entirely reliant on national courts for the enforcement of their immigration and social welfare rights.

13.59 Due to its unifying characteristic, Union citizenship has been a positive force for European-wide harmonisation and integration. Certain rights, proclaimed as citizenship rights of Union citizens, are also available to third country nationals. The right to petition the European Parliament and the right of application to the European Ombudsman are available to all persons, regardless of nationality, residence or citizenship. Directive 2003/109 on the status of non-EU nationals who are long-term residents creates a single status for long-term nationals that ensures equal treatment throughout the Union. The Directive requires Member Sates to recognise long-term resident status after five years of continuous legal residence (and provided that any absences from the Member State are for periods of less than six consecutive months and not exceeding 10 months in total). In order to obtain this status, the individual must prove that he/she is self-sufficient, i.e. does not need to have recourse to the social assistance system of the Member State concerned, and has sickness insurance. The Member States may require the satisfaction of further integration conditions, such as a language test. Third country nationals who qualify under the Directive will receive a permanent residence permit which is valid for five years and automatically renewable. In addition, with limited exceptions, they will enjoy equal treatment with nationals regarding:

- access to and conditions of employment;
- educational and vocational training, recognition of qualifications and study grants;
- welfare;
- social assistance;
- social benefits, tax relief and access to goods and services;
- freedom of association and union membership; and
- access to the entire territory of the Member State concerned.

Long-term residents will also benefit from enhanced protection against expulsion, as discussed above (**Chapter 12**).

13.60 A long-term resident can also exercise his/her right of residence in another Member State for a period exceeding three months, subject to the requirement that he/she is exercising one of the four freedoms, e.g., the exercise of an economic activity or for purposes of education. Family members may also accompany the resident to the second Member State as long as they were a family unit in the first Member State. Otherwise, Directive 2003/86 on the right to family reunification will apply.

13.61 It is important to note, however, that according to Protocols annexed to the TEU and TFEU, the United Kingdom, Ireland and Denmark do not take part in the Directive and, as such, are not bound by it or subject to its application. Therefore, third country nationals residing in these Member States will be subject to national rules regarding long-term residence and will not acquire the right to reside in a second EU Member State as described above.

FURTHER READING

Bogaert, S. van den, 'Not a wholly internal situation' (2000) *European Law Review* 554.

Commission Green Paper on a European Citizens' Initiative COM 2009/622

Costello, C., 'Metock: Free movement and "normal family life" in the Union' (2009) 46 *Common Market Law Review* 587.

Currie, S., 'The transformation of Union citizenship', in Currie, S. and Dougan, M., *50 Years of the European Treaties: Looking Back and Thinking Forward* (Oxford: Hart Publishing, 2009).

Doppelhammer, 'Expulsion: a test case for European citizenship?' (1999) *European Law Review* 621.

Dougan, M., 'The constitutional dimension to the case law on Union citizenship' (2006) 31 *European Law Review* 613–641.

Dougan, M., 'Expanding the frontiers of Union citizenship by dismantling the territorial boundaries of the national welfare states?' in Barnard, C. and Odudu, O. (eds), *The Outer Limits of EU Law* (Oxford: Hart Publishing, 2009).

Dougan, M., 'Free movement: the workseeker as citizen' (2001) *Cambridge Yearbook of European Legal Studies* 93.

Halibronner, K., 'Union citizenship and access to social benefits' (2005) 42 *Common Market Law Review* 1245.

Kunoy, B., 'A union of national citizens: the origin of the Court's *Arant-Gardisme* in the *Chen* case' (2006) 43 *Common Market Law Review* 179.

de Mei, A.P., van der, Bogaert, S.C.G. van den & Groot, G.R., 'De arresten Ruiz Zambrano en McCarthy: Het Hof van Justitie en het effectieve genot van EU-burgerschapsrechten' (2011) *Nederlands Tijdschrift voor Europees Recht*, 17 (6) 188–199.

Newdick, C., 'Citizenship, free movement and health care: cementing individual rights by corroding social solidarity' (2006) 43 *Common Market Law Review* 1645–1668.

O'Keeffe, D. and Horspool, M., 'European citizenship and the free movement of persons', *The Irish Jurist* (Round Hall: Sweet & Maxwell, 1996).

O'Leary, S., 'The free movement of persons and services' in Craig and de Búrca (eds), *The Evolution of EU Law* (Oxford: OUP, 1999).

Peers, S., 'Implementing equality? The Directive on long term resident third country nationals' (2004) 29 *European Law Review* 437–460.

Shaw, J., 'From the Margins to the centre: education and training law and policy' in Craig and de Búrca (eds), *The Evolution of EU Law* (Oxford: OUP, 1999).

Shaw, J., 'A view of the citizenship classics: *Martínez Sala* and subsequent cases on citizenship of the Union' in Azoulai, L. and Maduro, M.P., *The Past and Future of EU Law: The Classics of EU Law Revisited on the 50th Anniversary of the Rome Treaty* (Oxford: Hart Publishing, 2010).

Timmermans, C., '*Martínez Sala* and *Baumbast* revisited' in Azoulai, L. and Maduro, M.P., *The Past and Future of EU Law: The Classics of EU Law Revisited on the 50th Anniversary of the Rome Treaty* (Oxford: Hart Publishing, 2010).

SELF-TEST QUESTIONS

1   'Free movement of persons means that any citizen of an Member State should have the right to travel anywhere in the European Union and live there on equal terms with nationals.' To what extent does this reflect the current position in EU law?

2   'The restriction of full free movement of persons entitlements to economic activities is an anachronism and will prevent full integration of the Internal Market'. Explain, illustrate and criticise.

3   Hans, a German baker, wants to study nutrition in England. He arrives at Heathrow with his partner, Maria, who is Russian. Hans tells the customs authorities he has come to look for work as a baker. He is given a six-month permit to stay, as is Maria as a visitor. Hans finds work immediately. Maria finds part-time work as a waitress in a local restaurant. After about five months, Maria and Hans split up; Hans leaves his job and applies to the local college to be admitted to a course in nutrition and is accepted. He applies to the local authority for a tuition grant and for a maintenance grant. Both are refused. Maria receives a letter from the immigration authorities informing her that her permit is coming to an end and that she will have to leave. Advise both Hans and Maria. Can EU law help them?

4   A husband and wife (the Shustermans), both third country nationals, moved from their home in the United States to Poland where they had a child who acquired Polish nationality. After working without a work permit for some time, Mrs Shusterman lost her job. Mr Shusterman did not work, and instead stayed home with the baby. Mrs Shusterman's attempt to claim unemployment benefit was refused because she did not possess a work permit. The Shustermans are now worried that they will be forced to leave Poland and return home. Can EU law help the Shustermans stay in Poland?

14

Competition law and policy

SUMMARY

- Article 101 TFEU: the structure
- The *de minimis* principle
- Article 101(3) TFEU: conditions for exemption
- Block exemptions
- Article 102 TFEU: abuse of a dominant position
- Meaning of abuse
- Application and enforcement of EU competition rules: Regulation 1/2003
- Merger control
- State aid

The aims of competition law

14.1 From the inception of the European Economic Community (EEC) competition policy has always been considered an important element in the creation of the common market. Before the Treaty of Lisbon, Article 3 EC stated that the activities of the Community necessary to obtain the objectives in Article 2 EC, included 'a system ensuring that competition in the internal market is not distorted'. This Treaty provision with its unequivocal commitment to the principle of 'undistorted competition' has been relied on by the Court of Justice in its application of the competition law provisions. However, in the negotiations for the drafting of the Lisbon Treaty, the French President, Nicolas Sarkozy, wanted this sentence removed and the relevant Treaty Article post Lisbon, Article 3(3) TEU, now states that the 'Union shall establish an internal market. It shall work for….a highly competitive social market'.

Reference to the fact that the internal market includes 'a system ensuring that competition is not distorted' is now relegated to a Protocol on the Internal Market and Competition annexed to the Treaties. Whilst Article 51 TEU states that Protocols to the Treaties 'shall form an integral part thereof', it will be interesting to see if this relegation of the principle of undistorted competition to a Protocol has any impact on the application of competition law in the European Union by the Courts.

Note that under Article 3(1)b TFEU 'the establishing of the competition rules necessary for the functioning of the internal market' falls under the exclusive competence of the European Union.

14.2 The enforcement of the competition rules is necessary both to protect and encourage competition in that market (and thus influence the nature of that market), and also to ensure that the integration of that market, achieved by dismantling national barriers to trade, was not threatened by compartmentalisation of the market along national lines because of the activities of private companies. As the Court of Justice said in Joined Cases 56 and 58/64 *Consten and Grundig v Commission* (1966) (see further **14.53**), 'agreement[s] ... which might tend to restore the national divisions in trade between Member States might be such as to frustrate the most fundamental object of the Community'. The importance of the objective of integration of the market is a significant feature of EU competition law, which distinguishes it from other competition regimes. In addition to that objective, EU competition policy also pursues the aim of protecting consumer welfare (by ensuring that cartels or dominant companies cannot restrict output and/or maintain supra-competitive prices). Neelie Kroes, the former Commissioner, stated in 2005 that 'our aim is simple: to protect competition in the market as a means of enhancing consumer welfare and ensuring an efficient allocation of resources'.

14.3 In a market where an undertaking enjoys a monopoly or near monopoly, and by definition there is little competition, it is able to restrict output and to raise prices. This allows it to enjoy supra-competitive profits. Market power of a dominant undertaking also enables it to exclude competitors from the market by, for example, temporarily cutting prices, so as to undercut a competitor and drive it out of the market before again raising its own prices. A company that enjoys such power in the market will have little incentive to improve products or service to the consumer.

14.4 Where a number of companies collude by, for example, maintaining a price cartel, setting prices artificially high, their behaviour has a similar effect to that of the monopolist. They are able to maintain high prices, and if they successfully stifle competition, there will be no incentive to innovate or improve quality. A common objective of anti-competitive collusion between competitors is to divide up markets (often along national lines) as this allows different undertakings to set prices and conditions in their allocated territories without fear of competition. Competition law seeks to prevent such behaviour. The benefits of a successful competition policy therefore include lower prices, better quality goods, a wider choice of products and the stimulation of productive efficiency and innovation by undertakings; the benefits of all of these will be enjoyed by the consumer. In its Notice on the Application of Article 81(3) EC (2004) (now Article 101(3) TFEU) the Commission includes the statement that:

> the objective of [Article 101 TFEU] is to protect competition on the market as a means of enhancing consumer welfare and of ensuring an efficient allocation of resources. Competition and market integration serve these ends since the creation and preservation

of an open single market promotes an efficient allocation of resources throughout the Community for the benefit of consumers.

At the same time, however, the Union must have regard to the maintenance of the competitiveness of the Union's industries in the global market (Article 173 TFEU (ex Article 157 EC)).

Overview of the Treaty Articles

14.5 The Treaty Articles with which we are principally concerned are Articles 101 and 102 TFEU (ex Articles 81 and 82 EC), but this chapter also covers the law on mergers in outline. To avoid repetition, these Articles will be referred to by their TFEU numbering only in this chapter.

14.6 Articles 101 and 102 TFEU prohibit two separate forms of anti-competitive behaviour: Article 101(1) TFEU prohibits anti-competitive collusion between undertakings which, to an appreciable extent, prohibits, restricts or distorts competition within the EU. Article 102 TFEU, by prohibiting abuse of a dominant position by one or more undertakings, controls 'abusive' behaviour by an undertaking, or undertakings, which have significant market power. In both cases, for EU law to apply at all, there must be the possibility of an effect on trade between Member States. Article 101(3) TFEU provides for the possibility of exemption for behaviour caught by Article 101(1) where an agreement (or other collusive behaviour), despite its uncompetitive effect, fulfils certain conditions. If no exemption is granted under Article 101(3), then the agreement is void under Article 101(2). Article 102 TFEU contains no possibility of exemption within the wording of the Treaty Article but the Court of Justice (see Case T–30/89 *Hilti* at **14.121**) has developed the principle of objective justification. Where behaviour is objectively justified, it will not constitute an abuse.

14.7 Where undertakings are found to have infringed either of these provisions, they are subject to fines, currently up to 10 per cent of annual turnover, and are also liable to damages actions brought by parties adversely affected by the anti-competitive behaviour.

Role of the Commission

14.8 The Commission has always had the main responsibility for the development of competition policy as well as for implementation and enforcement of the Competition law provisions. This is one of its tasks as 'guardian of the Treaties' (see **3.32**). The responsibilities of the Commission in regard to Competition law are carried out by the Competition Directorate, currently headed by Commissioner Joaquín Almunia. The powers of the Commission to enforce competition law were originally laid out in Regulation 17/62, which has now been repealed and replaced by Regulation 1/2003, which enacted a radical reform of the implementation and enforcement of competition law. The Regulation came into effect on 1 May in 2004, at the same moment as the accession of 10 new Member States. The new regime decentralised the primary responsibility for day-to-day enforcement of EU competition law to a network of national competition authorities (NCAs) although the Commission maintains overall control of EU competition policy. One of the aims of the reform was to enable the Commission to concentrate on uncovering the most egregious and harmful anti-competitive practices, in particular international cartels. Mario Monti, former Competition Commissioner, stated in 2000 that 'of all restrictions of competition, cartels contradict most radically the principle of a market economy based on competition, which constitutes the very foundation of the Community' and continued that such cartels are 'cancers on the open market economy, which forms the very basis of our Community'. It is estimated that the average increase in price from price fixing is 10 per cent of the selling price allied to a 20 per cent reduction in production; in some recent cases in EU law, prices have been shown to have been increased by the cartel participants by 30 per cent (graphite electrodes) and 50 per cent (citric acid).

Summary of procedure

14.9 In many of the cases in this chapter, the initial investigation was carried out by the Commission. The Commission investigates a possible breach of the European Union competition rules, sometimes alerted by a complaint, sometimes as a result of its own enquiries, and issues 'a statement of objections'. The final decision can only be made in regard to allegations set out in the statement of objections, thus allowing the undertaking to respond to all of the possible grounds for an infringement. The undertakings have the right of access to the Commission's file (Article 27(2) Regulation 1/2003), in other words, access to all the information gathered by the Commission. There is then an oral hearing where the defendant undertakings may present their case; complainants are also represented. If the Commission decides that there is an infringement of the law, that determination is framed as a formal decision (per Article 288 TFEU, ex Article 249 EC) and must include full reasons for the findings, as required under Article 296 TFEU (ex Article 253 EC). The decision is agreed by the whole Commission either on a written procedure or, if it is contentious, during a meeting of the College of Commissioners.

14.10 If the undertaking is found to be in breach of either Article 101 or Article 102, fines may be imposed. As noted above (**14.4**), profits from cartel behaviour can be very large and, in order to ensure that anti-competitive behaviour ends up being unprofitable, the level of fines imposed has been dramatically increased. The undertaking is able to seek judicial review of the Commission decision, originally by bringing an action in the Court of Justice but since 1989 judicial review for individual applicants has been in the General Court (previously the Court of First Instance). Undertakings which have been found by the Commission to be in breach of EU competition law automatically have standing under Article 263 TFEU, as do complainants (Case 26/76 *Metro* (1977)). The majority of cases which go to review are challenges to the quantum of the fines. The judgment of the General Court in the judicial review proceedings can then be appealed, on a point of law only, to the Court of Justice, within two months.

Notice that this means that there can be a very long time period, four years or more, between the original finding of the Commission and the final resolution of the case because of the backlog of cases both in the General Court and the Court of Justice. Cases brought by private complainants or national competition authorities can result in a reference under Article 267 TFEU (ex Article 234 EC) to the Court of Justice; in the Treaty of Nice provision was made for the possibility of the General Court taking references from national courts under Article 267 in certain (unspecified) areas and it was thought that this might include competition law where the General Court has developed considerable expertise, but this has not happened.

The importance of the economic context

4.11 The last point to raise in this overview is that competition law is different from other forms of Union law; the application of competition law provisions can depend on economic analysis of relevant markets and market behaviour. The context in which they are applied is affected by economic theories which are not static but change; an example of a shift in economic thinking influencing the application of competition law is the more benevolent attitude adopted by the Commission to vertical agreements (agreements between entities at different levels of the supply chain, such as manufacturer and distributor) in recent times, especially when the undertakings concerned have little market power. This is evidence of a more economics based approach to the application of Article 101, directed to considering the *effects* of competition policy on consumer welfare and the efficient allocation of resources. In its Green Paper on Vertical Restraints the Commission stated that:

> the heated debate among economists concerning vertical restraints has calmed somewhat and a consensus is emerging. Vertical restraints are no longer regarded as per se suspicious or per se pro-competitive. Economists are less willing to make sweeping statements. Rather, they rely more on the analysis of the facts of a case in question [paragraph 10].

14.12 In the *British Airways* case, the General Court made a clear statement of the new approach:

> the protection of competition is not an aim in itself. As a means of both enhancing consumer welfare, and of ensuring an efficient allocation of resources, competition helps to prevent other welfare-reducing effects. Society as a whole, including consumers, in this way benefits from competition [Case T-219/99 *British Airways v Commission*].

14.13 This chapter concentrates on the provisions dealing with the actions of private undertakings. However, the Treaty also deals with the distortive effect on competition arising from the granting of special and exclusive rights to public undertakings or undertakings entrusted with public services (Article 106 TFEU (ex Article 86 EC)), anti-dumping rules and rules on state aids (Articles 107–109 TFEU (ex Articles 87–89 EC)).

Article 101 TFEU

14.14 Article 101(1) TFEU prohibits all agreements between undertakings, decisions by associations of undertakings and concerted practices which may affect trade between Member States and which have as their object or effect the prevention, restriction or distortion of competition within the Common Market. The Article itself provides a non-exhaustive list of examples of agreements which fall within the provision.

This list includes agreements or practices which:

(a) directly or indirectly fix purchase or selling prices or any other trading conditions;

(b) limit or control production, markets, technical development or investment;

(c) share markets or sources of supply;

(d) apply dissimilar conditions to equivalent transactions with other trading parties, thereby placing them at a competitive disadvantage;

(e) make the conclusion of contracts subject to acceptance by the other parties of supplementary obligations which, by their nature or according to commercial usage, have no connection with the subject of the contracts.

14.15 Article 101(2) TFEU provides that any agreement or decision in breach of Article 101(1) TFEU shall be automatically void. The Court of Justice of the European Union has held that the whole agreement does not have to be held void because of a breach of Article 101; the offending clauses can be severed (*Consten and Grundig* (see **14.53**)). Article 101(3) TFEU, provides the possibility of exemption for agreements which fall within Article 101(1) provided that all four of the requirements which it sets out are met. When this is the case, Article 101(1) is declared to be inapplicable.

Key elements of Article 101(1)

14.16 As with many of the other provisions that you have by now considered, the key elements of Article 101 are not defined in the Treaty itself and the Commission and EU courts have provided the definitions. To found a breach of Article 101, it is necessary to establish that there is:

- either an *agreement* between *undertakings*, or a *decision by an association of undertakings*, or a *concerted practice* between undertakings;
- which *may affect trade between Member States*; and
- that the agreement, decision by an association of undertakings or concerted practice has as *its object or effect* the *prevention, restriction or distortion of competition* within the internal market.

14.17 After consideration of the definitions of the italicised terms, the additional requirement for establishment of a breach of Article 101 TFEU, that the agreement should not be *de minimis* (see below **14.75** and **14.76**) will be discussed.

Undertakings

14.18 In the absence of a legislative definition, the Commission and the Court have stated that 'the concept of undertaking encompasses every entity engaged in an economic activity regardless of the legal status of the entity and the way in which it is financed' (Case C–41/90 *Höfner and Elser* (1991)). This is clearly a very wide definition encompassing many different bodies. Examples of undertakings for the purposes of EU competition law include limited companies, partnerships, trade associations, agricultural cooperatives, sole traders, even opera singers and state companies engaged in all economic sectors.

14.19 However, the courts have made it clear that state bodies which purchase goods for use in the public health systems of the Member States are not undertakings and therefore not subject to actions under Articles 101 and 102 when they purchase goods from public funds for use in the national health systems where patients are treated under social welfare provision. In C–205/03 P *FENIN* (2006) the Court of Justice clarified that the purchasing of goods is *not* an economic activity (according to the definition in *Höfner and Elser* (above at **14.18**)) when the goods are not offered for resale but used to perform a public function.

FENIN was an association of the majority of the undertakings which sold medical goods and equipment, particularly medical instruments, that were used in Spanish hospitals. It was alleging abuse of a dominant position by the state body, SNS, which bought 80 per cent of FENIN's members' products.

The Court of Justice stated that 'it is the activity consisting in offering goods and services on a given market that is the characteristic feature of an economic activity'. Although the organisations whose actions were being challenged under Article 102 by FENIN were large purchasers of goods, 'the nature of the purchasing activity must be determined according to whether or not the subsequent use of the purchased goods amounts to an economic activity'.

The Court held that SNS 'operates according to the principle of solidarity in that it is funded from social security contributions and other state funding and provides services free of charge to its members on the basis of universal cover...the SNS management bodies do not, therefore, act as undertakings in their activity of managing the health system'.

14.20 In Case C–264/01 *AOK Bundesverband* (2004), the Court of Justice held that sickness funds in Germany were not acting as undertakings or associations of undertakings when purchasing medical products because in carrying out this activity, 'they fulfil an exclusively social function, which is founded on the principle of national solidarity and is entirely non-profit-making'.

Groups of companies

14.21 The question whether a parent company and its subsidiaries are one entity or separate undertakings is clearly highly significant as this determines whether or not agreements between them will be scrutinised under Article 101 TFEU. This issue was considered in Case C–73/95P *Viho Europe v Commission* ('*Parker Pen*') (1996). The case was a challenge to the arrangements between Parker Pen and its subsidiaries concerning the distribution of Parker goods in different territories.

Viho was a company incorporated in the Netherlands which marketed office equipment. It had attempted to purchase Parker products from Parker's subsidiary in Germany which refused to sell to Viho but instead referred Viho to Parker's Netherlands subsidiary. Viho complained to the Commission, arguing that Parker's arrangements with its subsidiaries, whereby each subsidiary was restricted to distributing Parker products in its allocated territory, were contrary to Article 101. The case turned on whether Parker and its subsidiaries constituted a single entity, despite the fact that the subsidiaries had separate legal personality, or whether these arrangements were agreements between independent undertakings.

The Court of Justice concluded that 'Parker and its subsidiaries...form a single economic unit within which the subsidiaries do not enjoy real autonomy in determining their course of action in the market, but carry out the instructions issued to them by the parent company controlling them'. Parker owned 100 per cent of the shares of its subsidiaries and the sales and marketing activities of the subsidiaries were directed by the parent company as were the setting of sales targets, the management of costs, cash flow and stocks, pricing strategy and marketing. The subsidiaries were therefore not separate autonomous undertakings as they did not freely determine their conduct on the market but carried out the instructions given directly or indirectly by the parent company by which they were controlled.

14.22 The Guidelines on the applicability of Article 101 of the Treaty on the Functioning of the European Union to horizontal co-operation agreements (see further below at **14.41**) summarise the law as follows:

> *Companies that form part of the same 'undertaking' within the meaning of Article 101(1) are not considered to be competitors for the purposes of these guidelines. Article 101 only applies to agreements between independent undertakings. When a company exercises decisive influence over another company they form a single economic entity and, hence, are part of the same undertaking [paragraph 11].*

14.23 In Case C–97/08 *AKZO Nobel v Commission* (2009) the question was whether the Commission could address a Decision to a parent company that it was liable for a breach of Article 101 when it was a subsidiary which had participated in a cartel. The

Court of Justice held that 'where a parent company has a 100% shareholding in its subsidiary there is a rebuttable presumption that that parent company exercises a decisive
influence over the conduct of its subsidiary'. The Commission will then 'be able to hold
the parent company jointly and severally liable for payment of the fine imposed on the
subsidiary unless the parent company proves that the subsidiary... acts autonomously
on the market'.

Where the undertakings are based outside the EU

4.24 Undertakings based outside the European Union fall within the scope of Article 101(1)
TFEU even if the collusion takes place outside the EU, provided that implementation of
the agreement or concerted practice is within the EU. In the *Woodpulp* case, a number
of producers of wood pulp from countries including Finland (not at the time part of
the EU although part of the EEA), the US, Canada and Sweden were found by the
Commission to have concerted prices. The illegal collusion which was alleged to have
occurred took place outside the EU but was alleged to have been implemented within
the EU. Although the substantive finding was largely overturned by the Court of Justice
(see below **14.48**), the Court confirmed that it is possible for non-EU undertakings
which collude outside the EU to be held liable under the EU competition rules for a
concerted practice which took effect within the EU (see Joined Cases 89, 104, 114, 116–
117 and 125–129/85 *Ahlstrom* (*Woodpulp*) (1988)).

Agreements

14.25 This term has also been interpreted widely. An 'agreement' for the purposes of Article
101 includes informal, oral written agreements. A gentleman's agreement is sufficient:
Case 41/69 *ACF Chemiefarma NV v Commission* (1970). This is helpful for the enforcement of competition law since otherwise undertakings could evade the reach of Article
101 by avoiding formal agreements. Failure to prove the existence of an agreement in
any event has little impact given the extension of the prohibition to concerted practices
(see **14.34**).

Tacit acceptance of terms of agreement

14.26 In relation to distribution systems set up by manufacturers, a number of cases established that the tacit acceptance by established distributors of terms set by the manufacturer implies acceptance, tacit or express, of the manufacturer's refusal to supply
certain traders or to exclude traders from a distribution network.

14.27 C–107/82 *AEG-Telefunken* (1983) concerned a selective distribution system. In a selective distribution system a manufacturer of particular types of goods, including electrical goods, may limit retailing of those goods to undertakings which meet certain
qualitative criteria (*Metro*). The imposition of these criteria is held not to breach Article
101(1) but any company which complies with the criteria must be allowed to join the
network of distributors. AEG-Telefunken had refused to supply certain undertakings

which met the required criteria because these particular distributors would not comply with AEG's pricing policy and would therefore undermine the maintenance of high prices for AEG's goods. The refusal to supply undertakings which complied with the criteria for the selective distribution system would be a breach of Article 101 if it could be established to be an agreement or concerted practice. The Court of Justice upheld the Commission's decision that this refusal to supply, in the context of contractual relations between AEG and its existing distributors amounted to an agreement or concerted practice between the producer and its distributors. In this case, it was also in the interests of the established distributors that undertakings which would undercut the price were excluded. AEG's argument that its refusal to supply was a 'unilateral act' and hence a possible violation of Article 102 only, not Article 101, was rejected by the Court. It said that the refusal to supply formed:

> part of the contractual relations between the undertaking and resellers in the case of the admission of a distributor, approval is based on the acceptance, tacit or express, by the contracting parties of the policy pursued by AEG which requires inter alia the exclusion from the network of all distributors who are qualified for admission but are not prepared to adhere to that policy.

14.28 In Joined Cases 25 and 26/84 *Ford v Commission* (1985) the Court of Justice held that Ford's cessation of supply of right-hand drive cars to its German dealers in order to prevent customers in the United Kingdom from importing lower priced cars from Germany was an agreement or concerted practice contrary to Article 101 (it is not necessary for the Commission to establish whether collusion is an agreement or a concerted practice, see below **14.37**). The court held that Ford's decision not to supply formed 'part of the contractual relations between the undertaking and its dealers'. In Case T–62/98 *Commission v Volkswagen* (2000) the General Court of the European Union established that it 'is an agreement within the meaning of that provision if it forms part of a set of continuous business relations governed by a general agreement drawn up in advance'.

Unilateral conduct

14.29 However, in Joined Cases C–2 and 3/01 P *Commission v Bayer* (2004), the Court of Justice annulled a Commission decision holding that there was a breach of Article 101, on the grounds that the Commission had not established that there was an agreement within the context of arrangement within a distribution system; unilateral behaviour by the manufacturer was not sufficient to create an agreement under Article 101(1). Bayer had reduced its supplies of the drug Adalat to French and Spanish wholesalers which were re-exporting the drugs ('parallel imports') to the United Kingdom where prices were significantly higher (40 per cent). Bayer wanted to keep these markets separate so that it could maintain the higher price level in the United Kingdom. The Commission had decided that there was an agreement between the wholesalers and Bayer not to export to the United Kingdom, even though there was evidence that the wholesalers had, in fact, done their utmost to obtain supplies for re-export to 'get round' the restrictions imposed by Bayer. The then Court of First Instance annulled the Commission's decision against Bayer on the grounds that it had not established that there was an agreement. Approving the decision, the Court of Justice held that 'the mere fact that a measure adopted by the manufacturer, which has the object or effect of restricting competition, falls within the context of continuous business relations between the manufacturers and its wholesalers, is not sufficient for a finding that...an agreement exists'.

4.30   Unilateral behaviour will, therefore, not suffice to create an agreement under Article 101(1) unless there is at least tacit acquiescence, a 'concurrence of wills' on the part of both parties. In Case C–74/04 *Commission v Volkswagen* (2006), a series of letters and circulars from Volkswagen to its German distributors exhorting them not to sell the VW Passat at discounted prices was held not to be an agreement under Article 101(1), applying *Bayer*.

Parallel traders

14.31   One of the means of achieving the integration of the market and the reduction or elimination of price differentials between Member States is through the activities of the 'parallel importer'. This is the undertaking which perceives a difference in price between two areas and therefore imports goods across the price divide to undercut sellers in the higher-priced market, driving prices down for the consumers. This is the positive side of such activities. From the other point of view, the distributor allocated a territory into which he/she has introduced a new product, may well have incurred costs in establishing the brand (increasing inter-brand competition, see *Consten and Grundig,* **14.53** below); such undertakings will have little incentive to bear these cost if they can subsequently be undercut by the 'free rider' importing goods and selling them more cheaply.

Decisions by associations of undertakings

14.32   Associations of undertakings (such as trade associations) may coordinate the activities of their members, and thereby obtain an anti-competitive effect without having recourse to an actual agreement. This is the reason for their inclusion in Article 101(1). The phrase 'decisions by associations of undertakings' has been interpreted by the Court to encompass a non-binding recommendation for target prices by a trade association to its members (Case 8/72 *Vereeniging van Cementhandelaren v Commission* (1972)). The Commission has also turned its attention to restrictive rules of professional bodies. In Decision 95/188/EC *Spanish Association of Industrial Property Agents* (1995), the setting of prices for patent renewal services was a breach of Article 101 because it restricted competition between patent agents. The Commission did not impose a fine because this was its first decision against a professional body under Article 101.

14.33 In Case C–309/99 *Wouters* (2002), the Court held that individual members of the Dutch Bar association were 'undertakings' and that the Bar Association was an 'association of undertakings'. The Commission has issued a Communication on Competition in Professional Services, which effectively warns the professions that their restrictive practices may be scrutinised for compliance with Article 101.

Concerted practices

14.34 Concerted practice concerns collusion between undertakings where not even an informal, oral agreement has been reached between them but where rather, there is a consensus, an understanding, between the undertakings that they will not compete.

14.35 This concept is very useful as it makes collusion illegal even where there is no evidence of an agreement, and it means that undertakings which collude to coordinate their behaviour, perhaps in regard to setting prices or to share markets, cannot escape the reach of Article 101 simply by avoiding reaching an 'agreement'. The concept of concerted practice has been extended very broadly. For example, exchange of information between competitors in the context of an understanding that the companies would not compete, is sufficient to found a concerted practice.

14.36 The definition of a 'concerted practice' was given in Joined Cases 48, 49 and 51–57/69 *ICI (Dyestuffs)* (1972), where the Court of Justice defined it as 'a form of co-operation between undertakings which, without having reached the stage where an agreement properly so-called has been concluded, knowingly substitutes practical co-operation between them for the risks of competition'.

Is a plan necessary for a concerted practice?

14.37 In Cases 40–48, 50, 54–56, 11, 113–114/73 *Suiker Unie* (1975) the question was whether the cooperation needed to be within the context of a plan and the Court of Justice held not; the 'criteria of "coordination" and "cooperation" laid down by the case law of the court…in no way require the working out of an actual plan'. The case law on concerted practices makes it clear that positive contact between parties (e.g. meetings, discussions, exchanges of information) which has the object of influencing market behaviour and removing in advance the risks of uncertainty by maintaining or altering the conduct of the undertakings and which leads to conditions of competition not corresponding to the normal competitive forces of the market is illegal. The Court of Justice in *Suiker Unie* continued that 'coordination' and 'cooperation' should be 'understood in the light of the concept inherent in the provisions of the Treaty relating to competition that each economic operator must determine independently the policy which he intends to adopt'. Therefore Article 101 'strictly preclude[s] any direct or indirect contact between such operators, the object or effect whereof is either to influence the conduct on the market of an actual or potential competitor or to disclose to such a competitor the course of conduct which they themselves have decided to adopt or contemplate adopting on the market'.

14.38 The objective of Article 101 is that undertakings should compete for market share because this competition protects the welfare of the consumer by driving down prices. Competitors should not share information as this enables them to coordinate behaviour to the detriment of competition.

14.39 In Joined Cases T–202, 204 and 207/98 *Tate and Lyle and Others v Commission* (2001) it was held by the then Court of First Instance that where a number of companies attended a meeting with an anti-competitive purpose, the fact that only one of those companies present, the market leader (British Sugar), gave information on its future prices did not prevent there being a prohibited agreement or concerted practice for the purposes of Article 101. The purpose of such meetings was to restrict competition by the coordination of pricing policies. The fact that only one of the participants at the meetings in question revealed its intentions did not preclude an agreement or concerted practice. The exchange of any information about future pricing strategy could amount to a concerted practice because 'each participant could not fail to take account, directly or indirectly, of the information obtained' at such meetings, when 'determining its future conduct in the market'. Taking part in a meeting with an anti-competitive purpose meant that the participants were intending to eliminate uncertainty about the future conduct of their competitors.

14.40 This case confirms the 'joint classification' approach confirming that it is not necessary for the Commission to characterise an infringement of Article 101(1) as either an agreement or a concerted practice. In a long, complex infringement involving a number of participants it is often difficult to make a clear distinction.

14.41 With regard to exchanges of information between competitors, the Commission has recently published Guidelines on the applicability of Article 101 of the Treaty on the Functioning of the European Union to horizontal co-operation agreements (2011), which include a section on 'General Principles on the Competitive Assessment of Information Exchange', see below at **14.91**.

There must be 'conduct' in the market resulting from concertation. Does this conduct need to have anti-competitive effects?

14.42 In C–199/92 *Hüls AG v Commission* (*Polypropylene*) (1999) the Court of Justice conceded that a concerted practice requires, besides undertakings concerting with each other, 'subsequent conduct on the market, and a relationship of cause and effect between the two'. But the Court continued that a concerted practice would be caught under Article 101 'even in the absence of anti-competitive effects on the market'. This was because, unless the undertakings could prove the contrary, the onus being on them to do so, 'the presumption must be that the undertakings taking part in the concerted practice and remaining active on the market take account of the information exchanged with their competitors for the purposes of determining their conduct on that market'.

14.43 Therefore, once the Commission has established concertation the burden shifts to the economic operators to prove that there had been no resulting conduct on the market, since the presumption is that they cannot avoid taking into account any information they have discovered, and therefore any conduct subsequent to concertation must have anti-competitive effects.

14.44 A recent case, C–8/08 *T-Mobile v Netherlands BV and others v Raadvanbestuur van de Nederlandse Mededingingsautoriteit* (2009), reaffirms this principle and also established that this presumption applies 'even if the concerted action is the result of a meeting held by the participating undertakings on a single occasion'.

The case concerned a meeting in 2001 between the five operators of mobile telephone networks in the Netherlands. It was impossible that a sixth network provider could be established because no further licences had been issued. Post-paid mobile phone accounts, where the customer is invoiced for their call charges after a particular period has elapsed, are organised through dealers. The undertakings met on a single occasion and discussed, *inter alia*, a reduction of the remuneration they would pay to dealers for their services in regard to post-paid subscriptions.

14.45 It is not easy for the Commission to uncover the kind of cooperation created by concerted practices. In the early case of Case 48/69 *ICI v Commission* (*Dyestuffs*), the Commission established a concerted practice with reference to unusual market behaviour. Ten dye manufacturing companies shared 80 per cent of the European market; this market broke down into five separate national markets with distinct price structures. In 1964, companies in Italy, the Netherlands, Belgium and Luxembourg increased their prices by 15 per cent over a few days. In the last months of 1964, a number of companies announced future price increases and on 1 January 1965, all the companies except those in France (where there was a price freeze) and Italy, simultaneously raised prices by 10 per cent for those products which had not increased in price in 1964. Companies in markets, such as Germany, where prices had not increased in 1964, now also raised prices by 15 per cent. Similar near simultaneous price rises were again implemented by all the companies in 1967. The Court stated that 'although parallel behaviour may not of itself be identified with a concerted practice, it may however amount to strong evidence of such a practice if it leads to conditions of competition which do not correspond to the normal conditions of the market'. This parallel behaviour by the companies provided very strong *prime facie* evidence of concertation by the companies concerned, underpinned by evidence of communication between them prior to the price increases.

Oligopoly

14.46 Parallel behaviour (i.e. undertakings acting identically on the market) does not in itself constitute a concerted practice but it provides strong evidence thereof. However, before the conclusion can be drawn that there has been concertation, it has to be ascertained whether there is any other possible explanation for the parallel conduct. Parallel behaviour in the market may also be caused by market conditions, where undertakings are part of an oligopoly.

14.47 A monopolistic market is one where one company dominates and is able to restrict output and thereby set uncompetitive prices. At the other end of the spectrum, in a market with a large number of competing companies (an atomistic or dispersed market), competition will be strong. In between lies the oligopoly which is a market structure in which a relatively small number of companies (between two and six) operate. The rational response to such market conditions, without any collusion, is for the companies to mirror each other's behaviour. In an oligopoly therefore, without any agreement or understanding between them, the companies may adopt similar behaviour in the market. For example, because it is easy for customers to switch suppliers, a price cut by one must be followed by similar cuts by the others and therefore is uneconomic for all of them; they all end up receiving less for their goods or services. This is more likely to occur where the companies are trading in a homogenous product and where barriers to entry and price transparency are high (an example is the retail market for petrol). The result is 'tacit co-ordination' where the companies mirror each other's behaviour. Such behaviour may lead to uncompetitive conditions prevailing on the market as the companies can establish supra-competitive prices or limit output but it is acknowledged to be a rational response to market conditions and is not illegal under Article 101. Therefore, it must be discounted as an explanation for parallel behaviour before a finding of an illegal concerted practice can be sustained. In the *Dyestuffs* case (see **14.45**) the Court of Justice made it clear that parallel behaviour by members of an oligopoly arising from rational responses to a competitor's behaviour was legal. In determining that there was indeed a concerted practice the Court of Justice referred to the large number of producers involved and concluded that the market therefore could not be oligopolistic. In addition, the division of the relevant market into five national markets with different price levels and structure also made it 'improbable that a spontaneous and equal price increase would occur on all the national markets'.

14.48 In *Woodpulp* (see **14.24**), the Commission's finding of a concerted practice was overturned by the Court of Justice. This was after the Court had commissioned two economists to analyse the market, and the judgment of the Court relied, in part, on the fact that the economists decided that the Commission had overlooked the possibility that 'the parallelism of prices and price trends may be satisfactorily explained by the oligopolistic tendencies of the market' (Joined Cases 89, 104, 114, 116–7, 125–129/85 *A Ahlström Oy v Commission* (*Woodpulp*) (1988) at paragraph 126). More significantly, the Court held that establishment of a concerted practice required it to be 'the only plausible explanation' for the parallel conduct. The onus of proof is therefore on the Commission to establish that concertation is the only explanation for the parallel behaviour.

Vertical agreements

14.49 Originally it was thought that Article 101 only applied to horizontal agreements, however, the Court of Justice has determined that it does also control vertical agreements.

14.50   Vertical agreements are agreements between undertakings at different levels of trade or industry, for example, those between a producer or manufacturer of goods and a distributor. Horizontal agreements are agreements between undertakings at the same level of trade or industry who compete with each other, for example, agreements between two or more manufacturers, or two or more wholesalers of goods.

14.51   From an economic perspective, vertical agreements pose less of a threat to competition than horizontal agreements. Unlike agreements or collusion between competitors which would rarely be anything other than anti-competitive in effect, such vertical agreements can actually increase or encourage competition. They are often economically beneficial as they permit the penetration of new products into areas where they have not previously been sold, thus increasing the choice of products available to the consumer and so increasing competition between different brands; this is known as 'inter-brand' competition.

14.52   However, the aim of avoiding the fragmentation of the market has led the Court and the Commission to be vigilant also in regard to vertical agreements. In recent years, as we will see below (**14.93**), the earlier stance of the Commission has been softened and it has developed a more economics based, and more lenient approach to the treatment of vertical agreements where the parties do not have significant market power.

14.53   *Consten and Grundig* (see **14.2**) is a highly significant case for a number of reasons, the first of which is its clarification that Article 101 applied to vertical agreements. The agreement in this case was an exclusive distributorship, which is an example of a vertical agreement between non-competitors. Grundig had agreed with Consten that the latter would be the exclusive dealer for Grundig's products in France. This was what is known then as an exclusive distribution agreement. Such an agreement produces benefits for both parties. The distributor undertakes to establish the brand, to promote the products and to provide after-sales and technically competent sales staff. This is expensive, and the distributor will want to demand prices reflecting the level of service provided, so, in return, the distributor requires some sort of protection from parallel importers. This is called the 'free-rider' problem, where another retailer who has not incurred the costs entailed in establishing the brand imports them into the country and undercuts the exclusive distributor.

Consten's obligations towards Grundig (not dealing with competing brands, promoting the products, minimum purchase requirements, arranging after-sales service, etc.) were balanced by the fact that Consten received absolute territorial protection for the products. Grundig itself would not compete with Consten, nor supply any other distributor in France. Furthermore, Consten enjoyed reinforced protection through intellectual property rights on the products in its contract territory. Grundig granted to Consten, as part of their agreement, the right to be the exclusive user in France of the GINT trademark. This, the Court of Justice said, was 'intended to make it possible to keep under surveillance and to place an obstacle in the way of parallel imports'. When such an importer did, indeed, try to import products into France which had been bought in Germany, undermining the arrangement between Consten and Grundig, they sued the company on various grounds, including trademark infringement. The question then arose as to whether the agreement itself was in breach of Article 101.

4.54   Until this case it was not clear whether Article 101 applied only to agreements between competitors operating at the same level in the economic process but also to 'non-competing persons operating at different levels'. The Court of Justice decided that 'no distinction can be made where the Treaty does not make any distinction' and therefore vertical agreements are also caught by Article 101.

Object or effect

4.55   The second, and very significant, point determined in this case relates to the meaning of 'object or effect the prevention, restriction or distortion of competition'. In *Consten and Grundig*, the agreement had actually increased competition between similar brands (inter-brand competition) by introducing a new brand of electrical goods into France; could it then be said to have as its object or effect 'the prevention, restriction or distortion of competition'? The response of the Court of Justice was that an agreement that restricts competition between distributors of products of the same make (intra-brand competition) cannot escape being caught by Article 101. By attempting to 'seal off' the French territory from parallel imports by the grant of the GINT trademark, Grundig intended to isolate the French market for Grundig goods, to give absolute territorial protection to Consten; this would defeat one of the aims of European Union competition law, to integrate the market. The object of the agreement was therefore the 'distortion' of competition in the internal market, contrary to Article 101. It is significant that this is an early case. In the 1960s, the market was very much less integrated than it is today and such integration was a major focus of the Commission's policy.

The case establishes that the wording 'object or effect' is disjunctive, so where, as here, the agreement had as its *object* 'the prevention, restriction or distortion of competition' there was no requirement to establish an *effect*. Even if the 'effect' of the agreement overall was to increase inter-brand competition, this did not prevent it from being caught by Article 101 since its object was to restrict intra-brand competition.

The object of prevention, restriction or distortion of competition

14.56   Agreements which have as their 'object' the prevention, restriction or distortion of competition' are 'per se' illegal. These agreements contain the following types of clauses, described as the hard-core restrictions.

In horizontal agreements between competitors, agreements or concerted practices which fix prices, allocate markets, impose quotas or limit output.

In vertical agreements between non-competitors, agreements which grant a distributor absolute territorial protection are prohibited. This can be by export bans imposed on all distributors, by prohibition of passive sales (where a customer from another territory approaches the seller, who has made no effort to market or sell in that area) or by the granting of trademark rights in a given territory.

Such clauses render exemptions based on the *de minimis* principle or the application of the block exemptions (see **14.88-14.93**) inapplicable. (Note that a narrow exception to the prohibition of bans on passive sales has been introduced in the new Guidelines on Vertical Restraints, see below at **14.92**.)

In case C–8/08 *T-Mobile v Netherlands BV and others v Raad van bestuur van de Nederlandse Mededingingsautoriteit* (2009), discussed above (**14.44**), the Court of Justice states that a concerted practice

> pursues an anti-competitive object for the purposes of Article 81(1) EC where, according to its content and objectives and having regard to its legal and economic context, it is capable in an individual case of resulting in the prevention, restriction or distortion of competition within the common market.

Therefore the potential to prevent, restrict or distort competition is sufficient. The Court confirmed that, where the object is to restrict competition, it was not necessary 'for there to be actual prevention, restriction or distortion of competition or a direct link between the concerted practice and consumer prices'.

14.57 Case C–209/07 *The Competition Authority v Beef Industry Development Society (BIDS)* (2008) concerned a plan devised by *BIDS*, made up of the ten principal veal and beef processors in Ireland to reduce over capacity in the veal and beef processing industry in Ireland. The rationalisation was to be achieved by agreements between some processors who would withdraw from the market, the 'goers', in return for compensation by the 'stayers', The case concerned an agreement between BIDs and Barry Brothers, a veal and beef processor. The Court held that the question of whether an agreement is an agreement by object is not determined by the subjective intentions of the parties, (although that may be taken into account; see *T-Mobile*):

> even supposing it to be established that the parties to an agreement acted without any subjective intention of restricting competition, but with the object of remedying the effects of a crisis in their sector, such considerations are irrelevant for the purposes of applying that provision [Art 101(1)]. Indeed, an agreement may be regarded as having a restrictive object even if it does not have the restriction of competition as its sole aim but also pursues other legitimate objectives'.

Such matters were to be considered under Article 101(3).

14.58 A recent judgment of the Court of Justice on parallel trade, reaffirms that prohibitions on restrictions on parallel trade are a restriction 'by object', in which case, it is unnecessary to consider the effect of the agreement. The Court of Justice reiterated that the anti-competitive object and effect of an agreement were not cumulative but alternative conditions for assessing whether an agreement fell within Article 101(1).

The case concerned parallel trade in pharmaceuticals where prices paid by national health authorities are set at different levels in different Member States. Prices in Spain were significantly lower than the prices paid in other Member States including the United Kingdom. To prevent parallel traders exporting drugs bought more cheaply in Spain to the UK, GSK operated a dual pricing system for wholesalers in Spain, depending on whether the drugs were for domestic resale to Spanish hospitals or pharmacies or for export to other Member States. The prices at which the drugs are sold at retail level are subject to control by the Member States, so the prices paid by the end user were not affected by the parallel trade. The General Court held that this was not a restriction 'by object' because it did not 'reduce the welfare of the final consumer of the products in question.'

The Court of Justice overruled this finding, reaffirming the orthodox view that all agreements aimed at limiting or prohibiting parallel trade are restrictions 'by object' and that 'that principle … applies to the pharmaceuticals sector'.

The Court continued that 'for a finding that an agreement has an anti-competitive object, it is not necessary that final consumers be deprived of the advantages of effective competition in terms of supply or price'.

The effect of prevention, restriction or distortion of competition

14.59 In *Consten and Grundig* (see **14.2** and **14.53**), it was the absolute territorial protection that was anathema. Case 56/65 *Société Technique Minière v Maschinenbau* (1966) also concerned an exclusive distributorship but here there was no attempt in the contract to 'seal off' the allocated territory by grant of trademarks or by export bans. As the agreement did not have the 'object' of the prevention, restriction or distortion of competition, its 'effect' on competition had to be determined. The Court of Justice recognised the possible pro-competitive aspects of such exclusive distributorship agreements and stated that the effect on competition had to be considered 'within the actual context in which it would occur in the absence of the agreement in dispute'. So the effect on competition had to be considered by comparison with the competitive situation had the agreement not been implemented. The Court stated that 'it may be doubted whether there is an interference with competition if the said agreement seems really necessary for the penetration of a new area by an undertaking'. When determining the question as to whether an exclusive distributorship agreement containing the clause 'granting an exclusive right of sale' was prohibited because it had as its object or effect the prevention, restriction or distortion of competition, the precise purpose of the agreement, in the economic context in which it is to be applied, had to be considered.

14.60 A number of factors had to be taken into account such as:

- the nature and quantity, limited or otherwise, of the products covered by the agreement;
- the position and importance of the grantor and the concessionaire on the market for the products concerned;

- the isolated nature of the disputed agreement or, alternatively, its position in a series of agreements;

- the severity of the clauses intended to protect the exclusive dealership;

- the opportunities allowed for other commercial competitors in the same products by way of parallel re-exportation and importation.

14.61 *Société Technique Minière* is one of a number of cases where the courts seem to have balanced the pro and anti-competitive effects of the agreement in their analysis as to whether or not the agreement falls within Article 101(1) at all rather than applying Article 101(3) to assess whether the agreement is, on balance, good or bad for competition.

Is there a 'rule of reason' in EU competition law?

14.62 As discussed earlier in the chapter, the structure of Article 101 is that agreements and practices which are prohibited because they infringe Article 101(1) may be exempted under Article 101(3) and it is in the analysis under Article 101(3) that the pro- and anti-competitive effects of the agreement are to be considered. This contrasts with the approach in the US where there is no exemption mechanism and, therefore, when determining whether an agreement is a restraint of trade and therefore infringes section 1 of the Sherman Antitrust Act 1890, it is necessary to balance the agreement's pro- and anti-competitive effects. The agreement is unlawful where the anti-competitive effects outweigh the pro-competitive effects. This is called the 'rule of reason'. In a number of cases the European courts had appeared to balance the pro- and anti-competitive effects of an agreement (where it was not the *object* of the agreement to restrict competition) in the analysis undertaken under Article 101(1), which led to discussion of the possibility of a 'rule of reason' approach in EU competition law.

14.63 In Case T–112/99 *Métropole Télévision (M6) v Commission* (2001), the then Court of First Instance (now the General Court), addressed the question of whether there is a 'rule of reason' in EU competition law directly for the first time and confirmed the two-stage approach, rejecting the existence of a rule of reason in EU competition law: 'judgments of the Court of Justice and the CFI have been at pains to indicate that the existence of a rule of reason in Community competition law is doubtful'. The CFI continued that those cases where the courts had shown a flexible approach to the application of Article 101(1) (e.g. Cases 56/65 *STM* (1966), 258/78 *Nungesser* (1982), 161/84 *Pronuptia* (1986) and Joined Cases T–374, 375, 384 and 388/94 *European Night Services v Commission* (1998)) 'cannot be interpreted as establishing the existence of a rule of reason in Community competition law'. However, Article 101(1) could not be applied, 'wholly abstractly and without distinction' to any agreement restricting freedom of action of one or more parties. Rather, in assessing the applicability of Article 101(1):

Account should be taken of the actual conditions in which the agreement functions to determine whether it has the effect of restricting competition, in particular the economic context in which the undertakings operate, the products or services covered by the agreement and the actual structure of the market concerned.

Therefore a certain measure of economic analysis can take place in the initial application of Article 101(1) but 'it is only in the precise framework of [Article 101(3)] that the pro- and anti-competitive aspects of a restriction may be weighed'.

4.64 In a recent case Case T–328/03 *O2* the General Court reiterated the approach set out in *Société Technique Minière* to determining whether an agreement has 'the effect' of restricting competition, requiring a comparison between the competitive situation with and without the agreement.

The Commission had found a roaming agreement between O2 and T-mobile, which enabled O2 to operate in the German 3G market while it built its own network to be in breach of Article 101(1). It had then exempted the agreement, finding it would improve competition in the relevant market, but had exempted it for a shorter period than that stipulated by the parties to the agreement. The General Court annulled the decision, as the Commission had not considered the competitive situation in the absence of the agreement, and thus had incorrectly determined that Article 101(1) applied.

The Court stated that:

the examination required in the light of Article [101(1)] consists essentially in taking account of the impact of the agreement on existing and potential competition…and the competition situation in the absence of the agreement (*Société Technique Minière*), those two factors being intrinsically linked.

Ancillary restraints

14.65 It is apparent in the case law of the courts that restrictions which are objectively necessary to the main agreement and essential for its operation, will be considered with the agreement under Article 101. A restriction which is 'directly related and necessary to the implementation of a main operation' (*Métropole*, paragraph 104) will not fall within Article 101(1) or will be exempted, in accordance with the decision on the main agreement: see e.g. Case 42/84 *Remia* (1985) and Case C–250/92 *Gøttrup-Klim* (1994) where a restriction on members of a cooperative forbidding them from belonging to other cooperatives was not caught by Article 101(1) 'as long as the…provision is restricted to what is necessary to ensure that the cooperative functions properly'.

14.66 In two cases, a non-economic objective has resulted in a decision of association of undertakings which has restrictive effects on competition from falling within the scope of Article 101(1).

14.67   In C–309/99 *Wouters* (2002) the Court considered a restriction imposed by the Dutch Bar Association preventing lawyers from entering partnerships with accountants. The case came to the Court of Justice by an Article 267 TFEU reference.

The reason for the rule was that rules of professional conduct for members of the Bar required them to act for clients in complete independence, to avoid all risk of conflict of interest and to observe strict professional secrecy. Accountants were not covered by similar professional rules, in particular the requirement for professional secrecy; indeed their duties included auditing accounts to convey their opinion of the reliability of those accounts to third parties. There was therefore an incompatibility between the roles of the two professions.

The Court held that the rule did not infringe Article 101(1), despite 'the effects restrictive of competition that are inherent in it [as] it was necessary for the proper practice of the legal profession, as organised in the Member State concerned'.

14.68   In Case C–519/04P *Meca-Medina v Commission* (2006) (see **11.16**), a non-economic objective was again held to preclude the application of Article 101(1). The case concerned two year bans imposed on two swimmers by the International Swimming Federation (FINA) under rules of the International Olympic Committee, for taking nandrolone, a banned substance. The Court held that the purpose of the rules was to ensure the organisation and proper conduct of competitive sport and therefore, as the rules pursued 'a legitimate objective', and were not disproportionate, they did not constitute a restriction of competition within Article 101(1).

14.69   In these cases, a restriction on competition was outweighed by a non-competition objective. Richard Whish has suggested that they are conceptually similar to the cases discussed above in **14.65** but whereas those cases are concerned with 'commercial ancillarity' where 'restrictions necessary to achieve a legitimate commercial purpose fall outside Article [101(1)]', these cases are concerned with 'regulatory' ancillarity where the restrictions are ancillary to the legitimate objectives pursued by the regulatory body and hence do not infringe Article 101(1).

14.70   In the light of some of the case law, it is difficult to accept that there is no balancing of the pro- and anti-competitive effects under Article 101.

However, the Commission has reiterated the two-stage approach to Article 101 in its Notice—Guidelines on the application of Article 81(3) of the Treaty (now Article 101 TFEU) (2004):

> *The assessment under Article 81 thus consists of two parts. The first step is to assess whether an agreement between the undertakings, which is capable of affecting trade between Member States, has an anti-competitive object or actual or potential anti-competitive effects. The second step, which only becomes relevant when an agreement is found to be restrictive of competition, is to determine the pro-competitive benefits produced by that agreement and to assess whether these pro-competitive effects outweigh the*

anti-competitive effects. The balancing of anti-competitive and pro-competitive effects is conducted exclusively within the framework laid down by Article 81(3).

14.71 The confirmation of this approach will be particularly important if uniformity is to be maintained in the future. With decentralisation an increasing number of cases will be decided at the national level and the formalism of the approach under Article 101(3) is more likely to be conducive to uniformity of approach than the less prescriptive approach where economic analysis is carried out under Article 101(1).

Effect on trade between Member States

14.72 In order to be in breach of Article 101(1) the agreement, decision or concerted practice must affect intra-Union trade. This requirement applies equally to Article 102 and effectively defines the boundaries of the jurisdiction of European Union law. The basic test defining the circumstances in which an agreement falls within Article 101(1) TFEU was first stated by the Court in Case 56/65 *Société Technique Minière v Maschinenbau* (1966), as follows:

> It must be possible to foresee with a sufficient degree of probability on the basis of a set of objective factors of law or of fact that the agreement in question may have an influence, direct or indirect, actual or potential, on the pattern of trade between Member States.

14.73 The test is similar to the one applied in *Dassonville* (see **10.6**) with regard to Article 34 TFEU (ex Article 28 EC) but it is wider in scope as it refers to a mere effect (even potential) and not to the hindrance to trade between Member States.

In *Consten and Grundig*, decided two weeks later, the parties, argument that their agreement had increased trade between Member States did not prevent the application of Article 101(1): 'the fact that an agreement encourages an increase, even a large one, in the volume of trade between states is not sufficient to exclude the possibility that the agreement may "affect" such trade in the abovementioned manner'. The Commission has issued a Notice: Guidelines on the effect on trade concept contained in Articles 81 and 82 of the Treaty (2004).

14.74 An agreement which extends over the national territory of only one Member State may infringe Article 101(1) as it reinforces the partitioning of the Common Market along national lines. Thus, the Article has consistently been applied to collusion between undertakings in the same Member State: Case 8/72 *Vereeniging van Cementhandelaren v Commission* (1972).

The de minimis *principle*

14.75 It is a well-established principle that an agreement which would potentially fall within Article 101(1) is not caught by the prohibition if it does not have an appreciable effect on competition. This principle was first established by the Court of Justice in Case

5/69 *Völk* (1969). There the Court stated that an agreement falls outside the scope of Article 101(1) TFEU when it has an insignificant (*de minimis*) effect on the market. In 2001, the Commission issued the Notice on agreements of minor importance which do not appreciably restrict competition under Article 81(1) of the Treaty establishing the European Community (*de minimis*) [now Article 101(1) TFEU] (2001), superseding earlier versions. It provides guidance as to when an agreement does not fall within Article 101(1) EC because it is '*de minimis*'.

14.76 The *de minimis* Notice states that agreements between undertakings 'which are actual or potential competitors' (i.e. 'horizontal agreements') where the aggregate share of the undertakings does not exceed 10 per cent of the relevant market will not contravene Article 101(1). In the case of vertical agreements between undertakings which are 'not actual or potential competitors' the threshold of the market share is increased to 15 per cent. Where it is difficult to determine whether the agreement is one between competitors or non-competitors, the 10 per cent threshold will apply.

14.77 The 2001 Notice lowers the *de minimis* market share threshold to five per cent for both competitors and non-competitors in markets where competition is restricted by the 'cumulative foreclosure effect' of parallel networks of agreements having similar effects on the market. Such an effect is unlikely to exist where less than 30 per cent of the market is covered by such networks of agreements.

14.78 Exemption from the application of Article 101(1) does not apply in cases of particularly serious breaches of competition law. The Notice sets out the hard-core restrictions which, if included in the agreement, will make the application of the *de minimis* principle invalid. Examples of when the exemption will not apply include horizontal agreements which fix prices, clauses which allocate markets or customers and vertical agreements which restrict the territories into which the distributor/buyer may sell goods or services (see above, **14.56**).

The Notice also states that agreements between small and medium-sized undertakings are rarely capable of appreciably affecting trade between Member States and are unlikely to fall within Article 101(1).

Individual exemption

14.79 Agreements or decisions which fall within the prohibition of Article 101(1) TFEU are void under Article 101(2) TFEU, unless it is possible to sever the offending clause: *Consten and Grundig*. However, Article 101(3) TFEU provides for the 'exemption' of agreements which otherwise would be void under Article 101(1) if certain conditions are met, as follows.

Conditions for exemption

14.80 Article 101(3) TFEU sets out four conditions for exemption; the first two are 'positive' concerning the pro-competitive effects of the agreement, whilst the last two conditions ensure that competition is not entirely eliminated and that the restrictions are proportionate. All four conditions must be fulfilled.

The positive conditions are that the agreement:

- contributes to the improvement of the production or distribution of goods or to the promotion of technical or economic progress; and
- allows consumers to receive a fair share of the resulting benefit.

The negative conditions are that the agreement:

- imposes no restrictions on competition that are not indispensable to obtaining the benefit; and
- does not create the possibility for the undertakings involved to eliminate competition in respect of a substantial part of the products in question.

Both sets of conditions must be satisfied before exemption can be granted.

14.81 The system in operation until 2004 was that under Article 4(1) and 9(1) of Regulation 17/62 the Commission had exclusive competence to grant such exemptions after prior notification. Such an individual exemption could only be granted if the agreement had been notified to the Commission pursuant to Regulation 17/62 (now repealed) which set out the procedure for notification and established the rights of the parties within the procedure.

14.82 Notification resulted in immunity from fines even if the agreement was subsequently found to contravene Article 81(1) EC (now Article 101(1) TFEU).

14.83 The Commission, in order to reduce the quantity of applications, has issued a number of 'block exemptions'. Block exemptions are regulations which set out a number of requirements and prohibited clauses for contracts, which, when fulfilled, automatically lead to exemption for particular classes of agreements which comply with their terms (see below at **14.88**). In particular, in recognition of the beneficial effects of many vertical agreements, the Commission has adopted a single block exemption for vertical agreements offering a 'safe haven' for vertical agreements where the participating parties have a market share of less than 30 per cent of the market (Commission Regulation 330/2010; see **14.92**).

Regulation 1/2003

14.84 Regulation 1/2003 came into force on 1 May 2004. It marked a major development in the operation of competition law in the EU. The Regulation decentralised the application of the competition law rules to a network of national competition authorities, NCAs, which was established in the Member States and removed the Commission's monopoly over the application of Article 101(3). The Regulation makes Article 101(3) directly effective and applicable by the national competition authorities and the national courts thus the whole Article can now be applied at a national level. However, the Commission retains a major role and will concentrate its resources on uncovering the worst and most damaging cartels and other abuses. The Commission, in accordance with the principle of subsidiarity, will also deal with cases with major cross-border effects, where the effects are beyond the scope of NCAs, e.g. large cartels.

14.85 By abolishing the prior notification procedure the Regulation makes undertakings responsible for deciding whether their agreement will be caught by Article 101(1) or exempted under Article 101(3). Clearly their legal advisors will have Commission decisions, Commission Notices and case law of the European Courts to guide them in this evaluation. In particular, the Commission has issued a Notice on the application of Article 101(3): see **14.70**.

14.86 In 2009 the Commission issued a five year Report on the effectiveness of the Regulation. The Report concludes that the system works well, and that competition is being adequately enforced in Member States. Certainly some national competition authorities have been more effective than the Commission itself. Finally the question of the rights of companies investigated is raised, and the suggestion is made that these are more effectively protected on the national level than at the EU level. The Report is inconclusive as to changes that should be made.

14.87 Regulation 1/2003 is discussed further below in regard to the application and the enforcement of Articles 101 and 102 (see **14.134-14.148**).

Block exemptions

14.88 Because the mechanism to obtain individual exemptions under Article 101(3) TFEU was slow and cumbersome, the Commission issued a number of regulations called block exemptions which allow exemption under Article 101(3) for particular categories of agreement provided that the agreement in question complied with the conditions set out in the block exemption. Originally, block exemption regulations followed a pattern according to which certain clauses were specifically permitted ('permission clauses') and certain other provisions, which always restrict or distort competition, were expressly forbidden and would take the whole agreement outside the scope of the block exemption ('hard-core' or prohibited clauses). The agreement had to be drawn up to comply with the required clauses which led to criticism that they imposed overly restrictive form requirements, reducing the autonomy of the parties to set their own terms, which limited their usefulness. The new approach, introduced with the adoption of Regulation 2790/99, is more flexible and economically based. Agreements which fall below specified market share thresholds (set at different levels for the different block exemptions) and do not contain 'hard core' restrictions can be exempted under the block exemption; it is no longer necessary for an agreement to be drafted in accordance with the 'permitted' clauses so the parties have greater freedom to set their own terms.

14.89 Originally there were a number of block exemptions for vertical agreements, covering exclusive distribution agreements (Regulation 1983/83), exclusive purchasing agreements (Regulation 1984/83) and franchising agreements (Regulation 4087/88) but these were all replaced by a single block exemption for vertical agreements, Regulation 2790/99, which has now been revised as Regulation 330/2010 on the application of Article 101(3) TFEU to categories of vertical agreements and concerted practices; this is discussed below (14.92).

.90 There are also block exemptions for horizontal agreements:

- Regulation 772/2004 on the application of Article 81(3) TFEU to categories of technology transfer;

- Regulation 1217/2010 on the application of Article 101(3) TFEU to categories of research and development agreements;

- Regulation 1218/2010 on the application of Article 101(3) TFEU to categories of specialisation agreements, replacing Regulation 2658/00.

The last two block exemptions were issued in 2010 and the Commission published revised Guidelines on horizontal cooperation at the same time: Guidelines on the applicability of Art.101 of the Treaty on the Functioning of the European Union to horizontal co-operation agreements (2011).

The new Guidelines include a section on 'General Principles on the Competitive Assessment of Information Exchange', which provide detailed guidance for the assessment of information exchange between competitors under Article 101, with illustrative examples.

14.91 Whilst recognising that information exchange may in some circumstances have pro-competitive effects, the Guidelines set out the dangers to competition from information exchange. In regard to when an exchange of information would be a restriction of competition, the Guidelines (which are long and detailed) point out that:

> information exchange between competitors of individualised data regarding intended future prices or quantities [would] be considered a restriction of competition by object [paragraph 74].

When the information exchange is not a restriction by object, whether it has the 'effect' of restricting information:

> must be analysed on a case by case basis, depending on a number of factors..., in particular the economic conditions on the relevant markets and the characteristics of the information exchange. The assessment of restrictive effects on competition compares the likely effects of the information exchange with the competitive situation that would prevail in the absence of that specific information exchange.

The structure of the market is also relevant:

> companies are more likely to achieve a collusive outcome in markets which are sufficiently transparent, concentrated, non-complex, stable and symmetric.

The Block exemption for Vertical Agreements and
Concerted Practices Regulation 330/2010

14.92 As noted above, Regulation 2790/99 reflected the new, more economically based and market-orientated approach to the assessment of vertical agreements, following criticism of the treatment of vertical agreements in EU law. The new approach was described in the Commission's Guidelines on Vertical Restraints in EC Competition Policy (2000), which were revised in 2010 and accompanied Regulation 330/2010 on the application of Article 101(3) TFEU to categories of vertical agreements and concerted practices.

This block exemption applies to all vertical agreements (including selective distribution agreements) covering both services and goods, whether they are goods intended for resale or goods sold to end customers.

Its main objective is to allow companies which do not have market power (measured as having less than 30 per cent of the market) to benefit from a 'safe haven within which they are no longer obliged to assess the validity of their agreements with Community competition rules'. The Guidelines on Vertical Restraints which accompany the Regulation are long and detailed and provide guidance to undertakings in carrying out an evaluation of their position in regard to Article 101.

14.93 Regulation 330/2010 9, Article 1 sets out definitions: a 'vertical agreement' means an agreement or concerted practice entered into between two or more undertakings each of which operates, for the purposes of the agreement or the concerted practice, at a different level of the production or distribution chain, and relating to the conditions under which the parties may purchase, sell or resell certain goods or services; a 'vertical restraint' means a restriction of competition in a vertical agreement falling within the scope of Article 101(1) of the Treaty.

Article 2 states that 'Pursuant to Article 101(3) of the Treaty and subject to the provisions of this Regulation, it is hereby declared that Article 101(1) of the Treaty shall not apply to vertical agreements. This exemption shall apply to the extent that such agreements contain vertical restraints.'

Article 3 introduces a cap of 30 per cent market share on the availability of the block exemption. It states that the exemption provided under Article 2 applies on condition that the market share held by the supplier does not exceed 30 per cent of the relevant market on which it sells the contract goods or services and the market share of the buyer does not exceed 30 per cent of the relevant market on which it purchases the contract goods or services. Over this threshold, an individual exemption is possible if the conditions are fulfilled.

Article 4 sets out the prohibited list of provisions (hard-core restrictions) which will preclude the block exemption from applying (see **14.56** above). These include restrictions of passive sales and the imposition of fixed or minimum resale prices, although maximum prices and recommendations of a sale price are permitted.

Article 5 forbids direct or indirect non-compete clauses which exceed five years or which have an indefinite term or which prevent the buyer, after termination of the agreement, from manufacturing, purchasing, selling or reselling the goods or services. The inclusion of such clauses does not make the whole agreement ineligible for exemption, as is the case with the 'hard core' restrictions in Article 4, if they can be severed.

The Regulation is accompanied by revised Guidelines on Vertical Restraints (2010). The revised Guidelines contain a notable new departure, stating that bans on passive sales, one of the hard-core restrictions under the block exemption, may not fall within the scope of Article 101(1) at all for the first two years of operation of a new exclusive distributorship where substantial investment by the distributor is necessary to launch the products.

Agreements or practices, or parts thereof, which fall within Article 101(1) and are not exempted under Article 101(3) are void under Article 101(2).

Article 102 TFEU: abuse of a dominant position

The prohibition

14.94 Under Article 102 TFEU, any abuse by one or more undertakings of a dominant position within the internal market or in a substantial part of it is prohibited as incompatible with the internal market insofar as it may affect trade between Member States. This prohibition is followed by a non-exhaustive list of examples of abuse.

There are three essential elements in establishing a breach of Article 102 TFEU:

- determination of what is the relevant market;
- establishing that the company is dominant in that market, a process in which market share is an important but not the only factor; and
- proving that there has been abuse of that position.

It is then necessary to show that the abuse has affected trade within the Union.

Dominant position

14.95 A dominant position was defined in Case 27/76 *United Brands v Commission* (1978) as a:

Position of economic strength enjoyed by an undertaking which enables it to prevent effective competition being maintained on the relevant market by giving it the power to

behave to an appreciable extent independently of its competitors, customers, and ultimately, of its consumers.

14.96 In order to assess dominance within the meaning of Article 102 TFEU it is necessary to
examine the key factors of the relevant product and geographical market.

The relevant market

14.97 Dominance has to be assessed in relation to a particular, defined market. The correct
identification of the relevant market is critical, and can be controversial. Determining
the relevant market will clarify which producers can be regarded as actual or potential competitors leading to a clear view of the competitive constraints operating upon
the allegedly dominant company; thus the market power of the company can be
evaluated.

14.98 The relevant market has two main parameters: the product market and the geographic
market (the temporal market is also of significance and the Court of Justice has established that dominance must be sustained over a period of time: see Joined Cases 6,
7/73 *Commercial Solvents* (1974)). An important case on the definition of the relevant
market under Article 82 is Case 27/76 *United Brands v Commission* (1978).

The relevant product market

14.99 The essential concept used by the Court of Justice to determine the boundaries of a
particular product is that of interchangeability: those goods or services which are
interchangeable fall within one product market. The definition of this market therefore
requires an assessment of the extent to which products may be regarded as substitutes
for each other, an analysis of the 'cross-elasticity' of demand or supply.

Demand-side substitutability

14.100 In Case 27/76 *United Brands* (1978) one of the issues was the identification of the relevant product market. The question was whether the relevant product market was the
market for bananas, which was the product that United Brands traded, or the whole
fresh fruit market, as claimed by the company. The company's share of the latter was
relatively small so if the company could establish that the relevant market was all 'fresh
fruit' rather than a separate market comprising bananas alone, they would not be dominant. The Court considered the cross-elasticity of demand between bananas and fresh
fruit. An analysis of the market confirmed that consumers' buying habits in regard to
bananas were not significantly affected by the price and availability of other fresh fruit,
indicating low cross-elasticity of demand: consumers do not substitute other fresh fruit
for bananas when the price of that fresh fruit, which varies seasonally, is relatively low
compared to that of bananas. Bananas are unaffected by seasonal variations in production. The Court identified a significant group of consumers who had a constant need
for bananas: the very young, the old and the sick. The Court of Justice made reference
to the physical characteristics of bananas, to their appearance, taste, softness, seedless-
ness and ease of handling, which distinguishes them from other fruit. This case and

subsequent case law therefore establishes a test of cross-elasticity or substitutability of products for identification of the relevant product market, the test to be made with reference to physical characteristics, price and intended use (for the latter, see *Commercial Solvents* (see **14.98**)).

.101 The Commission has issued a Notice on the definition of relevant market for the purposes of Community competition law (1997).

.102 In regard to the definition of the relevant product market in relation to cross-elasticity of demand, the test developed by the Commission and set out in the Notice is to ask whether a hypothetical, small (5–10 per cent) permanent price increase would lead consumers to switch to another product. If it would do so to an extent that made the price increase uneconomic, those products are considered to be interchangeable and therefore part of the same product market: if an increase in price of one product causes a significant switch by consumers to the other then they are part of the same product market. This is called the SSNIP (Small but Significant Non-transitory Increase in Price) test.

Supply side substitutability

.103 In Case 6/72 *Continental Can v Commission* (1973) the Commission's identification of the relevant product market was overturned by the Court. The market here was assessed in relation to cross-elasticity of supply. Supply side substitutability comprises an analysis of whether suppliers are able to switch production to manufacture the relevant products and market them in the short term without incurring additional costs or risks in response to small permanent changes in relative prices. The test set out in the Notice is similar: if a manufacturer permanently raises the price of a product by a small amount, are manufacturers of other products able to compete by switching production to make that product, without incurring significant additional costs and risks? If they can, to an extent which has a 'disciplinary effect' on the company which raised prices, the goods or services they produce are part of the same product market.

4.104 In 2009, the Commission imposed a fine of €1,060,000,000 on Intel for violating antitrust rules on the abuse of a dominant market position contrary to Article 102. This is the largest fine ever recorded, although at only 4.5 per cent of Intel's turnover in 2008, it was well below the 10 per cent cap. Intel engaged in two illegal activities. Firstly it gave hidden rebates to computer manufacturers on the condition that they bought all their computer processing units (CPUs) from Intel, thereby excluding competitors from the market. Intel also made payments to major retailers on the condition that these stock only computers containing Intel CPUs. Secondly, Intel made direct payments to computer manufacturers to halt or delay the launch of products containing competitive CPUs and furthermore to limit the sales channels open to these products. The Commission plans to monitor Intel's implementation of orders. See IP/09/745.

The geographic market

4.105 The Court of Justice defined the geographic market in *United Brands* (see **14.100**) as 'an area where the objective conditions of competition applying to the product in question

[are] the same for all traders'. Three Member States had particular arrangements in regard to trade in bananas with overseas territories or, in the case of the United Kingdom, Commonwealth countries, and therefore the Court excluded them from the scope of the relevant geographic market.

14.106   The relevant geographic market comprises the area in which the undertakings concerned are involved in the supply of products or services and where the conditions of competition are sufficiently homogenous to be distinguished from neighbouring areas because the conditions of competition are appreciably different in those areas.

Dominance

14.107   Once the relevant market has been identified, the question of whether the undertaking is dominant in that market can be considered. The first and most important factor is that of market share.

14.108   In *Continental Can* (see **14.103**) the share of the German market held by Continental Can was 70–80 per cent. In *United Brands* (see **14.100**) the company was held to be dominant with a market share in the relevant market of only 40–45 per cent, but a significant factor was that its share was several times larger than that held by the next largest competitor. This is often a relevant factor in determining market power. In Case 62/86 *AKZO* (1991) the Court considered that a stable market share of 50 per cent or more raised a presumption of dominance. In C–95/04 *British Airways v Commission* (2007) British Airways was found to be dominant in the market for air travel agency services where it had a share of 39.7 per cent. It was significant that the nearest rival, Virgin, only had 5.5 per cent.

Barriers to entry

14.109   In assessing the dominance of an undertaking the issue of potential competition must be taken into account. This requires assessment of the prevailing barriers to entry for potential competitors which might enter the market; whether the barriers to entry of the particular market are high or low affects the constraints on the dominant company and will determine the ambit of its autonomy.

14.110   Examples of barriers to entry which have been taken into account by the Court in determining dominance are:

- legal provisions: Case 333/94P *Tetra Pak v Commission* (1996);
- superior technology: *United Brands* (**14.100**), Case 322/81 *Michelin v Commission* (1983), Case 85/76 *Hoffmann-La Roche* (1979);
- deep pocket: *United Brands* (**14.100**), Case 6/72 *Continental Can*;
- economies of scale, vertical integration and well-developed distribution systems: *United Brands* (**14.100**);

- a well developed sales network: Case 89/76 *Hoffmann-La Roche* (1979);

- product differentiation: *United Brands* (**14.100**)—advertising had established a high profile brand image for the Chiquita banana.

A firm's behaviour may provide evidence of dominance, e.g. a discriminatory rebate system as in Case 322/81 *Michelin* (1983).

Substantial part of the internal market

.111 A further requirement for a finding of a breach under Article 102 is that the dominance must be in a 'substantial part' of the internal market. The Court of Justice found that Southern Germany is sufficient to fulfil this requirement, which could be considered to operate as a *de minimis* threshold: see Joined Cases 40–48, 50, 54–56, 111 and 113–114/73 *Suiker Unie* (1975).

Joint/collective dominance

.112 Joint/collective dominance exists when two or more undertakings are linked in such a way that they adopt the same conduct in the market (Joined Cases T–68, 77, 78/89 *Italian Flat Glass* (1992)). In this case the then Court of First Instance annulled the Commission's finding of collective dominance against three companies because of errors in its decision, but the Court did accept the existence of the concept.

.113 In Joined Cases C–395 and 396/96 P *Compagnie Maritime Belge* (2000) the Court of Justice for the first time found collective dominance under Article 102. The Court held that 'a dominant position may be held by two or more economic entities legally independent of each other, provided that from an economic point of view they present themselves or act together on a particular market as a collective entity. That is how the expression collective dominant position . . . should be understood.' What was required to establish such a collective entity were 'links' or other 'factors which give rise to a connection between the undertakings concerned' which 'enabled them to act together independently of their competitors, their customers and consumers'.

The Court stated that the existence of an agreement or concerted practice between the undertakings does not necessarily create such economic links. However, an agreement or concerted practice between the undertakings *can* 'result in the undertakings concerned being so linked as to their conduct on a particular market that they present themselves on that market as a collective entity vis-à-vis their competitors'. The Court then made it clear that the 'tacit co-ordination' of oligopolies can be scrutinised in the context of Article 102: undertakings which have not created 'a link in law' such as an agreement, decision of association of undertakings or 'concerted practice' may nevertheless be collectively dominant based on 'on other connecting factors' which 'depend on an economic assessment and, in particular, on an assessment of the structure of the market in question'. Thus the parallel behaviour ('tacit co-ordination' see above **14.47**) by an oligopoly which is legal under Article 101 may fall to be scrutinised under Article

102 to see whether it constitutes collective dominance. Behaviour which constitutes abuse of the collective dominant position is then necessary before there is a breach of the Article.

The concept of collective dominance in merger control

14.114 When undertakings wish to merge, they may be subject to control by the Commission under Regulation 139/2004 depending on whether the merger has a European Union dimension (see further below **14.161**). The Merger Regulation can be applied to mergers which will create or strengthen a collective dominant position and case law on the meaning of the term, in fact in regard to joint dominance of two undertakings, has developed in regard to the application of the Merger Regulation (see Joined Cases C–68/94 and C–30/95 *France v Commission (Kali & Salz)* (1998) and Case T–102/96 *Gencor v Commission* (1997)). In Case T-342/99 *Airtours v Commission* (2002), a challenge to a Commission decision prohibiting a merger on the grounds that it would create a collective dominant position, the then Court of First Instance held that there are three cumulative conditions for the establishment of collective dominance (see further **14.180**).

14.115 Three cumulative conditions must be met for a finding of collective dominance: first, each member of the dominant oligopoly must have the ability to know how the other members are behaving in order to monitor whether or not they are adopting the common policy; second, the situation of tacit coordination must be sustainable over time, that is to say, there must be an incentive not to depart from the common policy on the market; thirdly, the foreseeable reaction of current and future competitors, as well as of consumers, must not jeopardise the results expected from the common policy.

14.116 It seems that the assessment of collective dominance is now the same whether it is conducted in regard to Article 102 or the application of the Merger Regulation.

14.117 In regard to Article 102, the establishment of collective dominance is the first step before the consideration of whether there has been an abuse by the undertaking whilst under the Merger regime, the question is whether a merger will create or strengthen a collective dominant position; if it will, the merger may be prohibited by the Commission.

14.118 Note that in Case T–228/97 *Irish Sugar v Commission* (1999), the General Court confirmed a finding of 'vertical' collective dominance between Irish Sugar plc and a distributor of sugar, Sugar Distributors Ltd.

The meaning of abuse

14.119 Article 102 TFEU does not prohibit dominance. It is the abuse of a dominant position which is illegal under Article 102 TFEU. The Article provides an illustrative and non-exhaustive list of examples of abuses which includes imposing directly or indirectly unfair pricing, limiting production, discrimination in contractual terms and the imposition of supplementary obligations.

120 The Court of Justice held that abuse is an objective concept: Case 85/76 *Hoffmann-La Roche* (1979). Article 102 has been defined as covering practices which are likely to affect the structure of a market where, as a result of the presence of a dominant undertaking, competition has been weakened and which, by having recourse to methods different from those governing normal competition on the basis of performance, have the effect of hindering the maintenance or development of the level of competition still existing on the market: *United Brands* (above) and Case 322/81 *Michelin* (1983).

.121 Article 102 prohibits practices which may be allowed in normal competitive circumstances but are not permissible because of the dominance of an undertaking. A dominant undertaking is effectively entrusted with a 'special responsibility' not to harm competition in general. However, a claim of abuse can be rebutted by providing 'objective justifications'. This principle was confirmed in, for example, Case T–30/89 *Hilti* (1991), (but rejected on the facts, Court of First Instance judgment upheld on appeal Case C–53/92P). See also Cases 468–478/06 *Sot Lelos Kai Sia EE v GlaxoSmithKline AEVE Farmakeftikon Proionton* (2008).

.122 In Case 6/72 *Continental Can v Commission* (1973) the Court of Justice took a purposive approach to Article 102. It established that the Article not only applies to behaviour which is 'exploitative' or damaging to consumers, but also applies to anti-competitive behaviour targeted at excluding or weakening competitors in the market. It therefore catches behaviour which is detrimental to, or weakens the competitive market structure.

.123 Since that case, the provision has been interpreted as penalising various forms of unfair competition or exclusionary behaviour as well as exploitation of the dominant position to the detriment of the consumer.

.124 In summary, two main categories of abuse can be identified: anti-competitive abuses, also described as exclusionary abuses, which exclude competitors from the market thereby reducing competition, and exploitative abuses, where the dominant company exploits its market power. These categories can overlap and are difficult to distinguish.

Anti-competitive or exclusionary abuse

4.125 Since *Continental Can* (above) the Court has construed Article 102 as prohibiting conduct which substantially reduces competition by making it difficult for competitors to enter the market or to maintain or increase market share. The main forms of this type of abuse are:

- predatory pricing whereby a company seeks to eliminate a competitor by setting its prices at a particularly low level with the intention of raising prices once the competitor is eliminated: Case C–62/86 *AKZO* (1991), Case T–83/91 *Tetra Pak* (1994), Case T–340/03 *France Telecom SA* (2007);

- tying-in and bundling, which refers to making the conclusions of contracts subject to acceptance by the other parties of supplementary obligations which by their nature or according to commercial usage have no connection with the subject of such contracts: Case C–53/92P *Hilti* (1994), Case 85/76 *Hoffmann-La Roche* (1979), Case 311/84 *Telemarketing* (1985), Case T–201/04 *Microsoft v Commission* (2007): Microsoft was found to have abused its 'super-dominant' position by bundling the Windows Media Player with the Windows operating system (see **14.132**);

- offering rebates and discounts: Case C–53/92P *Hilti* (1994) and 322/81 *Michelin v Commission* (1994); this case established that whilst a dominant supplier can give discounts which relate to savings in cost, for example discounts for large orders, it cannot give discounts, rebates or incentives to encourage loyalty; Case 85/76 *Hoffmann-La Roche* (1979), Case C–95/04 *British Airways v Commission* (2007): in this case British Airways was found in breach of Article 102 for offering commission payments, incentives and loyalty-inducing targets schemes to travel agents;

- refusal to supply which, however, can also be seen as a form of unfair competition (see below at **14.128**).

14.126 Exclusionary abuses have been described in the DG Competition Discussion Paper on the Application of Article 82 EC (now Article 102 TFEU) as follows:

> *Behaviours by dominant firms which are likely to have a foreclosure effect on the market, i.e. which are likely to completely or partially deny profitable expansion in or access to a market to actual or potential competitors and which ultimately harm consumers. Foreclosure may discourage entry or expansion of rivals or encourage their exit [p 4].*

14.127 The Commission paper Guidance on the Commission's enforcement priorities in applying Article 82 (now 102 TFEU) to abusive exclusionary conduct by dominant undertakings (2008) sets out an economic and effects-based approach to exclusionary conduct and mirrors the approach already taken in cases such as *Microsoft* (**14.132**) and Case T–339/04 *Wanadoo* (2007). The document provides comprehensive guidance to stakeholders, in particular the business community and competition law enforcers at national level, as to how the Commission uses an effects-based approach to establish its enforcement priorities under Article 102 in relation to exclusionary conduct. It is guidance on the Commission's enforcement priorities rather than a statement of what the law in regard to exclusionary abuse actually is. The Guidance cites the protection of consumers as its main priority:

> *In applying Article 82 to exclusionary conduct by dominant undertakings, the Commission will focus on those types of conduct that are most harmful to consumers. Consumers benefit from competition through lower prices, better quality and a wider choice of new or improved goods and services. The Commission, therefore, will direct its enforcement to ensuring that markets function properly and that consumers benefit from the efficiency and productivity which result from effective competition between firms. [paragraph 5].*

This therefore means an 'effects based' analysis—the effect on consumer welfare has to be assessed.

The Guidelines state that the Commission need not establish that the dominant under-taking's conduct actually harmed competition, only that there is convincing evidence that harm is likely.

Exploitative abuse

.128 Exploitative abuse occurs where the dominant undertaking takes advantage of its position by imposing unfair trading conditions. The most common examples of these exploitative abuses include:

- unfair prices and unfair trading conditions; this type of abuse is referred to in Article 102(a). Unfair pricing may be either low or high pricing. The test for unfair pricing is controversial and there have been few cases under this heading;

- price discrimination; for example, when an undertaking sells the same product at different prices to different customers despite the costs on delivery being the same. This conduct is expressly prohibited by Article 102(c) which prohibits applying dis-similar conditions to equivalent transactions: in *United Brands* (**14.100** above), one of the abuses was the company's practice of delivering bananas to ripener/distributors (companies which buy green bananas to ripen and sell on) in Germany and Ireland and charging different prices in the two countries despite the costs incurred being similar;

- refusal to supply; this form of abuse, which is not explicitly prohibited by Article 102 has nevertheless been thoroughly analysed in the case law of the European Courts and the Commission. It is possible for a dominant company to show that there is some objective justification for its refusal to supply which means that its behaviour would not be an abuse under Article 102.

Refusal to supply

4.129 Refusal to supply was originally applied in cases in which the refusal was addressed to previous customers (*Commercial Solvents, United Brands*). Cases 468–478/06 *Sot Lelos Kai Sia EE v GlaxoSmithKline AEVE Farmakeftikon Proionton* (2008) is an interesting recent case where there was a refusal to supply an existing customer. GlaxoSmithKline refused to supply a Greek wholesaler engaged in parallel trade in pharmaceuticals; regulation in Greece meant that prices for the pharmaceuticals were set low in Greece relative to other Member States. Whilst the Court of Justice held that refusal to supply the 'ordinary' orders of an existing customer in order to prevent parallel trade was an abuse of a dominant position under Article 102, it also recognised that a refusal to supply quantities that were 'out of the ordinary' might be objectively justified as it was 'permissible for that company to counter in a reasonable and proportionate way the threat to its own commercial interests potentially posed by the activities of an undertaking which wishes to be supplied in the first Member State with significant quantities of products that are essentially destined for parallel export'.

The question of whether the orders were in fact 'ordinary' with regard both to the size of the orders in relation to the requirements of the market for the drugs in the Member

State and the previous orders from the wholesaler was for the national court to ascertain (the case was an Article 267 reference).

14.130 An abuse of a dominant position because of a refusal to supply it was, controversially, applied in a situation where there was no previous commercial relationship between the parties in Joined Cases T–69, 70, 76–77 and 91/89 *Magill TV Guide* (1991). The principle in this case developed into what is known as the 'essential facilities doctrine' (see *Sealink/B & I—Holyhead*: interim measures (1992)). This is where a dominant company controls and uses an essential facility and other companies are unable to compete without access to this facility. Where the dominant company then refuses access, it will be in breach of Article 102 unless there is objective justification. This can also apply where a company owns an essential facility and uses its power on that market to strengthen its position in another related market. So in *Sealink* itself, the complaint was that Sealink which owned the Holyhead port in North Wales from which it operated a ferry service, allocated inconvenient sailing slots to its rival ferry operator, B & I. In Case C–7/97 *Oscar Bronner* (1998) a reference was made to the Court which ruled that for a breach of Article 102, access to the essential facility must be 'indispensable', lack of access should have the effect of eliminating all competition in the market and the refusal should be incapable of objective justification. This was not the case in *Bronner* itself.

Refusal to supply: intellectual property rights

14.131 Case C–418/01 *IMS Health GmbH & Co v NDC Health GmbH & Co KG* (2004) arose from an Article 267 TFEU (ex Article 234 EC) reference to the Court of Justice and, like the *Magill* case above (14.130), concerned refusal to supply in the context of intellectual property rights. The case concerned refusal to grant a licence for a data system which was protected by copyright. In such a case, the Court of Justice held that for a refusal to supply to be abusive, three cumulative conditions had to be fulfilled: the refusal prevented the emergence of a new product for which there was a potential consumers' demand; the refusal was unjustified; and it would exclude any competition on the secondary market. The secondary (or downstream) market is the market 'on which the product or service in question is used for the production of another product or the supply of another service' (paragraph 42). This case was an Article 267 reference, so the application of the test to the facts was left to the national court.

14.132 In Case T–201/04 *Microsoft v Commission* (2007) the then Court of First Instance substantially upheld a finding of abuse of a dominant position by Microsoft, for its refusal to supply interoperability information to competitors so that their work group servers could achieve interoperability with Windows PCs. The General Court held that it was only in 'exceptional circumstances' that 'the refusal by an undertaking holding a dominant position to license a third party to use a product covered by an intellectual property right was an abuse of a dominant position within Article 101.' Those circumstances were that:

> in the first place, the refusal relates to a product or service indispensable to the exercise of a particular activity on a neighbouring market; in the second place, the refusal is of such a

kind as to exclude any effective competition on that neighbouring market; in the third place, the refusal prevents the appearance of a new product for which there is potential consumer demand.

In regard to this final criterion, the Court's approach in the case itself was not stringent, holding that whilst the refusal to supply in this case did not prevent the appearance of 'a new product', that was not the 'only parameter which determines whether a refusal to license an intellectual property right is capable of causing prejudice to consumers within the meaning of [Article 102(b) TFEU]'. It was sufficient that the refusal to supply 'limited technical development to the prejudice of consumers'. In addition, the supply of interoperability information was likely to result in Microsoft's competitors developing work group server operating systems which would be different from the Microsoft systems 'with respect to parameters which consumers consider important'.

Microsoft's claim that the refusal to supply was objectively justified by the need to protect its incentives to innovate was rejected.

14.133 Note that Article 102 TFEU does not provide for any possibility of exemption.

Application and enforcement of EU competition law: Regulation 1/2003

14.134 As discussed above (14.84), the Commission's powers to enforce Articles 101 and 102 were originally set out in Regulation 17/62, which has now been repealed and replaced by Regulation 1/2003. This Regulation also governs the operation of the network of competition authorities, which is at the heart of the modernisation and decentralisation of EU competition law.

14.135 Decentralisation of the application of the competition rules had become essential to relieve the Commission of part of an ever-increasing workload, and allowed it to concentrate its resources on investigating the most serious infringements of the competition provisions. Central to the new regime was the principle that the Commission and the National Competition Authorities 'form … a network of public authorities applying the Community competition rules in close co-operation' (recital 15 Regulation 1/2003). The result has been to give national authorities greater powers: they are well placed to take action as they are better acquainted with local markets and national operators and are closer to complainants (paragraph 46 of the White Paper). The requirement that undertakings wishing to invoke Article 101(3) had to notify the Commission in advance placed them under a heavy burden of work and cost. The ex-post system leaves the responsibility for assessing whether an agreement is compatible with the EU competition rules with the undertakings themselves; years of operation of the rules has ensured that undertakings and national courts are well acquainted with the principles governing the application of Articles 101 and 102 and the Commission has given additional assistance by issuing a raft of Notices (see below **14.151**). Companies are now able to invoke the direct effect of Article 101(3) as an argument in their defence before the national courts.

Provisions of Regulation 1/2003

14.136 Article 2 of the Regulation specifies the burden of proof: it is for the party or authority alleging an infringement of competition law to prove it. In regard to the application of Article 101(3), the undertaking or association of undertakings wishing to rely on Article 101(3) has the burden of proving that it has fulfilled the conditions set out in that provision.

14.137 Article 3 enshrines the principle of supremacy of EU competition law, requiring EU competition law to be applied where there is an effect on trade between Member States, thus ensuring that conduct is being judged in the same way, by the same rules, irrespective of which Member State it takes place in. This is intended to create a 'level playing field' (recital 8 of the Regulation).

14.138 The question as to whether the EU competition provisions or national law takes precedence is clarified by Article 3 of the Regulation. Article 3(1) requires national competition authorities, when applying national competition law to conduct which affects trade between Member States and which falls under Article 101(1) or is an abuse under Article 102, also to apply EU law. Article 3(2) of the Regulation then makes it clear that national competition law may *not* prohibit agreements, decisions by associations of undertakings or concerted practices which would be legal under Union law, either where the conduct does not fall within Article 101(1) or where it would be exempted under Article 101(3) (including by application of a block exemption). However, in regard to Article 102, national authorities are permitted to apply stricter national law controlling 'unilateral conduct'.

14.139 Article 9 of the Regulation allows the Commission to take 'commitments' from undertakings that they will take action to meet the concerns raised by the Commission. The Commission can make these binding on the undertaking and subsequently will take no action unless there is a change of circumstances or the undertaking does not comply with those commitments. This mirrors the similar practice under the Merger Regulation. The Commission has made extensive use of this new power to accept legally binding commitments under Regulation 1/2003, for example, in the 2005/670/EC *Coca-Cola* decision.

The network of national competition authorities and the application of Articles 101 and 102

14.140 Regulation 1/2003 empowers Member States' courts (Article 6) and national competition authorities (NCAs) (Article 5) to apply Articles 101 and 102. The Commission and the national competition authorities (NCAs) form a network of competition authorities. Each Member State designates the competition authority or authorities responsible for the application of Articles 101 and 102 in its own territory (Article 35).

Article 5 empowers the competition authorities of the Member States to apply Articles 101 and 102, allowing them to require that the infringement be brought to an end, to order interim measures, to accept commitments and to impose fines and periodic penalties as well as any other penalty provided for in their national law. Article 6 allows national courts to apply Articles 101 and 102. It is recognised that enforcement systems will differ between different Member States.

Cooperation between the Commission and the NCAs

4.141   A number of provisions in Regulation 1/2003 facilitate cooperation between the Commission, the national competition authorities and the national courts: the Commission and the competition authorities of the Member States shall 'apply the EU competition rules in close cooperation'.

Exchange of information

4.142   The Commission must supply the NCAs with the most important documents relating to its decisions as to whether there has been an infringement of the competition provisions, on the granting of interim relief (Article 8) or on accepting commitments (Article 11(2)). The NCAs must inform the Commission when commencing a formal investigation (Article 11(2)). They should also inform the Commission 'not later than 30 days' before the adoption of any decision requiring an infringement to be brought to an end, before 'accepting commitments and before withdrawing the benefit of a block exemption' (Article 11(4)). Information is to be shared, including confidential information, with certain limitations as to use (Article 12(1)).

Ensuring uniformity

4.143   The Commission may, on its own initiative, submit written observations to national courts 'where the coherent application of [Article 101 or Article 102 TFEU] so requires' and may, with the permission of the court, submit oral observations (Article 15(3)).

4.144   Where NCAs and national courts rule on agreements, decisions or practices under Articles 101 or 102 which are already the subject of a Commission decision, they cannot take decisions which conflict with decisions of the Commission (Article 16).

The role of the Commission

14.145   The Commission has a power enshrined in Article 10 of the Regulation to take a decision 'where the Community public interest... so requires', declaring that Article 101(1) does not apply, either because the conditions of Article 101(1) are not fulfilled or because the conditions of Article 101(3) are satisfied. It may also declare that Article 102 is not applicable. This may be used by the Commission where there is uncertainty about the lawfulness of a certain type of agreement (perhaps of a novel nature) to provide guidance to the market. The Commission should also take action if the 'Community interest requires the adoption of a Commission decision to develop Community competition policy when a new competition issue arises or to ensure effective enforcement'.

14.146 The Commission has discretion as to whether to pursue an investigation following a complaint being made to it. It was held in Case T–24/90 *Automec v Commission* (1992) that 'the Commission…cannot be compelled to carry out an investigation' under the EU competition provisions but can set priorities. However, if the Commission decides not to pursue an investigation, it must give reasons, as required by Article 296 TFEU (ex Article 253 EC) explaining why it concluded 'that there was insufficient Community interest to justify investigation of the case'.

NCAs may consult the Commission on a particular case (Article 11(5)).

14.147 The Commission has issued a Notice on the handling of complaints by the Commission under Articles 81 and 82 of the EC Treaty (now Articles 101 and 102 TFEU) (2004) which sets out the criteria for assessment of the Union interest in the investigation of a case (paragraph 44). It states that:

> the Commission and NCAs, the public enforcers, may focus their action on the investigation of serious infringements of [Articles 101 and 102] which are often difficult to detect [paragraph 2].

Allocation of cases

14.148 Regulation 1/2003 is 'based on a system of parallel competences in which all competition authorities have the power to apply [Articles 101 or 102 TFEU]'. Cases can therefore be dealt with by a single NCA, several NCAs acting in parallel or by the Commission.

14.149 Where the Commission initiates proceedings, the NCAs will no longer have competence to apply Articles 101 and 102 (Article 11(6)). If a NCA is already acting on a case, the Commission must consult it before initiating proceedings. The Notice on cooperation within the network of competition authorities (2004) sets out criteria for the allocation of cases. The NCA in a particular Member State is best 'placed to deal with agreements or practices that substantially affect competition mainly within its territory'.

14.150 Parallel action by two or three NCAs may be appropriate where an agreement or practice has substantial effects on competition in their respective territories and the action of only one NCA would not be sufficient to bring the entire infringement to an end and/ or to sanction it adequately (paragraph 12). Where the agreements or practices effect competition in more than three Member States the Commission should normally take action. Cases can be reallocated. This should be done within two months of information being sent to the network as required by Article 11(3) of Regulation 1/2003.

.151 A number of Notices and a Regulation have been issued by the Commission to facilitate the application of these rules:

- Regulation No 773/2004 relating to the conduct of proceedings by the Commission pursuant to Articles 81 and 82 of the EC Treaty [now Articles 101 and 102 TFEU];

- Commission Notice on the cooperation between the Commission and the courts of the EU Member States in the application of Articles 81 and 82 EC [now Articles 101 and 102 TFEU] (2004);

- Commission Notice on cooperation within the network of Competition Authorities (2004);

- Commission Notice on the handling of complaints by the Commission under Articles 81 and 82 of the EC Treaty (2004);

- Commission Notice on informal guidance relating to novel questions concerning Articles 81 and 82 of the EC Treaty that arise in individual cases (guidance letters) (2004);

- Commission Notice Guidelines on the effect on trade concept contained in Articles 81 and 82 of the Treaty (2004).

Action before the national courts

4.152 The complainant, perhaps consumers or an undertaking adversely affected by anti-competitive activities of one or more undertakings, may choose to take action against the undertaking alleged to have infringed EU competition law in the national courts, rather than filing a complaint to the Commission or the NCAs.

4.153 Articles 101 and 102 TFEU are directly effective and give rise to rights and obligations on the part of individuals; national courts have a duty to protect and enforce these rights. Article 101(2) makes the offending agreements (or parts thereof) null and void. Where questions of interpretation arise as to the correct interpretation of EU competition rules, national courts can make a reference to the Court of Justice under Article 267 TFEU (ex Article 234 EC) and also can now request advice or information from the Commission (Article 15).

4.154 In paragraph 16 of the 'Notice on the handling of complaints by the Commission', the Commission sets out the advantages for the complainant of taking action in the national court including the fact that the national courts can award damages; are better placed than the Commission to adopt interim measures; may combine a claim under EU competition law with other claims under national law; and normally have the power to award legal costs to the successful applicant.

14.155 The role of the national courts has become much more important with the shift in the enforcement of EU competition law to the national level. In Case C–453/99

Courage Ltd v Crehan (2001) the Court of Justice decided that Article 101 precludes the application of the English rule that a party to an illegal contract cannot recover damages from the other party. The party seeking damages, however, must not have significant responsibility for the breach of Article 101. This judgment should encourage actions for damages under Article 101 in the national courts.

Leniency Notice

14.156   In 1996 the Commission adopted a 'Leniency Notice' which sets out the Commission's policy giving immunity or reduced fines to companies which came forward with information about cartels. This followed on from the success of such a policy in the United States. The notice was revised in 2002 to make 'whistle blowing' more attractive to companies and in 2006 it was revised again: the Notice on immunity from fines and reduction of fines in cartel cases (the 'Leniency Notice') (2006). The 2006 notice was adopted 'to provide more guidance to applicants and to increase the transparency of the procedure'.

14.157   Under the current regime, complete immunity from fines is given (i) to the first member of a cartel which informs the Commission about an undetected cartel, giving sufficient information for the Commission to launch an inspection of premises of the implicated companies and (ii) to the first member of a cartel to provide the Commission with the necessary evidence to establish an infringement where the Commission has had sufficient information to launch an inspection but not enough evidence for a successful prosecution. This immunity can only be granted where no undertaking has qualified for immunity under (i).

14.158   Other companies which provide evidence which contributes 'significant added value' to the information which the Commission holds, and which end their involvement in the cartel, will be given reduced fines on a sliding scale (downwards) as further companies come forward.

14.159   The 2006 Notice introduces an innovation which is a 'marker' system whereby an application for immunity can be accepted by the submission of only limited information. The applicant is then granted time to adduce further information and evidence to qualify for exemption. This will mean that companies can more easily submit preliminary information in order to qualify first for immunity.

Merger control

14.160   The Treaty on the Functioning of the European Union does not contain express provisions regulating mergers. There is Court of Justice case law in which both Article 102 and Article 101 have been applied to mergers: see respectively Case 6/72 *Continental Can v Commission* (1973) and Joined Cases 142 and 156/84 *BAT Co Ltd—R J Reynolds Industries Inc v Commission* (1987).

Merger Regulation 139/2004

.161 In 1989 the Council adopted a long-standing Commission proposal for a regulation on the control of concentrations of undertakings: Regulation 4064/89. This Regulation has now been replaced by Regulation 139/2004.

Regulation 139/2004 retains the general schema of the original Regulation. The Regulation requires compulsory notification for concentrations with a Community dimension. An implementing Regulation concerning procedural issues has also been adopted: Regulation 802/2004 implementing Council Regulation (EC) 139/2004 on the control of concentrations between undertakings.

.162 The concept of concentration encompasses mergers, acquisitions and 'full function' joint ventures. A transaction amounts to a concentration when it involves 'a lasting change in the control of the undertakings concerned and therefore in the structure of the market' (recital 20 ECMR). The term 'concentration' is defined in Article 3 and the Commission has adopted a Notice on the concept of concentration (1998) which sets out in detail the means by which control is deemed to be acquired for the purposes of the Regulation.

Types of mergers

4.163 Mergers can be: horizontal, between undertakings producing the same products; vertical, between undertakings operating at different levels of the same product market: or conglomerate, where the parties to the proposed merger do not participate in the same product market.

4.164 Non-horizontal merger guidelines applying to vertical and conglomerate mergers were published by the Commission in October 2008 while guidelines on horizontal mergers had been published in 2004 (see Further Reading below).

Joint ventures

4.165 A joint venture falls within the definition of a 'concentration' when it performs all the functions of an autonomous economic entity on a lasting basis (Article 3(4) Regulation 139/2004). This concept is explained in more detail in the Commission Notice on the concept of full function joint ventures (1998).

'A Community dimension'

4.166 A concentration will have a Community dimension when the participating undertakings meet specified thresholds of turnover. The thresholds in the original Regulation were set very high, so relatively few concentrations came within their scope. In 2004 an additional, lower, set of thresholds was added in an attempt to bring more concentrations within the scope of application of control by the Union. These thresholds have been retained in the present Regulation and are set out in Article 1(2) and (3) of the

Regulation. However, a concentration which satisfies the thresholds will not have a Community dimension if each of the undertakings concerned achieves more than two-thirds of its aggregate Union-wide turnover within one and the same Member State, the rationale being that in such a case, the relevant Member State is more suitably placed to assess such a concentration (Article 1(2)).

'The one-stop shop'

14.167 The system put in place by the original Regulation and continued under the new Regulation is inspired by the principle of the 'one-stop shop' whereby concentrations falling within the Regulation thresholds (as set out in Article 1(2) and (3)), need be notified to the Commission only, thus preventing the need for multiple filings in different Member States. However, if the concentration does not have a Community dimension, because it does not meet the required turnover thresholds, national rules apply (these are not harmonised). The idea of setting thresholds is to create an easily applied formula, a 'bright line jurisdictional test' to determine whether the concentration is to be assessed at a national or EU level. It is recognised that application of the thresholds will not always provide an appropriate outcome so there are mechanisms within the Regulation allowing concentrations to be referred either way; these have been made more flexible under the new Regulation.

Exceptions to the general principle

Referral from the Commission to the authorities of a Member State by application of the Member State concerned: Article 9

14.168 The general principle that concentrations falling within the Regulation thresholds should be notified to the Commission only, is subject to a number of exceptions. Under Article 9, notified concentrations may be referred back to the Member State by the Commission where a concentration threatens significantly to affect competition in a market within that Member State which 'presents all the characteristics of a distinct market' (Article 9(2)a) or where the concentration affects competition within a Member State which presents the characteristics of a distinct market and 'does not constitute a substantial part of the [internal market]' (Article 9(2)b). The decision as to whether there is such a 'distinct market' and whether there is a threat to competition is determined by the Commission; the Commission then has discretion as to whether to refer the whole or part of the case back to the Member State concerned. If it decides there is not a 'distinct market' it will deal with the matter itself.

Referral from the Authorities of a Member State by application of the undertakings concerned: Article 4(4)

14.169 Undertakings may request a referral of whole or part of a concentration from the Commission to a Member State where it may significantly affect competition in a market within that Member State which presents all the characteristics of a distinct market. The Commission informs all the Member States of this submission and the Member State concerned has 15 days to respond; unless the Member State disagrees, the Commission can then decide, if it agrees that there is such a distinct market and that competition may be significantly affected, whether to refer the concentration in whole or in part to the Member State concerned.

Referral from national authorities to the Commission by application of the undertakings concerned: Article 4(5)

.170   Where a concentration (as defined in Article 3) does not fall to be considered by the Commission because it does not have a Community dimension as determined by application of the thresholds under Article 1, the undertakings themselves can nonetheless request (by reasoned submission prior to notification), a referral to the Commission. The concertation must be capable of being reviewed under the national competition law of at least three Member States (Article 4(5)). All Member States are notified and the disagreement of one Member State (within 15 days of notification) is sufficient to ensure that the transfer does not occur.

Referral from one or more Member States to the Commission: Article 22

4.171   One or more Member States may request the Commission to examine a concentration (as defined in Article 3) which does not have a Union dimension within the meaning defined in Article 1 because it affects trade between Member States and threatens to 'significantly affect competition within the territory of the Member State or States making the request' (Article 22(1)). If the Commission decides that the proposed concentration does meet these criteria, it can decide to consider the proposed concentration itself (Article 22(3)).

4.172   The Commission has issued a Notice to assist Member States and notifying parties in applying for referrals: Commission Notice on case referral in respect of concentrations (2005).

4.173   Proposed concentrations with a Community dimension must be notified to the Commission before their implementation (Article 4(1)) and implementation must be suspended pending the outcome of the Commission's investigation (Article 7(1)).

4.174   Under Article 21(4) of the Regulation, Member States are permitted to 'take appropriate measures to protect legitimate interests other than those taken into consideration by this regulation'. This allows a Member State to scrutinise and possibly prohibit a merger which affects sensitive interests such as 'public security, plurality of the media and prudential rules'.

The substantive test

14.175   During the consultation following the Commission's review of Council Regulation 4064/89, the question of whether the existing substantive test should be retained or changed was the subject of much debate. The test in the *old* Regulation (now annulled and replaced) required that there should be the creation or strengthening of a dominant position which significantly impeded competition in the internal market. In the United States and a number of other jurisdictions the test for intervention is whether the effect of a merger may substantially lessen competition (SLC) and, when the adoption of a new Merger Regulation was under review, a number of academics and Member States (in particular the United Kingdom and Ireland) were in favour of adopting the same test. There is, in any case, an argument for harmonising the applicable standard.

The SIEC test: Significant Impediment to Effective Competition

14.176 The test that was adopted for EU Merger control is the SIEC test: Significant Impediment to Effective Competition. It is set out in Article 2(3) which reads as follows: 'A concentration which would significantly impede effective competition, in the [internal market] or in a substantial part of it, in particular as the result of the creation or strengthening of a dominant position, shall be declared incompatible with the [internal market]'. This new formulation significantly broadens the scope of the test under the present EU merger regime from the position under Regulation 4064/89. The Commission now has power to intervene even where there is no creation or strengthening of a dominant position.

14.177 It was already clear that the EU merger regime would apply not only to the creation or strengthening of the dominant position of a single firm, but also to the creation of joint or collective dominance of a duopoly or oligopoly (see below at 14.18.2)). Whilst dominance is still likely to be the trigger under Regulation 139/2004, the Commission is now empowered to intervene where the merger might not result in the creation of a dominant position either of one company or joint or collective dominance of an oligopoly. In an oligopoly where there are no coordinated effects (parallel behaviour) which are required to establish collective dominance, the merging of two of the undertakings may nonetheless reduce competition by the reduction of competitive pressure on the remaining members of the oligopoly. Under the old Regulation, which had required the creation or strengthening of a dominant position, this situation, where no collective dominant position is created or strengthened, was not caught by the merger regime.

14.178 Further explanation and guidance on the application of the Merger Regulation to oligopolies is provided in the Notice on the assessment of horizontal mergers (see Further Reading below).

Joint/collective dominance

14.179 In Cases C–68/94 and C–30/95 *France v Commission (Kali & Salz)* (1998) the Court of Justice established that joint dominant positions fall within the scope of the Merger Regulation even though the Regulation does not explicitly say so. In Case T–102/96 *Gencor v Commission* (1997) (the first Commission decision actually proscribing a merger on the grounds that it would create a joint dominant position), the then Court of First Instance clarified that a position of collective dominance could be held by undertakings in an oligopoly.

.180 In T–342/99 *Airtours plc v Commission* (2002), the then Court of First Instance annulled the Commission decision prohibiting the proposed merger between Airtours and First Choice. This was one of three Commission decisions prohibiting mergers overturned by the Court between June and October 2003, giving rise to unprecedented criticism of the Commission. The Commission prohibited a merger between Airtours and First Choice on the ground that the merger would create a collective dominant position. As discussed above (see **14.114**), this case set out the criteria for the establishment of collective dominance. The General Court held that the three cumulative conditions for the establishment of collective dominance are: first, there must be sufficient market transparency so that each member of the dominant oligopoly has the ability to know how the other members are behaving in order to monitor whether or not they are adopting a common policy. Secondly, the implementation of the common policy must be sustainable over time, so there must be adequate deterrents or punishment mechanisms to ensure that members of the oligopoly do not depart from the common policy. And, third, it is necessary to establish that the foreseeable reaction of 'current and future competitors, as well as consumers, would not jeopardise the results expected from the common policy'.

4.181 Applying these criteria to the position after the proposed merger, the General Court held that the Commission had failed to establish that a collective dominant position would be created; the decision was 'vitiated by a series of errors of assessment as to factors fundamental to any assessment of whether a collective dominant position might be created'.

4.182 Before the adoption of the new Regulation, therefore, case law had clarified that the creation of both joint dominance and collective dominance of an oligopoly were caught by EU merger control and the judgment in Case T–342/99 *Airtours* (2002) set out stringent criteria for assessing whether a merger may lead to the creation of a collective dominant position. There is case law of the European Courts on collective dominance both under Article 102 and the merger regime. However, the nature of the assessment is different because the application of Article 102 involves an analysis of whether a collective dominant position has been established whilst under the Merger Regulation the Commission is determining whether a collective dominant position will be created in the future by the merger.

14.183 Under Article 29 of Regulation 139/2004, 'substantial and likely efficiencies' should be taken into account in determining the impact of the concentration on competition in the internal market. The Article states that 'it is possible that the efficiencies brought about by the concentration counteract the effects on competition, and in particular the potential harm to consumers…and that, as a consequence, the concentration would not significantly impede effective competition in the [internal market]'. The factors to be taken into account by the Commission are set out in the Guidelines, paragraphs 77–88.

14.184 The Guidelines also contain criteria (paragraph 90) to be taken into account in the case of failing firms when it can be the case that the disappearance of the firm would cause greater harm to competition than the proposed merger:

> *89. The Commission may decide that an otherwise problematic merger is nevertheless compatible with the [internal market] if one of the merging parties is a failing firm. The basic requirement is that the deterioration of the competitive structure that follows the merger cannot be said to be caused by the merger. This will arise where the competitive structure of the market would deteriorate to at least the same extent in the absence of the merger.*

> *90. The Commission considers the following three criteria to be especially relevant for the application of a 'failing firm defence'. First, the allegedly failing firm would in the near future be forced out of the market because of financial difficulties if not taken over by another undertaking. Second, there is no less anti-competitive alternative purchase than the notified merger. Third, in the absence of a merger, the assets of the failing firm would inevitably exit the market.*

Market share threshold

14.185 The Guidelines state that the Commission is unlikely to find 'concern' in horizontal mergers, where the market share post-merger of the new entity is below 25 per cent of the market.

14.186 In its Guidelines on the assessment of non-horizontal mergers (2004), the Commission indicates that it is unlikely to need to assess non-horizontal mergers, where the market share post-merger of the new entity in each of the markets concerned is below 30 per cent of the market.

Time limits

14.187 The strength of the EU merger regime has been the short, legally enforceable deadlines for review. The new Regulation has introduced some flexibility into this regime. Mergers are notified to the Commission using the prescribed form (called a 'Form CO'), which is done electronically.

14.188 Once the proposed merger has been notified to the Commission, the initial investigation (Phase I) must be completed within 25 working days. This can be extended to 35 days if the Commission receives a request from a Member State for a referral under Article 9(2) or where the undertakings concerned offer commitments. At the end of Phase I, a decision is taken as to whether the proposed merger is or is not compatible with the internal market; if it is, and this can be in the light of the commitments offered by the undertaking(s), then the case is cleared. If, however, the Phase I assessment raises serious doubts as to its compatibility with the internal market then a more in-depth Phase II assessment is launched. Most cases do not warrant a Phase II investigation. Less than

3 per cent do so; in 2007, 402 cases were notified, 15 went into Phase II and only one was prohibited (Case M.4439—*Ryanair/Aer Lingus* (2007)). In Phase II, the Commission has 90 working days to rule in favour of or against the proposed merger with the possibility of an extension of 15 days where the undertakings offer commitments after the 54th day after initiation of proceedings. Recognising the pressure that these time limits have created, there is also now the possibility of an extension of up to 20 days where the case is a complex one, at the request of, or with the agreement of, the parties.

1.189 Mergers which by their nature are not problematic may be notified to the Commission with a request that they are assessed using a simplified procedure. The requirements for such treatment are set out in the 'Notice on a simplified procedure for treatment of certain concentrations' (2000) and the application thereof is usually because of the small market shares of the undertakings concerned. Typically a case qualifies if the market share post-merger would be less than 15 per cent (horizontally) or 25 per cent (vertically) or if it qualifies for any other reason as set out in the notice.

1.190 The Commission has issued Best Practices on the conduct of EC merger control proceedings (2004). In order to improve decision-making in merger cases in particular, the Commission has also created a post of Chief Competition Economist who will, with his team, participate in merger and other competition investigations.

FURTHER READING

Al-Dabbah, M., 'Conduct, dominance and abuse in market relationships' (2000) *ECL Review* 45.

Baker, S. and Wu, L., 'Applying the market definition guidelines of the EC Commission' (1998) *ECL Review* 273.

Baxter, S. and Dethmers, F., 'Collective Dominance under EC Merger control—after Airtours and the introduction of unilateral effects is there still a future for collective dominance?' (2006) *ECL Review* 148.

Carle, J., 'The new leniency notice' (2002) 6 *ECL Review* 265–272.

Commission Communication, Guidance on the Commission's enforcement priorities in applying Article 82 of the EC Treaty [now Article 102 TFEU] to abusive exclusionary conduct by dominant undertakings [2009] OJ C045/07, see also IP/08/1877.

Commission Communication, Report on the Functioning of Regulation 1/2003 COM(2009) 206 final.

Commission, DG Competition Discussion Paper on the Application of Article 82 EC, see IP/05/1626.

Commission Guidelines on the assessment of horizontal mergers under the Council Regulation on the control of concentrations between undertakings [2004] OJ C31/05.

Commission Guidelines on the assessment of non-horizontal mergers under the Council Regulation on the control of concentrations between undertakings [2008] OJ C265/07.

Commission Notice on case referral in respect of concentrations [2005] OJ C56/02.

Commission Notice on Immunity from Fines and Reduction of Fines in Cartel Cases [2006] OJ C298/11.

Commission Notice on the concept of full-function joint ventures under Council Regulation (EEC) No 4064/89 on the control of concentrations between undertakings [1998] OJ C66/01.

Commission Notice, Guidelines on the effect on trade concept contained in Articles 81 and 82 of the Treaty [now Articles 101 and 102 TFEU] [2004] OJ C101/07.

Commission Notice, The definition of relevant market for the purposes of Community competition law [1997] OJ C372/05.

Ehlermann, C., 'The modernization of EC antitrust policy: a legal and cultural revolution?' (2000) *Common Market Law Review* 537–590.

Furse, M., *Competition Law of the EC and UK* (5th edn, Oxford: OUP, 2006).

Griffiths, M., 'A glorification of de minimis—the regulation on vertical agreements' (2000) *Common Market Law Review* 241.

Institut Economique Molinari, 'DG Competition Discussion Paper on the Application of Article 82 of the Treaty to Exclusionary Abuses—A Comment' (accessible at <http://ec.europa.eu/competition/antitrust/art82/024_en.pdf>); see also IP/05/1626.

Jones, A. and Sufrin, B., *EC Competition Law: Text, Cases and Materials* (3rd edn, Oxford: OUP, 2007).

Jones, A., 'Woodpulp: concerted practice and/or conscious parallelism?' (1993) *ECL Review* 273.

Klimisch, A. and Krueger, B., 'Decentralised application of EC competition law' (1999) *ECL Review* 463.

Korah, V., *Cases and Materials on EC Competition Law* (3rd edn, Oxford: Hart Publishing, 2006).

Korah, V., *Introductory Guide to EC Competition Law and Practice*, (9th edn, Oxford: Hart Publishing, 2007).

Monti, G., 'The scope of collective dominance under Article 82' (2001) 38 *Common Market Law Review* 131.

Rivas, R. and Horspool, M., *Modernisation and Decentralisation of Competition Law* (Kluwer, 2000).

Soames, 'An analysis of the principles of concerted practice and collective dominance: a distinction without a difference?' (1996) *ECL Review* 24.

Whish, R., 'Regulation 2790/99: The Commission's new style block exemption for vertical agreements' (2000) 37 *Common Market Law Review* 887–924.

Whish, R., 'The enforcement of EC competition law in the domestic courts of member states' (1994) *ECL Review* 60.

Whish, R., *Competition Law* (6th edn, Oxford: OUP, 2008).

Ysewyn, J. and Caffarra, C., 'Two's company, three's a crowd: the future of collective dominance after the *Kali & Salz* judgment' (1998) *ECL Review* 468.

SELF-TEST QUESTIONS

1   What elements have to be proved in order to establish a breach of Article 101? Cite
appropriate cases.

2   What is a block exemption?

3   What are the key factors to define a relevant market?

4   Explain the concept of 'abuse' under Article 102 with examples from relevant case law.

5   What routes are open to a company which believes that a competitor/supplier is breaching EU competition law?

6   What is the effect of Regulation 1/2003 on the application of EU competition law? Explain
its effect on the application of Article 101(3).

7   What is the role of a national competition authority?

15

Environmental law and policy

SUMMARY

This chapter reviews environmental law and policy in the European Union, considering the Union powers and the international context. It covers:

- The framework for EU environmental law and policy: institutional and constitutional aspects
- Principles of environmental law and policy, including sustainability
- Union air and water pollution legislation
- Integrated pollution prevention and control
- Trade in endangered species
- Nature conservation
- Enforcement and citizen participation
- Enforcement of environmental law
- Civil and criminal liability
- International agreements

The framework for Union environmental law and policy

15.1 European Union environmental law has had a significant impact on the direction of environmental policy, both at European Union level and within each Member State. The body of Union law instruments setting standards of environmental protection is itself large, and is still growing. The principles upon which EU environmental law is founded influence the development of policy on many levels, internationally and locally.

15.2 The European Union has been markedly proactive in the development of environmental standards and policy, and in driving forward the level of environmental protection in each of the Member States. Environmental policy then is a good illustration of the development of influence of the European Union as a body, the addition of environmental powers representing an important marker in the shift of focus from the more limited economic sphere of activity that typified the original Community Treaties to the broader aspirations and ambitions of the organisation today.

15.3 Environmental law is simultaneously part of the Union's objective to establish a single market and a reflection of the broader social aims of that objective.

Evolution of environmental policy

15.4 The original EEC Treaty did not include environmental law competences, and for a time the development of initiatives affecting environmental protection in the Member States was confused: it was generally understood that legislation introduced to construct a European internal market potentially impacted upon the environment, or impacted upon environmental protection policy operating in the Member States, but it was not clear that environmental legislation was in all cases properly single or common market law. There were additionally a range of widespread concerns, from fears that market rules, either harmonising measures or the free movement rights, would jeopardise environmental standards enacted by the Member States, to concerns about the appropriateness of Union measures affecting the environment at a time when the Member States had not all agreed the Union should include environmental powers. By developing clear competence for environmental policy and environmental protection legislation in the Treaties, these circles were to some extent squared. The tension, however, remains between the market orientated measures encouraging economic growth and the desire to protect the environment. If there is recognition that measures aimed at developing the internal market have potential environmental impact, there is still a question about the appropriateness of environmental policy developed centrally. Environmental policy is an area where the relationship between centralisation and standardisation compared to diversity is most interesting.

15.5 The defining moments in the development of EU environmental law and policy fall into five main periods. In 1957 the original Treaty of Rome setting up the European Economic Communities made no mention of the environment. Reference to environmental issues was made in the First Common Market Directive (64/548/EEC) in 1967 which contained clear environmental consideration of the labelling of dangerous goods. In 1972 the UN Stockholm Environment Conference was held which not only highlighted the cause but provided impetus for the enactment of the EEC's first Environmental Action Programme in 1973. The second period—prior to the Single European Act—is defined by environmental action without Treaty basis. Between 1973 and 1986 initiatives such as directives were enacted in fields like water, air and waste pollution, while in 1980, the Court of Justice ruled for the first time that internal market measures can lawfully pursue environmental objectives. In 1985, in Case 240/83 *Procureur de la Republique v ABDHU*, the Court of Justice first held that environmental protection is 'one of the Community's essential objectives' (see **15.9** below).

15.6 Crucially, in 1987, the Single European Act, the first proper reforming measure of the 1957 Treaty establishing the EEC, introduced the Environmental Title into the

Treaty. From 1987 until 1993 this was followed by a rapid expansion of environmental legislation, mostly in furtherance of the internal market programme. Moreover, in 1988 the Court of Justice ruled that environmental protection is a mandatory requirement that can affect the free movement of goods. In the next year, a separate Directorate General was established for the Environment, while work began following an agreement to create a European Environment Agency, which itself began work in 1993. In 1992 the Seminal Fifth Environmental Action Programme was announced, which stressed 'shared responsibility' and greater flexibility in rule-making, while the precautionary principle, long one of the main tenets of European environmental action, was added to the Treaty of Rome by the Maastricht Treaty. The fourth period saw a focus on an economic, social and environmental European union. In 1997 the Amsterdam Treaty reformed the Treaty of Rome once again and incorporated the principle of sustainable development as an objective of the European Union. Meanwhile, the requirement that environmental protection be integrated into all areas of Union policy, formerly a provision in the Environment Title of the Treaty, was relocated as an overarching principle of the Treaty in its first Articles. The fifth period to date includes preparations for enlargement of the Union and the ramifications of the Treaty of Lisbon. In 2001 the EU developed its Sustainable Development Strategy, and since then sustainability has grown in stature as an overarching principle of European governance. Sustainable development is not only mentioned in the preamble to the Treaty on the Functioning of the European Union as an aspiration, but is repeatedly mentioned throughout the Treaty (Articles 3(3), 3(5), 21(2)(d) and (f), TEU and Articles 11, 119 and 140 TFEU). Additionally, several of those provisions refer to EU relations with the international community, and seek to integrate environmental protection within EU foreign policy. There is then, in some respects, a sixth period with the development of EU environmental policy on the global scale. However, this picture is mixed. The EU has a clear commitment to environmental causes, but international tensions are often created where it moves at a pace beyond that agreeable to the rest of the global community. International criticism of the EU 'going it alone' is to some extent counterbalanced by EU frustrations over limited progress in multilateral political negotiations. In striking some form of balance the EU both negotiates multilaterally yet also acts alone at times in specific areas. Whether combining these actions can form a coherent—meaning successful—whole for EU international environmental policy is unclear. This is perhaps inevitable given the varied nature of international fora, participants and impetus across sectors, when compared to the EU's internal organisation, even with different Member States' views and attitudes to compliance. But for these reasons any sixth period is labelled here as developing and not yet defined.

15.7 In the period prior to 1986, when the Single European Act introduced the Environment Title into the Treaty, there were no express provisions in the Treaty on environmental matters. This did not prevent the enactment of environmental legislation and the institutions made frequent use of powers in Article 100 EEC (on market legislation, now Article 115 TFEU) and Article 235 EEC (on implied powers, now Article 352 TFEU) as the legal basis for such legislation.

15.8 Following the 1967 Directive on labelling dangerous products, the Union addressed environmental issues on the premise that legislation affecting environmental standards could affect business and businesses' costs, and that commonly agreed environmental initiatives removed non-tariff barriers to intra-Union trade. The legislation was seen as part and parcel of the creation of a level playing field where different requirements could produce hurdles for some participants in the internal market. At the same time, environmental concerns were rising as the awareness of resource depletion and initial doubts as to global warming took hold. In 1970 the Commission declared the necessity of drawing up a Community Action Programme on the Environment. The United Nations Stockholm Conference was followed by a joint declaration by all the Member States of what was then the European Community on the environment. Four Action Programmes on the Environment were agreed and, in conjunction with the Action Programmes, an extensive body of substantive environmental rules. The European Union itself has subsequently become a party to a number of (international) environmental treaties (see **15.91**).

15.9 By 1985, the amount of environmental legislation had become voluminous and the Court of Justice concluded that environmental protection had become an 'essential objective' of Community law (in Case 240/83 *Procureur de la Republique v ABDHU* (1985)). That being so, the environment had clearly become a sphere of policy and legislative action that was not always well premised on the internal market or other Union powers cited as the basis for the legislation. Product standards for car engines that minimised pollution could be properly understood as market harmonisation measures with an environmental, and perhaps supplementary, consequence. But legislation on bathing waters was difficult to link back to the construction of a European market.

15.10 The Single European Act dealt with these difficulties by creating a formal Treaty basis for environmental legislation, and thereby clearly making environmental policy a legitimate area of activity. Title VII on Environment in the EEC Treaty, created three new Articles: 130r, 130s and 130t (now amended and renumbered as Articles 191–193 TFEU). At the same time, specific mention was made of the environment in the provisions providing for legislation in the field of the internal market, making it clear that this power could also properly be used to create legislation with an environmental protection consequence. The EEC Treaty had added a competence to produce 'single market' harmonisation legislation (the new Article 100a EEC (now Article 114 TFEU)) to the existing power for 'common market' legislation, and Article 100a specifically referred to environmental protection in providing a mechanism for Member States to continue to apply high environmental protection standards that might be lessened by the effect of the market harmonisation legislation.

15.11 The overall result however was a little unsatisfactory since the positive of having alternative bases for environmental legislation (single market harmonisation measures under the then Article 100a EEC; and environmental policy legislation under Article 130s EEC (now Article 192 TFEU)) had to be set against different procedures applying to the adoption of legislation under Article 100a EEC compared to those in operation with Article 130s EEC legislation. The important distinction, ultimately, between the two legal bases for legislation related to whether or not an individual state could block the legislation. Under Article 130s EEC the requirement was for unanimity in Council, whereas single market measures under Article 100a could be agreed by qualified majority vote. The processes under which the Council comes to decisions, and by which legislation is adopted, are considered in more detail in **Chapter 4**. The Court of Justice, then, was required to deal with institutional disputes and disputes as to whether the use of Article 100a or Article 130s was appropriate to the environmental legislation at issue. In Case C–300/89 *Commission v Council (Titanium Dioxide)* (1991), the Council and Commission disputed whether the proposed Directive on procedures for harmonising the programmes for the reduction and eventual elimination of pollution caused by waste from the titanium dioxide industry was a single market measure, or an environmental policy measure. In truth, it was probably both. However, the choice of legal basis was important because of the implications for decision-making in Council. The Court of Justice held that the Directive had dual aims and therefore its 'centre of gravity' had to be determined. Since the Directive's objective was the elimination of disparities in competition it should have been passed under Article 100a (now Article 114). It was then a single market measure and could be agreed by qualified majority vote. However, in Case C–155/91 *Commission v Council* (1993), the Court of Justice decided that the protection of the environment was the principal objective of a Directive on waste disposal (Directive 91/156) and, even though it would have an impact on the functioning of the internal market, the Directive had to be based on Article 175 EC (now Article 192 TFEU).

15.12 Disputes as to whether measures aiming at protecting the environment should be market measures or environmental policy measures were not exactly engaging for citizens as a whole, particularly when the only real difference at issue was with regards to a choice between already complicated decision-making and adoption procedures. At the same time, the requirement of unanimity for decisions and legislation based on the Environmental Title of the Treaty to some extent inhibited the aspiration to develop environmental policy ensuring a high standard of protection. Environmental legislation required protracted negotiations and the result was generally diluted provisions, because of the difficulty of achieving a common position in a Council with each Member having a veto.

15.13 The enactment of the Maastricht Treaty saw the elevation of environmental policy and protection to one of the fundamental objectives of the EU. Furthermore, it saw the introduction of the precautionary principle into the principles of environmental protection referred to in Article 130r EEC (now Article 191 TFEU, see **15.34**). Environmental protection requirements were to be 'integrated into the definition and implementation of other community policies' in an attempt to require the cross-reference of all policy areas with environmental policy.

15.14 The Amsterdam Treaty, agreed in 1997, made further relevant amendments to the framework of Union environmental law by simplifying decision-making procedures that applied to environmental policy, thereby dealing with the problem noted at **15.12**. Article 192 TFEU now permits the adoption of environmental legislation following qualified majority vote in Council. However, unanimity voting remained the rule for provisions which were primarily of a fiscal nature, measures concerning town and country planning, land use and management of water resources.

15.15 The Amsterdam amendments also saw the enshrinement of the sustainable development concept within the preamble and the objectives of both the Community Treaty and the Treaty on European Union. The Amsterdam reforms introduced a new Article 6 EC (now Article 11 TFEU), which adopted identical wording to Article 130r EEC, calling for environmental protection requirements to be integrated into the definition and implementation of other policies, but transferred the provision from the Environment Title to the overarching provisions at the start of the Treaty and added the words 'in particular with a view to promoting sustainable development'. Article 11 TFEU and its relationship with the general principles of Union law is considered in **Chapter 6**. Finally, the Amsterdam Treaty amended the European Community Treaty to make clear that all proposals by the Commission relating to the environment should be based on a high level of environmental protection.

15.16 The European Union's Sixth Action Programme on the Environment: 'Environment 2010: Our future, Our choice' will expire in mid-2012, with no seventh action programme fully formulated as yet. The Sixth Action Programme set out to identify overall objectives and priority actions for the Union's future environment policy. The priority areas for action, which the Commission identifies and defines in this programme as facing the greatest problems, are: tackling climate change; protecting and restoring nature and bio-diversity; achieving a quality of environment where the levels of man-made contaminants, including different types of radiation, do not give rise to significant impacts on, or risks to, human health; and ensuring the sustainable use of natural resources and management of wastes.

Institutional structure

15.17 The institutions of the Union are considered in earlier chapters. The Commission, Council, Parliament and the Court of Justice all have a role to play in the development and implementation of environmental policy. Work in the development of environmental policy is further supported by the European Environment Agency, and, where appropriate, the European Ombudsman and the European Investment Bank.

15.18 The Commission, as the body responsible for implementing EU policies, for the enforcement of Union law and with certain investigatory powers, draws up the environmental action programmes and in accordance with its right of legislative initiative drafts proposed environmental legislation. It is, on the one hand, the driving force behind new environmental policies; whilst on the other hand it is responsible for enforcing the economic aims of the Union. As noted above (**15.6**), the Commission has an Environmental Directorate General. The Commission has also decided to create a further Directorate General for Climate Action, and the two commissioners will no doubt work together closely. However, since the environment should form a component of other policies, there are Commission officials in other Directorates that also deal with environmental issues, for example in the Energy and Transport Directorate General.

5.19 The Council, as the political body made up of representatives from each Member State, is constituted by Environment Ministers when the Council agrees environmental measures.

5.20 The European Parliament has traditionally been a significant mouthpiece of concern over environmental issues and it has a vigorous Committee on the environment. Parliament has generally opposed the use of 'soft law' rules of environmental law and has pushed for greater transparency in the relevant decision-making processes.

5.21 The Court of Justice has widely been seen as a driving force in the development of Union environmental policy and the enforcement of environmental law. It has interpreted environmental directives purposively, as much as according to the spirit of their environmental objectives as the letter of the law, and the Court has been particularly vigilant in striving to ensure that environmental law is properly implemented in the Member States, while at the same time using the proportionality principle to counterbalance environmental obstacles to the free movement of goods. All this is considered in **Chapters 6** and **10.**

15.22 The European Environmental Agency was established by Regulation 1210/90/EEC and is based in Copenhagen. Its principal tasks are to monitor, gather information, establish the European environment information and observation network, provide the Union and the Member States with objective information and record, collate and assess data on the state of the environment. Such information might be used to form the basis for new European legislation in this field. A report detailing this information is published every three years by the Agency.

15.23 The Agency has no enforcement or policing powers in relation to environmental legislation, despite efforts on the part of the Parliament to give the Agency such a role. Instead, the Agency takes its remit as one of trying to improve compliance within the Members States rather than as a Union body trying to police environmental legislation.

15.24 The Agency is an autonomous entity, having separate legal personality and run by a management board. It has an Executive Director and a scientific committee.

Sources of European Union environmental law

15.25 European Union environmental law is contained in: (i) the Treaties; (ii) secondary legislation based upon Article 192 TFEU, and from other Union policy areas where the effect of the legislation impacts upon environmental protection standards;

(iii) International Treaties to which the Union is a party; and (iv) the judgments and principles set out by the Court of Justice.

15.26 The Treaty on the Functioning of the European Union is the source of the environmental principles, discussed below (see **15.32–15.45**) and the sustainability and integration requirements set out in Article 11 TFEU. Since each of these provisions relates mostly to the development of policy, the Treaty Articles are not directly effective.

15.27 Where there are regulations in the field of environmental protection, these also are rarely directly effective. The regulations that exist give effect to international treaties, agricultural policy, administrative matters (such as setting up the European Environment Agency) and the eco-auditing and eco-labelling schemes.

15.28 Directives can be an important source of environmental law, and the Court of Justice has found provisions in environmental directives directly effective in a twin-track approach to ensuring the common application of Union law, and maximising the standard of environmental protection ensured. However, environmental directives are often drafted in such a way as to lack detail, contain vague commitments and wide-ranging derogations aimed at softening the impact on Member States that might be particularly hard hit. In essence, the directives themselves are often frameworks or structures for other policy or legal initiatives, and it is then generally difficult to find within them rights that can be enforced by individuals by virtue of the direct effect doctrine (see **Chapter 7**). In such situations, the Court of Justice has focused upon the obligation imposed upon the state rather than the question of whether individual rights have been created. In Case C–129/96 *Inter-EnvironnementWallonie ASBL v Region Wallone* (1997) a problem with the interpretation of waste under Directive 75/442/EEC was considered, with the Walloon region of Belgium interpreting the term differently to the definition of waste set out in the Directive. The Court focused upon the obligation on the Belgian state to comply with the provisions of a directive, rather than the question of whether any rights for individual citizens were created by the legislation, insisting on the definition of waste in the Directive rather than that used in the Walloon region. The Directive was not yet in force, the period for implementation not having expired. However, the Court ruled that the obligation under the Directive extended to a requirement not to act in such a way as to inhibit the Directive's objectives before the Directive was in force, thus extending the obligation on the Member State to comply with the spirit and terms of a directive from the time it is adopted and whether or not environmental directives create actionable rights for individuals.

15.29 Since many environmental directives contain vague requirements, and extensive derogations, it can be difficult to assess whether a Member State has fully complied with the requirements. That being so, the directive is a useful form of legislation for environmental protection measures, since it requires implementation and since it leaves the choice of how to implement the environmental initiative to the Member State. Most Union environmental law comes in the form of directives.

15.30 Decisions, defined as secondary legislation by Article 288 TFEU as binding in their entirety upon those to whom they are addressed, are rare in environmental law, being limited mainly to matters of monitoring and information gathering. The institutions may also use recommendations or opinions; however, these are not binding and only have persuasive effect and are seldom used in the environmental area.

5.31 The case law of the Court of Justice is itself a source of environmental law, the Court having developed relevant principles from the Treaties and the traditions in the Member States. In Case 302/86 *Commission v Denmark (Danish Bottles)* (1988, see also **10.37**) the Court accepted environmental protection as a justification for a bottle recycling scheme that impeded the trade in drinks while insisting on the proportionality of measures aiming at environmental protection, and in particular ruling measures that went beyond what was necessary to achieve the environmental objective could not continue. In this case then, the requirement that containers be part of the deposit and return system was held to be reasonable to ensure the recycling scheme worked, the recycling scheme itself contributing to environmental protection. However, the requirement that only specific containers could be used and be part of a scheme was deemed disproportionate since the recycling of other containers could also contribute to environmental protection and banning their use went beyond what was necessary to protect the environment. Then, in Case T–13/99 *Pfizer Animal Health SA v Council* (2002), the Court of First Instance (now the General Court) held that a cost/benefit analysis is a particular expression of the principle of proportionality in cases involving risk management. A cost/benefit analysis is therefore relevant to an assessment of the proportionality of an environmental protection measure.

Environmental principles

15.32 Environmental law is particularly apposite to legal principles, and there are various principles set out in the Treaty that apply to the development of environmental law and policy. The general principles of Union law are discussed in **Chapter 6**, and as is noted above (**15.21**) the proportionality principle must be considered in the evaluation of any environmental protection measure. Subsidiarity is also particularly relevant to environmental rules, it being generally understood that environmental rules should always be considered in terms of local impact. Article 191 TFEU expands on this and adds some principles specific to environmental law.

Article 191(2) TFEU states:

> *Union policy…shall be based on the precautionary principle and on the principles that preventive action should be taken, that environmental damage should as a priority be rectified at source and that the polluter should pay.*

15.33 None of these principles are further defined in the Treaty but they have been applied with varying degrees of success in the Court of Justice and national courts. The institutions are working together towards a better understanding of what is required by environmental principles with the development of European Principles for the

Environment. The aim of the initiative for European Principles for the Environment is to harmonise environmental principles, practices and standards associated with the financing of projects. Taking the principles set out in Article 191 TFEU, and others drawn from Union environmental legislation, project sponsors sign up to the European Principles for the Environment to ensure environmental protection is factored into the development of any project, and to develop common and shared understanding of what is meant and required by the environmental principles operating in Union law.

Precautionary principle

15.34 The precautionary principle was added to the list of environmental principles last, and only became a formal part of the Environment Title in 1993. The requirements associated with precaution are not completely clear. The Convention on the protection of the marine environment in the North-East Atlantic describes the precautionary principle as a principle 'by virtue of which preventive measures are taken when there are reasonable grounds for concern that substances or energy introduced directly or indirectly into the environment may bring about damage to human health, harm living resources... even where there is no conclusive evidence of a causal relationship between the inputs and effects'. The principle was noted in the Declaration of the UN Conference in Rio de Janeiro in 1992, where precaution was defined as:

> *Where there are threats of serious or irreversible damage, lack of full scientific certainty shall not be used as a reason for postponing cost-effective measures to prevent environmental degradation.*

The precautionary principle is understood to require a consideration of risk, and perhaps an avoidance of action even where scientific research has not yet fully shown the cause of the environmental impairment.

15.35 The presumption to be taken is against the discharge or use of potentially harmful or accumulative substances even where the exact nature of the risk is not known; where there is evidence of possible risk rather than actual risk, the precautionary principle indicates that steps should still be taken to prevent the risk. However, in *R v Secretary of State for Trade and Industry, ex p Duddridge and Others* (1996) the Court of Appeal in the United Kingdom, when asked to consider the requirements associated with precaution and assessing risk before any action it was held that Article 191 TFEU (ex Article 174 EC) did not place any direct obligation on any organ of national government.

15.36 The General Court of the European Union (formerly the Court of First Instance) has been more specific about the application of the precautionary principle. In Case T–13/99 *Pfizer Animal Health SA/NV v Council* (2002) the principle was relied on to justify the banning of an antibiotic developed by Pfizer on the basis that there was some potential for harm to human beings. Case C–180/96 *UK v Commission* (1996) gives another example of its use. Here the United Kingdom challenged, unsuccessfully, a Commission decision to take emergency interim measures against British beef in the light of the spread of bovine spongiform encephalopathy (BSE, or 'mad cow disease') amid concerns about the potential for harm to humans. The Court of Justice noted the Community law requirement that needed to be read in conjunction with precautionary measures in this context of a 'high level of health protection' and rejected the UK's contention that the emergency measures were unjustified. Interestingly, in the context of World Trade Organisation law, the US has perpetually challenged what it considers to be overly restrictive measures, which the EU has taken in relation to hormone-treated meat. Considering the international origins of the precautionary principle in 1992 such differences of opinion regarding application, both in the EU and at international level, are likely to be unavoidable.

Preventive principle

5.37 It is somewhat unclear the extent to which the prevention principle has content independent from the precautionary principle. As with the precautionary principle, the preventive principle is not defined or explained elsewhere in the Treaty. However, both principles are, in practice, almost always used together.

It has existed in the Treaties since 1987 and the SEA and is of overriding importance in every serious environmental policy, since it allows or requires action to be taken at an early stage. It emerged in the first Action Programme and is based on the maxim that prevention is better than a cure.

5.38 Directive 85/337/EEC is a prime example of the preventive principle in operation in environmental law. The Directive requires the assessment of the effects of projects on the environment, the projects listed as prompting an impact assessment including developments around transport infrastructure, housing and industrial or commercial buildings. The Directive requires an assessment of the environmental effects of major construction projects to be assessed before they are approved and given the go-ahead to be built.

15.39 The Chemicals Directive 67/548/EEC is another example. The current version of the Directive requires new chemicals to be tested not only for their health effects but also for their effect on the environment in general before being launched on the market.

The principle that environmental degradation should be rectified at source—the proximity principle

15.40 The proximity principle advocates that environmental damage should be rectified as close to its source as possible. Its effect was considered by the Court of Justice in Case C–2/90 *Commission v Belgium* (1992) where a decree by the Walloon Regional Executive banning the import of waste into the region was, in relation to waste other than hazardous waste, held to be effective. The Court cited the proximity principle as an appropriate reference point for such an environmental protection measure.

Polluter pays principle

15.41 The polluter pays principle was introduced into the Treaty in 1987, although it has been referred to in Union documents on policy since 1973. In origin, the principle is economic. It is understood as requiring the cost of environmental impairment, damage and clean-up should not be left unpaid, or external to production, and thereby picked up by society at large, or by general taxation. The person who caused the pollution should bear the cost. The economics of the principle are that thereby the pollution costs become internalised into the production process, and the result is that a true cost is then charged rather than a charge that ignores the hidden pollution costs. As environmental protection requirements became more generally accepted, and as concerns about pollution rose, the polluter pays principle moved out of its purely economic context and took on a slightly different role in the policy attempts to combat pollution. From the point of view of the economic principle, the pollution does not much matter so long as it is charged for. However, the polluter pays principle as an environmental principle suggests the implementation of the principle would entail charging for pollution to limit it.

15.42 The polluter pays principle underlies a great deal of EU legislation. This principle is enshrined in Article 191 TFEU. It gives encouragement to the use of economic and fiscal instruments aimed at influencing the behaviour of producers and promoting technologies and processes which are consistent with resource conservation. Moreover, in the context of waste (see **15.54–15.60**), the Court of Justice observed of the possibility to hold liable 'one or several previous holders...who are neither the producers nor the possessors of the waste' (Case C–1/03 *Paul Van de Walle and Others v Texaco Belguim SA* (2004)). This allowed for extension of the financial burden associated with clean-up (proper disposal or recovery) to all those who could be considered to have *caused* the waste. This, the Court stated, was achieved through applying Directive 75/442/EEC 'in accordance with the polluter pays principle' and can generally be seen as encouraging responsibility, coordination and good practice throughout the handling chain. However, the great utility and popularity of the polluter pays principle does not mean that the requirements of the principle are any more certain than the requirements of the other environmental principles. The willingness of the Court of Justice to apply the principle widely must be understood in the context that often the identification of a polluter is somewhat difficult—indeed, it is impossible in relation to groundwater or coastal water, pollution, forest decline, soil erosion, desertification, climate change and urban smog. In reality, in all Member States and at Union level, there are many situations where pollution clean-up is a task for public authorities, and the question of historic pollution is not one that has been resolved by reference to getting polluters to pay more (see **15.89**, and *ERG*).

Therefore, where the polluter pays principle is not as effective as it might be, and where there are little incentives for private investment, Member States may grant particular companies aid to promote environmental protection. To regulate the award of such aid, the Commission has developed a policy on state aid for environmental protection which is contained in its Guidelines on State Aid for Environmental Protection.

There are some concerns that the use of state aid diametrically opposes the polluter pays principle as the producer is not bearing the cost of the pollution that it has created. Nevertheless, given that is not always possible to identify the polluter and the need to create the right sorts of incentives for greater private investment in innovation, research and development in the field of environmental protection, a combination of policies is important. It should be noted that state aid measures are short term and are only needed where private investment is not forthcoming. One of the advantages of using state aid is that it can encourage private investors to go beyond meeting the minimum levels of environmental protection and setting the standard higher, for example by committing to using greater renewable energy sources than is presently required of them.

Emissions trading

15.43 Emissions trading is a cornerstone of the Union's climate change strategy. The trading system rewards companies that reduce their emissions and penalises those that exceed limits. Directive 2003/87/EC established a scheme for greenhouse gas emission allowance trading within the Union. It provides that, for each five-year period, each Member State should develop a national action plan (NAP) stating the total quantity of allowances it intends to allocate for that period and how these will be allocated. The scheme was introduced and began operation in 2005, and includes around 12,000 factories and plants responsible for about half the EU's emissions of CO_2. Member State governments are responsible for setting limits on the amount of carbon dioxide emitted by energy-intensive industries, and if these want to emit more greenhouse gases they then have to purchase emissions permits from less polluting industries. The EU emissions trading scheme expanded significantly from 1 January 2012 so as to include commercial aviation. The Court of Justice recently upheld the inclusion, in Directive 2008/101/EC, not only of flights within the EU but also international flights which 'depart from or arrive at an aerodrome situated in the territory of a Member State' (Case C–366/10 *Air Transport Association of America v Secretary of State for Energy and Climate Change* (2011)). More industries are also expected to be added to the scheme in the future, including petrochemical companies. Furthermore, the development and integration of a global trading system will also hopefully allow EU countries to offset emissions by purchasing permits from other non-EU states.

15.44 In 2006 Poland and Estonia notified the Commission of their NAPs for the period 2008–2012. In 2007 the Commission declared these incompatible with the aims of the Directive and declared that proposed allocations should be reduced by 26.7 per cent and 47.8 per cent by each country respectively. In Case T–183/07 *Poland v Commission* (2009) and T–263/07 *Estonia v Commission* (2009) both countries sought the annulment of the Commission Decision before the General Court (then Court of First Instance) on the grounds that the Commission had exceeded its powers in rejecting their NAPs. The General Court agreed with the Member States. It stated that the administrative measures must be adopted in compliance with the competences accorded to various administrative bodies and that in principle, according to Article 288 TFEU, when the Directive in question does not prescribe the form and methods for achieving a particular result, the choice of appropriate method is left to the Member State. The Court also referred to the principle of subsidiarity, and held that by rejecting the NAPs on the basis of reasoning based on doubts as to the reliability of data used by the Member States, the Commission exceeded its powers. The Commission has no power under the Directive to replace the data provided by the Member States, and to assume such would be according competence to the Commission not provided for in the Directive. Furthermore, by imposing allowance ceilings above which any NAP would be deemed incompatible with the Directive, the Commission substituted its decisions for those of the Member States.

15.45 The application of Directive 2003/87 to certain industries but not others was questioned in Case C–127/07 *Société Arcelor Atlantique* (2008). While the steel sector was included within the scope of the Directive, the plastics and aluminium sectors were not, thus financially disadvantaging the steel sector against other non-ferrous metal industries. A case was brought arguing that the principle of equal treatment had been breached in not treating competing sectors in a similar manner. The Court stated that Community policy on the environment aims 'at a high level of protection and is based in particular on the precautionary principle, the principle that preventative action should be taken, and the polluter pays principle'. Considering that CO_2 emissions by the steel sector far outweighed those of the other sectors, the Court found that a difference in treatment was justified in the first stage of the implementation of the trading scheme in order to reduce the administrative burden of effective implementation.

European Union environmental law by sector

15.46 Environmental law is both about the application of key principles to policy activity, and specific rules applicable to set standards or combat certain types of behaviour. European Union environmental law is extensive and difficult to define and isolate, because many measures have environmental impact or a relationship with environmental policy. However, the Union has a specific body of rules clearly aimed at environmental protection. There are few substantive environmental areas where the EU has not legislated. In broad terms, water, waste and air are all included so basic laws have been established in all these fields. But the EU has also taken a radical approach to the development of new forms of control and major pieces of legislation include the Directives on Environmental Liability, Strategic Environmental Assessment, as well as producer responsibility directives such as the End of Life Vehicle Directive and the Waste from Electrical and Electronic Equipment Directive. Further details on the specifics of EU environmental law can to be obtained in the many dedicated works in this field (see Further Reading).

Air and water pollution

Air

5.47 When the Union first began to adopt laws relating to air quality, its measures were aimed at particular sources and forms of air pollution with the recognition that air pollutants have a significant impact on environmental quality and human health. It adopted laws to limit and control emissions from specific sources, such as vehicles and factories, and set standards for certain fuels to ensure that they did not contain substances which would lead to air pollution. However, these laws did not really aim to ensure good air quality in general and air quality has been the focus of more recent legislation. The 2005 Communication on a Thematic Strategy on Air Pollution sets out objectives for air pollution and proposes legislative measures for the period to 2020 that would modernise existing legislation and focus on particular pollutants. A public consultation on how best to improve EU air quality legislation was also held, and was recently closed by the Commission on 15 October 2011 having sought the views of a wide range of concerned parties.

General air quality

5.48 Directive 96/62/EC on ambient air quality assessment and management provides a basis for ensuring that air quality standards are set and complied with for a number of substances. This Directive does not create any precise air quality objectives but sets out a framework and basic principles for air quality. It has been amended, generally as the health impact of air pollution has become better understood, but the framework approach needs to be read in conjunction with the ambient air quality Directive's 'daughter directives'; measures that have been adopted to lay down the permitted concentrations for specific pollutants. Daughter directives also contain requirements relating to the passing of information on to the public.

5.49 Member States have to comply with the standards laid down in the daughter directives. In areas where there is a risk of these standards being breached, action plans are drawn up to indicate short term measures to reduce the risk and limit the duration of the breach. Case C–232/07 *Dieter Janecek v FriestaatBayern* (2008) notes however that 'an integrated reduction of pollution' is sought and that Member States must thus act 'taking into account all the material circumstances and opposing interests'. A good example of the balancing process regarding air quality in general is the current position of the UK. In 2012 London will host the Olympic games, which will clearly increase pollution in the city both during and, through increased building activities, prior to the games. London could miss the targets set for it by the EU by as many as 10 years according to the UK Department for the Environment and Rural Affairs. The Commission had used its discretion not to bring proceedings in 2011, where a £300m fine was estimated as a possibility. With the economic boost that such an event can bring to Member States—one could also highlight Poland and the Euro 2012 football championships in this regard— perhaps earlier clarity in legislating, rather than later use of discretion in enforcing, is called for to avoid such uncertainties for Member States.

Water

15.50 The Water Framework Directive 2000/60/EC is the most important legislative instrument in this area. This Directive was adopted with the purposes of protecting the supply of surface water and groundwater, and to try to instil a principle of equitable access to water supplies. The aim is to prevent further deterioration and to protect and enhance the status of aquatic ecosystems, and to promote sustainable water use. The Water Framework Directive also aims at the progressive reduction of pollution of groundwater.

The Directive embodies the concept of integrated water and river basin management. It replaced seven previously existing directives. The measures provided for in the river basin management plan are intended to prevent deterioration of surface water and groundwater and preserve protected areas. The Framework Directive sets out various objectives to this effect.

The Directive also lists substances which are deemed to present a significant risk to the aquatic environment and sets forth measures to control such substances. It also contains certain specific provisions.

15.51 Further to the Water Framework Directive, there are numerous directives relating to water for specific purposes and which govern the use of such water. Directive 98/83/EC regulates water intended for human consumption in conjunction with Directive 75/440/EEC on drinking water; Directive 2006/7/EC sets values with regards to bathing water as from the start of 2008, finally replacing the old bathing waters regime under Directive 76/160/EEC; Directive 2006/11/EC regulates pollution caused by certain dangerous substances discharged into the aquatic environment; Directive 2006/118/EC prevents groundwater pollution; Directive 2006/44/EC protects the quality of waters to support fish life in conjunction with Directive 2006/113/EC on water for shellfish; and Directive 91/271/EEC protects the environment from the adverse effects of discharges of urban waste water and waste water from certain industrial sectors.

Integrated pollution, prevention and control

15.52 Traditionally, laws relating to the control of environmental pollution have treated each sector of the environment separately. However, this approach created the danger that separate controls on emissions to air, water and soil encourage pollution to be shifted between different environmental media rather than ensuring protection of the environment as a whole.

15.53 In 1996, the EU adopted an approach which aimed to prevent or minimise emissions of substances, vibrations, heat and noise to air, water and soil, and at the same time to take waste management into account. Directive 96/61/EC on integrated pollution, prevention and control sets out a framework of permits for certain industries. The main type of industry coverage are energy, production and processing metals, the mineral industry, the chemical industry, waste management and other activities. The final components of the integrated pollution, prevention and control regime came into force in October 2007.

The IPPC Directive minimises pollution from a range of industrial sources. All industries require a permit and applications must provide the national authorities with specified information. The permits contain the conditions required by the Directive and, in particular, emissions limit values based on the best available techniques. Furthermore, applications for permits are to be made available to the public to allow them to comment before the national authority makes a decision. Decisions on permits and the results of monitoring releases are also to be made available to the public.

Waste: definition, movement and disposal

Definition and movement of waste

5.54 European Union law on waste set out a framework for waste management within the Member States. A basic requirement for permits for waste disposal facilities, including landfill and incineration, is laid down by Directive 2006/12/EC on waste and specific wastes, including waste (Directive 75/442/EEC), waste oils (Directive 75/439/EEC), packaging (Directive 94/62/EC), PCBs (Directive 96/59/EC), sewage sludge (Directive 86/278/EEC), batteries and accumulators (Directive 2006/66/EC), batteries and wastes from the titanium dioxide industry (Directive 78/176/EEC), are separately regulated. Directive 91/689/EEC sets out rules on hazardous waste, and 2006/116/Euratom regulates the supervision and control of radioactive waste and spent fuel.

15.55 The directives on waste lay down general provisions on the management and disposal of waste and hazardous waste. Waste is defined as 'any substance or object which the holder discards or intends or is required to discard'. The Court of Justice has made it clear that even reusable or recyclable items can be regarded as waste in terms of the directives.

15.56 In Joined Cases C–304, 330, 342 and C–224/95 *Criminal Proceedings against Tombesi and Others* (1997) the Court gave an extremely wide definition of waste, stating that the term includes:

> …substances and objects which are capable of economic reutilization, even if the materials in question may be the subject of a transaction or quoted on public or private commercial lists. In particular, a deactivation process intended merely to render waste harmless, landfill tipping in hollows or embankments and waste incineration constitute disposal or recovery operations falling within the scope of…Community rules [on waste]. The fact that a substance is classified as a re-usable residue without its characteristics or purpose being defined is irrelevant in that regard. The same applies to the grinding of a waste substance.

Furthermore, in Case C–129/96 *Inter-Environment Wallonie* (see **15.28** above), the Court ruled that the concept of waste does not, in principle, exclude any kind of residue, industrial by-product or other substance arising from production processes. A substance will not, therefore, be excluded from the definition of waste by the mere fact that it directly or indirectly forms an integral part of an industrial production process.

15.57 The above definition (**15.56**) grew even wider in Case C–263/05 *Commission v Italy* (2007) where the Court stated (at paragraph 50):

> In view of the obligation…to give the concept of waste a broad meaning…goods, materials or raw materials resulting from a manufacturing process which is not designed to produce them may be regarded as by-products which the holder does not wish to discard only where their re-use (including, as the case may be, in order to meet the needs of economic operators other than the producer) is not merely a possibility, but a certainty and where such re-use does not require any prior processing and forms an integral part of the process of production.

The requirement for certainty of re-use is combined with the exclusion of the possibility of certainty where some form of processing is required prior to the materials' ultimate use in a potential new process of production. This means that potentially valuable materials can be considered as waste even though the likelihood of them becoming discarded in the longer term is slight. This is so as that definition of an object as waste is not based on its quintessential characteristics, but on its relationship with a future hypothetical process (of which there may be many possible options).

15.58 The Court of Justice revisited this area in Case C–188/07 *Commune de Mesquer v Total France SA and Total International Ltd* (2008) in which it considered whether oil accidentally spilled at sea following a shipwreck is 'waste' for the purposes of Directive 75/442/EEC on waste. The case concerned the sinking of the Erika off the Atlantic coast of France in 1999 and the subsequent spilling of her cargo of oil into the sea. The event caused pollution of the waters and coastline and the town of Mesquer sued the companies responsible for the transportation of the oil, Total, for reimbursement of the cost of cleaning and anti-pollution operations on the French coast. The action was brought under Directive 75/442/EEC, and the town claimed that the oil spilled at sea was 'waste' under the Directive. The Court of Justice found that the oil, mixed with sediment and water, was indeed waste because it was a substance which the holder did not intend to produce and which was discarded, albeit involuntarily, during transport. The Court held that the oil during transport, prior to the spillage, was not waste, and noted that the meaning of this term depends on the meaning of the term 'discard', as stated in Case C–129/96 *Wallonie* (see **15.28**). Furthermore, these terms must be interpreted in the light of the Directive (Cases C–418/97 and C–419/97 *Chemie Nederland* (2000)) which pursues the protection of human health and the environment against harmful effects caused by the collection, transport, treatment, storage and tipping of waste, based on Article 191(2) TFEU (ex Article 174 EC). This provides that Union policy on the environment is to aim at a high level of protection and is to be based on the precautionary principle and the principle that preventive action should be taken. Finally, the Court noted that to meet these aims, the concept of waste cannot be interpreted restrictively. The Court also found that the owner of the ship carrying the oil, who had the substance in his possession and produced the waste, is to be regarded as the 'holder' of the substance within the meaning of the Directive, and is therefore liable for the cost of clean-up operations. However, it is for the national court to determine whether the company that chartered the ship may be held responsible for not taking adequate precautions, or indeed whether the producer of the product may be found liable. The Court finally stated that, in accordance with the polluter pays principle, such a producer cannot be liable to bear costs unless he has contributed by his conduct to the risk that the pollution caused by the shipwreck will occur.

15.59   The main regulatory requirements in the directives are that waste disposal must be properly planned by the national authorities and that all waste disposal or waste recovery installations must be licensed by the national authorities. Collection or transportation of waste must, as a minimum, be registered with the national authorities; and where hazardous waste is being collected, transported or stored temporarily, it must be properly packaged and labelled in accordance with the Union rules in force.

15.60   Inspections of all waste and hazardous waste disposal, recovery, collection and transport operations are to be carried out to ensure that they are complying with the requirements in the directives. Protecting the environment and human health are, of course, a vital component of these directives but the Court has stated, in the context of storing leftover stone, that (Case C–9/00 *PalinGranit Oy* (2002)):

> The fact, even if proven, that the stone does not pose any real risk to human health or the environment are not relevant criteria for determining whether the stone is to be regarded as waste.

This reveals that prevention, reduction and recovery are key aims which must be understood as standing alone and which are not to be judged purely in reference to any *specific* human or environmental harm.

Incineration and disposal of waste

15.61   Municipal waste incinerators burn domestic refuse, as well as trade refuse and other wastes which are similar to domestic waste. Directive 2000/76/EC relates to incinerators and lays down detailed operating and emission standards which incinerators must meet. These must be open for review by the public.

A permit will only be granted to an incinerator of hazardous waste if the permit application shows that the plant is designed, equipped and will be operated so that preventive measures against environmental pollution are taken.

15.62   There are further provisions for the disposal of 'end of life' vehicles (Directive 2000/53/EC), waste electrical and electronic equipment (Directive 2002/96/EC) and waste from extractive industries (Directive 2006/21/EC) with the main objective of waste prevention.

Trade in endangered species

15.63 Regulation 338/97/EC on the protection of species of wild fauna and flora implements the CITES, the 1973 Convention on International Trade in Endangered Species of Wild Flora and Fauna. It regulates the import, export and re-export of live and dead wild animals and plants. Its aim is to protect endangered species by imposing controls on international trade in those species. The European Union is a party to CITES and this Regulation governs trade between the Union and third countries.

Permits and certificates are required for the import or export of thousands of listed animals and plants and will only be issued by national authorities where specific conditions are fulfilled. Member States must designate customs offices to carry out the checks and formalities for import into and export from the Union and must ensure that these are adequately equipped and staffed to handle live animals and plants.

The Commission may, in certain circumstances, establish restrictions on the import of certain species and a list of such restrictions will be published in the Official Journal every three months.

15.64 To protect the Union's indigenous species, Regulation 2551/97/EC suspends the introduction into the Union of certain species of wild flora and fauna which would pose a threat to indigenous species within the European Union.

Nature conservation

15.65 The Union has a comprehensive range of legislation protecting European bird, animal and plant species and their habitats (Directives 92/43/EEC on habitats and 79/409/EEC on wild birds), protecting forests from the dangers of air pollution and fire (Regulation 2152/2003/EC) and limiting the size of drift nets used by fishing vessels in order to prevent marine mammals from being caught accidentally (Regulations 812/2004/EC and 88/98/EC).

15.66 The European Union is also party to a number of international agreements which aim to protect flora, fauna and their habitats throughout the world. Union nature conservation measures also regulate Union trade in certain endangered species (see **15.63**), and trade in furs of certain animals and in furs caught by means of leghold traps (Regulation 3254/91/EC, although a proposal exists to replace this measure).

15.67 Two principal laws protect natural resources within the European Union and form the basis of the Union's biodiversity strategy: Directive 79/409/EEC on wild birds and Directive 92/43/EEC on habitats. The Habitats Directive is part of the attempt to create an ecological network of special protected areas known as 'Natura 2000'. The two directives together aim to provide protection for the bird, animal and plant species themselves and also to conserve their habitats by providing for the establishment of protected areas.

5.68 The Wild Birds Directive protects all species of wild birds in the territories of the Member States by prohibiting the killing or capture of all such birds, the destruction of, and damage to, nests and eggs, egg collection and the deliberate disturbance of birds and the keeping of species whose hunting and capture is prohibited. The Directive also prohibits the use of snares, explosives, nets and hunting from aircraft; and the sale of live or dead birds. There are derogations and exceptions to such prohibitions, set out in the Directive itself.

5.69 The Wild Birds Directive requires measures to be taken to preserve sufficient diversity and area of habitats for all species covered by the Directive. It also requires the classification of Special Protection Areas (SPAs) to ensure protection of bird species. Such classification must follow ornithological criteria defined in the Directive. Cases on the Wild Birds Directive have mainly related to enforcement problems. However, Case C–44/95 *R v Secretary of State for the Environment, ex parte RSPB* (1996) provided some useful assistance with defining the requirements associated with SPAs. Here the Court of Justice was asked to consider the criteria for deciding whether an area should be designated as an SPA, and therefore become an area protected from development. The Court ruled that the only criteria guiding a Member State in the designation and definition of SPA boundaries are ornithological, and the economic benefits of development should not be taken into account in making the decision as to designation. Excluding an area designation as an SPA on economic grounds was not permissible.

15.70 In all SPAs, Member States must take steps to avoid the deterioration of habitats and significant disturbance of the species for which the areas have been designated. Member States should assess the environmental impact and implications of any proposed development plans. If there is a development project, which is detrimental to the environmental habitat, but which must go ahead due to an overriding public interest, then the opinion of the Commission must be sought. The Commission Opinion of 18/12/1995 reported in the Official Journal is an interesting illustration of the process. Germany had sought the Commission's Opinion on whether building a major connecting road through a number of SPAs, in the presence of many rare and endangered birds, would be allowed on the grounds of imperative reasons of overriding public interest (IROPI). The Commission weighed up the necessity and importance of the road, and the compensation measures to be taken to compensate for damage to the SPAs. It held that the adverse effects were justified by IROPI and gave an Opinion accepting the basis for the road and the impact on the designated SPAs.

15.71 Member States cannot escape the obligations to protect habitats by failing to designate an area as an SPA (Case C–355/90 *Commission v Spain* (*Santoña Marshes*) (1993)).

15.72 The Habitats Directive 92/43/EEC requires the establishment of a system of strict protection for listed species of animals and plants in a system similar to that used with the Wild Birds Directive, with the designation of Special Areas of Conservation (SACs) as the equivalent of the Birds Directive's SPAs. The Member States are required to prohibit the deliberate capture or killing in the wild; deliberate disturbance during breeding, migration, hibernation and rearing periods; and the deliberate destruction or taking of eggs from the wild and deterioration or destruction of breeding sites for these species. The Court of Justice recently reiterated that this obligates Member States 'not only to adopt a comprehensive legislative framework but also to implement concrete and specific protection measures' (Case C–383/09 *Commission v France* (2011)). In relation to plants, Member States are required to prohibit the deliberate picking, collecting, cutting, uprooting or destruction of listed plants species in the wild. Keeping, transporting selling or exchanging any live or dead specimens of plants or animals is also prohibited. The Directive does, however, allow certain derogations.

For the less endangered species of plants and animals, full prohibition is not necessarily required, but the Member States must take measures to prevent overexploitation.

Furthermore, Member States should also assess the desirability of reintroducing certain native wild species into the wild.

15.73 The network of the most important bird, animal and plant habitats, known as 'Natura 2000', is designed to ensure that the habitats of protected species are conserved. The network is set up of the SPAs for wild birds and SACs for plant and animal species.

International agreements on the protection of species and their habitats

15.74 The European Union is a party to several international agreements which aim to protect species and their habitats. These include the convention on the conservation of migratory species of wild animals (Decision 82/461/EEC on the conclusion of the Bonn Convention); the convention on the conservation of European wildlife and habitats (Decision 82/72/EEC on the Bern Convention); the convention on the protection of the Alps (Decision 96/191/EC); and the convention on the conservation of Antarctic marine living resources (Decision 81/691/EC on the Canberra Convention).

Environmental protection implementation and enforcement: access to environmental information and citizen participation in environmental decision-making process

Treaty enforcement

15.75 As noted above the Commission is the guardian of the Treaties and has the obligation to ensure the application of Union law as set out in the Treaty (see **15.25** and **15.32**).

Under Article 258 TFEU, the Commission brings Member States before the Court of Justice to enforce Union law, and the European Union is unique in having a system whereby states can be required to uphold environmental law in this way. However, the limitations of the centralised enforcement of environmental law under Article 258 TFEU are considerable.

Although Union law obligations are formally owned by the central governments of the Member States, environmental law obligations are frequently devolved or delegated to administrative agencies over which government control is likely to be indirect. There is, for all the challenges of centralised enforcement in such a system, no gap in scope however, as the state is deemed responsible for all breaches of such law and the Commission can take action against the central government in respect of breaches elsewhere in the system. However, as the Commission cannot take action against private polluters, Article 58 TFEU actions are going to focus upon administrative processes such as reporting requirements, or on the formal level of the implementation of directives, rather than litigation over particular environmental incidents or environmental quality. The Commission relies very heavily on complaints from third parties, and in particular upon individuals for detecting infringements of Union environmental law that might prompt an Article 258 TFEU action.

Access to environmental information

15.76 The Aarhus Convention of the United Nations Economic Commission for Europe on Access to Environmental Information, participation in environmental decisions and access to justice in environmental matters applies to Union level decision-making and provides a framework for the examination of public participation in decision-making. The Convention's title indicates three pillars: access to information; participation in environmental decision-making and access to justice in environmental matters.

15.77 Access to information is the most detailed pillar of the Aarhus Convention, which includes a right of access to information without having to state or show any interest in the information requested. Regulation 1049/2001/EC provides a right of access to environmental information, within specified time limits and a requirement for reasoned decisions. The Regulation also lays down grounds for refusing access to documents where there are competing public interests.

15.78 The Aarhus Convention also provides for public participation in decision-making. This occurs at three stages: (i) decisions on specific activities; (ii) plans, programmes and policies relating to the environment; and (iii) the preparation of executive regulations and/or generally applicable legally binding normative instruments. The Convention assumes public participation far beyond familiar techniques of consulting neighbours. The Treaty of Amsterdam introduced a duty on the Commission to consult widely before issuing proposals, in the context of the European Governance project.

Environmental Impact Assessment

15.79 An Environmental Impact Assessment (EIA) procedure is required for certain types of development before development consent. The purpose of the assessment is to ensure that decision-makers consider environmental impacts before deciding whether to proceed with new projects. The requirement for an EIA is set out in Directive 85/337/EEC, as amended (see also 15.80). The procedure requires the developer to compile an Environmental Statement describing the likely significant effects of the development on the environment and proposed mitigation measures. The ES must be circulated to statutory consultation bodies and made available to the public for comment. Its contents, together with any comments, must be taken into account by the competent authority, e.g. the local planning authority, before it may grant consent.

Strategic Environmental Assessment

15.80 The limitations of the EIA requirements were to some extent addressed by the introduction of Strategic Environmental Assessment (SEA) in Directive 2001/42/EC on the assessment of the effects of certain plans and programmes on the environment. The SEA process ensures that significant environmental effects arising from policies, plans and programmes are identified and assessed to enable the effects to be mitigated and monitored, and so that opportunities for public involvement are provided. This complements the project focus of EIA, and deals with the issue where individual projects create minimal environmental impact but where a series of such projects taken together have an environmental impact that would otherwise not be considered. The strategic assessment provides for such a collective consideration of related policies and programmes. The SEA is closely related to the attempts to achieve sustainable development values in public planning and policy making.

The SEA Directive focuses on programmes which are likely to have significant effects on the environment. Authorities which prepare and/or adopt programmes likely to have significant environmental effects must prepare a report on the likely environmental effects, consult environmental authorities and the public, and take the report and the results of the consultation into account during the preparation process and before the plan or programme is adopted. They must also make information available on the plan or programme as adopted on how the environmental assessment was taken into account.

Environmental litigation

Environmental litigation against the Commission and Council

15.81 Environmental litigation against the Commission and Council is founded on two authorities: the Third Pillar of the Aarhus Convention, which imposes obligations in respect of 'access to justice'; and also Article 263 TFEU (ex Article 230 EC), which provides for claims against the Union institutions (considered in **Chapter 8**). It will be recalled that Member States are 'privileged' applicants with a general right of access to the Court, while ordinary private litigants can only challenge a decision addressed to that person or a more general measure that is of direct and individual concern. The stringency of the standing rules in the Court of Justice has a particular impact on the possibility of bringing a case against the Commission or the Council by any non-privileged applicant. In Case C–321/95 P *Stichting Greenpeace Council v Commission* (1998) (see **8.54**), Greenpeace, together with local individuals and groups, attempted to challenge a Commission's decision to grant funding to Spain for the construction of two power stations, arguing a breach of environmental law in the funding decision. Standing was denied to both Greenpeace and the local residents on the basis that neither was individually concerned by the decision. Greenpeace was denied standing on the basis that the members it claimed to represent lacked standing. And none of the local residents was affected in a way that distinguished them from all the people who live or pursue an activity in the areas concerned. Such an outcome poses particular challenges in the context of environmental law, where it is difficult to see how any complainant can demonstrate the necessary individual concern to bring an action in the Court of Justice. A well-established environmental interest group, such as Greenpeace, is in a good position to represent all those interests questioning a legislative act with an environmental impact where no individual is specifically and particularly affected, however, the Court has taken a restrictive line on interest groups and standing.

Keeping to its strict line of standing, the Court of Justice again considered the matter of standing of individuals in Case C–362/06 P *MarkkuSahlstedt and Others v Commission* (2009). Under the 'Habitats Directive', Council Directive 92/43/EC on the conservation of natural habitats and of wild flora and fauna, each Member State must propose a list of sites of ecological importance to the Commission, who then publishes a European-wide list of such 'special areas of conservation' (SACs). Each Member State must then take special measures to protect the environment in these areas. Certain landowners and farmers with land in designated sites in the Boreal biogeographical area in Finland brought an action before the General Court of the European Union to annul the Commission Decision designating the area a SAC. The General Court (then the Court of First Instance) declared the action was inadmissible and held that the applicants were not directly concerned by the contested decision, within the meaning of Article 263(4) TFEU (ex Article 230 EC). While the Commission Decision was binding as to the result to be achieved, the manner in which this was carried out was left to the discretion of the competent national authorities. The Applicants then appealed to the Court of Justice. In his Opinion of 23 October 2008, Advocate General Bot concluded that the appeal was well founded and that the landowners were individually concerned by the Commission's decision. However, the Court of Justice declined to follow the Advocate General, and ruled that the applicants were not individually concerned. The Court stated that applicants other than the addressees of a decision can claim to be individually concerned only if that decision affects them by reason of certain attributes which are peculiar to them or by reason of circumstances in which they are differentiated from all other persons. It concluded that the contested decision was of general application because it applies to all economic operators who, in whatever capacity, carry on or are likely to carry on activities in those areas concerned which could jeopardise the conservation objectives of the Habitats Directive. Of interest in this case are not only the strict rules of standing for individuals, but the substitution of the reasoning of the Court of Justice for that of the General Court. The latter held that the applicants were not 'directly' concerned, while the Court of Justice held that they were not 'individually' concerned.

Environmental litigation against Member States

15.82 The Commission's main source of information on possible omissions in the application of European Union environmental law is mostly from citizens, and the Commission has a complaints system to enable citizens to raise concerns. As was noted above (see 15.75), the Commission can bring formal proceedings under Article 258 TFEU against a Member State. The Commission has a very large discretion on deciding whether to take action under Article 258 TFEU and an individual has no standing to bring infringement proceedings or to compel the Commission to act. Where the Commission does decide to prosecute a Member State for failures with regards environmental law, the Court of Justice will not annul the national measure nor pronounce any rectifying measures to be taken. The Court leaves it up to the Member State to comply with the judgment.

15.83 Following Article 258 TFEU (ex Article 226 EC) proceedings, penalties can be imposed under Article 260 TFEU (ex Article 228 EC). In CaseC–387/97 *Commission v Greece (Chania Waste)* (2000) the Court imposed a daily fine of £20,000 against Greece, judging the failure to implement management plans in an area of Crete for toxic waste as serious a breach as actual unlawful disposal of non-toxic waste, and noting Greece's failure to act despite previous Article 258 TFEU rulings. Then in Case 278/01 *Commission v Spain (Spanish Bathing Water)* (2003), penalty payments were imposed on Spain for breaching the Bathing Waters Directive (see 8.22 above) in relation to the quality of various inshore waters and for failures to respond to previous Article 258 TFEU judgments in this regard. Because compliance with the Bathing Waters Directive was assessed annually, the Court ruled that the penalty payment should also be determined annually.

15.84 Equally, citizens themselves may play a more direct role in enforcement. In contrast to the restrictive approach taken to public and non-governmental organisation (NGO) standing in matters concerning challenges to EU institutions, the Court of Justice recently took a more relaxed approach in the context of the EIA Directive and a challenge by an NGO to the decision of a local authority in Germany to grant a partial permit for the construction of a coal-fired power station. In Case C–115/09 *Bund fürUmwelt und Naturschutz Deutschland, LandesverbandNordhein-Westfalenv Bezirksregierung Arnsberg* (2011) the Court of Justice based its decision on Article 10a of Directive 2003/35, amending the EIA Directive, which expressly recognises that NGOs too have 'rights capable of impairment' and provides more generally for 'wide access to justice'. The consequence is that national legislation which does not permit NGOs (and therefore also individuals) promoting environmental protection to rely before the courts 'on the infringement of a rule flowing from EU environment law' is precluded. This can be contrasted with the outcome of Case C–321/95 P *Stichting Greenpeace Council v Commission* (1998) (see **15.81**), also concerning the EIA Directive but in the context of a challenge to a Commission decision. The latter decision did, however, predate Directive 2003/35/EC amending the EIA Directive so as to align it with principles in the Aarhus Convention concerning access to justice.

15.85 In the context of habitats, the Court of Justice has held Article 9(3) of the Aarhus Convention, concerning access to justice, not to be directly effective. But the Court stated significantly that 'if the effective protection of EU environmental law is not to be undermined, it is inconceivable that Article 9(3) of the Aarhus Convention be interpreted in such a way as to make it in practice impossible or excessively difficult to exercise rights conferred by EU law' (Case C–240/09 *Lesoochranárskezoskupenie VLK v Slovakia* (2011)). The matter at hand was a Member State decision, and notably general application of the Third Pillar of the Aarhus Convention has not yet limited the unsuccessful trend for litigants regarding standing when challenging the EU institutions (see **15.81** and Case C–362/06 P *MarkkuSahlstedt and Others v Commission* (2009)).

Civil and criminal liability

15.86 Civil liability refers to the liability of any legal or natural person for environmental harm. There are a number of (non-Union) treaties which establish rules on civil liability for environmental damage, such as the Paris Convention (1960) on third party liability and insurance against nuclear risks; the Vienna Convention (1963) on operator liability for nuclear damage; the Civil Liability Convention (1992) on the liability of the owner of a ship for pollution damage caused by oil escaping from the ship; and the Fund Convention (1992) which provides additional compensation for victims of oil pollution and transfers some of the economic consequences to the owners of the oil cargo as well as the shipowner.

15.87 The distinction between state and civil liability is becoming increasingly difficult to draw, as treaties and other international acts have established an obligation for the state to provide public funds where an operator cannot meet certain costs of environmental damage.

15.88 Generally, civil liability regimes have been developed in relation to specific activities which are considered to be ultra-hazardous and rules have now been in force for some time for damage caused by nuclear activities.

15.89 Directive 2004/35/EC on environmental liability with regard to the prevention and remedying of Environmental Damage is limited to coverage for environmental damage and it only applies to environmental damage caused by the operation of any of the activities expressly identified in an annex to the Directive. The Directive is centred on the requirement that the Member State must in respect of prevention and remediation, either require the operator to take the necessary measures or do so itself. However, the risk that taxpayers will ultimately foot the bill in pursuit of a 'high level' of environmental protection within the Union perhaps helps to explain the ruling in Case C–370/08 *ERG and Others* (2010). Here the Court permitted national legislation within the framework of Directive 2004/35/EC to operate on the:

> …basis of the presumption that there is a causal link between the pollution found and the activities of the operator or operators concerned due to the fact that their installations are located close to that pollution.

The Court did say that this presumption must be based on 'plausible evidence'. But, somewhat circularly, cited correlation of pollutant types and proximity of location between operator and pollution as meeting this test.

15.90 A protracted process underpinned the agreement of Directive 2009/123/EC, an instrument which amends Directive 2005/35/EC to include criminal penalties to buttress the substantive provisions. There was an institutional dispute leading to two Court rulings in Case C–176/03 *Commission v Council* (2005) and Case C–440/05 *Commission v Council* (2007), and a competency dispute harking back to previous debates about environmental measures (see **15.44**) and particularly the *Titanium Dioxide* judgment (**15.11** above). The Court of Justice reaffirmed that the choice of a legal basis for any Union measure must rest on objective factors which are amenable to judicial review, and in this context that the aim and content of environmental law measures affecting criminal liability should be an Environment Title matter, giving rise to a Directive. This led to the agreement of Directive 2009/123/EC and concluded the long-running dispute between the Commission and the Council regarding the inclusion of provisions on harmonising criminal penalties for breaches of EU law and environment law.

The European Union, the environment and international organisations and conventions

15.91 The European Union is party to many international agreements which aim to protect species and their habitats, as was noted above (**15.74**). Environmental treaties have become increasingly numerous since the 1990s. The 1992 Rio Conference, also known as the Earth Summit, led to the adoption of several groundbreaking environmental treaties, including the United Nations Framework Convention on Climate Change (1992) and the Convention on Biological Diversity (1992). Furthermore, the Kyoto Protocol to the 1992 Climate Change Convention was adopted in 1997. The Kyoto Protocol's objective is to reduce greenhouse gases thought to cause climate change. The European Union, along with the Member States, are signatories of these treaties, and the Union is required to reduce greenhouse gas emissions to the levels specified for it and its Member States in the Kyoto Protocol.

5.92 There are additionally various international environmental organisations established at global, regional, sub-regional and bilateral levels to which the European Union is a party. The EU has ratified approximately 30 international environmental agreements which have therefore become part of EU environmental law.

5.93 For instance, the Court of Justice made reference to international environmental agreements, and in particular the Kyoto Protocol, when it approved of a German requirement to make use of renewable energy sources in electricity production in Case C–379/98 *PreussenElektra AG v Schleswag AG* (2001) (see **Chapter 10**). The Court found that the international obligations to which the Community was a party, along with other factors, permitted some fairly major obstacles to free intra-Community trade in electricity because these obstacles were justified by a policy encouraging the use of renewable sources for electricity.

FURTHER READING

Bell, S. and McGillivray D., *Environmental Law* (7th edn, Oxford: OUP, 2008).

Cheyne, I., 'The definition of waste in EC law' (2002) 14 (1) 13(2) *Journal of Environmental Law* 61.

Commission, Community Guidelines on State Aid for Environmental Protection OJ 2008/C 82/01

Commission, Staff Working Paper on the implementation of EU Air Quality Policy and preparing for its comprehensive review (Brussels, 14.03.2011SEC(2011) 342 final) (available at <http://ec.europa.eu/environment/air/pdf/sec_2011_342.pdf>).

Davies, P., *European Union Environmental Law* (Aldershot: Ashgate, 2004).

Gillies, D., *A Guide to EC Environmental Law* (London: Earthscan, 1999).

Gormley, L., 'Free movement of goods and the environment' in Holder (ed), *The Impact of EC Environment Law in the UK* (London: Wiley, 1997) 289.

Haigh, N., *Manual of Environmental Policy: The EC and Britain* (Leeds: Money Publishing, looseleaf updated).

Jans, J. and Vedder, H., *European Environmental Law* (3rd edn, Groningen: Europa, 2008).

Kramer, L., *Casebook on EC Environmental Law* (Oxford: Hart Publishing, 2002).

Kramer, L., *EU Environmental Law* (6th edn, London: Sweet & Maxwell, 2006).

Lee, M., *EU Environmental Law* (Oxford: Hart Publishing, 2005).

Scotford., E., 'Trash or treasure: policy tensions in EC waste regulation' (2007) 19(3) *Journal of Environmental Law* 367.

Scott, J., 'The Multi-level Governance of Climate Change', in Craig, P. and De Búrca, G., (eds), *The Evolution of EU Law* (2nd edn, Oxford: OUP, 2011) 805.

Scott, J., *EC Environmental Law* (London: Longmans, 1998).

SELF-TEST QUESTIONS

1   How has the focus of the European Union changed in regard to environmental policy since that envisaged in the original EEC?

2   Are the environmental principles (as set out in Article 191 TFEU) all capable of legal application in the same way?

3   'The Polluter Pays Principle is fatally flawed since we do not know who the polluter is nor what it means to pay.' Discuss.

4   What characteristics of European Union law hinder efforts to ensure proper application of Union environmental law?

5   To what extent do the Rio Declaration and its content on the precautionary principle embody coherent environmental values?

6   How can a polluter pay for destroying a rare species?

7   To what extent does Environmental Impact Assessment embody the precautionary principle?

8   To what extent does European Union Environmental Policy challenge the economic basis of Union law?

16

Discrimination law: from sex discrimination in employment to a general equality principle

SUMMARY

- The general principle of non-discrimination
- Articles 18, 19 and 157 TFEU
- The meaning of 'equal pay' and 'equal work'
- Temporal and direct effect of Article 157 TFEU
- Secondary legislation on equal pay and equal treatment
- Pensions
- Justification for direct and indirect discrimination

Introduction

16.1 Equality—or non-discrimination—is one of the general principles of Union law (see **Chapter 6**). Nationality discrimination is prohibited under Article 18 TFEU as being one of the primary expressions of the objectives of the Union legal system. In addition, in the regulation and liberalisation of goods movement, discrimination in favour of domestic products is outlawed under Articles 28–30 and 114 TFEU (in terms of taxes and charges) and under Articles 34 and 35 TFEU (in terms of quantitative restrictions and measures with equivalent effect).

16.2 However, prohibited discrimination is not limited to nationality. Sex discrimination has always been prohibited, in one form or another, in the Treaty. Article 157 TFEU, which provides that men and women should receive equal pay, establishes the principle on a purely economic basis. The initial need for sex discrimination legislation was motivated by the aim of preventing the distortion of competition and the avoidance of 'social dumping'. France, in particular, raised concerns that French law at the time had relatively advanced protection for women. The social aim of the provision against sex discrimination could be inferred from the preamble to the Treaty of Rome, and the Treaty on European Union now states that the improvement of living and working conditions of the peoples of the Union is an essential objective. This demonstrates the combination of economic and social objectives, which was confirmed by the Court of Justice in Case 43/75 *Defrenne v Sabena (No 2)* (1976), where it said:

> This double aim, which is at once economic and social, shows that the principle of Equal Pay forms part of the foundations of the Community. (See **16.31** for further detail on *Defrenne (No 2)*.)

16.3 Other forms of discrimination were not always addressed by the Treaty, not only in terms of sex discrimination arising outside the context of pay, but also other forms of discrimination such as race, age, disability, religion and sexual orientation. However, gradually, equality and non-discrimination have achieved the status of general principles of Union law. Confirmation of this came from the Treaty of Amsterdam which added a new Article to the Treaty, providing:

> *Without prejudice to the other provisions of this Treaty and within the limits of the powers conferred by it upon the Community, the Council, acting unanimously on a proposal from the Commission and after consulting the European Parliament, may take appropriate action to combat discrimination based on sex, racial or ethnic origin, religion or belief, disability, age or sexual orientation.*

This provision, now Article 19 TFEU (ex Article 13 EC), is an enabling provision, surrounded by all the safeguards limiting Union competence, and requiring the consultation procedure. It is doubtful if Article 19 could have direct effect as it does not seem to fulfil the Court's criteria (see **Chapter 7, Section I**). Nevertheless, the Article is a clear indication that the principle of non-discrimination was being confirmed as a general principle of Union law, covering an extensive array of discrimination and going far beyond the specific forms of economic-based discrimination originally contained in the Treaty.

16.4 After the Amsterdam Treaty entered into force in 1999 the Commission was quick to propose a number of directives based on what is now Article 19 TFEU. The first directive to be adopted was Council Directive 2000/43/EC implementing the principle of equal treatment between persons irrespective of racial or ethnic origin. That this Directive was achieved so quickly is indicative of the unanimous view of the Member States that this form of discrimination needed to be part of Union competence. This was followed by Council Directive 2000/78/EC establishing a general framework for equal treatment in employment and occupation. This Directive deals with all the remaining forms of discrimination listed under Article 19 TFEU. It refers to the 'rights, freedoms and principles set out in the Charter of Fundamental Rights of the European Union' as contained in Article 6 TEU, to the European Human Rights Convention (ECHR) and to the general principles which result from 'the constitutional traditions common to the Member States'. It also refers to a number of United Nations instruments. Directive 2000/78 states that the 'principle of equal treatment' means that 'there shall be no direct or indirect discrimination whatsoever' on the grounds of religion or belief, disability, age or sexual orientation. Indirect discrimination may be objectively justified by a legitimate aim and if it is proportionate. In some fields, there are a number of exceptions, such as for the armed forces in respect of age and disability, and in respect of state social security schemes. The Directive also provides that different treatment may not constitute discrimination if, by the nature of the particular occupation, a certain characteristic is a genuine and determining occupational requirement, and so long as the objective is legitimate and the requirement is proportionate (Article 4(1)). For example, in respect of age, difference in treatment may be justified by legitimate aims such as employment policy and labour market and vocational training objectives, so long as the means of achieving such aims are appropriate and necessary (Article 5). The Directive applies to both private and public sector employment situations. The implementation date was December 2003, and Member States then had an additional three-year period to implement the provisions on age and disability, so that the Directive had to be in force in its entirety by January 2007. Thus, the development of Union legislation demonstrates that, from the relatively narrow bases of non-discrimination as to nationality and the principle of equal pay for men and women, a broader and more generalised standard of equal treatment in employment in the law of the European Union has been clearly established. We discussed the scope of this standard and relationship with the concept of the general principles in **Chapter 6**. It is clear that the general principle of equality is wider than the specific protection afforded to categories of people in employment situations, and even wider than the nationality discrimination provisions upon which much of the internal market is founded.

16.5   In this chapter, the discussion is focused on discrimination prohibited in employment, an expression of the 'double…economic and social' aim of Union law, as first identified by the Court in *Defrenne* (see **16.2** and **16.31**). We will first look, in particular, at sex discrimination, which, as it developed both in respect of abundant case law and of legislation, has already contributed much to the development of the more general principle of equal treatment. We will then consider the other forms of discrimination which have been included in the directives made under Article 19 TFEU (see **16.86–16.95**).

Article 157 TFEU and Treaty changes relevant to sex equality

16.6   Article 157 TFEU (ex Article 141 EC) provides for men and women to receive equal pay for equal work (to avoid repetition, this Article will generally be referred to by its TFEU numbering only in this chapter). It is clear that the Court considers this standard to be of fundamental importance to the operation of Union law, and it is one of the bases from which the general equality principle was developed. The expansive interpretation given by the Court to the Article, to the concept of 'pay' and to the directives adopted pursuant to the Article, has led to a far greater development of Union sex discrimination law than was originally anticipated.

16.7 As well as the broad interpretation given to the original text of the Article and the secondary legislation, the Treaty of Amsterdam added two paragraphs to the Article (Article 157(3) and (4)) TFEU so as to indicate an acknowledgement and acceptance of the Court's stance, and to show a commitment on the part of the Member States to go even further.

16.8 The Treaty of Lisbon removed the reference to the codecision procedures as set out in paragraph (3), and, interestingly, reworded paragraph 4 to remove the phrase 'positive discrimination'. Article 157(4) TFEU now states:

> *With a view to ensuring full equality in practice between men and women in working life, the principle of equal treatment shall not prevent any Member State from maintaining or adopting measures providing for specific advantages in order to make it easier for the underrepresented sex to pursue a vocational activity or to prevent or compensate for disadvantages in professional careers.*

16.9 The TFEU also sets out the aims of the Union in establishing equality. Article 8 TFEU states:

> *In all its activities, the Union shall aim to eliminate inequalities, and to promote equality, between men and women.*

Article 153(1) TFEU further aims to promote 'equality between men and women with regard to labour market opportunities and treatment at work'. The TEU also states its aims with regard to equality in Articles 2, 3, 9 and 21 TEU which respect the principle.

16.10 At this point it must be noted that the terms 'equality' and 'non-discrimination' appear to be used interchangeably in the Treaties. The term 'discrimination' is more often used when seeking to define the grounds on which the particular discrimination is prohibited. An example is Article 10 TFEU, which states the Union's aims of combating 'discrimination based on sex, racial or ethnic origin, religion or belief, disability, age or sexual orientation'.

16.11 An important development made by the Treaty of Lisbon is the inclusion of Part Two of the TFEU. Entitled 'Non-Discrimination and Citizenship of the Union' the section is reserved for the various principles respected by the Union, along with provisions concerning citizenship, on which see **Chapter 13**. Article 18 TFEU prohibits any discrimination on grounds of nationality (echoed in Articles 45, 49 and 56 TFEU), while Article 19 TFEU restates the list of prohibited discriminations in Article 10 TFEU with the added category of sex, which is set out in full in Article 157 TFEU. Articles 2 and 3 TEU also state the commitment of the Union to combating discrimination and achieving equality.

16.12 Additionally, the Protocol on Social Policy, which was attached to the Treaty of Maastricht provides for the conclusion of an Agreement on social policy and the implementation of the 1989 Community Charter on the Fundamental Social Rights of Workers. Paragraph 16 of the Protocol concerns equal treatment for men and women:

> Action should be intensified to ensure the implementation of the principle of equality for men and women as regards, in particular, access to employment, remuneration, working conditions, social protection, education, vocational training and career development.

16.13 At Amsterdam, the United Kingdom 'opt-out' from the Protocol on Social Policy annexed to the Maastricht Treaty was lifted. With the Treaty of Lisbon, the Protocol has now become part of the Treaty in Articles 153–156 TFEU. Directives adopted under the Social Protocol therefore apply to all Member States.

16.14 Lastly, Council Directive 96/34 on Parental Leave, extended to the United Kingdom by Directive 97/75 after Amsterdam, is based on the Social Policy Agreement and is a good example of the sorts of provisions intended. This Directive extends the principle of equal treatment of men and women to the possibility of reconciling occupational and family obligations. It provides for an individual and non-transferable right for men and women to parental leave on the grounds of birth or adoption of a child for at least three months until a given age up to the age of eight, to be defined by the Member States.

The meaning of 'pay' in Article 157 TFEU

16.15 Without resorting to the Equal Pay Directive 75/117 (see **16.36**), the Court has interpreted 'pay' in Article 157 TFEU to include 'any consideration, whether in cash or in kind, provided by an employer to employees or to retired employees'. In Case 12/81 *Garland v British Rail Engineering Ltd* (1982) the employer granted a benefit in the form of a grant of special travel facilities only to male employees after retirement. This benefit was granted *independently* of any contractual entitlement. The Court stated that the legal nature of the benefit was not important for the purpose of Article 157 TFEU, provided it was granted *in respect of the applicant's employment*. As such, female employees should also receive the grant.

16.16 The definition of pay does not, however, include state pensions, as was made clear in Case 80/70 *Defrenne v Belgium (No 1)* (1971), in which Ms Defrenne lost her claim that Belgian state social security benefits should come within the definition of 'pay' covered by Article 157 TFEU. The Social Security Directive 79/7 expressly excludes statutory pensions from its provisions. However, occupational pensions are included, i.e. those pensions which are part of a private social security scheme, even if those benefits are not part of a normal employment contract, but are provided gratuitously by the employer. In Case 170/84 *Bilka-Kaufhaus v Weber von Hartz* (1986) part-time employees, who were mainly female, could only join such a scheme if they had worked for a total of 15 out of 20 years. This scheme was provided by the employer in addition to the existing social security schemes and was therefore contractual and not statutory in origin. The Court held that the benefit constituted pay, since it represented consideration paid by the employer to the employee in respect of employment. Moreover, it was discriminatory as a far larger proportion of women than men were part-time employees.

16.17 Statutory schemes are in the field of welfare provision, which is not within Union competence. In the past 20 years, more and more moves have been made, particularly in the United Kingdom but gradually in other EU countries, to induce employees to 'contract out' of state pensions in favour of private schemes which fall within the scope of the definition of pay.

In Case C–147/02 *Alabaster* (2004) the Court made it clear that benefit paid to a pregnant woman during her maternity leave is to be treated like pay (see further **16.82**).

The meaning of 'equal work' in Article 157 TFEU and justifications for derogation from equal treatment

16.18 Equal work in Article 157 TFEU covers a broad range of employment activities. People employed in the same jobs are clearly within the scope of the equal work category, and different pay for a man and a woman doing the same work breaches Article 157 TFEU. When someone is paid more than another employee of the opposite sex, even though both are doing the same job, this is 'direct discrimination' since the difference of treatment directly arises from the gender differences. In Case C–100/95 *Kording* (1997) the Court defined direct discrimination as the 'application of different rules to comparable situations or the application of the same rule to different situations'. However, the equal work scope of Article 157 TFEU is not limited to such direct situations. Part-time workers have also been held to be doing equal work to full-timers, the rationale being that, although the different treatment of part-time workers is not considered direct discrimination, it is an example of 'indirect discrimination'. In such a situation, the different pay offered to part-time workers is presumably made because of the differences the employer sees between full-timers and part-timers. But the effect of such treatment is discriminatory because part-time workers are predominantly female across the EU while full-time workers are either not predominantly female or are mostly male. This was certainly the case when the Court first considered this matter. Thus, the meaning of equal work for the purposes of Article 157 is not limited to those situations where people are doing exactly the same job, but includes part-time variants of the standard full-time employment contract and all those categories that may fall into 'work' and that take account of indirectly discriminatory treatment.

16.19 In Case 170/84 *Bilka-Kaufhaus v Weber von Hartz* (1986) (new) the Court found that discrimination can be justified under certain circumstances, provided that the measure concerned satisfies a test of proportionality. In this case, a German department store had an occupational pension scheme which part-time, mainly female, employees could only join if they had worked for a total of 15 out of 20 years. Weber argued that women were more likely to take part-time jobs as they had to look after their families. Bilka responded that the justification for the difference in treatment was that part-time workers were less useful to the store; they were unlikely, for example, to work evenings or Saturdays.

The Court held that the difference in treatment did constitute indirect discrimination, however, it provided a three-fold test for measures which might justify their discriminatory effect:

- the measure corresponds to a real need of the enterprise, which might be economic;

- the measure is *appropriate*, i.e. suitable for attaining the objective pursued by the enterprise; and

- the measure is *necessary*.

These factors together constitute a test of proportionality. The Court found that, in this case, the test was satisfied and that the discrimination which had occurred was objectively justified on economic grounds. Therefore, the part-time work was defined as being equal to the full-time work, and so fell within the scope of Article 157 TFEU. However, this particular policy concerning the occupational pension scheme did not fall foul of the prohibition on discrimination because it was objectively justified.

16.20 This does not necessarily mean that objectively justified grounds other than economic ones would be excluded, such as administrative efficiency in an enterprise not engaged in commerce or business (see *Rainey v Greater Glasgow Health Board* (1987)). In Case C–144/04 *Werner Mangold v Rüdiger Helm* (2005) (see also **7.17**, **16.86** and **16.87**) the Court considered a justification regarding permitted age discrimination and concluded that policies aimed at getting older unemployed people into work could objectively justify different treatment of individuals on grounds of age. However, in the case in question, the Court held that direct discrimination on grounds of age could not be justified by the argument that younger persons could react more easily to the loss of their jobs and could be expected to be more flexible. Justifications under employment and labour market policy have also failed to justify direct discrimination on grounds of age, as in Case C–555/07 *Kücükdeveci*, discussed later (see **16.89**). There are a range of permissible objective justifications for indirect discrimination, and these are considered in more detail below (at **16.62–16.69**).

16.21 Equal work has also been held to include the same tasks performed by employees working either different shift hours or different numbers of hours. Some employers had suggested that employees who worked different patterns of hours could be treated differently, with some paid more than others. In Case 96/80 *Jenkins v Kingsgate (Clothing Production) Ltd* (1981), Kingsgate employed 35 men and 54 women full-time, and five women and one man part-time (30 hours a week). The Employment Appeal Tribunal referred a question to the Court on whether the principle of equal pay contained in Article 157 TFEU and in Directive 75/117 required that pay for work at hourly rates should be the same *irrespective* of the number of hours worked each week. There was some concern that the commercial benefit for the employer to encourage workers to work the maximum possible number of hours would be ignored by holding otherwise, and that this justified a higher rate of pay to workers who worked more hours. The Court stated that a difference in pay between full-time and part-time workers did not amount to discrimination unless it is merely an indirect way of reducing part-time workers' pay on the ground that the group is composed exclusively or predominantly of women. Thus the onus is on the employer to show the necessity for such a difference in pay, but also on the national court both to consider the extent of indirect discrimination and to test whether the effect on one sex is adverse in the case before it.

16.22 In *Equal Opportunities Commission v Secretary of State for Employment* (1994) the House of Lords accepted that part-time work was equal work when compared with full-time employment in the same task, and that different treatment of part-time workers was generally indirectly discriminatory towards women. In the judgment, the Lords considered the proof that was required before objective justification of indirect discrimination was accepted. The UK statute at issue in this case, the Employment Protection (Consolidation) Act 1978, only gave protection to workers in respect of unfair dismissal and redundancy payments if they worked for between eight and 16 hours for more than five years. Those working more than 16 hours a week would qualify after two years.

The Equal Opportunities Commission brought an action on the grounds that these provisions were contrary to Article 157 TFEU, and Directives 75/117 and 76/207 (the major secondary legislation on sex discrimination then in force, see **16.35**). The UK Government argued that there was objective justification of the indirect discrimination in the form of an avoidance of burdens on employers to try to encourage the employment of part-timers. Their Lordships held that the burden of proof was on the government to objectively justify discrimination and this burden had not been discharged. The government had not shown any evidence that the United Kingdom had a significantly higher number of part-time workers than other Member States, which would have been good evidence for the success of the policy. The provisions of the 1978 Act were, therefore, contrary to EU law. Subsequent to this case, the law was changed to deal with unfair dismissal and part-time workers. It is fair to say that the House of Lords' decision was very 'European' and far-reaching However, what if the situation changed and the United Kingdom *did* have more part-timers than other Member States? With how many Member States would the comparison be relevant? How far back would the government have to look in its statistics?

16.23 In Case C–127/92 *Enderby v Frenchay Health Authority and Secretary of State for Health* (1993) the Court of Justice clarified the role of statistics in the objective justification of discriminatory measures, stating:

> There is a prima facie case of sex discrimination where valid statistics disclose an appreciable difference in pay between two jobs of equal value, one of which is carried out almost exclusively by women and the other predominantly by men. It is for the national court to assess whether the statistics appear to be significant in that they cover enough individuals and do not illustrate purely fortuitous or short-term phenomena.

16.24 Statistics again came to the fore in Case C–167/97 *R v Secretary of State for Employment, ex p Seymour-Smith and Perez* (1999) which also concerned the different entitlement to protection against unfair dismissal available to full and part-time workers in the

United Kingdom. The Court held that where a measure adopted by a Member State is not based directly on sex, it is necessary to establish that its impact is significant enough to amount to discrimination. The national court must verify whether the statistics available indicate that a considerably smaller percentage of women than men fulfil the requirement imposed by the measure. Even if the statistics show a lesser, but persistent and relatively constant, disparity over a long period, this may amount to indirect discrimination, which may be justified by objective factors. The onus is on the Member State to show: that the rule reflects a legitimate aim of its social policy; that that aim is unrelated to any discrimination based on sex; and that it could reasonably be considered that the means chosen were suitable for attaining that aim.

16.25 The Court has also held that there may be some circumstances in which the difference in treatment between male and female workers does not constitute discrimination. For example, in Case C–218/98 *Abdoulaye v Régie Nationale des Usines Renault* (1999) the Court held that the principle of equal pay does not preclude the making of a lump-sum payment exclusively to those female workers who take maternity leave where that payment is designed to offset the occupational disadvantages which arise from their absence from work.

16.26 Similarly, where national legislation grants an employment termination payment to workers who end their employment relationship prematurely in order to take care of their children owing to a lack of childcare facilities for them, Union law does not require this payment to be related to the payments made in other employment termination situations. In Case C–249/97 *Gruber v Silhouette International Schmied* (1999) the payment made to a woman who felt compelled to leave work because of the lack of childcare facilities was less than the payment received, for the same actual period of employment, by workers who gave notice of resignation for an important reason related to working conditions in the undertaking or to the employer's conduct. The Court ruled that these payments could not be compared with one another since the situations covered were different in substance and origin.

16.27 Even if there is a difference in pay between male and female workers, there is no discrimination on grounds of sex if those two categories of workers do not carry out the same work. In the light of this, the Court has held that work is not the same where the same activities are performed over a considerable length of time by persons the basis of whose qualification to exercise their profession is different (Case C–309/97 *Angestelltenbetriebsrat der Wiener Gebietskrankenkasse v Wiener Gebietskrankenkasse* (1999)).

16.28 The scope of permissible comparisons was restricted by the Court in Case C–320/00 *Lawrence v Regent Office Care* (2002), the 'dinner ladies' case. Female school catering and cleaning staff had changed employers because the local authority they worked for had transferred their jobs to a private company, which paid them less. This meant that they were paid less than their male comparators who were still working for the local authority and whose work had been rated by a job evaluation study to be of equal value. In fact, they had won their case at the time claiming equal pay with them. The Court said that Article 157 TFEU did not limit its applicability to employees working for the same employer. Nevertheless, in the present case there was no single body which was responsible for the inequality and thus nobody could bring about equal treatment. It was, therefore, not possible to make a proper comparison between the female catering and cleaning staff and their male counterparts and, as a consequence, Article 157 did not apply. In Case C–256/01 *Allonby v Accrington & Rossendale* (2004) the Court repeated the argument that where the work could not be attributed to a single source the Article could not apply. In this case, Ms Allonby had become a contractor for the college where she had previously worked, and was therefore self-employed through an intermediary company. In applying the above rule, the Court held that she could not compare her pay with the pay of her colleagues who were still employed by the college, even though she was still employed by the college indirectly.

16.29 Permissible comparisons were also at issue in Case C–220/02 *Österreichischer Gewerkschaftsbund* (2004). Here (mostly) men were permitted, by Austrian law, to include periods of compulsory military service, or civilian service equivalents, in the periods of employment used to calculate employment termination payments made by private employers. The inclusion of periods of accepted absence meant that the termination payments made were calculated according to a period longer than the actual period worked. At issue in the case was the fact that the periods of absence permitted as parental leave, taken mostly by women, were not permitted under Austrian law to be included at the same generous rate in the calculation of a termination payment as the compulsory military/civilian service periods of absence. It was held that even though the termination payment was to be regarded as pay within the scope of Article 157 TFEU and Community secondary legislation, the situations were not comparable: parental leave covered the interest of the worker and the family but military service concerned the collective interest of the nation. This therefore fell outside of the scope of equal work protected by the Article.

16.30 In Case C–423/04 *Richards v Secretary of State for Work and Pensions* (2006) the Court considered permissible comparisons for the grant of a pension to a male–female transsexual. The Member State refused to grant a pension to a male–female transsexual of the same age as a female who had not undergone gender reassignment surgery. However, the Advocate General stated that the correct comparator for analysis was, indeed, a female who has not undergone gender reassignment surgery. The existing derogation from the Directive on Equal Treatment in matters of Social Security (see 16.47) is intended to determine the pensionable ages for men and women and not the sex of the person concerned. The Court agreed with the Advocate General and found that Article 4(1) of Directive 79/7 EEC precluded such legislation.

Does Article 157 TFEU have direct effect?

16.31 In *Defrenne (No 2)* Article 157 TFEU was held by the Court to be directly effective, but only in respect of direct discrimination. The circumstances in which discrimination occurred had to be easily discernible. Ms Defrenne, a retired flight attendant, sued the Belgian airline Sabena for damages to compensate her for pay she had received during her period of employment that was lower than that paid to comparable male flight attendants. She based her claim on Article 157 TFEU as there was no provision in Belgian law which could help her.

The Court of Justice held that the Article was sufficiently precise and unconditional, at least in part, so that it could be given direct effect in national courts. It limited this effect to 'direct and overt discrimination which may be identified solely with the aid of criteria based on equal work and equal pay'. It also drew a distinction, however, between this and, at paragraph 18:

> Indirect and disguised discrimination which can only be identified by reference to the more explicit implementing provisions of a [Union] or national character.

16.32 Since then, the Court has moved towards finding that indirect discrimination, too, is actionable by virtue of its direct effect. The Court ruled in Case 69/80 *Worringham and Humphreys v Lloyds Bank* (1981) that the Article had direct effect in respect of 'all forms of discrimination which may be identified solely with the aid of the criteria of equal work and equal pay'. This included claims based on indirect discrimination, and it was confirmed by the Court on several subsequent occasions that such claims could use Article 157 directly (also confirmed in Case 170/84 *Bilka-Kaufhaus v Weber von Hartz*, see **16.19**). Collective agreements, generally reached between employers and a trade union, have also been held to be subject to the directly effective nature of Article 157. In Case C–187/00 *Kutz-Bauer* (see also **16.63**) the Court ruled that, in the case of a breach of Directive 76/207 by legislative provisions or by provisions of collective agreements introducing discrimination contrary to that Directive, the national courts must set aside that discrimination, using all the means at their disposal. In particular this must be done by applying those provisions for the benefit of the class placed at a disadvantage. Also, the national courts are not required to request or await the setting aside of the provisions by the legislature, by collective negotiation or otherwise.

16.33 Article 157 TFEU would now seem to have direct effect in most circumstances, and may be used in courts both horizontally, i.e. against a private employer such as *Sabena*, and vertically against a state employer. This is different to some Treaty Articles, such as Article 34 TFEU, which have been held by the Court not to have horizontal direct effect (see **10.2**).

Temporal effect of Article 157 TFEU

16.34 In *Defrenne (No 2)* (see **16.31**) the Court held that the direct effect of Article 157 TFEU could not be relied upon in order to support claims in respect of pay periods prior to the date of the judgment (8 April 1976). The only exception to this applied to workers who had already instituted a claim at that time. In Case C–262/88 *Barber v Guardian Royal Exchange* (1990) the Court stipulated that the direct effect of the Article could not be relied upon in order to claim entitlement to a pension with effect from a date prior to that of the judgment in this case (17 May 1990), except in the case of those who had, before that date, instituted legal proceedings or raised an equivalent claim under the applicable national law. For more on the temporal limits in the domain of equal treatment, see **16.53** onwards.

Secondary legislation

16.35 After the Community adopted a Social Action Programme in 1974, a number of directives were adopted pursuant to what is now Article 157 TFEU. The principal directives currently in force are:

- Directive 2006/54, which consolidates the Equal Pay Directive (Directive 75/117/EEC), the Equal Treatment Directive (Directive 76/207/EEC) and the Directive on Occupational Social Security Schemes: (Directive 86/378/EEC). Most of its provisions do not substantially amend the previous directives, and it is to some extent a 'tidying-up' exercise;

- Social Security Directive (Directive 79/7/EEC).

These directives express in much clearer language what Article 157 means to do. It should be noted, however, that, even where these directives have direct effect, this will only be vertical direct effect against the state or an emanation of the state (see Case 152/84 *Marshall v Southampton Area Health Authority* (1986) (see **7.18**). It will not be against a private employer.

Equal Pay Directive 75/117

16.36 Until it was replaced by Article 4 of Directive 2006/54, secondary legislation on equal pay for equal work existed (in addition to Article 157 TFEU itself) in the form of Directive 75/117. The Court stated that Directive 75/117 is merely:

Designed to facilitate the practical application of the principle of equal pay outlined in Article 119 of the Treaty [now Article 157 TFEU] [Case 96/80 *Jenkins v Kingsgate* (1981)].

Article 4 of Directive 2006/54 requires the elimination of both direct and indirect discrimination in all aspects and conditions of remuneration for the same work or for work to which equal value is attributed.

Article 4 of the Directive also refers to job classification systems to facilitate the determination of pay rates.

Equal Treatment Directive 76/207

.37 Equal treatment goes beyond the prohibition on pay discrimination referred to in Article 157 TFEU. Directive 2006/54 updates the series of equal treatment rules originally introduced in Directive 76/207 and, as a result, sex discrimination has been widened to include many other factors, such as promotion, vocational training and working conditions (Article 1 of the Directive). The Directive also refers to both direct and indirect discrimination (Article 2), and provides definitions for both harassment and sexual harassment.

5.38 Article 2 of the Directive includes sexual harassment in the list of actionable sex discrimination incidents. Harassment is defined in 2(c) as:

> *unwanted conduct related to the sex of a person occurs with the purpose or effect of violating the dignity of a person, and of creating an intimidating, hostile, degrading, humiliating or offensive environment.*

Sexual harassment is also defined in 2(d) as:

> *any form of unwanted verbal, non-verbal or physical conduct of a sexual nature occurs, with the purpose or effect of violating the dignity of a person, in particular when creating an intimidating, hostile, degrading, humiliating or offensive environment.*

6.39 The Directive also provides an updated definition of indirect discrimination (see **16.62–16.69**):

> *Where an apparently neutral provision, criterion or practice would put persons of one sex at a particular disadvantage compared with persons of the other sex, unless that provision, criterion or practice is objectively justified by a legitimate aim, and the means of achieving that aim are appropriate and necessary. [Article 2(1)b]*

16.40 In Case 152/84 *Marshall v Southampton Area Health Authority* (1986), Article 5(1) of the old Equal Treatment Directive, which applied to working conditions, including conditions covering dismissal, was held to be directly effective. In Case 222/84 *Johnston v Chief Constable of the Royal Ulster Constabulary* (1986), the prohibition on discrimination in conditions of employment and on discrimination with regard to vocational guidance and training (i.e. Articles 3 and 4 of the old Directive), were also held to have direct effect. Mrs Johnston had been dismissed from the Royal Ulster Constabulary because she was considered to be unsuitable for firearms training as she was a woman. The Chief Constable of the RUC, against whom Mrs Johnston had brought a claim for sex discrimination, relied on a statutory provision which provided that a certificate signed by the Secretary of State certifying that an act was done for the purpose of safeguarding national security or protecting public safety or public order, was conclusive evidence of that fact.

16.41 Article 14(2) of the current Directive allows for a derogation on the basis of occupational activities in which 'by reason of their nature or the context in which they are carried out, the sex of the worker constitutes a determining factor'. This could include, for example, midwives. Alternatively, in Case C–273/97 *Sirdar v The Army Board* (1999) the Court held that the exclusion of women from service in special combat units such as the British Royal Marines may be justified under what is now Article 14(2) of the Directive by reason of the nature of the activities in question and the context in which they are carried out. The Court held that, subject to the principle of proportionality, the competent authorities could exercise discretion as to whether to maintain the exclusion concerned in the light of social developments, provided this was justified in view of the specific conditions for deployment of those assault units and in particular the rule of inter-operability. The Court further defined the scope of such justified exclusions in Case C–285/98 *Kreil* (2000). Here, the applicant claimed before the national court that the German army (the *Bundeswehr*) had refused to engage her in its maintenance branch. That refusal was founded on the German Basic Law, which imposes a general exclusion of women from military posts involving the use of arms and allows them access only to the medical and military-music services. When asked whether such an exclusion was compatible with Directive 76/207 (then in force), the Court held that this Directive precluded the application of national provisions such as those of German law which impose a blanket ban on the use of arms by women. The Court acknowledged that it is for the Member States to take decisions on the organisation of their armed forces. However, it did not follow that such decisions were bound to fall entirely outside the scope of Community law. In fact, some specific cases are covered by certain provisions of the Treaty, but the latter does not contain a general exception concerning all measures adopted by a Member State to safeguard public security. Any limitation of access by women to military posts must therefore comply with the principle of proportionality inasmuch as a derogation from an individual right must be appropriate and necessary to achieve the public security objective pursued. The exclusion at issue, which applied to almost all military posts in the Bundeswehr, could not be regarded as a derogating measure justified by the specific nature of the posts in question or by the particular context in which the activities in question were carried out. Subsequently, Case C–186/01 *Dory* (2001), concerned the question whether the limitation of compulsory military service to men is compatible with the principle of equal treatment. The Court held, adopting its reasoning in *Sirdar* and *Kreil,* that it was up to the Member States to ensure its defence in part by compulsory military service. The delay in careers for men is an inevitable consequence of that choice but this does not mean that that choice comes within the scope of Union law.

16.42 Article 24 of the current Directive (and 6 of the old Equal Treatment Directive) prohibits victimisation by an employer (by means of dismissal or other adverse treatment) of an employee who has instituted a complaint or brought legal proceedings to enforce compliance with the principle of equal treatment. This principle first originated in cases such as Case C–185/97 *Coote v Granada Hospitality Ltd* (1998). Ms Coote had brought an action against Granada Hospitality alleging she had been dismissed because of her pregnancy. The claim was settled and she left. Later, she asked her former employers for a reference, who refused because of the case she had brought against them. The Court held that Article 6 of the old Equal Treatment Directive, which requires Member

States to ensure effective judicial protection against instances of unequal treatment, includes measures to ensure judicial protection for workers whose employer, after the employment relationship has ended, refuses to provide references as a reaction to legal proceedings brought to enforce compliance with the principle of equal treatment. To decide otherwise would mean that such retaliatory measures on the part of the employer might deter workers who considered themselves the victims of discrimination from pursuing their claims by judicial process and, as a consequence, seriously jeopardise implementation of the aim pursued by the Directive.

6.43 In Case 407/98 *Abrahamsson v Anderson & Fogelqvist* (2000) considered at **6.44**, the Court considered the relationship between Article 141(4) EC (now Article 157(4) TFEU), which permits positive discrimination, or 'measures providing for specific advantages', and Article 3 of the old Equal Treatment Directive. Article 3 of the current Directive now uses the term 'positive action' and specifically states that 'Member States may maintain or adopt measures...with a view to ensuring full equality in practice between men and women in working life'. In *Abrahamsson,* Swedish legislation had provided for the creation of posts aimed at women since they were under-represented at a senior level in universities. The candidates for such posts were to be selected if they had sufficient qualifications, even if other candidates of the opposite sex would normally have been chosen because of better qualifications. However, the difference in qualifications should not be so great that such application would breach the requirement of objectivity. A professorial appointment at Göteborg University went to the female candidate who was considerably less qualified than the male candidate. The Court ruled that both Directive 76/207 and Article 157 TFEU precluded national legislation which was so unclear in scope and application, and disproportionate to the aim pursued, that it resulted in the appointment of a candidate from one preferred gender, purely on the basis of sufficient qualifications. If, however, a candidate presented 'equivalent or substantially equivalent merits', the appointment might be lawful, subject to an objective assessment. The reference in the current Directive, Article 3, to positive action does not change the difficulty of establishing proportionality of such measures. Further, the requirement that positive action initiatives should be considered by reference to the standard of equality under the Directive and the Treaty (i.e. consideration of the impact on those not targeted as the beneficiaries of the initiative) is also unaffected by the new provision in the current Directive.

16.44 In Case C–409/95 *Marschall* (1997), (see **6.44**), the Court was more favourable toward a national policy that sought to advantage women in certain work situations, since the policy concerned permitted well-qualified men also to be considered. Moreover, it specifically made possible male applicants' success despite the clear bias towards women. In Case C–158/97 *Badeck* (2000) the Court ruled in favour of a rule laying down binding targets for an advancement plan for women who were under-represented in posts in the academic service. However, there had to be a guarantee that candidatures were the subject of an objective assessment which took account of the specific personal situations of all candidates. A rule providing that half the training places should go to women and that half the places on representative bodies should go to women, if there were enough candidates, was also compatible with the then Equal Treatment Directive, although it is difficult to see how this is reconcilable with the proportionality requirement in *Abrahamsson*. In Case C–319/03 *Briheche* (2004) the Court ruled that the Equal Treatment Directive precluded a national provision which reserved the exemption from an age limit for obtaining access to public sector employment to widows who have not remarried and who are obliged to work, excluding widowers in the same situation. Such a provision automatically and unconditionally gives priority to the candidatures of certain categories of women and excludes widowers who have not remarried and who are in the same situation.

16.45 Therefore, the relationship between the Equal Treatment Directive—even with the inclusion of Article 3 of the Directive, a provision not in place at the time of these judgments–and Article 157(4) TFEU is difficult, since the positive discrimination seemingly encouraged by Article 157(4) struggles when it comes up against the equality principle as expressed in the Directive.

16.46 Subsequent to the Equal Treatment Directive, a number of directives were adopted providing for equal treatment of the self-employed, part-time workers and self-employed women during pregnancy and motherhood. For example, the Part-time Workers' Directive 97/81 based on a framework agreement between the social partners is aimed at eliminating discrimination against part-time workers and to assist the development of opportunities for part-time working on a basis acceptable to both workers and employers. Clause 4 of the Framework Agreement states that part-time workers should not be treated in a less favourable manner than comparable full-time workers unless this can be objectively justified. An objective justification would allow Member States to make access to employment subject to requirements as to period of service, time worked or an earnings threshold. With regard to the protection of pregnant workers there is Council Directive 86/613/EEC on the Application of the Principle of Equal Treatment between Men and Women engaged in an Activity, including Agriculture, in a Self-employed Capacity, and on the Protection of Self-employed Women during Pregnancy and Motherhood. A directive was also introduced under the health and safety provisions of the Treaty (now Article 154 TFEU) concerning the health and safety of pregnant women and of those who have recently given birth or are breastfeeding (Council Directive 92/85/EEC on the Introduction of Measures to encourage Improvements in the Safety and Health at Work of pregnant workers and workers who have recently given birth or are breastfeeding). The extent to which the Equal Treatment Directive covers discrimination on grounds of pregnancy is considered from **16.70** below.

Social Security Directive 79/7

16.47 The concept of equal treatment was further extended by the Social Security Directive. It covers statutory schemes protecting against risks arising from sickness, invalidity, old age, accidents at work and occupational diseases and unemployment (Article 3(1) of the Directive). It does *not*, however, cover survivors' or family benefits and Article 7(1)(a) of the Directive also excludes:

> *...the determination of pensionable age for the purposes of granting old-age and retirement pensions and the possible consequences thereof for other benefits.*

16.48 These exceptions have been interpreted very narrowly by the Court. In Case 150/85 *Drake v Chief Adjudication Officer* (1986) an invalidity allowance payable to a married man but not to a married woman caring for a severely disabled person was found to fall within the scope of protection offered by the Directive. The Article 7(1) exception did not apply because the carer would have been part of the working population and thus the benefit was covered by the risk provided for in the Directive. (See also Joined Cases C–87, 88 and 89/90 *Verholen v Sociale Verzekeringsbank Amsterdam* (1991) whereby the Court ruled that the provisions of the Directive were not confined to individuals who came within the scope of the Directive *ratione personae* (at paragraph 22), but could also be invoked by others who had been affected by the discriminatory provisions.) In Case 102/88 *Ruzius-Wilbrink* (1989) part-time workers were held to fall within the protection of the Directive. Invalidity benefits payable to part-time workers were linked to their previous earnings, whereas full-time workers were entitled to a 'minimum subsistence income' irrespective of their previous earnings. This was indirect discrimination, as the percentage of women working part-time in the Netherlands was much higher than that of men. As this was indirect discrimination, it could be justified by objective factors unrelated to sex.

16.49 However, the general standard of equal protection set out in Article 4 of the Directive was held by the Court not to justify limiting the application of the derogation in Article 7 of the Directive in all circumstances. In Case C–9/91 *R v Secretary of State for Social Security, ex p Equal Opportunities Commission* (1992) the Equal Opportunities Commission brought an action for a declaration that the Social Security Act 1975 was in breach of the Social Security Directive because it maintained different contribution periods for male and female workers under a state pension scheme and permitted different treatment between men and women with respect to the moment at which they become entitled to a pension. The Court held that the Directive's Article 7 derogation included different statutory pensionable ages, and other 'forms of discrimination…necessarily linked to that difference'. The result of this case was to render the relationship between the standard of equal protection and permitted forms of discrimination in pensions a little unclear.

16.50 Clarification was obtained in *Barber v Guardian Royal Exchange Assurance Group* (1990). Mr Barber sought to challenge his employer's contracted out pension scheme which operated as a substitute for the statutory social security schemes. The parties in such a scheme exercise statutory rights to replace the state pension scheme with that of a pension paid by the employer. The scheme was payable at different ages for men and women, so that when Mr Barber was made redundant at 52, if he had been a woman, he would have been able to receive a pension. Instead, as a man, he had to wait until he was 55. The Court held that although the pension was 'contracted out' and therefore in lieu of a statutory scheme, the scheme nevertheless constituted 'pay' within Article 157 TFEU. They reasoned that pensions are 'deferred pay' and received by reason of the existence of the employment relationship. Thus there must be equality as to the age at which it is received. The fact that the benefits are payable at different ages resulted in an overall difference of pay between men and women. This was contrary to Article 157, even if the difference between the pensionable ages for men and women was based on the one provided for by the national statutory scheme.

16.51 The consequence of *Barber* was to open up further the concept of pay to include a pension scheme which is not supplementary to a statutory scheme but actually is in lieu of such a scheme, i.e. a contracted out scheme. Just because a scheme is in lieu of a statutory scheme will not mean that it will fall outside Article 157. This had the effect of requiring Member States to bring statutory schemes into line with occupational schemes which were contracted out.

16.52 Difficulties arose with this judgment. The direct effect of Article 157 TFEU with respect to pensions had always been doubted because of all the complexities. Different life expectancies of men and women and other factors leading to complicated actuarial calculations seemed to point to an absence of the criteria for direct effect. Moreover, this ruling effectively bypassed the Social Security Directive and was clearly far-reaching in its effect. The economic impact of having to adapt national legislation would clearly be grave and 'for reasons of legal certainty' (at 44) the Court therefore limited the retroactive effect of the ruling. It said:

> In those circumstances, overriding considerations of legal certainty preclude legal situations which have exhausted all their effects in the past from being called in question where that might upset retroactively the financial balance of many contracted-out pension schemes…
>
> It must therefore be held that the direct effect of Article 119 [now Article 157 TFEU] of the Treaty may not be relied upon in order to claim entitlement to a pension with effect from a date prior to that of this judgment, except in the case of workers or those claiming under them who have before that date initiated legal proceedings or raised an equivalent claim under the applicable national law.

This wording caused confusion. Did the ruling only apply to benefits payable after the judgment or to service periods after the date of judgment?

The *Barber* Protocol

16.53 The answer to the above question came when the Maastricht Treaty on European Union (1993) was adopted. This Treaty included a Protocol to the EC Treaty, which became known as the '*Barber* Protocol' and which was in line with the later judgment of the Court in Case C–109/91 *Ten Oever v Stichting Bedrijfspensioenfonds voor het Glazenwassers-en Schoonmaakbedrijf* (1993). In this case, the Court made it clear that the ruling applied to periods of employment after the date of the *Barber* judgment, subject to an exception in favour of workers who had initiated proceedings before that date.. The Protocol provided that benefits attributable to periods of employment prior to the date of the *Barber* judgment did not constitute pay, subject to the exception for those who had already started proceedings before 17 May 1990. However, the *Barber* Protocol only applies to occupational schemes themselves, not to access thereto. In Case C–57/93 *Vroege v NCIV Instituut voor Volkshuisvesting BV* (1994) the Court held that the Protocol did not apply to the right to join an occupational pension scheme; in Case C–128/93 *Fisscher v Voorhuis Hengelo BV en Stichting Bedrijfspensioenfonds voor de Detailhandel* (1994) national rules relating to time limits for bringing actions under national law were accepted even though this operated against workers asserting their right under Union law to join an occupational pension scheme; and in Case C–435/93 *Dietz v Stichting Thuiszorg Rotterdam* (1996) the Court confirmed it had been clear since *Bilka Kaufhaus* that what is now Article 157 TFEU prohibits discrimination in the award of benefits by an occupational pension scheme which results from discrimination as regards the right to join such a scheme, so that employers and pension schemes could not reasonably have considered such discrimination permissible. (See also Case C–78/98 *Preston v Fletcher* discussed further at **16.56**). See also point 18 of the recital in Directive 2006/54.

16.54 Although the distinction between pay and occupational pensions had been eroded by the above cases, in Case C–152/91 *Neath v Hugh Steeper Ltd* (1993) and Case C–200/91 *Coloroll Pension Trustees Ltd v James Richard Russell* (1994) the Court drew back somewhat from the broad definition of pay ruling that employers' contributions to so-called 'defined-benefit' occupational pension schemes did not fall within the concept of pay.

Time limits and the secondary legislation

16.55 In **Chapter 7** the manner in which directives operate is discussed. In Case C–208/90 *Emmott v Minister for Social Welfare* (1991) (see also **7.103**) the Court stated that a Member State in breach of its obligations under a directive may not rely on an individual's delay in initiating proceedings in order to defend a claim based on rights conferred upon him by a directive. This meant that national time limits cannot begin to run in advance of the claim being made. Instead, the time limits only start once the national law has properly implemented the relevant directive. However, this ruling was qualified in Case C–338/91 *Steenhorst-Neerings v Bestuur van de Bedrijfsvereniging voor Detailhandel, Ambachten en Huisvrouwen* (1993). Mrs Steenhorst-Neerings had claimed sex discrimination in respect of disability benefits payable to her. A national rule limited the retroactive effect of such a claim to 12 months. The Court drew a distinction between this rule and the time limit ruling in *Emmott*. The rule in this case served simply to ensure sound administration, in that it enabled dates prior to that of the judgment to be excluded, except for those who had, before that date, instituted legal proceedings or raised an equivalent claim with the authorities to ascertain both the degree of disability and whether conditions of eligibility were satisfied.

16.56 A distinction with *Emmott* was also made in Case C–410/92 *Johnson v Chief Adjudication Officer (No 2)* (1994). The Court confirmed the distinction made in *Steenhorst-Neerings* between a time bar which had the result of depriving the applicant of any opportunity whatever to rely on her right to equal treatment under the Directive, (as was the case in *Emmott)*, and a rule which 'merely limited to one year the retroactive effect of claims for benefits for incapacity for work' (at paragraph 35). In Case C–188/95 *Fantask A/S v Industrieministeriet (Erhvervsministeriet)* (1997) (see **7.16**), the Court confirmed that *Emmott* was justified by the special circumstances of the case, where the time limit meant that the applicant was deprived of any opportunity to rely on her right to equal treatment under a directive. However it also held that Community law did not prevent a Member State, which has not properly transposed a directive, from relying on a national limitation period which was no less favourable than a Community one and which did not make the exercise of Community law virtually impossible or excessively difficult. Further confirmation came in Case C–78/98 *Preston v Fletcher* (2000) whereby a six-month time limit on the bringing of a claim for retroactive membership of an occupational pension scheme for a part-time worker was found to be legitimate as an application of the principle of legal certainty. Further, the time-limit complied with the principle of effectiveness as long as the national procedural rule did not make it impossible or excessively difficult to exercise the right. Nonetheless, the principle of effectiveness would preclude a procedural rule which restricted periods of service to be taken into account up to two years prior to the date of claim (see further **Chapter 7, Section III** on national procedural rules). Thus, on the basis of this case law, it is probably right to say that *Emmott* must be seen as a one-off case.

Burden of proof

16.57 In Case 109/88 *Handels- og Kontorfunktionaerernes Forbund i Danmark v Dansk Arbejdsgiverforening (acting for Danfoss)* (1989) the Court said that Directive 75/117, the Directive then in force on equal pay, had to be interpreted as meaning that, when a pay system lacks transparency, this shifts the burden of proof on to the employer to show that there is no discrimination. Moreover, adjustments to the national rules relating to the burden of proof had to be made in such circumstances in order to ensure the effective application of the principle of equal pay. In Case C–400/93 *Specialarbejderforbundet i Danmark v Dansk Industri, acting for Royal Copenhagen A/S* (1995) the point about transparency and the burden of proof was restated:

> The mere finding that in a piecework pay scheme the average pay of a group of workers consisting predominantly of women is appreciably lower than the average pay of a group consisting predominantly of men does not suffice to establish discrimination as the difference may be due to differences in individual output.

However, the burden of proof was on the employer when such a scheme totally lacked transparency.

5.58 Council Directive 97/80 (replaced by Directive 2006/54, Article 19) on the burden of proof in cases of discrimination based on sex, as amended, now provides that when a claimant has established discrimination, it shall be for the respondent to prove that there has been no breach of the equal treatment principle. The same conditions for reversal of the burden of proof apply to the General Framework Discrimination Directive 2000/78/EC (see **16.86**) and to subsequent directives. In Case C–196/02 *Nikoloudi* (2005) the Court held that where an employee's benefits depend on length of service, it may be indirectly discriminatory for the employer to disregard part-time service or to count part-time service on a pro-rata basis, unless the policy can be objectively justified. Moreover, the Court stressed that where employees plead that the principle of equal treatment has been infringed to their detriment and establish substantiated facts, Union law, in particular Directive 97/80 is to be interpreted so that it shall be for the respondent to prove that there has been no breach of that principle.

6.59 In Case C–17/05 *BF Cadman v Health & Safety Executive* (2006), possibly one of its most significant discrimination rulings in recent years, the Court of Justice preserved the capacity of employers to differentiate pay between workers at the same grade, based on a length of service criterion. The claimant in the main proceedings, Bernadette Cadman discovered in 2001 that the annual salaries of four men employed as inspectors at the same grade as herself were up to £13,000 higher. The claimant had worked for the Health and Safety Executive for nine years, whereas her male colleagues had been employed for a longer period.

The Employment Tribunal found in the claimant's favour, and held that, in accordance with Section 1 of the Equal Pay Act 1970, her salary should be modified to be equal with that of others working at the same grade. The Employment Appeal Tribunal (EAT) reversed that decision, citing Case 109/88 *Danfoss* (1989), which ruled that where unequal pay arises among full-time workers when length of service is used as a criterion, no special justification is required. The EAT considered that *Danfoss* remained good authority for full-time employees, whilst Mrs Cadman's claim related to part-time employment. Despite this, the Court was uncertain whether the approach in *Danfoss* remained appropriate, in the light of subsequent Court of Justice rulings that have, arguably, evidenced 'second thoughts' on the question (for example, Case C–184/89 *Nimz* (1991)).

The Court was asked to consider whether and in what circumstances Article 157 TFEU requires an employer to provide justification for recourse to the criterion of length of service as a determinant of pay where the use of that criterion gives rise to disparities between the men and women concerned. In response, the Court of Justice recalled the general rule outlined in *Danfoss*, whereby the Court had confirmed that rewarding the experience that enables workers to better perform their duties is a legitimate objective of pay policy, and that recourse to the length of service criterion is generally appropriate to attain that objective. Therefore, in the absence of any doubt as to its appropriateness, employers did not need to specifically justify having recourse to that criterion. However, in case of doubt, the employer would have to justify and prove that experience enabled the worker to perform their duties better in that particular job.

The effect of the judgment could be that the pay of women who change jobs or take career breaks whilst not covered by an employment contract, could be adversely affected if the requirement of experience is genuinely linked to greater skill in the job. This could affect many employees in a society where frequent job changes, particularly for women, are increasingly common. However, if a serious doubt arose as to the appropriateness of the use of the criterion, the burden of proof would still be on the employer to justify differential pay. Also, this would not affect employees under contract who take maternity leave without terminating their employment.

16.60   In Case C–307/05 *Del Cerro Alonso v Osakidetza-Servicio Vasco de Salud* (2007), the Court was asked to interpret clause 4(1) of the Framework Agreement on fixed-term work, concluded on 18 March 1999 (set out in the Annex to Council Directive 1999/70/EC). Mrs Del Cerro Alonso had worked for more than 12 years as an administrative assistant as a member of the 'temporary regulated staff'. In 2004, she became a member of the 'permanent regulated staff', and requested that her previous 12 years of service be taken into account in the determination of her pay. Her employer accepted this request. She then made another request that these benefits be recognised retroactively for a period of one year prior to the actual recognition and payment of the three-yearly allowances. However, since this retroactive recognition was available only to permanent regulated staff, and since the applicant was previously a member of temporary regulated staff, she was not entitled to the benefits. The Court held that the concept of 'employment conditions' referred to in clause 4(1) of the Framework Agreement could act as a basis for the claim, and precluded any difference in treatment between fixed term and permanent workers with regard to a length of service allowance.

Direct and indirect discrimination and justification

16.61   *Direct* sex discrimination cannot be justified. There are specific instances of different treatment between men and women provided for in the directives implementing Article 157 TFEU which permit derogation from the general principle but these are narrowly defined and context specific. The Court has never ruled that direct discrimination cannot be justified, although some suggestions have from time-to-time been made. For example Advocate General van Gerven in Case C–132/92 *Birds Eye Walls Ltd v Roberts* (1993) invited the Court to consider that 'such discrimination in a case such as *Webb* [see **16.77-16.78**] might nevertheless be justified having regard to the specific circumstances of the case'. However, when responding to the case, the Court ruled there was no infringement of the Article and thus avoided the question.

Justification of indirect discrimination

16.62   *Indirect* discrimination may be justified by objective factors unrelated to sex. These objective factors were defined by the Court in *Bilka* (see **16.16** and **16.19**). In Case 171/88 *Rinner-Kühn v FWW Spezial-Gebäudereinigung GmbH* (1989) the claimant worked as an office cleaner for 10 hours a week. German legislation excluded workers who normally worked for no more than 10 hours a week from being paid sick pay. The proportion of women working these shorter hours was considerably greater than that of men. The Court held that such a legislative provision must, in principle, be regarded as contrary to the aim of Article 157 TFEU, but may be justified by objective considerations unrelated to sex. Although the German Government alleged (at paragraphs 13 and 14) that part-time workers such as these were not as integrated in, or as dependent on, the undertaking employing them as other workers, the Court held that such considerations, insofar as they were generalisations about certain categories of workers, could not be accepted as objective justification. It would be different, however, if the Member State could show that the means chosen met a necessary aim of social policy and that they were suitable and requisite for attaining that aim. In Case C–189/91 *Kirshammer-Hack v Nurhan Sidal* (1993) the Court ruled that in the context of equal treatment, legislation favouring small enterprises which were exempt from applying the general rules on unfair dismissal to part-time workers could constitute objective justification. Objective justification is to be decided by the national court.

16.63 In Cases C–399/92, C–409/92, C–425/92, C–34/93, C–50/93 and C–78/93 *Stadt Lengerich v Helmig* (1994) the Court ruled that there was no indirect discrimination if overtime rates were paid to part-time workers only where the normal working hours for full-time workers had been exceeded. In Case C–187/00 *Kutz-Bauer* (2003) (see above at **16.32**) the case concerned a scheme enabling older workers to take part-time employment in the public service in which they had been employed. The collective agreement provided, however, that this possibility was only available until the date on which the person concerned first became eligible for statutory retirement. The Court ruled that the Directive precluded such a collective agreement imposing such conditions unless there was an objective justification:

> [w]here the class of persons eligible for such a pension at the age of 60 consists almost exclusively of women whereas the class of persons entitled to receive such a pension only from the age of 65 consists almost exclusively of men.

16.64 Also, in Case 300/06 *Voß* (2007) the remuneration of a female part-time teacher was questioned. Her overtime pay was less than that paid for equivalent hours worked by full-time teachers. As such, she received less for working the same number of hours as a full-time employee. The Court held that this was precluded by Article 157 TFEU (then Article 141 EC) as the part-time workers in question were predominantly female.

16.65 The Court has stressed that budgetary considerations of the Member States may never justify a difference in treatment. For example, Cases C–4/02 and C–5/02 *Schönheit and Becker* (2003) concerned legislation which could entail a reduction in the pension of civil servants who have worked part-time for at least part of their working life, a category which included a considerably higher number of women than of men. This was not acceptable unless objectively justified. Such objective justification was not available if the effect of reducing a worker's retirement pension was justified by the fact that the pension is consideration for less work or on the ground that its aim was to prevent civil servants employed part-time from being at an advantage in comparison to those employed full-time.

16.66   The Court has held repeatedly that the broad margin of discretion which the Member States enjoy in matters of social policy may not have the effect of frustrating the implementation of a fundamental principle of Union law such as that of equal treatment for men and women (see Case C–167/97 *Seymour-Smith and Perez*, at paragraph 75, noted above at **16.24** and *Kutz-Bauer*, noted above at **16.32** at pararaph 57). In Case C–77/02 *Steinicke* (2003), Ms Steinicke worked part-time for the German civil service and wanted to increase her amount of hours to full-time, exploiting a provision in German law which sought to encourage older workers into employment. Her request to increase her hours was rejected because she did not fulfil the requirement of German policy that she should have worked full-time for three of the five years immediately preceding the period of part-time work for older employees. Other arguments were also made concerning the budgetary impact of including applicants such as Ms Steinicke. The Court said (at paragraph 67):

> To concede that budgetary considerations may justify a difference in treatment between men and women which would otherwise constitute indirect discrimination on grounds of sex would mean that the application and scope of a rule of [Union] law as fundamental as that of equal treatment between men and women might vary in time and place according to the state of the public finances of Member States. [*Roks and Others*, paragraph 36, and *Kutz-Bauer*, paragraph 60]

16.67   In Case C–25/02 *Rinke* (2003), the Court had to decide whether Directives 86/457 and 93/16 which laid down the requirement that certain components of medical training, (which confer the right to use the title 'general medical practitioner'), must be undertaken full-time, constitutes indirect discrimination on grounds of sex within the meaning of the Equal Treatment Directive. Since the statistical data available showed that the percentage of women working part-time was much higher than that of men, the Court had to examine whether the requirements in question were objectively justified. The Court held that the requirement of full-time training is justified because the view of the legislature—that this requirement enables doctors to acquire the experience necessary—was reasonable.

16.68   In Case C–19/02 *Hlozek* (2004) an Austrian provision entitling men to a bridging allowance, (i.e. an advance payment of a pension), at 55 when women were entitled to this bridging allowance at 50 was considered. The Court ruled that Union law did not preclude the application of a social plan providing for a difference in the treatment of male and female workers in terms of the age at which they are entitled to a bridging allowance, since, under the national statutory scheme governing early retirement pensions, they are in different situations with regard to the factors relevant to the grant of that allowance. The different circumstances relevant to this policy, and accepted as objective justifications here, relate to the likelihood of unemployment.

5.69 In Case C–285/02 *Elsner-Lakeberg* (2004) overtime pay was the same for full-time and part-time workers. However, the Court stated (at paragraph 17) that:

> Although that pay may appear to be equal inasmuch as the entitlement to remuneration for additional hours is triggered only after three additional hours have been worked by part-time and full-time teachers, three additional hours is in fact a greater burden for part-time teachers than it is for full-time teachers. A full-time teacher must work an additional three hours over his regular monthly schedule of 98 hours, which is approximately 3% extra, in order to be paid for his additional hours, whilst a part-time teacher must work three hours more than his monthly 60 hours, which is 5% extra. Since the number of additional teaching hours giving entitlement to pay is not reduced for part-time teachers in a manner proportionate to their working hours, they receive different treatment compared with full-time teachers as regards pay for additional teaching hours.

Therefore the Court ruled: Article 157 TFEU (then Article 141 EC) and Article 1 of Council Directive 75/117, then in force, precluded national legislation which provides that teachers, part-time as well as full-time, do not receive any remuneration for additional hours worked when the additional work does not exceed three hours per calendar month, if that different treatment affects considerably more women than men and if there is no objective justification.

Discrimination on grounds of pregnancy

16.70 Is discrimination on the grounds of pregnancy direct discrimination? The Court has stated in a number of cases that a refusal to employ or a dismissal of a woman because she is pregnant amounts to direct discrimination. There are, however, some limitations. In Case C–177/88 *Dekker v Stichting Vormingscentrum voor Jonge Volwassenen (VJV-Centrum) Plus* (1990) and Case 179/88 *Handels- og Kontorfunktionaerernes Forbund i Danmark (acting for Hertz) v Dansk Arbejdsgiverforening (acting for Aldi Marked K/S)* (1990), two cases decided on the same day, the Court set out the principle.

Mrs Dekker applied for a post as a training instructor with a youth training centre. She was pregnant when she applied and so informed the selection committee. Although the committee recommended her as the most suitable candidate, the training centre refused to take her on. This was because their insurers would not reimburse the sickness benefits the centre would have to pay during Mrs Dekker's maternity leave because she was pregnant at the time of the application. Mrs Dekker claimed compensation, arguing that the refusal of employment was contrary to the provisions of the Dutch equal treatment law which implemented the Equal Treatment Directive 76/207. The Dutch courts held that the law had been violated but rejected her claim on the grounds that the employer had raised an acceptable ground for justification under Dutch law. Upon referral by the Dutch Supreme Court, the Court of Justice ruled as follows:

> Whether a refusal to employ results in direct discrimination on grounds of sex depends on whether the most important reason for the refusal is a reason which applies without

> distinction to employees of both sexes or whether it applies exclusively to one sex. As employment can only be refused because of pregnancy to women, such refusal is direct discrimination…

The employer had, therefore, acted in breach of Articles 2(1) and 3(1) of the old Equal Treatment Directive and the discrimination could not be justified by the financial detriment which the employer would suffer during the woman's maternity leave. The provisions breached in the old Directive are now covered by Article 14 of the current Directive.

16.71 In *Hertz*, Mrs Hertz had had repeated absences from her work due to an illness arising out of her pregnancy and confinement but which appeared after her maternity leave. This resulted in her dismissal on grounds of absence. The Court held that in this case there was no breach of the Equal Treatment Directive as the illness was treated as such, and the applicant's position was therefore comparable to that of a man who would have been dismissed under the same conditions. The Court did, however, state that dismissal of a woman on grounds of pregnancy constituted direct discrimination in the same way as a refusal to recruit a pregnant woman. A woman is, therefore, protected from dismissal because of her absence during maternity leave from which she benefits under national law.

16.72 In Case C–400/95 *Larsson v Føtex Supermarked* (1997), the Court concluded, in passing, that where a woman is absent owing to illness resulting from pregnancy or childbirth, and that illness arose during pregnancy and persisted during and after maternity leave, her absence not only during maternity leave but also during the period extending from the start of her pregnancy to the start of her maternity leave cannot be taken into account for the purpose of computing the period justifying her dismissal under national law. This rule was reiterated in Case C–394/96 *Brown v Rentokil Ltd* (1998) in which the Court stated that the principle of non-discrimination required protection throughout the period of pregnancy in addition to the period of maternity leave protected by the Equal Treatment Directive. The Directive therefore precluded dismissal of a female worker at any time during her pregnancy for absences due to incapacity for work caused by an illness resulting from that pregnancy.

16.73 In Case 232/09 *Danosa* (2010), the Court held that legislation under which a member of the board of directors of a capital company may be dismissed without any account being taken of the fact she is pregnant is contrary to Article 10 of the Pregnancy Directive. In its decision, the Court reiterated that, by virtue of the principle of non-discrimination and the provisions of Directive 76/207, protection against dismissal must be afforded to women not only during their maternity leave, but also throughout the period of the pregnancy. Consequently, even if the board member concerned is not a 'pregnant worker' under Directive 92/85, her removal on account of pregnancy can only affect women and, as such, constitutes direct discrimination on grounds of sex.

16.74 In Cases C–109/00 *Tele Danmark* (2001) and C–320/01 *Busch* (2003) the Court considered a duty to inform the employer of a pregnancy. In *Tele Danmark* it held that a worker cannot be dismissed on the ground of pregnancy where she was recruited for a fixed period; and where she failed to inform the employer that she was pregnant even though she was aware of this when the contract of employment was concluded; and where, because of her pregnancy, she was unable to work during a substantial part of the term of that contract. In *Busch* the claimant had a three-year period of parental leave following having her first child and had agreed with her employer to return to work before the end of the three years. She was at this time already pregnant again. The German courts considered the conflicting requirements of German laws preventing pregnant women from undertaking certain employment tasks (the *Mutterschutzgesetz*, also considered in **16.80**), compared to the right of pregnant women not to have to disclose their pregnancy. It was held that the Equal Treatment Directive precludes a requirement that an employee who, with the consent of her employer, wishes to return to work before the end of her parental leave must inform her employer that she is pregnant, even though there are legislative limits upon what an employer could require pregnant women to do while at work.

16.75   In Case C–191/03 *McKenna* (2005) the Court ruled on pregnancy-related illness and sick pay schemes and decided that pregnancy-related illness can be treated in the same way as any other illness causing sick leave. It will not constitute unlawful discrimination to apply the same sick leave scheme to employees off sick for reasons related to their pregnancy. The condition is that an employee is treated in the same way as a male worker who is absent on the grounds of illness and that the amount of payment made is not so low as to undermine the objective of protecting pregnant workers.

16.76   In Case 104/09 *Roca Álvarez* (2010) the Court found that a national measure which provided for 'breastfeeding' leave only in favour of women and their spouses, whilst excluding employed fathers, was contrary to both Directive 76/207 and Article 157(4). The positions of a male and a female worker, as mother and father of a child, were comparable in terms of their possible need to reduce their working time so as to look after a child. Furthermore, the Court observed that the granting of 'breastfeeding' leave has gradually become detached from the fact of breastfeeding and has, instead, moved more towards the act of feeding and devoting time to the child, both of which are activities which can be carried out just as well by the father as by the mother. The measure could not, therefore, be justified by the need to ensure the biological condition of the mother or the protection of the special relationship between her and her child.

16.77   While there is no justification for direct sex discrimination, there are circumstances in which different treatment on grounds of sex will not amount to direct discrimination. In Case C–32/93 *Webb v EMO Cargo (UK) Ltd* (1994) the House of Lords referred to the Court the case of a woman who had been hired on an indefinite contract to replace a pregnant worker, who had then herself become pregnant. The employer had dismissed her, alleging her pregnancy made her unable to do the job for which she was hired, namely to provide maternity cover. Although she acted as a temporary replacement it was anticipated that Mrs Webb would stay in employment after the other worker returned. The Employment Appeal Tribunal (EAT) and the Court of Appeal had dismissed her complaint on the grounds that her position should be compared with that of a man with a condition as nearly comparable as possible, and that a man appointed to a post he was unable to do (for medical or other reasons) would be similarly treated. The House of Lords took the view that the dismissal would constitute direct discrimination but that the motive for the dismissal should be examined, in this case that the applicant was unavailable to do the work she had been recruited specifically to do. It therefore considered the situation of a man in a comparable situation. Upon reference to the Court of Justice asking for an interpretation of the Equal Treatment Directive the Court stated:

> Dismissal of a woman on grounds of pregnancy constitutes direct discrimination on grounds of sex. Since pregnancy is not in any way comparable with a pathological condition, and even less so with unavailability for work on non-medical grounds, there can be no question of comparing the situation of a woman who finds herself incapable by reason of pregnancy of performing the task for which she was recruited with that of a man similarly incapable for medical or other reasons.

The Pregnancy Directive (Directive 92/85), which was not in force when the national courts decided this case, had also to be taken into account when considering the need for special protection to be given to pregnant women and those on maternity leave. *Webb* concerned an employment contract for an indefinite term and this was referred to by the Court in its ruling; the Directive precluded:

> *The dismissal of an employee who is recruited for an unlimited term with a view, initially, to replacing another employee.*

The House of Lords, in its judgment applying the Court's ruling, considered this to be an important factor: Mrs Webb's appointment on a permanent contract, and subsequent dismissal on grounds of pregnancy, was unjustifiable.

16.78   Perhaps *Webb* represents the high water mark of the Court's case law in this respect. There is still no clear answer as regards temporary, fixed-term contracts and those which concern a specific task. The Pregnancy Directive does not set a qualifying period and the only exception is contained in Article 10(1), which provides that in '…exceptional cases not connected with their condition which are permitted under national legislation and/or practice…' dismissal may be permitted. The employer must cite the grounds for such a dismissal in writing.

16.79   Since the adoption of the Pregnancy Directive, the difficulty for the national courts to interpret situations such as that of *Webb* has been eliminated. Indeed, the principle has only grown in importance in respect of other types of discrimination, e.g. in respect of terms and conditions of employment. In Case C–342/93 *Gillespie v Northern Health and Social Services Board* (1996), which concerned the Equal Pay Directive, the Court ruled that the Equal Treatment Directive did not apply and that, therefore, there was neither a requirement that women should continue to receive full pay during maternity leave, nor did it lay down any specific criteria for the amount of benefit payable to them during that period.

6.80   In Case C–421/92 *Habermann-Beltermann v Arbeiterwohlfahrt, Bezirksverband Ndb/ Opf eV* (1994) the Court found direct discrimination because of the existence of an indefinite contract. A German law on the protection of mothers prohibited pregnant women from carrying out night work. The Court drew a distinction between fixed term and permanent contracts. The national prohibition on night work was only for a limited period and, therefore, it would undermine the effectiveness of the Equal Treatment Directive to allow the employment contract to be found void or invalid. Case C–207/98 *Mahlburg* (2000) concerned a refusal to appoint a pregnant woman to an indefinite contract on the basis of a statutory prohibition to employ women from the outset and during pregnancy. The Court ruled that the Equal Treatment Directive precluded such a refusal; its provisions aimed at protecting pregnant women could not result in less favourable treatment in regard to their access to employment.

6.81   Since the adoption of the Pregnancy Directive (Directive 92/85) dismissal of workers during the minimum maternity leave prescribed in Article 10 of the Directive would no longer need to be examined under the Equal Treatment Directive. The situation in *Habermann-Beltermann* would thus no longer need to be objectively justified. In Case C–411/96 *Boyle v Equal Opportunities Commission* (1998) the Court gave, for the first time, an interpretation of the Pregnancy Directive with a series of answers relating to the interpretation of the provisions in Article 157 TFEU, of the Directive as well as of the then in force Directives on Equal Pay and Equal Treatment. Those replies determine the rights of female workers before, during and after their maternity leave and concern the payments to which they are entitled, the time when they must commence their maternity leave, the accrual of rights to annual leave and pension rights and the relationship between maternity leave and sick leave. The case concerned a clause in a contract of employment for staff of a public body which made the application of a maternity scheme (which was more favourable than the statutory scheme) conditional on the woman's return to work after the birth of the child. Failure to return would mean that she was required to repay the difference between the contractual maternity pay and the statutory payments in respect of that leave. The Court held this did not constitute discrimination. In Case C–342/01 *Merino Gómez* (2004) the Court confirmed its judgment in *Boyle,* stating that the purposes of annual and maternity leave are different. It added (at paragraph 39) that it would be no different if the period of maternity leave coincided with the general period of annual leave fixed, by a collective agreement, for the entire workforce.

16.82   However, in Case C–147/02 *Alabaster* (2004) the Court was concerned with the question whether a pay rise should be taken into account when calculating statutory maternity pay. Mrs Alabaster, commenced maternity leave in January 1996. Shortly before that she received a pay increase backdated as from December 1995, but the method of calculation was such that the pay increase could not be taken into account in her maternity pay. The Court found that Directive 92/85 did not help in answering the questions asked by the national court. It nevertheless established some general principles applicable to the case: the benefit was to be treated as pay (see also Case C–342/93 *Gillespie* (**16.79**)) and, as such, the principle of equal treatment meant that a woman who receives a pay increase before the start of her maternity leave must be entitled to have the increase taken into consideration in the calculation of the earnings-related element of her statutory maternity pay. The Court did not, however, express a view on the precise manner in which the principle was to be implemented as this was a matter for the national court.

16.83 Case C–284/02 *Sass* (2004) concerned statutory maternity leave in Germany. The period of maternity had been much longer under the old legislation in the German Democratic Republic (GDR), where it was 20 weeks, whereas under the current legislation it was eight weeks. Where legislation granted women maternity leave of more than 14 weeks that did not preclude this leave from being considered to be maternity leave as referred to in Article 8 of Directive 92/85. The purpose of the eight weeks' maternity leave provided for by the present law, and that of the 20 weeks' maternity leave provided for by the GDR legislation taken by Mrs Sass, were largely the same. Therefore, the Court said (at paragraph 58) that, if the national court reached the conclusion that the maternity leave provided for by the GDR legislation was such statutory leave intended to protect women who have given birth, the whole of that leave must be counted towards the qualifying period to be completed in order to be classified in a higher salary grade. This was in order to prevent a woman who has taken such leave from being placed in a worse position, because of her pregnancy and her maternity leave, than a male colleague who started work in the former GDR on the same day as she did.

16.84 Directive 2006/54 provides safeguards to women returning to work after maternity leave, stating that they will be able to return to their job on terms and conditions which are no less favourable to them than before and to benefit from any improvement in working conditions to which they should have been entitled in their absence (Article 15 of the Directive). It also incorporates the principle laid down in *Coote* (see **16.42**) that judicial and/or administrative procedures should be available for all persons who considered themselves to be wronged by the failure to apply the principle of equal treatment to them, even after the relationship in which the discrimination is alleged to have occurred has ended. Member States should ensure real and effective compensation, including removing any upper limit on compensation and reparation. In Article 16 the Directive embodies the same conditions for those on paternity or adoption leave if the Member State recognises such distinct rights.

16.85 Lastly, and on a slightly different note, in the interesting case of *Mayr*, Case C–506/06 (2008) the Court was asked to determine at what stage a woman undergoing IVF treatment to become pregnant was to be classed as a pregnant worker for the purposes of statutory protection. While Council Directive 92/85/EEC could not be interpreted as extending protection to women whose ova had been fertilised but not yet implanted, the Court held this scenario was within the scope of the old Equal Treatment Directive, and therefore the dismissal of a worker who was at an advanced stage of IVF treatment was precluded inasmuch as the dismissal was based purely on the grounds of the IVF treatment.

Discrimination on grounds of age, disability and sexual orientation: discrimination as a 'general principle'

6.86 The general equality principle and those specific rules prohibiting discrimination in specific situations should not be seen as operating in distinct or separate boxes: the boundary between the two is vague. In Case C–144/04 *Werner Mangold v Rüdiger Helm* (2005) the Court considered, for the first time, discrimination legislation based on age and merged the standard into the general equality principle. (See also **6.1, 7.17, 7.20, 16.87**)

This case concerned a German law on fixed-term contracts which permitted such contracts to be concluded without any restrictions when the employee was over 52 years old. This meant the employee, who was a party to the contract and who was above the age of 52, could have the contract terminated without compensation. The date of implementation of the directive on which this legislation was based (Directive 1999/70 concerning the Framework Agreement on Fixed-Term Work) had not yet expired, and Article 6 of the General Framework Directive on discrimination in employment (Directive 2000/78) had not yet come into force. The age limit in the original German Act had been set at 58 but had been lowered in January 2003 to 52. Mr Mangold, while aged 56, had concluded a fixed-term contract with Mr Helm, to take effect on 1 July 2003 for a seven-month period. Mr Mangold contended that the fixed term of the contract was forced upon him because the German law made it 'easier to conclude fixed-term contracts of employment with older workers... since the employee is more than 52 years old'.

The Court noted that, although the implementation date of the Directive had not yet expired, in accordance with its judgment (paragraph 45) in Case C–129/96 *Inter-Environnement Wallonie* (1997):

A Member State to which a directive is addressed may not, during the period prescribed for transposition, adopt measures that may seriously compromise the attainment of the result prescribed by the directive.

The Court answered the questions referred to it with a clear statement of the effect of the general principle of equality that broadens the terms of the specific non-discrimination legislative provisions. The Court accepted that the Framework Agreement on Fixed-Term Work allowed domestic legislation to lower the age above which fixed-term contracts may be concluded without restriction if it was 'for reasons connected with the need to encourage employment...'. It concluded, however, that any provision of national law that conflicted with its broad understanding (based on the general principle of equality) of the effect of the age discrimination legislation had to be set aside.

16.87   The Court went so far in *Mangold* (above at **16.86**) that it looked beyond the provisions of the Directive and stated that 'the source of the actual principle underlying the prohibition of those forms of discrimination' was to be found 'in various international instruments and in the constitutional traditions common to the Member States'. The Court also concluded that the full effectiveness of Community law in combating discrimination had to be guaranteed by the national court, to the extent of the national court setting aside any provision of national law in conflict with Union law 'even where the period prescribed for transposition of that directive had not yet expired'. This is a logical step from the ruling that the results of the non-discrimination Directive should not be compromised by the fact that the Directive had not yet been implemented (see further **7.13**). However, this is still quite a jump from the usual basis upon which unimplemented directives operate and is perhaps, yet again, a further expression of the significance with which the Court of Justice reads the equality general principle. Paragraphs **16.61–16.69** cover in more detail the justifications that can permit certain forms of discrimination to continue, but in the context of this case it should be noted that the Court accepted the objective of the legislation at issue, i.e. to promote the vocational integration of unemployed older workers who had difficulties finding work. So, policies aimed at promoting the employment of unemployed older workers can, in certain cases, result in discrimination on grounds of age. Still, the particulars of this factual situation meant that the justification of seeking to get older workers back to work was not accepted here: the Court held that as the age of the worker concerned was 'the only criterion for the application of the fixed-term contract of employment' regardless of any other considerations; this did not comply with the principle of proportionality (also considered in **Chapter 6**).

16.88   Case C–411/05 *Palacios de la Villa* (2007) concerned Directive 2000/78/EC's provisions on age discrimination. A collective agreement provided for automatic termination of the employment relationship where a worker had reached 65 years of age and was entitled to a social security retirement pension. The Court held that such a rule could be justified:

> The prohibition on any discrimination on grounds of age, as implemented by Directive 2000/78, must be interpreted as not precluding national legislation… pursuant to which compulsory retirement clauses contained in collective agreements are lawful where such clauses provide as sole requirements that workers must have reached retirement age, set at 65 by national law, and must have fulfilled the conditions set out in the social security legislation for entitlement to a retirement pension under their contribution regime, where
>
> • the measure, although based on age, is objectively and reasonably justified in the context of national law by a legitimate aim relating to employment policy and the labour market, and
>
> • it is not apparent that the means put in place to achieve that aim of public interest are inappropriate and unnecessary for the purpose [in other words, that proportionality was observed.]

In this case, legitimate aims relating to employment policy and the labour market that aimed to increase general employment levels, were held to justify discrimination.

6.89 Subsequently, (in a judgment confirming *Mangold)*, the Court was again asked to rule on the scope of justifications to age discrimination. In Case C–555/07 *Kücükdeveci* (2010) (see **6.10** and **7.22**), Ms Kücükdeveci was employed from the age of 18 by a private German company called Swedex. Ten years after she started working for them she was dismissed, and given the notice period of someone who had been working for the company for only three years. The reason for this was that German legislation stated that periods of employment prior to the age of 25 should not be taken into account when calculating length of employment. Ms Kücükdeveci challenged this decision before the German courts, which asked the Court of Justice whether the law constituted illegal age discrimination according to EU primary law and Directive 2000/78. The German court also asked whether, if the first question was answered in the affirmative, the national court should disapply the national law in the dispute between two private individuals. The Court reiterated its stance in *Mangold* that it is a general principle of Union law that all discrimination on grounds of age is prohibited, and Directive 2000/78 'gives specific expression' to that principle. The German Government claimed that young workers can generally react more easily and more rapidly to the loss of their jobs and therefore greater flexibility can be demanded of them. Further, shorter notice periods for younger workers also facilitates their recruitment by increasing the flexibility of personnel management. The Court took these justifications to be offered within the meaning of Article 6(1) of Directive 2000/78 and thus went on to question whether the means of achieving such a legitimate aim were 'appropriate and necessary'. The Court found that the measures were not appropriate and necessary because they applied to all employees who joined the undertaking before the age of 25. Further, the legislation disproportionately affected those joining vocational work with few qualifications, as opposed to those who chose to study for longer and entered the workforce at a later stage. The Court also proposed the horizontal direct effect of the Directive, although for more on this see **Chapter 7**.

16.90 In Case 149/10 *Chatzi* (2010), the Court referred to the general principle of equal treatment when it held that a national measure, when read in light of the principle, could oblige the national legislature to establish a parental leave regime which ensures that the parents of twins receive treatment that takes due account of their particular needs— in this case, more than one entitlement to parental leave. In such a case, it is left to the national courts to determine whether the national rules meet such a requirement.

16.91 Furthermore, the test in *Kücükdeveci* was applied in Case 45/09 *Rosenbladt* (2010). The Court ruled that Article 6(1) of Directive 2000/78 does not preclude a national provision which provides that clauses on automatic termination of employment contracts on the ground that the employee has reached the age of retirement are valid (compare with Case 341/08 *Peterson* (2010)). Case 499/08 *Andersen* (2010) concerned a Danish law which granted a severance allowance to workers who had been employed in the same undertaking for at least 12 years. The same legislation also provided that the severance allowance was not payable to workers who, on termination of employment, may draw money from an old age pension scheme which they had joined before turning 50. According to the Court, such a national measure was contrary to Directive 2000/78 since the measure concerned operated a difference of treatment which was based directly on age. Such a measure could not be justified by employment policy and labour market objectives since it went beyond what is necessary to attain those aims by excluding from entitlement not only all workers who are going to receive a pension, but also all those who are eligible for a pension but who wish to continue their career. Conversely, in Case 229/08 *Wolf* (2010) the Court held that although national legislation which sets a maximum age of 30 to intermediate career posts in the fire service, constitutes a difference in treatment on grounds of age, it could be objectively justified under Article 4(1) of Directive 2000/78. The legislation did not go beyond what is necessary in order to ensure operational capacity and proper functioning of the professional fire service since the possession of especially high physical capacities may be regarded as a genuine and determining occupational requirement and closely related to the age of the persons in that career.

16.92 The joint social and economic aims of Article 157 TFEU (according to dicta in *Defrenne (No 2)*) had previously been reconsidered in Case C–50/96 *Deutsche Telekom v Schröder* (2000), where a dispute arose over participation in an occupational pension scheme. The social aim of ensuring fairness to individual women and men was contrasted with the economic aim of ensuring equal conditions for competing employers. The social aim would suggest German law could apply the equal pay principle retroactively, so as to permit part-time workers access to an occupational pension scheme. The economic aim would suggest that Germany—in order to ensure that its firms were not operating under less favourable conditions than those of Member State competitors—should not. The Court ruled that 'economic aim..., namely the elimination of distortions of competition between undertakings established in different Member States, is secondary to the social aim...which constitutes the expression of a fundamental human right'.

16.93 Further indication of the presence of a general equality principle can be found in the case law of the Court concerning disability and sexual orientation. Case C–13/05 *Sonia Chacón Navas v Eurest Colectividades SA* (2006) concerned Directive 2000/78/EC in respect of the concept of disability. A Spanish court questioned the Court on the interpretation of Articles 2(1) and 3(1)(c) of the Directive concerning discrimination in regard to disability, where Mrs Chacón had been dismissed on grounds of sickness. The Court ruled that the concept of disability could not be extended to include sickness, and in answer to the Spanish court's questions ruled as follows:

(1) A person dismissed by his employer solely on account of sickness did not fall within the general framework of the Directive.

(2) The prohibition, as regards dismissal, of discrimination on grounds of disability contained in Articles 2(1) and 3(1)(c) of the Directive precluded dismissal on grounds of disability. In light of the obligation to provide reasonable accommodation for people with disabilities, dismissal was not justified by the fact that

the person concerned was not competent, capable and available to perform the essential functions of his post.

(3) Sickness could not as such be regarded as a ground in addition to those in relation to which Directive 2000/78 prohibits discrimination.

Conversely, in Case C–303/06 *Coleman v Attridge Law* (2008), Ms Coleman was dismissed from her job due to time off to care for her disabled son. She claimed discrimination on the grounds of disability. The Court held that Directive 2000/78 should be interpreted as prohibiting direct discrimination on grounds of disability even when the person facing the discrimination is not the disabled person. Ms Coleman was the primary carer for her son, and was therefore able to rely on the Directive.

6.94 Lastly, in Cases C–117/01 *K.B. v National Health Service Pensions Agency and Secretary of State for Health* (2004) and C–267/06 *Tadao Maruko v Versorgungsanstalt der Deutschen Bühnen* (2008), the Court further extended the principle of equal treatment to include discrimination on grounds of sexual orientation. In *KB* the Court of Justice held that Article 157 could preclude a national measure which prevented a female-to-male transsexual partner of a female member of the NHS from fulfilling the marriage requirement necessary to be able to benefit from a survivor's pension under the NHS Pension Scheme (see **6.5**). Similarly, in *Maruko,* the Court concluded that Articles 1 and 2 of the Equal Treatment Directive could preclude a national measure which prevented an individual from receiving a survivor's pension on the grounds that the individual concerned was a life partner from a same sex couple, and not a spouse. For more on the general principle of non discrimination on grounds of age, disability or sexual orientation see **6.34**.

6.95 To date, case law on discrimination under Article 19 TFEU has been sparse and, with the accession of new Member States, the adjustments needed to implement the directives, and the differing cultures in respect of various forms of discrimination throughout the European Union, probably account for the relatively small number of cases that have come to the Court. Where such cases have been referred, the Court has very largely left it to the referring court to determine the final outcome.

FURTHER READING

Bell, M. and Waddington, L., 'Reflecting on inequalities in European equality law' (2003) 28 *European Law Review* 349–369.

Curtin, D., 'Scalping the Community legislator: occupational pensions and "Barber"' (1990) *Common Market Law Review* 475.

European Union Agency for Fundamental Rights and European Court of Human Rights – Council of Europe, 'Handbook on European non-discrimination law' (2011).

Fontanelli, F., 'General principles of the EU and a glimpse of solidarity in the aftermath of *Mangold* and *Kücükdeveci*' (2011) 17(2) *European Public Law* 225–240.

More, G., 'The principle of equal treatment: from market unifier to fundamental right?' in Craig and de Búrca (eds), *The Evolution of EU Law* (Oxford: OUP, 1999).

Schlachter, M., 'Mandatory retirement and age discrimination under EU law' (2011) 27 *Journal of Comparative Labour Law and Industrial Relations* 287–299.

Whittle, R., 'The framework Directive for equal treatment in employment and occupation: an analysis from a disabililty rights perspective' (2002) 27 *European Law Review* 303–326.

SELF-TEST QUESTIONS

1   What is the difference between direct and indirect discrimination? How is objective justi-fication relevant to either?

2   Are pensions pay?

3   'The case law of the Court of Justice on matters of sex discrimination considerably expanded the scope of Article 157 TFEU. More recently, in applying the principle of equal-ity, the Court has shown uncharacteristic restraint.' Discuss.

TABLE OF EQUIVALENCES

Numbering pre-Amsterdam	Previous (Amsterdam) numbering of the Treaty on European Union	Current (Lisbon) numbering of the Treaty on European Union
Title I	**Title I**	**Title I**
Article A	Article 1	Article 1
		Article 2
Article B	Article 2	Article 3
Article C	Article 3 (repealed)[1]	
		Article 4
		Article 5[2]
Article D	Article 4 (repealed)[3]	
Article E	Article 5 (repealed)[4]	
Article F	Article 6	Article 6
Article F.1(*)	Article 7	Article 7
		Article 8
Title II	**Title II**	**Title II**
Article G	Article 8 (repealed)[5]	Article 9
		Article 10[6]
		Article 11
		Article 12
Title III	**Title III**	**Title III**
Article H	Article 9 (repealed)[7]	Article 13
		Article 14[8]
		Article 15[9]
		Article 16[10]
		Article 17[11]
		Article 18
		Article 19[12]
Title IV	**Title IV**	**Title IV**
Article I	Article 10 (repealed)[13]	Article 20[14]
	Articles 27a to 27e (replaced)	
	Articles 40 to 40b (replaced)	
	Articles 43 to 45 (replaced)	
Title V(***)	**Title V**	**Title V**
		Chapter 1 — General provisions on the Union's external action
		Article 21
		Article 22

Numbering pre-Amsterdam	Previous (Amsterdam) numbering of the Treaty on European Union	Current (Lisbon) numbering of the Treaty on European Union
		Chapter 2 — Specific provisions on the common foreign and security policy
		Section 1 - common provisions
		Article 23
Article J.1	Article 11	Article 24
Article J.2	Article 12	Article 25
Article J.3	Article 13	Article 26
		Article 27
Article J.4	Article 14	Article 28
Article J.5	Article 15	Article 29
	Article 22 (moved)	Article 30
	Article 23 (moved)	Article 31
Article J.6	Article 16	Article 32
Article J.7	Article 17 (moved)	Article 42
Article J.8	Article 18	Article 33
Article J.9	Article 19	Article 34
Article J.10	Article 20	Article 35
Article J.11	Article 21	Article 36
Article J.12	Article 22 (moved)	*Article 30*
Article J.13	Article 23 (moved)	*Article 31*
Article J.14	Article 24	Article 37
Article J.15	Article 25	Article 38
		Article 39
	Article 47 (moved)	Article 40
Article J.16	Article 26 (repealed)	
Article J.17	Article 27 (replealed)	
	Article 27a (replaced)[15]	*Article 20*
	Article 27b (replaced)[15]	*Article 20*
	Article 27c (replaced)[15]	*Article 20*
	Article 27d (replaced)[15]	*Article 20*
	Article 27e (replaced)[15]	*Article 20*
Article J.18	Article 28	Article 41
		Section 2 — Provisions on the common security and defence policy
Article J.7	*Article 17 (moved)*	Article 42
		Article 43
		Article 44
		Article 45
		Article 46
Title VI(***)	**Title VI[16]**	
Article K.1	Article 29 (replaced)[17]	
Article K.2	Article 30 (replaced)[18]	

Numbering pre-Amsterdam	Previous (Amsterdam) numbering of the Treaty on European Union	Current (Lisbon) numbering of the Treaty on European Union
Article K.3	Article 31 (replaced)[19]	
Article K.4	Article 32 (replaced)[20]	
Article K.5	Article 33 (replaced)[21]	
Article K.6	Article 34 (repealed)	
Article K.7	Article 35 (repealed)	
Article K.8	Article 36 (replaced)[22]	
Article K.9	Article 37 (repealed)	
Article K.10	Article 38 (repealed)	
Article K.11	Article 39 (repealed)	
Article K.12	Article 40 (replaced)[23]	*Article 20*
	Article 40 A (replaced)[23]	*Article 20*
	Article 40 B (replaced)[23]	*Article 20*
Article K.13	Article 41 (repealed)	
Article K.14	Article 42 (repealed)	
Title VIa(**)	**Title VII** [24]	**Title VII**
Article K.15(*)	Article 43 (replaced)[24]	*Article 20*
	Article 43 A (replaced)[24]	*Article 20*
	Article 43 B (replaced)[24]	*Article 20*
	Article 44[24]	*Article 20*
Article K.16(*)	Article 44 A (replaced)[24]	*Article 20*
Article K.17(*)	Article 45 (replaced)[24]	*Article 20*
Title VII	**Title VIII**	**Title VIII**
Article L	Article 46	
		Article 47
Article M	Article 47 (replaced)	*Article 40*
Article N	Article 48	Article 48
Article O	Article 49	Article 49
		Article 50
		Article 51
		Article 52
Article P	Article 50 (repealed)	
Article Q	Article 51	Article 53
Article R	Article 52	Article 54
Article S	Article 53	Article 55

(*) New Article introduced by the Treaty of Amsterdam.
(**) New Title introduced by the Treaty of Amsterdam.
(***) Title restructured by the Treaty of Amsterdam.

(1) Replaced, in substance, by Article 7 of the Treaty on the Functioning of the European Union ('TFEU') and by Articles 13(1) and 21, paragraph 3, second subparagraph of the Treaty on European Union ('TEU').

(2) Replaces Article 5 of the Treaty establishing the European Community ('TEC').

(3) Replaced, in substance, by Article 15.

(4) Replaced, in substance, by Article 13, paragraph 2.

(5) Article 8 TEU, which was in force until the entry into force of the Treaty of Lisbon (hereinafter 'current'), amended the TEC. Those amendments are incorporated into the latter Treaty and Article 8 is repealed. Itsnumber is used to insert a new provision.

(6) Paragraph 4 replaces, in substance, the first subparagraph of Article 191 TEC.

9.5.2008 EN Official Journal of the European Union C 115/361

(1) Tables of equivalences as referred to in Article 5 of the Treaty of Lisbon. The original centre column, which set out the intermediate numbering as used in that Treaty, has been omitted.

(7) The current Article 9 TEU amended the Treaty establishing the European Coal and Steel Community. This latter expired on 23 July 2002. Article 9 is repealed and the number thereof is used to insert another provision.

(8) — Paragraphs 1 and 2 replace, in substance, Article 189 TEC;

— paragraphs 1 to 3 replace, in substance, paragraphs 1 to 3 of Article 190 TEC;

— paragraph 1 replaces, in substance, the first subparagraph of Article 192 TEC;

— paragraph 4 replaces, in substance, the first subparagraph of Article 197 TEC.

(9) Replaces, in substance, Article 4.

(10) — Paragraph 1 replaces, in substance, the first and second indents of Article 202 TEC;

— paragraphs 2 and 9 replace, in substance, Article 203 TEC;

— paragraphs 4 and 5 replace, in substance, paragraphs 2 and 4 of Article 205 TEC.

(11) — Paragraph 1 replaces, in substance, Article 211 TEC;

— paragraphs 3 and 7 replace, in substance, Article 214 TEC.

— paragraph 6 replaces, in substance, paragraphs 1, 3 and 4 of Article 217 TEC.

(12) — Replaces, in substance, Article 220 TEC.

— the second subparagraph of paragraph 2 replaces, in substance, the first subparagraph of Article 221 TEC.

(13) The current Article 10 TEU amended the Treaty establishing the European Atomic Energy Community. Those amendments are incorporated into the Treaty of Lisbon. Article 10 is repealed and the number thereof is used to insert another provision.

(14) Also replaces Articles 11 and 11a TEC.

(15) The current Articles 27a to 27e, on enhanced cooperation, are also replaced by Articles 326 to 334 TFEU.

(16) The current provisions of Title VI of the TEU, on police and judicial cooperation in criminal matters, are replaced by the provisions of Chapters 1, 5 and 5 of Title IV of Part Three of the TFEU.

(17) Replaced by Article 67 TFEU.

(18) Replaced by Articles 87 and 88 TFEU.

(19) Replaced by Articles 82, 83 and 85 TFEU.

(20) Replaced by Article 89 TFEU.

(21) Replaced by Article 72 TFEU.

(22) Replaced by Article 71 TFEU.

(23) The current Articles 40 to 40 B TEU, on enhanced cooperation, are also replaced by Articles 326 to 334 TFEU.

(24) The current Articles 43 to 45 and Title VII of the TEU, on enhanced cooperation, are also replaced by Articles 326 to 334 TFEU.

Numbering pre-Amsterdam	Numbering of the Treaty establishing the European Community as adopted at Amsterdam	Numbering of the Treaty on the Functioning of the European Union
PART ONE	PART ONE — PRINCIPLES	PART ONE — PRINCIPLES
Article 1	Article 1 (repealed)	
		Article 1
Article 2	Article 2 (repealed)[25]	
		Title I — Categories and areas of union competence
		Article 2
		Article 3
		Article 4
		Article 5
		Article 6
		Title II — Provisions having general application
		Article 7
Article 3	Article 3, paragraph 1 (repealed)[26]	
Article 3	Article 3, paragraph 2	Article 8
Article 3a	Article 4 (moved)	*Article 119*
Article 3b	Article 5 (replaced)[27]	
		Article 9
		Article 10
Article 3c(*)	Article 6	Article 11
	Article 153, paragraph 2 (moved)	Article 12
		Article 13[28]
Article 4	Article 7 (repealed)[29]	
Article 4a	Article 8 (repealed)[30]	
Article 4b	Article 9 (repealed)	
Article 5	Article 10 (repealed)[31]	
Article 5a(*)	Article 11 (replaced)[32]	*Articles 326 to 334*
	Article 11a (replaced)[32]	*Articles 326 to 334*
Article 6	Article 12 (repealed)	*Article 18*
Article 6a(*)	Article 13 (moved)	*Article 19*
Article 7 (repealed)		
Article 7a	Article 14 (moved)	*Article 26*
Article 7b (repealed)		
Article 7c	Article 15 (moved)	*Article 27*
Article 7d(*)	Article 16	Article 14
	Article 255 (moved)	Article 15
	Article 286 (moved)	Article 16
		Article 17
PART TWO	PART TWO — CITIZENSHIP OF THE UNION	PART TWO — NON-DISCRIMINATION AND CITIZENSHIP OF THE UNION

Numbering pre-Amsterdam	Numbering of the Treaty establishing the European Community as adopted at Amsterdam	Numbering of the Treaty on the Functioning of the European Union
	Article 12 (moved)	Article 18
	Article 13 (moved)	Article 19
Article 8	Article 17	Article 20
Article 8a	Article 18	Article 21
Article 8b	Article 19	Article 22
Article 8c	Article 20	Article 23
Article 8d	Article 21	Article 24
Article 8e	Article 22	Article 25
PART THREE	**PART THREE — COMMUNITY POLICIES**	**PART THREE — POLICIES AND INTERNAL ACTIONS OF THE UNION**
		Title I — The internal market
	Article 14 (moved)	Article 26
	Article 15 (moved)	Article 27
Title 1	Title I — Free movement of goods	Title II — Free movement of goods
Article 9	Article 23	Article 28
Article 10	Article 24	Article 29
Article 11 (repealed)		
Chapter 1	Chapter 1 — The customs union	Chapter 1 — The customs union
Section 1 (deleted)		
Article 12	Article 25	Article 30
Articles 13-26 (repealed)		
Article 27 (repealed)	Article 26	Article 31
Article 28	Article 27	Article 32
	Part Three, Title X, Customs cooperation (moved)	Chapter 2 — Customs cooperation
Article 29	*Article 135 (moved)*	Article 33
	Chapter 2 — Prohibition of quantitative restrictions between Member States	Chapter 3 — Prohibition of quantitative restrictions between Member States
Article 30	Article 28	Article 34
Articles 31-33 (repealed)		
Article 34	Article 29	Article 35
Article 35		
Article 36	Article 30	Article 36
Article 37	Article 31	Article 37
Title II	Title II — Agriculture	Title III — Agriculture and fisheries
Article 38	Article 32	Article 38
Article 39	Article 33	Article 39

Numbering pre-Amsterdam	Numbering of the Treaty establishing the European Community as adopted at Amsterdam	Numbering of the Treaty on the Functioning of the European Union
Article 40	Article 34	Article 40
Article 41	Article 35	Article 41
Article 42	Article 36	Article 42
Article 43	Article 37	Article 43
Articles 44-45 (repealed)		
Article 46	Article 38	Article 44
Article 47 repealed		
Title II	Title III — Free movement of persons, services and capital	Title IV — Free movement of persons, services and capital
Chapter 1	Chapter 1 — Workers	Chapter 1 — Workers
Article 48	Article 39	Article 45
Article 49	Article 40	Article 46
Article 50	Article 41	Article 47
Article 51	Article 42	Article 48
Chapter 2	Chapter 2 — Right of establishment	Chapter 2 — Right of establishment
Article 52	Article 43	Article 49
Article 53 (repealed)		
Article 54	Article 44	Article 50
Article 55	Article 45	Article 51
Article 56	Article 46	Article 52
Article 57	Article 47	Article 53
Article 58	Article 48	Article 54
	Article 294 (moved)	Article 55
Chapter 3	Chapter 3 — Services	Chapter 3 — Services
Article 59	Article 49	Article 56
Article 60	Article 50	Article 57
Article 61	Article 51	Article 58
Article 62 (repealed)		
Article 63	Article 52	Article 59
Article 64	Article 53	Article 60
Article 65	Article 54	Article 61
Article 66	Article 55	Article 62
Chapter 4	Chapter 4 — Capital and payments	Chapter 4 — Capital and payments
Articles 67-73a (repealed)		
Article 73b	Article 56	Article 63
Article 73c	Article 57	Article 64
Article 73d	Article 58	Article 65
Article 73e (repealed)		

Numbering pre-Amsterdam	Numbering of the Treaty establishing the European Community as adopted at Amsterdam	Numbering of the Treaty on the Functioning of the European Union
Article 73f	Article 59	Article 66
Article 73h (repealed)		
	Article 60 (moved)	*Article 75*
Title IIIa(**)	Title IV — Visas, asylum, immigration and other policies related to free movement of persons	Title V — Area of freedom, security and justice
		Chapter 1 — General provisions
Article 73i(*)	Article 61	Article 67[33]
		Article 68
		Article 69
		Article 70
		Article 71[34]
	Article 64, paragraph 1 (replaced)	Article 72[35]
		Article 73
	Article 66 (replaced)	Article 74
	Article 60 (moved)	Article 75
		Article 76
		Chapter 2 — Policies on border checks, asylum and immigration
Article 73j(*)	Article 62	Article 77
Article 73k(*)	Article 63, points 1 et 2, and Article 64, paragraph 2[36]	Article 78
Article 73k(*)	Article 63, points 3 and 4	Article 79
		Article 80
Article 73l(*)	Article 64, paragraph 1 (replaced)	*Article 72*
		Chapter 3 — Judicial cooperation in civil matters
Article 73m(*)	Article 65	Article 81
Article 73n(*)	Article 66 (replaced)	Article 74
Article 73o(*)	Article 67 (repealed)	
Article 73p(*)	Article 68 (repealed)	
Article 73q (*)	Article 69 (repealed)	
		Chapter 4 — Judicial cooperation in criminal matters
		Article 82[37]
		Article 83[37]
		Article 84
		Article 85[37]
		Article 86

Numbering pre-Amsterdam	Numbering of the Treaty establishing the European Community as adopted at Amsterdam	Numbering of the Treaty on the Functioning of the European Union
		Chapter 5 — Police cooperation
		Article 87[(38)]
		Article 88[(38)]
		Article 89[(39)]
Title IV	Title V — Transport	Title VI — Transport
Article 74	Article 70	Article 90
Article 75	Article 71	Article 91
Article 76	Article 72	Article 92
Article 77	Article 73	Article 93
Article 78	Article 74	Article 94
Article 79	Article 75	Article 95
Article 80	Article 76	Article 96
Article 81	Article 77	Article 97
Article 82	Article 78	Article 98
Article 83	Article 79	Article 99
Article 84	Article 80	Article 100
Title V	Title VI — Common rules on competition, taxation and approximation of laws	Title VII — Common rules on competition, taxation and approximation of laws
Chapter 1	Chapter 1 — Rules on competition	Chapter 1 — Rules on competition
Section 1	Section 1 — Rules applying to undertakings	Section 1 — Rules applying to undertakings
Article 85	Article 81	Article 101
Article 86	Article 82	Article 102
Article 87	Article 83	Article 103
Article 88	Article 84	Article 104
Article 89	Article 85	Article 105
Article 90	Article 86	Article 106
Section 2 (deleted)		
Article 91 (repealed)		
Section 3	Section 2 — Aids granted by States	Section 2 — Aids granted by States
Article 92	Article 87	Article 107
Article 93	Article 88	Article 108
Article 94	Article 89	Article 109
	Chapter 2 — Tax provisions	Chapter 2 — Tax provisions
Article 95	Article 90	Article 110
Article 96	Article 91	Article 111
Article 97 (repealed)		
Article 98	Article 92	Article 112
Article 99	Article 93	Article 113

Numbering pre-Amsterdam	Numbering of the Treaty establishing the European Community as adopted at Amsterdam	Numbering of the Treaty on the Functioning of the European Union
	Chapter 3 — Approximation of laws	Chapter 3 — Approximation of laws
Article 100a	*Article 95 (moved)*	Article 114
Article 100	*Article 94 (moved)*	Article 115
Articles 100b-d (repealed)		
Article 101	Article 96	Article 116
Article 102	Article 97	Article 117
		Article 118
	Title VII — Economic and monetary policy	Title VIII — Economic and monetary policy
	Article 4 (moved)	Article 119
	Chapter 1 — Economic policy	Chapter 1 — Economic policy
Article 102a	Article 98	Article 120
Article 103	Article 99	Article 121
Article 103a	Article 100	Article 122
Article 104	Article 101	Article 123
Article 104a	Article 102	Article 124
Article 104b	Article 103	Article 125
Article 104c	Article 104	Article 126
Chapter 2	Chapter 2 — monetary policy	Chapter 2 — monetary policy
Article 105	Article 105	Article 127
Article 105a	Article 106	Article 128
Article 106	Article 107	Article 128
Article 107	Article 108	Article 130
Article 108	Article 109	Article 131
Article 108a	Article 110	Article 132
Article 109	Article 111, paragraphs 1 to 3 and 5 (moved)	*Article 219*
Article 109	Article 111, paragraph 4 (moved)	*Article 138*
		Article 133
Chapter 3	Chapter 3 — Institutional provisions	Chapter 3 — Institutional provisions
Article 109a	Article 112 (moved)	Article 283
Article 109b	Article 113 (moved)	Article 284
Article 109c	Article 114	Article 134
Article 109d	Article 115	Article 135
		Chapter 4 — Provisions specific to Member States whose currency is the euro
		Article 136
		Article 137
	Article 111, paragraph 4 (moved)	Article 138

Numbering pre-Amsterdam	Numbering of the Treaty establishing the European Community as adopted at Amsterdam	Numbering of the Treaty on the Functioning of the European Union
	Chapter 4 — Transitional provisions	Chapter 5 — Transitional provisions
Article 109e	Article 116 (repealed)	
		Article 139
Article 109f	Article 117, paragraphs 1, 2, sixth indent, and 3 to 9 (repealed)	
Article 109f	Article 117, paragraph 2, first five indents (moved)	*Article 141, paragraph 2*
	Article 121, paragraph 1 (moved)	
	Article 122, paragraph 2, second sentence (moved)	
	Article 123, paragraph 5 (moved)	Article 140[40]
Article 109g	Article 118 (repealed)	
	Article 123, paragraph 3 (moved)	
	Article 117, paragraph 2, first five indents (moved)	Article 141[41]
	Article 124, paragraph 1 (moved)	Article 142
Article 109h	Article 119	Article 143
Article 109i	Article 120	Article 144
Article 109j	Article 121, paragraph 1 (moved)	*Article 140, paragraph 1*
Article 109j	Article 121, paragraphs 2 to 4 (repealed)	
Article 109k	Article 122, paragraphs 1, 2, first sentence, 3, 4, 5 and 6 (repealed)	
Article 109k	Article 122, paragraph 2, second sentence (moved)	*Article 140, paragraph 2, first subparagraph*
Article 109l	Article 123, paragraphs 1, 2 and 4 (repealed)	
Article 109l	Article 123, paragraph 3 (moved)	*Article 141, paragraph 1*
Article 109l	Article 123, paragraph 5 (moved)	*Article 140, paragraph 3*
Article 109m	Article 124, paragraph 1 (moved)	Article 142
Article 109m	Article 124, paragraph 2 (repealed)	
Title VIa(**)	Title VIII — Employment	Title IX — Employment
Article 109n(*)	Article 125	Article 145
Article 109o(*)	Article 126	Article 146
Article 109p(*)	Article 127	Article 147
Article 109q(*)	Article 128	Article 148

Numbering pre-Amsterdam	Numbering of the Treaty establishing the European Community as adopted at Amsterdam	Numbering of the Treaty on the Functioning of the European Union
Article 109r(*)	Article 129	Article 149
Article 109s(*)	Article 130	Article 150
Title VIII	Title IX — Common commercial policy (moved)	Part Five, Title II, common commercial policy
Article 110	Article 131 (moved)	*Article 206*
Article 111 (repealed)		
Article 112	Article 132 (repealed)	
	Article 133 (moved)	Article 207
	Article 134 (repealed)	
Title VIIa(**)	Title X — Customs cooperation (moved)	Part Three, Title II, Chapter 2, Customs cooperation
Article 116(*)	Article 135 (moved)	Article 33
Title VIII	Title XI — Social policy, education, vocational training and youth	Title X — Social policy
Chapter 1(***)	Chapter 1 — social provisions (repealed)	
Article 117	Article 136	Article 151
		Article 152
Article 118	Article 137	Article 153
Article 118a	Article 138	Article 154
Article 118b	Article 139	Article 155
Article 118c	Article 140	Article 156
Article 119	Article 141	Article 157
Article 119a	Article 142	Article 158
Article 120	Article 143	Article 159
Article 121	Article 144	Article 160
Article 122	Article 145	Article 161
Chapter 2	Chapter 2 — The European Social Fund	Title XI — The European Social Fund
Article 123	Article 146	Article 162
Article 124	Article 147	Article 163
Article 125	Article 148	Article 164
Chapter 3	Chapter 3 — Education, vocational training and youth	Title XII — Education, vocational training, youth and sport
Article 126	Article 149	Article 165
Article 127	Article 150	Article 166
Title IX	Title XII — Culture	Title XIII — Culture
Article 128	Article 151	Article 167
Title X	Title XIII — Public health Title	XIV — Public health
Article 129	Article 152	Article 168
Title XI	Title XIV — Consumer protection	Title XV — Consumer protection

Numbering pre-Amsterdam	Numbering of the Treaty establishing the European Community as adopted at Amsterdam	Numbering of the Treaty on the Functioning of the European Union
Article 129a	Article 153, paragraphs 1, 3, 4 and 5	Article 169
	Article 153, paragraph 2 (moved)	*Article 12*
Title XII	Title XV — Trans- European networks Title XVI — Trans-European networks	
Article 129b	Article 154	Article 170
Article 129c	Article 155	Article 171
Article 129d	Article 156	Article 172
Title XIII	Title XVI — Industry Title XVII — Industry	
Article 130	Article 157	Article 173
Title XIV	Title XVII — Economic and social cohesion	Title XVIII — Economic, social and territorial cohesion
Article 130a	Article 158	Article 174
Article 130b	Article 159	Article 175
Article 130c	Article 160	Article 176
Article 130d	Article 161	Article 177
Article 130e	Article 162	Article 178
Title XV	Title XVIII — Research and technological development	Title XIX — Research and technological development and space
Article 130f	Article 163	Article 179
Article 130g	Article 164	Article 180
Article 130h	Article 165	Article 181
Article 130i	Article 166	Article 182
Article 130j	Article 167	Article 183
Article 130k	Article 168	Article 184
Article 130l	Article 169	Article 185
Article 130m	Article 170	Article 186
Article 130n	Article 171	Article 187
Article 130o	Article 172	Article 188
		Article 189
Article 130p	Article 173	Article 190
Article 130q (repealed)		
Title XVI	Title XIX — Environment	Title XX — Environment
Article 130r	Article 174	Article 191
Article 130s	Article 175	Article 192
Article 130t	Article 176	Article 193
		Titre XXI — Energy
		Article 194
		Title XXII — Tourism

Numbering pre-Amsterdam	Numbering of the Treaty establishing the European Community as adopted at Amsterdam	Numbering of the Treaty on the Functioning of the European Union
		Article 195
		Title XXIII — Civil protection
		Article 196
		Title XXIV — Administrative cooperation
		Article 197
Title XVII	Title XX — Development cooperation (moved)	Part Five, Title III, Chapter 1, Development cooperation
Article 130u	Article 177 (moved)	*Article 208*
Article 130v	Article 178 (repealed)[(42)]	
Article 130w	Article 179 (moved)	*Article 209*
Article 130x	Article 180 (moved)	*Article 210*
Article 130y	Article 181 (moved)	*Article 211*
	Title XXI — Economic, financial and technical cooperation with third countries (moved)	*Part Five, Title III, Chapter 2, Economic, financial and technical cooperation with third countries*
	Article 181a (moved)	*Article 212*
PART FOUR	**PART FOUR — ASSOCIATION OF THE OVERSEAS COUNTRIES AND TERRITORIES**	**PART FOUR — ASSOCIATION OF THE OVERSEAS COUNTRIES AND TERRITORIES**
Article 131	Article 182	Article 198
Article 132	Article 183	Article 199
Article 133	Article 184	Article 200
Article 134	Article 185	Article 201
Article 135	Article 186	Article 202
Article 136	Article 187	Article 203
Article 136a	Article 188	Article 204
		PART FIVE — EXTERNAL ACTION BY THE UNION
		Title I — General provisions on the union's external action
		Article 205
	Part Three, Title IX, Common commercial policy (moved)	Title II — Common commercial policy
	Article 131 (moved)	Article 206
	Article 133 (moved)	Article 207
		Title III — Cooperation with third countries and humanitarian aid
	Part Three, Title XX, Development cooperation (moved)	Chapter 1 — development cooperation
	Article 177 (moved)	Article 208[(43)]
	Article 179 (moved)	Article 209

Numbering pre-Amsterdam	Numbering of the Treaty establishing the European Community as adopted at Amsterdam	Numbering of the Treaty on the Functioning of the European Union
	Article 180 (moved)	Article 210
	Article 181 (moved)	Article 211
	Part Three, Title XXI, Economic, financial and technical cooperation with third countries (moved)	Chapter 2 — Economic, financial and technical cooperation with third countries
	Article 181a (moved)	Article 212
		Article 213
		Chapter 3 — Humanitarian aid
		Article 214
		Title IV — Restrictive measures
	Article 301 (replaced)	Article 215
		Title V — International agreements
		Article 216
	Article 310 (moved)	Article 217
	Article 300 (replaced)	Article 218
	Article 111, paragraphs 1 to 3 and 5 (moved)	Article 219
		Title VI — The Union's relations with international organisations and third countries and the Union delegations
	Articles 302 to 304 (replaced)	Article 220
		Article 221
		Title VII — Solidarity clause
		Article 222
PART FIVE	**PART FIVE — INSTITUTIONS OF THE COMMUNITY**	**PART SIX — INSTITUTIONAL AND FINANCIAL PROVISIONS**
Title I	Title I — Institutional provisions	Title I — Institutional provisions
Chapter 1	Chapter 1 — The institutions	Chapter 1 — The institutions
Section 1	Section 1 — The European Parliament	Section 1 — The European Parliament
Article 137	Article 189 (repealed)[44]	
Article 138	Article 190, paragraphs 1 to 3 (repealed)[45]	
Article 138	Article 190, paragraphs 4 and 5	Article 223
Article 138a	Article 191, first paragraph (repealed)[46]	
Article 138a	Article 191, second paragraph	Article 224

Numbering pre-Amsterdam	Numbering of the Treaty establishing the European Community as adopted at Amsterdam	Numbering of the Treaty on the Functioning of the European Union
Article 138b	Article 192, first paragraph (repealed)[47]	
Article 138b	Article 192, second paragraph	Article 225
Article 138c	Article 193	Article 226
Article 138d	Article 194	Article 227
Article 138e	Article 195	Article 228
Article 139	Article 196 Article 229	Article 229
Article 140	Article 197, first paragraph (repealed)[48]	
Article 140	Article 197, second, third and fourth paragraphs	Article 230
Article 141	Article 198	Article 231
Article 142	Article 199	Article 232
Article 143	Article 200	Article 233
Article 144	Article 201	Article 234
		Section 2 — The European Council
		Article 235
		Article 236
Section 2	Section 2 — The Council	Section 3 — The Council
Article 145	Article 202 (repealed)[49]	
Article 146	Article 203 (repealed)[50]	
Article 147	Article 204 Article 237	
Article 148	Article 205, paragraphs 2 and 4 (repealed)[51]	
Article 148	Article 205, paragraphs 1 and 3	Article 238
Article 149 (repealed)		
Article 150	Article 206	Article 239
Article 151	Article 207	Article 240
Article 152	Article 208	Article 241
Article 153	Article 209	Article 242
Article 154	Article 210	Article 243
Section 3	Section 3 — The Commission	Section 4 — The Commission
Article 155	Article 211 (repealed)[53]	
		Article 244
Article 156	Article 212 (moved)	*Article 249, paragraph 2*
Article 157	Article 213	Article 245
Article 158	Article 214 (repealed)[55]	
Article 159	Article 215	Article 246
Article 160	Article 216	Article 247
Article 161	Article 217, paragraphs 1, 3 and 4 (repealed)[56]	
Article 161	Article 217, paragraph 2	Article 248

Numbering pre-Amsterdam	Numbering of the Treaty establishing the European Community as adopted at Amsterdam	Numbering of the Treaty on the Functioning of the European Union
Article 162	Article 218, paragraph 1 (repealed)[57]	
Article 162	Article 218, paragraph 2	Article 249
Article 163	Article 219	Article 250
Section 4	Section 4 — The Court of Justice	Section 5 — The Court of Justice of the European Union
Article 164	Article 220 (repealed)[58]	
Article 165	Article 221, first paragraph (repealed)[59]	
Article 165	Article 221, second and third paragraphs Article 251	
Article 166	Article 222	Article 252
Article 167	Article 223	Article 253
Article 168	Article 224[60]	Article 254
		Article 255
Article 168a	Article 225	Article 256
	Article 225a	Article 257
Article 169	Article 226	Article 258
Article 170	Article 227	Article 259
Article 171	Article 228	Article 260
Article 172	Article 229	Article 261
	Article 229a	Article 262
Article 173	Article 230	Article 263
Article 174	Article 231	Article 264
Article 175	Article 232	Article 265
Article 176	Article 233	Article 266
Article 177	Article 234	Article 267
Article 178	Article 235	Article 268
		Article 269
Article 179	Article 236	Article 270
Article 180	Article 237	Article 271
Article 181	Article 238	Article 272
Article 182	Article 239	Article 273
Article 183	Article 240	Article 274
		Article 275
		Article 276
Article 184	Article 241	Article 277
Article 185	Article 242	Article 278
Article 186	Article 243	Article 279
Article 187	Article 244	Article 280
Article 188	Article 245	Article 281
		Section 6 — The European Central Bank
		Article 282
	Article 112 (moved)	Article 283
	Article 113 (moved)	Article 284

Numbering pre-Amsterdam	Numbering of the Treaty establishing the European Community as adopted at Amsterdam	Numbering of the Treaty on the Functioning of the European Union
Section 5	Section 5 — The Court of Auditors	Section 7 — The Court of Auditors
Article 188a	Article 246	Article 285
Article 188b	Article 247	Article 286
Article 188c	Article 248	Article 287
Chapter 2	Chapter 2 — Provisions common to several institutions	Chapter 2 — Legal acts of the Union, adoption procedures and other provisions
		Section 1 — The legal acts of the Union
Article 189	Article 249	Article 288
		Article 289
		Article 290[(61)]
		Article 291[(61)]
		Article 292
		Section 2 — Procedures for the adoption of acts and other provisions
Article 189a	Article 250	Article 293
Article 189b	Article 251	Article 294
Article 189c	Article 252 (repealed)	
		Article 295
Article 190	Article 253	Article 296
Article 191	Article 254	Article 297
		Article 298
Article 191a(*)	Article 255 (moved)	*Article 15*
Article 192	Article 256	Article 299
		Chapter 3 — The Union's advisory bodies
		Article 300
Chapter 3	Chapter 3 — The Economic and Social Committee	Section 1 — The Economic and Social Committee
Article 193	Article 257 (repealed)[(62)]	
Article 194	Article 258, first, second and fourth paragraphs	Article 301
Article 195	Article 258, third paragraph (repealed)[(63)]	
Article 196	Article 259	Article 302
Article 197	Article 260	Article 303
Article 198	Article 261 (repealed)	
	Article 262	Article 304
Chapter 4	Chapter 4 — The Committee of the Regions	Section 2 — The Committee of the Regions
Article 198a	Article 263, first and fifth paragraphs (repealed)[(64)]	

Numbering pre-Amsterdam	Numbering of the Treaty establishing the European Community as adopted at Amsterdam	Numbering of the Treaty on the Functioning of the European Union
Article 198a	Article 263, second to fourth paragraphs	Article 305
Article 198b	Article 264	Article 306
Article 198c	Article 265	Article 307
Chapter 5	Chapter 5 — The European Investment Bank	Chapter 4 — The European Investment Bank
Article 198d	Article 266	Article 308
Article 198e	Article 267	Article 309
Title II	Title II — Financial provisions	Title II — Financial provisions
Article 199	Article 268	Article 310
Article 200 (repealed)		
		Chapter 1 — The Union's own resources
Article 201	Article 269	Article 311
Article 201a	Article 270 (repealed)[(65)]	
		Chapter 2 — The multiannual financial framework
		Article 312
		Chapter 3 — The Union's annual budget
Article 203	*Article 272, paragraph 1 (moved)*	Article 313
Article 202	Article 271 (moved)	*Article 316*
Article 203	Article 272, paragraph 1 (moved)	*Article 313*
Article 203	Article 272, paragraphs 2 to 10	Article 314
Article 204	Article 273	Article 315
Article 202	*Article 271 (moved)*	Article 316
		Chapter 4 — Implementation of the budget and discharge
Article 205	Article 274	Article 317
Article 205a	Article 275	Article 318
Article 206	Article 276	Article 319
Article 206a (repealed)		
		Chapter 5 — Common provisions
Article 207	Article 277	Article 320
Article 208	Article 278	Article 321
Article 209	Article 279	Article 322
		Article 323
		Article 324
		Chapter 6 — Combating fraud

Numbering pre-Amsterdam	Numbering of the Treaty establishing the European Community as adopted at Amsterdam	Numbering of the Treaty on the Functioning of the European Union
Article 209a	Article 280	Article 325
		Title III — Enhanced cooperation
	Articles 11 and 11a (replaced)	Article 326[66]
	Articles 11 and 11a (replaced)	Article 327[66]
	Articles 11 and 11a (replaced)	Article 328[66]
	Articles 11 and 11a (replaced)	Article 329[66]
	Articles 11 and 11a (replaced)	Article 330[66]
	Articles 11 and 11a (replaced)	Article 331[66]
	Articles 11 and 11a (replaced)	Article 332[66]
	Articles 11 and 11a (replaced)	Article 333[66]
	Articles 11 and 11a (replaced)	Article 334[66]
PART SIX	**PART SIX — GENERAL AND FINAL PROVISIONS**	**PART SEVEN — GENERAL AND FINAL PROVISIONS**
Article 210	Article 281 (repealed)[67]	
Article 211	Article 282	Article 335
Article 212(*)	Article 283	Article 336
Article 213	Article 284	Article 337
Article 213a(*)	Article 285	Article 338
Article 213b(*)	Article 286 (replaced)	*Article 16*
Article 214	Article 287	Article 339
Article 215	Article 288	Article 340
Article 216	Article 289	Article 341
Article 217	Article 290	Article 342
Article 218(*)	Article 291	Article 343
Artilce 219	Article 292	Article 344
Article 220	Article 293 (repealed)	
Article 221	Article 294 (moved)	Article 55
Article 222	Article 295	Article 345
Article 223	Article 296	Article 346
Article 224	Article 297	Article 347
Article 225	Article 298	Article 348
Article 226 (repealed)		
Article 227	Article 299, paragraph 1 (repealed)[68]	
Article 227	Article 299, paragraph 2, second, third and fourth subparagraphs	Article 349
Article 227	Article 299, paragraph 2, first subparagraph, and paragraphs 3 to 6 (moved)	*Article 355*
Article 228	Article 300 (replaced)	*Article 218*
Article 228a	Article 301 (replaced)	*Article 215*
Article 229	Article 302 (replaced)	*Article 220*
Article 230	Article 303 (replaced)	*Article 220*

Numbering pre-Amsterdam	Numbering of the Treaty establishing the European Community as adopted at Amsterdam	Numbering of the Treaty on the Functioning of the European Union
Article 231	Article 304 (replaced)	*Article 220*
Article 232	Article 305 (repealed)	
Article 233	Article 306	Article 350
Article 234	Article 307	Article 351
Article 235	Article 308	Article 352
		Article 353
Article 236(*)	Article 309	Article 354
Article 237 (repealed)		
Article 238	Article 310 (moved)	Article 217
Article 239	Article 311 (repealed)[69]	
	Article 299, paragraph 2, first subparagraph, and paragraphs 3 to 6 (moved)	Article 355
Article 240	Article 312 Article 356	
Articles 241-246 (repealed)		
Final Provisions	Final Provisions	
Article 247	Article 313	Article 357
		Article 358
Article 248	Article 314 (repealed)[70]	

(*) New Article introduced by the Treaty of Amsterdam.

(**) New Title introduced by the Treaty of Amsterdam.

(***) Chapter 1 restructured by the Treaty of Amsterdam.

(25) Replaced, in substance, by Article 3 TEU.

(26) Replaced, in substance, by Articles 3 to 6 TFEU.

(27) Replaced, in substance, by Article 5 TEU.

(28) Insertion of the operative part of the protocol on protection and welfare of animals.

(29) Replaced, in substance, by Article 13 TEU.

(30) Replaced, in substance, by Article 13 TEU and Article 282, paragraph 1, TFEU.

(31) Replaced, in substance, by Article 4, paragraph 3, TEU.

(32) Also replaced by Article 20 TEU.

(33) Also replaces the current Article 29 TEU.

(34) Also replaces the current Article 36 TEU.

(35) Also replaces the current Article 33 TEU.

(36) Points 1 and 2 of Article 63 EC are replaced by paragraphs 1 and 2 of Article 78 TFEU, and paragraph 2 of Article 64 is replaced by paragraph 3 of Article 78 TFEU.

(37) Replaces the current Article 31 TEU.

(38) Replaces the current Article 30 TEU.

(39) Replaces the current Article 32 TEU.

(40) — Article 140, paragraph 1 takes over the wording of paragraph 1 of Article 121.

  — Article 140, paragraph 2 takes over the second sentence of paragraph 2 of Article 122.

  — Article 140, paragraph 3 takes over paragraph 5 of Article 123.

(41) — Article 141, paragraph 1 takes over paragraph 3 of Article 123.

— Article 141, paragraph 2 takes over the first five indents of paragraph 2 of Article 117.

(42) Replaced, in substance, by the second sentence of the second subparagraph of paragraph 1 of Article 208 TFUE.

(43) The second sentence of the second subparagraph of paragraph 1 replaces, in substance, Article 178 TEC.

(44) Replaced, in substance, by Article 14, paragraphs 1 and 2, TEU.

(45) Replaced, in substance, by Article 14, paragraphs 1 to 3, TEU.

(46) Replaced, in substance, by Article 11, paragraph 4, TEU.

(47) Replaced, in substance, by Article 14, paragraph 1, TEU.

(48) Replaced, in substance, by Article 14, paragraph 4, TEU.

(49) Replaced, in substance, by Article 16, paragraph 1, TEU and by Articles 290 and 291 TFEU.

(50) Replaced, in substance, by Article 16, paragraphs 2 and 9 TEU.

(51) Replaced, in substance, by Article 16, paragraphs 4 and 5 TEU.

(53) Replaced, in substance, by Article 17, paragraph 1 TEU.

(55) Replaced, in substance, by Article 17, paragraphs 3 and 7 TEU.

(56) Replaced, in substance, by Article 17, paragraph 6, TEU.

(57) Replaced, in substance, by Article 295 TFEU.

(58) Replaced, in substance, by Article 19 TEU.

(59) Replaced, in substance, by Article 19, paragraph 2, first subparagraph, of the TEU.

(60) The first sentence of the first subparagraph is replaced, in substance, by Article 19, paragraph 2, second subparagraph of the TEU.

(61) Replaces, in substance, the third indent of Article 202 TEC.

(62) Replaced, in substance, by Article 300, paragraph 2 of the TFEU.

(63) Replaced, in substance, by Article 300, paragraph 4 of the TFEU.

(64) Replaced, in substance, by Article 300, paragraphs 3 and 4, TFEU.

(65) Replaced, in substance, by Article 310, paragraph 4, TFEU.

(66) Also replaces the current Articles 27a to 27e, 40 to 40b, and 43 to 45 TEU.

(66) Also replaces the current Articles 27a to 27e, 40 to 40b, and 43 to 45 TEU.

(67) Replaced, in substance, by Article 47 TEU.

(68) Replaced, in substance by Article 52 TEU.

(69) Replaced, in substance by Article 51 TEU.

(70) Replaced, in substance by Article 55 TEU.

Index

A

Aarhus Convention, environmental law,
    15.76–8, 15.84, 15.85
    see also Environmental law and policy
Abortion cases, 6.68, 7.88–9, 11.15
Abuse of dominant position, Article 102 TFEU
    (ex Article 82 EC), 14.94
  abuse, meaning of, 14.119–33
    anti-competitive and exclusionary
      abuse, 14.125–7
    exploitative abuse, 14.128
    refusal to supply, 14.129–33
  dominance, 14.107–118
    barriers to entry, 14.109–11
    joint collective dominance, 14.112–13
    merger control, and, 14.114–18
  dominant position, 14.95–106
    geographic market, 14.105–6
    relevant market, 14.97–104
Access to Commission documents, 6.85
Acquis communautaire, 1.9
Acte clair doctrine, 4.41–2, 7.54
Acte éclairé, 4.43–9
Acts *sui generis,* 5.25–31
Administrative justice and good governance,
    principles of, 6.73
Adonnino Report, 1.11, 2.6, 13.2
Advocates General, role of, 4.3, 4.6
Age discrimination, 16.3, 16.4, 16.20, 16.86–9,
    16.91
  equality, general principles of law, 6.3, 6.4,
    6.10, 6.36, 6.43, 16.86–9, 16.91
Air pollution, environmental law, 15.47–9
    see also Environmental law and policy
Almunia, Joaquin, 14.8
Amendment procedure, 5.3
Amsterdam Treaty, 1.13, 2.13–16, 2.44, 2.51,
    2.52
Ancillary restraints, competition law,
    14.65–71
    see also Competition law
Animal health inspections, 9.23
Annulment actions *see* **Judicial review**
Anti-competitive collusion, Article 101 TFEU
    (ex Article 81), 14.14, 14.15

  agreements, 14.25–31
    parallel traders, 14.31
    tacit acceptance of, 14.26–8
    unilateral conduct, 14.29–30
    vertical and horizontal
      agreements, 14.49–54
  concerted practices, 14.34–48
    oligopoly, 14.46–8
  decisions, 14.32–33
  groups of companies, 14.21–3
  object or effect, 14.55–61
  undertakings, definition of, 14.18–20
    based outside the EU, 14.24
  see also Abuse of dominant position;
      Block exemptions; Competition law;
      Merger Control
Anti-dumping regulations, judicial review,
    locus standi, 8.53
Aristotle, 6.34
Ashton, Baroness, 2.29, 3.12
Assent procedure, 2.27, 3.47, 5.42, 5.44
    see also Legislative procedure
Asylum, 2.51, 2.52, 4.7
Austria
  Union law, application by, 7.90
    see also Member States

B

Barriers to entry, abuse of dominant
    position, 14.109–110
Barroso, José Manuel, 3.23
Betting and lotteries, 11.30, 11.44–8, 11.51
    see also Freedom to provide services
Block exemptions, 14.83, 14.88–93
Bonaparte, Napoleon, 1.2
Briand, Francois, 1.2
Brussels Treaty, 1.7
Budgetary procedure, 3.50, **5.42,** 5.45
    see also Legislative procedure
Bulgaria, 1.1, 12.149, 12.150

C

Cartels, 14.2, 14.4, 14.8, 14.23, 14.10, 14.84,
    14.156–8